University Casebook Series

March, 1986

ACCOUNTING AND THE LAW, Fourth Edition (1978), with Problems Pamphlet (Successor to Dohr, Phillips, Thompson & Warren)

George C. Thompson, Professor, Columbia University Graduate School of Business.
Robert Whitman, Professor of Law, University of Connecticut.
Ellis L. Phillips, Jr., Member of the New York Bar.
William C. Warren, Professor of Law Emeritus, Columbia University.

ACCOUNTING FOR LAWYERS, MATERIALS ON (1980)

David R. Herwitz, Professor of Law, Harvard University.

ADMINISTRATIVE LAW, Seventh Edition (1979), with 1983 Problems Supplement (Supplement edited in association with Paul R. Verkuil, Dean and Professor of Law, Tulane University)

Walter Gellhorn, University Professor Emeritus, Columbia University.
Clark Byse, Professor of Law, Harvard University.
Peter L. Strauss, Professor of Law, Columbia University.

ADMIRALTY, Second Edition (1978), with Statute and Rule Supplement

Jo Desha Lucas, Professor of Law, University of Chicago.

ADVOCACY, see also Lawyering Process

AGENCY, see also Enterprise Organization

AGENCY—PARTNERSHIPS, Third Edition (1982)

Abridgement from Conard, Knauss & Siegel's Enterprise Organization, Third Edition.

ANTITRUST: FREE ENTERPRISE AND ECONOMIC ORGANIZATION, Sixth Edition (1983), with 1983 Problems in Antitrust Supplement and 1985 Case Supplement

Louis B. Schwartz, Professor of Law, University of Pennsylvania.
John J. Flynn, Professor of Law, University of Utah.
Harry First, Professor of Law, New York University.

BANKRUPTCY (1985)

Robert L. Jordan, Professor of Law, University of California, Los Angeles.
William D. Warren, Professor of Law, University of California, Los Angeles.

BUSINESS ORGANIZATION, see also Enterprise Organization

BUSINESS PLANNING, Temporary Second Edition (1984)

David R. Herwitz, Professor of Law, Harvard University.

BUSINESS TORTS (1972)

Milton Handler, Professor of Law Emeritus, Columbia University.

UNIVERSITY CASEBOOK SERIES—Continued

CHILDREN IN THE LEGAL SYSTEM (1983)

Walter Wadlington, Professor of Law, University of Virginia.
Charles H. Whitebread, Professor of Law, University of Southern California.
Samuel Davis, Professor of Law, University of Georgia.

CIVIL PROCEDURE, see Procedure

CLINIC, see also Lawyering Process

COMMERCIAL LAW (1983) with 1986 Bankruptcy Supplement

Robert L. Jordan, Professor of Law, University of California, Los Angeles.
William D. Warren, Professor of Law, University of California, Los Angeles.

COMMERCIAL LAW, CASES & MATERIALS ON, Fourth Edition (1985)

E. Allan Farnsworth, Professor of Law, Columbia University.
John Honnold, Professor of Law, University of Pennsylvania.

COMMERCIAL PAPER, Third Edition (1984)

E. Allan Farnsworth, Professor of Law, Columbia University.

COMMERCIAL PAPER (1983) (Reprinted from COMMERCIAL LAW)

Robert L. Jordan, Professor of Law, University of California, Los Angeles.
William D. Warren, Professor of Law, University of California, Los Angeles.

COMMERCIAL PAPER AND BANK DEPOSITS AND COLLECTIONS (1967), with Statutory Supplement

William D. Hawkland, Professor of Law, University of Illinois.

COMMERCIAL TRANSACTIONS—Principles and Policies (1982)

Alan Schwartz, Professor of Law, University of Southern California.
Robert E. Scott, Professor of Law, University of Virginia.

COMPARATIVE LAW, Fourth Edition (1980)

Rudolf B. Schlesinger, Professor of Law, Hastings College of the Law.

COMPETITIVE PROCESS, LEGAL REGULATION OF THE, Third Edition (1986), with Selected Statutes Supplement

Edmund W. Kitch, Professor of Law, University of Virginia.
Harvey S. Perlman, Dean of the Law School, University of Nebraska.

CONFLICT OF LAWS, Eighth Edition (1984)

Willis L. M. Reese, Professor of Law, Columbia University.
Maurice Rosenberg, Professor of Law, Columbia University.

CONSTITUTIONAL LAW, Seventh Edition (1985), with 1985 Supplement

Edward L. Barrett, Jr., Professor of Law, University of California, Davis.
William Cohen, Professor of Law, Stanford University.

CONSTITUTIONAL LAW, CIVIL LIBERTY AND INDIVIDUAL RIGHTS, Second Edition (1982), with 1985 Supplement

William Cohen, Professor of Law, Stanford University.
John Kaplan, Professor of Law, Stanford University.

CONSTITUTIONAL LAW, Eleventh Edition (1985), with 1985 Supplement (Supplement edited in association with Frederick F. Schauer, Professor of Law, University of Michigan)

Gerald Gunther, Professor of Law, Stanford University.

UNIVERSITY CASEBOOK SERIES—Continued

CONSTITUTIONAL LAW, INDIVIDUAL RIGHTS IN, Fourth Edition (1986), (Reprinted from CONSTITUTIONAL LAW, Eleventh Edition), with 1985 Supplement (Supplement edited in association with Frederick F. Schauer, Professor of Law, University of Michigan)

Gerald Gunther, Professor of Law, Stanford University.

CONSUMER TRANSACTIONS (1983), with Selected Statutes and Regulations Supplement

Michael M. Greenfield, Professor of Law, Washington University.

CONTRACT LAW AND ITS APPLICATION, Third Edition (1983)

The late Addison Mueller, Professor of Law, University of California, Los Angeles.
Arthur I. Rosett, Professor of Law, University of California, Los Angeles.
Gerald P. Lopez, Professor of Law, University of California, Los Angeles.

CONTRACT LAW, STUDIES IN, Third Edition (1984)

Edward J. Murphy, Professor of Law, University of Notre Dame.
Richard E. Speidel, Professor of Law, Northwestern University.

CONTRACTS, Fourth Edition (1982)

John P. Dawson, Professor of Law Emeritus, Harvard University.
William Burnett Harvey, Professor of Law and Political Science, Boston University.
Stanley D. Henderson, Professor of Law, University of Virginia.

CONTRACTS, Third Edition (1980), with Statutory Supplement

E. Allan Farnsworth, Professor of Law, Columbia University.
William F. Young, Professor of Law, Columbia University.

CONTRACTS, Second Edition (1978), with Statutory and Administrative Law Supplement (1978)

Ian R. Macneil, Professor of Law, Cornell University.

COPYRIGHT, PATENTS AND TRADEMARKS, see also Competitive Process; see also Selected Statutes and International Agreements

COPYRIGHT, PATENT, TRADEMARK AND RELATED STATE DOCTRINES, Second Edition (1981), with 1985 Case Supplement, 1986 Selected Statutes Supplement and 1981 Problem Supplement

Paul Goldstein, Professor of Law, Stanford University.

COPYRIGHT, Unfair Competition, and Other Topics Bearing on the Protection of Literary, Musical, and Artistic Works, Fourth Edition (1985), with 1985 Statutory Supplement

Ralph S. Brown, Jr., Professor of Law, Yale University.
Robert C. Denicola, Professor of Law, University of Nebraska.

CORPORATE ACQUISITIONS, The Law and Finance of (1986)

Ronald J. Gilson, Professor of Law, Stanford University.

CORPORATE FINANCE, Second Edition (1979), with 1984 Supplement

Victor Brudney, Professor of Law, Harvard University.
Marvin A. Chirelstein, Professor of Law, Columbia University.

CORPORATE READJUSTMENTS AND REORGANIZATIONS (1976)

Walter J. Blum, Professor of Law, University of Chicago.
Stanley A. Kaplan, Professor of Law, University of Chicago.

UNIVERSITY CASEBOOK SERIES—Continued

CORPORATION LAW, BASIC, Second Edition (1979), with 1983 Case and Documentary Supplement

Detlev F. Vagts, Professor of Law, Harvard University.

CORPORATIONS, see also Enterprise Organization

CORPORATIONS, Fifth Edition—Unabridged (1980), with 1984 Supplement

The late William L. Cary, Professor of Law, Columbia University.
Melvin Aron Eisenberg, Professor of Law, University of California, Berkeley.

CORPORATIONS, Fifth Edition—Abridged (1980), with 1984 Supplement

The late William L. Cary, Professor of Law, Columbia University.
Melvin Aron Eisenberg, Professor of Law, University of California, Berkeley.

CORPORATIONS, Second Edition (1982), with 1982 Corporation and Partnership Statutes, Rules and Forms

Alfred F. Conard, Professor of Law, University of Michigan.
Robert N. Knauss, Dean of the Law School, University of Houston.
Stanley Siegel, Professor of Law, University of California, Los Angeles.

CORPORATIONS COURSE GAME PLAN (1975)

David R. Herwitz, Professor of Law, Harvard University.

CORRECTIONS, SEE SENTENCING

CREDITORS' RIGHTS, see also Debtor-Creditor Law

CRIMINAL JUSTICE ADMINISTRATION, Third Edition (1986).

Frank W. Miller, Professor of Law, Washington University.
Robert O. Dawson, Professor of Law, University of Texas.
George E. Dix, Professor of Law, University of Texas.
Raymond I. Parnas, Professor of Law, University of California, Davis.

CRIMINAL LAW, Third Edition (1983)

Fred E. Inbau, Professor of Law Emeritus, Northwestern University.
James R. Thompson, Professor of Law Emeritus, Northwestern University.
Andre A. Moenssens, Professor of Law, University of Richmond.

CRIMINAL LAW AND APPROACHES TO THE STUDY OF LAW (1986)

John M. Brumbaugh, Professor of Law, University of Maryland.

CRIMINAL LAW, Second Edition (1986)

Peter W. Low, Professor of Law, University of Virginia.
John C. Jeffries, Jr., Professor of Law, University of Virginia.
Richard C. Bonnie, Professor of Law, University of Virginia.

CRIMINAL LAW, Third Edition (1980)

Lloyd L. Weinreb, Professor of Law, Harvard University.

CRIMINAL LAW AND PROCEDURE, Sixth Edition (1984)

Rollin M. Perkins, Professor of Law Emeritus, University of California, Hastings College of the Law.
Ronald N. Boyce, Professor of Law, University of Utah.

UNIVERSITY CASEBOOK SERIES—Continued

CRIMINAL PROCEDURE, Second Edition (1980), with 1985 Supplement

Fred E. Inbau, Professor of Law Emeritus, Northwestern University.
James R. Thompson, Professor of Law Emeritus, Northwestern University.
James B. Haddad, Professor of Law, Northwestern University.
James B. Zagel, Chief, Criminal Justice Division, Office of Attorney General of Illinois.
Gary L. Starkman, Assistant U. S. Attorney, Northern District of Illinois.

CRIMINAL PROCESS, Third Edition (1978), with 1985 Supplement

Lloyd L. Weinreb, Professor of Law, Harvard University.

DAMAGES, Second Edition (1952)

Charles T. McCormick, late Professor of Law, University of Texas.
William F. Fritz, late Professor of Law, University of Texas.

DEBTOR–CREDITOR LAW (1984) with 1986 Supplement

Theodore Eisenberg, Professor of Law, Cornell University.

DEBTOR–CREDITOR LAW, Second Edition (1981), with Statutory Supplement

William D. Warren, Dean of the School of Law, University of California, Los Angeles.
William E. Hogan, Professor of Law, New York University.

DECEDENTS' ESTATES (1971)

Max Rheinstein, late Professor of Law Emeritus, University of Chicago.
Mary Ann Glendon, Professor of Law, Boston College.

DECEDENTS' ESTATES AND TRUSTS, Sixth Edition (1982)

John Ritchie, Emeritus Dean and Wigmore Professor of Law, Northwestern University.
Neill H. Alford, Jr., Professor of Law, University of Virginia.
Richard W. Effland, Professor of Law, Arizona State University.

DOMESTIC RELATIONS, see also Family Law

DOMESTIC RELATIONS, Successor Edition (1984) with 1985 Supplement

Walter Wadlington, Professor of Law, University of Virginia.

ELECTRONIC MASS MEDIA, Second Edition (1979)

William K. Jones, Professor of Law, Columbia University.

EMPLOYMENT DISCRIMINATION (1983) with 1985 Supplement

Joel W. Friedman, Professor of Law, Tulane University.
George M. Strickler, Professor of Law, Tulane University.

ENERGY LAW (1983)

Donald N. Zillman, Professor of Law, University of Utah.
Laurence Lattman, Dean of Mines and Engineering, University of Utah.

ENTERPRISE ORGANIZATION, Third Edition (1982), with 1982 Corporation and Partnership Statutes, Rules and Forms Supplement

Alfred F. Conard, Professor of Law, University of Michigan.
Robert L. Knauss, Dean of the Law School, University of Houston.
Stanley Siegel, Professor of Law, University of California, Los Angeles.

ENVIRONMENTAL POLICY LAW 1985 Edition, with 1985 Problems Supplement (Supplement in association with Ronald H. Rosenberg, Professor of Law, College of William and Mary)

Thomas J. Schoenbaum, Professor of Law, University of Georgia.

UNIVERSITY CASEBOOK SERIES—Continued

EQUITY, see also Remedies

EQUITY, RESTITUTION AND DAMAGES, Second Edition (1974)

Robert Childres, late Professor of Law, Northwestern University.
William F. Johnson, Jr., Professor of Law, New York University.

ESTATE PLANNING, Second Edition (1982), with 1985 Case, Text and Documentary Supplement

David Westfall, Professor of Law, Harvard University.

ETHICS, see Legal Profession, and Professional Responsibility

ETHICS AND PROFESSIONAL RESPONSIBILITY (1981) (Reprinted from THE LAWYERING PROCESS)

Gary Bellow, Professor of Law, Harvard University.
Bea Moulton, Legal Services Corporation.

EVIDENCE, Fifth Edition (1984)

John Kaplan, Professor of Law, Stanford University.
Jon R. Waltz, Professor of Law, Northwestern University.

EVIDENCE, Seventh Edition (1983) with Rules and Statute Supplement (1984)

Jack B. Weinstein, Chief Judge, United States District Court.
John H. Mansfield, Professor of Law, Harvard University.
Norman Abrams, Professor of Law, University of California, Los Angeles.
Margaret Berger, Professor of Law, Brooklyn Law School.

FAMILY LAW, see also Domestic Relations

FAMILY LAW Second Edition (1985)

Judith C. Areen, Professor of Law, Georgetown University.

FAMILY LAW AND CHILDREN IN THE LEGAL SYSTEM, STATUTORY MATERIALS (1981)

Walter Wadlington, Professor of Law, University of Virginia.

FEDERAL COURTS, Seventh Edition (1982), with 1985 Supplement

Charles T. McCormick, late Professor of Law, University of Texas.
James H. Chadbourn, late Professor of Law, Harvard University.
Charles Alan Wright, Professor of Law, University of Texas.

FEDERAL COURTS AND THE FEDERAL SYSTEM, Hart and Wechsler's Second Edition (1973), with 1981 Supplement

Paul M. Bator, Professor of Law, Harvard University.
Paul J. Mishkin, Professor of Law, University of California, Berkeley.
David L. Shapiro, Professor of Law, Harvard University.
Herbert Wechsler, Professor of Law, Columbia University.

FEDERAL PUBLIC LAND AND RESOURCES LAW (1981), with 1983 Case Supplement and 1984 Statutory Supplement

George C. Coggins, Professor of Law, University of Kansas.
Charles F. Wilkinson, Professor of Law, University of Oregon.

FEDERAL RULES OF CIVIL PROCEDURE, 1984 Edition

FEDERAL TAXATION, see Taxation

FOOD AND DRUG LAW (1980), with Statutory Supplement

Richard A. Merrill, Dean of the School of Law, University of Virginia.
Peter Barton Hutt, Esq.

UNIVERSITY CASEBOOK SERIES—Continued

FUTURE INTERESTS (1958)

Philip Mechem, late Professor of Law Emeritus, University of Pennsylvania.

FUTURE INTERESTS (1970)

Howard R. Williams, Professor of Law, Stanford University.

FUTURE INTERESTS AND ESTATE PLANNING (1961), with 1962 Supplement

W. Barton Leach, late Professor of Law, Harvard University.
James K. Logan, formerly Dean of the Law School, University of Kansas.

GOVERNMENT CONTRACTS, FEDERAL, Successor Edition (1985)

John W. Whelan, Professor of Law, Hastings College of the Law.

**GOVERNMENT REGULATION: FREE ENTERPRISE AND ECONOMIC ORGANI-
ZATION, Sixth Edition (1985)**

Louis B. Schwartz, Professor of Law, University of Pennsylvania.
John J. Flynn, Professor of Law, University of Utah.
Harry First, Professor of Law, New York University.

HINCKLEY JOHN W., TRIAL OF: A Case Study of the Insanity Defense

Peter W. Low, Professor of Law, University of Virginia.
John C. Jeffries, Jr., Professor of Law, University of Virginia.
Richard C. Bonnie, Professor of Law, University of Virginia.

INJUNCTIONS, Second Edition (1984)

Owen M. Fiss, Professor of Law, Yale University.
Doug Rendleman, Professor of Law, College of William and Mary.

INSTITUTIONAL INVESTORS, 1978

David L. Ratner, Professor of Law, Cornell University.

INSURANCE, Second Edition (1985)

William F. Young, Professor of Law, Columbia University.
Eric M. Holmes, Professor of Law, University of Georgia.

**INTERNATIONAL LAW, see also Transnational Legal Problems, Transnational
Business Problems, and United Nations Law**

**INTERNATIONAL LAW IN CONTEMPORARY PERSPECTIVE (1981), with Essay
Supplement**

Myres S. McDougal, Professor of Law, Yale University.
W. Michael Reisman, Professor of Law, Yale University.

**INTERNATIONAL LEGAL SYSTEM, Second Edition (1981), with Documentary
Supplement**

Joseph Modeste Sweeney, Professor of Law, Tulane University.
Covey T. Oliver, Professor of Law, University of Pennsylvania.
Noyes E. Leech, Professor of Law, University of Pennsylvania.

**INTRODUCTION TO LAW, see also Legal Method, On Law in Courts, and
Dynamics of American Law**

INTRODUCTION TO THE STUDY OF LAW (1970)

E. Wayne Thode, late Professor of Law, University of Utah.
Leon Lebowitz, Professor of Law, University of Texas.
Lester J. Mazor, Professor of Law, University of Utah.

UNIVERSITY CASEBOOK SERIES—Continued

JUDICIAL CODE and Rules of Procedure in the Federal Courts with Excerpts from the Criminal Code, 1984 Edition

Henry M. Hart, Jr., late Professor of Law, Harvard University.
Herbert Wechsler, Professor of Law, Columbia University.

JURISPRUDENCE (Temporary Edition Hardbound) (1949)

Lon L. Fuller, Professor of Law Emeritus, Harvard University.

JUVENILE, see also Children

JUVENILE JUSTICE PROCESS, Third Edition (1985)

Frank W. Miller, Professor of Law, Washington University.
Robert O. Dawson, Professor of Law, University of Texas.
George E. Dix, Professor of Law, University of Texas.
Raymond I. Parnas, Professor of Law, University of California, Davis.

LABOR LAW, Tenth Edition (1986), with 1986 Statutory Supplement

Archibald Cox, Professor of Law, Harvard University.
Derek C. Bok, President, Harvard University.
Robert A. Gorman, Professor of Law, University of Pennsylvania.

LABOR LAW, Second Edition (1982), with Statutory Supplement

Clyde W. Summers, Professor of Law, University of Pennsylvania.
Harry H. Wellington, Dean of the Law School, Yale University.
Alan Hyde, Professor of Law, Rutgers University.

LAND FINANCING, Third Edition (1985)

The late Norman Penney, Professor of Law, Cornell University.
Richard F. Broude, Member of the California Bar.
Roger Cunningham, Professor of Law, University of Michigan.

LAW AND MEDICINE (1980)

Walter Wadlington, Professor of Law and Professor of Legal Medicine, University of Virginia.
Jon R. Waltz, Professor of Law, Northwestern University.
Roger B. Dworkin, Professor of Law, Indiana University, and Professor of Biomedical History, University of Washington.

LAW, LANGUAGE AND ETHICS (1972)

William R. Bishin, Professor of Law, University of Southern California.
Christopher D. Stone, Professor of Law, University of Southern California.

LAW, SCIENCE AND MEDICINE (1984)

Judith C. Areen, Professor of Law, Georgetown University.
Patricia A. King, Professor of Law, Georgetown University.
Steven P. Goldberg, Professor of Law, Georgetown University.
Alexander M. Capron, Professor of Law, Georgetown University.

LAWYERING PROCESS (1978), with Civil Problem Supplement and Criminal Problem Supplement

Gary Bellow, Professor of Law, Harvard University.
Bea Moulton, Professor of Law, Arizona State University.

LEGAL METHOD (1980)

Harry W. Jones, Professor of Law Emeritus, Columbia University.
John M. Kernochan, Professor of Law, Columbia University.
Arthur W. Murphy, Professor of Law, Columbia University.

UNIVERSITY CASEBOOK SERIES—Continued

LEGAL METHODS (1969)

Robert N. Covington, Professor of Law, Vanderbilt University.
E. Blythe Stason, late Professor of Law, Vanderbilt University.
John W. Wade, Professor of Law, Vanderbilt University.
Elliott E. Cheatham, late Professor of Law, Vanderbilt University.
Theodore A. Smedley, Professor of Law, Vanderbilt University.

LEGAL PROFESSION, THE, Responsibility and Regulation (1985)

Geoffrey C. Hazard, Jr., Professor of Law, Yale University.
Deborah L. Rhode, Professor of Law, Stanford University.

LEGISLATION, Fourth Edition (1982) (by Fordham)

Horace E. Read, late Vice President, Dalhousie University.
John W. MacDonald, Professor of Law Emeritus, Cornell Law School.
Jefferson B. Fordham, Professor of Law, University of Utah.
William J. Pierce, Professor of Law, University of Michigan.

LEGISLATIVE AND ADMINISTRATIVE PROCESSES, Second Edition (1981)

Hans A. Linde, Judge, Supreme Court of Oregon.
George Bunn, Professor of Law, University of Wisconsin.
Fredericka Paff, Professor of Law, University of Wisconsin.
W. Lawrence Church, Professor of Law, University of Wisconsin.

LOCAL GOVERNMENT LAW, Second Revised Edition (1986)

Jefferson B. Fordham, Professor of Law, University of Utah.

MASS MEDIA LAW, Second Edition (1982), with 1985 Supplement

Marc A. Franklin, Professor of Law, Stanford University.

MENTAL HEALTH PROCESS, Second Edition (1976), with 1981 Supplement

Frank W. Miller, Professor of Law, Washington University.
Robert O. Dawson, Professor of Law, University of Texas.
George E. Dix, Professor of Law, University of Texas.
Raymond I. Parnas, Professor of Law, University of California, Davis.

MUNICIPAL CORPORATIONS, see Local Government Law

NEGOTIABLE INSTRUMENTS, see Commercial Paper

NEGOTIATION (1981) (Reprinted from THE LAWYERING PROCESS)

Gary Bellow, Professor of Law, Harvard Law School.
Bea Moulton, Legal Services Corporation.

NEW YORK PRACTICE, Fourth Edition (1978)

Herbert Peterfreund, Professor of Law, New York University.
Joseph M. McLaughlin, Dean of the Law School, Fordham University.

OIL AND GAS, Fourth Edition (1979)

Howard R. Williams, Professor of Law, Stanford University.
Richard C. Maxwell, Professor of Law, University of California, Los Angeles.
Charles J. Meyers, Dean of the Law School, Stanford University.

ON LAW IN COURTS (1965)

Paul J. Mishkin, Professor of Law, University of California, Berkeley.
Clarence Morris, Professor of Law Emeritus, University of Pennsylvania.

UNIVERSITY CASEBOOK SERIES—Continued

PATENTS AND ANTITRUST (Pamphlet) (1983)

Milton Handler, Professor of Law Emeritus, Columbia University.
Harlan M. Blake, Professor of Law, Columbia University.
Robert Pitofsky, Professor of Law, Georgetown University.
Harvey J. Goldschmid, Professor of Law, Columbia University.

PERSPECTIVES ON THE LAWYER AS PLANNER (Reprint of Chapters One through Five of Planning by Lawyers) (1978)

Louis M. Brown, Professor of Law, University of Southern California.
Edward A. Dauer, Professor of Law, Yale University.

PLANNING BY LAWYERS, MATERIALS ON A NONADVERSARIAL LEGAL PROCESS (1978)

Louis M. Brown, Professor of Law, University of Southern California.
Edward A. Dauer, Professor of Law, Yale University.

PLEADING AND PROCEDURE, see Procedure, Civil

POLICE FUNCTION, Fourth Edition (1986)

Reprint of Chapters 1–10 of Miller, Dawson, Dix and Parnas's CRIMINAL JUSTICE ADMINISTRATION, Third Edition.

PREPARING AND PRESENTING THE CASE (1981) (Reprinted from THE LAWYERING PROCESS)

Gary Bellow, Professor of Law, Harvard Law School.
Bea Moulton, Legal Services Corporation.

PREVENTIVE LAW, see also Planning by Lawyers

PROCEDURE—CIVIL PROCEDURE, Second Edition (1974), with 1979 Supplement

The late James H. Chadbourn, Professor of Law, Harvard University.
A. Leo Levin, Professor of Law, University of Pennsylvania.
Philip Shuchman, Professor of Law, Cornell University.

PROCEDURE—CIVIL PROCEDURE, Fifth Edition (1984)

Richard H. Field, late Professor of Law, Harvard University.
Benjamin Kaplan, Professor of Law Emeritus, Harvard University.
Kevin M. Clermont, Professor of Law, Cornell University.

PROCEDURE—CIVIL PROCEDURE, Fourth Edition (1985)

Maurice Rosenberg, Professor of Law, Columbia University.
Hans Smit, Professor of Law, Columbia University.
Harold L. Korn, Professor of Law, Columbia University.

PROCEDURE—PLEADING AND PROCEDURE: State and Federal, Fifth Edition (1983), with 1985 Supplement

David W. Louisell, late Professor of Law, University of California, Berkeley.
Geoffrey C. Hazard, Jr., Professor of Law, Yale University.
Colin C. Tait, Professor of Law, University of Connecticut.

PROCEDURE—FEDERAL RULES OF CIVIL PROCEDURE, 1986 Edition

PRODUCTS LIABILITY (1980)

Marshall S. Shapo, Professor of Law, Northwestern University.

PRODUCTS LIABILITY AND SAFETY (1980), with 1985 Case and Documentary Supplement

W. Page Keeton, Professor of Law, University of Texas.
David G. Owen, Professor of Law, University of South Carolina.
John E. Montgomery, Professor of Law, University of South Carolina.

PROFESSIONAL RESPONSIBILITY, Third Edition (1984), with 1986 Selected National Standards Supplement

Thomas D. Morgan, Dean of the Law School, Emory University.
Ronald D. Rotunda, Professor of Law, University of Illinois.

PROPERTY, Fifth Edition (1984)

John E. Cribbet, Dean of the Law School, University of Illinois.
Corwin W. Johnson, Professor of Law, University of Texas.

PROPERTY—PERSONAL (1953)

S. Kenneth Skolfield, late Professor of Law Emeritus, Boston University.

PROPERTY—PERSONAL, Third Edition (1954)

Everett Fraser, late Dean of the Law School Emeritus, University of Minnesota.
Third Edition by Charles W. Taintor, late Professor of Law, University of Pittsburgh.

PROPERTY—INTRODUCTION, TO REAL PROPERTY, Third Edition (1954)

Everett Fraser, late Dean of the Law School Emeritus, University of Minnesota.

PROPERTY—REAL AND PERSONAL, Combined Edition (1954)

Everett Fraser, late Dean of the Law School Emeritus, University of Minnesota.
Third Edition of Personal Property by Charles W. Taintor, late Professor of Law, University of Pittsburgh.

PROPERTY—FUNDAMENTALS OF MODERN REAL PROPERTY, Second Edition (1982), with 1985 Supplement

Edward H. Rabin, Professor of Law, University of California, Davis.

PROPERTY—PROBLEMS IN REAL PROPERTY (Pamphlet) (1969)

Edward H. Rabin, Professor of Law, University of California, Davis.

PROPERTY, REAL (1984)

Paul Goldstein, Professor of Law, Stanford University.

PROSECUTION AND ADJUDICATION, Third Edition (1986)

Reprint of Chapters 11–26 of Miller, Dawson, Dix and Parnas's CRIMINAL JUSTICE ADMINISTRATION, Third Edition.

PSYCHIATRY AND LAW, see Mental Health, see also Hinckley, Trial of

PUBLIC REGULATION OF DANGEROUS PRODUCTS (paperback) (1980)

Marshall S. Shapo, Professor of Law, Northwestern University.

PUBLIC UTILITY LAW, see Free Enterprise, also Regulated Industries

REAL ESTATE PLANNING (1980), with 1980 Problems, Statutes and New Materials Supplement

Norton L. Steuben, Professor of Law, University of Colorado.

REAL ESTATE TRANSACTIONS, Second Edition (1985), with 1985 Statute, Form and Problem Supplement

Paul Goldstein, Professor of Law, Stanford University.

UNIVERSITY CASEBOOK SERIES—Continued

RECEIVERSHIP AND CORPORATE REORGANIZATION, see Creditors' Rights

REGULATED INDUSTRIES, Second Edition, 1976

William K. Jones, Professor of Law, Columbia University.

REMEDIES (1982), with 1984 Case Supplement

Edward D. Re, Chief Judge, U. S. Court of International Trade.

RESTITUTION, Second Edition (1966)

John W. Wade, Professor of Law, Vanderbilt University.

SALES, Second Edition (1986)

Marion W. Benfield, Jr., Professor of Law, University of Illinois.
William D. Hawkland, Chancellor, Louisiana State Law Center.

SALES AND SALES FINANCING, Fifth Edition (1984)

John Honnold, Professor of Law, University of Pennsylvania.

SALES LAW AND THE CONTRACTING PROCESS (1982)

Reprint of Chapters 1–10 of Schwartz and Scott's Commercial Transactions.

SECURED TRANSACTIONS IN PERSONAL PROPERTY (1983) (Reprinted from COMMERCIAL LAW)

Robert L. Jordan, Professor of Law, University of California, Los Angeles.
William D. Warren, Professor of Law, University of California, Los Angeles.

SECURITIES REGULATION, Fifth Edition (1982), with 1985 Cases and Releases Supplement and 1985 Selected Statutes, Rules and Forms Supplement

Richard W. Jennings, Professor of Law, University of California, Berkeley.
Harold Marsh, Jr., Member of California Bar.

SECURITIES REGULATION (1982), with 1985 Supplement

Larry D. Soderquist, Professor of Law, Vanderbilt University.

SECURITY INTERESTS IN PERSONAL PROPERTY (1984)

Douglas G. Baird, Professor of Law, University of Chicago.
Thomas H. Jackson, Professor of Law, Stanford University.

SECURITY INTERESTS IN PERSONAL PROPERTY (1985) (Reprinted from Sales and Sales Financing, Fifth Edition)

John Honnold, Professor of Law, University of Pennsylvania.

SENTENCING AND THE CORRECTIONAL PROCESS, Second Edition (1976)

Frank W. Miller, Professor of Law, Washington University.
Robert O. Dawson, Professor of Law, University of Texas.
George E. Dix, Professor of Law, University of Texas.
Raymond I. Parnas, Professor of Law, University of California, Davis.

SOCIAL SCIENCE IN LAW, Cases and Materials (1985)

John Monahan, Professor of Law, University of Virginia.
Laurens Walker, Professor of Law, University of Virginia.

SOCIAL WELFARE AND THE INDIVIDUAL (1971)

Robert J. Levy, Professor of Law, University of Minnesota.
Thomas P. Lewis, Dean of the College of Law, University of Kentucky.
Peter W. Martin, Professor of Law, Cornell University.

UNIVERSITY CASEBOOK SERIES—Continued

TAX, POLICY ANALYSIS OF THE FEDERAL INCOME (1976)

William A. Klein, Professor of Law, University of California, Los Angeles.

TAXATION, FEDERAL INCOME, Successor Edition (1985)

Michael J. Graetz, Professor of Law, Yale University.

TAXATION, FEDERAL INCOME, Fifth Edition (1985)

James J. Freeland, Professor of Law, University of Florida.
Stephen A. Lind, Professor of Law, University of Florida.
Richard B. Stephens, Professor of Law Emeritus, University of Florida.

TAXATION, FEDERAL INCOME, Volume I, Personal Income Taxation, Second Edition (1986), Volume II, Taxation of Partnerships and Corporations, Second Edition (1980), with 1985 Legislative Supplement

Stanley S. Surrey, late Professor of Law, Harvard University.
Paul R. McDaniel, Professor of Law, Boston College Law School.
Hugh J. Ault, Professor of Law, Boston College Law School.
Stanley A. Koppelman, Boston University

TAXATION, FEDERAL WEALTH TRANSFER, Second Edition (1982) with 1985 Legislative Supplement

Stanley S. Surrey, late Professor of Law, Harvard University.
William C. Warren, Professor of Law Emeritus, Columbia University.
Paul R. McDaniel, Professor of Law, Boston College Law School.
Harry L. Gutman, Instructor, Harvard Law School and Boston College Law School.

TAXATION, FUNDAMENTALS OF CORPORATE, Cases and Materials (1985)

Stephen A. Lind, Professor of Law, University of Florida.
Stephen Schwarz, Professor of Law, University of California, Hastings.
Daniel J. Lathrope, Professor of Law, University of California, Hastings.
Joshua Rosenberg, Professor of Law, University of San Francisco.

TAXATION, FUNDAMENTALS OF PARTNERSHIP, Cases and Materials (1985)

Stephen A. Lind, Professor of Law, University of California, Hastings.
Stephen Schwarz, Professor of Law, University of California, Hastings.
Daniel J. Lathrope, Professor of Law, University of California, Hastings.
Joshua Rosenberg, Professor of Law, University of San Francisco.

TAXATION, PROBLEMS IN THE FEDERAL INCOME TAXATION OF PARTNERSHIPS AND CORPORATIONS, Second Edition (1986)

Norton L. Steuben, Professor of Law, University of Colorado.
William J. Turnier, Professor of Law, University of North Carolina.

TAXATION, PROBLEMS IN THE FUNDAMENTALS OF FEDERAL INCOME, Second Edition (1985)

Norton L. Steuben, Professor of Law, University of Colorado.
William J. Turnier, Professor of Law, University of North Carolina.

TAXES AND FINANCE—STATE AND LOCAL (1974)

Oliver Oldman, Professor of Law, Harvard University.
Ferdinand P. Schoettle, Professor of Law, University of Minnesota.

TORT LAW AND ALTERNATIVES, Third Edition (1983)

Marc A. Franklin, Professor of Law, Stanford University.
Robert L. Rabin, Professor of Law, Stanford University.

UNIVERSITY CASEBOOK SERIES—Continued

TORTS, Seventh Edition (1982)

William L. Prosser, late Professor of Law, University of California, Hastings College.
John W. Wade, Professor of Law, Vanderbilt University.
Victor E. Schwartz, Professor of Law, American University.

TORTS, Third Edition (1976)

Harry Shulman, late Dean of the Law School, Yale University.
Fleming James, Jr., Professor of Law Emeritus, Yale University.
Oscar S. Gray, Professor of Law, University of Maryland.

TRADE REGULATION, Second Edition (1983), with 1985 Supplement

Milton Handler, Professor of Law Emeritus, Columbia University.
Harlan M. Blake, Professor of Law, Columbia University.
Robert Pitofsky, Professor of Law, Georgetown University.
Harvey J. Goldschmid, Professor of Law, Columbia University.

TRADE REGULATION, see Antitrust

TRANSNATIONAL BUSINESS PROBLEMS (1986)

Detlev F. Vagts, Professor of Law, Harvard University.

TRANSNATIONAL LEGAL PROBLEMS, Third Edition (1986) with Documentary Supplement

Henry J. Steiner, Professor of Law, Harvard University.
Detlev F. Vagts, Professor of Law, Harvard University.

TRIAL, see also Evidence, Making the Record, Lawyering Process and Preparing and Presenting the Case

TRIAL ADVOCACY (1968)

A. Leo Levin, Professor of Law, University of Pennsylvania.
Harold Cramer, of the Pennsylvania Bar.
Maurice Rosenberg, Professor of Law, Columbia University, Consultant.

TRUSTS, Fifth Edition (1978)

George G. Bogert, late Professor of Law Emeritus, University of Chicago.
Dallin H. Oaks, President, Brigham Young University.

TRUSTS AND SUCCESSION (Palmer's), Fourth Edition (1983)

Richard V. Wellman, Professor of Law, University of Georgia.
Lawrence W. Waggoner, Professor of Law, University of Michigan.
Olin L. Browder, Jr., Professor of Law, University of Michigan.

UNFAIR COMPETITION, see Competitive Process and Business Torts

UNITED NATIONS LAW, Second Edition (1967), with Documentary Supplement (1968)

Louis B. Sohn, Professor of Law, Harvard University.

WATER RESOURCE MANAGEMENT, Second Edition (1980), with 1983 Supplement

Charles J. Meyers, Dean of the Law School, Stanford University.
A. Dan Tarlock, Professor of Law, Indiana University.

WILLS AND ADMINISTRATION, Fifth Edition (1961)

Philip Mechem, late Professor of Law, University of Pennsylvania.
Thomas E. Atkinson, late Professor of Law, New York University.

WORLD LAW, see United Nations Law

University Casebook Series

CASES AND MATERIALS

ON

COMMERCIAL PAPER

THIRD EDITION

By

E. ALLAN FARNSWORTH
Alfred McCormack Professor of Law, Columbia University

Mineola, New York
THE FOUNDATION PRESS, INC.
1984

Library of Congress Cataloging in Publication Data

Farnsworth, E. Allan (Edward Allan), 1928–
   Cases and materials on commercial paper.

   (University casebook series)
   Includes index.
   1. Negotiable instruments—United Stated—Cases.
I. Title.   II. Series.
KF957.A4F3   1984   346.73'096   84–7997
ISBN 0–88277–178–7   347.30696

Farnsworth Cs.Com'l Paper 3rd Ed. UCB

2nd Reprint—1986

To
JEANNE, KAREN,
TED and PAM

*

PREFACE

This book, like its predecessors, is intended for use in a separate course on commercial paper or negotiable instruments. Substantially the same material is also contained in Farnsworth and Honnold, Cases and Materials on Commercial Law, which is designed for an integrated course in commercial law.

The book's structure is similar to that of the last edition. The book is divided into three parts: Good Faith Purchase; Payment by Check; Other Uses of Commercial Paper. (This final part is limited to the draft in the documentary exchange and to accommodation parties. The subject of the promissory note in the secured sale of goods is dealt with in Chapter 2 in connection with good faith purchase.) The organization is largely functional except for the first part. That part presents a comparative examination of good faith purchase in the setting not only of commercial paper but of goods and simple contract rights as well. Good faith is one of the important recurring themes in commercial law, and useful comparisons and contrasts emerge from such a presentation.

Much of the material in this edition is new, with many cases selected from the substantial body of recent litigation under the Code. Except for a few landmark decisions, historical background is provided by explanatory text. Recent years have also seen the establishment of significant protection for consumers and efforts to adapt the law to new payment systems. This edition includes materials designed to introduce students to these new developments. Students will want to obtain the Official Text of the Code with Comments to supplement this casebook.

The use of problems also calls for a few words of explanation. Problems are often employed at the outset of a topic to help students get off on the right foot and quickly come to grips with basic issues. These analytical, introductory problems are followed by cases that show judicial response to situations where the text of the Code does not provide a compelling answer, and sometimes by problems of the more conventional sort that add refinements to the basic presentation. Instructors who do not wish to use the problems can focus their attention on the cases without seriously impairing the continuity of the materials. Prototype transactions and forms illustrate the mechanics of check collections, documentary sales, and letters of credit. When practicable, problems have been framed in terms of the prototypes in order to examine legal problems in a realistic commercial context.

PREFACE

My thanks go to Professor John Honnold of the University of Pennsylvania Law School for consent to incorporation of materials prepared by him for our integrated edition on commercial law, to friends in business and banking for advice and forms so graciously given, to Mr. Steven P. Eichel and Mr. Donald J. Guiney for help in research and editing, and to Ms. Brenda Fox for secretarial assistance.

E. ALLAN FARNSWORTH

New York
June, 1984

SUMMARY OF CONTENTS

*

TABLE OF CONTENTS

PART III.   OTHER USES OF COMMERCIAL PAPER

TABLE OF CASES

The principal cases are in italic type; the cited cases are in roman type. The references are to Pages.

CASES AND MATERIALS

ON

COMMERCIAL PAPER

*

GENERAL INTRODUCTION

DEVELOPMENT OF COMMERCIAL LAW

(1) Historical Background. The following summary traces the development of the tribunals and sources of law that determine commercial disputes. It will serve as a background for later discussion of the development of the law itself. The subject is divided into three parts.

(a) English Law. The Uniform Commercial Code refers to the law merchant as a source of law. (See UCC 1–103.) Malynes' classic work, *Lex Mercatoria,* first published in England in 1622, included in the law merchant such subjects as banks and bankers, bills of exchange, letters of credit, buying and selling commodities by contract, insurance and admiralty. To Malynes, a seventeenth century merchant, this was a comprehensive body of authority that had been created not by kings or judges but by the customs of merchants, that was international rather than national in character, and that was distinct from the common law of England. How had the law merchant come to have this status in England by 1622?

Soon after the Norman invasion, local courts which became known as piepowder courts [1] were created as incident to the royal charters that authorized medieval fairs. The jurisdiction of these courts included commercial cases. The law was declared by a jury of merchants, the defendant's right to resort to compurgation was limited, and the procedure was summary enabling the participants to move on as their trade demanded.

In 1353 the Statute of the Staples [2] was enacted, regulating dealing in staple commodities, particularly wool which was of great economic and political importance. It created staple courts in certain boroughs with jurisdiction over commercial matters, and provided that the law merchant rather than the common law should govern. A mayor of the staple, who was required to be versed in the law

---

1. From *pie poudre* (dusty foot) in reference to the shoes of itinerant merchant litigants. See generally Honnold, The Influence of the Law of International Trade on the Development and Character of English and American Commercial Law, in Sources of the Law of International Trade (1964) 70 (C. Schmitthoff ed. 1964); Coquillette, Legal Ideology and Incorporation II: Sir Thomas Ridley, Charles Molloy, and the Literary Battle for the Law Merchant, 1607–1676, 61 B.U.L.Rev. 315, 346–70 (1981); Trakman, The Evolution of the Law Merchant: Our Commercial Heritage (pts. 1 & 2), 12 J.Mar.L. & Com. 1, 153 (1981).

2. Stat. 27 Edward III, Stat. 2 (1353).

1

merchant, presided and cases were tried before a merchant jury. With the advent of these courts a decline in the fair courts began and when, in 1477, legislation limited the jurisdiction of the piepowder courts to causes arising out of the fair at which the court sat, merchants began to take their cases in greater numbers to the staple courts, which were not so limited.

In the sixteenth century, control of the staple courts was given to officers of the king's court, and the common law courts began their interference in commercial cases. The merchants, unwilling to submit to the common law, retreated to the courts of admiralty, which then had a substantial commercial jurisdiction and which applied the law merchant. However, by the second half of the seventeenth century the common law courts, led by Lord Coke, had wrenched jurisdiction in all but the most maritime mercantile matters from the admiralty courts. At this point, common law lawyers and judges assumed roles which had previously been played by merchants and civilians. In 1690 Sir Josiah Child in his Discourse About Trade complained of ". . . his Majesties Court of Kings-Bench, where after great expences of Time and Money, it is well if we can make our own Council (being common lawyers) understand one half of our case, we being amongst them as in a foreign country, our Language strange to them, and theirs as strange to us."

The judges at Westminster were not versed in the problems of merchants and common law procedure was not conducive to the prompt adjudication of disputes. Their antipathy toward freedom of assignment was particularly distressing to merchants, many of whom resorted to commercial arbitration to stay out of court. In such cases as did come before the common law courts in the seventeenth century, testimony as to the customs of the law merchant began to be accepted, at first only in controversies where both litigants were merchants and, in the latter half of the seventeenth century, in cases involving nonmerchants. But by the turn of the century the practice changed and the court itself declared the custom which was then deemed to be a part of the common law. This simplified pleading and proof, for it was no longer necessary to establish by evidence the custom of merchants in each case, but it also lessened the influence of mercantile practices upon English courts. Nevertheless, custom played a leading role under Lord Mansfield, a Scot, Chief Justice of the King's Bench from 1756 to 1788, and England's greatest commercial judge.[3] Mansfield familiarized himself with commercial usages, selected a group of merchants that sat as a special jury to advise him on controversies between merchants, and thus translated custom into judicial precedent. Karl Llewellyn attributed the fact that more of

3. Mansfield's work in commercial law is detailed in C. Fifoot, Lord Mansfield Chapter 4 (1936). For a briefer account see W. Holdsworth, Some Makers of English Law 160–75 (1938). Mansfield's Scottish background is not irrelevant, for it may explain his receptiveness to civil law doctrines prevalent in Scotland.

the law merchant was absorbed into the law of negotiable instruments than into the law of sales to the accident that the significant mercantile sales cases of this time did not come before Mansfield.[4]

For a century after Mansfield's death the then common law of commercial transactions grew as case law, with relatively few statutory enactments. In 1882, however, the Bills of Exchange Act, drafted by Sir Mackenzie Chalmers, was enacted by Parliament. A decade later, Chalmers performed a similar service for the law of sales, resulting in the enactment of the Sale of Goods Act in 1893. This act, like its predecessor, was intended as a restatement of English law and in turning the case law of sales into statutory form, he followed advice, prompted by the difficulty of getting innovations through Parliament, that he should "reproduce as exactly as possible the existing law." [5] Both statutes are now in effect in England and much of the Commonwealth and are of importance in foreign trade as well as historically.

(b) American Unification. During the nineteenth century, commercial law in America had developed in part under the influence of England, with variations caused by differing treatment of the problem of reception. By 1890 every state had at least one statute on negotiable instruments, seven states led by California had comprehensive codes, and the result was chaotic. There was talk of federal legislation. A year later, under the leadership of New York, the National Conference of Commissioners on Uniform State Laws came into being and in 1895 it appointed John J. Crawford, of the New York bar, to draft a Uniform Negotiable Instruments Law, which it recommended for adoption in 1896.[6] It closely followed the Bills of Exchange Act in many respects. By 1924 every state had enacted it, with occasional variations in a few sections.

In 1902 the Commissioners appointed Professor Samuel Williston to draft a uniform law of sales. The Uniform Sales Act was approved by the Commissioners in 1906 and shows the strong influence of Chalmers' Sale of Goods Act, both in substance and language. It was enacted in over thirty states, the principal exceptions being in the South. There followed the Uniform Warehouse Receipts Act (1906) drafted by Professor Williston and Barry Mohun, the Uniform Bills of Lading Act (1909) drafted by Professor Williston, the Uniform Conditional Sales Act (1918) drafted by Professor Bogert, and the Uniform Trust Receipts Act (1933) drafted by Professor Llewellyn.

4. Llewellyn, Across Sales on Horseback, 52 Harv.L.Rev. 725, 742 (1939).

5. M. Chalmers, Sale of Goods Act p. x (13th ed. 1957) (introduction to the First Edition).

6. An expenditure of not more than two thousand dollars was authorized for the project. Report of the Fifth Annual Conference of Commissioners 14 (1895). Mr. Crawford's fee as draftsman was one thousand dollars. Report of the Sixth Annual Conference of Commissioners 7 (1896). The discussion of the draft at the 1896 Convention of the Commissioners lasted for only three days. 19 A.B.A. Reports 407 (1896).

Some legislation came from other sources. The Federal Bills of Lading or Pomerene Act (49 U.S.C. §§ 81–124), which is still in effect, was enacted by Congress in 1916 to govern bills of lading in exports and interstate shipments, and followed the wording of the uniform act in most respects. The Bank Collection Code, which was drafted in 1929 under the auspices of the American Bankers Association, supplemented the Negotiable Instruments Law in almost twenty states. Statutes on such subjects as bulk sales and factors' liens were first adopted by a few states on their own initiative and then borrowed by others so that they tended to follow uniform patterns. These uniform laws and related statutes are discussed in the notes in this casebook when an understanding of their provisions is important in solving problems under the Uniform Commercial Code.

(c) The Uniform Commercial Code. During the half-century after the first uniform acts, a number of proposals were made for change, and some states passed amendments to certain sections. A federal sales act was proposed in Congress in 1940, but the Commissioners succeeded in having it postponed. Work began in that year on a Uniform Revised Sales Act and in 1945 this project was expanded to concentrate upon a comprehensive Uniform Commercial Code. The American Law Institute joined forces with the National Conference of Commissioners in this effort, with Professor Karl Llewellyn as Chief Reporter, and Soia Mentschikoff as Associate Chief Reporter. A final Official Draft with extensive comments was prepared at a cost of over $400,000, was approved by the two sponsoring organizations in 1952, and was promptly enacted by Pennsylvania in April 1953, effective July 1, 1954.[7]

The Code is divided into the following articles: Article 1, General Provisions; Article 2, Sales; Article 3, Commercial Paper; Article 4, Bank Deposits and Collections; Article 5, Letters of Credit; Article 6, Bulk Transfers; Article 7, Warehouse Receipts, Bills of Lading and Other Documents of Title; Article 8, Investment Securities; Article 9, Secured Transactions; Sales of Accounts and Chattel Paper; Article 10, Effective Date and Repealer.[8] All but Article 8 are dealt with in this book.

In many areas the Code took an entirely new approach to problems. The New York Law Revision Commission began to study it in 1953 and in response to criticism, the sponsors of the Code published in 1955 a number of amendments in Supplement Number 1 to the 1952 Official Draft. The Commission held public hearings and retained consultants to study the draft,[9] and in 1956, after three years and the expenditure of some $300,000, it reported to the state legisla-

---

7. For further details and references see Honnold's account in New York Law Revision Commission, Study of Uniform Commercial Code, Vol. 1, 348 (1955).

8. A new Article 11, Effective Date and Transition Provisions, was added in

connection with the 1972 Amendments to Article 9.

9. The studies fill three volumes and were published in 1955. See fn. 7 supra. The hearings fill two volumes and were published in 1954.

ture that the Code was not satisfactory and would require comprehensive reexamination and revision. Contemporaneous revision by the Editorial Board produced the 1956 Recommendations for the Uniform Commercial Code and these Recommendations became the 1957 Official Edition, which was published with comments and minor revisions early in 1958.

By late 1961, thirteen states, including Pennsylvania, had adopted the 1958 Official Text of the Code, and the New York Law Revision Commission recommended its adoption in New York. It was enacted in 1962. Adoptions of the Code then proceeded at an accelerating pace and the Code has now been adopted by all states (Louisiana has adopted only Articles 1, 3, 4, 5, 7 and 8), by Congress for the District of Columbia and by the Legislature of the Virgin Islands. A list of these jurisdictions with effective dates is contained in the official edition of the Code.[10]

New York made, as did other states, a number of changes in the 1958 Official Text.[11] In order to curb this tendency away from uniformity, a Permanent Editorial Board for the Uniform Commercial Code was established in 1961 to pass upon amendments made or proposed by the states. Its Report No. 1 (1962) contains amendments of which it approved, and these were incorporated in the 1962 Official Text. Its Report No. 2 (1964) discusses those of which it did not approve. And its Report No. 3 (1967) proposed three more "official" and four "optional" amendments, and explained its rejection of many other amendments. Nevertheless, hundreds of changes were made by the various states in enacting the Code. Merely counting the changes grossly exaggerates the divergencies among the various enacted versions of the Code, but it drives home the fact that a careful practicing lawyer must work from statutory materials that embody the version of the Code actually enacted in the particular state.

In Report No. 3, the Board observed that by 1966, 337 non-uniform, non-official amendments had been made to the various sections of Article 9. California had been particularly active in this respect, but some sections had been amended in a non-uniform fashion by as many as 30 jurisdictions. Because of this and in the light of published criticism of Article 9, the Board appointed a Committee to conduct a "restudy in depth." The Committee worked from 1967 to

10. Courts have occasionally given the Code an anticipatory impact by applying its principles before its effective date. See, e.g., Williams v. Walker-Thomas Furniture Co., 121 U.S.App.D.C. 315, 350 F.2d 445 (1965) (adoption of UCC 2–302 subsequent to contracts in suit was "persuasive authority for following the rationale of the cases from which the section is explicitly derived"). Cf. United States v. Gleaners & Farmers Co-operative Elevator Co., 481 F.2d 104 (7th Cir.1973) (1972 Amendments to Article 9, even though not adopted, "aided" court in interpreting UCC 9–204); Domain Industries v. First Security Bank & Trust Co., 230 N.W.2d 165 (Iowa, 1975) (1972 Amendments to Article 9 "only clarified what was always the intended meaning").

11. See Penney, New York Revisits the Code: Some Variations in the New York Enactment of the Uniform Commercial Code, 62 Colum.L.Rev. 992 (1962).

1970, and then submitted what were to become, after revision, the 1972 Amendments to Article 9. They have been adopted by over two-thirds of the states.[12] Another committee of the Code's Permanent Editorial Board has prepared a revision of Article 8 for the "certificateless society," resulting in the 1977 amendments, adopted by a few states. The same committee has begun work on a revision of Articles 3 and 4 for the "checkless society."

(2) **Use of the Code and Comments.** The Code makes much less of an attempt than did the earlier legislation in Britain and the United States, to follow existing formulations of the law. Very little of the language of the Negotiable Instruments Law and the Uniform Sales Act is retained, and in some respects the Code takes a drastically new approach to the law. Professor Williston stated that some of the changes in the law of Sales under the Code "are not only iconoclastic but open to criticisms that I regard so fundamental as to preclude the desirability of enacting [the Sales Article] of the proposed Code." Professor Corbin was among those who took a different view.[13] We shall have a chance to consider the soundness of many of the changes made by the Code.

One question in working with the Code is the extent to which recourse is to be had to prior drafts as an aid to interpretation. The 1952 edition of the Code attempted to close the door on such legislative history by providing in UCC 1–102(3)(g): "Prior drafts of text and comments may not be used to ascertain legislative intent." The drafting process had, of course, been in the hands of the sponsors of the Code and not the state legislatures which ultimately enacted it. The explanation given in the Comments for the provision was, however, somewhat different from this: "Frequently matters have been omitted as being implicit without statement and language has been changed or added solely for clarity. The only safe guide to intent lies in the final text and comments."

Subsection (3)(g) was deleted as the result of the revisions leading to the 1957 and 1958 editions of the Code. The Comments to the 1956 Recommendations of the Editorial Board for the Uniform Commercial Code state that "paragraph (3)(g) was deleted because the changes from the text enacted in Pennsylvania in 1953 are clearly legitimate legislative history." Is this intended to suggest that changes made prior to the 1952 edition adopted in Pennsylvania are *not* clearly legit-

---

12. For a case giving interpretative effect to the 1972 amendments, see PPG Industries, Inc. v. Hartford Fire Insurance Co., 531 F.2d 58 (2d Cir.1976) (although 1972 amendment of UCC 9–306(1) "has not yet been adopted in New York, it is a persuasive indication of the effect which § 9–306 was originally intended to have"). For a summary of such cases, see In re Sexton, 16 B.R. 240 (Bkrtcy. Tenn.1981).

13. Compare Williston, The Law of Sales in the Proposed Uniform Commercial Code, 63 Harv.L.Rev. 561 (1950) with Corbin, The Uniform Commercial Code— Sales; Should it be Enacted? 59 Yale L.J. 821 (1950). See also Mellinkoff, The Language of the Uniform Commercial Code, 77 Yale L.J. 185 (1967), where the author states that "for all its substantive contributions, the UCC is a slipshod job of draftsmanship."

imate legislative history? And to what extent *should* changes made by a drafting group, unconnected to the legislature, be considered as legitimate legislative history? For an example of the use of legislative history, see Industrial National Bank v. Leo's Used Car Exchange, p. 188 infra.

A comparable question is the extent to which, in interpreting the Code, recourse should be had to the Comments that follow each section. A hazard for the lazy mind, and a help for the responsible lawyer, the Comments raise troublesome problems about their place in the Code system which need to be faced at the outset.

The most obvious point about the Comments is the one which, curiously enough, is most often overlooked: The text of the Code was enacted by the legislature; the Comments were not. One is tempted to ignore this point because the Comments, written in an explanatory and non-statutory style, are easier to read. *Facilis est descensus Averno.* But the tempter will whisper: The drafters wrote these Comments, did they not? If they say what the Code does, that is bound to be right, is it not? Why bother then with this prickly statutory language? (You may find it easier to resist these temptations if you put yourself, in your mind's eye, in the role of a judge to whom this argument has been made and then imagine your comments to that hapless attorney.)

The problem of the force of the Comments is sufficiently important to justify some background. The 1952 edition of the Code included as UCC 1–102(3)(f) a significant provision about the Comments: "The Comments of the National Conference of Commissioners on Uniform State Laws and the American Law Institute may be consulted in the construction and application of this Act but, if text and comment conflict, text controls."

The 1956 Recommendations of the Editorial Board for the Uniform Commercial Code deleted UCC 1–102(3)(f), and did not substitute any new provision on the status of the Comments. The question immediately arises: Does this deletion imply the rejection of the idea behind the deleted provision so that reference to the Comments has become illegitimate? An answer appears in the Comments to the 1956 Recommendations. The reasons for this and other changes were only briefly stated; the explanation for this change was as follows: "paragraph (3)(f) was deleted because the old comments were clearly out of date and it was not known when new ones could be prepared." [14]

Revised Comments accompanied the 1957 and 1958 versions of the Code, but without any statutory provision referring to them. But the

---

14. 1956 Recommendations 3. Perhaps we face here an engineering problem: How high can the comments lift themselves by their own boot-straps? See Braucher, The Legislative History of the Uniform Commercial Code, 58 Colum. L.Rev. 798, 808–10 (1958).

role of the Comments is discussed in the Comments themselves. Thus, the Comment to the Title of the Code (1962 Official Text, page 1) in part reads: "This Comment and those which follow are the Comments of the National Conference of Commissioners on Uniform State Laws and the American Law Institute. Uniformity throughout American jurisdictions is one of the main objectives of this Code; and that objective cannot be obtained without substantial uniformity of construction. To aid in uniform construction these Comments set forth the purpose of various provisions of this Act to promote uniformity, to aid in viewing the Act as an integrated whole, and to safeguard against misconstruction." This Comment continues with interesting material on the legislative history of the Code, but does not indicate to what extent the revision of the Comments was brought before the sponsoring organizations or reviewed by the draftsmen. Apparently this revision of the Comments was considered part of the final editorial work and entrusted to the faithful few who were carrying the Code project to its conclusion.

Embarrassing questions multiply if one subjects the Comments to the standards often imposed for recourse to legislative history. In some states the revised Comments had not yet been drafted at the time of the Code's adoption. In others it is highly doubtful that the Comments were laid before the legislators in the form of a committee report explaining the legislation which the legislators were asked to adopt.

It would be very wrong, however, to conclude that the Comments are without value to lawyers and to courts. Professor Williston's treatise on Sales was given heavy weight by courts in construing the Uniform Sales Act on the ground that it reflected the intent of the drafter, though it was written subsequent to the drafting of the Act;[15] courts have repeatedly quoted the Comments in construing the Code. Surely the Comments may be given at least as much weight as an able article or treatise construing the Code. It is equally clear that the Comments do not approach the weight of legislation; if the statutory provisions adopted by the legislature contradict or fail to support the Comments, the Comments must be rejected.[16] The point is significant, for we shall see instances, easily understood in the light of the Comments' bulk and the many successive revisions of the Code, where the Comments contradict the statute. More frequent are instances of enthusiastic discussion of significant problems

---

15. See Braucher, note 14 supra at 809. The Code sponsors criticized this use of Professor Williston's treatise as a "delegation to private persons of essentially legislative power." Id. at note 73. Is this criticism applicable to the use of the Comments to the Code?

16. See also Consolidated Film Industries v. United States, 547 F.2d 533 (10th Cir.1977) (refusing to follow Comment 5 to UCC 9–302 "in preference to the words of the statute and particularly so in view of the fact that Utah has not chosen to adopt it"); In re Bel Air Carpets, 452 F.2d 1210 (9th Cir.1971) (refusing to follow part of Comment 2 to UCC 2–702).

on which the statute is silent. (See, e.g., the Comment to the Title quoted above.)

A thorough job of construing the Code calls for using the Comments to make sure one has found the pertinent language of the statute, as a double-check on a tentative construction, and as a secondary aid where the language of the statute is ambiguous. However, the editors warn their students that they sternly reject any reference to Comments until *after* the pertinent statutory language has been carefully examined in the light of the statutory definitions and the statutory structure. Nuances concerning the precise weight which may be given the Comments must await further litigation testing the issue. For further helpful discussion, see Skilton, Some Comments on the Comments to the Uniform Commercial Code, 1966 Wis.L.Rev. 597.

Statutes first [handwritten marginal note]

A word of caution is also in order concerning the "Definitional Cross References" which are contained in the Comments. A careful lawyer will not rely on the completeness of these references in the Comments. For a thorough job the lawyer will check Article 1, which contains important provisions applicable to the Code as a whole; Section 1–201 contains the definitions (in alphabetical order) of forty-six terms used throughout the Code. In addition, the lawyer will check the definitions specially applicable to the article involved; in nearly every article there is a helpful section, e.g., UCC 2–103, 3–102, containing an "index of definitions." [17]

(3) General Principles and the Code. If the Code is more than a collection of statutes on separate though related subjects, it should be possible to discern some general principles that run throughout its various articles. The most likely candidate is the principle of good faith. UCC 1–203, which is applicable throughout the Code provides: "Every contract or duty within this Act imposes an obligation of good faith in its performance or enforcement."

The pervasive character of this requirement makes it important to understand the nature of the "obligation of good faith." Article 1 (UCC 1–201(19)) restricts "good faith" to "honesty in fact in the conduct or transaction concerned." This is the sense in which the term is used, for example, in Article 3. Article 2, however, contains a different definition: UCC 2–103(1)(b) provides that " 'Good faith' in the case of a merchant means honesty in fact and the observance of reasonable commercial standards of fair dealing in the trade." For the professional who comes within the definition of merchant in UCC 2–104(1), then, there is a special standard. And it will be noted that this

---

17. It should be observed, however, that only terms set out in quotation marks are generally included in the definitional cross references. Contrast "receipt" of goods (which is so set out in UCC 2–103(1)(c) and which is therefore included in the definitional cross references to, e.g., UCC 2–503, 2–509) with "acceptance" of goods (which is not so set out in UCC 2–606 and which is therefore not included in the definitional cross references to, e.g., UCC 2–607, 2–608). But cf. UCC 2–103(2), where "acceptance" is included in an "index of definitions."

is not merely the standard for protection of a purchaser in "good faith"; the requirement applies to every step of "performance or enforcement." [18]   Both the Code and Comments are strangely silent, however, on what is meant by "reasonable commercial standards of fair dealing in the trade."

A related provision is UCC 2–302, which deals with "unconscionable" contracts and clauses.   The most difficult problem under this section is the lack of any definition in the Code of the key concept of "unconscionability."   Comment 1 to UCC 2–302 seeks to meet this gap.   At one point, however, it refers to the "basic test" of whether the clause is "onesided"; at another the Comment states that "the principle is one of the prevention of oppression and unfair surprise (cf. Campbell Soup Co. v. Wentz, 172 F.2d 80 (3d Cir.1948)), and not of disturbance of allocation of risks because of superior bargaining power."   Can these two comments be reconciled? [19]   The Comment in addition states that "the underlying basis of the section is illustrated by the results in cases such as the following. . . ."   It then summarizes the holdings of ten cases.   Five of these involved narrow construction of clauses disclaiming implied warranties of quality; the Code deals with this problem specifically in UCC 2–316.   The remaining five cases limited the impact of clauses restricting remedies for breach, a problem covered in UCC 2–719.   Cf. UCC 2–718 (agreements for unreasonably large liquidated damage are void as a penalty).   Thus, even if these Comments are influential in construing the Code, the possible scope of Section 2–302, in areas not duplicated by UCC 2–316, 2–718 and 2–719, is left for case-law development.   We shall see the beginnings of this development at various places in this book.

Note, however, that the "unconscionability" rule of UCC 2–302 differs from the "good faith" rule of UCC 1–203 in that it appears in the article on Sales, and not the one on General Provisions.   Does this mean that the principle of "unconscionability" would have no relevance to, for example, a contract between a bank and its customer that was governed by Article 4, not Article 2?

The possibilities latent in these two general ideas, "good faith" (including "fair dealing") and "unconscionability" can best be appreciated in the light of rather similar concepts which are important in continental law.   One of these bars the "abuse of rights," which in its development in French law seems to be related to the exercise of

---

18. A literal (but certainly unintended) reading of UCC 2–103(1) would apply this broad requirement of "good faith" only to provisions of Article 2 that mention "good faith," and not to the general "good faith" requirement of Article 1 (UCC 1–203) when that requirement governs Article 2 transactions.

19. The conflicts in the drafting process that helped produce this ambiguity are exposed in Leff, Unconscionability and the Code—The Emperor's New Clause, 115 U.Pa.L.Rev. 485 (1967).   See also Ellinghaus, In Defense of Unconscionability, 78 Yale L.J. 757 (1969).

rights for an improper motive.[20] Broader and more suggestive of the rules of the Code is Section 242 of the German Civil Code: "The obligor is bound to perform the obligation in such a way as is required by the principles of *bona fides* with due regard to existing usage." Another helpful analogy is the famous provision of Article 2 of the Swiss Civil Code that "every person is bound to exercise his rights and fulfill his obligations according to the principles of good faith. The law does not protect the manifest abuse of a right."

Unlike judges in these civil law systems, Anglo-American judges have no generalized principle for the control of abuse of rights, and in dealing with the problem have had to expand limited precedents or categories like "forfeitures" and "penalties." True, civil law judges have difficulty in determining whether any given situation calls for the application of the general rule. But Professor Schlesinger makes the significant observation that in the common law, "When a case arises which does not fit into any of our narrower mental compartments, a common law court must either refuse relief or take the difficult, seemingly revolutionary step of expanding or exploding the existing compartments. In the same situation, a civil law court may find it easier to innovate, because it can rationalize the result as the mere 'application' of an established general principle." [21] The Uniform Commercial Code presents the interesting possibility that general principles have been made available for the control of conduct and of contracts that are not unlike the rules enunciated in the civil law systems.[22]

Is it wise to create different contract rules for contracts that fall within the Code than for other agreements? Is adoption of the Code likely to apply pressure for the drafting of a general code of contract law? Or will the ideas developed in the Code permeate the rest of the law of contracts? In this connection it is of interest that the Restatement (Second) of Contracts contains a section (§ 205) entitled "Duty of Good Faith and Fair Dealing" and one (§ 208) entitled "Unconscionable Contract or Term," both inspired by the comparable Code provision.[23]

20. See Gutteridge, Abuse of Rights, 5 Cambr.L.J. 22 (1933); L. Josserand, De l'Abus des Droits (1927); Note, 109 U.Pa. L.Rev. 401, 415–18 (1961).

21. R. Schlesinger, Comparative Law 530 (3d ed. 1970).

22. See Farnsworth, Good Faith Performance and Commercial Reasonableness Under the Uniform Commercial Code, 30 U.Chi.L.Rev. 666 (1963). On good faith generally, see Burton, Breach of Contract and the Common Law Duty to Perform in Good Faith, 94 Harv.L.Rev. 369 (1980); Burton, Good Faith Performance of a Contract Within Article 2 of the Uniform Commercial Code, 67 Iowa L. Rev. 1 (1981); Burton, More on Good Faith Performance: A Reply to Professor Summers, 69 Iowa L.Rev. 497 (1984); Gillette, Limitations on the Obligation of Good Faith, 1981 Duke L.J. 619; Muris, Opportunistic Behavior and the Law of Contracts, 65 Minn.L.Rev. 521 (1981); Summers, "Good Faith" in General Contract Law and the Sales Provisions of the Uniform Commercial Code, 54 Va.L.Rev. 195 (1968); Summers, The General Duty of Good Faith—Its Recognition and Conceptualization, 67 Cornell L.Rev. 810 (1982).

23. See generally Patterson & Schlesinger, Problems of Codification of Commercial Law, in 1 N.Y.L.Rev.Comm.,

(4) Special Legislation to Protect Consumers. In many of the
countries that have a commercial code the code's applicability depends on whether the transaction is classified as "commercial" by criteria derived either from the parties' status as "merchants" or from
the nature of the transaction as "mercantile." Lawyers schooled in
such a legal setting may be startled to learn that our Uniform Commercial Code extends to transactions among ordinary consumers and
that, with only a few exceptions, the rules are the same for both commercial and consumer transactions.

It must quickly be added that these general rules may lead to different results in commercial and in consumer settings. One example
is the rule of UCC 2–315 which gives the buyer special protection
when he relies "on the seller's skill or judgment"; similar flexibility
is inherent in the Code's rules on "good faith" and "unconscionability" that have just been discussed (pp. 9–11, supra). The point is that
the application of these rules does not depend on placing the parties
or the transaction in a "commercial" or "consumer" category.

One of the striking legal developments of the past two decades
has been the enactment of legislation designed to give special protection to "consumers." With respect to basic rules of law embraced
within the Uniform Commercial Code, Congress in the past has usually played a subsidiary role; in the field of consumer protection it has
taken the lead. In 1960 Senator Paul Douglas introduced his first
legislative proposal for "Truth in Lending." This proposal stimulated
countermeasures for state enactment, including the preparation by
the National Conference of Commissioners on Uniform State Laws of
a Uniform Consumer Credit Code (the "U3C"). The Uniform Consumer Credit Code was first promulgated in 1968 and provided the
basis for legislation in a number of states; a revised version was issued in 1974. In 1973 a Model Consumer Credit Act was issued by
The National Consumer Law Center. In the meantime, Congress
moved ahead with legislation based on Senator Douglas's early proposals: In 1968 Congress passed the Consumer Credit Protection Act;
Title I is the Truth in Lending Act. A more recent development is
the sweeping regulation of seller's warranties in the interests of consumers that became effective in 1975, under the Magnuson-Moss
Warranty Act.

(5) Uniform Laws for International Transactions. Important
steps have been taken to unify the law applicable to international
trade. Trade with the larger part of the world—the continent of Eu-

---

Study of the Uniform Commercial Code
37 (1955).

Consider also the possible influence on
the Code of common law principles pursuant to UCC 1–103. See Hillman, Construction of the Uniform Commercial
Code: UCC Section 1–103 and "Code"
Methodology, 18 B.C.Ind. & Com.L.Rev.

655 (1977); Nickles, Problems of Sources
of Law Relationships Under the Uniform
Commercial Code (pts. 1 & 2), 31 Ark.L.
Rev. 1, 171 (1977); Summers, General
Equitable Principles Under Section 1–103
of the Uniform Commercial Code, 72 Nw.
U.L.Rev. 906 (1978).

rope, the American republics to the south and much of Asia and Africa—carries Americans into legal systems that stem from unfamiliar roots; the differences in legal concepts are, of course, complicated by linguistic barriers.

Sales. One field for unification is the law applicable to the international sale of goods. As early as 1930 work toward this goal was under way in Europe, and in April 1964 a diplomatic conference at the Hague approved conventions establishing a Uniform Law on the International Sale of Goods and a Uniform Law on the Formation of Contracts for the International Sale of Goods. By 1972 sufficient ratifications, primarily by countries of Western Europe, had occurred to bring the conventions into force.

These two conventions broke the ground for international unification, but the lack of world-wide collaboration in their preparation stood in the way of general adoption. In 1966 the General Assembly of the United Nations provided for the creation of the United Nations Commission on International Trade Law (UNCITRAL). UNCITRAL's membership, limited to 36 states, is allocated among the regions of the world: Africa, 9; Asia, 7; Eastern Europe, 5; Latin America, 6; Western Europe and Others, 9. (This last region, the industrial West, includes Australia, Canada and the United States.) The United States has been a member from the outset, and has played an active role in UNCITRAL's work.

UNCITRAL promptly began work on a new international law that would meet the objections to the 1964 Conventions. By 1978 the Commission had unanimously approved a new draft Convention dealing with matters covered by both of the earlier laws. In 1980 a diplomatic conference of 62 states, after five weeks of intensive work, approved the United Nations Convention on Contracts for the International Sale of Goods. The Convention will go into force after adoption by ten states. In 1983, with the support of the American Bar Association, CISG was submitted for ratification to the United States Senate.[24]

Negotiable Instruments. A second field for unification involves the rules governing important negotiable instruments used in international payments—bills of exchange, promissory notes, checks. In this field, UNCITRAL is preparing conventions setting forth uniform rules applicable to a special negotiable instrument for use in international payments. The instrument would bear a legend stating that it was subject to the uniform rules and the rules would be brought into play if such an instrument were used.

24. For an introduction to CISG, see Farnsworth, The Vienna Convention: An International Law for the Sale of Goods, 1983 Southwestern Legal Foundation Symposium: Private Investors Abroad 121; Winship, New Rules for International Sales, 68 A.B.A.J. 1230 (1982). A definitive treatment can be found in J. Honnold, Uniform Law for International Sales (1982).

Other Fields. UNCITRAL has also been active in unification in other fields, notably arbitration and ocean carrier liability. The Commission's work is described in the UNCITRAL yearbooks. For further background material, see Symposium, UNCITRAL's First Decade, 79 Am.J.Comp.L. 201 (1979).

(6) Reference Materials. The most useful tool for research on the Code is the Uniform Commercial Code Reporting Service and Case Digest. This service gives local variations of the Code and Comments and brings together with a digest and index the rapidly growing body of case-law under the Code. Another helpful guide is W. Willier & H. Hart, Uniform Commercial Code Reporter-Digest.

On the Code as a whole, see J. White & R. Summers, Handbook of the Law Under the Uniform Commercial Code (2d ed. 1980); R. Braucher & R. Riegert, Introduction to Commercial Transactions (1977); R. Alderman & R. Dole, A Transactional Guide to the Uniform Commercial Code (2d ed. 1983). For an extremely brief treatment, see Stone, Uniform Commercial Code in a Nutshell (1975). On commercial paper, see F. Hart & W. Willier, Commercial Paper Under the Uniform Commercial Code (looseleaf); W. Hawkland, Commercial Paper (2d ed. 1979); E. Peters, A Negotiable Instruments Primer (2d ed. 1974); C. Weber & R. Speidel, Commercial Paper in a Nutshell (3d ed. 1982).

Part I

GOOD FAITH PURCHASE

INTRODUCTION

Introduction. This course, like the first-year course in contracts, is primarily concerned with consensual exchange transactions. In contracts, however, the emphasis was on the creation, scope and enforcement of rights to and duties of performance. Here the emphasis is on the transfer of personal property. Part I asks two questions about such transfers. First, to what extent does a good faith purchaser of property take free of conflicting claims of ownership to that property. Second, if the property consists of a right of some kind, to what extent does a good faith purchaser of that right take it free of the obligor's defenses with respect to it. Two types of property will be considered in connection with the first question: goods and rights evidenced by commercial paper (promissory notes). The latter will be considered again in connection with the second question.

Chapter 1

FREEDOM FROM CLAIMS OF OWNERSHIP

Prefatory Note. A key problem posed by the transfer of property is the extent to which an innocent transferee, who has given something in exchange for property, takes free of conflicting claims of ownership asserted by persons other than the transferor, e.g., a claim that the property was stolen or obtained by fraud from the rightful owner. According to Professor Grant Gilmore: "The triumph of the good faith purchaser has been one of the most dramatic episodes in our legal history. In his several guises, he serves a commercial function: he is protected not because of his praiseworthy character, but to the end that commercial transactions may be engaged in without elaborate investigation of property rights and in reliance on the possession of property by one who offers it for sale. . . ." Gilmore, The Commercial Doctrine of Good Faith Purchase, 63 Yale L.J. 1057 (1954).

15

Although our principal concern will be with the doctrine of good faith purchase in typical commercial situations, the doctrine also finds application in more exotic settings. Consider in this connection the case of the Afo-A-Kom, a statue sacred to the people of Kom, an isolated kingdom that is part of the United Republic of Cameroon, from whom it was stolen. In 1973, the Afo-A-Kom was located in the hands of a New York art dealer, who reportedly was offering it for sale for some $65,000. Following a report in the New York Times, the dealer agreed to return it "in deep sympathy with . . . the people of Kom," after having been paid, it was said, some $25,000 raised by private contribution to cover his costs of acquiring it and of shipping it back to Africa. Could he have been compelled to return it? If so, would he have been legally entitled to be reimbursed in the amount that he is said to have paid? Are more facts necessary? What facts? What conflicting policies does this example suggest? Might the civil law, from which the law of the United Republic of Cameroon is derived, resolve this conflict differently from the common law? (The question of which law governs is beyond the scope of this course.) [1]

The freedom of the "good faith purchaser" from claims of ownership is developed in the following series of problems involving goods and intangibles. The sources suggested for their solution are both contemporary (notably the provisions of the Code) and historical (notably seminal cases from past centuries that fashioned the principles embodied in the Code). (Where Code sections are cited, *read the relevant Comments as well and be sure to find other related sections* including those indexed under the definitional cross references.) As you look through the problems, ask yourself: To what extent would the Code suffice without some understanding of the history behind it, i.e., to what extent did the drafters of the Code assume at least some familiarity of traditional principles?

SECTION 1. GOODS

Problem 1. O owned cotton worth $100,000. A stole it and sold it to P, who paid A $100,000 for it, not suspecting that it was stolen. O sued P to replevy the cotton.

(a) What result? Does P have a right to be reimbursed by O for the $100,000 P paid for it? See UCC 2–403; Mowrey v. Walsh, infra; Law Reform Committee, Twelfth Report, infra; Explanatory Report on Draft Uniform Law, infra.

(b) Would it make a difference if A is in the cotton business?

---

1. For discussion of this and other international art thefts, see Bator, An Essay on the International Trade in Art, 34 Stan.L.Rev. 275, 277–82 (1982).

yes it would. 2-403
(2)

who is B? —merchant?

(c) Would it make a difference if A had sold it to B who had sold it to P? (As to P's recourse against B, see UCC 2–312.) Can you think of additional facts that would change the result in the case? [1] For a suggestion that O's rights against P might be prejudiced in some circumstances by obtaining an uncollectible judgment against A, see Linwood Harvestore v. Cannon, 427 Pa. 434, 235 A.2d 377 (1967).

Problem 2. O owned cotton worth $100,000. A fraudulently induced O to sell it to him. A sold it to P, who paid A $100,000 for it, not suspecting the fraud. O sues P to replevy the cotton.

(a) What result? See UCC 2–403; Mowrey v. Walsh, infra. (A consideration of the effect of UCC 2–702 is best left to a course on sales.) What result if O sues P in conversion? Would it make any difference if P is in business? In the cotton business? See UCC 1–201(19), 2–103(1)(b), 2–104(1).

(b) What result if P had paid A only $60,000? See Hollis v. Chamberlin, 243 Ark. 201, 419 S.W.2d 116 (1967) (buyer paid $500 for camper unit and did not know seller but "did know that the camper unit looked new and was worth at least $1,000 . . . and . . . apparently asked no questions concerning [seller's] title"); Liles Brothers & Son v. Wright, 638 S.W.2d 383 (Tenn.1982) (operator of septic tank service, who knew of thefts of equipment in his area, paid $11,000 for new backhoe worth about $20,000, took blank bill of sale, and did not receive usual warranty papers from seller who offered him "a good deal on *any* kind of equipment that he wanted"); cf. Cooper v. Pacific Automobile Insurance Co., 95 Nev. 798, 603 P.2d 281 (1979) (owner of bar bought used Cadillac in sale that "was for cash; was consummated in the nighttime and on a weekend; and, took place at a bar," and buyer "made no effort to verify any of the information given to him"). Would it make any difference if P had promised to pay $100,000, but has not yet paid anything? See UCC 1–201(44).

(c) What result if P, instead of buying the cotton from A, had taken it as security for a loan that P had extended to A six months earlier? See UCC 1–201(32), (33), (44).

(d) What result if P had bought the cotton at a sheriff's execution sale on levy by a judgment creditor? See UCC 1–201(32), (33); Mazer v. Williams Brothers Co., 461 Pa. 587, 337 A.2d 559 (1975).

Problem 3. O owned cotton worth $100,000. A fraudulently induced O to sell it to him for $100,000 payable in 10 days, having obtained 10 days credit by falsely representing that he was B, a responsible dealer in cotton. A sold the cotton to P, who paid A $100,000 for it, not suspecting the fraud. A did not pay for the cotton at the end of 10 days, and O sues P to replevy it. What result? See UCC 2–403; Cundy v. Lindsay, infra.

---

1. With respect to the availability to P of the defense that O had himself stolen the cotton, see Lieber v. Mohawk Arms, 64 Misc.2d 206, 314 N.Y.S.2d 510 (1970), involving the theft from an ex-GI of Hitler's personal belongings.

Problem 4. O owned cotton worth $100,000. A fraudulently induced O to sell it to him by giving O his check in that amount drawn on a bank in which he had no account. A sold the cotton to P, who paid A $100,000 for it, not suspecting the fraud. The check was dishonored, and O sues to replevy the cotton. What result? Would it make a difference if O had noted on his check, "This is a cash sale"? See UCC 2–403.

MOWREY v. WALSH

Supreme Court of New York, 1828.
8 Cowen 238.

Trover for cotton cloths; tried at the Washington Circuit, November 14th, 1826, before Walworth, C. Judge.

The case at the trial was briefly this: On the 16th of January, 1826, a person calling himself Samuel Stevens, came to the plaintiff's factory in Easton, Washington county, and presented a forged paper, purporting to be signed by Isaac Bishop, mentioning Stevens as a person who wished to purchase cotton goods, as one who might safely be trusted, and assuming to pay whatever amount the plaintiffs might supply him with. The plaintiffs' clerk sold to Stevens the cotton cloths in question, amounting to 172 dollars and 38 cents; and gave him a bill of the goods, which (goods) he took to Lansingburgh the next day, and sold to the defendant, for considerable less than the prices charged at the factory. The defendant's clerk testified, however, that the price was a fair one. The plaintiffs afterwards demanded the goods of the defendant, who refused to surrender them; and the present action was brought.

The judge charged that the goods were obtained fraudulently, but not feloniously; and, that if the defendant purchased them *bona fide,* and without notice of the fraud, (a matter which he left to the jury upon the evidence,) the plaintiffs could not recover.

Verdict for the defendant.

A motion was now made, in behalf of the plaintiffs, for a new trial.

SAVAGE, CH. J. It seemed to be conceded upon the argument that if the goods were taken feloniously, no title passed from the vendors; and they might pursue and take their goods wherever found. Such is the law in England, unless the stolen goods are sold fairly in market overt.[2] (2 Bl.Com. 449.) And as we have, in this state, no such market, (1 John. 471,) sales here can have no other effect than mere private sales in England. It follows that, in this state, any sale of stolen goods does not divest the title of the owner.

---

2. See Note 4, p. 24 infra. [Ed.]

It is proper, therefore, to inquire whether the goods in question were feloniously taken.

Larceny is defined, by East, to be the wrongful, or fraudulent taking or carrying away by any person, of the mere personal goods of another, from any place, with a felonious intent to convert them to his (the taker's) own use, and make them his own property, without the consent of the owner. (2 East's P.C. 553.) It is, therefore, important, in cases of delivery of possession by the owner, to inquire whether he intended to part with the possession or with the property; for if the latter, by whatever fraudulent means he was induced to give the credit, it cannot be felony. (2 East's P.C. 668.) . . .

The delivery of the goods in question to Stevens was clearly intended as an absolute sale. It was not, therefore, a case of larceny.

The jury have found that the goods were fairly purchased by the defendant of Stevens, without any notice of the fraud; and in my opinion the testimony fully warrants their finding.

The question then arises, upon a case where the goods are obtained by fraud from the true owner, and fairly purchased of, and the price paid to the fraudulent vendee, without notice, by a stranger, which is to sustain the loss, the owner or the stranger? . . .

Parker v. Patrick, (5 T.R. 175), seems to be in point for the defendant. In that case, goods had been fraudulently obtained from the defendant, and pawned, for a valuable consideration, and without notice, to the plaintiff. After conviction of the offender, the defendant obtained possession of his goods, but by what means does not appear. It was contended that the plaintiff, the innocent pawnee, could not recover; as he derived title through a fraud, and was like a person deriving title from a felon. But Lord Kenyon thought the cases distinguishable; and the plaintiff had a verdict. A motion to set aside this verdict was refused; the court saying that the statute of 21 H. 8 ch. 21, did not extend to the case of goods obtained by fraud, but only to a felonious taking of them. By that statute, the owner of stolen goods is entitled to restitution, on conviction of the felon. But as that statute did not apply to a fraudulent obtaining of goods, the owner was not entitled to restitution. The question, then, was purely at common law; and the innocent pawnee was allowed to recover against the owner, whose goods had been obtained from him by fraud. According to that decision, had the plaintiffs in this case succeeded in getting their goods in any other way than by voluntary delivery from the defendant, he would be entitled to recover against them. The same principle was adopted by this court in M'Carty v. Vickery, (12 John. 348,) where it was decided, that after a delivery of goods sold, the vendor cannot bring trespass, although the sale was procured by fraud. The court say the property was changed.

Hollingsworth v. Napier, (3 Caines, 182,) was like Parker v. Patrick. The defendant had sold the cotton to Kinworthy, for cash payable on delivery. The defendant, in fact, delivered it by giving an order on the storekeeper without receiving payment. Kinworthy sold it *bona fide* to the plaintiff, though there were some suspicious circumstances. The plaintiff took possession, and the defendant afterwards took and sold it. The plaintiff recovered a verdict; and this court refused to set it aside. Kinworthy's purchase was palpably fraudulent, and so considered by the court.

The plaintiff's counsel relies on a case lately tried in the English common pleas: Tamplin v. Addy, sheriff of Warwickshire. In that case, goods were fraudulently purchased of the plaintiffs by one Staunton. After the delivery of the goods to Staunton, they were levied on by the defendant under an execution, and sold. Best, Ch. J., does indeed lay down the broad proposition, that if the goods were obtained by fraud, the right remained in the original owner, no matter into whose hands they found their way. That proposition was advanced at *nisi prius*; but is certainly at variance with settled principles of law.

It is, no doubt, true, if confined to the parties in the fraud. But it does not extend to an innocent purchaser. Perhaps, too, it may be correct in the particular case. The judgment creditor had not advanced money upon these goods, and his loss placed him in no worse situation than he was in before the fraud. But surely, in point of equity, there is a great difference between the fraudulent purchaser and an innocent one. The case of Noble v. Adams, (7 Taunt. 59,) decides, that between the parties, a fraudulent purchase gives no title; but the case of Parker v. Patrick was admitted to be good law by the counsel for the party defrauded.

The case of Bristol v. Wilsmore, (1 B. & C. 514,) was not cited on the argument; but it is in point to shew the true principle which supports the *nisi prius* decision of Ch. J. Best. The principle is this: that the fraudulent purchaser having no title, and the sheriff having no power to seize and sell any thing but the title of such purchaser, the sheriff's sale did not divest the title of the true owner, the defendant in the execution having no right or title to be sold. (And see Van Cleef v. Fleet, 15 John. 147.)

On the whole, therefore, I am of opinion that the innocent purchaser for valuable consideration must be protected; and the motion for a new trial must be denied.

New trial denied.

NOTES

(1) **"Merchants" and "Good Faith."** In the opinion in Mowrey v. Walsh, the trial judge is said to have charged "that if the defendant purchased them bona fide, and without notice of the fraud, . . . the plaintiffs could not recover." Assuming that the defendant dealt in cotton goods, would the plaintiff have had grounds for objection to this charge under the Code? See UCC 2–103(1)(b), 2–104(1). As to

who is a merchant, see Dolan, The Merchant Class of Article 2: Farmers, Doctors, and Others, 1977 Wash.U.L.Q. 1; McDonnell, Purposive Interpretation of the Uniform Commercial Code: Some Implications for Jurisprudence, 126 U.Pa.L.Rev. 795, 801–09 (1978); Newell, The Merchant of Article 2, 7 Valparaiso L.Rev. 307 (1973).

(2) **Voidable Title.** The seminal case in this area is the English case of Parker v. Patrick, decided in 1793 and cited and followed in Mowrey v. Walsh.[3] In its one sentence per curiam opinion the court gave only the reason mentioned by the New York court for distinguishing fraud and theft—the existence of a statute as to the latter. By the time of White v. Garden, 10 Common Bench, 919, 138 Eng. Rep. 364 (Q.B.1851), however, doctrine had developed to the point that the court could write that where fraud was involved, "the transaction is not absolutely void, except at the option of the seller; that he may elect to treat it as a contract, and he must do the contrary before the buyer has acted as if it were such, and re-sold the goods to a third party."

Professor Gilmore has summarized the historical development: "The initial common law position was that equities of ownership are to be protected at all costs: an owner may never be deprived of his property rights without his consent. That worked well enough against a background of local distribution where seller and buyer met face to face and exchanged goods for cash. But as the marketplace became first regional and then national, a recurrent situation came to be the misappropriation of goods by a faithless agent in fraud of his principal. Classical theory required that the principal be protected and that the risks of agency distribution be cast on the purchaser. The market demanded otherwise.

"The first significant breach in common law property theory was the protection of purchasers from such commercial agents. The reform was carried out through so-called Factor's Acts, which were widely enacted in the early part of the 19th century. Under these Acts any person who entrusted goods to a factor—or agent—for sale took the risk of the factor's selling them beyond his authority; anyone buying from a factor in good faith, relying on his possession of the goods, and without notice of limitations on his authority, took good title against the true owner. In time the Acts were expanded to protect people, i.e., banks, who took goods from a factor as security for loans made to the factor to be used in operating the factor's own business. The Factor's acts, as much in derogation of the common law as it is possible for a statute to be, were restrictively construed and consequently turned out to be considerably less than the full grant of mercantile liberty which they had first appeared to be. Oth-

---

3. For a discussion of Mowrey v. Walsh in its historical context, see Weinberg, Markets Overt, Voidable Titles, and Feckless Agents: Judges and Efficiency in the Antebellum Doctrine of Good Faith Purchase, 56 Tul.L.Rev. 1, 23–32 (1981).

er developments in the law gradually took the pressure off the Factor's Acts, which came to be confined to the narrow area of sales through commission merchants, mostly in agricultural produce markets.

"Even while they were cutting the heart out of the Factor's Acts, the courts were finding new ways to shift distribution risks. Their happiest discovery was the concept of 'voidable title'—a vague idea, never defined and perhaps incapable of definition, whose greatest virtue, as a principle of growth, may well have been its shapeless imprecision of outline. The polar extremes of theory were these: if *B* buys goods from *A*, he gets *A*'s title and can transfer it to any subsequent purchaser; if *B* steals goods from *A*, he gets no title and can transfer none to any subsequent purchaser, no matter how clear the purchaser's good faith. 'Voidable title' in *B* came in as an intermediate term between the two extremes: if *B* gets possession of *A*'s goods by fraud, even though he has no right to retain them against *A*, he does have the power to transfer title to a good faith purchaser.

"The ingenious distinction between 'no title' in *B* (therefore true owner prevails over good faith purchaser) and 'voidable title' in *B* (therefore true owner loses to good faith purchaser) made it possible to throw the risk on the true owner in the typical commercial situation while protecting him in the noncommercial one. Since the law purported to be a deduction from basic premises, logic prevailed in some details to the detriment of mercantile need, but on the whole voidable title proved a useful touchstone.

"The contrasting treatment given to sales on credit and sales for cash shows the inarticulate development of the commercial principle. When goods are delivered on credit, the seller becomes merely a creditor for the price: on default he has no right against the goods. But when the delivery is induced by buyer's fraud—buyer being unable to pay or having no intention of paying—the seller, if he acts promptly after discovering the facts, may replevy from the buyer or reclaim from buyer's trustee in bankruptcy. The seller may not, however, move against purchasers from the buyer, and the term 'purchaser' includes lenders who have made advances on the security of the goods. By his fraudulent acquisition the buyer has obtained voidable title and purchasers from him are protected." Gilmore, The Commercial Doctrine of Good Faith Purchase, 63 Yale L.J. 1057–60 (1954).[4]

Suppose that the defrauded owner discovers the fraud after the fraudulent buyer has disappeared with the goods. How can the owner avoid the passage of title so as to prevail over a subsequent good faith purchaser? Cases on this point are rare. See Car and Universal Finance Co. v. Caldwell, [1965] 1 Q.B. 525.[5]

4. Reproduced with permission of the Yale Law Journal.

5. That case was singled out for criticism in both the English and Ontario studies discussed in Note 4, p. 39 infra. Here is the Ontario view. "Under existing law, a rogue who has a 'voidable' title can transfer good title to a *bona*

(3) Nemo Dat v. Possession Vaut Titre. "It is necessary in every legal system to reconcile the conflict that arises when a seller purports to transfer title of goods that he does not own, or that are subject to an undisclosed security interest, to a person who buys them in good faith and without notice of the defect in title. The alternative means of resolving this conflict are usually stated in terms of a policy favouring security of ownership, as opposed to a policy that favours the safety of commercial transactions. Few, if indeed any, legal systems have committed themselves fully to the adoption of one or other solution. Between these extremes there lies a range of compromise solutions that depend on the nature of the goods, the persons involved, and the type of transaction." 2 Ontario Law Reform Commission, Report on Sale of Goods 283 (1979).[6]

The common law begins with the principle that a buyer acquires no better title to goods than the seller had, a principle embodied in the maxim *nemo dat quod non habet* (one cannot give what one does not have). To this principle the common law admits a number of exceptions, the most significant of which has been the doctrine of voidable title for cases of fraud.

The civil law, however, begins with a very different principle under which the good faith purchaser of goods is generally protected against the original owner, a principle expressed in the phrase *possession vaut titre* (possession is equivalent to title). Civil law systems have therefore no need for a doctrine of voidable title for cases of fraud. But most such systems make an exception for cases of theft, allowing the original owner of stolen goods to reclaim them from a good faith purchaser within a statutory period of, in French law, three years. Some of these systems, however, protect the good faith

fide third party purchaser for value, unless the sale is avoided prior to the disposition of the goods to the third party. In the *Caldwell* case, the Court held that, where the fraudulent buyer has disappeared, a substitutional form of notice, such as notification of the police or Automobile Association, is sufficient to rescind the sale. The Law Reform Committee drew attention to the hardship that this decision may cause to third parties, and recommended that the rule should be changed to require notice of rescission to the rogue. It is not easy to see how this recommendation will relieve the hardship to the third party since, *ex hypothesi*, he will not know of the rescission. The Committee thought the third party would be sufficiently protected in the great majority of cases, since it will usually be impractical for the original owner to communicate with the rogue. It seems curious that the third party's position should depend on the accessibility of the rogue.

"It appears to us that the Committee failed to come to grips with a more fundamental question: namely, whether it should be necessary that rescission be accompanied by the recovery of possession, and whether, in the meantime, the buyer should retain his power to transfer good title. . . . [We recommend a] provision to the effect that a purported avoidance of such a contract shall not affect the position of a third party who has purchased the goods in good faith, unless the goods are recovered by the owner before they are delivered to the third party by the person in possession of the goods." 2 Ontario Law Reform Commission, Report on Sale of Goods 287–88 (1979).

6. For an economic analysis of the problem, see Weinberg, Sales Law, Economics, and the Negotiability of Goods, 9 J. Legal Stud. 569 (1980).

purchaser who has acquired stolen goods at a fair or at a market or from a merchant who deals in similar goods by requiring the purchaser to return the goods to the original owner only on reimbursement of the purchase price. See International Institute for the Unification of Private Law (UNIDROIT), Draft Uniform Law on the Protection of the Bona Fide Purchaser of Corporeal Movables with Explanatory Report 5–9 (1968).

(4) Market Overt.   English law makes an exception to the principle of *nemo dat* by protecting the good faith purchaser of stolen goods where the goods "are sold in market overt according to the usage of the market." Sale of Goods Act § 22(1). A market overt is an open and public market. In Wheelwright v. Depeyster, 1 Johns. 471, 480 (N.Y.1806), Kent rejected a contention based on the notion of a market overt: "I know of no usage or regulation within this State, no Saxon institution of *market-overt,* which controls or interferes with the application of the common law."

(5) Statute of Limitations.   When is the original owner of stolen goods barred by the statute of limitations from reclaiming them? The Supreme Court of New Jersey faced this question in O'Keeffe v. Snyder, 83 N.J. 478, 416 A.2d 862 (1980), in which the noted artist Georgia O'Keeffe sought in 1976 to replevy from a Princeton art gallery three of her pictures that had allegedly been stolen in 1946 from a New York art gallery.

At the outset, the Supreme Court decided that O'Keeffe's claim was governed by the New Jersey statute of limitations, which required that an action for replevin be commenced within six years after the accrual of the cause of action. (O'Keeffe had contended her claim was governed by the New York statute of limitations, since it had been so interpreted that it did not begin to run until after refusal upon demand for the return of the goods.)

The Supreme Court then rejected the conclusion of the Appellate Division, based on New Jersey precedents, "that an action might have accrued more than six years before the date of suit if possession by the defendant or his predecessors satisfied the elements of adverse possession." Instead, it applied a discovery rule, under which "O'Keeffe's cause of action accrued when she first knew, or reasonably should have known through the exercise of due diligence, of the cause of action, including the identity of the possessor of the paintings . . .. The discovery rule shifts the emphasis from the conduct of the possessor to the conduct of the owner. The focus of the inquiry will no longer be whether the possessor has met the tests of adverse possession, but whether the owner has acted with due diligence in pursuing his or her personal property . . .. Under the doctrine of adverse possession, the burden is on the possessor to prove the elements of adverse possession . . .. Under the discovery rule, the burden is on the owner as the one seeking the benefit of the rule to establish facts that would justify deferring the beginning of the period of limitations."

The Supreme Court also concluded that subsequent transfer of the stolen property did not constitute "separate acts of conversion that would start the statute of limitations running anew. . . . The majority and better view is to permit tacking, the accumulation of consecutive periods of possession by parties in privity with each other." The court recognized, however, that "subsequent transfers . . . may affect the degree of difficulty encountered by a diligent owner seeking to recover his goods. To that extent, subsequent transfers and their potential for frustrating diligence are relevant in applying the discovery rule."

A vigorous dissent argued that the majority opinion placed too heavy a burden on the original owner and that "by making it relatively more easy for the receiver or possessor of an artwork with a 'checkered background' to gain security and title than for the artist or true owner to reacquire it, it seems as though the Court surely will stimulate and legitimize art thievery." After remand by the Supreme Court but before trial, the case was settled.

For a fascinating case involving an international controversy over the ownership of two paintings by Albrecht Dürer that had disappeared from Germany after the Second World War (the "discovery of the century," according to an official of the Metropolitan Museum of Art), see Kunstsammlungen zu Weimar v. Elicofon, 678 F.2d 1150 (2d Cir.1982). The court applied New York law, under which "an innocent purchaser of stolen goods becomes a wrongdoer only after refusing the owner's demand for their return." Where, as under New York law, "the demand requirement is *substantive,* that is, where a demand and refusal are requisite elements of the cause of action, it accrues and the statute of limitation begins to run only after such demand and refusal."

The court rejected the contention that the rule treats good faith purchasers as worse than thieves "since for a thief the statute of limitations begins to run immediately upon the theft while a *bona fide* purchaser must wait, possibly indefinitely, for a demand from the owner." The court thought that "familiar principles of equitable estoppel will prevent a wrongdoer from asserting the statute of limitations defense" and, in any case, "we are charged only with applying New York law, not with remaking or improving it."

CUNDY V. LINDSAY, 1878 L.R. 3 A.C. 459 (H.L.). Alfred Blenkarn hired a room on the top floor of a house down the street from the firm of W. Blenkiron & Son. He wrote letters appearing to come from "Blenkiron & Co." but giving his address down the street, ordering linen handkerchiefs on credit from Lindsay & Co. Lindsay, who knew of the respectability of W. Blenkiron & Sons, but not the address, sent handkerchiefs to "Blenkiron & Co." at Blenkarn's address. Blenkarn sold some of them to Cundy, a good faith purchaser, who resold them in the course of their business. Blenkarn failed to pay Lindsay and was ultimately prosecuted and convicted. Lindsay then sued Cundy in conversion. From a judgment for Lindsay, Cundy appealed.

"THE LORD CHANCELLOR (LORD *Cairns*): . . . Now, my Lords, there are two observations bearing upon the solution of that question which I desire to make. In the first place, if the property in the goods in question passed, it could only pass by way of contract . . . . The second observation is this, . . . the whole history of the whole transaction lies upon paper. The principal parties concerned, the Respondents and *Blenkarn*, never came in contact personally—everything that was done was done by writing. What has to be judged of, and what the jury in the present case had to judge of, was merely the conclusion to be derived from that writing, as applied to the admitted facts of the case.

"Now, my Lords, discharging that duty and answering that inquiry, what the jurors have found . . . that by the form of the signatures to the letters which were written by *Blenkarn*, by the mode in which his letters and his applications to the Respondents were made out, and by the way in which he left uncorrected the mode and form in which, in turn, he was addressed by the Respondents; that by all those means he led, and intended to lead, the Respondents to believe, and they did believe, that the person with whom they were communicating was not *Blenkarn*, the dishonest and irresponsible man, but was a well known and solvent house of *Blenkiron & Co.*, doing business in the same street. . . . Now, my Lords, stating the matter shortly in that way, I ask the question, how is it possible to imagine that in that state of things any contract could have arisen between the Respondents and *Blenkarn*, the dishonest man? Of him they knew nothing, and of him they never thought. With him they never intended to deal. Their minds never, even for an instant of time rested upon him, and as between him and them there was no *consensus* of mind which could lead to any agreement or any contract whatever. As between him and them there was merely the one side to a contract, where, in order to produce a contract, two sides would be required. With the firm of *Blenkiron & Co.* of course there was no contract, for as to them the matter was entirely unknown, and therefore the pretence of a contract was a failure."

[Affirmed.]

NOTES

(1) **Impostors.** Four decades after Cundy v. Lindsay, the New York Court of Appeals heard a very similar case, Phelps v. McQuade, 220 N.Y. 232, 115 N.E. 441 (1917). Walter J. Gynne falsely represented to Phelps that he was Baldwin J. Gwynne, a man of financial

responsibility, and Phelps delivered jewelry to Walter on credit, which Walter sold to McQuade. When the fraud was discovered, Phelps sued McQuade in replevin to recover the jewelry. The Court of Appeals affirmed a judgment for McQuade. It distinguished Cundy v. Lindsay on the ground that it involved impersonation by mail rather than face to face impersonation. "The fact that the vendor deals with the person personally rather than by letter is immaterial, except in so far as it bears upon the question of intent. Where the transaction is a personal one, the seller intends to transfer title to a person of credit, and he supposes the one standing before him to be that person. He is deceived. But in spite of that fact his primary intention is to sell his goods to the person with whom he negotiates. Where the transaction is by letter the vendor intends to deal with the person whose name is signed to the letter. He knows no one else. He supposes he is dealing with no one else. And while in both cases other facts may be shown that would alter the rule, yet in their absence, in the first, title passes; in the second, it does not." Does UCC 2–403(1)(a) make an exception for impersonation by mail?[7] Is it as explicit in this regard as UCC 3–405(1)(a)? Is the difference between these two sections significant?

(2) **The "Cash Sale" Doctrine.** UCC 2–403(1)(b) and (c) are intended to stamp out the "cash sale" doctrine, exemplified by Young v. Harris-Cortner Co., 152 Tenn. 15, 268 S.W. 125 (1924). Young, a farmer, sold cotton to McNamee, a middleman, who resold to Harris-Cortner, cotton merchants. McNamee paid by a check drawn on insufficient funds, and when it was dishonored because of lack of funds, Young sued Harris-Cortner to replevy the cotton. Young prevailed. "Looking to the intention of the parties, which is the governing principle, we are satisfied that Young purposed to transfer title to the cotton only upon receiving cash therefor . . ... We are therefore of the opinion that title to said ten bales of cotton never passed from Young to McNamee. . . . A farmer brings his cotton, tobacco, or wheat to town for sale and sells same, and, as a general rule, is paid by check, although all of such sales are treated as cash transactions. If, in such a case, the purchaser can immediately resell to an innocent party and convey good title, it would follow that vendors would refuse to accept checks and would require the actual money, which would result in great inconvenience and risk to merchants engaged in buying such produce since it would require them to keep on hand large sums of actual cash." Does the "cash sale" doctrine seem more in keeping with an agricultural or an industrial economy?

---

7. In the study discussed in Note 4, p. 39 infra, the Ontario Law Reform Commission recommended "a provision stating that a purchaser shall be deemed to have a voidable title notwithstanding that the transferor was deceived as to the identity of the purchaser or the presence of some other mistake affecting the validity of the contract of sale." 2 Ontario Law Reform Commission, Report on Sale of Goods 287 (1979).

Problem 5. O owned cotton worth $100,000. O placed it in storage with A, who both stores cotton and buys and sells it. A wrongfully sold the cotton to P, who did not suspect A's wrongdoing, for $100,000. O sues P to replevy the cotton.

(a) What result? See UCC 2–403, 1–201(9); Porter v. Wertz, infra; Simonds-Shields-Theis Grain Co. v. Far-Mar-Co., 575 F.Supp. 290 (W.D.Mo.1983) (owner entrusted soybeans to independent trucker who also sold soybeans).

(b) What result if P had promised to pay $100,000, but has not yet paid it when O claims the cotton?

(c) What result if P, instead of buying the cotton from A, had taken it as security for a loan that P had extended to A six months earlier? See In re Sitkin Smelting & Refining, Inc., 639 F.2d 1213 (5th Cir.1981). Compare Problem 2(c) (p. 17).

(d) What result if A had wrongfully delivered the cotton to B, who is in the cotton business, as security for a loan that B had extended to A six months earlier and B had sold the cotton to P, who suspected nothing, for $100,000. See Leary & Sperling, The Outer Limits of Entrusting, 35 Ark.L.Rev. 50, 55–60, 66–71 (1981).

PORTER v. WERTZ

New York Supreme Court, Appellate Division, First Department, 1979.
68 A.D. 2d 141, 416 N.Y.S.2d 254.

BIRNS, JUSTICE: Plaintiffs-appellants, Samuel Porter and Express Packaging, Inc. (Porter's corporation), owners of a Maurice Utrillo painting entitled "Chateau de Lion-sur-Mer", seek in this action to recover possession of the painting or the value thereof from defendants, participants in a series of transactions which resulted in the shipment of the painting out of the country. The painting is now in Venezuela.

Defendants-respondents Richard Feigen Gallery, Inc., Richard L. Feigen & Co, Inc. and Richard L. Feigen, hereinafter collectively referred to as Feigen, were in the business of buying and selling paintings, drawings and sculpture.

The amended answer to the complaint asserted, *inter alia*, affirmative defenses of statutory estoppel (UCC, § 2–403) and equitable estoppel.[1] The trial court, after a bench trial, found statutory estoppel inapplicable but sustained the defense of equitable estoppel and dismissed the complaint.

---

1. The defense of equitable estoppel was not contained in the original answer. At the close of the trial, Feigen moved to amend the answer to include that defense. We are not at all certain that amendment of the pleading should have been allowed at that point. In any event, as the defense was raised, we will consider it.

On this appeal, we will consider whether those defenses, or either of them, bar recovery against Feigen. We hold neither prevents recovery.[2]

Porter, the owner of a collection of art works, bought the Utrillo in 1969. During 1972 and 1973 he had a number of art transactions with one Harold Von Maker who used, among other names, that of Peter Wertz.[3] One of the transactions was the sale by Porter to Von Maker in the spring of 1973 of a painting by Childe Hassam for $150,000, financed with a $50,000 deposit and 10 notes for $10,000 each. At about that time, Von Maker expressed an interest in the Utrillo. Porter permitted him to have it temporarily with the understanding that Von Maker would hang it in his (Von Maker's) home,[4] pending Von Maker's decision whether to buy the painting. On a visit to Von Maker's home in Westchester in May 1973, Porter saw the painting hanging there. In June 1973, lacking a decision from Von Maker, Porter sought its return, but was unable to reach Von Maker.

The first note in connection with Von Maker's purchase of the Childe Hassam, due early July 1973, was returned dishonored, as were the balance of the notes. Porter commenced an investigation and found that he had not been dealing with Peter Wertz—but with another man named Von Maker. Bishop reports, dated July 10 and July 17, 1973, disclosed that Von Maker was subject to judgments, that he had been sued many times, that he had an arrest record for possession of obscene literature, and for "false pretenses", as well as for "theft of checks", and had been convicted, among other crimes, of transmitting a forged cable in connection with a scheme to defraud the Chase Manhattan Bank and had been placed on probation for three years. Porter notified the FBI about his business transactions concerning the notes. He did not report that Von Maker had defrauded him of any painting, for, as will be shown, Porter did not know at this time that Von Maker had disposed of the Utrillo.

2. We note that the appeal is from the trial court's determination that equitable estoppel constitutes a bar to the action. However, because the enactment of statutory estoppel (UCC, § 2–403) was intended to embrace prior uniform statutory provisions and case law thereunder (so as "to continue unimpaired all rights acquired under the law of agency or of apparent agency or ownership or other estoppel"), and to state a unified and simplified policy on good faith purchase of goods (see Practice Commentary, Alfred A. Berger and William J. O'Connor, Jr., McKinney's Cons.Laws of N.Y., Book 62½, p. 395), we find it necessary to enter into some discussion of section 2–403 of the Uniform Commercial Code.

3. As will be seen, Peter Wertz was a real person, at least an acquaintance of Von Maker; who permitted Von Maker to use his name. Von Maker's true name was Harold Maker, presumably he was born in New Jersey. Apparently Maker added the prefix "Von" to his name to indicate nobility of birth.

4. It is questioned as to where Porter believed Von Maker was living at the time. Respondents claim Porter knew only that Von Maker had a townhouse in Manhattan, whereas Porter testified he was aware Von Maker had two residences, one of them being in Westchester County. There is no support in the record for the trial court's finding that the painting was to be hung only in the Manhattan townhouse.

Porter did, however, have his attorney communicate with Von Maker's attorney. As a result, on August 13, 1973, a detailed agreement, drawn by the attorneys for Porter and Von Maker, the latter still using the name Peter Wertz, was executed. Under this agreement the obligations of Von Maker to Porter concerning several paintings delivered by Porter to Von Maker (one of which was the Utrillo) were covered. In paragraph 11, Von Maker acknowledged that he had received the Utrillo from Porter together with a certain book [5] on Utrillo, that both "belong to (Porter)", that the painting was on consignment with a client of Von Maker's, that within 90 days Von Maker would either return the painting and book or pay $30,000 therefor, and that other than the option to purchase within said 90-day period, Von Maker had "no claim whatsoever to the Utrillo painting or Book."

Paragraph 13 provided that in the event Von Maker failed to meet the obligations under paragraph 11, i.e., return the Utrillo and book within 90 days or pay for them, Porter would immediately be entitled to obtain possession of a painting by Cranach held in escrow by Von Maker's attorney, and have the right to sell that painting, apply the proceeds to the amount owing by Von Maker under paragraph 11, and Von Maker would pay any deficiency. Paragraph 13 provided further that "[t]he above is in addition to all [Porter's] other rights and remedies which [Porter] expressly reserved to enforce the performance of [Von Maker's] obligations under this Agreement."

We note that the agreement did not state that receipt of the Cranach by Porter would be in full satisfaction of Porter's claim to the Utrillo and book. Title to the Utrillo and book remained in Porter, absent any payment by Von Maker of the agreed purchase price of $30,000. Indeed, no payment for the Utrillo was ever made by Von Maker.

At the very time that Von Maker was deceitfully assuring Porter he would return the Utrillo and book or pay $30,000, Von Maker had already disposed of this painting by using the real Peter Wertz to effect its sale for $20,000 to Feigen. Von Maker, utilizing Sloan and Lipinsky, persons in the art world, had made the availability of the Utrillo known to Feigen. When Wertz, at Von Maker's direction, appeared at the Feigen gallery with the Utrillo, he was met by Feigen's employee, Mrs. Drew-Bear. She found a buyer for the Utrillo in defendant Brenner. In effecting its transfer to him, Feigen made a commission. Through a sale by Brenner the painting is now in Venezuela, S.A.

We agree with the conclusion of the trial court that statutory estoppel does not bar recovery.

5. The book, entitled "Petrides on Utrillo", was purchased by Porter in 1971 in Paris for the sum of $200.00.

The provisions of statutory estoppel are found in section 2–403 of the Uniform Commercial Code. Subsection 2 thereof provides that "any entrusting of possession of goods to a merchant who deals in goods of that kind gives him power to transfer all rights of the entruster to a buyer in the ordinary course of business." Uniform Commercial Code, section 1–201, subdivision 9, defines a "buyer in [the] ordinary course of business" as "a person who in good faith and without knowledge that the sale to him is in violation of the ownership rights or security interest of a third party in the goods buys in ordinary course from a person in the business of selling goods of that kind . . . ."

In order to determine whether the defense of statutory estoppel is available to Feigen, we must begin by ascertaining whether Feigen fits the definition of "[a] buyer in [the] ordinary course of business." (UCC, § 1–201[9].) Feigen does not fit that definition, for two reasons. First, Wertz, from whom Feigen bought the Utrillo, was not an art dealer—he was not "a person in the business of selling goods of that kind." (UCC, § 1–201[9].) If anything, he was a delicatessen employee.[6] Wertz never held himself out as a dealer. Although Feigen testified at trial that before he (Feigen) purchased the Utrillo from Wertz, Sloan, who introduced Wertz to Feigen told him (Feigen) that Wertz was an art dealer, this testimony was questionable. It conflicted with Feigen's testimony at his examination before trial where he stated he did not recall whether Sloan said that to him.[7] Second, Feigen was not "a person . . . in good faith" (UCC, § 1–201[9]) in the transaction with Wertz. Uniform Commercial Code, section 2–103, subdivision (1)(b), defines "good faith" in the case of a merchant as "honesty in fact and the observance of reasonable commercial standards of fair dealing in the trade." Although this definition by its terms embraces the "reasonable commercial standards of fair dealing in the trade", it should not—and cannot—be interpreted to permit, countenance or condone commercial standards of sharp trade practice or indifference as to the "provenance", i.e., history of ownership or the right to possess or sell an object d'art, such as is present in the case before us.

We note that neither Ms. Drew-Bear nor her employer Feigen made any investigation to determine the status of Wertz, i.e., wheth-

---

6. Wertz is described as a seller of caviar and other luxury food items (because of his association with a Madison Avenue gourmet grocery) and over whom the Trial Term observed, Von Maker "cast his hypnotic spell . . . and usurped his name, his signature and his sacred honor."

7. Feigen's explanation for his changed version was that after his examination before trial and before the trial, his memory was "jogged" by Lipinsky, who had introduced Sloan to Feigen.

In connection with Feigen's claim that Wertz was a dealer, it is observed that on a previous appeal, Porter v. Wertz, et al., defendants, and Richard Feigen Gallery, Inc., et al., appellants, 56 A.D.2d 570, 392 N.Y.S.2d 10, this court unanimously affirmed an order of Special Term denying appellants' motion for summary judgment in that there was an issue of fact as to whether Wertz was a dealer or a collector. If a dealer, appellants claimed, as they do now, the applicability of UCC, § 2–403(2).

er he was an art merchant, "a person in the business of selling goods of that kind." (UCC, § 1–201[9].) Had Ms. Drew-Bear done so much as call either of the telephone numbers Wertz had left, she would have learned that Wertz was employed by a delicatessen and was not an art dealer. Nor did Ms. Drew-Bear or Feigen make any effort to verify whether Wertz was the owner or authorized by the owner to sell the painting he was offering. Ms. Drew-Bear had available to her the Petrides volume on Utrillo which included "Chateau de Lion-sur-Mer" in its catalogue of the master's work.[8] Although this knowledge alone might not have been enough to put Feigen on notice that Wertz was not the true owner at the time of the transaction, it could have raised a doubt as to Wertz's right of possession, calling for further verification before the purchase by Feigen was consummated. Thus, it appears that statutory estoppel provided by Uniform Commercial Code, section 2–403(2), was not, as Trial Term correctly concluded, available as a defense to Feigen.

We disagree with the conclusion of the trial court that the defense of equitable estoppel (see Zendman v. Harry Winston, Inc., 305 N.Y. 180, 111 N.E.2d 871) raised by Feigen bars recovery.

We pause to observe that although one may not be a buyer in the ordinary course of business as defined in the Uniform Commercial Code, he may be a good-faith purchaser for value and enjoy the protection of pre-Code estoppel (see Tumber v. Automation Design & Mfg. Corp., 130 N.J.Super. 5, 13, 324 A.2d 602, 616; UCC, § 1–103). We now reach the question whether the defense of equitable estoppel has been established here.

In general terms:

> Equitable estoppel or estoppel in pais is the principle by which a party is absolutely precluded, both at law and in equity, from denying, or asserting the contrary of, any material fact which, by his words or conduct, affirmative or negative, intentionally or through culpable negligence, he has induced another, who was excusably ignorant of the true facts and who had a right to rely upon such words or conduct, to believe and act upon them thereby, as a consequence reasonably to be anticipated, changing his position in such a way that he would suffer injury if such denial or contrary assertion were allowed. An estoppel in pais can arise only when a person, either by his declarations or conduct, has induced another person to act in a particular manner. The doctrine prohibits a person, upon principles of honesty and fair and open dealing, from asserting rights the enforcement of which would, through his omissions

8. Page 32 of that book clearly contained a reference to the fact that that painting, at least at the time of publication of the book in 1969, was in the collection of Mrs. Donald D. King of New York, supposedly the party from whom Porter obtained it.

or commissions, work fraud and injustice. (21 N.Y. Jur., Estoppel, § 15 [citing cases].)

As the Court of Appeals reiterated in Zendman v. Harry Winston, Inc., supra, an " 'owner may be estopped from setting up his own title and the lack of title in the vendor as against a *bona fide* purchaser for value where the owner has clothed the vendor with possession and other indicia of title (46 Am. Jur., Sales, § 463).' " Indeed, "[t]he rightful owner may be estopped by his own acts from asserting his title. If he has invested another with the usual evidence of title, or an apparent authority to dispose of it, he will not be allowed to make claim against an innocent purchaser dealing on the faith of such apparent ownership (Smith v. Clews, 114 N.Y. 190, 194, 21 N.E. 160, 161)."

In Zendman v. Harry Winston, Inc., supra, a diamond merchant in New York City sent a ring to Brand, Inc., a corporation which conducted auctions on the boardwalk in Atlantic City, New Jersey, with a memorandum reciting that the ring was for examination only and that title was not to pass until the auctioneer had made his selection, and had notified the sender of his agreement to pay the indicated price and the sender had indicated acceptance thereof by issuing a bill of sale. The ring was placed in a public show window at the auctioneer's place of business, remaining there for more than a month, before being sold to the plaintiff at a public auction. Under circumstances where it was demonstrated that the defendant had permitted other pieces of jewelry it owned to be exhibited and sold by the auctioneer, it was held that the defendant by his conduct was estopped from recovering the ring from the plaintiff.

In the case at bar, Porter's conduct was not blameworthy. When the first promissory note was dishonored, he retained Bishop's investigative service and informed the FBI of the financial transactions concerning the series of notes. His attorney obtained a comprehensive agreement covering several paintings, within which was the assurance (now proven false) by Von Maker that he still controlled the Utrillo. Although Porter had permitted Von Maker to possess the painting, he conferred upon Von Maker no other indicia of ownership. Possession without more is insufficient to create an estoppel (Zendman v. Harry Winston, Inc., supra, 305 N.Y. at 186–187, 111 N.E.2d 874–875).

We find that the prior art transactions between Porter and Von Maker justified the conclusion of the trial court that Porter knew that Von Maker was a dealer in art. Nevertheless, the testimony remains uncontradicted, that the Utrillo was not consigned to Von Maker for business purposes, but rather for display only in Von Maker's home (compare Zendman v. Harry Winston, Inc., supra). In these circumstances, it cannot be said that Porter's conduct in any way contributed to the deception practiced on Feigen by Von Maker and Wertz.

Finally, we must examine again the position of Feigen to determine whether Feigen was a purchaser in good faith.

In purchasing the Utrillo, Feigen did not rely on any indicia of ownership in Von Maker. Feigen dealt with Wertz, who did not have the legal right to possession of the painting. Even were we to consider Wertz as the agent of Von Maker or merge the identities of Von Maker and Wertz insofar as Feigen was concerned, Feigen was not a purchaser in good faith. As we have commented, neither Ms. Drew-Bear nor Feigen made, or attempted to make, the inquiry which the circumstances demanded.

The Feigen claim that the failure to look into Wertz's authority to sell the painting was consistent with the practice of the trade does not excuse such conduct. This claim merely confirms the observation of the trial court that "in an industry whose transactions cry out for verification of . . . title . . . it is deemed poor practice to probe . . . ." Indeed, commercial indifference to ownership or the right to sell facilitates traffic in stolen works of art. Commercial indifference diminishes the integrity and increases the culpability of the apathetic merchant. In such posture, Feigen cannot be heard to complain.

In the circumstances outlined, the complaint should not have been dismissed. Moreover, we find (CPLR 4213[b] and 5712[c][2]) that plaintiffs-appellants are the true owners of the Utrillo painting and are entitled to possession thereof, that defendants-respondents wrongfully detained that painting and are obligated to return it or pay for its value at the time of trial (CPLR 7108[a]; 10 Fuchsberg, New York Damages Law, § 934; 7A Weinstein-Korn-Miller, N.Y. Civ. Prac., par. 7108.02 and cases cited).

In view of the inconclusive nature of the evidence at trial as to damages (the painting apparently being irretrievable), that sole issue remains to be determined. Further, plaintiffs-appellants may have obtained the proceeds from a sale of the Cranach (as to which we have no information) and that could be a credit against those damages.

Accordingly, the judgment of the Supreme Court, New York County, entered June 22, 1978, should be reversed and vacated, on the law and the facts, the complaint reinstated, judgment entered in favor of plaintiffs-appellants on liability, and the matter remanded for an assessment of damages, with costs and disbursements to plaintiffs-appellants. . . .

––––––––––

PORTER v. WERTZ

Court of Appeals of New York, 1981.
53 N.Y.2d 696, 439 N.Y.S.2d 105, 421 N.E.2d 500.

MEMORANDUM. The judgment appealed from an order of the Appellate Division brought up for review should be affirmed . . . with costs. We agree with the Appellate Division's conclusion that subdivision (2) of section 2–403 of the Uniform Commercial Code does not insulate defendants from plaintiff Porter's lawful claim to the Utrillo painting. . . . The "entruster provision" of the Uniform Commercial Code is designed to enhance the reliability of commercial sales by merchants (who deal with the kind of goods sold on a regular basis) while shifting the risk of loss through fraudulent transfer to the owner of the goods, who can select the merchant to whom he entrusts his property. It protects only those who purchase from the merchant to whom the property was entrusted in the ordinary course of the merchant's business.

While the Utrillo painting was entrusted to Harold Von Maker, an art merchant, the Feigen Gallery purchased the painting not from Von Maker, but from one Peter Wertz, who turns out to have been a delicatessen employee acquainted with Von Maker. It seems that Von Maker frequented the delicatessen where Peter Wertz was employed and that at some point Von Maker began to identify himself as Peter Wertz in certain art transactions. Indeed, Von Maker identified himself as Peter Wertz in his dealings with Porter.

Defendants argued that Feigen reasonably assumed that the Peter Wertz who offered the Utrillo to him was an art merchant because Feigen had been informed by Henry Sloan that an art dealer named Peter Wertz desired to sell a Utrillo painting. Feigen therefore argues that for purposes of subdivision (2) of section 2–403 of the Uniform Commercial Code it is as though he purchased from a merchant in the ordinary course of business. Alternatively, he claims that he actually purchased the Utrillo from Von Maker, the art dealer to whom it had been entrusted, because Peter Wertz sold the painting on Von Maker's behalf. Neither argument has merit.

Even if Peter Wertz were acting on Von Maker's behalf, unless he disclosed this fact to Feigen, it could hardly be said that Feigen relied upon Von Maker's status as an art merchant. It does not appear that the actual Peter Wertz ever represented that he was acting on behalf of Von Maker in selling the painting.

As to the argument that Feigen reasonably assumed that Peter Wertz was an art merchant, it is apparent from the opinion of the Appellate Division that the court rejected the fact finding essential to this argument, namely, that Peter Wertz had been introduced to Feigen by Henry Sloan as an art merchant. The court noted that in his examination before trial Richard Feigen had testified that he could not recall whether Henry Sloan had described Peter Wertz as an art dealer and concluded that this substantially weakened the probative force of Feigen's trial testimony on this point. Indeed, Peter Wertz testified that Von Maker had not directed him to the Feigen Gallery but had simply delivered the painting to Wertz and asked him to try to find a buyer for the Utrillo. Wertz had been to several art galleries before he approached the Feigen Gallery. Thus, the Appellate Division's finding has support in the record.

Because Peter Wertz was not an art dealer and the Appellate Division has found Feigen was not duped by Von Maker into believing that Peter Wertz was such a dealer, subdivision (2) of section 2–403 of the Uniform Commercial Code is inapplicable for three distinct reasons: (1) even if Peter Wertz were an art merchant rather than a delicatessen employee, he is not the same merchant to whom Porter entrusted the Utrillo painting; (2) Wertz was not an art merchant; and (3) the sale was not in the ordinary course of Wertz' business because he did not deal in goods of that kind (Uniform Commercial Code, § 1–201, subd. [9]).

Nor can the defendants-appellants rely on the doctrine of equitable estoppel. It has been observed that subdivision (1) of section 2–403 of the Uniform Commercial Code incorporates the doctrines of estoppel, agency and apparent agency because it states that a purchaser acquires not only all title that his transferor had, but also all title that he had power to transfer (White & Summers, Uniform Commercial Code, § 3–11, p. 139).

An estoppel might arise if Porter had clothed Peter Wertz with ownership of or authority to sell the Utrillo painting and the Feigen Gallery had relied upon Wertz' apparent ownership or right to transfer it. But Porter never even delivered the painting to Peter Wertz, much less create apparent ownership in him; he delivered the painting to Von Maker for his own personal use. It is true, as previously noted, that Von Maker used the name Peter Wertz in his dealings with Porter, but the Appellate Division found that the Feigen Gallery purchased from the actual Peter Wertz and that there was insufficient evidence to establish the claim that Peter Wertz had been described as an art dealer by Henry Sloan. Nothing Porter did influenced the Feigen Gallery's decision to purchase from Peter Wertz a delicatessen employee. Accordingly, the Feigen Gallery cannot protect its defective title by a defense of estoppel.

The Appellate Division opined that even if Von Maker had duped Feigen into believing that Peter Wertz was an art dealer, subdivision (2) of section 2–403 of the Uniform Commercial Code would still not protect his defective title because as a merchant, Feigen failed to purchase in good faith. Among merchants good faith requires not only honesty in fact but observance of reasonable commercial standards. (Uniform Commercial Code, § 2–103, subd. [1], par. [b]). The Appellate Division concluded that it was a departure from reasonable commercial standards for the Feigen Gallery to fail to inquire concerning the title to the Utrillo and to fail to question Peter Wertz' credentials as an art dealer. On this appeal we have received *amicus* briefs from the New York State Attorney-General urging that the court hold that good faith among art merchants requires inquiry as to the ownership of an *object d'art,* and from the Art Dealers Association of America, Inc., arguing that the ordinary custom in the art business is not to inquire as to title and that a duty of inquiry would cripple the art business which is centered in New York. In view of our disposition we do not reach the good faith question.

NOTES

(1) **Questions.** Would it have made a difference if Feigen had bought the Utrillo from Von Maker rather than from Wertz? Why?

Does it make a difference under UCC 2–403(2) if the original owner of the goods does not know that the person to whom the owner entrusts them is a merchant who deals in goods of that kind? See Atlas Auto Rental Corp. v. Weisberg, 54 Misc.2d 168, 281 N.Y.S.2d 400 (1967); Leary & Sperling, The Outer Limits of Entrusting, 35 Ark.L.Rev. 50, 83–85 (1981). But cf. Antigo Co-op Credit Union v. Miller, 86 Wis.2d 90, 271 N.W.2d 642 (1978).

Suppose that Feigen had been duped by Von Maker into believing that Wertz was an art dealer. Suppose that Feigen had been duped by Wertz, who held himself out as an art dealer. Compare UCC 2–104(1) with UCC 2–403(2). In Sea Harvest v. Rig & Crane Equipment Corp., 181 N.J. Super. 41, 46, 436 A.2d 553, 556 (1981), the court said: "A buyer's misunderstanding that the seller was in the business of selling does not improve the former's position." Do you agree with this reading of the Code?

(2) **"Entrusting" and Buyers in Ordinary Course.** The Code's sharpest break with the traditional law of good faith purchase is found in UCC 2–403(2). Suppose an owner leaves a diamond ring for repair with a jeweler who both repairs and sells jewelry. The jeweler wrongfully sells the ring to a good faith purchaser. Who has the right to the ring—the original owner or the good faith purchaser?

The common law favored the original owner. Merely entrusting possession to a dealer was not sufficient to clothe the dealer with the authority to sell. "If it were otherwise people would not be secure in sending their watches or articles of jewelry to a jeweler's establishment to be repaired or cloth to a clothing establishment to be made into garments." Levi v. Booth, 58 Md. 305, 315 (1882).

During the nineteenth century, however, many states enacted "factor's acts" under which an owner of goods who entrusted them to an agent (or "factor") for sale took the risk that the agent might sell them beyond his authority. A good faith purchaser from the agent, relying on the agent's possession of the goods and having no notice that he exceeded his authority, took good title against the original owner. (See the discussion by Gilmore at p. 21 supra.) But the factor's acts did not protect the good faith purchaser where, as in the example of the diamond ring, the owner entrusted the goods to another for some purpose other than that of sale. A mere bailee could not pass good title to a good faith purchaser.

Here UCC 2–403(2) goes well beyond the factor's acts, since it applies to "[a]ny entrusting," i.e., "any delivery" under (3), regardless of the purpose. Who is entitled to the diamond ring under the Code? Would it make a difference in the result if the jeweler sold the ring from his home through an advertisement in the newspaper? Contrast the narrow scope of "buyer in ordinary course" under UCC 1–201(9) with the definitions of "purchase" and "purchaser" under UCC 1–201(32) and (33). See Comment 3 to UCC 2–403.[1] See generally Note, 38 Ind. L.J. 675 (1963); Note, 20 Wm. & Mary L.Rev. 513 (1979); Comment, 72 Yale L.J. 1205 (1963).

In a remarkable recantation, Professor Gilmore has expressed doubt about the wisdom of the Code's expansion of the rights of good faith purchasers. "If, in the 1940's, we had paid any attention to what the courts had been doing for fifty or seventy-five years past, we might have come up with something like this: the good faith purchase idea was an intuitive judicial response to economic conditions that ceased to exist after 1850 or thereabouts. During the second half of the nineteenth century, the courts, losing their enthusiasm for the good faith purchase idea, began cutting back instead of further expanding it." Gilmore, The Good Faith Purchase Idea and the Uniform Commercial Code: Confessions of a Repentant Draftsman, 15 Ga.L.Rev. 605, 615 (1981).

(3) **Entrusting of Cars and Certificates of Title.** Because of the value and mobility of motor vehicles, state statutes have established certificate of title systems for their transfer. Such certificates were originally developed as a police measure to impede the sale of stolen vehicles. Certificate of title statutes usually provide for the issuance of a certificate describing the vehicle in detail and identifying the

---

1. According to Professor Gilmore: "For some reason, the security transferees who were protected in the voidable title subsection by the use of the term 'purchaser' do not qualify for protection under the entrusting subsection. I have no idea why the draftsmen chose thus to narrow the protected class." Gilmore, The Good Faith Purchase Idea and the Uniform Commercial Code: Confessions of a Repentant Draftsman, 15 Ga.L.Rev. 605, 618 (1981).

According to the Ontario Law Reform Commission, which was "attracted to the distinction": "The supporting theory is, presumably, grounded on either of the following premises: namely, that commerce will not be impeded if lenders are required to assume the risk of a merchant-borrower exceeding his actual authority; or, that lenders are in as good a position as are entrusters, or perhaps even better, to protect themselves against a dishonest merchant." 2 Ontario Law Reform Commission, Report on Sale of Goods 314–15 (1979).

It has also been suggested that transfers for security are transfers "in which the price or consideration received for the goods . . . is likely to be considerably less than the amount normally received in a sale of the same goods in other transactions." Leary & Sperling, The Outer Limits of Entrusting, 35 Ark.L. Rev. 50, 65 (1981).

owner, and state that transfer of title to the vehicle is to be completed by delivery of the certificate signed by the owner. Thus, if a car is stolen, the original owner who retains the certificate will generally prevail over a good faith purchaser who takes the car without the certificate.[2]

But what if the original owner entrusted the car to a dealer who wrongfully sold it to a buyer in ordinary course? Will retention of the certificate protect the original owner despite the rule of UCC 2–403(2)? Courts that have faced this question have generally held that UCC 2–403(2) prevails over the certificate of title statute. See Atwood Chevrolet-Olds v. Aberdeen Municipal School District, 431 So. 2d 926 (Miss.1983) (buyer in ordinary course who did not get certificate prevailed over owner of bus chassis who entrusted it to dealer after assembly); Godfrey v. Gilsdorf, 86 Nev. 714, 476 P.2d 3 (1970) (buyer in ordinary course prevailed over owner who entrusted car but not certificate to used car dealer). But cf. Ellsworth v. Worthey, 612 S.W.2d 396 (Mo.App.1981) (consumer-buyer was not buyer in ordinary course in view of fact that he took car without certificate); Mattek v. Malofsky, 42 Wis.2d 16, 165 N.W.2d 406 (1969) (dealer-buyer was not buyer in ordinary course in view of fact that he took car without certificate). Is this justified by the prevailing practice of having the dealer handle the paperwork involved in the transfer of the certificate of title, with the buyer not receiving the certificate until after taking delivery of the car?

(4) Efforts at Reform. Since the drafters of the Code reexamined the doctrine of good faith purchase, there have been three other notable studies of the subject: by the English Law Reform Committee, by the Ontario Law Reform Commission, and by the International Institute for the Unification of Private Law at Rome.

In a 1966 report on good faith purchase, the English Law Reform Committee rejected the idea that courts be given the power to apportion loss in controversies involving good faith purchasers because "it would introduce into a field of law where certainty and clarity are particularly important that uncertainty which inevitably follows the grant of a wide and virtually unrestrained judicial discretion." The Committee reaffirmed the principle of *nemo dat*, but a majority recommended a major change in the rule on market overt, which the Committee characterized as "capricious in its application." Under the Committee's recommendation, the rule "should be replaced by a provision that a person who buys goods by retail at trade premises or by public auction acquires a good title provided he buys in good faith and without notice of any defect or want of title on the part of the apparent owner . . . . By 'trade premises' we mean premises open to the public at which goods of the same or a similar description

---

2. Certificate of title statutes also generally provide for perfection of security interests in the vehicle by notation on the certificate itself. Problems arising out of the relationship between such statutes and Article 9 of the Code are of great practical importance.

to those sold are normally offered for sale by retail in the course of business carried on at those premises . . . ." There was a strong dissent to this recommendation on the ground that it would encourage trafficking in stolen goods. (English) Law Reform Committee, Twelfth Report (Transfer of Title to Chattels) Cmnd. 2958, par. 9, 31, 33 (1966). The Committee's major recommendations, including the one just described, have not been implemented.

In 1979 the Ontario Law Reform Commission took up the subject of good faith purchase in the course of its report on revision of the Ontario Sale of Goods Act. The Commission reaffirmed the principle of *nemo dat*, as the English Law Reform Committee had done. It found it "a little surprising that the English Law Reform Committee should have voted in favour of extending its modernized *market overt* concept to stolen goods" and rejected that recommendation, noting that "restricting protection to those who purchase at retail premises would create a new set of anomalies." Instead, the Ontario Commission recommended "that the revised Act contain an additional exception to the *nemo dat* rule, along the lines of UCC 2–403(2) and (3), in the case of entrustment to a merchant." 2 Ontario Law Reform Commission, Report on Sale of Goods 312–13 (1979).

The Ontario Commission also considered whether an owner who has been deprived of title to goods because of one of the exceptions to the *nemo dat* rule should be entitled to recover the goods on reimbursing the good faith purchaser for the purchase price (see Note 3, p. 23 supra), "a principle . . . recognized in French and Quebec law in the case of lost or stolen goods acquired in a commercial sale . . . . The argument put to us has been that an owner may have a particular attachment to an article, and that the third party will not ordinarily be prejudiced by being required to surrender the goods, so long as his reliance interests are protected. Once again, what may appear to be a simple proposition is considerably complicated by several factors. First, the goods may have passed through a number of hands. Secondly, the goods may have been altered or improved since leaving the owner's hands. While we have concluded that a right of recovery should be recognized, and so recommend, we are of the view that, in light of the above-mentioned factors, the right of recovery should be subject to the following qualifications. The right of recovery should not apply where the owner originally entrusted the goods to a merchant who sold them in the ordinary course of his business. It should only apply where the court considers it fair to make such an order. Further, the terms of the order should be in the court's discretion, but in making such an order no account should be taken of any expectation losses suffered by the third person in whose hands the goods are located." Id. at 314. The Commission's proposals have not yet been enacted, but they have been incorporated in a Draft Uniform Sale of Goods Act prepared by the Uniform Law Conference of Canada. See Uniform Law Conference of Canada, Proceedings of the Sixty-Third Annual Meeting 185–321 (1981).

The International Institute for the Unification of Private Law published in 1968 a draft proposal for a uniform international law on the protection of good faith purchasers of goods. This draft adopted the principle of *possession vaut titre* in the case of stolen goods that were bought in good faith "under normal conditions from a dealer who usually sells goods of the same kind." International Institute for the Unification of Private Law (UNIDROIT), Draft Uniform Law on the Protection of the Bona Fide Purchaser of Corporeal Moveables with Explanatory Report art. 10(2) (1968). A committee of governmental experts studied this draft and prepared a 1974 revision, which receded from this extreme position because a majority feared that it might encourage trafficking in stolen goods, particularly works of art. The revised text therefore provides that the "transferee of stolen moveables cannot invoke his good faith." Uniform Law on the Acquisition in Good Faith of Corporeal Moveables art. 11, in Uniform Law Review (UNIDROIT), No. I, p. 79 (1975). The draft Uniform International Law was prepared on the assumption that it would be submitted to a diplomatic conference and the final text submitted to governments for ratification, but no diplomatic conference has yet been held.

Problem 6. A, who is in the cotton business, sold cotton to O, who paid A $60,000 and promised to pay the balance of $40,000 when O took delivery of the cotton in two weeks. The bill of sale recited: "A hereby sells and conveys to O all right and title to cotton [giving description] and agrees to take good care and custody of said cotton until final delivery." A week later, A sold the same cotton to P, who took delivery without knowing of the sale to O and promised to pay A $90,000 in 30 days. O sues P to replevy the cotton.

(a) What result? See UCC 2–403, 1–201(9). (If P has not yet paid A the $90,000, what would you advise O to do?)

(b) Suppose that P also left A in possession of the cotton and O got wind of the sale and took delivery. P sues O to replevy the cotton. What result? Does P run any risk if he leaves A in possession of the cotton? (Note that UCC 2–403 does not require that a good faith purchaser of goods take possession in order to be protected. In contrast, UCC 1–201(20) requires that a good faith purchaser of a note take possession in order to be a holder. Are the two situations distinguishable? Which rule is easier to justify?)

Problem 7. A, who is in the cotton business, sold a used cotton gin to O, who paid A $60,000 and promised to pay the balance of $40,000 when O took delivery of the machine in two weeks. The bill of sale recited: "A hereby sells and conveys to O all right and title to cotton gin [giving description] and agrees to take good care and custody of said machine until final delivery." A week later, A sold the same machine to P, who took delivery without knowing of the sale to O. O sues P to replevy the machine. What result? For additional circumstances that might justify a decision for P on the ground of "apparent authority" or "estoppel" under UCC 1–103, see Tumber v. Automation Design & Manufacturing Corp., 130 N.J.Super. 5, 324 A.2d 602 (1974).

SECTION 2.   COMMERCIAL PAPER

Prefatory Note. Without the advantage of some business background, the law student is likely to find the law of negotiable commercial paper, at least at the outset, the most esoteric and intractable area of commercial law. The student is to some extent familiar with the law of sales from a course in contracts, but the forms, the functions, and even the terminology of commercial paper remain to be explored. Because they can be fully understood only in the light of some six centuries of development, it is the purpose of this brief introduction to present at least some of the highlights of that development. The Code classifies negotiable instruments under three main headings: "drafts," "checks" and "notes." (UCC 3–104(2)).[1] Their origins will be separately discussed.

Origin of the Draft. The draft, or bill of exchange as it is often called,[2] grew out of the practices of fourteenth-century merchants who sought to avoid the hazards and the publicity of transporting money. It thus began as a device for the transmission of funds. If a London merchant received goods on credit from a Venetian merchant, the London merchant would send to the Venetian an acknowledgement of the debt together with his promise to pay it at a fixed date at one of the fairs where trade was centered in medieval Europe.[3] The London merchant then chose a London banker who was going to that fair and gave him an authority to pay the debt in the London merchant's name when it fell due. The Venetian merchant chose a Venetian banker going to the same fair and authorized him to receive payment. All of the principal trading cities of Western Europe would be represented at the fair and each banker would have many payments to make and to receive from many other bankers. Probably the debts owed by the Venetian banker to the London banker would not exactly equal those owed by the London banker to the Venetian banker so that they could not be extinguished by set-off. But if the Venetian should still have an adverse balance as against London, the Venetian might well have a favorable balance as against, say, Gene-

---

1. The Code also mentions a fourth type of negotiable instrument, the "certificate of deposit," a written acknowledgment by a bank of the receipt of a deposit. See UCC 3–104(2)(c).

2. The terms "draft" and "bill of exchange" are synonymous. The latter was used throughout the Negotiable Instruments Law. The Code uses the former.

3. The example which follows is adapted from P. Huvelin, Le Droit des Marchés et des Foires 557–58 (1897), as translated in 8 W. Holdsworth, History of English Law 129–30 (1925).

va. To settle his adverse balance to London, he would draw an order (*draft*) upon a debtor from Geneva directing him to pay a specified amount to the London creditor. By this means accounts could be settled with the exchange of a minimum amount of money.

From these orders, the draft developed so that it was no longer necessary for bankers to meet at a fair. If a London buyer wished to pay a Venetian seller for goods, the London buyer would find a London banker who had an account with a correspondent in Venice. The London buyer would then pay the London banker, the sum to be remitted to Venice. The London banker (as *drawer*) would then draw on the Venetian correspondent (as *drawee*), ordering him to pay the sum to the Venetian seller (as *payee*). The letter would then be given to the London buyer (as *remitter*), who would send it to the Venetian seller. The Venetian seller would then present it to the Venetian banker to receive payment.

Origin of the Check. The London "bankers" mentioned in the foregoing examples were probably Lombard or Florentine money changers rather than bankers in the modern sense, for, although private banking had originated in Venice in the fourteenth century, it was not until the seventeenth century that banking began in England. At that time the goldsmiths of Lombard Street in London were experiencing a decline in their trade in gold and silver plate with the dwindling landed class, and sought to augment their business by accepting for safekeeping the valuables of their customers. The merchants of London, however, preferred to deposit their funds at the king's mint in the Tower of London until Charles I, in 1640, forcibly borrowed about £200,000. Thereafter the merchants patronized the goldsmiths in increasing numbers. The latter began to lend the money on deposit, thus becoming true bankers, whose loans were made from the deposits of others, as opposed to moneylenders, whose loans were made from their own capital. The legal relationship between goldsmith and customer changed from bailor-bailee to debtor-creditor, that which exists today between a bank and its depositors.

The merchant looked to the goldsmith banker not only as a depository but also as an intermediary for making payment to his creditors. The draft or bill of exchange provided a pattern. At first the merchant probably addressed a letter to the goldsmith, directing payment to the creditor. Later the form become that of a check. Printed checks came into use in the second half of the eighteenth century. The word "check" itself dates from about the same period and is derived from "the name of the counterfoil of an Exchequer or other bill, the purpose of which was to check forgery or alteration." [4] In the nineteenth century the English adopted the spelling "cheque," while the traditional spelling has been retained in the United States.

4. 2 J. Murray, A New English Dictionary 320 (1893).

Origin of the Note. The draft and the check, at least as they are used in the foregoing examples, are both instruments for the safe and convenient transmission of funds, in place of money. Marius however, mentions another use for the draft, as an instrument of credit rather than for transmission of funds. Two parties only are involved, a debtor and a creditor. Suppose that a buyer buys goods from a seller, who is unable or unwilling to finance the transaction himself until the buyer pays. The seller, as creditor, may draw a draft on the buyer, as debtor, payable to the order of the seller at the end of a fixed time. The seller then presents it to the buyer who accepts it by signing his name across the draft itself, indicating his agreement to pay. Then "the drawer, before the Bill falls due, doth negotiate the parcell, with another man, and so draws in the money at the place where he liveth, and makes only an Assignment on the Bill, payable to him of whom he hath received the value." [5] The buyer has the goods, the seller gets his money immediately upon negotiating the draft, and the new holder of the draft finances the transaction. In modern parlance the seller has "discounted" the draft, receiving its face value less a discount equal to interest from the time of the discount until maturity. Today, however, it might seem simpler for the buyer (as *maker*) merely to execute a promissory note, promising to pay the sum to the seller (as *payee*), and this form of instrument did become popular among the goldsmith bankers in the late seventeenth century. The promissory note could then be transferred by means of the indorsement of the seller, as payee to a third party who would purchase it and finance the transaction.[6]

Uses of the Note. "I shall not undertake to explain how or why the commercial system of a century ago lost the use of notes to evidence the credit-price of freshly delivered goods. It is enough here that the practice went into decline, and that between merchants goods are now delivered typically on purely 'open' credit (resulting in a 'book account,' and 'account receivable'), often with the buyer, if he is financially strong, paying within ten days against a large 'cash discount.' The giving of a commercial note between dealers has come to be the gesture with which a stale account, long overdue, is promised

---

5. Page 3 of 1655 edition.

6. The fact that the note was transferable at all was only grudgingly conceded. As will be recalled from the study of contracts, the assignability of simple contract rights had at first met with objection. However, by the beginning of the eighteenth century it was well established that a *draft* payable to order was freely transferable and that suit could be brought by the transferee, as indorsee, in his own name. Yet in Buller v. Crips, 6 Mod.Rep. 29, 87 Eng. Rep. 793 (1704) Lord Holt refused to allow the indorsee of a *promissory note* payable to order to maintain an action against the maker under the custom of merchants, calling "the notes in question . . . only an invention of the goldsmiths in Lombard-Street, who had a mind to make a law to bind all those that did deal with them." But while the courts lagged behind the custom, the legislature was not slow to act, and in 1704, Parliament enacted the Statute of Anne, "An Act for Giving like Remedy upon Promissory Notes, as is now used upon Bills of Exchange . . . ." The act overruled Buller v. Crips, making promissory notes as freely transferable as drafts.

really to be met next time. Such a note smells." Llewellyn, Meet Negotiable Instruments, 44 Colum.L.Rev. 299, 321–22 (1944). However the note came to have commercial significance in three other important areas.

First, and most important for the purposes of this casebook, is the use of the note in a secured sale. The consumer purchaser of an automobile on credit will be asked by the seller to execute a security agreement, perhaps called a conditional sale contract, under which the purchaser, in return for payment of a financing charge, has the right to make installment payments over a period of time and the seller's rights include that of repossession of the car, which is security for the balance of the purchase price, in the event of the buyer's default. Together with the security agreement the seller may ask the purchaser to execute a negotiable promissory note. The seller's rights under the security agreement will then be assigned and the note negotiated to a finance company or bank which will finance the transaction. Much the same pattern is followed in the installment financing of industrial equipment. The note is also commonly used in secured transactions involving real estate, but the problems thus raised can best be studied in the context of a course in real estate transactions.

A second significant use of the note is in connection with the loan of money, a function that is epitomized by the banker's "collateral note." Here, as in the case of the secured sale, the creditor is intent upon security and the loan may be secured by a pledge of stock or in a variety of other ways. The bank that takes the note may, instead of financing the transaction itself, choose to negotiate the note to a Federal Reserve bank for rediscount. Some of the problems arising out of such notes are considered in Chapter 7, Accommodation Parties.

A third important use of the note is the corporate bond, which is a long-term promissory note. However, the difficulty of dealing with investment paper such as bonds under the general rules for negotiable instruments led the drafters of the Code to treat it separately in Article 8, Investment Securities.

Irving Trust

Promissory Note - Commercial

Date: _____ , 19___

Note Amount: $_____

In this Note, the words "the Bank" mean Irving Trust Company, _____
(address of branch)

1. Payment of Note Amount.

For value received, the undersigned promise(s) to pay to the order of the Bank the Note Amount:

☐ on _____ .

☐ on demand.

☐ in _____ payments, consisting of _____ payments of $_____ each, followed by a payment of
$_____ . Payments will be due on the same day of each _____
(If other than each month, specify names of months)
beginning _____ .

2. Payment of Interest.

a. The undersigned will pay interest on the unpaid portion of the Note Amount for each day from the date of this Note until the Note Amount is paid in full at a rate per annum equal to:

☐ _____ %.

☐ the rate of interest publicly announced (or if not publicly announced, established and available for quotation) from time to time by the Bank as its prime rate, as in effect on such day, plus _____ %. The applicable interest rate shall be adjusted automatically as of the opening of business on the effective date of each change in such prime rate.

☐ _____

_____

If no box is checked this Note has been discounted and the Note Amount includes interest computed at the rate of _____ % per annum.

b. Interest shall be payable on the same day of each _____ , beginning
(If other than each month, specify names of months)
_____ , and when the Note Amount is due.

c. Overdue portions of the Note Amount shall bear interest for each day from the due date thereof until paid in full at a rate per annum equal to the rate of interest otherwise payable thereon, plus 2%, such interest to be payable on demand.

d. Interest shall be computed on the basis of a 360 day year, but shall be charged for the actual number of days elapsed in the year.

3. **Payment of Costs and Expenses.**

The undersigned will pay all costs and expenses, including attorneys' fees and disbursements, incurred by the Bank in connection with the administration, enforcement or attempted enforcement of this Note.

4. **Place and Means of Payment; Holidays.**

Payment of the Note Amount and interest shall be made at the Bank's office specified above in lawful money of the United States of America and in immediately available funds. Whenever any payment to be made pursuant to this Note shall be due on a Saturday, Sunday or other day on which banks are authorized to close under the laws of the State of New York, such payment may be made on the next succeeding business day and any extension of time shall be included in computing interest, if any, with respect to such payment.

5. **Acceleration.**

a. The Bank may without notice to or demand upon the undersigned declare all amounts payable pursuant to this Note immediately due and payable, whereupon the same shall become so due and payable, if:

(i) The undersigned (or, if more than one, any of the undersigned) or any guarantor or endorser of this Note (A) defaults in the payment when due of, or otherwise defaults in the performance of, any obligation to the Bank; (B) has made or makes to the Bank any representation or warranty that proves to have been incorrect or misleading in any material respect when made; (C) fails to pay when due any other indebtedness for borrowed money, the maturity of any such indebtedness is accelerated or an event occurs which, with notice or lapse of time or both, would permit acceleration of such indebtedness; (D) if an individual, dies or becomes incompetent; (E) if not an individual, is dissolved or is a party to any merger or consolidation or sells or otherwise disposes of all or substantially all of its assets without the written consent of the Bank; (F) challenges, or institutes any proceedings, or any proceedings are instituted, to challenge, the validity, binding effect or enforceability of this Note, any guaranty or endorsement of this Note or any other obligation to the Bank; (G) makes any payment on account of any indebtedness subordinated to this Note in contravention of the terms of such subordination; (H) fails to furnish information upon request of, or permit inspection of its books and records by, the Bank; (I) creates, without the written consent of the Bank, a security interest in or lien upon, or an attachment or levy is made upon, any of its assets, or a judgment is rendered against it; or (J) is, or is a member of any co-partnership which is, expelled from or suspended by any stock or securities exchange or other exchange; or

(ii) The Bank at any time and for any reason in good faith deems itself to be insecure or the risk of nonpayment or nonperformance of this Note or any guaranty or endorsement of this Note to be increased.

b. All amounts payable pursuant to this Note shall be immediately due and payable, without presentment, demand, protest or notice of any kind, if the undersigned (or, if more than one, any of the undersigned) or any guarantor or endorser of this Note (i) becomes insolvent or unable to meet its debts as they mature or is generally not paying its debts as they become due, or suspends or ceases its present business, or a custodian, as defined in Title 11 of the United States Code, of substantially all of its property shall have been appointed or taken possession, or (ii) commences, or has commenced against it, a case under such Title 11, or any proceeding under any other federal or state bankruptcy, insolvency or other law relating to the relief of debtors, the readjustment, composition or extension of indebtedness or reorganization.

Demand for payment may be made whether or not any of the foregoing events shall have occurred if the Note Amount is payable on demand.

6. **General.**

If the undersigned are more than one, they shall be jointly and severally liable hereunder. The words "it" or "its" as used herein shall be deemed to refer to individuals and to business entities.

7. **Waivers; Governing Law.**

The undersigned waive(s) presentment, protest, notice of dishonor and the right to assert in any action or proceeding with regard to this Note any offsets or counterclaims which the undersigned may have. No failure or delay by the Bank in exercising any right hereunder shall operate as a waiver thereof, nor shall any single or partial exercise of any right preclude other or further exercises thereof or the exercise of any other right. This Note shall be governed by and interpreted and enforced in accordance with the laws of the State of New York.

                      _____
                       (Name of Company)

                       By: _____
                       Title:

                       By: _____
                       Title:

_____
(Name of Company)

By: _____
Title:

By: _____
Title:

C6064/00 (8-81) Rev. 8-82

PROMISSORY NOTE (COMMERCIAL)

[Front]

Guaranty of Payment

The undersigned (if more than one, jointly and severally) (a) unconditionally guarantee(s) the payment when due, without any setoff or other deduction, of all amounts payable pursuant to the Note on the reverse side, (b) waive(s) all acts and other things upon which, but for such waiver, this guaranty would or might be conditioned, including, but not limited to, any presentment, demand for payment, protest, notice of dishonor, and exercise of any right or remedy, and (c) consent(s), without notice to the undersigned, to all acts, omissions and other things that would or might, but for such consent, impair or otherwise affect this guaranty, including, but not limited to, any extension, regardless of length and whether preceded by another or others, any renewal, modification or acceleration, any substitution or release of any collateral or party liable for payment, any failure to call for, take, hold, protect or perfect, continue the perfection of or enforce any security interest in or other lien upon, any collateral and any failure to exercise, delay in the exercise, exercise or waiver of, or forbearance or other indulgence with respect to, any right or remedy.

PROMISSORY NOTE (COMMERCIAL)

[Reverse]

[D616]

Problem 8. O owned $100,000 in $100 bills. A stole it and gave it to P, who did not suspect the theft, in payment for cotton. O sues P to replevy the money. What result? Does Article 2 or 3 of the Code apply? See UCC 2–105(1), 3–103(1); Miller v. Race, infra.

Problem 9. O was the owner of a negotiable promissory note, made by M, who promised "to pay on demand to bearer $100,000." A stole it from O and gave it to P, who did not suspect the theft, in return for $100,000. O sues P to replevy the note.

(a) What result? See UCC 3–305, 3–302, 1–201(20), 3–202, 3–111; Miller v. Race, infra.

(b) What result if P had paid only $60,000 for the note? See UCC 1–201(19); Stewart v. Thornton, 116 Ariz. 107, 568 P.2d 414 (1977) (note "was discounted one-third").

(c) What result if P had promised to pay $100,000 but has not yet paid it? See UCC 3–303 and Comment 3.

(d) What result if P had given his check for $100,000, which is still in the hands of A?

(e) To what extent would P be a holder in due course if P had promised to pay $90,000 and had paid only $80,000 before learning of the theft? See O. P. Ganjo v. Tri-Urban Realty Co., 108 N.J.Super. 517, 261 A.2d 722 (1970).[7] Would it make a difference if P had then paid the remaining $10,000? (Where does the Code deal with the effect of value given after notice?)

Problem 10. O was the owner of a negotiable promissory note, made by M, who promised "to pay on demand to the order of O $100,000." A stole it from O, forged O's indorsement, and sold it to P, who did not suspect the theft, for $100,000. O sues P to replevy the note.

(a) What result? See UCC 3–305, 3–306, 3–302, 1–201(20), 3–202, 3–110, 3–404. (As to A's liability to P, see UCC 3–414(1), 3–417(2)(a).)

(b) What result if, before the theft, O had indorsed the note on the back by signing "O"? See UCC 3–204.

(c) What result if, before the theft, O had indorsed the note on the back by writing "Pay to the order of B, (signed) O."?[8]

---

7. In resolving the ambiguity inherent in the phrase "to the extent that the agreed consideration has been performed" (UCC 3–303(a)), is it significant that the comparable provision of the Negotiable Instruments Law read "to the extent of the amount theretofore paid" (NIL 54)? Varying interpretations of the latter phrase are discussed in Britton, Bills and Notes § 111 (1961).

8. Those with a penchant for the daedal may wonder at this point about the case in which a note made by M to the order of O is stolen by A, who forges O's name on a special indorsement to B and delivers it to B, who specially indorses and delivers it to C, who does the same to D. If the note is dishonored, what are D's rights against B? Some may be satisfied with the answer that the practical importance of the problem is negligible because both forgery and such multiple negotiation are rare. Others may wish to pursue the implications of the "new bill" doctrine, according to which, as Lord Holt put it in 1704, "the indorsement may be said to be tantamount to the drawing of a new bill." Buller v. Crips, 6 Mod.Rep. 29, 30, 87 Eng.Rep. 793, 794 (1704). Cf. Cormack and Browne, Indorsements After Maturity and the "New Bill" Doctrine, 30 Ill.L. Rev. 46 (1935). As to whether the "new bill" doctrine survived enactment of the Code, see UCC 1–103.

Problem 11. O was the owner of a promissory note made by M, who promised "to pay to the order of O $100,000." A fraudulently obtained it from O, who did not indorse the note. A gave it to P, who did not suspect the fraud, in payment for cotton delivered by P to A. O sues P to replevy the note. What result? See UCC 3–306. Would the result be different if P had promised to deliver cotton to A but has not yet done so?

MILLER v. RACE

Court of King's Bench 1758.
1 Burr. 452, 97 Eng.Rep. 398.

It was an action of trover against the defendant, upon a bank note,[9] for the payment of twenty-one pounds ten shillings to one William Finney or bearer, on demand.

The cause came on to be tried before Lord Mansfield at the sittings in Trinity term last at Guildhall, London: and upon the trial it appeared that William Finney, being possessed of this bank note on the 11th of December 1756, sent it by the general post, under cover, directed to one Bernard Odenharty, at Chipping Norton in Oxfordshire; that on the same night the mail was robbed, and the bank note in question (amongst other notes) taken and carried away by the robber; that this bank note, on the 12th of the same December, came into the hands and possession of the plaintiff, for a full and valuable consideration, and in the usual course and way of his business, and without any notice or knowledge of this bank note being taken out of the mail.

It was admitted and agreed, that, in the common and known course of trade, bank notes are paid by and received of the holder or possessor of them, as cash; and that in the usual way of negotiating bank notes, they pass from one person to another as cash, by delivery only and without any further inquiry or evidence of title, than what arises from the possession. It appeared that Mr. Finney, having notice of this robbery, on the 13th December, applied to the Bank of England, "to stop the payment of this note:" which was ordered accordingly, upon Mr. Finney's entering into proper security "to indemnify the bank."

Some little time after this, the plaintiff applied to the bank for the payment of this note; and for that purpose delivered the note to the defendant, who is a clerk in the bank: but the defendant refused either to pay the note, or to re-deliver it to the plaintiff. Upon which this action was brought against the defendant.

9. Bank of England notes did not become legal tender until 1833. 3 & 4 Wm. IV, c. 98, § 6. [Ed.]

The jury found a verdict for the plaintiff, and the sum of 21*l.* 10s. damages, subject nevertheless to the opinion of this Court upon this question—"Whether under the circumstances of this case, the plaintiff had a sufficient property in this bank note, to entitle him to recover in the present action?"

.   .   .

LORD MANSFIELD now delivered the resolution of the Court.

After stating the case at large, he declared that at the trial, he had no sort of doubt, but this action was well brought, and would lie against the defendant in the present case; upon the general course of business, and from the consequences to trade and commerce: which would be much incommoded by a contrary determination.

It has been very ingeniously argued by Sir Richard Lloyd for the defendant. But the whole fallacy of the argument turns upon comparing bank notes to what they do not resemble, and what they ought not to be compared to, viz. to goods, or to securities, or documents for debts.

Now they are not goods, not securities, nor documents for debts, nor are so esteemed: but are treated as money, as cash, in the ordinary course and transaction of business, by the general consent of mankind; which gives them the credit and currency of money, to all intents and purposes. They are as much money, as guineas themselves are; or any other current coin, that is used in common payments, as money or cash.

They pass by a will, which bequeaths all the testator's money or cash; and are never considered as securities for money, but as money itself. Upon Ld. Ailesbury's will, 900*l.* in bank-notes was considered as cash. On payment of them, whenever a receipt is required, the receipts are always given as for money; not as for securities or notes.

So on bankruptcies, they cannot be followed as identical and distinguishable from money: but are always considered as money or cash.

It is a pity that reporters sometimes catch at quaint expressions that may happen to be dropped at the Bar or Bench; and mistake their meaning. It has been quaintly said, "that the reason why money can not be followed is, because it has no ear-mark:" but this is not true. The true reason is, upon account of the currency of it: it can not be recovered after it has passed in currency. So, in case of money stolen, the true owner can not recover it, after it has been paid away fairly and honestly upon a valuable and bona fide consideration: but before money has passed in currency, an action may be brought for the money itself. There was a case in 1 G. 1, at the sittings, Thomas v. Whip, before Ld. Macclesfield: which was an action upon assumpsit, by an administrator against the defendant, for money had and received to his use. The defendant was nurse to the intestate during his sickness; and, being alone, conveyed away the money. And Ld. Macclesfield held that the action lay. Now this must be esteemed a finding at least.

Apply this to the case of a bank-note. An action may lie against the finder, it is true; (and it is not at all denied:) but not after it has been paid away in currency. And this point has been determined, even in the infancy of bank-notes; for 1 Salk. 126, M. 10 W. 3, at Nisi Prius, is in point. And Ld. Ch. J. Holt there says that it is "by reason of the course of trade; which creates a property in the assignee or bearer." (And "the bearer" is a more proper expression than assignee.)

Here, an inn-keeper took it, bona fide, in his business from a person who made an appearance of a gentleman. Here is no pretence or suspicion of collusion with the robber: for this matter was strictly inquired and examined into at the trial; and is so stated in the case, "that he took it for a full and valuable consideration, in the usual course of business." Indeed if there had been any collusion, or any circumstances of unfair dealing, the case had been much otherwise. If it had been a note for 1000*l.* it might have been suspicious: but this was a small note for 21*l.* 10s. only: and money given in exchange for it.

Another case cited was a loose note in 1 Ld.Raym. 738, ruled by Ld. Ch. J. Holt at Guildhall, in 1698; which proves nothing for the defendant's side of the question: but it is exactly agreeable to what is laid down by my Ld. Ch. J. Holt, in the case I have just mentioned. The action did not lie against the assignee of the bank-bill; because he had it for valuable consideration.

In that case, he had it from the person who found it: but the action did not lie against him, because he took it in the course of currency; and therefore it could not be followed in his hands. It never shall be followed into the hands of a person who bona fide took it in the course of currency, and in the way of his business.

The case of Ford v. Hopkins, was also cited: which was in Hil. 12 W. 3, coram Holt Ch. J. at Nisi Prius, at Guildhall; and was an action of trover for million-lottery tickets. But this must be a very incorrect report of that case: it is impossible that it can be a true representation of what Ld. Ch. J. Holt said. It represents him as speaking of bank-notes, Exchequer-notes, and million lottery tickets, as like to each other. Now no two things can be more unlike to each other than a lottery-ticket, and a bank-note. Lottery tickets are identical and specific: specific actions lie for them. They may prove extremely unequal in value: one may be a prize; another, a blank. Land is not more specific than lottery-tickets are. It is there said, "that the delivery of the plaintiff's tickets to the defendant, as that case was, was no change of property." And most clearly it was no change of the property; so far, the case is right. But it is here urged as a proof "that the true owner may follow a stolen bank-note, into what hands soever it shall come."

Now the whole of that case turns upon the throwing in bank-notes, as being like to lottery-tickets.

But Ld. Ch. J. Holt could never say "that an action would lie against the person who, for a valuable consideration, had received a bank note which had been stolen or lost, and bona fide paid to him:" even though the action was brought by the true owner: because he had determined otherwise, but two years before; and because bank-notes are not like lottery-tickets, but money.

The person who took down this case, certainly misunderstood Lord Ch. J. Holt, or mistook his reasons. For this reasoning would prove, (if it was true, as the reporter represents it,) that if a man paid to a goldsmith 500*l.* in bank-notes, the goldsmith could never pay them away.

A bank-note is constantly and universally, both at home and abroad, treated as money, as cash; and paid and received, as cash; and it is necessary, for the purposes of commerce, that their currency should be established and secured.

Lord Mansfield declared that the Court were all of the same opinion, for the plaintiff; and that Mr. Just. Wilmot concurred.

Rule—That the postea be delivered to the plaintiff.

NOTES

(1) Good Faith. It is tautological that a good faith purchaser must take in good faith. But what is "good faith" ? UCC 1–201(19) says that it means "honesty in fact in the conduct or transaction concerned," the traditional subjective definition that is sometimes characterized as that of the "pure heart and empty head." However, the merchant who claims to be a good faith purchaser under UCC 2–403 must also meet an objective standard. For the purposes of Article 2, "Good faith in the case of a merchant means honesty in fact *and* the observance of *reasonable commercial standards of fair dealing in the trade*" (UCC 2–103(1)(b)).

The standard of good faith applicable to commercial paper has had a checkered career. In Miller v. Race, Lord Mansfield observed that Miller had taken the note "bona fide . . . 'in the usual course of business.'" In Gill v. Cubitt, 3 B. & C. 466, 107 Eng.Rep. 806 (K.B.1824), Bayley, J. of the Court of King's Bench concluded that "the course of business must require . . . a proper and reasonable degree of caution necessary to preserve the interest of trade." It thus appeared that the absence of simple negligence was required. But in Crook v. Jadis, 5 B. & Ad. 909, 110 Eng.Rep. 1028 (K.B.1834), decided only a decade after Gill v. Cubitt, the same court decided that the absence of gross negligence was enough. Two years later, in Goodman v. Harvey, 4 A. & E. 870, 111 Eng.Rep. 1011 (1836), Lord

Denman declared: "I believe we are all of opinion that gross negligence only would not be a sufficient answer, where the party has given consideration for the bill. Gross negligence may be evidence of mala fides, but is not the same thing. We have shaken off the last remnant of the contrary doctrine." The result in the United States was confusion; some courts following Gill v. Cubitt, others adopting Goodman v. Harvey. In Goodman v. Simonds, 61 U.S. (20 How.) 343, 15 L.Ed. 934 (1857), the Supreme Court of the United States determined to follow Goodman v. Harvey, repudiating Gill v. Cubitt, and nearly all American jurisdictions were in accord by the time of the enactment of the Negotiable Instruments Law. The Negotiable Instruments Law did not define good faith, so that the earlier cases such as Goodman v. Simonds, remained authoritative under it.

The drafters of Article 3 originally laid down a standard of good faith that was not unlike the merchant's standard of good faith in Article 2. In the 1952 edition of the Code, UCC 3–302(1)(b) read: "(b) in good faith including observance of the reasonable commercial standards of any business in which the holder may be engaged; and . . . ."

The comment to this section explained: ". . . The 'reasonable commercial standards' language added here and in comparable provisions elsewhere in the Act, e.g., Section 2–103, merely makes explicit what has long been implicit in case-law handling of the 'good faith' concept. A business man engaging in a commercial transaction is not entitled to claim the peculiar advantages which the law accords to the good faith purchaser—called in this context holder in due course—on a bare showing of 'honesty in fact' when his actions fail to meet the generally accepted standards current in his business, trade or profession. The cases so hold; this section so declares the law."

The present version of UCC 1–201(19) was adopted in the 1957 edition of the Code. The reason given for the change was: ". . . to make clear that the doctrine of an objective standard of good faith, exemplified by the case of Gill v. Cubitt, 3 B. & C. 446 (1824), is not intended to be incorporated . . . ." 1956 Recommendations of the Editorial Board for the Uniform Commercial Code. Was the change necessary to accomplish this result?

In Funding Consultants v. Aetna Casualty & Surety Co., 187 Conn. 637, 447 A.2d 1163 (1982), the payee of a $68,000 noninterest bearing negotiable note (the "Preisner note"), payable in four annual installments, sold the note to a holder for $5,000 and a $35,000 noninterest bearing negotiable note (the "Funding note"), payable in bimonthly installments over less than a year. The Supreme Court of Connecticut held that, in determining whether the holder took in "good faith" under the Code, the trial court erred in excluding expert testimony "to show what a commercial bank would have paid for the Preisner note and what the effective rate of return on the [holder's] investment would have been . . . . It is not unreasonable to offer a lay jury expert assistance in the proper calculation of values that are not obvious on the face of the instruments to be compared . . . . [T]here is no inconsistency between a subjective standard of good faith and a reasonable inquiry into the actual known circumstances surrounding a purchase of negotiable paper. The price actually paid, the present value of the instrument actually bought, are elements which may be considered in determining a holder's good faith."

(2) **Notice.** UCC 3–302(1) requires that the purchaser of commercial paper take not only "in good faith" but "without notice that it is overdue or has been dishonored or of any defense against or claim to it on the part of any person." Although it is traditional to state the requirement of lack of notice separately in the case of commercial paper, it is frequently not separately stated for the purchaser of goods. See UCC 2–403(1).

"Notice" is defined by the Code in UCC 1–201(25). The last three sentences were added by the 1957 edition. Is there any vestige of an objective standard in UCC 1–201(25)? [10] Often the same facts may be used both to show lack of good faith and to show notice. In view of your answer to the preceding question, which of these two approaches would be more advantageous to the one being sued on the instrument? Of course good faith and notice do not always overlap in this way. For a case in which notice but not good faith was involved, see First National Bank of Odessa v. Fazzari, p. 62 infra. Note also that the incompleteness or irregularity of the instrument is material on the issue of notice rather than good faith. See UCC 3–304(1)(a). Is the test of that subsection subjective or objective? See generally Blum, Notice to Holders in Due Course and Other Bona Fide Purchasers Under the Uniform Commercial Code, 22 B.C.L.Rev. 203 (1981).

(3) **Value.** In order to show that he is a good faith purchaser, not merely a donee, the person in possession of personal property must show that he gave value. See, e.g., UCC 2–403(1), 3–302(1). A general definition of "value" appears in UCC 1–201(44), subparagraph (d) of which makes it clear that one gives "value" if one gives "any consideration sufficient to support a simple contract." But under subparagraphs (b) and (c), "value" is a broader concept than "consideration," for one can also give value by giving something that would not, because of the pre-existing duty rule, be consideration. The argument for this view was stated by Mr. Justice Story, in connection with

10. The Negotiable Instruments Law defined notice in a purely subjective manner, as "actual knowledge . . . or knowledge of such facts that his action in taking the instrument amounted to bad faith." NIL 56. Inspired by this, New York and Virginia made a non-uniform amendment to UCC 3–304, adding a subsection (7) that provides: "In any event, to constitute notice of a claim or defense, the purchaser must have knowledge of the claim or defense or knowledge of such facts that his action in taking the instrument amounts to bad faith."

the good faith purchase of commercial paper, in Swift v. Tyson, 41 U.S. (16 Pet.) 1, 20 (1842) [11] :

> . . . And why upon principle should not a pre-existing debt be deemed such a valuable consideration? It is for the benefit and convenience of the commercial world to give as wide an extent as practicable to the credit and circulation of negotiable paper, that it may pass not only as security for new purchases and advances, made upon the transfer thereof, but also in payment of and as security for pre-existing debts. The creditor is thereby enabled to realize or to secure his debt, and thus may safely give a prolonged credit or forbear from taking any legal steps to enforce his rights. The debtor also has the advantage of making his negotiable securities of equivalent value to cash. But establish the opposite conclusion, that negotiable paper cannot be applied in payment of or as security for pre-existing debts, without letting in all the equities between the original and antecedent parties, and the value and circulation of such securities must be essentially diminished, and the debtor driven to the embarrassment of making a sale thereof, often at a ruinous discount to some third person, and then by circuity to apply the proceeds to the payment of his debts. What, indeed, upon such a doctrine would become of that large class of cases, where new notes are given by the same or by other parties, by way of renewal or security to banks, in lieu of old securities discounted by them, which have arrived at maturity? Probably more than one-half of all bank transactions in our country, as well as those of other countries, are of this nature. The doctrine would strike a fatal blow at all discounts of negotiable securities for pre-existing debts.

But, for the purposes of Articles 3 and 4, the general definition of "value" in UCC 1–201(44) is subject to the modifications imposed by UCC 3–303, 4–208 and 4–209.

UCC 3–303(b) preserves the departure from the pre-existing debt rule justified by Mr. Justice Story. But subparagraph (a) substantially narrows the definition of "value" for the purposes of Article 3 by providing that the purchaser only "takes the instrument for value . . . to the extent that the agreed consideration has been performed." Generally, as Comment 3 expresses it, "An executory promise to give value is not itself value . . . ." In terms familiar

---

11. Ironically, Swift v. Tyson is better known today for the rule of choice of law that was given its quietus in Erie Railroad Co. v. Tompkins, 304 U.S. 64, 58 S.Ct. 817, 82 L.Ed. 1188 (1938), than for the rule of commercial paper that survived. Devotees of the "federal common law" will recall Clearfield Trust Co. v. United States, 318 U.S. 363, 63 S.Ct. 573, 87 L.Ed. 838 (1943), in which it was concluded that "the rights and duties of the United States on commercial paper which it issues are governed by federal rather than local law." For later applications of the Clearfield doctrine, see Note, 66 Iowa L.Rev. 391 (1981). That the Code is a source of federal common law, see United States v. Conrad, 589 F.2d 949, 953 (8th Cir.1978); Note, 20 B.C.L.Rev. 680, 680–81 (1979).

to the law of contracts, the *expectation* to which an executory promise gives rise is not enough; there must be actual *reliance* in the form of performance of that promise. Subparagraph (c) makes a limited exception to this, notably in the case where the executory promise is embodied in a negotiable instrument. A further exception made in UCC 4–208(1)(b) will be considered later.

Dean Frederick Beutel criticized the Code for its various definitions of "value," Beutel, The Proposed Uniform [?] Commercial Code Should Not Be Adopted, 61 Yale L.J. 334, 339–41 (1952). Professor Gilmore replied: "In effect the Code says that value is any consideration sufficient to support a simple contract (including extension of credit) except that for the purpose of determining when a person . . . is a holder in due course of a negotiable instrument, the extension of credit is not enough: the consideration must be executed. Is the exception necessary? There was considerable sentiment among members of the drafting staff in favor of abolishing the exception and thereby achieving a uniformity in this important concept which the earlier Acts had failed to do. This proposal met the massed opposition of the legal profession as represented in the Conference and the Institute." Gilmore, The Uniform Commercial Code: A Reply to Professor Beutel, 61 Yale L.J. 364, 369 (1952). See also Lawrence, Misconceptions About Article 3 of the Uniform Commercial Code: A Suggested Methodology and Proposed Revisions, 62 N.C.L.Rev. 115, 134–136 (1984).

(4) **Contract Rights.** In a case involving a good faith purchaser of a bill of exchange that had been stolen after the payee had indorsed it in blank, Lord Mansfield distinguished negotiable instruments from ordinary contract rights. "The holder of a bill of exchange, or promissory note, is not to be considered in the light of an assignee of the payee. An assignee must take the thing assigned, subject to all the equity to which the original party was subject. If this rule applied to bills and promissory notes, it would stop their currency." Peacock v. Rhodes, 2 Dougl. 633, 99 Eng.Rep. 402 (K.B. 1781). But should not the assignee of a contract right who has purchased it in good faith have at least the protection accorded by the doctrine of voidable title in the case of fraud?

The modern rule applicable to such an assignee is set out in the Restatement (Second) of Contracts § 343, entitled "Latent Equities."

> If an assignor's right against the obligor is held in trust or constructive trust for or subject to a right of avoidance or equitable lien of another than the obligor, an assignee does not so hold it if he gives value and becomes an assignee in good faith and without notice of the right of the other.

Comment *c* to that section includes an interesting comparison to the Code rules on the same subject.

> The rule of this Section is negated with respect to negotiable instruments and documents of title which are transferred but

not duly negotiated by Uniform Commercial Code §§ 3–306, 7–504, 8–301. But compare § 9–308 (chattel paper).

Is this a fair reading of UCC 3–306? Of UCC 7–504?

What does § 343 mean by "value"? Comment *d* to § 338, after reviewing the various definitions of "value" found in the Code, concludes:

> The extent to which by analogy this statutory rule [of UCC 1–201(44)] may be applicable to purchases of contractual rights not subject to the statutory provisions is beyond the scope of this Restatement.

BOARD OF INLAND REVENUE v. HADDOCK
(THE NEGOTIABLE COW)

A.P. Herbert, The Uncommon Law 112–117, 1936.[12]

"Was the cow crossed?"

"No, your worship, it was an open cow."

These and similar passages provoked laughter at Bow Street to-day when the Negotiable Cow case was concluded.

Sir Joshua Hoot, K.C. (appearing for the Public Prosecutor): [Sir Joshua stated, for Sir Basil String, the justice sitting, the history of Mr. Albert Haddock's dispute with the Collector of Taxes.] On the 31st of May the Collector was diverted from his respectable labours by the apparition of a noisy crowd outside his windows. The crowd, Sir Basil, had been attracted by Mr. Haddock, who was leading a large white cow of malevolent aspect. On the back and sides of the cow were clearly stencilled in red ink the following words:

"To the London and Literary Bank, Ltd.

"Pay the Collector of Taxes, who is no gentlemen, or Order, the sum of fifty-seven pounds (and may he rot!).

£57/0/0 "ALBERT HADDOCK."

Mr. Haddock conducted the cow into the Collector's office, tendered it to the Collector in payment of income-tax and demanded a receipt. . . . The Collector then endeavoured to endorse the cheque—

Sir Basil String: Where?

Sir Joshua: On the back of the cheque, Sir Basil, that is to say on the abdomen of the cow. The cow, however, appeared to resent endorsement and adopted a menacing posture. The Collector, abandoning the attempt, declined finally to take the cheque. . . .

12. Reproduced with permission of the Estate of Sir Alan Herbert.

Mr. Haddock, in the witness-box, said that he had tendered a cheque in payment of income-tax, and if the Commissioners did not like his cheque they could do the other thing. A cheque was only an order to a bank to pay money to the person in possession of the cheque or a person named on the cheque. There was nothing in statute or customary law to say that that order must be written on a piece of paper of specified dimensions. A cheque, it was well known, could be written on a piece of notepaper. He himself had drawn cheques on the backs of menus, on napkins, on handkerchiefs, on the labels of wine-bottles; all these cheques had been duly honoured by his bank and passed through the Bankers' Clearing House. He could see no distinction in law between a cheque written on a napkin and a cheque written on a cow. The essence of each document was a written order to pay money, made in the customary form . . . . There were funds in his bank sufficient to meet the cow; the Commissioners might not like the cow, but, the cow having been tendered, they were estopped from charging him with failure to pay. . . .

Sir Basil String (after hearing of further evidence):

[The court's discussion of the law is omitted.]

In my judgment Mr. Haddock has behaved throughout in the manner of a perfect knight, citizen, and taxpayer. The charge brought by the Crown is dismissed. . . . What is the next case, please?

NOTE

Consistency. Before proceeding to the next chapter, review your answers to the problems in this chapter to see if the rules relating to good faith purchase of goods and commercial paper are consistent. Is the treatment of "value" consistent? Compare Problem 2 (p. 17), Problem 5 (p. 28), Problem 9 (p. 50), and Problem 11 (p. 51). Is the treatment of "good faith" consistent? Compare Problem 2 (p. 17), Problem 5 (p. 28), and Problem 9 (p. 50).

Can you think of adequate explanations for the variations that you find? Do the provisions that you have studied on good faith purchase (notably UCC 2–403(1), 3–305(1)) have helpful similarities in format and style that encourage you in the notion that the Code is a "code" rather than a collection of related statutes? For a survey of holder in due course problems, see McDonnell, Freedom from Claims and Defenses: A Study in Judicial Activism Under the Uniform Commercial Code, 17 Ga.L.Rev. 569 (1983).

Chapter 2

FREEDOM FROM DEFENSES; OTHER CONSEQUENCES

Introduction. The preceding chapter was concerned with the purchaser's freedom from conflicting *claims* of ownership with respect to the property. Where the property consists of an obligation of some kind, further questions arise concerning the purchaser's freedom from *defenses* of the obligor with respect to that obligation. The simplest questions are those arising out of the assignment of an ordinary contract right. The familiar rule is stated by the Code in UCC 9–318(1) and by the Restatement (Second) of Contracts in § 336(1).

> By an assignment the assignee acquires a right against the obligor only to the extent that the obligor is under a duty to the assignor; and if the right of the assignor would be voidable by the obligor or unenforceable against him if no assignment had been made, the right of the assignee is subject to the infirmity.

This chapter explores analogous questions arising out of the transfer of commercial paper.

SECTION 1. DEFENSES TO COMMERCIAL PAPER IN GENERAL

Problem 1. By fraudulent representations B sold A a machine for A's factory for $100,000, payable in 30 days. B assigned the right to payment to the C finance company, which did not know of the fraud and paid B $100,000 less a discount. On discovery of the fraud, A tendered the machine back to C and refused to pay anything.

(a) Can C recover the $100,000 from A? See UCC 9–318(1); Restatement (Second) of Contracts § 336(1), supra.[1]

1. As to B's liability to C, Restatement (Second) of Contracts § 333(1) provides: "Unless a contrary intention is manifested, one who assigns . . . a right by assignment . . . for value warrants to the assignee . . . that the right, as assigned, actually exists and is subject to no limitations or defenses good against the assignor other than those stated or apparent at the time of the assignment. . . ."

(b) What result if the contract between A and B contained a waiver-of-defense clause—an agreement that A will not assert against an assignee any claim or defense that A may have against B? See UCC 9–206, 3–305. (Would a *promise* by C to pay B $100,000 less a discount be value under UCC 9–206(1)? See Note 3, p. 56 supra.)

Problem 2. By fraudulent representations, B sold A a machine for A's factory for $100,000, payable in 30 days. In connection with the sale, A executed a negotiable promissory note, promising "to pay to the order of B, $100,000" in 30 days. B assigned the right to payment and negotiated the note to the C finance company, by indorsing it "Pay to the order of C, (signed) B." C did not suspect the fraud and paid B $100,000 less a discount. On discovery of the fraud, A tendered the machine back to C and refused to pay anything. Can C recover the $100,000 from A? See UCC 3–305; First National Bank of Odessa v. Fazzari, infra; Universal C.I.T. Credit Corp. v. Ingel, infra.

Problem 3. Would the answer to the preceding problem be different if the body of the promissory note read as follows:

> For value received, I promise to pay to the order of B, $100,000, payable $50,000 in six months after date and $50,000 in twelve months after date, with interest at six per cent per annum on payments overdue, with the privilege of discharging this note by payment of principal less a discount of five per cent within thirty days from the date hereof. The entire principal of this note shall become due and payable on demand should the holder at any time deem itself insecure.

See UCC 3–106, 3–109, 1–208. (Does the note provide for a discount "if paid before . . . the date fixed for payment"? Comment 1 to UCC 3–106 says, "It is sufficient that at any time of payment the holder is able to determine the amount then payable from the instrument itself with any necessary computation." Does the note meet this test?)

FIRST NATIONAL BANK OF ODESSA v. FAZZARI

Court of Appeals of New York, 1961.
10 N.Y.2d 394, 223 N.Y.S.2d 483, 179 N.E.2d 493.

FOSTER, JUDGE. On December 16, 1957 defendant executed a six-month promissory note to the order of John Wade, Jr. The instrument was payable at the Glen National Bank, Watkins Glen, N.Y., in the amount of $400, with interest. Apparently defendant was unable to read or write English. It was found below that the payee, Wade, prepared the note and induced defendant to sign it upon the misrepresentation that it was a statement of wages earned by Wade while working for defendant, and that it was necessary for income tax purposes. Defendant was not in debt to Wade, and there was no consideration given for the note. The note was signed at the home of defendant in Watkins Glen. At the time, his wife and daughter were present in the house, and his wife, who was able to read, was in an adjoining room. Defendant did not request his wife to read the instrument.

Subsequently defendant learned that the instrument he had signed might have been a note. He consulted his attorney who advised him to notify all of the banks in Schuyler County, and to advise them not to accept the note. In January of 1958, defendant orally informed the cashier of the plaintiff bank in Odessa that he "had been tricked" and that he did not intend to sign a note. He instructed the cashier not to "cash a note" for John Wade, and "not to give him any money under my name". The cashier told him "not to worry" and defendant departed. The cashier, Gilbert, recalled the incident, and testified that defendant told him not to give any money to anyone under Fazzari's name. Gilbert acknowledged that he probably did tell defendant "not to worry", but testified that at the time the note was presented to him for discount he had forgotten the incident.

We thus have an element presented in this case not present in any of the "forgotten notice" cases so far as we have been able to discover. Not only was notice given to the very cashier who subsequently discounted the note, but the defendant was assured that he had no cause to be concerned about the bank's discounting the note. The phrase "not to worry" would present no other realistic meaning to the average person.

On April 10, 1958 the note was presented to the First National Bank of Odessa by Wellington R. Doane, a customer of the bank and an indorsee of the payee, Wade. Doane indorsed the instrument in blank, and the plaintiff bank, by its cashier, Gilbert, accepted it for value, paying $400 by cashier's check. It was found by the trial court that the cashier, at the time of the negotiation of the note to the bank, had forgotten defendant's prior visit to the bank and the oral notice he had given.

After nonpayment and protest, the plaintiff bank brought this action against defendant. At the close of the evidence the trial court awarded judgment to the plaintiff, holding that the bank was a holder in due course under section 91, Consol.Laws, c. 38, of the Negotiable Instruments Law [NIL 52], since its agent had forgotten the prior notice and had acted in good faith in accepting the note. The Appellate Division reversed, holding that the notice, once given, was binding on the bank (Negotiable Instruments Law, § 91, subd. 4) [NIL 52(4)]; that the bank was not a holder in due course; and that the maker's defense, therefore, was valid.

Thus the status of the bank is determinative here. The courts below found fraud in the factum; that is, defendant was induced to sign something entirely different than what he thought he was signing. *In the absence of negligence on the part of the maker,* such fraud constitutes a real defense and is sufficient against a holder in due course [citations omitted]. But the courts below have determined as a fact that defendant was negligent in not asking his wife to read over the instrument prior to signing. We cannot say this finding was erroneous as a matter of law, particularly since defendant, an experienced business man, on prior occasions, asked that documents of obvious legal import be read to him before signing. Defendant also knew that he had paid Wade $500 in wages, and yet signed a purported statement of wages in the amount of $400.

The facts as determined by the trial court have been affirmed. The sole question presented is this: Did the bank, the purchaser of a negotiable promissory note, qualify as a holder in due course, and defeat the effect of a prior oral notice of infirmity in the note, by showing that it had forgotten the notice at the time of purchase?

Section 91 of the Negotiable Instruments Law [NIL 52] provides:

"A holder in due course is a holder who has taken the instrument under the following conditions:

"1. That it is complete and regular upon its face;

"2. That he became the holder of it before it was overdue, and without notice that it had been previously dishonored, if such was the fact;

"3. That he took it in good faith and for value;

"4. That at the time it was negotiated to him he had no notice of any infirmity in the instrument or defect in the title of the person negotiating it."

Section 95 [NIL 56] provides: "To constitute notice of an infirmity in the instrument or defect in the title of the person negotiating the same, the person to whom it is negotiated must have had actual knowledge of the infirmity or defect, or knowledge of such facts that his action in taking the instrument amounted to bad faith."

The bank contends that the cashier did not have notice of the infirmity *at the time of the negotiation,* and thus the bank met each of the conditions of sections 91 and 95 [NIL 52, 56], and we are asked to apply the doctrine of forgotten notice. This doctrine was first enunciated in Raphael v. Bank of England (17 C.B. 161, 84 Eng.Com.Law 160) cited with approval by this court in Magee v. Badger (34 N.Y. 247, 249). In the Raphael case notice of a robbery of a certain note was given to a bank, but thereafter the bank accepted the note for value and contended that it had forgotten the notice. It was held that a jury question existed as to whether the bank had forgotten the notice or omitted inadvertently to look for the notice, and that such a lapse of memory and omission to look for the notice, if established, would constitute mere negligence, not *mala fides.* Mere negligence, it was held, would not destroy the bank's status as a holder in due course. In Lord v. Wilkinson (56 Barb. 593 [Sup.Ct., Broome County,

1870]) the doctrine of forgotten notice was adopted by a court of this State, and Raphael v. Bank of England specifically was followed. In the Lord case the facts again were strikingly similar to those herein involved. In Graham v. White-Phillips Co., 296 U.S. 27, 56 S.Ct. 21, 80 L.Ed. 20, the United States Supreme Court, construing the Illinois Negotiable Instruments Law (containing the same provisions as the New York law), followed the Lord and Raphael cases, and referred specifically thereto. That case involved forgotten notice of stolen bonds, and it was held that the negligent omission to look for the notice, or to recall it, did not destroy the status of the defendant as a holder in due course.

The rule was followed in Merchants Nat. Bank v. Detroit Trust Co. (258 Mich. 526, 242 N.W. 739, 85 A.L.R. 350, cited with approval in Graham v. White-Phillips Co., supra) and in State Bank of Benkelman v. Iowa-Des Moines Nat. Bank & Trust Co. (223 Iowa 596, 273 N.W. 160; see, also, Seybel v. National Currency Bank, 54 N.Y. 288, wherein this court virtually approved the doctrine; contra, Northwestern Nat. Bank v. Madison & Kedzie State Bank, 242 Ill. App. 22, holding notice, once given, is binding on the bank). The doctrine is not without its critics, who favor an objective test of notice. Thus, it is said, notice once given should bind the purchaser, for such a rule would impose upon the banks no more difficult administrative responsibility than they are under in many analogous situations (see e.g., Britton, Bills and Notes [1943], p. 449; Merrill, The Wages of Indifference, 10 Temp.L.Q. 147; Unforgettable Knowledge, 34 Mich. L.Rev. 474; The Anatomy of Notice, 3 U. of Chi.L.Rev. 416; 10 Tul.L. Rev. 302; cf. 40 Harv.L.Rev. 315; 45 Yale L.J. 539).

Perhaps the doctrine is in accord with the general rule in New York, that "The rights of the holder [of a negotiable instrument] are to be determined by the simple test of honesty and good faith, and not by speculations in regard to the purchaser's diligence or negligence" (Manufacturers & Traders Trust Co. v. Sapowitch, 296 N.Y. 226, 230, 72 N.E.2d 166; Magee v. Badger, 34 N.Y. 247, 249). "The requirement of the statute is good faith, and bad faith is not mere carelessness. It is nothing less than guilty knowledge or willful ignorance" (Manufacturers & Traders Trust Co. v. Sapowitch, supra, 296 N.Y. p. 229, 72 N.E.2d p. 168 . . .). The doctrine, of course, is based on a policy of freedom of negotiability.

The Appellate Division was of the opinion that since the doctrine was adopted prior to the enactment of the Negotiable Instruments Law (Lord v. Wilkinson, supra) its rationale should be rejected. We are not prepared to reject the doctrine summarily and to hold that once notice is given it is fixed and immutable for all time as to negotiable instruments, particularly in the case where a blanket notice is broadcast with relation to stolen bonds and other securities (Kentucky Rock Asphalt Co. v. Mazza's Adm'r, 264 Ky. 158, 165, 94 S.W.2d 316). But we also think that the doctrine should be applied with great caution in the case where a simple promissory note is involved. A lapse of memory is too easily pleaded and too difficult to controvert to permit the doctrine to be applied automatically irrespective of the circumstances surrounding each transaction and the relationship of the parties. Under the peculiar facts of this case a strict application of the doctrine would be unrealistic and not in the interests of substantial justice. As we have heretofore said, something more than the naked fact of notice is involved here. The defendant was practically assured that his notice would be honored and that the note would not be discounted by the plaintiff bank. Under such circumstances, the bank should be precluded from invoking the doctrine of "forgotten notice."

The judgment should be affirmed.

NOTES

(1) The Code. What result in the Fazzari case under the Code? See UCC 1–201(25), 3–302, 3–305. Note that there were no conflicting "claims" of ownership under UCC 3–305(1) since it was not argued that the bank was not the owner of the instrument. Rather there was a "defense" of fraud under UCC 3–305(2) asserted by the maker of the note. In order to be free from that defense under the Code the bank would have to establish four things. First, the bank would have to show that the note was negotiable, that is that it met the requisites of negotiability laid down by UCC 3–104. Second, it would have to show that it took the note by negotiation so as to become a holder of it under UCC 1–201(20), 3–202(1). Third, it would have to show that it complied with the requirements for holding in due course under UCC 3–302. And fourth, it would have to show that the maker's defense was one of those defenses known as *personal* defenses, to which the holder in due course is immune rather than one of those exceptional defenses known as real defenses, to which the holder in due course is subject under UCC 3–305(2). As to which of these four was there a controversy in the Fazzari case? Which would be the bank's weakest point under the Code?

(2) Who Benefits From Negotiability? Take the simple situation in which a buyer, as maker, executes a negotiable promissory note for the price of goods to the order of the seller, as payee, who then indorses it to a financing agency, as holder in due course. In considering who benefits from the negotiability of the note, it is best to concentrate on the normal case, in which the buyer asserts no defense on the note, rather than the abnormal case (popular with editors of casebooks), such as the Fazzari case, in which the buyer does assert a defense. Obviously the financing agency benefits by being freed from most defenses in the abnormal case. But in the normal case, the seller and the buyer benefit as well because of the resulting expansion of the "market" for commercial paper. The seller, who "dealt" with the buyer, would not have been protected by UCC 3–

305(2) if the seller had retained the note. However, the seller benefits indirectly from the protection that that section affords the financing agency to which the seller negotiates it because such financing agencies, freed from most of the buyer's defenses, are more willing to finance such transactions and to do so on more favorable terms. This, in turn, enables the seller to sell to more buyers on credit and to offer them more favorable terms. And this benefits the buyer since it increases the opportunity to buy on credit and to obtain more favorable terms. On this reasoning, a buyer's ability to relinquish most defenses as against a financing agency by signing a negotiable promissory note, may make credit available when it would otherwise be denied or may make credit available to him at more favorable terms than would otherwise be available. Are there instances in which society should restrict a buyer's freedom to obtain these advantages in return for the relinquishment of most defenses?

UNIVERSAL C.I.T. CREDIT CORP. v. INGEL

Supreme Judicial Court of Massachusetts, 1964.
347 Mass. 119, 196 N.E.2d 847.

SPIEGEL, JUSTICE. This is an action of contract on a promissory note by the assignee of the payee against the maker. The case was first tried in the District Court of Fitchburg, to which it had been remanded by the Superior Court. There was a finding for the plaintiff in the sum of $1,630.12. At the request of the defendants, the case was retransferred to the Superior Court for trial by jury. Upon conclusion of the evidence the court allowed a motion by the plaintiff for a directed verdict to which the defendants excepted. They also excepted to the exclusion of certain evidence.

At the trial the plaintiff introduced in evidence the note,[1] a completion certificate signed by the defendants, and the District Court's

1.

"This Is A Negotiable Promissory Note

$1890.00
(Total Amount of Note)
    Fitchburg, Mass., 6/22, 1959
    (City, State)   (Date)

I/WE JOINTLY AND SEVERALLY PROMISE TO PAY TO ALLIED ALUMINUM ASSOCIATES, INC. OR ORDER THE SUM OF EIGHTEEN HUNDRED NINETY DOLLARS IN 60 SUCCESSIVE MONTHLY INSTALMENTS OF $31.50 EACH, EXCEPT THAT THE FINAL INSTALMENT SHALL BE THE BALANCE THEN DUE ON THIS NOTE. COMMENCING THE 25 DAY OF JULY, 1959, AND THE SAME DATE OF EACH MONTH THEREAFTER UNTIL PAID, with interest after maturity at the highest lawful rate, and a reasonable sum (15% if permitted by law) as attorney's fees, if this note is placed in the hands of any attorney for collection after maturity. Upon nonpayment of any instalment at its maturity, all remaining instalments shall at the option of the holder become due and payable forthwith. Charges for handling late payments, of 5¢ per $1 (maximum $5), are payable on any instalment more than 10 days in arrears. . . . *Notice of Proposed Credit Life Insurance:* Group credit life insurance will be obtained by the holder of this instrument, without additional charge to customer, subject to acceptance by the insurer, Old Republic Life Insurance Company, Chica-

finding for the plaintiff. The defendants admitted the authenticity of the signatures on the note and the completion certificate. As a witness for the defendants, one Charles D. Fahey testified that he was the plaintiff's Boston branch manager at the time the defendants' note was purchased, and that the plaintiff purchases instalment contracts regarding automobile and property improvement purchases. He described the procedures by which purchases of commercial paper are arranged by the plaintiff; these procedures included a credit check on the "customer," i.e., the maker of the note which the plaintiff is planning to purchase. The defendants attempted to introduce through Fahey a credit report obtained by the plaintiff on Allied Aluminum Associates, Inc. (Allied), the payee of the note. The defendants excepted to the exclusion of this evidence. They offered to prove that the excluded report, which was dated "3–31–59," contained the following statement: "The subject firm is engaged in the sale of storm windows, doors, roofing, siding, and bathroom and kitchen remodeling work. The firm engages a crew of commission salesmen and it is reported they have been doing a good volume of business. They are reported to employ high pressure sales methods for the most part. They have done considerable advertising in newspapers, on radio, and have done soliciting by telephone. They have been criticized for their advertising methods, and have been accused of using bait advertising, and using false and misleading statements. The Boston Better Business Bureau has had numerous complaints regarding their advertising methods, and have reported same to the Attorney General. *FHA has had no complaints other than report of this from Better Business Bureau and have warned the firm to stop their practice.*"

The defendants excepted to the exclusion of testimony by the defendant Dora Ingel concerning certain of her negotiations with Allied. An offer of proof was made which indicates that this testimony might have been evidence of fraud or breach of warranty on the part of

go, Illinois. Such insurance will cover only the individual designated and signing below as the person to be insured (who must be an officer if customer is a corporation, a partner if partnership), except that no individual 65 years of age or older on the date the indebtedness is incurred will be eligible for such insurance. Such insurance will become effective, upon acceptance by the insurer, as of the date the indebtedness is incurred, and will terminate when the indetedness terminates or upon such default or other event as terminates the insurance under the terms of the group policy. The amount of such insurance will be equal to the amount of customer's indebtedness hereunder at any time but not to exceed $10,000; proceeds will be applicable to reduction or discharge of the indebtedness.

The provisions of this paragraph are subject to the terms of the group policy and the certificate to be issued.

PLEASE PRINT MAILING ADDRESS

Customer acknowledges receipt of a completed copy of this promissory note, including above Notice.

ALBERT T. INGEL

Customer (Person on whose life group credit life insurance will be obtained, if applicable.)

DORA INGEL

(Additional Customer, if any)

ORIGINAL"

Allied. They also excepted to the exclusion of a letter [2] from the plaintiff to the defendant Albert.

I.

The defendants contend that the note was nonnegotiable as a matter of law and, therefore, any defence which could be raised against Allied may also be raised against the plaintiff. They argue that the note contained a promise other than the promise to pay, failed to state a sum certain, and had been materially altered.

It appears that the note was a form note drafted by the plaintiff. The meaning of Fahey's general testimony that the note and the completion certificate were "together" when given by the plaintiff to Allied is unclear. However, we see nothing in this testimony to justify the inference urged upon us by the defendants that in this case the note and completion certificate were "part of the same instrument" and that an additional obligation in the completion certificate rendered the note nonnegotiable under G.L. c. 106, § 3–104(1)(b). Similarly, we are not concerned with any variance between the written contract (entered into by Allied and the defendants) and the note, since there is nothing in the note to indicate that it is subject to the terms of the contract. We are equally satisfied that the insurance clause in the note does not affect negotiability under § 3–104(1)(b) since it is clear that the "no other promise" provision refers only to promises by the maker.

The provision in the note for "interest after maturity at the highest lawful" rate does not render the note nonnegotiable for failure to state a sum certain as required by § 3–104(1)(b). We are of opinion that after maturity the interest rate is that indicated in G.L. c. 107, § 3,[3] since in this case there is no agreement in writing for any other

2.

"October 27, 1959

Identification 'B'

Mr. Albert Ingel
115 Belmont
Fitchburg, Massachusetts
            Re: 200–12–51767

Dear Sir,

We are sorry to learn that the Aluminum Siding on which we hold your promissory note, is giving you cause for complaint. Our part in the transactions consisted of extending the credit which you desired, and arranging to accept prepayment of the advance on terms convenient to you. We did not perform any of the work, and any questions in connection with materials and workmanship should be adjusted with the dealer from whom you made your purchase. There-fore, we have passed your report along to Allied Aluminum and we are confident that everything reasonably possible will be done to correct any faulty conditions which may exist.

In the meantime, we shall appreciate your continuing to make payments on your note as they fall due so that your account may be kept in current condition.

Very truly yours,
UNIVERSAL C.I.T. CREDIT CORPORATION
C. KEVENY
Collection Man"

3. "If there is no agreement or provision of law for a different rate, the interest of money shall be at the rate of six dollars on each hundred for a year, but, except as provided in sections seventy-eight, ninety, ninety-two, ninety-six and one hundred of chapter one hundred and forty, it shall be lawful to pay, reserve or

rate after default. This being the case, we do not treat this note differently from one payable "with interest." The latter note would clearly be negotiable under G.L. c. 106, § 3–118(d).

The note in question provides that payment shall be made "commencing the 25 day of July, 1959." It appears that there is an alteration on the face of the note in that "July" was substituted for "June," the "ly" in the former word being written over the "ne" in the latter. The alteration has no effect in this case, where the defendants admitted that they had paid a particular sum on the note and where the sum still owing (assuming the note to be enforceable on its face) is not in dispute. See Mindell v. Goldman, 309 Mass. 472, 473–474, 35 N.E.2d 669.

We thus conclude that the note in question is a negotiable instrument.[4]

II.

The finding of the District Court which the plaintiff offered in evidence is, under G.L. c. 231, § 102C, prima facie evidence upon such matters as are put in issue by the pleading at the trial in the Superior Court. Lubell v. First Nat. Stores, Inc., 342 Mass. 161, 164, 172 N.E.2d 689. The defendants' answer denies that the plaintiff is "a holder in due course" of the note on which the action is brought; accordingly, this must be regarded as a matter "put in issue by the pleadings." We are satisfied that the finding of the District Court was prima facie evidence that the plaintiff took the note for value and without notice, and notwithstanding the provisions of G.L. c. 106, § 3–307(3), the burden was on the defendants to rebut the plaintiff's prima facie case. See Cook v. Farm Service Stores, Inc., 301 Mass. 564, 566, 17 N.E.2d 890.

III.

The trial judge correctly excluded the evidence offered by the defendants to show that the plaintiff and Allied had worked together on various aspects of the financing and that the plaintiff was aware of complaints against Allied by previous customers. We are of opinion that there was nothing in this evidence by which the plaintiff had "reason to know" of any fraud. The letter of October 27, 1959, from the plaintiff to the defendant Albert was also properly excluded; it is immaterial that the plaintiff may have found out about Allied's allegedly fraudulent representations after the note had been purchased.

Exceptions overruled.

contract for any rate of interest or discount. No greater rate than that before mentioned shall be recoverd in a suit unless the agreement to pay it is in writing."

4. By G.L. c. 255, § 12C, inserted by St.1961, c. 595, certain notes given in connection with the sale of consumer goods were made nonnegotiable.

NOTES

(1) **Requisites of Negotiability.** Promissory notes, which are often relatively elaborate and may contain hand tailored provisions to suit the particular transaction, are more likely to run afoul of the requisites of negotiability than are checks and other drafts, which are usually relatively simple in form. The creditor who is the payee of a note will want to bind the debtor with numerous obligations in addition to the clean-cut promise to pay money. The creditor wants to be able to declare the entire debt due if the debtor defaults on any obligation or if the debtor's financial position becomes shaky. The creditor who takes a security interest in personal property wants to bind the debtor not to make off with the collateral and also to keep it insured, undamaged, and free from liens.

This need to secure a wide assortment of promises from the debtor came into collision with the traditional rules on the proper scope of negotiability—a tradition epitomized by Chief Justice Gibson's famous dictum that a negotiable instrument must be "a courier without luggage." [5] The fences that were erected to confine the doctrine of negotiability took the form of the "formal requisites" for negotiable instruments set forth in painful detail in the Negotiable Instruments Law and carried forward, with significant modifications, in Article 3 of the Code. See UCC 3–104–3–114.

Why have such complex "formal requisites"? Why not permit the parties to a contract to make it a negotiable instrument simply by so stating in the contract itself? Professor Chafee advanced the following explanation: "Although the law usually cares little about the form of a contract and looks to the actual understanding of the parties who made it, the form of a negotiable instrument is essential for the security of mercantile transactions. The courts ought to enforce these requisites of commercial paper at the risk of hardship in particular cases. A businessman must be able to tell at a glance whether he is taking commercial paper or not. There must be no twilight zone between negotiable instruments and simple contracts. If doubtful instruments are sometimes held to be negotiable, prospective purchasers of queer paper will be encouraged to take a chance with the hope that an indulgent judge will call it negotiable. On the same principle, if trains habitually left late, more people would miss trains than under a system of rigid punctuality." Chafee, Acceleration Provisions in Time Paper, 32 Harv.L.Rev. 747, 750 (1919).[6] Is this the only reason for confining the attributes of negotiability to a limited class of paper? If the "security of mercantile transactions" is the only object, why have such complex requisites?

Contrast with Chafee's remarks the following comment by Professor Gilmore: "Few generalizations have been more fully repeated, or

---

5. Overton v. Tyler, 3 Pa. 346, 45 Am. Dec. 645 (1846).

6. Reproduced with permission of The Harvard Law Review Association.

by generations of lawyers more devoutly believed, than this: negotiability is a matter rather of form than substance. It is bred in the bone of every lawyer that an instrument to be negotiable must be 'a courier without luggage.' It must conform to a set of admirably abstract specifications which, for our generation, have been codified in Section 1 of the Negotiable Instruments Law and spelled out in the nine following sections. These rules are fixed, eternal and immutable. No other branch of law is so clear, so logical, so inherently satisfying as the law of formal requisites of negotiability. To determine the negotiability of any instrument, all that need be done is to lay it against the yardstick of NIL sections 1–10: if it is an exact fit it is negotiable; a hair's breadth over or under and it is not.

"Few generalizations, legal or otherwise, have been less true; the truth is, in this as in every other field of commercial law, substance has always prevailed over form. 'The law' has always been in a constant state of flux as it struggles to adjust itself to changing methods of business practice; what purport to be formal rules of abstract logic are merely *ad hoc* responses to particular situations.

"Nevertheless, the cherished belief in the sacrosanct nature of formal requisites serves, as do most legal principles, a useful function. The problem is what types of paper shall be declared negotiable so that purchasers may put on the nearly invincible armor of the holder in due course. The policy in favor of protecting the good faith purchaser does not run beyond the frontiers of commercial usage. Beyond those confines every reason of policy dictates the opposite approach. The formal requisites are the professional rules with which professionals are or ought to be familiar. As to instruments which are amateur productions outside any concept of the ordinary course of business, or new types which are just coming into professional use, it is wiser to err by being unduly restrictive than by being over liberal. The formal requisites serve as a useful exclusionary device and as a brake on a too rapid acceptance of emerging trends. . . .

"As long as the law distinguishes between commercial and noncommercial property on the basis of form, there will have to be borderline or fringe litigation. On the whole a continuing trickle of such litigation is not obnoxious; it produces a clearer state of the law than does the law of sales where the doctrines say one thing and mean another, a situation not productive of certainty and predictability." Gilmore, The Commercial Doctrine of Good Faith Purchase, 63 Yale L.J. 1057, 1068–69, 1072 (1954).[7]

According to Dean Mentschikoff, the Associate Chief Reporter for the Code, "the classification of these pieces of paper [bills of exchange, notes, checks] as negotiable instruments should be dependent on commercial use and the nature of the current markets to be pro-

7. Reproduced with permission of the Yale Law Journal.

tected." Mentschikoff, Highlights of the Uniform Commercial Code, 27 Mod.L.Rev. 167, 176 (1964).

Do the Code provisions seem to take "commercial usage" and current markets into account? In times of rapidly changing interest rates, the parties to a loan may want to provide for a variable or "floating" interest rate, for example one tied to a published rate. Would such a provision affect the negotiability of a note? See UCC 3–106(1).[8]

(2) Acceleration Clauses. Under UCC 3–109(1)(c), negotiability is not impaired by the fact that the instrument is payable "at a definite time subject to any acceleration." It may seem surprising that such a provision was thought to be necessary since, as Comment 4 to UCC 3–109 points out: "So far as certainty of time of payment is concerned a note payable at a definite time but subject to acceleration is no less certain than a note payable on demand, whose negotiability has never been questioned. It is in fact more certain, since it at least states a definite time beyond which the instrument cannot run." Nevertheless, under the Negotiable Instruments Law courts generally held that at least some types of acceleration clauses impaired negotiability.

NIL 2(3) provided that where payment was by instalments the sum payable was "a sum certain" in spite of "a provision that upon default in payment of any instalment or of interest the whole shall become due." From this it was argued that negotiability was destroyed by other types of acceleration clauses which did not condition the holder's right to accelerate the time for payment on some event within the control of the debtor. Typical of the clauses condemned by this argument were those giving the holder the power to accelerate "at will" or "when he deems himself insecure."

The comments to an early draft of Article 3 of the Code gave the following explanation for this line of decisions: "It seems evident that the courts which give uncertainty of time of payment as a reason for denying negotiability are in reality objecting to the acceleration clause itself. This objection may be founded on abuses of the clause. The signer of an acceleration note, unlike the signer of a demand note, does not expect to be called upon to pay before the ultimate date. Normally he understands the acceleration clause to be for the protection of the holder against his own insolvency or similar contingencies, and he expects that the note will not be accelerated without good reason. An unscrupulous creditor can accelerate it without rea-

---

8. A statute enacted in Louisiana in 1981 provides that in "accordance with regulations promulgated by the commissioner of financial institutions . . . a supervised financial organization may vary from time to time the interest rate it charges on a promissory note by setting forth in the promissory note the terms and conditions under which the rate may change" and that this shall not "destroy the negotiability of the promissory note." La.Stat.Ann.—Rev.Stat. 6:25.1. See also Rev.Stat. 9:3504, which provides for negotiable promissory notes evidencing adjustable rate mortgage loans.

son, and a note prematurely called may ruin the debtor. . . . Inquiry among banks has led to the conclusion that the privilege of acceleration at the option of the holder has real advantage to the creditor, who frequently must act on the basis of confidential information or evidence as to the condition of the debtor which does not amount to definite proof. The effect of denying negotiability to acceleration paper is not to remedy any abuses arising in connection with the acceleration clause, which remains in effect even if the instrument be treated as a simple contract. It is merely to open the paper to defenses which have nothing to do with acceleration." Commercial Code, Comments and Notes to Article III 43–44 (Tent.Draft No. 1, 1946). See also Comment 4 to UCC 3–109.

The Code, therefore, makes the power to accelerate irrelevant to the issue of negotiability. See UCC 3–105(1)(c). But UCC 1–208 limits the holder's power to accelerate "at will" or "when he deems himself insecure" by requiring "good faith." What does good faith mean in this sense? See UCC 1–201(19). How easy would it be for the maker to prove lack of good faith? See Note, 13 U.Mich.J.L.Ref. 623 (1980). Does UCC 1–208 limit the power of the holder of a note payable on demand to demand payment? Why? See Comment to UCC 1–208; Fulton National Bank v. Willis Denney Ford, 154 Ga.App. 846, 269 S.E.2d 916 (1980).

One reason for including a clause permitting acceleration "should the holder of this note deem the debt insecure" is suggested by State National Bank of Decatur v. Towns, 36 Ala.App. 677, 62 So.2d 606 (1952). In that case the bank which held such a note as payee was served, before the maturity date of the note, with a writ of garnishment by which a judgment creditor of the maker sought satisfaction from the maker's bank account. However the bank was held to be entitled to accelerate the maturity date under the clause and set off its debt ahead of the judgment creditor. "By the garnishment the judgment plaintiff acquired only the rights to the judgment defendant. As to the judgment defendant the bank, as a result of the acceleration clause in the note, had a right of set off against any claim of the judgment defendant in a suit against it." The note held by the bank also contained a clause purporting to give the bank a "lien" on the maker's account, but the court did not rely on this, pointing out that a bank has a right to set off a general deposit against a debt of the depositor if the debt is matured. See Note 2, p. 122 infra.

(3) Reference to Other Documents. The effects of other documents upon negotiability are dealt with in UCC 3–105(1)(c), (e) and 3–119(1). UCC 3–105(1)(c) was amended in 1962 by adding the words "or refers to a separate agreement for rights as to prepayment or acceleration." "This change was made to meet a criticism of the [New York Clearing House Association] that the 1958 Official Text appears to preclude a very common provision in notes that allows acceleration or prepayment in accordance with the terms of a loan agreement or mortgage of a particular date. This provision is of primary concern to banks who wish to discount or pledge commercial paper with Federal Reserve Banks or other large banking institutions. [Footnote:] Although negotiability is not required in specific terms by the Federal Reserve Act . . . or the Federal Reserve Board's regulations, the definitions of promissory notes, drafts, and bills of exchange contained in Regulation A have been so interpreted. See 9 Fed.Reserve Bull. 559 (1923)." Penney, New York Revisits the Code: Some Variations in the New York Enactment of the Uniform Commercial Code, 62 Colum.L.Rev. 992, 994–95 (1962).[8]

(4) **Negotiability Revisited.** A quarter of a century after expressing the thoughts in Note 1 supra, Professor Gilmore had these harsh words for the Code. "As a general rule, anything—including negotiability—which was good enough for Lord Mansfield was good enough for Llewellyn. That attitude, unfortunately, carried through to the drafting of Article 3 of the Code, which can be described as the N.I.L. doubled in spades or negotiability *in excelsis.* Article 3 gravely takes up each of the pressure points which developed in the N.I.L. case law and resolves the issue in favor of negotiability. [In a footnote he gives examples including the provisions of UCC 3–109 on acceleration clauses and of UCC 3–105 on notes with security agreements, discussed in Notes 2 and 3 supra.] . . . What Article 3 really is is a museum of antiquities—a treasure house crammed full of ancient artifacts whose use and function have long since been forgotten. Another function of codification, we may note, is to preserve the past, like a fly in amber." Gilmore, Formalism and the Law of Negotiable Instruments, 13 Creighton L.Rev. 441 (1979).

(5) **Non-negotiable Instruments.** Under the Negotiable Instruments Law, unless the instrument complied with the requisites of negotiability, none of the statutory provisions was applicable. In many instances the rules were the same for instruments that were not negotiable, but this was not because the statute controlled but because the statute was, in part, a codification of common law rules, some of which applied to non-negotiable instruments as well. In addition, in a few instances, courts applied the statutory provisions to non-negotiable instruments by analogy. Here the Code departs from the Negotiable Instruments Law in two significant respects. First, while NIL 1 provided that an instrument had to comply with the stated requisites "to be negotiable" UCC 3–104 says only that it must comply "to be a negotiable instrument within this Article." According to Comment 1 to that section this language "leaves open the possibility that some writings may be made negotiable by other statutes or by judicial decision." Second, UCC 3–805, which has no counterpart in the Negotiable Instruments Law, creates a special class of non-negotiable instrument to which all of Article 3 applies with the very important

8. Reproduced with permission of the
Columbia Law Review.

exception that "there can be no holder in due course of such an instrument."

SECTION 2. DEFENSES TO COMMERCIAL PAPER IN CONSUMER TRANSACTIONS

The Nature of the Problem. The situation in which Albert and Dora Ingel found themselves (p. 67 supra) was a common one in which a consumer buyer purchases goods from a retail seller and signs documents that the seller transfers to a financing agency, usually a finance company or a bank. The goods prove to be defective. If it were the seller who claimed payment from the buyer, the buyer would have a defense, either by rejecting (UCC 2–601) them if they have not already been accepted, or by revoking acceptance (UCC 2–608) or setting off damages for breach of warranty against the price (UCC 2–714, 2–717) if they have been accepted. But are these remedies still available when the claim against the buyer is made by the financing agency to whom the seller's rights have been transferred?

Of course, even if the buyer must pay the price to the financing agency, he still has a claim against the seller. The buyer's interest in asserting a claim against the one who demands the price grows out of the following considerations, which are particularly strong in consumer transactions. (1) *The inertia of litigation.* Setting up a defense as a defendant is easier than starting an action, even though the "burden of proof" with regard to the seller's breach may fall on the buyer in either case. In practice, this consideration has its greatest impact on the settlement value of the buyer's claim, since a reduction in price is much easier to negotiate than a cash refund. (2) *The strain of current cash outlay.* The buyer may not have the resources to pay the full amount for defective goods and wait until a legal action against the seller can reach trial, which in many jurisdictions may take years, and finally be converted into a judgment. (3) *The risk of the seller's insolvency.* The seller may be insolvent or judgment proof. The seller may have been a fly-by-night operator, or driven into sharp practice by financial pressure, or forced to the wall by keen competition, poor management or a business recession.

Conversely, these advantages to the buyer in preserving defenses against the financing agency, suggest the importance to it of freeing itself from these defenses. In addition, its interest is magnified to the extent that buyers interpose spurious defenses in an attempt to scale down or avoid their obligation to pay for what they buy.

For several decades, opposing interests struggled over whether a financing agency should be permitted to insulate itself from defenses that a consumer buyer would have had against the seller, either by using a negotiable instrument (as in the Ingel case) or a waiver-of-defense clause (as in Problem 1(b), p. 62 supra). The result was a substantial revision of the traditional concept of good faith purchase as applied to consumer transactions.

Judicial Intervention. The first victories for the consumer oriented view came in the courts, which began to hold by the early 1950s that a financing agency that was closely connected with a retailer could not be a holder in due course and was not protected by a waiver-of-defense clause. These courts twisted traditional notions of good faith and notice to reach what they regarded as a just result. According to the Supreme Court of Arkansas, in an early seminal case, the finance company "was so closely connected . . . with the deal that it can not be heard to say that it, in good faith, was an innocent purchaser" of a note given by a buyer for a car. Commercial Credit Co. v. Childs, 199 Ark. 1073, 1077, 137 S.W.2d 260, 262 (1940). According to the Supreme Court of Florida, where a finance company had been involved in the transaction it "had such notice of . . . infirmity" in a note given by a grocer for a freezer. The court also stated the policy behind such decisions. "We believe the finance company is better able to bear the risk of the dealer's insolvency than the buyer and in a far better position to protect his interests against unscrupulous and insolvent dealers." Mutual Finance Co. v. Martin, 63 So.2d 649, 653 (Fla.1953). The nature of the transaction made it difficult for the financing agency to divorce itself from the seller sufficiently to avoid being characterized as "closely connected." Since the relationship is ordinarily a continuing one, there is typically a master agreement and some arrangement for a fund to be retained by the financing agency to secure its right of recourse against the seller.[1] In addition, the financing agency will insist that the standard forms for contracts with buyers as well as for assignments be its own. But though the requisite close connection could usually be shown, the buyer had to show it in each case, and in this respect these decisions fell short of giving the buyer optimum protection.

Legislative Intervention. By the early 1970's most states had enacted statutes applicable to consumer transactions [2] prohibiting nego-

---

1. Under recourse financing, the dealer is liable to the financing agency in the event of the buyer's default. But the assignment of a simple contract right does not of itself operate as a warranty that the obligor is solvent or will perform his obligation. See Restatement (Second) of Contracts § 333(2). Therefore, if recourse financing is intended, an express provision to that effect must be added to the language of assignment or to the master agreement under which the assignment is made. An indorser of commercial paper, however, engages that if the obligor refuses to pay he, the indorser, will pay the instrument to his in-

dorsee (UCC 3–414(1)), if the indorsee takes prescribed steps such as giving prompt notice of dishonor. (These steps will be studied in Chapter 3.) If a promissory note is used, nothing further need be said if recourse financing is intended. If non-recourse financing is intended, language such as "without recourse" must be added to the indorsement (UCC 3–414(1)).

2. Definitions of "consumer" differ, but Uniform Consumer Credit Code § 1.301 is typical. Its definition of "consumer credit sale" requires: that the buyer be a person other than an organi-

tiable instruments and waiver-of-defense clauses, limiting their effectiveness, or depriving them of effect altogether. Thus the Uniform Consumer Credit Code, as promulgated in 1974 (see p. 12 supra), provides:

Section 3.307   [Certain Negotiable Instruments Prohibited.]

With respect to a consumer credit sale or consumer lease, [except a sale or lease primarily for an agricultural purpose,] the creditor may not take a negotiable instrument other than a check dated not later than ten days after its issuance as evidence of the obligation of the consumer.

Section 3.404   [Assignee Subject to Claims and Defenses.]

(1) With respect to a consumer credit sale or consumer lease [, except one primarily for an agricultural purpose], an assignee of the rights of the seller or lessor is subject to all claims and defenses of the consumer against the seller or lessor arising from the sale or lease of property or services, notwithstanding that the assignee is a holder in due course of a negotiable instrument issued in violation of the provisions prohibiting certain negotiable instruments (Section 3.307).

(2) A claim or defense of a consumer specified in subsection (1) may be asserted against the assignee under this section only if the consumer has made a good faith attempt to obtain satisfaction from the seller or lessor with respect to the claim or defense and then only to the extent of the amount owing to the assignee with respect to the sale or lease of the property or services as to which the claim or defense arose at the time the assignee has notice of the claim or defense. Notice of the claim or defense may be given before the attempt specified in this subsection. Oral notice is effective unless the assignee requests written confirmation when or promptly after oral notice is given and the consumer fails to give the assignee written confirmation within the period of time, not less than 14 days, stated to the consumer when written confirmation is requested.

(3) For the purpose of determining the amount owing to the assignee with respect to the sale or lease:

(a) payments received by the assignee after the consolidation of two or more consumer credit sales, except pursuant to open-end credit, are deemed to have been applied first to the payment of the sales first made; if the sales

zation; that the credit be granted pursuant to a seller credit card or by a seller who regularly engages in credit transactions of the same kind; that the goods, services, or interest in land sold be purchased primarily for a personal, family, household or agricultural purpose; that the debt be payable in installments or a finance charge is made; and that, with respect to a sale of goods or services, the amount financed not exceed $25,000.

consolidated arose from sales made on the same day, payments are deemed to have been applied first to the smallest sale; and

(b) payments received for an open-end credit account are deemed to have been applied first to the payment of finance charges in the order of their entry to the account and then to the payment of debts in the order in which the entries of the debts are made to the account.

(4) An agreement may not limit or waive the claims or defenses of a consumer under this section.

Note that under such statutes it is no longer necessary to show that the financing agency and the seller were closely connected.

For discussion of the justification for such legislation, see Banta, Negotiability in Consumer Sales: The Need for Further Study, 53 Neb.L.Rev. 195 (1974); Rohner, Holder in Due Course in Consumer Transactions: Requiem, Revival or Reformation?, 60 Cornell L.Rev. 503 (1975); Schwartz, Optimality and the Cutoff of Defenses Against Financers of Consumer Sales, 15 B.C.Ind. & Com.L.Rev. 499 (1974); Note, 78 Yale L.J. 618 (1969).

Direct Loans. Neither the judicial decisions nor the statutes described above deal with a developing practice in which the seller refers the buyer to a financing agency that makes a direct loan to the buyer.[3] The loan is secured by an interest in the goods purchased by the buyer and the financing agency makes sure that the loan is applied to purchase the goods by making its check payable jointly to the buyer and the seller. Should the buyer refuse payment of the loan on the ground of a defense against the seller, the financing agency's response is that its contract with the buyer is entirely separate from the seller's contract with the buyer and was fully performed when it gave the buyer the money. Statutes protecting consumers in the case of direct loans are newer and less common than those described above. The Uniform Consumer Credit Code contains an example.

Section 3.405 [Lender Subject to Claims and Defenses Arising From Sales and Leases.]

(1) A lender, except the issuer of a lender credit card, who, with respect to a particular transaction, makes a consumer loan to enable a consumer to buy or lease from a particular seller or lessor property or services [, except primarily for an agricultural purpose,] is subject to all claims and defenses of

---

3. This practice is known, picturesquely as "dragging the body" to suggest that the seller "drags" the buyer to the financing agency's office.

the consumer against the seller or lessor arising from that sale or lease of the property or services if:

(a) the lender knows that the seller or lessor arranged for the extension of credit by the lender for a commission, brokerage, or referral fee;

(b) the lender is a person related to the seller or lessor, unless the relationship is remote or is not a factor in the transaction;

(c) the seller or lessor guarantees the loan or otherwise assumes the risk of loss by the lender upon the loan;

(d) the lender directly supplies the seller or lessor with the contract document used by the consumer to evidence the loan, and the seller or lessor has knowledge of the credit terms and participates in preparation of the document;

(e) the loan is conditioned upon the consumer's purchase or lease of the property or services from the particular seller or lessor, but the lender's payment of proceeds of the loan to the seller or lessor does not in itself establish that the loan was so conditioned; or

(f) the lender, before he makes the consumer loan, has knowledge or, from his course of dealing with the particular seller or lessor or his records, notice of substantial complaints by other buyers or lessees of the particular seller's or lessor's failure or refusal to perform his contracts with them and of the particular seller's or lessor's failure to remedy his defaults within a reasonable time after notice to him of the complaints.

(2) A claim or defense of a consumer specified in subsection (1) may be asserted against the lender under this section only if the consumer has made a good faith attempt to obtain satisfaction from the seller or lessor with respect to the claim or defense and then only to the extent of the amount owing to the lender with respect to the sale or lease of the property or services as to which the claim or defense arose at the time the lender has notice of the claim or defense. Notice of the claim or defense may be given before the attempt specified in this subsection. Oral notice is effective unless the lender requests written confirmation when or promptly after oral notice is given and the consumer fails to give the lender written confirmation within the period of time, not less than 14 days, stated to the consumer when written confirmation is requested.

(3) For the purpose of determining the amount owing to the lender with respect to the sale or lease:

(a) payments received by the lender after consolidation of two or more consumer loans, except pursuant to open-end credit, are deemed to have been applied first to the payment of the loans first made; if the loans consolidated arose from loans made on the same day, payments are deemed to have been applied first to the smallest loan; and

(b) payments received for an open-end credit account are deemed to have been applied first to the payment of finance charges in the order of their entry to the account and then to the payment of debts in the order in which the entries of the debts are made to the account.

(4) An agreement may not limit or waive the claims or defenses of a consumer under this section.

Note the complexity introduced by the requirement that the lender be closely connected with the seller. Would it be practicable to allow consumers to assert defenses against the lender in all cases? What of the consumer who obtains a loan from his savings bank, giving a passbook as security?

FTC Initiative. In 1976, Federal Trade Commission rule 433 took effect. Its stated purpose is to deny protection to financing agencies in transactions involving consumer goods and services.[4] But because the FTC has no jurisdiction over banks and it was thought undesirable to regulate some financing agencies but not others, the rule was not made applicable to financing agencies. Instead the rule makes it an unfair and deceptive trade practice for the *seller* to fail to incorporate in a contract of sale a legend that will preserve the buyer's defenses against the financing agency.

If the transaction is one in which the seller assigns the contract with the buyer to a financing agency, the contract must include the following legend in ten-point type:

NOTICE

ANY HOLDER OF THIS CONSUMER CREDIT CONTRACT IS SUBJECT TO ALL CLAIMS AND DEFENSES WHICH THE DEBTOR COULD ASSERT AGAINST THE SELLER OF GOODS OR SERVICES OBTAINED PURSUANT HERETO OR WITH THE PROCEEDS HEREOF. RECOVERY HEREUNDER BY THE DEBTOR SHALL NOT EXCEED AMOUNTS PAID BY THE DEBTOR HEREUNDER.

If the seller receives the proceeds from a direct loan made to the buyer by a financing agency to which the seller "refers consumers" or with whom the seller "is affiliated . . . by common control, contract, or business arrangement," the loan contract must include a similar legend.

Would the financing agency be affected in any of the situations covered by FTC rule 433 if the legend were not included? Is UCC 9–

4. The rule defines a consumer as: "A natural person who seeks or acquires goods or services for personal, family, or household use."

206 relevant? On these and other legal issues raised by this "half step by the FTC," see Garner & Dunham, FTC Rule 433 and the Uniform Commercial Code: An Analysis of Current Lender Status, 43 Mo.L.Rev. 199 (1978).

Claims Against Financing Agency. We have thus far been concerned with the buyer's right to assert a defense against the financing agency in order to reduce the buyer's obligation to pay that agency. What of claims by the buyer against the financing agency to recover payments already made in ignorance of such a defense?

Even in the case of an assignee of a simple contract right, the question is not free from dispute. But there is authority that if, after a defense or claim has arisen but before learning of it, the buyer mistakenly and even negligently renders performance to the assignee when not required to do so, the buyer may have restitution if the assignee has not changed position in reliance on the performance. Compare Farmers Acceptance Corp. v. DeLozier, 178 Colo. 291, 496 P.2d 1016 (1972) (where contractor's progress payments to assignee exceeded amount to which subcontractor was entitled because of breach, contractor could recover excess from assignee where there was no showing of reliance by further loans), with Michelin Tires (Canada) Limited v. First National Bank of Boston, 666 F.2d 673 (1st Cir. 1981) (where owner's progress payments to assignee were based on fraudulent invoices, owner could not recover from innocent assignee). Statutes such as the Uniform Consumer Credit Code do not appear to be dispositive on this issue, though by preserving a buyer's defense against the financing agency they open the door to a claim to restitution of payments made in ignorance of that defense.

The legend required by FTC rule 433, however, states that the financing agency is subject to all "claims and defenses which the debtor could assert against the seller" and provides, that "recovery hereunder by the debtor shall not exceed amounts paid by the debtor hereunder." Does this give the buyer a right to restitution of payments made in ignorance of a defense in any of the situations covered by the rule? For discussion of this question, see Garner & Dunham, FTC Rule 433 and the Uniform Commercial Code: An Analysis of Current Lender Status, 43 Mo.L.Rev. 199, 232 (1978).

Credit Cards. Suppose that a buyer uses a credit card to pay for goods that turn out to be defective. Can the buyer, when billed by the issuing bank, set up defenses that would be good against the seller? Is it significant that a credit card system is not entirely lacking in control over the merchants that are allowed to put its decal on the door?

Congress dealt with this problem in Truth in Lending Act § 170, as added by the Fair Credit Billing Act of 1974 (15 U.S.C. § 1666i). That section generally subjects a card issuer "to all claims (other than tort claims) and defenses arising out of any transaction in which the credit card is used" up to "the amount of credit outstanding with respect to such transaction" at the time the cardholder first gives notice of the claim of defense.[5]　There are, however, three limitations.

First, the cardholder must have made "a good faith attempt to obtain satisfactory resolution of a disagreement or problem relative to the transaction from the person honoring the credit card."　Second, the amount of the initial transaction must exceed $50.　Third, the place where the initial transaction occurred must be in the same state as the mailing address previously provided by the cardholder or within 100 miles from that address.[6]　What are the justifications for these limitations?

SECTION 3.　OTHER CONSEQUENCES

Introduction.　The most dramatic consequence of the negotiability of commercial paper is the protection that may be afforded the good faith purchaser against claims and defenses, illustrated by the preceding materials in the first two chapters.　This protection is not, however, the only consequence.

Another consequence of the negotiability of commercial paper is that the party seeking to enforce such an instrument has advantages of pleading and proof.　For example, every negotiable instrument is presumed to have been issued for consideration, so that even when the instrument remains in the hands of the original payee, the burden is shifted to the obligor on the instrument to show that there was no consideration.[1]　See UCC 3–408, 3–307(2); Kinyon, Actions on Commercial Paper: Holder's Procedural Advantages Under Article Three, 65 Mich.L.Rev. 1441 (1967).　Two additional consequences are considered in the following two subsections.

5.　The amount of claims or defenses may not exceed the amount of credit outstanding with respect to the transaction at the time the cardholder first gives notice of the claim or defense.

6.　The second and third limitations do not apply in a few limited situations.

1.　By the beginning of the eighteenth century, it had been established that in an action upon the custom of merchants on a *draft* payable to order, the plaintiff need not prove consideration.　Yet in Clerke v. Martin, 2 Ld.Raym. 757, 1 Salk. 129, 92 Eng.Rep. 6 (1702), Lord Holt, Chief Justice of the Queen's Bench, refused to apply this rule in favor of the payee of a *promissory note* payable to order who sought recovery from the maker, describing "such notes [as] innovations .　.　. unknown to the common law, and invented in Lombard-Street, which attempted in these matters of bills of exchange to give laws to Westminster-Hall."　Clerke v. Martin was overruled two years later by the Statute of Anne, which provided that the holder of a note could maintain an action just as could the holder of a draft.　See footnote 6, p. 44, supra.

(A) Discharge

Prefatory Note. To what extent, in performing an obligation, must the obligor pay attention to the whereabouts of the writing that evidences it? An obligor on an ordinary contract right can safely deal with the original obligee in discharging the obligation, even if the right is evidenced by a writing, unless the obligor has received notice of an assignment. The Code so provides in UCC 9–318(3). The Restatement (Second) of Contracts § 338(1) puts it as follows:

> . . . notwithstanding an assignment, the assignor retains his power to discharge or modify the duty of the obligor to the extent that the obligor performs or otherwise gives value until but not after the obligor receives notification that the right has been assigned and that performance is to be rendered to the assignee.

The obligor on a negotiable instrument, however, cannot safely deal with the original obligee without paying attention to the writing that embodies the obligation.[1]

Problem 5. B sold A a machine for A's factory for $100,000, payable in 30 days. B assigned the right to payment to the C finance company, which paid B $100,000 less a discount. At the end of the 30 days, A, who did not know of the assignment, paid B $100,000. Can C recover the $100,000 from A? See UCC 9–318(3); Restatement (Second) of Contracts § 338(1), supra.[2]

Problem 6. B sold A a machine for A's factory for $100,000, payable in 30 days. In connection with the sale, A executed a negotiable promissory note, promising to "pay to the order of B, $100,000" in 30 days. B assigned the right to payment and negotiated the note to the C finance company by indorsing it "Pay to the order of C, (signed) B." At the end of the 30 days, A, who did not know of the assignment and negotiation, paid B $100,000. Can C recover the $100,000 from A? See UCC 3–603.

NOTE

Modification by Contract. Would it be possible, by an appropriate provision, to make the rule of UCC 3–603 applicable to the discharge of a debt under an ordinary contract? See UCC 3–805. Might there be disadvantages as well as advantages to doing this?

---

1. Note also that under UCC 3–605 the obligee on a negotiable instrument can, even without consideration, discharge an obligor on the instrument simply by cancelling, destroying, or mutilating it or by striking out the obligor's signature.

2. As to B's liability to C, Restatement (Second) of Contracts § 333(1)(a) provides: ". . . one who assigns . . . a right . . . for value warrants to the assignee . . . that he will do nothing to defeat or impair the value of the assignment . . . ."

Consider the financing agency that finances retail instalment sales without the use of a negotiable note. Buyers change their addresses and employees of financing agencies occasionally make mistakes. The rule of UCC 3–603 would protect the financing agency if it failed to notify the buyer of the transfer to it of the buyer's obligation. But what precautions would the cautious buyer then have to insist upon before paying each instalment?

Is there a better way to protect the financing agency if it fails to notify the buyer? Forms furnished to dealers by financing agencies frequently provide that instalments are to be payable at the office of the financing agency. Will such a clause adequately protect the financing agency if it fails to notify the buyer of the fact of assignment? Would the following clause be preferable: "I acknowledge, this day, receipt of a duplicate of this contract and admit notice of the intended assignment of this contract to Friendly Finance Company"?

(B) "SPENT" INSTRUMENTS

Prefatory Note. To what extent, after performing an obligation, does the obligor run a risk by leaving outstanding (without cancellation or some appropriate notation of performance) the writing that evidences it? In other words, to what extent can the good faith purchaser of the right to performance safely rely on the writing as an indication that the obligation has not already been discharged? The obligor on an ordinary contract right runs no risk by leaving the writing that evidences it outstanding, or to put it differently, the good faith purchaser who takes that right by assignment cannot safely rely on the writing as an indication that the obligation has not already been discharged. This is clear from Restatement (Second) of Contracts § 336(1):

> By an assignment the assignee acquires a right against the obligor only to the extent that the obligor is under a duty to the assignor; and if the right of the assignor would be voidable against the obligor or unenforceable against him if no assignment had been made, the right of the assignee is subject to the infirmity.

As might be expected, the rule is different for a negotiable instrument or document of title.

Problem 7. B sold A a machine for A's factory for $100,000, payable in 30 days. Before the 30 days were up, A paid B $100,000, but left the written contract of sale in B's hands without any notation on it. B then assigned the right to payment and delivered the written contract to the C finance company, which paid B $100,000 less a discount without knowing of A's payment to B. At the end of the 30 days, A refused to pay C. Can C recover the $100,000 from A? See Restatement (Second) of Contracts § 336(1), supra.[1]

Problem 8. B sold A a machine for A's factory for $100,000, payable in 30 days. In connection with the sale, A executed a negotiable promissory note, promising "to pay to the order of B $100,000" in 30 days. Before the 30 days were up, A paid B $100,000 but left the written contract of sale and the promissory note in B's hands without any notation on them. B then assigned the right to payment, negotiated the note, and delivered both the written contract and the note to the C finance company, which paid B $100,000 less a discount without knowing of A's payment to B. At the end of the 30 days, A refused to pay C. Can C recover the $100,000 from A? See UCC 3–602, 3–603, 3–305.

1. As to B's liability to C, see footnote 2, p. 84 supra.

Part II

PAYMENT OF THE PRICE: THE CHECK

INTRODUCTION

Of the three main types of commercial paper (notes, drafts and checks), the note has already been discussed in Chapters 1 and 2, the draft will be encountered in Chapter 6, and the check is the subject of the three chapters that follow.

Although the check has undergone the most dramatic growth of any negotiable instrument and has been most subjected to modern techniques of bulk handling and automation, both its form and its function remain remarkably close to those of the first checks over three centuries ago. See the typical example of a personal check at p. 96 infra. When is it payable? (See UCC 3–108). To whom is it payable? (See UCC 3–110, 3–111.)

The primary function of the check also remains essentially the same—it is ordinarily an instrument for the payment of the drawer's own debts. Today, if a buyer owes a seller for goods, he will in most instances pay by his own personal check made payable to the order of the seller as payee. The seller will take it to his bank and deposit it for collection. It will then be sent by the seller's bank, often through a chain of collecting banks, to the buyer's bank upon which it was drawn, the drawee bank. For a more detailed description of the check collection process, see p. 92 infra. Sometimes the payee will "cash" the check, that is transfer it for value, at a store or bank instead of depositing it in his bank, but particularly in a commercial setting this is the exception rather than the rule.

Payment of the drawer's own debt is not, however, the only function of the check, for checks today may take a number of forms and have a variety of purposes. You will recall the draft, described earlier (p. 42 supra), that was used by a London buyer to pay a Venetian seller. Its modern counterpart would be a bank draft, which might be used by a New York buyer, as remitter, to pay a San Francisco seller, drawn by the buyer's New York bank as drawer, upon its correspondent bank in San Francisco, as drawee. When it is received the San Francisco seller will probably deposit it in his own bank for collection, just as he would the buyer's personal check. Note that although this instrument is commonly called a "bank draft," it is a type of check (UCC 3–104(2)(b)). Can you think of any reasons why the seller might prefer it to the buyer's personal check? If the draw-ee in San Francisco should refuse to pay, would the seller, the payee, have recourse against the buyer, the remitter (UCC 3–802)? Against the New York drawer (UCC 3–413(2))? Against the San Francisco drawee (UCC 3–409)? [1]

Still another variety of check that the buyer might use to pay the seller is what is known as a cashier's or official check, a check drawn by a bank as drawer upon itself as drawee.

The great majority of the more than 40 billion checks drawn each year are properly honored upon presentment to the drawee bank and give rise to no legal problems. Less than one half of one per cent are dishonored, although in absolute terms this may amount to nearly a million checks a day. The most frequent reasons for dishonor are "insufficient funds" and "uncollected funds." Other reasons appear on the return item stamp which the drawee bank usually places on dishonored checks when they are returned (see p. 111 infra). In an even smaller number of instances checks are paid by the drawee bank by mistake—perhaps in violation of a stop order or in spite of a for-gery or alteration.

Nevertheless, most of the reported cases involving checks arise out of these unusual situations in which a drawee bank has either refused to pay a check, or has paid a check by mistake. These cases make up the bulk of Part II of this book. Llewellyn put it this way: "A course in Negotiable Instruments is in this like so many hours a week spent in an operating room, as giving light on the normal func-tioning of the human body. In the course the student meets only wrecked transactions. Yet the rules that govern the lawsuits are modelled upon the normal, natural *unwrecked* transaction; the rules seek as best may be to approximate the result which should have been, and which *would* have been, except for the wreck." Llewellyn, Meet Negotiable Instruments, 44 Colum.L.Rev. 299, 321 (1944).

Each of the three chapters in Part II deals with a general risk inherent in the use of checks. Chapter 3 is concerned with the risk of checks drawn on insufficient funds. Chapter 4 deals with the risk of attempts to countermand checks. Chapter 5 explores the risk of for-gery and alteration. But first, a brief description of the check sys-tem is in order.

"A successfully functioning check payment system is essential to the economic health of the nation. The 19th century saw the rise of checks and drafts as commonly used means of payment, facilitated by the growth of clearing houses which began with the founding of the New York Clearing House in 1853. The Federal Reserve Act of 1913 established the Federal Reserve as a new crucial element in the na-tion's check system. The Fed was empowered to create a clearing and settlement system among member banks handling checks. Start-

---

1. The bank draft is now little used. It fell into disfavor because it was not easily assimilated into automated check processing procedures.

ing in 1915 on a voluntary basis, the Fed gradually brought about a smoothly functioning nationwide system of clearing and collection of checks at par. The system, operated by a combination of commercial bank and Federal Reserve bank efforts, has served the nation well for nearly 70 years.

"A survey of households, completed in 1981 by Opinion Research Corporation, based on a representative national sample, showed that 79% of households have a regular checking account and 3% have a NOW account (but no other checking account). Thus, 82% of households have some form of checking account.

"The most recent intensive study of the checking system, guided by the Federal Reserve Bank in Atlanta, shows that 32 billion checks were written on commercial banks in the United States during 1979, and an additional one billion government checks and money orders. Every month, 20 checks were written on the average individual's checking account in 1979. The annual growth in the number of checks has been declining slowly since 1970, from slightly above 7% a year at the beginning of the 1970's, to a level approaching 5% in 1982.

"Although 32 billion checks were written in 1979, only 29% of them were presented initially at the bank on which they were written. The other 71% required processing by more than one bank, sometimes including processing by one or more Federal Reserve banks. the total number of 'processed checks' in 1979 was estimated to be 77 billion, indicating that the average check was processed by 2.4 banks. These multiple processings include handling of checks by correspondent commercial banks and Federal Reserve banks in addition to the bank of first deposit.

"Indicators of the performance of the check collection system show that the quality of its performance has been improving and its use of resources has been becoming more efficient. The system is still heavily labor intensive and unit cost is rising as labor costs increase. Space and transportation are important resources in the check collection system, and the costs of both have been rising faster than inflation." Association of Reserve City Banks, Report on the Payments System 12–13 (1982).[2]

2. Reproduced with permission of the Association of Reserve City Banks.

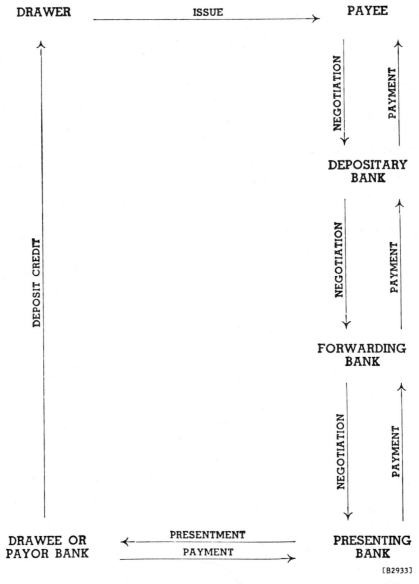

[B2933]

Consider a seller who receives checks in payment for goods. He will enter his daily receipts on his books and take the checks with a deposit slip (p. 99 infra) to his bank, the *depositary* bank (see UCC 4–105(a)), which will return to him a receipted copy of the deposit slip. The depositary bank will treat the checks as *cash items* since they are payable on presentation to the drawee and are handled in bulk rather than individually. It will credit the depositor's account provisionally, awaiting subsequent determination of whether the item will be finally paid, with the understanding that he is not to draw checks against the credit until the item which it represents has been collected. The provisional settlement will become final without any further entry, unless the item should be among the small fraction of checks which is dishonored, in which case the bank will charge back the provisional credit given for that item.

The depositary bank them *proves* the deposit, that is, checks the depositor's entries on the deposit slip and *sorts* the checks. Checks are classified as *on us* (drawn on the depositary bank itself) or *on others* (drawn on banks other than the depositary). Somewhat less than one third of all checks fall in the first category. The remaining items must be forwarded to other banks for payment.

Clearing House Items. A little more than one fifth of these remaining items go to local clearing houses. When checks first became common in London, bank clerks presented city items by making daily trips to each of the other banks. Soon they arranged meetings and exchanged checks on street corners, and later chose a public house when they transacted their business. In about 1773 the bankers of London rented a room in Lombard Street for the settlement of their accounts, thus establishing the London Clearing House. The New York Clearing House Association was organized in 1853 and similar institutions now exist in many cities. At the clearing house messengers from the seller's bank, the *presenting* bank (see UCC 4–105(e)), will present packages of checks to messengers from the *payor* (see UCC 4–105(b)) or *drawee* banks, and will receive in exchange packages of checks drawn on the seller's bank. *Not good* items may be returned through the clearing house by the banks on which they are drawn. Settlement of exchanges is made through the clearing house.

Transit Items. Most of the on-others checks consist of items drawn on out-of-town banks. When checks are forwarded they are accompanied by a *cash letter* with a list of the items enclosed. If the drawee bank is a correspondent of the depositary bank, the latter may send the check by mail directly to the drawee. Otherwise it may send it to an *intermediary collecting* bank (see UCC 4–105(c), (d)), which may present the check through the mail or through the clearing house, or may, after sorting the checks received, forward it to a second intermediary bank. The majority of transit items pass through the Federal Reserve System, which will be discussed at p. 157 infra.

Payment. Each bank thus receives checks drawn on it over its own counter, through the clearing house, and by mail. These checks are sorted, proved, examined for date, forgery, alteration and missing indorsements, checked for sufficiency of funds, stop orders, attachment or garnishment of the drawer's account, and finally posted, that is, charged to the drawer's account (see UCC 4–109). Payment may be effected in several ways. Where an on us item has been deposited by a customer, he expects the bank to pay by crediting his account. Similarly where a check has been presented by mail by a correspondent bank which has an account with the payor bank, payment may be made by crediting its account. Otherwise payment may be made by *remittance draft,* a check drawn by the payor bank on another bank to the order of the presenting bank.   Collection instructions requesting either *collection and credit* or *collection and remittance* may be found either in the cash letter or in a standing agreement.

The law relating to checks is discussed in H. Bailey, Brady on Bank Checks (5th ed. 1979); B. Clark, The Law of Bank Deposits, Collections and Credit Cards (rev.ed.1981); J. Clarke, H. Bailey, & R. Young, Bank Deposits and Collections (4th ed. 1972).

THE MECHANICS OF CHECK COLLECTIONS:
A PROTOTYPE [1]

Quaker Manufacturing Co., a Philadelphia manufacturer of containers, sells large quantities of cans to Empire Enterprises Co., a New York firm.   Quaker sells on open credit, under the terms shown on its Acknowledgement (FORM 1), and receives payment by check. On Monday, January 16, 1984 Empire mails its check (FORM 2) for $2,178.50 drawn on Irving Trust Company, its New York bank, to Quaker in payment for April purchases.   Quaker receives the check on Tuesday, January 17, and enters this payment in its books as part of its daily receipts.   On the same day it stamps its indorsement on the back of the check (FORM 2A), lists the check on a deposit slip (FORM 3) along with other checks received the same day, and takes the check with the deposit slip to its bank, The Philadelphia National Bank, for deposit.

Collection.   The Philadelphia National Bank, the depositary bank, returns a receipted copy of the deposit slip to Quaker.   It encodes the amount on the front (compare Form 23 with Form 2).   It handles Empire's check, along with other checks received for deposit, in bulk rather than individually, on the assumption that in all probability it will be paid when it is presented to Irving Trust Company.   Quaker's deposit is proved, that is the depositor's addition is checked by the bank, and the amount is then credited to its account.   (At this point much of the work may be done by automation.)   The credit is provisional, awaiting subsequent determination of whether the check is finally paid by Irving Trust Company, with the understanding that Quaker is not to draw checks against the credit until the item which it represents has been collected.   The provisional settlement will become final without any further entry, unless the item should be dishonored, in which case the bank would reverse the provisional credit previously given for the item.   The Empire check, along with all other deposited checks drawn on out-of-town banks, is handled by The Philadelphia National Bank's transit department, which sorts the checks according to place of payment.   Transit items, such as the Empire check are sent along with other checks drawn on banks in the

1. Thanks are due to Michael P. Scher, Esq. and Ms. Paulette Peters Simpson of Irving Trust Company and to Richard L. Krzyzanowski, Esq. of Crown Cork and Seal Company for their help in assembling and preparing the sample forms, and also to The Philadelphia National Bank for its cooperation.

New York City area to its New York correspondent, Citibank. During the sorting process, each check is indorsed by The Philadelphia National Bank on the back (FORM 2A). Along with the checks goes a transmittal form called a "cash letter" (FORM 4), with a machine listing of the amounts of the items sent.

When the cash letter and checks are received by Citibank, the total is credited, again provisionally, awaiting final payment of the checks, to the account of The Philadelphia National Bank. The total is proved and the checks are sorted by Citibank, which adds its indorsement to the back of the check (FORM 2A). Checks drawn on banks which are members of the New York Clearing House Association are sorted into packages for each drawee bank, and the Empire check is therefore placed with other checks received by Citibank that are drawn on Irving Trust Company. The package containing the Empire check is then presented to Irving Trust Company at the New York Clearing House at the 10 A.M. clearing on Wednesday, January 18. By this procedure Irving Trust Company, the drawee, has received the check drawn on it by Empire, the drawer, mailed by Empire to Quaker, the payee, in Philadelphia, deposited by Quaker in The Philadelphia National Bank, the depositary bank, forwarded by it to Citibank, the presenting bank, and presented by Citibank to Irving Trust Company.

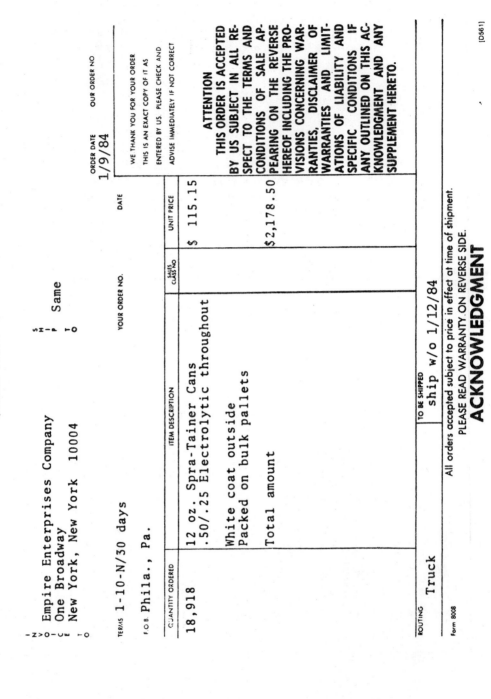

FORM 1

SELLER'S ACKNOWLEDGEMENT

[*Front*]

TERMS AND CONDITIONS

1. Prices for the goods sold hereunder will be Seller's list prices in effect on the date of shipment plus applicable taxes and governmental charges.

2. On all orders for private decorated or other specially manufactured products an under or over run of 10% of the quantity ordered will be considered as fulfillment of the order. The amount of all such orders must be accepted by the Purchaser within ninety days from first shipment against each order.

3. Seller will use its best efforts to make delivery of the goods ordered on the date or dates specified by the Purchaser, but Seller does not guarantee delivery on any date or dates so specified and shall be subject to no liability for any damage caused by delayed delivery.

4. **WARRANTIES, DISCLAIMER OF WARRANTIES AND LIMITATIONS OF LIABILITY.**

   (a) CONTAINERS

   Seller warrants that containers sold by it shall be free from defects in workmanship and materials. However, in no event shall Seller incur any liability under this warranty, where the containers are not packed, stored and distributed in accordance with good business practice, or where the alleged damage results from rust or outside corrosion occurring after receipt of containers by Purchaser, or from improper capping, closing, crimping, filling and gassing operations by Purchaser, or from the use of parts other than those supplied by Seller. Seller's liability under this warranty whether based on tort or contract is limited exclusively to the repayment of the purchase price of the defective containers. **PROVIDED THAT ANY CLAIMS OR ANY COURT ACTION ARISING UNDER THIS WARRANTY IS BROUGHT WITHIN ONE (1) YEAR AFTER SUCH CAUSE OF ACTION HAS ACCRUED.**

   IN VIEW OF THE ABOVE WARRANTY, SELLER MAKES NO OTHER WARRANTY, WHETHER OF MERCHANTABILITY, FITNESS OR OTHERWISE, EXPRESS OR IMPLIED IN FACT OR BY LAW AND SELLER SHALL HAVE NO FURTHER OBLIGATION OR LIABILITY WITH RESPECT TO THE CONTAINERS. SELLER SHALL IN NO EVENT BE LIABLE FOR ANY GENERAL, CONSEQUENTIAL OR INCIDENTAL DAMAGES.

   Purchaser waives all claims for shortages in the containers ordered and received hereunder unless they are submitted, in writing, within thirty (30) days after delivery.

   Subject to the above provisions, Seller shall not bring any other action arising under this agreement unless such action is brought within two (2) years after such cause of action has accrued.

   (b) OTHER PRODUCTS

   Seller shall in no event be liable for damages arising directly or indirectly from the use of goods sold hereunder. Seller's liability, in any event, shall be limited to the invoice price of goods sold, and in this respect, no claim will be allowed after 30 days from billing date.

5. Fires, strikes, differences with workmen, accidents, failure of usual sources of supply, priorities, or other Governmental regulations, or any contingencies beyond the control of Seller, whether related or unrelated to any of the foregoing, shall excuse any failure of performance on the part of the Seller, and similar causes unavoidable by Purchaser shall be sufficient excuse for failure to take goods ordered, beyond those in transit, or manufactured or in process of manufacture, until such contingencies are removed.

6. The Seller shall be entitled to refuse to honor any order or to ship any part of the goods sold if any indebtedness or liability of the Purchaser to the Seller under this or any other contract shall at that time be overdue. Seller may fix or change from time to time the terms of credit under which the goods ordered shall be shipped, and may decline to ship all or any part thereof until such credit terms are met. The interest is changeable on past due accounts.

7. The terms and conditions set forth herein and in any written supplement hereto represent the entire agreement between Purchaser and Seller with respect to the goods mentioned in Purchaser's order and supersede all prior agreements, oral or written in respect of the subject matter of said order.

8. This agreement shall be governed by the law of the State of Pennsylvania.

[B2878]

[Reverse]

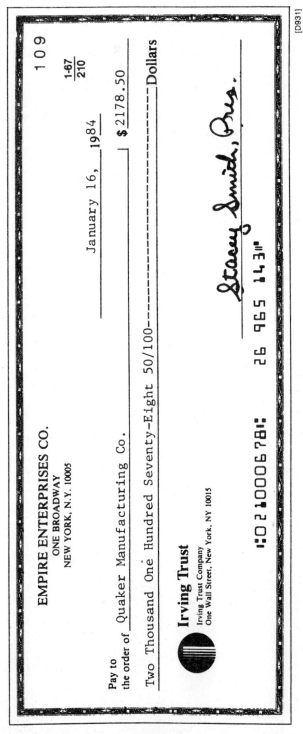

FORM 2
CHECK

[D932]

FOR DEPOSIT ONLY.
QUAKER MEG. CO.

PAY ANY BANK P.F.G.
THE PHILADELPHIA
NATIONAL BANK
PHILADELPHIA, PA.
3-1   3-1

1984 JAN 17

PAY ANY BANK, P.E.G.
CITIBANK, N.A.
NEW YORK NEW YORK
LOWER MAN
1-8
02

FORM 2A
BACK OF CHECK

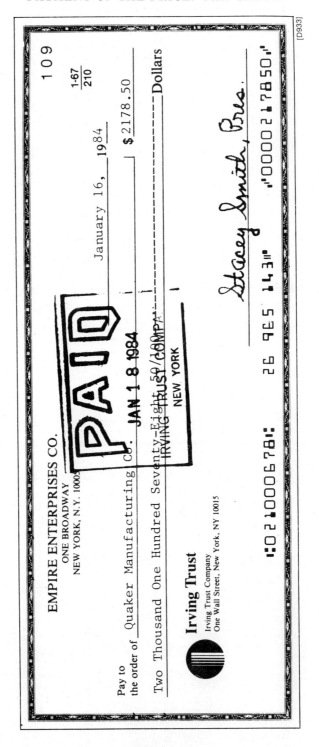

FORM 2B

PAID CHECK

CHECKING ACCOUNT DEPOSIT

PNB® PHILADELPHIA NATIONAL BANK

DATE January 17, 1984

DEPOSIT TO ACCOUNT OF

Quaker Manufacturing Co.

100 Market Street
Philadelphia, Pa.   19174

PRESS PEN FIRMLY FOR CLEAR COPIES
Please endorse each check with
your Name and Account Number

	DOLLARS	CENTS
CASH DEPOSIT		
LIST CHECKS BY BANK NO. *ENDORSE WITH NAME & A/C NO*		
3-5	376	11
2-3	1,500	00
1-67	2,178	50
5-39	3,153	07
8-26	10	00
TOTAL DEPOSIT	7,217	68

This deposit is accepted subject to verification by the Bank the laws
of the Commonwealth of Pennsylvania and the rules and regulations
of this Bank. For your protection the Bank recommends that cash
deposits not be made by mail

ORIGINAL

S 1203
8 72

[B29471]

⑈091⑈ ⑈205718⑈⑈

FORM 3
DEPOSIT SLIP

PNB THE PHILADELPHIA NATIONAL BANK   3-1 / 310

PHILADELPHIA, PA. 19101

[B2948]

January 17, 1984

```
*  ::  ::  ::  ::  ::  ::  ::
      589.46
      827.63
      159.35
    2,178.50
       62.33
      194.58
      121.32
      164.32
    4,297.49  *
```

FIRST NATIONAL CITY BANK
111 Wall Street
New York, New York 10015

FORM 4
CASH LETTER

Please Print or Type

Title of Account

Empire Enterprises Co.

Account Number
26-965-143

Number of Signatures Requested
Checks 1 | Loans 2

One Broadway, New York 13004

In Account With **Irving Trust**   Main Office

You are authorized to mail or to deliver by messenger to our address each month, statement of our checking account and cancelled vouchers.

Name (To Be Typed)	Title	Authorized Signature
Stacey Smith	Pres.	*Stacey Smith*
Kim Kaller	Tres.	*Kim Kaller*
Leslie Long	Sec'y.	*Leslie Long*

Secretary or other recording officer will please attest above signature(s) here.   Bank Approval

Title *Leslie Long* Secretary Date 6/30/83

2450/00 (Rev. 6—80)

[D617]

FORM 5

SIGNATURE CARD

Irving Trust

EMPIRE ENTERPRISES CO.
ONE BROADWAY
NEW YORK, N. Y. 10004

Account Number 26-965-143
Statement Closing Date 2-10-84

Page 1

PREVIOUS BALANCE	+ TOTAL CREDITS	- TOTAL DEBITS	- SERVICE CHRG	= NEW BALANCE
20,944.77	9,718.90	10,273.09	0.00	20,390.58

CHECKS AND OTHER DEBITS			CREDITS	DATE	BALANCE
94.50	202.18	472.25		1-12-84	20,175.84
20.62	319.12			1-13-84	19,836.10
			3,931.65	1-16-84	23,767.75
2.12	1,163.97			1-17-84	22,601.66
2,178.50				1-18-84	20,423.16
			4,736.50	1-25-84	25,159.66
50.80	125.76	2,581.40		1-30-84	22,401.70
1,143.25	1,250.50			2-02-84	20,007.95
			1,050.75	2-06-84	21,058.70
67.92	215.80	384.40		2-07-84	20,390.58

										Savings Codes	
AD	Loan Advance	EC	Error Correction	MT	Mortgage Payment	RI	Returned Item	SC	Service Charge	DP	Deposit
BV	Back Valued	FT	Funds Transfer	OC	Overdraft Charge	SC	Service Charge	SS	Social Security	ID	Interest Disbursement
CB	Checkbook Charge	IN	Interest	OD	Overdraft	SS	Social Security	ST	Savings Transfer	IN	Interest
CC	Certified Check	LS	List Posted	PT	Personal Trust Transfer	ST	Savings Transfer	VT	Visa Transaction	WD	Withdrawal
CM	Credit Memo	LT	Inst. Loan Payment	PY	Payment To Loan	VT	Visa Transaction				
DM	Debit Memo										

FORM 6
STATEMENT

Change of Address Order

To change your address please complete this form, then cut along dotted line and mail or bring to the bank.

New Address: Number and Street

City	State	Zip

New Phone Number

Customer's Signature

To Reconcile Your Statement and Checkbook

1. Add to your checkbook balance any credits appearing on the statement which you have not previously recorded. These items will be identified by symbols as shown on the front or described fully.

2. Deduct from your checkbook balance any bank charges or other debits appearing on the statement which you have not previously recorded. These items will be identified by symbols as shown on the front or described fully.

3. If your checks are serialized, examine the listing on the front of this statement and check off the items

against the entries in your checkbook. An asterisk in the listing indicates a gap where one or more checks are not on this particular statement.

If your checks are not serialized, arrange them by date or number and check them off against the entries in your checkbook.

4. List any checks or debits issued by you and not shown on the statement, and any bank charges since the statement date, in the area provided at the right.

Outstanding Checks and Debits	
Number	Amount
Bank charges since statement closing date	
Total	

5.	List last balance shown on statement	
+	Plus: Deposits and credits made after date of last entry on statement	
	Subtotal	
−	Minus: Total of outstanding checks and debits	
=	Balance: Which should agree with your checkbook	

Instructions for Keeping Your Savings Account Records

1. This space is provided for you to enter all deposits and withdrawals made during the next statement period.

2. Enter the last balance shown on the front side of this statement in the balance box.

3. Add to your balance all subsequent deposits and credits such as interest. Deduct all withdrawals.

4. Save your deposit receipts and withdrawal records and verify them with your next statement.

Date	Withdrawals	Deposits	Balance

Please Examine and Reconcile This Statement Promptly

Unless errors are reported within time periods indicated below, we will consider this statement to be correct.

Business Account Transactions: 15 days

Personal Checking and Savings Transactions: 30 days

Personal Electronic Transfers: 60 days

Preauthorized Credits

If you have arranged to have direct deposits, such as Social Security or salary payments, etc., made to your account, you can find out if the deposit has been made by calling the telephone number appearing on the front of the last page of this statement.

Transfer of Savings and Time Deposits

If this statement covers a Savings or Time Deposit account, you may transfer funds from the account to third parties only on the records of the Bank.

[D986]

[Reverse]

Payment. On Wednesday, January 18, the Empire check, along with other checks received by Irving Trust Company for payment, is sorted, proved, examined for date, alteration and missing indorsements, checked for sufficiency of funds, stop orders, and attachment or garnishment of Empire's account. The drawer's signature is checked against that on the signature card (FORM 5) which Empire filled out when it opened its account at Irving Trust Company. The check is then posted, that is, charged to Empire's account, and stamped "PAID" (FORM 2B). (The order of these steps may vary depending upon the degree of automation employed by the Irving Trust Company.)

At the end of the periodic banking cycle for Empire's account, all of the checks drawn by Empire and paid by Irving Trust Company during this period, including the check payable to Quaker, are returned to Empire with a statement showing all deposits and withdrawals during that period and the resulting balance (FORM 6). Empire compares these checks and the corresponding entries against its own records to verify the bank's statement.

Check-Like Instruments Drawn on Thrift Institutions. Congress enacted the Consumer Checking Account Equity Act of 1980, Pub.L. No. 96–221, §§ 301–313, 94 Stat. 132, to resolve a controversy between commercial banks and thrift institutions. The controversy involved the power of thrift institutions—mutual savings banks, savings and loan associations, and credit unions—to allow their customers to draw on such institutions instruments similar to checks.

The Act resolved the controversy in favor of the thrift institutions. It permits mutual savings banks and savings and loan associations to furnish negotiable orders of withdrawal (NOWs) to their noncommercial customers, and it permits credit unions to furnish share drafts to their members.

Although the power of thrift institutions to make these check-like instruments available to their customers is no longer in issue, questions remain as to the status of these instruments under the Uniform Commercial Code. This is particularly true for share drafts. Because credit unions do not have direct access to the Federal Reserve collection system, a share draft indicates on its face the name of a commercial bank that the draft is "payable through" (see UCC 3–120), in order to gain the advantage of the Federal Reserve collection system.

This book does not discuss these new check-like instruments. For more on the subject, see Leary, Is the U.C.C. Prepared for the Thrifts' NOWs, NINOWs, and Share Drafts?, 30 Cath.U.L.Rev. 159 (1981); Wilson, The "New Checks": Thrift Institution Check-Like Instruments and the Uniform Commercial Code, 45 Mo.L.Rev. 199 (1980).

CREDIT CARDS

The introduction of electronic fund transfer systems has been aided by the growing use of credit cards.[1] Although this book does

---

1. A credit card is to be distinguished from a debit card, an access device that enables the holder to transfer funds from an account. Sometimes, however, a credit card doubles as a debit card, enabling the holder to transfer funds from an account to that of a merchant. For the applicability of federal legislation to such cards, see B. Clark, The Law of Bank Deposits, Collections and Credit Cards § 9.3[2][c] (rev.ed.1981).

not offer a detailed treatment of credit cards, a little background will be helpful.

Extensive use of the credit card goes back to the 1950s, when Diner's Club, American Express, and Carte Blanche cards were introduced. By the beginning of the 1960s the banks had entered the field. In 1966 the Bank of America enlarged its credit card program by offering to license the operation of its card to other banks, giving rise to the system now known as VISA. In 1969 Interbank Card Association launched a competing nationwide program that resulted in the system now known as MasterCard. Since 1976, most banks have been members of both systems, providing merchants with services for both cards. Many banks offer both cards to their customers.

In 1980 Visa reported 657 million transactions on 65 million cards for a total value of $26 billion, and Mastercard reported 607 million transactions on 56 million cards for a total value of $23 billion. Although these totals are dwarfed by the $19,000 billion in payments by check in the same year, about 53% of all households have at least one bank card account. For these consumers, the bank card has been a means of becoming familiar with a plastic card as a device for access to a payment system.

A typical bank card transaction involves four parties: the cardholder, the issuing bank, the merchant, and the depositary bank. A consumer obtains a card by applying to a local bank. The cardholder's agreement with the issuing bank establishes a line of credit for the cardholder and states conditions for the use of the card. The cardholder agrees to pay the issuing bank for purchases made with the card prior to its surrender to the bank or the receipt by the bank of notice of its loss. The issuing bank is connected, through an interchange system, with thousands of other banks. Banks in the system solicit merchants to participate in the system. After joining the system, a merchant deals with the soliciting bank, which becomes the merchant's depositary bank. In its agreement with the merchant, the bank agrees to exchange credit available for withdrawal at a discounted rate for sales slips generated by cardholders using their cards.

When a cardholder uses a card the merchant may, depending on the size of the transaction, be required to seek credit authorization by a telephone connected with a computer to make sure, for example, that the card has not been lost and that the cardholder's credit limit will not be exceeded. The merchant then fills out and the cardholder signs a sales slip, which authorizes the issuing bank to pay the amount indicated and which restates the cardholder's promise to pay that total. The merchant imprints on the slip the information on the face of the card, identifying the cardholder and the issuing bank, and enters a description of the goods or services and the price. The merchant gives the cardholder a copy and deposits the slip with the depositary bank. The bank credits the merchant's account with the discounted amount and the information is then transmitted electronically to the issuing bank. The issuing bank enters this information on the cardholder's monthly bill. On receipt of the bill, the cardholder typically has the option of paying with a "free period" without any additional cost or deferring payment and paying a finance charge.

The relationship between the cardholder and the issuing bank that results from the use of the card is one of debtor and creditor. These transactions are subject to federal legislation, now found in the Consumer Protection Act, 15 U.S.C. § 1601 et seq. Of special importance are §§ 132–135 and §§ 161–171 (as added by the Fair Credit Billing Act of 1974). Some aspects of the legislation will be considered later.

ELECTRONIC FUND TRANSFERS

Recent years have at last begun to bear out the promise of electronic fund transfers (EFT) as a common means of payment. This long-heralded development has many advantages, including cutting the enormous cost of our present paper-based system of payment by check and reducing the "float" of items in the process of collection. It is not expected, however, that EFT will completely replace the use of checks, at least not in the near future. A lawyer must therefore be prepared to cope with the legal problems presented by a variety of different systems of payment.

The following materials emphasize problems arising out of the use of the check, a means of payment on which courts, legislatures, and scholars have lavished attention over the past century. The materials also consider those problems in the context of other payment systems. Thus, for example, the discussions of wrongful dishonor and of stopping payment refer to other payment systems as well as to checks. The materials do not, however, deal with problems that are largely peculiar to other payment systems, such as the provision of receipts and the resolution of errors in an EFT system.

Draw Orders. A check is the most common example of what has been called a "draw order." It is initiated by the transferor (Empire) and transmitted to the transferee (Quaker), and directs the transferor's bank (Irving Trust) to pay the transferee. The transferee obtains the money by instructing its bank (PNB) by means of a deposit slip to collect the money from the drawee, which pays the sum and debits the transferor's account. A draw order *pulls* funds back from the transferor's bank back to the transferee's bank.

The check collection process does not easily lend itself to EFT procedures. One possibility is what is called "check truncation." Instead of sending checks all over the country for collection, the information on the checks would be fed by the transferee's bank into an electronic system and transmitted to the transferor's bank, which would pay the check and remit the funds electronically to the transferee's bank. The check, or a photocopy of it, would be stored at the point of transmission. The transferor would receive a statement describing the transaction (much as the holder of a credit card now does) and could obtain a photocopy of the check if the need arose. One problem with such a system, of course, is that of verifying the transferor's signature as drawer of the check. This problem is avoided in a less ambitious type of check truncation, in which the check is sent to the transferor's bank but is not returned by that bank to the transferor, its customer. This less ambitious type of check truncation has been introduced by some banks.[1]

A more efficient system of draw orders can be devised, however, for a debtor's recurring payments to a single creditor, such as mortgage payments, insurance premiums, and loan payments. The debtor first gives the creditor authority to initiate periodic transfers. The creditor, as transferee then initiates these pre-authorized transfers by periodically sending the billing information to its bank. The bank will arrange the transfer of funds from the bank of the debtor, as transferee, through an Automated Clearing House (ACH), a computerized clearing facility that effects the paperless exchange of funds between banks. Instructions to transfer funds are on magnetic tape or in some other form that can be read by a computer. As will be pointed out shortly, ACHs perform other functions than those connected with such pre-authorized recurring payments.

Pay Orders. A more promising type of transaction for an EFTS involves what has been called a "pay order." Such an order is initiated by the transferor and is transmitted by the transferor to the drawee, directing the drawee to pay or to arrange payment to the transferee. Under a pay order, the transferor (Empire) instead of giving the transferee (Quaker) an order addressed to the drawee (Irving Trust), would instruct the drawee directly to arrange to have payment made to the transferee. If the transferee did not have an account with the transferor's bank, the drawee, that bank would remit the funds to the transferee's bank (PNB) for credit to the transferee's account. A pay order *pushes* funds from the transferor's bank to the transferee's bank. Such a system, known as a "giro system," has long been in existence in a number of European countries, sometimes through the postal system.

Pay orders in electronic form are well-established in this country for large transfers between banks. Four electronic fund transfer systems carry out or facilitate such transactions: (1) Fed Wire, the national Federal Reserve Wire Network; (2) Bank Wire, a private

---

1. Truncation has already occurred in connection with bank credit cards, when a shift was made from "country club" to "descriptive" billing. Although the sales slips formerly cleared through the system and were returned to the customer like checks, the transaction is now truncated and the slips remain with the merchant bank.

system introduced as an alternative to Fed Wire; (3) Clearing House Interbank Payment System (CHIPS), a private system operated by the New York Clearing House for dollar transfers arising out of international transfers; (4) Society for Worldwide Interbank Financial Transactions (S.W.I.F.T.), a private communications system, organized under Belgian law, designed to facilitate multicurrency payments. See Scott, Corporate Wire Transfers and the Uniform New Payments Code, 83 Colum.L.Rev. 1664 (1983).

Furthermore, the great bulk of ACH EFT volume consists of preauthorized recurring pay orders under direct deposit programs of both the federal government and the private sector. Most of the government transfers involve Social Security benefits and most of the private transfers involve payrolls. EFTS for pay orders by consumers are less developed in this country.

Some pay orders may be available to a consumer through an automated teller machine (ATM), an EFT terminal that is available twenty-four hours a day and may be placed at such off-premises locations as a supermarket or a shopping mall. The consumer activates the ATM by inserting a plastic debit card and entering a personal identification number (PIN). ATMs generally permit not only deposits and withdrawals, but also transfers between the customer's checking and savings accounts and at least some transfers to pay mortgages, credit cards, utility bills, and the like. An ATM can be on-line, connected directly to the bank's computer, or off-line, recording each transaction on a tape that must be returned to the bank for processing.

A more sophisticated system for consumer pay orders uses a point-of-sale (POS) terminal, located on a merchant's premises to enable consumers to pay for purchases from the merchant. The customer activates the POS terminal by a plastic debit card and PIN, just as in the case of an ATM. Under a single-institution POS plan, the customer must have an account at the same bank as the merchant, for there are no facilities for transfer of funds between banks. Under a multi-institutional POS plan, a number of banks share the system so that payments can be made from a customer with an account in one of those banks to a merchant with an account in another.

In addition, some banks have instituted bill paying by telephone, a type of electronic giro system. And home electronic banking, in which a customer may order a bank to pay bills by using a computer terminal in the home, is in its infancy.

The following table is from Association of Reserve City Banks, Report on the Payments System 13 (1982).[2]

---

2. Reproduced with permission of the Association of Reserve City Banks.

1980 PAYMENT SYSTEM ACTIVITY

Means of Payment	Amount (Billions)	Transactions (Millions)	Average Transaction
Fed Wire	$80,000	43	$1,800,000
CHIPS	37,000	13	2,800,000
Checks	19,000	34,000	570
ACH	164	239	686
Bank Cards	49	1,300	38

Note: At this time BankWire and S.W.I.F.T. are not value transfer systems, and are therefore not included in this tabulation. Coin and currency, and minor forms of retail EFT are omitted because of the lack of good information.

Legislation. In 1974, Congress established the National Commission on Electronic Fund Transfers to make a study and to recommend legislation "in connection with the possible development of public or private electronic fund transfer systems." 12 U.S.C. § 2401 et seq. In 1977, the Commission presented its report, EFT in the United States: Policy Recommendations and the Public Interest (The Final Report of the National Commission on Electronic Fund Transfers 1977). In 1978, Congress passed the Electronic Fund Transfer Act (EFT Act), 15 U.S.C. § 1693 et seq., as Title IX of the Consumer Credit Protection Act. Many, though not all, of the provisions of the EFT Act have been amplified by Regulation E of the Federal Reserve Board, 12 C.F.R. Part 205. There is also some state legislation on the subject.

According to Regulation E, "The Act establishes the basic rights, liabilities, and responsibilities of consumers who use electronic money transfer services and of financial institutions that offer these services." 12 C.F.R. 205.1(b). Its scope is thus limited in two important respects. First, the Act applies only to services used by or offered to *consumers,* and a "consumer" is defined as "a natural person." 12 C.F.R. § 205.2(e). The Act does not cover the large volume of electronic fund transfers initiated by businesses and banks. Second, the Act applies only to electronic money transfer services. An "electronic fund transfer" is defined to include "any transfer of funds . . . that is initiated through an electronic terminal, telephone, or computer or magnetic tape for the purpose of ordering, instructing, or authorizing a financial institution to debit or credit an account," including "point-of-sale transfers, automated teller machine transfers, direct deposits or withdrawals of funds, and transfers initiated by telephone." It does not, however, include transfer of funds by paper instruments such as checks. 12 C.F.R. § 205.2(g).

A much more ambitious project was mounted in 1977 by the Permanent Editorial Board of the Uniform Commercial Code—the drafting of a Uniform New Payments Code (UNPC). The UNPC is not primarily directed at consumer protection but would apply to transactions by businesses and banks as well as consumers. And it is not limited to electronic funds transfers but would apply to all payments, except cash, including those by check and credit card. According to UNPC 2: "This Code applies to any orders payable by or at, or transmitted by or to, an account institution, and Articles 3 and 4 of the Uniform Commercial Code do not apply even though the order meets the requirements of those Articles." The UNPC distinguishes between *draw* orders and *pay* orders. An order, such as a check, that is transmitted by the drawer to the *payee* is a draw order. An order that is transmitted by the drawer to the *drawee* is a pay order. See UNPC 51.

The UNPC would replace Articles 3 and 4 of the UCC as far as checks are concerned. It would also replace some federal legislation, including the EFT Act. This would, of course, require enactment on the federal level. Since the UNPC is still in the drafting stage, its prospects are uncertain. Nonetheless, the ideas it embodies are worthy of immediate attention and some are presented in the chapters that follow. Citations are to Draft No. 3 (June 2, 1983).

For a general discussion of EFT, see N. Penny & D. Baker, The Law of Electronic Fund Transfer Systems (1980).

Chapter 3

CHECKS DRAWN ON INSUFFICIENT FUNDS

Introduction. It has already been pointed out that the most common cause of dishonor is insufficient funds. What happens when a "bad" check "bounces"? [1] Most commonly the cause is a mistake by the drawer in calculating his bank balance or in drawing against uncollected checks, checks that he has already deposited in his account but on which he is not yet entitled to draw. The drawee bank will return the check with a return item ticket marked with the appropriate reason. If the check is presented a second time it will be paid by the drawee bank, or if the drawer is asked for payment it will be paid by him. But not all "bad" checks are so simply collected. This chapter is concerned in large part with the holder's recourse in such cases. (It will be assumed that the drawer does not assert that he is not liable on the check because of some defense; problems involving defenses are discussed in Chapter 4.) The final section of the chapter deals with the situation where the drawee has paid by mistake a check drawn on insufficient funds.

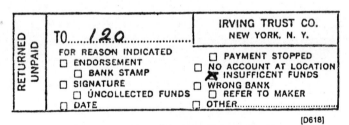

[D618]

RETURN ITEM STAMP

SECTION 1. LIABILITY ON DISHONOR

(A) LIABILITY OF DRAWEE TO DRAWER

---

1. For a discussion of a study of such checks, see Cavers, Science, Research, and the Law: Beutel's "Experimental Jurisprudence," 10 J.Legal Ed. 162 (1957). For another study, see Note, 50 N.C.L. Rev. 1079 (1972).

Prefatory Note. Before inquiring into the holder's recourse, we take a brief look at the problem of the dishonored check from the drawer's standpoint. Suppose that a check was drawn on sufficient funds and should have been honored, but was instead returned to the holder as a "bad" check. What recourse has he against the drawee? Or, to put the question differently, what legal sanctions stand behind the natural incentive of banks as competing businesses to keep the good will of their customers by honoring their properly drawn orders? What does the signature card (p. 101 supra) have to say about this?

Problem 1.[2] After drawing the Empire check, Stacey Smith stops payment on it, using the form on p. 183 infra, at a time when Empire has a balance of $4,000, and withdraws all but $1,000 from the account. When Quaker presents the check, the Irving Trust dishonors it, indicating on the return item stamp "insufficient funds." A criminal proceeding is instituted against Smith under a penal statute making it a crime to draw a check with knowledge that sufficient funds are not on deposit. After Smith's arrest and release on bail, the information is dismissed. Smith sues the Irving Trust alleging the above facts and claiming damages for harm to business reputation and credit and for legal expenses in connection with the criminal charges. On the Irving Trust's demurrer to the complaint, what decision? See UCC 4–402, 4–403, 4–104(1)(e), 1–103, 1–109; Loucks v. Albuquerque National Bank, infra. Consider, in formulating your answer, whether Smith was a "customer" and whether there was a "wrongful dishonor." Cf. Robbins v. Bankers Trust Co., 4 Misc.2d 347, 157 N.Y.S.2d 56 (1956); Johnson v. Grant Square Bank & Trust Co., 634 P.2d 1324 (Okl.App.1981). Would it be advisable for the Irving Trust to check "refer to maker" on all checks dishonored? See UCC 3–510(b). Can you think of any practical disadvantage of such a step?

Problem 2. Along with the Empire check for $2,178.50, three other checks drawn by Empire, for $200, $500, and $1,000, are presented in the same bundle at the Clearing House. Empire has only $2,200 in its account. What may the Irving Trust do without risking liability under UCC 4–402? Refuse to pay all of them? Refuse to pay some of them? If the Irving Trust processes checks by a computer that automatically rejects overdrafts, would the order in which the computer processes checks be important? See UCC 4–303(2); Reinisch v. Consolidated National Bank, 45 Pa.Super. 236 (1911).

---

2. The facts in most of the problems in Part II are those in the Prototype Transaction at p. 92, except as varied in the problem itself. Such variations in the facts in one problem are not to be made in the next problem unless so indicated.

LOUCKS v. ALBUQUERQUE NATIONAL BANK

Supreme Court of New Mexico, 1966.
76 N.M. 735, 418 P.2d 191.

[Loucks and Martinez were partners engaged in a business known as L & M Body Shop, and maintained a checking account in the partnership name in the Albuquerque National Bank. Martinez owed the bank $402, a personal debt unconnected with the partnership business, and the bank improperly charged this sum to the partnership account. Loucks and Martinez informed the bank that the charge was improper and that they had some outstanding checks against the partnership. The bank refused to recredit the account, which then had a balance of only $3.66, and after some unpleasantness the two partners closed it. The bank then refused to honor nine checks totalling $210.82. Both the partnership and the individual partners sued the bank for the $402, together with punitive damages, damage to business reputation and credit, and an ulcer sustained by Loucks allegedly because of the bank's wrongful acts. The trial judge dismissed all counts except that for recovery of the $402, permitting the jury to decide whether the deduction of that sum from the partnership account was wrongful. The jury found for the partnership on that issue, and all the plaintiffs appealed from the dismissal of the other claims.]

La Fel E. Oman, Judge, Court of Appeals. [The court quoted UCC 4–402.] It would appear that the first question to be resolved is that of the person, or persons, to whom a bank must respond in damages for a wrongful dishonor. Here, the account was a partnership account, and if there was in fact a wrongful dishonor of any checks, such were partnership checks.

We have adopted the Uniform Commercial Code in New Mexico. In § 50A–4–402, N.M.S.A.1953, quoted above, it is clearly stated that a bank "is liable to its customer." In § 50A–4–104(1)(e), N.M.S.A. 1953, entitled "Definitions and index of definitions" it is stated that:

"(1) In this article unless the context otherwise requires

"(e) 'Customer' means any person having an account with a bank or for whom a bank has agreed to collect items and includes a bank carrying an account with another bank; . . ."

This requires us to determine who is a "person" within the contemplation of this definition. Under part II, article I of the Uniform Commercial Code, entitled "General Definitions and Principles of Interpretation," we find the term "person" defined in § 50A–1–201(30), N.M.S.A.1953 as follows: " 'Person' includes an individual or an organization . . . ."

Subsection (28) of the same section expressly includes a "partnership" as one of the legal or commercial entities embraced by the term "organization."

It would seem that logically the "customer" in this case to whom the bank was required to respond in damages for any wrongful dishonor was the partnership. The Uniform Commercial Code expressly regards a partnership as a legal entity. This is consistent with the ordinary mercantile conception of a partnership. . . .

The Uniform Partnership Act, which has been adopted in New Mexico and appears as chapter 66, article I, N.M.S.A.1953, recognizes that a partnership has a separate legal entity for at least some purposes. See Attaway v. Stanolind Oil & Gas Company, 232 F.2d 790 (10th Cir.1956); I. Rowley, Partnership, § 1.3F at 22 (2d Ed. 1960); Jensen, Is a Partnership Under the Uniform Partnership Act an Aggregate or an Entity, 16 Vand.L.Rev. 377 (1963).

Suits may be brought in New Mexico by or against the partnership as such. Sections 21–6–5 and 21–1–1(4)(o), N.M.S.A.1953. A partnership is a distinct legal entity to the extent that it may sue or be sued in the partnership name. National Surety Co. v. George E. Breece Lumber Co., 60 F.2d 847 (10th Cir.1932). . . .

We have not overlooked the fact that tortious conduct may be tortious as to two or more persons, and that these persons may be the partnership and one or more of the individual partners. II Rowley, Partnership, § 49.2J at 278 (2d Ed. 1960).

The relationship, in connection with which the wrongful conduct of the bank arose, was the relationship between the bank and the partnership. The partnership was the customer, and any damages arising from the dishonor belonged to the partnership and not to the partners individually.

The damages claimed by Mr. Loucks as a result of the ulcer, which allegedly resulted from the wrongful acts of the defendants, are not consequential damages proximately caused by the wrongful dishonor as contemplated by § 50A–4–402, N.M.S.A.1953. In support of his right to recover for such claimed damages he relies upon the cases of Jones v. Citizens Bank of Clovis, 58 N.M. 48, 265 P.2d 366 and Weaver v. Bank of America Nat. Trust & Sav. Ass'n., 59 Cal.2d 428, 30 Cal.Rptr. 4, 380 P.2d 644. The California and New Mexico courts construed identical statutes in these cases. The New Mexico statute appeared as § 48–10–5, N.M.S.A.1953. This statute was repealed when the Uniform Commercial Code was adopted in 1961.

Assuming we were to hold that the decisions in those cases have not been affected by the repeal of the particular statutory provisions involved and the adoption of the Uniform Commercial Code, we are still compelled by our reasoning to reach the same result, because the plaintiffs in those cases were the depositor in the California case and the administratrix of the estate of the deceased depositor in the New Mexico case. In the present case, Mr. Loucks was not a depositor, as provided in the prior statute, nor a customer, as provided in our present statute. No duty was owed to him personally by reason of the debtor-creditor relationship between the bank and the partnership.

It is fundamental that compensatory damages are not recoverable unless they proximately result from some violation of a legally-recognized right of the person seeking the damages, whether such be a right in contract or tort.   Hedrick v. Perry, 102 F.2d 802 (10th Cir. 1939); 72 Am.Jur.2d, Damages, §§ 1, 2, and 11; 25 C.J.S. Damages §§ 18 and 19.

Insofar as the damage questions are concerned, we must still consider the claims for damages to the partnership. As above stated, the claim on behalf of the partnership for the recovery of the $402 was concluded by judgment for plaintiffs in this amount. This leaves (1) the claim of $5,000 for alleged damage to credit, reputation and business standing, (2) the claim of $1,800 for alleged loss of income, and (3) the claim of $14,404 as punitive damages.

The question with which we are first confronted is that of whether or not the customer, whose checks are wrongfully dishonored, may recover damages merely because of the wrongful dishonor. We understand the provisions of § 50A–4–402, N.M.S.A.1953 to limit the damages to those proximately caused by the wrongful dishonor, and such includes any consequential damages so proximately caused. If the dishonor occurs through mistake, the damages are limited to actual damages proved.[1]

It is pointed out in the comments to this section of the Uniform Commercial Code that:

. . .

"This section rejects decisions which have held that where the dishonored item has been drawn by a merchant, trader or fiduciary he is defamed in his business, trade or profession by a reflection on his credit and hence that substantial damages may be awarded on the basis of defamation 'per se' without proof that damage has occurred. . . . . " Uniform Commercial Code, § 4–402, Comment 3.

If we can say as a matter of law that the dishonor here occurred through mistake, then the damages would be limited to the "actual damages proved." Even if we are able to agree, as contended by defendants in their answer brief, that the defendants acted under a mistake of fact in ". . . that Mr. Kopp acting on behalf of the bank thought that the money was invested in the partnership and could be traced directly from Mr. Martinez to the L & M Paint and Body Shop," still defendants cannot rely on such mistake after both Mr. Martinez and Mr. Loucks informed them on March 15 and 18 that this was a personal obligation of Mr. Martinez and that the partnership had outstanding checks. At least it then became a question for

---

1. Does the text of UCC 4–402 clearly reject the rule of *per se* liability in cases where the dishonor does not occur "through mistake"?   Compare Elizarraras v. Bank of El Paso, 631 F.2d 366 (5th Cir.1980), with Yacht Club Sales & Service v. First National Bank, 101 Idaho 852, 623 P.2d 464 (1980). See Davenport, Wrongful Dishonor: UCC Section 4–402 and the Trader Rule, 56 N.Y.U.L.Rev. 1117 (1981). [Ed.]

the jury to decide whether or not defendants had wrongfully dishonored the checks through mistake.

The problem then resolves itself into whether or not the evidence offered and received, together with any evidence properly offered and improperly excluded, was sufficient to establish a question as to whether the partnership credit and reputation were proximately damaged by the wrongful dishonors. There was evidence that ten checks were dishonored, that one parts dealer thereafter refused to accept a partnership check and Mr. Loucks was required to go to the bank, cash the check, and then take the cash to the parts dealer in order to get the parts; that some persons who had previously accepted the partnership checks now refused to accept them; that other places of business denied the partnership credit after the dishonors; and that a salesman, who had sold the partnership a map and for which he was paid by one of the dishonored checks, came to the partnership's place of business, and ripped the map off the wall because he had been given "a bad check for it."

This evidence was sufficient to raise a question of fact to be determined by the jury as to whether or not the partnership's credit had been damaged as a proximate result of the dishonors. This question should have been submitted to the jury.

Damages recoverable for injuries to credit as a result of a wrongful dishonor are more than mere nominal damages and are referred to as ". . . compensatory, general, substantial, moderate, or temperate, damages, as would be fair and reasonable compensation for the injury which he [the depositor] must have sustained but not harsh or inordinate damages. . . ." 5A, Michie, Banks and Banking, § 243 at 576.

What are reasonable and temperate damages varies according to the circumstances of each case and the general extent to which it may be presumed the credit of the depositor would be injured. Valley National Bank v. Witter, 58 Ariz. 491, 121 P.2d 414. The amount of such damages is to be determined by the sound discretion and dispassionate judgment of the jury. Meinhart v. Farmers' State Bank, 124 Kan. 333, 259 P. 698, 701.

The next item of damages claimed on behalf of the partnership, which was taken from the jury, was the claim for loss of income in the amount of $1,800 allegedly sustained by the partnership as a result of the illness and disability of Mr. Loucks by reason of his ulcer. We are of the opinion that the trial court properly dismissed this claim for the announced reason that no substantial evidence was offered to support the claim, and for the further reason that the partnership had no legally-enforceable right to recover for personal injuries inflicted upon a partner.

Even if we were to assume that a tortious act had been committed by defendants which proximately resulted in the ulcer and the consequent personal injuries and disabilities of Mr. Loucks, the right to recover for such would be in him. An action for damages resulting from a tort can only be sustained by the person directly injured thereby, and not by one claiming to have suffered collateral or resulting injuries. Ware v. Brown, 29 Fed.Cas. 220 (No. 17,170) (S.D.Ohio 1869); Commercial Credit Company v. Standard Baking Co., 45 Ohio App. 403, 187 N.E. 251; General Home Improvement Co. v. American Ladder Co., 26 N.J.Misc. 24, 56 A.2d 116.

As was stated by Mr. Justice Holmes in Robins Dry Dock & Repair Co. v. Flint, 275 U.S. 303, 48 S.Ct. 134, 72 L.Ed. 290:

". . . no authority need be cited to show that, as a general rule, at least, a tort to the person or property of one man does not make the tort-feasor liable to another merely because the injured person was under a contract with that other, unknown to the doer of the wrong. . . . The law does not spread its protection so far."

[The court then affirmed the dismissal of the claim for punitive damages on the ground that there was no evidence of willful or wanton conduct on the part of the bank.]

It follows from what has been said that this cause must be reversed and remanded for a new trial solely upon the questions of whether or not the partnership credit was damaged as a proximate result of the dishonors, and, if so, the amount of such damages.

NOTES

(1) **Recovery by Non-customer.** Compare the denial of recovery to Loucks in the principal case with Macrum v. Security Trust & Savings Co., 221 Ala. 419, 129 So. 74 (1930), in which it was held that the manager of a corporation could recover damages that he suffered as the result of the wrongful dishonor of a check that he had drawn on behalf of the corporation on its account. Would the "principles of law" that allowed recovery in that case be "displaced" by UCC 4–402, or would they be "supplementary general principles of law" under UCC 1–103? What does the section caption to UCC 4–402 suggest concerning its intended coverage? Are section captions part of the Code? See UCC 1–109. Do you suppose that the drafters of the Code contemplated the problem in the Loucks and Macrum cases? Are there any dangers in codifying an area such as this?

For a case applying "a flexible and reasonable interpretation of the word 'customer'" and distinguishing Loucks where the corporate drawer was "nothing but a transparent shell, having no viability as a separate and distinct legal entity," see Kendall Yacht Corp. v. United California Bank, 50 Cal.App.3d 949, 123 Cal.Rptr. 848 (1975).

(2) **Wrongful Dishonor of Other Orders.** What rules govern the wrongful dishonor of orders other than checks?

Suppose, for example, that a bank receives a telex from a depositor ordering it to transfer a sum of money to a transferee's account, but the bank negligently fails to make the transfer. As a result, the transferee cancels its contract with the depositor. Is the bank liable to the depositor for the resulting loss? Is the answer to be found in the Uniform Commercial Code? In UCC 4–402? In UCC 4–103(5)? Is a telex an "item" under UCC 4–104? See Evra Corp. v. Swiss Bank Corp., 673 F.2d 951 (7th Cir.), cert. denied, ___ U.S. ___, 103 S.Ct. 377, 74 L.Ed.2d 511 (1982).

Suppose that a cardholder tries to use a credit card to purchase goods in an amount for which telephonic authorization is required, but authorization is mistakenly denied on the erroneous ground that the cardholder's dollar limit has been exceeded, and the cardholder is unable to make the purchase? Is the issuing bank liable to the cardholder for damages? Would it make a difference if the agreement between the cardholder and the issuing bank provided that the bank could cancel the credit privileges at any time without notice? See Smith v. Federated Department Stores, 165 Ga.App. 459, 301 S.E.2d 652 (1983). As to the impact of the Fair Credit Reporting Act, see Wood v. Holiday Inns, 508 F.2d 167 (5th Cir.1975).

Suppose that instead of using a credit card, a consumer attempts to pay for the goods using a point of sale system, but the consumer's order is wrongfully dishonored. Is the financial institution liable to the consumer for damages? EFT Act § 1693(h) lays down as a general rule that a financial institution is liable to a consumer "for all damages proximately caused" by its wrongful failure to observe the consumer's instruction to make an electronic funds transfer. The institution is not liable, however, if it "shows by a preponderence of the evidence": (1) that its failure resulted from a "circumstance beyond its control, that it exercised reasonable care to prevent such an occurrence, and that it exercised such diligence as the circumstances required," or (2) that its failure resulted from "a technical malfunction which was known to the consumer at the time he attempted to initiate an electronic fund transfer or, in the case of a preauthorized transfer, at the time such transfer should have occurred." Furthermore, if the failure "was not intentional and . . . resulted from a bona fide error, notwithstanding the maintenance of procedures reasonably adapted to avoid any such error, the financial institution shall be liable for actual damages proved."

(3) Dishonor of Stale Checks. Before the enactment of the Code, most states had adopted special statutes which relieved the drawee bank from liability for wrongful dishonor of a check presented more than a fixed period, six months or a year, after its date. The comparable provision of the Code is UCC 4–404, which uses a six month period.

Like its predecessors, UCC 4–404 is designed to save the drawee bank from the horns of a dilemma that it faces when a check is presented long after its date. At some point in time the check may be regarded as having become so stale that if the bank paid it, the drawer could resist a charge to his account, assuming, of course, that he has not received the benefit of it. But in a doubtful case how is the bank to tell whether the check is so stale that it should dishonor the check to avoid this risk, or not so stale so that the bank should pay the check to avoid risk of liability to the drawer for wrongful dishonor? UCC 4–404 solves the problem by amputating one of the horns of the dilemma, that is, by relieving the drawee bank of liability for wrongful dishonor in any doubtful case. What practice would you expect a drawee bank to follow with respect to ten month old checks presented to it? See Comment to UCC 4–404.

(B) LIABILITY OF DRAWEE TO HOLDER

Prefatory Note. The inquiry turns now to the problem of the dishonored check from the holder's standpoint, and first to the holder's rights against the drawee. What recourse has the holder of a check against a drawee bank that has dishonored the check?

Before the Negotiable Instruments Law there was authority for the proposition that a check operated as an assignment to the payee of a part of the claim which the drawer, as depositor, had against his bank. The result was, of course, to give the holder a right of action against the drawee bank on the assigned claim. This did not appeal to bankers who feared that banking practices in dealing with checks could not survive if checks were regarded as assignments. Take, for example, the rule that an obligor is not discharged by payment to one assignee if he has notice of a prior irrevocable assignment to another assignee. How would this affect a bank in the position of the drawee in Problem 2, p. 112 supra? Would it then be liable to the holders of earlier checks if it had first paid the holders of later checks? If the numbers on the checks were not consistent with the dates on the checks, which should the bank follow?

Happily for the bankers, the Negotiable Instruments Law laid to rest the argument that a check is, of itself, an assignment and the Code follows the Negotiable Instruments Law on this point. See UCC 3–409(1).

Two questions remain: (1) What difference does it make that a check is not, of itself, an assignment? (2) What additional facts may cause a check to operate as an assignment?

Problem 3. At the time that Empire draws the check at page 96 supra, it has $4,000 in its account in the Irving Trust. Irving Trust has not yet paid the check.

(a) If Empire discovers that the cans are defective, orders the Irving Trust not to pay, and the Irving Trust refuses to pay, what are Quaker's rights against Irving Trust?

(b) Can a judgment creditor of Empire attach any part of the $4,000 debt owed by Irving Trust? How much?

(c) Can a judgment creditor of Quaker attach any part of the $4,000 debt owed by Irving Trust? How much?

(d) If Empire goes into bankruptcy, can its trustee in bankruptcy claim any part of the $4,000 as an asset of Empire? How much? See State Bank of Southern Utah v. Stallings, infra.

STATE BANK OF SOUTHERN UTAH v. STALLINGS

Supreme Court of Utah, 1967.
19 Utah 2d 146, 427 P.2d 744.

ELLETT, JUSTICE: The appellants [Kaze & Gammon Construction Co.] as general contractors constructed a public school building. The defendant, Thomas A. Stallings was the electrical subcontractor and bought his merchandise from Westinghouse Supply Company. He owed Westinghouse some $8,000, $2,200 of which was past due.

Appellants made out a check to Stallings in the amount of $2,250 and requested Stallings to endorse it so the appellants could take it to Westinghouse and apply it on the delinquent account. Stallings claimed that Westinghouse had requested only $2,200 and refused to endorse the check, whereupon appellants gave their check to Stallings to be deposited in Stallings' checking account in the Hurricane Branch of the Bank of St. George, Stallings then gave his own check made payable to Westinghouse in the amount of $2,200 to the appellants to deliver to Westinghouse.

The respondent, State Bank of Southern Utah, had a couple of judgments against Stallings, and before the Westinghouse check could pass through the clearing house, the respondent had placed two garnishments against the Stallings account in the Hurricane Branch Bank.

The appellants intervened by some means not here questioned in the two cases from which the garnishments were issued and now claim that the check from Stallings was an assignment of $2,200 of the bank account when and if the $2,250 check from the appellants was deposited.

The trial court allowed the intervention and then gave a summary judgment against the intervenor and a garnishee judgment against the Hurricane Branch Bank of St. George. The appellants do not contend that the assignment of the $2,200 was made to them. They say it was an assignment out of the $2,250 given by them and was assigned to Westinghouse. They claim an interest by reason of the fact that unless Stallings pays Westinghouse, they as general contractors will have to pay the bill themselves.

If appellants are correct in their contention, then the trial court was in error in giving a garnishee judgment, and Westinghouse should be here doing the appealing in order to protect its rights.

However, Westinghouse has made no intervention and is not a party to the proceedings in this court.

We do not think the giving of the check operated as an assignment in this case. Section 3–409 in Chapter 154 of Laws of Utah 1965 provides as follows:

> (1) A check or other draft does not of itself operate as an assignment of any funds in the hands of the drawee available for its payment, and the drawee is not liable on the instrument until he accepts it.

. . .

In the Idaho case of Kaesemeyer v. Smith, 22 Idaho 1, 123 P. 943, at page 947, 43 L.R.A., N.S., 100, the court in speaking of a situation like the one before us said:

> The check given to Carscallen was a mere direction to the bank to pay a certain sum of money to the person named therein. By the giving of such check the amount of the same did not become the property of the payee of the check nor place such fund beyond the control of Smith. Until the check was presented to the bank, Smith could have countermanded its payment and could have given different directions for the disposition of the money remaining in the bank to his credit, and could even have personally demanded payment, and the bank could have been required to pay the same, and by so doing its indebtedness to Smith would have been discharged.

This court has heretofore spoken concerning what constituted an assignment. In the case of Milford State Bank v. Parrish et al., 88 Utah 235, 53 P.2d 72, the court said at page 238 of the Utah Reports, 53 P.2d at page 73:

> The evidence relating to this primary and controlling question is brief and free from conflict. The law as to what constitutes an equitable assignment is well settled. The application of the law and the facts is sometimes difficult.

In the case of Nickerson v. Hollet (National Bank of Goldendale, Intervener) 149 Wash. 646, 272 P. 53, Tolman, J., quotes the law and cites authority as follows:

> In order to work an equitable assignment there must be an absolute appropriation by the assignor of the debt or fund sought to be assigned to the use of the assignee. The intention of the assignor must be to transfer a present interest in the debt or fund or subject matter; if this is done the transaction is an assignment; otherwise not. 5 C.J. 909.

> The assignor of a chose in action must part with the power of control over the thing assigned; if he retains control it is fatal to the claim of the assignee, 5 C.J. 912. See, also, Hossack v. Graham, 20 Wash. 184, 55 P. 36.

In this case there can be no question but that Stallings had the power to stop payment on the check.

Of course, the assignor and the assignee may by agreement make an assignment by means of a check. See Merchants' National Bank of St. Paul v. State Bank, 172 Minn. 24, 214 N.W. 750; Slaughter v. First National Bank, Tex.Civ.App., 18 S.W.2d 754. However, no such agreement was ever made by the parties to the alleged assignment. Stallings and Westinghouse never spoke to each other about the check. The appellants planned the transactions but did not foresee the consequences. Had they wished an assignment, they could have taken the Stallings check to the bank and had it certified.

We feel sorry for appellants, but the law, like the north wind, cannot be altered to suit the needs of the mangy fleece. We hold that there was no assignment of the $2,200 represented by the Stallings check and that the garnishment being served before the check was presented for payment gives priority to the garnishment. See Commercial Bank of Tacoma v. Chilberg et al., 14 Wash. 247, 44 P. 264.

The judgment of the lower court is affirmed with costs to the respondent. [Dissenting opinion omitted.]

NOTES

(1) **Counselling.** Could Kaze & Gammon have protected themselves by having Stallings write appropriate language on his check? What language would you suggest? Would it be enough if he wrote: "The above amount is on deposit and will be kept there subject to this check"? See El Dorado National Bank v. Butler County State Bank, 120 Kan. 109, 242 P. 475 (1926).

(2) **Agricultural Marketing Finance.** Considerable litigation has arisen in agricultural regions from variations on the following typical fact situation. Dealer purchases commodities from farmers and resells them to commission houses. To finance his business Dealer makes an agreement with Bank whereby Bank promises Dealer to honor his checks drawn in payment for such purchases and Dealer agrees to deposit immediately the proceeds from his resale. Dealer's turnover is rapid and normally the proceeds are deposited before the checks are presented. However, should checks arrive before the deposit of proceeds to cover them, Bank agrees to honor these overdrafts. After the agreement, Farmer presents one of Dealer's checks given in payment for goods, but Bank refuses to pay it and applies Dealer's balance to outstanding debts owed to Bank, under the general rule that where a bank holds the matured debt of its depositor it may apply his deposit in payment of it. Farmer sues Bank. On what theories might he recover? Would it be sufficient for Farmer to show that the check was an assignment of Dealer's rights against Bank? Might he claim rights as a third party beneficiary? As the beneficiary of a trust? Is it arguable that this was a "special deposit" not subject to set-off? Compare Bradley Grain Co. v. Farmers & Merchants National Bank, 274 S.W.2d 178 (Tex.Civ.App.1954), with Ballard v. Home National Bank, 91 Kan. 91, 136 P. 935 (1913). For a case raising similar questions in the context of a construction

contract, see Mid-Continent Casualty Co. v. Jenkins, 431 P.2d 349 (Okl.1967).

In answering these questions, it may be useful to know a little about the bank's right of setoff, "the common law, equitable right of a bank to apply the general deposits of a depositor against the matured debts of the depositor. This right grows out of the contractual debtor-creditor relationship created between the depositor and the bank at the time the account is opened, and it rests on the principle that it would be inequitable to permit the debtor-depositor to carry an open account that induces the bank to extend credit, and then allow the debtor to apply the funds to other purposes because he had not expressly agreed to apply them to the debt." TeSelle, Banker's Right of Setoff—Banker Beware, 34 Okla.L.Rev. 40, 40 (1981).

The right is often misleadingly termed a "banker's lien." "The so-called 'lien' of the bank on the depositor's account or funds on deposit is not technically a lien, for the bank is the owner of the funds and the debtor of the depositor, and the bank cannot have a lien on its own property. The right of the bank to charge the depositor's fund with his matured indebtedness is more correctly termed a right of set-off, based on general principles of equity." Gonsalves v. Bank of America, 16 Cal.2d 169, 173, 105 P.2d 118, 121 (1940).

It has been held that "the act of setoff is not complete until three steps have been taken: (1) the decision to exercise the right, (2) some action which accomplishes the set off and (3) some record which evidences that the right of setoff has been exercised." Baker v. National City Bank of Cleveland, 511 F.2d 1016 (6th Cir.1975).

This right of set-off exists, however, only where the deposit is "general," not "special." "From the special deposit approach, stated broadly, funds deposited for a special purpose known to the bank, or under special agreement, cannot be set off by the bank . . . . A deposit is special rather than general when there is specific direction, or agreement express or implied, that it be special or where there are circumstances sufficient to create a trust by operation of law." Kaufman v. First National Bank of Opp, 493 F.2d 1070, 1072 (5th Cir. 1974).

Problem 4. A gave the First Bank B's personal check for $500 payable to First Bank plus a small fee and received a "Personal Money Order" like that shown on p. 124 infra, with the amount "five hundred dollars" imprinted on it by machine. A filled in his own name as payee and indorsed it to Dealer in payment for a stereo. When Dealer presented it for payment, First Bank refused to pay it because B's check had been dishonored for insufficient funds. Is First Bank liable to Dealer? See UCC 3–401; Sequoyah State Bank v. Union National Bank of Little Rock, infra. What is the answer to "the question of whether the purchaser may stop payment"? Would First Bank be liable to Dealer if a blank personal money order were stolen from its safe, filled in by the thief, and taken by Dealer in payment of a stereo?

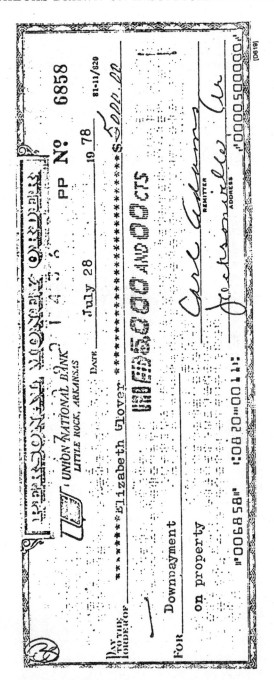

PERSONAL MONEY ORDER

[*A copy is retained by the bank and a record copy is given to the customer. The latter contains a space to enter the date and the name of the payee. It may also contain a provision such as: "Purchaser agrees that no request for refund or to stop payment or otherwise will be made to this Bank with respect to the said Money Order unless the customer's RECORD is submitted therewith."*]

SEQUOYAH STATE BANK v. UNION NATIONAL BANK

Supreme Court of Arkansas, 1981.
274 Ark. 1, 621 S.W.2d 683.

ADKISSON, CHIEF JUSTICE. The only issue in this case is whether Union Bank by its own initiative can stop payment on a personal money order it had issued in exchange for a hot check and, thereby, cause Sequoyah Bank, a holder in due course, to bear the loss. Under these circumstances the loss must be borne by Union Bank which issued the negotiable instrument to be circulated in commerce.

We do not decide the question of whether the purchaser may stop payment, but we do hold that after the sale of a personal money order, the issuing bank cannot stop payment on the instrument.

A personal money order is issued with unfilled blanks for the name of the payee, the date, and the signature of the purchaser. Only the amount is filled out at the time of issue, usually by checkwriter impression as was done in this case.

The Uniform Commercial Code apparently did not directly contemplate the use of money orders and made no specific provision for them. Mirabile v. Udoh, 92 Misc.2d 168, 399 N.Y.S.2d 869 (1977). It was recognized in Mirabile that it is the custom and practice of the business community to accept personal money orders as a pledge of the issuing bank's credit. We may consider this custom and practice in construing the legal effect of such instruments. See Ark.Stat. Ann. § 85–1–103 (Add.1961).

Appellee relies on the cases of Garden Check Cashing Service, Inc. v. First National City Bank, 25 A.D.2d 137, 267 N.Y.S.2d 698 (1966), aff'd. 18 N.Y.2d 941, 223 N.E.2d 566, 277 N.Y.S.2d 141 (1966) and Krom v. Chemical Bank New York Trust Co., 63 Misc.2d 1060, 313 N.Y.S.2d 810 (1970), rev'd. 38 A.D.2d 871, 329 N.Y.S.2d 91 (A.D.1972) which held that a purchaser of a personal money order may stop payment on it. However, the only cited case to specifically address the issue of whether the issuing bank, on its own initiative, may stop payment on a personal money order is Rose Check Cashing Service, Inc. v. Chemical Bank N.Y. Trust Co., 40 Misc.2d 995, 244 N.Y.S.2d 474, 477 (1963). In holding that the issuing bank could not stop payment and therefore must suffer the loss the court stated:

> All of these differences between the instrument at issue and an ordinary check would seem to indicate that the bank would honor the order to pay no matter who signed the face of the instrument, assuming of course an otherwise valid negotiation of the instrument.

> . . .

In the instrument in suit, the drawer *purchases* the instrument from the bank. The transaction is in the nature of a sale. No deposit is created. The funds to pay the instrument, immediately come within the bank's exclusive control and ownership.

. . .

The bank's contention that the instrument is a check is inconsistent with its own acts. The bank (drawee) stamped "Stop Payment" on the instrument in suit on its own order. Nowhere in the Negotiable Instruments Law is there any provision that a drawee [bank] may "Stop Payment" of a check unless ordered to do so by the drawer.

Appellee also denies liability on the instrument based upon Ark. Stat.Ann. § 85–3–401(1) which states that "No person is liable on an instrument unless his signature appears thereon." Subdivision (2) of this same section provides that a signature may be "any word or mark used in lieu of a written signature." The authenticity of the instrument involved here is not in question. The issuance of the money order with the bank's printed name evidences the appellee's intent to be bound thereby. *Mirabile*, supra.

Appellee also relies on Ark.Stat.Ann. § 85–3–409 for the proposition that it is not liable on the personal money order since it did not accept it. In our opinion, however, the appellee accepted the instrument in advance by the act of its issuance. Rose Check Cashing Service Inc. v. Chemical Bank New York Trust Co., 43 Misc.2d 679, 252 N.Y.S.2d 100 (1964).

The personal money order constituted an obligation of Union from the moment of its sale and issuance. The fact that Union was frustrated in retaining the funds because instead of cash it accepted a check drawn on insufficient funds is no reason to hold otherwise. We note by analogy that the Uniform Commercial Code on sales Ark. Stat.Ann. § 85–2–403(1)(b) provides that a purchaser of goods, who takes delivery in exchange for a check which is later dishonored, transfers good title to the goods.

Union placed the personal money order in commerce for a consideration it accepted as adequate and was, thereafter, liable on it. Banks are not allowed to stop payment on their depositor's checks and certainly should not be allowed to stop payment on personal money orders. See Note, Personal Money Orders and Teller's Checks: Mavericks Under the UCC, 67 Colum.L.Rev. 524 (1967).

Reversed.

DUDLEY, JUSTICE, dissenting. This case involves a personal money order, not a bank money order, not a certificate of deposit and not a certified check. A personal money order is for the convenience of anyone who does not have an ordinary checking account and needs a safe, inexpensive and readily acceptable means of transferring funds. The bank simply sells to the individual a check-sized form which has the amount impressed into the face of the paper, an identification number and the name of the issuing bank. No authorized representative of the bank signs the instrument. When the purchaser of the instrument decides to pass it, he dates it, enters the name of the payee and signs the instrument.

Ark.Stat.Ann. § 85–3–104(1)(a) (Add.1961) requires that a writing be signed by the drawer or maker in order to be negotiable. Any item which is an order to pay is considered a "draft" and any draft drawn on a bank and payable on demand is a "check." § 85–3–104(2) (a), (b). Since the only signature on a personal money order is that of the purchaser, since the instrument takes the form of an order to pay, and since it is drawn on a bank and payable on demand, it is clearly within the classification of a check. The absence of the bank's signature as a "maker" and the absence of any express "undertaking" to pay by the bank, § 85–3–102(1)(c) and § 85–3–104(2)(d) preclude a finding that the instrument is a note. Aside from "draft," "check" and "note" the only other form of negotiable instrument recognized by the Uniform Commercial Code is a "certificate of deposit" and that requires an acknowledgment that the bank will repay it. § 85–3–104(2)(c). Under these code provisions a personal money order must be classified as a check. There is no other code classification of negotiable commercial paper. § 85–3–104. For the sake of clarity in the law of commercial paper this personal money order should be classified as a check.

However, the matter of classification is not nearly as important as the issue of liability. No authorized representative of appellee bank signed this check. Section 85–3–401 states: *"No person is liable on an instrument unless his signature appears thereon."* Section 85–3–409(1) states that a check or other draft is not an assignment of funds held by the drawee (appellee Union Bank) and *the drawee is not liable until it accepts the check or draft.* Appellee did not accept this instrument. It stopped payment. The language of these statutes, a part of the Uniform Commercial Code, is unmistakable.

The majority opinion holds:

> The personal money order constituted an obligation of Union from the moment of its sale and issuance.

I respectfully submit that statement is supported by absolutely no authority and it creates an unnecessary legal quagmire. Assume that a purchaser of a personal money order has not filled in the name of the payee or has not signed the check and it is lost or stolen. The purchaser then wants to stop payment before it is negotiated to a third party. The majority has stated that it was an obligation of the bank from the moment of sale and issuance. Fairness and logic dictate that the purchaser should not be allowed to stop payment and leave the bank liable. Yet, § 85–4–403(1) provides:

> Customer's right to stop payment—Burden of proof of loss. A customer may by order to his bank stop payment of any item payable for his account but the order must be received at such time and in such manner as to afford the bank a reasonable

opportunity to act on it prior to any action by the bank with respect to the item described in Section 4–303.

Comment 4 to this statute makes it abundantly clear that personal money orders are intended to be covered by this broad language.

One of the three explanations given for the holding is:

The issuance of the money order with the bank's printed name evidences the appellee's intent to be bound thereby.

That notion will echo because the name of the drawee bank is printed on every ordinary check in circulation.

The other two explanations are that banks should not be allowed to stop payment and business custom. Both explanations are dead letters. Assume, for the sake of argument only, that banks should not be allowed to stop payment. That occurrence takes place after the sale and issuance of the instrument. The majority has held that liability attached upon issuance. Therefore this subsequent event logically cannot have any effect on liability. It very simply is not a reason for a decision that liability attached at the time of issuance. Business custom is not proven. There is not one single word in the transcript or abstract about business custom. Even if this defense had been proven it would be an estoppel defense, or a defense which accrues after the sale and, once again, it would not be a reason for a decision that liability attached at the time of issuance.

The master purpose of the Uniform Commercial Code is to clarify the law governing commercial transactions. The tragedy of this case is that both the purpose and the Code are emaciated [sic] for no reason.

NOTES

(1) **Personal Money Orders.** "Personal money orders were first issued in 1937 and have grown steadily in popularity since 1944, when the price of the competing Post Office Money Order was raised. Personal money orders are attractive to people who have no ordinary checking account, for they offer a safe, inexpensive, and readily acceptable means of transferring funds, in a form that has the prestigious appearance of a personal check. Moreover, banks favor the instruments because they are simpler, faster, and less expensive to issue than cashier's checks and bank money orders; because they attract potential customers for other bank services; and because they can create a substantial deposit balance for the bank's use." Note, 67 Colum.L.Rev. 524, 525–26 (1967). With which opinion in the Sequoyah case do you agree as to result? As to the reading of the Code? As to treatment of "custom"? See UCC 1–205(2). For criticism of the case, see Murphey, Acceptance and Dishonor: "Payable Through" Drafts and Personal Money Orders, 5 U.Ark. Little Rock L.J. 519, 541–48 (1982). In what ways, if any, should a creditor be better off because of having received a personal money order instead

of a personal check from a debtor? See Note 2, p. 260 infra; Note, p. 272 infra.

As to the issuer's liability on unsigned traveller's checks, see Ashford v. Thos. Cook & Son (Bankers) Limited, 52 Hawaii 113, 471 P.2d 530 (1970); Hawkland, American Travellers Checks, 15 Buffalo L.Rev. 501 (1966).

(2) Remitters. Buyer, who wishes to make payment to Seller by a cashier's check or bank draft, may have it made payable to Buyer's own order and later indorse it to Seller, or may have it made payable to Seller's order. In this latter case Buyer is known as a "remitter." Although not a holder or a transferee from the payee without indorsement, Buyer has purchased the instrument from the bank and is the owner until its delivery to the payee. Suppose that Seller refuses to take the instrument or that Buyer changes his mind and decides not to give it to Seller. What are Buyer's rights against the bank from which he bought it? Remitters have been allowed recovery in such situations, but there may be a dispute as to whether the action is one on the instrument or one to recover the amount paid for the instrument. The difference is particularly important in foreign remittance transactions, where the remitter arranges with a domestic bank to have its foreign correspondent pay in foreign currency to the remitter's foreign creditor. If the remitter's action is on the instrument, he will bear the risk of depreciation of the foreign currency. If the remitter can recover the amount paid for the instrument, the bank must bear this risk. On this problem see Kerr Steamship Co. v. Chartered Bank of India, Australia & China, 292 N.Y. 253, 54 N.E.2d 813 (1944); Note, 57 Yale L.J. 1426 (1948); cf. Bunge Corp. v. Manufacturers Hanover Trust Co., 31 N.Y.2d 223, 286 N.E.2d 903 (1972).[1]

ACCEPTANCE AND CERTIFICATION

UCC 3–409 provides: "A check or other draft does not of itself operate as an assignment . . . , and the drawee is not liable on the instrument until he accepts it." Acceptance is defined in UCC 3–410 as "the drawee's signed engagement to honor the draft as presented." The acceptor's contract is set out in UCC 3–413(1). Acceptance has always been commonly written on the instrument itself and the drawee's signature alone, on the face of the bill, has been considered sufficient. Under UCC 3–410 the acceptance "must be written on the draft."[2] The problem of the acceptance that varies the terms of the draft is dealt with in UCC 3–412.

1. Note the loose use of the term "remitter" on the Personal Money Order form to refer to the drawer.

2. For a case holding that a bank may nevertheless be liable on a theory of promissory estoppel where a bank employee said over the telephone that a check would be paid if represented, see Bigger v. Fremont National Bank & Trust Co., 215 Neb. 580, 340 N.W.2d 142 (1983).

In the case of a check, the counterpart of acceptance is commonly certification by a stamp similar to the one below. Under UCC 3–411(1), "Certification of a check is acceptance." Upon certification the drawee bank charges the amount of the check to the drawer's account and transfers it to the "certified check" account on its books. It therefore will not certify a postdated check before its date. The practice of certifying checks does not exist in England and has been common in this country for only a century. On the history of the certified check, see Steffen & Starr, A Blue Print for the Certified Check, 13 N.C.L.Rev. 450, 463–67 (1935).

[D620]

CERTIFICATION

(C) LIABILITY OF DRAWER AND INDORSERS TO HOLDER

DISHONOR AND NOTICE OF DISHONOR

"Secondary" Parties. Buyer's obligation under a contract of sale is usually to pay money, but the medium of payment is not commonly specified. In the absence of such a specification, Buyer must pay in "legal tender." Since a check is not legal tender, Seller has the right to refuse a check. However, if Buyer tenders a check, drawn upon ample funds in a solvent bank, Seller is deemed to have waived his right unless he objects on the specific ground that the check is not legal tender. Were he to so object, Buyer could probably make a conforming tender. See UCC 2–511(2). Restatement (Second) of Contracts § 249.

Usually Seller will take Buyer's check. Because, as was seen in the preceding section, the holder of an uncertified check generally has no rights against the drawee, it becomes especially important to ask what rights the holder has against the drawer and any indorsers in the event that the check is dishonored. First, what are the holder's rights on the underlying obligation for which the instrument was given? Second, what are the holder's rights on the instrument itself? The first question is dealt with in UCC 3–802, where the usual rule that a check is conditional payment is restated in more helpful terms of suspension of the underlying obligation. The second question is dealt with in UCC 3–413(2), which sets out the drawer's contract, and in UCC 3–414(1), which sets out the indorser's contract.[1] (See also the final sentence of UCC 4–207(2) for the similar obligation imposed on a customer or collecting bank transferring an item for collection.) These contracts of the drawer and indorser are similar in that each is conditional "upon dishonor and any necessary notice of dishonor and protest." [2] Their liability thus differs from that of the maker of a note and acceptor of a bill whose contracts are not so conditioned under UCC 3–413(1). The drawer or indorser is therefore a "secondary party" according to UCC 3–102(1)(d).

Dishonor. "Dishonor," the first of these conditions, is defined in UCC 3–507(1). It usually consists of the maker's or drawee's refusal to pay, but in the case of a draft may also consist in the drawee's refusal to accept.[3] Presentment of a draft for acceptance as opposed to payment is, however, required only in the cases enumerated in UCC 3–501(1)(a), and even presentment for payment may be delayed or dispensed with under certain conditions under UCC 3–511. Presentment is dealt with in more detail in UCC 3–501 to 3–507, 3–511. Would it be enough to charge Empire on its check if Quaker tele-

1. UCC 3–403 deals with questions that arise when an agent signs on behalf of a principal. Suppose, for example, that the president of Empire had signed the check on page 96 "Stacey Smith" instead of "Stacey Smith, Pres." Would Smith be personally liable as drawer if the check were dishonored? Suppose Smith had signed "By Stacey Smith"? Would parol evidence be admissible to resolve these questions? Compare Colonial Baking Co. of Des Moines v. Dowie, 330 N.W.2d 279 (Iowa, 1983), with Valley National Bank v. Cook, 136 Ariz. 232, 665 P.2d 576 (App.1983).

2. Protest, which is of little practical importance in connection with checks, is dealt with in UCC 3–501, 3–502, 3–509, 3–511. Protest is usually made by a notary public, who executes a certificate of protest.

In most civil law countries, protest is generally required in the case of any dishonor of a negotiable instrument. The Code, like its predecessors (the Negotiable Instruments Law and the British Bills of Exchange Act), retains the requirement of protest for international drafts, preserving uniformity in international transactions and affording foreign drawers satisfactory evidence of dishonor. Thus UCC 3–501(3) requires protest of any dishonor "to charge the drawer and indorsers of any draft which on its face appears to be drawn or payable outside of . . . the United States."

However, since a check does not commonly indicate where it was drawn, protest of a check is rarely required by the Code. Furthermore, protest is dispensed with in those cases where notice of dishonor is dispensed with (UCC 3–511), and—like notice and presentment—protest can be waived (UCC 3–511(2)(a), (5)).

Even where protest is not required by law, collecting banks often send large checks, e.g., $1,000 or over, with instructions to protest if dishonored in order to have formal evidence of dishonor. But see UCC 3–510. The same practice may also be followed with other drafts and with notes (UCC 3–501(3)).

3. Note also that Comment 2 to UCC 3–510 makes a distinction between a dishonor and a justifiable refusal to pay a check. See UCC 3–504(1); see also Problem 1, p. 112 supra.

phoned the Irving Trust and was told that there were no funds to pay it? See Kirby v. Bergfield, 186 Neb. 242, 182 N.W.2d 205 (1970).

Notice of Dishonor. "Notice of dishonor," the second condition, is treated in UCC 3–501, 3–502, 3–508, 3–510, 3–511. The purpose of requiring that notice be given to secondary parties is to enable such a party promptly to seek recourse against prior parties and others who may in turn be liable to him in the event of dishonor. The penalty for failure to give the required notice to a secondary party is generally discharge of that party under UCC 3–501, 3–502. However, in some situations notice to a party secondarily liable is not required under UCC 3–511. It is hardly surprising that a drawer who has, for example, stopped payment is not entitled to notice of dishonor according to UCC 3–511(2)(b). Notice of dishonor can also be waived under UCC 3–511(2)(a), (5). Where a check is dishonored after presentment by a collecting bank as the agent of the holder, the presenting bank may give notice of dishonor to the holder or to the bank that forwarded the check to it (UCC 3–508(1)).

In general, the presenting bank must act within the time specified in UCC 3–508(2). That the Code is not the only guide to proper banking procedures, however, is shown by the following case.

WELLS FARGO BANK v. HARTFORD NATIONAL BANK & TRUST CO, 484 F.Supp. 817 (D.Conn.1980). [On November 22, 1971, John D. Porter as agent for Great Western Industries opened a checking account with Lincoln First Bank in New York state by depositing a $25,000 check payable to Lincoln's order and drawn on Great Western's account with First National Bank of Nevada. Instead of using the Federal Reserve collection system, Lincoln chose to use private collection channels which promised earlier availability of funds. It therefore sent the check to Hartford National Bank & Trust Co. (HNBT), which sent it on to its California correspondent, Wells Fargo Bank. On November 23, Wells Fargo mailed the check to the Nevada bank's Las Vegas branch. Inexplicably, the check was not received until December 8, 15 days later. An additional delay occurred because the Las Vegas branch had to forward the check to the Reno branch. The Reno branch promptly discovered that the check was drawn on insufficient funds. Late in the afternoon of Friday, December 10, the Nevada bank succeeded in telephoning Wells Fargo and notifying it of this fact. On Monday, December 13, the Nevada bank mailed the dishonored check to Wells Fargo, which did not receive it until Friday, December 17. On receiving the check, Wells Fargo immediately wired notice of dishonor to HNBT and mailed the dishonored check to it. HNBT claimed not to have received the telegram, but admitted that it received the check in the mail on Monday, December 21. On the same day, HNBT mailed the check to Lincoln and notified it by telegram of the dishonor, but since the notice did not indicate the drawer's name, Lincoln's first chance to identify the check came when it received the check on December 27. Lincoln had already allowed Great Western to make withdrawals against the $25,000 check and, claiming that the notice of dishonor came too late, refused to accept the return of the check. After attempting unsuccessfully to collect from the now bankrupt drawer, Wells Fargo sued HNBT, claiming a right on HNBT's indorsement under UCC 3–414(1), a right on HNBT's engagement under 4–207(2),[1] and a right of "charge-back" to HNBT under UCC 4–212(1).[2] Both Wells Fargo and HNBT moved for summary judgment.

BLUMENFELD, JR. [The court noted that in order to recover under any of its theories, Wells Fargo must show that it gave HNBT timely notice of the Nevada bank's dishonor of the check.]

U.C.C. § 3–508(2) provides that "[a]ny necessary notice must be given by a bank before its midnight deadline." "Midnight deadline," in turn, is defined as "midnight on [the bank's] next banking day following the banking day on which it receives the relevant item or notice . . .." U.C.C. § 4–104(1)(h). Thus, in order to determine whether Wells Fargo gave HNBT a timely notice of Nevada's dishonor, it is first necessary to establish "the banking day on which [Wells Fargo received] the relevant item or notice . . .."

As indicated above, Wells Fargo received a notice of Nevada's dishonor by telephone on Friday afternoon, December 10, 1971. It sent no notice to HNBT before the midnight deadline on its next banking day, Monday, December 13. Wells Fargo first received written notice from Nevada on Friday, December 17, when the dishonored check arrived in the mail. Notice of dishonor was then sent to HNBT prior to midnight on Monday, December 21, the next banking day following receipt of the *written* notice. Therefore, the first question this court must decide is whether oral notice from the payor bank, Nevada, can trigger the obligation of the collecting bank, Wells Fargo, to give notice to its customer, HNBT.

At first reading, section 3–508(3) would seem to resolve this question. That section provides, "Notice may be given in any reasonable manner. It may be oral or written . . . ." By virtue of section 4–102(1), section 3–508(3) applies to bank collections unless it conflicts with a specific provision of Article 4. In such a case, the Article 4 provision governs the transaction.

Wells Fargo argues that section 4–301 supersedes section 3–508 with respect to notice from payor banks and that therefore only written notice from such banks triggers the presenting bank's obligation to pass the notice of dishonor down through the chain of collection.[3]

---

1. Insofar as Wells Fargo's claim was based on UCC 3–414(1), whether notice of dishonor was "necessary" is dealt with in UCC 3–501(2)(a). Where does the Code deal with whether notice of dishonor was "necessary" under UCC 4–207(2)? [Ed.]

2. The right of charge-back is discussed below. [Ed.]

3. U.C.C. § 4–301, which discusses notice of dishonor by payor banks, provides only for written notice. Moreover, the use of the word "sent" in section 4–301(3)

This position appears to be meritorious and has been adopted by several courts. This court, however, need not rule on the specific question.

Lincoln has raised an issue which dispenses with the need to determine whether oral or written notification is required by the terms of the statute itself. In an introductory section to Article 4, the U.C.C. provides:

> "The effect of the provisions of this Article may be varied by agreement except that no agreement can disclaim a bank's responsibility for its own lack of good faith or failure to exercise ordinary care or can limit the measure of damages for such lack or failure; but the parties may by agreement determine the standards by which such responsibility is to be measured if such standards are not manifestly unreasonable.

> "Federal Reserve regulations and operating letters, clearing house rules, and the like, have the effect of agreements under subsection (1), whether or not specifically assented to by all parties interested in items handled."

U.C.C. § 4–103(1), (2).

In its affidavits, Lincoln established that the transaction in question was governed by the terms of the Federal Reserve Operating Circular No. 6.[4] At the time of the transaction this operating circular provided that payor banks can—in fact, must—give notice by "wire" when they dishonor items with values in excess of $1,000.[5] "Wire" is

further suggests that only written notice from a payor bank constitutes dishonor. See U.C.C. § 1–201(38). Since "an item is dishonored at the time . . . it is returned or notice sent in accordance with [§ 4–301]," Wells Fargo argues that only the written notice from Nevada triggered its obligation to give HNBT notice of dishonor.

4. The affidavit of David M. Stratton, Vice President of Operations for Lincoln, makes clear that the terms of the circular governed this transaction. Although the transaction did not involve the Federal Reserve Bank, Mr. Stratton attests that: "It is now and was in November-December, 1971, the practice in commercial banking to follow Federal Reserve procedures for giving notice of dishonor, regardless of whether the item is sent through the Federal Reserve System or, as in this case, through a correspondent collecting bank." Affidavit of David M. Stratton, ¶ 10, November 8, 1979.

Thus, the terms of the Operating Circular supersede the statutory provisions of article 4 in two distinct ways. The regulations are applicable as agreements "whether or not specifically assented to

by all parties" under section 4–103(2). See Security Bank and Trust Co. v. Federal National Bank and Trust Co., 554 P.2d 119 (Okl.App.1976) (Federal Reserve operating letter requiring notice by wire supersedes section 4–301, which requires written notice from payor banks). Alternatively, the conduct of the parties can be said to have evinced an "agreement" under section 4–103(1). As the official comments to this section make clear, the word "agreement" is intended to incorporate the statutory definition set forth in U.C.C. § 1–201(3), which includes those agreements implied from commercial practice. Cf. Delbrueck & Co. v. Manufacturers Hanover Trust Co., 609 F.2d 1047, 1051, (2d Cir.1979) ("The practices associated with banking transactions can be conclusive evidence of the legal effect of those transactions"). . . .

5. Federal Reserve Operating Circular No. 6, 17(c) (September 1, 1967) provides:

"WIRE ADVICE of nonpayment of any item of $1,000 or over, unless it has not been paid because of a missing, irregular, or unsatisfactory endorsement or unless it bears on its face the legend,

expressly defined to include "telephonic" notices.[6] Thus, since this operating circular governed the transaction here in dispute, it is clear that Nevada's telephonic notice was an adequate notice of dishonor, and Wells Fargo was not entitled to wait for written notice.

As is indicated above, Wells Fargo's failure to give timely notice essentially precludes it from prevailing under any of the three counts in its complaint.

[Summary judgment for Wells Fargo against HNBT denied; summary judgment for HNBT against Wells Fargo granted.]

NOTES

(1) **Extent of Liability.** Would HNBT have been discharged if, in spite of Wells Fargo's delay, the full amount of the check could have been recovered from the drawer? In Appliance Buyers Credit Corp. v. Prospect National Bank, 708 F.2d 290 (7th Cir.1983), the court held that under UCC 4–103(5) the measure of damages for failure to give timely notice under UCC 4–212(1) "is the amount of the item reduced by an amount which could not have been realized by the use of ordinary care" and that the party seeking to take advantage of the failure to give notice has the burden of establishing the loss caused by that failure.

(2) **Federal Reserve Regulations and Operating Letters.** Federal Reserve Board Regulation J, which "governs the collection of checks and other . . . items by Federal Reserve Banks," empowers each Federal Reserve Bank to "issue operating circulars governing the details of its handling of items and other matters deemed appropriate by the Reserve Bank." It provides that both Regulation J and the operating circular "are binding on the sender of an item, on each collecting bank, paying bank, and nonbank payor, to which a Reserve Bank (or a subsequent collecting bank) presents or sends an item, and on other parties interested in the item, including the owner." 12 C.F.R. §§ 210.1, 210.3(a), (b). See Comment 3 to UCC 4–103.[1]

(3) **Presentment and Check Truncation.** To make it clear that presentment of a check at an off-premises electronic check-processing center would be a "presentment" under the Code, UCC 4–204(3) was inserted in the Code in 1962. It expressly permits presentment "by a presenting bank at a place where the payor bank has requested that presentment be made." See also Comment 4 to UCC 4–204. Does

'DO NOT WIRE NONPAYMENT,' of a Federal Reserve Bank or of a preceding bank endorser. Include in the advice of nonpayment, the amount of the item, the reason for nonpayment, the date of our cash letter, the name of the drawer or maker, and the names of the two endorsers immediately preceding the Federal Reserve Bank or their A.B.A. transit numbers, if any."

6. "For the purposes of this operating circular, the term 'wire' includes telephone, telegraph, and cable."

Id. 17 n. 4.

1. With respect to the applicability of Regulation J and operating circulars, compare footnote 4 to the Wells Fargo case with footnote 7, p. 163 infra.

this language cover the kind of electronic presentment required for a system of check truncation at the depositary bank, as described at page 106 supra.

CONSEQUENCES OF DELAY

Discharge of Drawer by Delay in Presentment. The check has traditionally been regarded as an instrument that contemplates prompt presentment for payment. Take the case of a check for $1,000 drawn on an account with sufficient funds. If promptly presented, it will be paid and the amount charged to the drawer's account. Suppose the holder delays presentment, however, and during the delay the drawee bank becomes insolvent. When the check is then presented, it will be dishonored, leaving the drawer with a claim against his insolvent bank that is $1,000 greater than it would have been had the check been paid. In that circumstance, it would be unjust to require the drawer to pay the full amount of the check to the holder, and seek reimbursement from the insolvent bank.

UCC 3–502(1)(b) therefore provides that in this situation the drawer "may discharge his liability by written assignment to the holder of his rights against the drawee . . . bank." Under UCC 3–503(2), a reasonable time for the ordinary uncertified personal check is presumed to be thirty days. Only if the drawee bank fails after the thirty day period will the drawer be discharged.

The likelihood of discharge of the drawer by delay in presentment is therefore remote. Furthermore, if the drawer's account is fully insured by the Federal Deposit Insurance Corporation the drawer will not lose any of his deposit and this problem will presumably not arise.

The Federal Deposit Insurance Corporation was established by Congress in 1933 and now finds its authority in the Federal Deposit Insurance Corporation Act of 1950, 12 U.S.C. §§ 1811–1832. It has not only afforded protection to depositors of failed banks, but has contributed to the striking reduction in bank failures. During the three years 1930–32, more than 5,100 banks suspended business, as compared to 100, all of which were insured, during the three years 1981–83. Deposits in virtually all commercial banks are insured by the FDIC. Each depositor is insured up to $100,000 which may be paid in cash or by making available a deposit in a new bank or in another insured bank. Holders of certified checks, cashiers' checks, and remittance drafts are treated as depositors. 12 Code Fed.Reg. § 330. However, the holder of an uncertified check is not protected and the deposit of the check for collection does not result in an insured deposit in the depositary bank until the item has been collected.

Discharge of Indorser by Delay in Presentment. Under UCC 3–502(1)(a), an indorser is discharged by delay in presentment, regardless of whether the delay has caused any loss to the indorser. Delay is much more likely to result in the discharge of an indorser than in the discharge of a drawer. Furthermore, UCC 3–503(1)(e) requires that, in order to hold an indorser, presentment must be made "within a reasonable time after such party becomes liable thereon," and UCC 3–503(2) goes on to provide that in the case of the ordinary uncertified personal check the reasonable time for an indorser is seven days, as distinguished from thirty days for the drawer.

Discharge of Drawer and Indorser by Delay in Notice of Dishonor. Under UCC 3–502(1), delay in giving notice of dishonor has the same consequences as delay in presentment.

OTHER BASES OF LIABILITY

Liability on the Underlying Obligation. Since a check is ordinarily taken as conditional rather than absolute payment, the question arises whether an action can be brought on the underlying obligation for which the check was given even though liability on the instrument has been lost, as by delay in presentment or notice of dishonor. UCC 3–802(1)(b) takes the position that a discharge on the instrument is a discharge on the underlying obligation as well.

Liability on Warranties. The sale of a negotiable instrument, like the sale of a chattel, also gives rise to implied warranties. These warranties are found in UCC 3–417, 4–207. Although the holder will usually prefer to sue the transferor on the more extensive engagement of the indorser spelled out in UCC 3–414(1), the warranties are important in at least three situations. (1) Where an instrument payable to bearer is negotiated by delivery without indorsement, the transferor does not make the indorser's engagement but does make implied warranties to his immediate transferee. (2) Where an instrument is negotiated by indorsement that includes such words as "without recourse" the transferor does not make the indorser's engagement, but does make implied warranties to the transferee and subsequent holders (see also UCC 3–417(3)). (3) Where an instrument is negotiated by the usual indorsement which includes no such qualification, so that the transferor makes the indorser's engagement, but because of a failure to fulfill the conditions of dishonor, notice of dishonor or protest is discharged from this engagement, the transferor may still be liable to the transferee or subsequent holders on warranties that are not so conditioned.[1] But note the scope of the warranties. Do they cover the common case where a check is dishonored because of insufficient funds? Note the analogy to warranties in the sale of goods. Do the warranties of Articles 3 and 4 apply only to "sales" of negotiable instruments or to gifts as well? Is privity of contract required for an action for their breach?

---

1. The warranties may also be important in a fourth situation. As was seen in footnote 3, p. 131 supra, a justifiable refusal to pay a check is not a dishonor according to Comment 2 to UCC 3–510. Therefore, if a bank refused to pay a check because of a forgery or alteration, the refusal would not be a dishonor and the only recourse would be under the warranties. See UCC 3–504(1).

Right of Charge-Back or Refund. A bank, such as Philadelphia National, that takes a check from a depositor, such as Quaker, for collection, giving it a provisional credit, has yet another ground on which to proceed against its depositor should the check be dishonored. UCC 4–212(1) gives the collecting bank a right to "revoke the settlement given by it" and "charge back the amount of any credit given for the item to its customer's account or obtain refund from its customer." In order to preserve this right, however, it must either return the item or send notification of the facts to its customer "by its midnight deadline or within a longer reasonable time after it learns the facts." [2] See UCC 4–104(1)(h) and compare UCC 3–508(2). See also Lufthansa German Airlines v. Bank of America National Trust & Savings Association, 478 F.Supp. 1195 (N.D.Cal.1979), affirmed 652 F.2d 835 (9th Cir.1981); First Security Bank of Utah v. Ezra C. Lundahl, Inc., 22 Utah 2d 433, 454 P.2d 886 (1969).

In any event, under UCC 4–212(1) a bank's right of charge-back ends when it receives a final settlement for the item. Thus in Boggs v. Citizens Bank & Trust Co., 32 Md.App. 500, 363 A.2d 247 (1976), it was held that a depositary bank had no right to charge back to its depositor's account the amount of a check that—seven months after payment by the drawee and receipt of final settlement by the depositary bank—had been returned to the depositary bank with a claim that the signature of the depositor's indorser had been forged. The case was remanded for a trial on the depositor's claim that the depositary bank had wrongfully dishonored her checks as a result of the charge-back.

Statute of Limitations. The liability of a party to a check may, of course, be affected by the running of the statute of limitations, as well as in the ways mentioned above. The Code deals with this subject in UCC 3–122. Does UCC 3–122(3) apply to the indorser's liability for breach of warranty under UCC 3–417(2) as well as his engagement under UCC 3–414(1)? See Comment 1 to UCC 3–122. [3]

Problem 5. A grocer delivers groceries, and occasionally cash, to customers, taking in return personal checks drawn by them. What risks, if any, does the grocer run by failing to deposit these checks for collection for two weeks? For two months? See UCC 3–802, 3–413, 3–501, 3–502, 3–507, 3–503, 3–511, 3–417(2).

Problem 6. A grocer delivers groceries, and occasionally cash, to customers, taking in return their pay checks, drawn by their em-

2. In Wells Fargo Bank v. Hartford National Bank & Trust Co., supra, was it arguable that Wells Fargo's wire notice on December 19 was "within a longer reasonable time after it learns the facts"? In a footnote, omitted in the edited version set out above, the court noted that "nothing produced suggests that any extension of time beyond the midnight deadline would constitute a 'longer reasonable time,' as those words are in U.C.C. § 4–212(1)."

3. For a case allowing a depositary bank restitution of money that it had mistakenly paid on a check deposited by a "knowing wrongdoer," who at least suspected that the check would be dishonored, see Great Western Bank & Trust v. Nahat, 138 Ariz. 260, 674 P.2d 323 (App.1983). The court held that the bank was not barred by its failure to comply with UCC 4–212(1).

ployers to their order, and specially indorsed by them to him. What risks, if any, does he run by failing to deposit these checks for collection for two weeks? For two months? See UCC 3–414. Are there any circumstances suggested by either Problem 5 or this problem in which the grocer may end up in a worse position, as a result of having taken a negotiable instrument, than he would have been in by selling on open credit? If so, can you think of an explanation?

CERTIFICATION

Effect of Certification on Liability of Drawer and Indorsers. Ordinarily, the drawee's acceptance of a draft merely adds his liability to that of the drawer and any indorsers. Under UCC 3–411(1), however, "where a holder procures certification the drawer and all prior indorsers are discharged." The notion behind this provision is the same as that behind UCC 3–502(1)(b)—the check is regarded as an instrument that contemplates prompt presentment for payment. If the holder chooses to prolong its circulation by having it certified rather than paid, he must pay the price of relinquishing the liability of secondary parties. Usually, the holder will prefer payment to certification anyway, but there are, for example, instances in which the holder's agent, who is in possession of a check but is not authorized to indorse it, has it certified on behalf of the holder before remitting it. UCC 3–411(1) does not apply to the situation in which the drawer himself procures the certification before giving it to the payee.

Refusal to Certify as a Dishonor. Yet another consequence of the notion that a check is an instrument that contemplates prompt presentment is that the drawee bank's refusal to certify is not a dishonor since it is not presumed that the drawer would undertake that it would be certified. The drawer is therefore not liable to the holder under UCC 3–413(2) if the bank refuses to certify the check. (What would you advise the holder to do in that situation?) The derivation of this proposition under the Code requires a close reading of UCC 3–507(1) and 3–501(1) and an acceptance of the Code's curious use of language under which presentment of a check for certification is neither a "necessary" nor an "optional" presentment.

More important to bankers is the corollary found in UCC 3–411(2), that "Unless otherwise agreed a bank has no obligation to certify a check." It therefore runs no risk of liability for wrongful dishonor under UCC 4–402 if it refuses to certify. Why would such a rule appeal to bankers? Consider the fact that banks often charge the holder a fee for certifying. Does the rule of UCC 3–411(2) affect the advisability of this practice? Consider the fact that banks have traditionally included in their certification language such as "Payable only as originally drawn and when properly endorsed." Does the rule of UCC 3–411(2) affect the advisability of this practice? See p. 274, infra.

Automation and Certification. "In automated systems, processing certified checks becomes an unnecessarily expensive procedure because cashier's checks seem to provide an entirely satisfactory substitute for them. Certified checks are demanded because they signify that funds are on hand at the bank. However, if such checks were processed by machine in the normal manner, when presented for payment, they would make double deductions from the depositors' accounts. To avoid this, certified checks must be handled manually, as exceptions to the machine system. Hence, banks mutilate the customer's MICR number when making the certification to cause a machine rejection. In sharp contrast, cashiers' checks flow smoothly and normally through the new systems. The elimination of check certification is not yet possible. Many statutes and official regulations provide for the acceptance of such checks but not cashiers' checks. Efforts probably should be initiated to secure official acceptance of cashiers' checks routinely and to discourage the use of certified checks." Freed, Some Implications of the Use of Computers in the Banking Business, 19 Bus.Law. 355, 362 (1964).[4] See also, Windsor, The Certified Check: A Special Handling Item in Automation, 81 Banking L.J. 480 (1964). Does the rule of UCC 3–411(2) have any bearing upon this suggestion?

Problem 7.   Assume that Empire, instead of mailing its check to Quaker, delivers it in New York to Quaker's sales representative. If the representative, who is not authorized to indorse the check, takes the precaution of having Irving Trust certify it before forwarding it to Philadelphia, how does this affect Quaker's recourse on the instrument should it ultimately be dishonored? See UCC 3–411, 3–413.

Problem 8.   If, under the facts in Problem 7, Irving Trust had refused to certify the check, would it thereby have become liable to Empire under UCC 4–402 for wrongful dishonor? See UCC 3–411. Would Empire thereby have become liable to Quaker under UCC 3–413(2)? Read UCC 3–411(2) with care (Are we concerned with the bank's "obligation" here?) and then see UCC 3–507(1) and 3–501(1).

SECTION 2.   DRAWEE'S RECOURSE AFTER PAYMENT BY MISTAKE

(A) BASIC RULES

Prefatory Note.   In the absence of a contrary agreement with the depositor, American banks do not make a practice of paying overdrafts. But if the drawee bank should, either intentionally or by mistake, pay an overdraft it is clear that it can recover the amount from the drawer. According to UCC 4–401, a bank may charge any properly payable item to its customer's account "even though the charge creates an overdraft." The provision restates what was a rule of

---

4. Reproduced with permission of the American Bar Association.

case law before the Code, "since the draft itself authorizes the payment for the drawer's account and carries an implied promise to reimburse the drawee." Comment 1 to UCC 4–401; see also UCC 3–105(2)(b). For an interesting discussion of whether this rule allows a bank to recover on a husband's overdraft against a wife who, though a cosignatory on a joint account, neither participated in the transaction creating the overdraft nor received funds as a result of it, see Cambridge Trust Co. v. Carney, 115 N.H. 94, 333 A.2d 442 (1975), noted in 1976 B.Y.U.L.Rev. 499; United States Trust Co. v. McSweeney, 91 A.D.2d 7, 457 N.Y.S.2d 276 (1982).[1]

But what if the overdrawn drawer is judgment proof so that recourse against him is of no avail? What alternatives are open to the drawee? Where does the loss ultimately fall?

Problem 9. When the Empire check is presented, Empire has only $1,000 in its account at the Irving Trust. If Irving Trust nevertheless pays the check as a courtesy to Empire, can it recover the balance of $1,178.50 from Empire? From Quaker? Would your answer be different if Irving Trust pays the check by mistake, without realizing that it was an overdraft? See UCC 4–401, 4–213, 3–418, 3–417, 3–302(2); Kirby v. First & Merchants National Bank, infra. If, instead of *paying* an overdraft by mistake, Irving Trust had *certified* an overdraft by mistake, would its mistake justify it in refusing to pay Quaker? See UCC 3–413, 3–418, 3–417.

KIRBY v. FIRST & MERCHANTS NATIONAL BANK

Supreme Court of Virginia, 1969.
210 Va. 88, 168 S.E.2d 273.

GORDON, JUSTICE. On December 30, 1966, defendant Margaret Kirby handed the following check to a teller at a branch of plaintiff First & Merchants National Bank:

	Check
NEUSE ENG. AND DREDGING CO.	Number _____
	68–728
	514
	12–29–1966

Pay to the
order of _____ William J. Kirby & Margaret Kirby _____ $ 2,500.00
_____ Twenty-Five Hundred _____ Dollars

FIRST & MERCHANTS
NATIONAL BANK
Virginia Beach, Virginia   NEUSE ENG. & DREDGING CO.
. . . 0514 . . . 0728   /s/ W. R. Wood

---

1. As to the personal liability of one lawyer for another lawyer's overdraft on the account of the professional corporation of which they were the only share- holders, see First Bank & Trust Co. v. Zagoria, 250 Ga. 844, 302 S.E.2d 674 (1983).

The back of the check bore the signatures of the payees, Mr. and Mrs. Kirby.

Mrs. Kirby, who also had an account with the Bank, gave the teller the following deposit ticket: [1]

The teller handed $200 in cash to Mrs. Kirby, and the Bank credited her account with $2,300 on the next business day, January 3, 1967. The teller or another Bank employee made the notation "Cash for Dep." under Mr. and Mrs. Kirby's signatures on the back of the Neuse check.

On January 4 the Bank discovered that the Neuse check was drawn against insufficient funds. Instead of giving written notice, a Bank officer called Mr. and Mrs. Kirby on January 5 to advise that the Bank had dishonored the check and to request reimbursement. Mr. and Mrs. Kirby said they would come to the Bank to cover the check, but they did not. On January 10 the Bank charged Mrs. Kirby's account with $2,500, creating an overdraft of $543.47.

On January 18 the Bank instituted this action to recover $543.47 from Mr. and Mrs. Kirby. At the trial a Bank officer, the only witness in the case, testified:

"Q. Did you cash the check [the Neuse check for $2,500] before you credited this deposit [the deposit of $2,300 to Mrs. Kirby's account]?

"A. Yes, sir.

"Q. So the bank, in effect, cashed the check for $2,500.00 and then gave the defendant a credit of $2,300.00 to their [sic] account and gave them [sic] $200.00 in cash?

"A. Correct.

". . .

---

1. The handwriting in the upper-left portion of the deposit ticket corresponds with Mrs. Kirby's handwriting on the back of the check. The record does not indicate what persons added the other handwritten information on the ticket.

The symbol "68–728–514" designates a check drawn on First & Merchants by a depositor who has an account with a branch of that Bank in the Norfolk-Virginia Beach area. The word following the symbol is "partial".

"Q. So you cashed the check for $2,500.00?

"A. Yes, sir."

The trial court, sitting without a jury, entered judgment for the plaintiff First & Merchants, and the defendants Mr. and Mrs. Kirby appeal. The question is whether the Bank had the right to charge Mrs. Kirby's account with $2,500 on January 10 and to recover from Mr. and Mrs. Kirby the overdraft created by that charge ($543.47).

U.C.C. § 4–213 [2] provides:

"(1) An item [3] is finally paid by a payor bank when the bank has done any of the following, whichever happens first:

"(a) paid the item in cash;".

So if First & Merchants paid the Neuse check in cash on December 30, it then made final payment and could not sue Mr. or Mrs. Kirby on the check except for breach of warranty.[4]

When Mrs. Kirby presented the $2,500 Neuse check to the Bank on December 30, the Bank paid her $200 in cash and accepted a deposit of $2,300. The Bank officer said that the Bank cashed the check for $2,500, which could mean only that Mrs. Kirby deposited $2,300 in cash.

And the documentary evidence shows that cash was deposited. The deposit of cash is evidenced by the word "currency" before "2,300.00" on the deposit ticket and by the words "Cash for Dep." on the back of the check.[5] The Bank's ledger, which shows a credit of $2,300 to Mrs. Kirby's account rather than a credit of $2,500 and a debit of $200, is consistent with a cashing of the Neuse check and a

---

2. The Uniform Commercial Code ("U.C.C.") has been codified as Titles 8.1 through 8.10 of the Code of Virginia. References to the U.C.C. are to that Code as adopted in Virginia, but citations will omit the title number 8. E.g., U.C.C. § 4–213 means Va.Code Ann. § 8.4–213.

3. The Uniform Commercial Code gives "item" its generally accepted meaning: " 'Item' means any instrument for the payment of money even though it is not negotiable but does not include money." U.C.C. § 4–104(1)(g).

4. As shown by the quotation in the text, U.C.C. § 4–213, which deals with bank deposits and collections, provides without qualification that a payor bank's payment of an item in cash is final. The Code recognizes, however, that a bank may recover a payment when a presenter's warranty is breached, e.g., when an indorsement is forged. U.C.C. §§ 3–417(1), 4–207(1). And under the established law before adoption of the Uniform Commercial Code, a bank could also recover a payment in case of fraud or bad faith on the part of the person re-

ceiving the payment. 3 Paton's Digest of Legal Opinions, Overdrafts § 4:1 (1944). In this case there is no evidence of breach of a presenter's warranties or of fraud or bad faith.

Unlike U.C.C. § 4–213, U.C.C. § 3–418, which deals with commercial paper generally, implies that payment of an instrument is final only in favor of a holder in due course or a person who has changed his position in reliance on the payment. First & Merchants neither relied on U.C.C. § 3–418, nor based its right to recover on an assertion that Mr. and Mrs. Kirby were not holders in due course and did not change their position. See U.C.C. § 3–307 and comment. Moreover, insofar as U.C.C. §§ 3–418 and 4–213 conflict, U.C.C. § 4–213 prevails. U.C.C. § 4–102(1).

5. Since no dollar amount was inserted after "checks" on the deposit ticket, the notation "6–28–728–514 partial" was apparently inserted to identify the source of the currency being deposited. See n. 1 supra.

depositing of part of the proceeds. We must conclude that First & Merchants paid the Neuse check in cash on December 30 and, therefore, had no right thereafter to charge Mrs. Kirby's account with the amount of the check.

The trial court apparently decided that Mr. and Mrs. Kirby were liable to the Bank because they had indorsed the Neuse check. But under U.C.C. § 3–414(1) an indorser contracts to pay an instrument only if the instrument is dishonored. And, as we have pointed out, the Bank did not dishonor the Neuse check, but paid the check in cash when Mrs. Kirby presented it.

As a practical matter, the contract of an indorser under U.C.C. § 3–414(1) does not run to a drawee bank. That contract can be enforced by a drawee bank only if it dishonors a check; and if the bank dishonors the check, it has suffered no loss.

The warranties that are applicable in this case are set forth in U.C.C. §§ 3–417(1) and 4–207(1): warranties made to a drawee bank by a presenter and prior transferors of a check. Those warranties are applicable because Mrs. Kirby presented the Neuse check to the Bank for payment. U.C.C. § 3–504(1); Bunn, Snead & Speidel, An Introduction to the Uniform Commercial Code § 3.4(B) (1964). And those warranties do not include a warranty that the drawer of a check has sufficient funds on deposit to cover the check.

The rule that a drawee who mistakenly pays a check has recourse only against the drawer was firmly established before adoption of the Uniform Commercial Code:

> "The drawer of a check, and not the holder who receives payment, is primarily responsible for the drawing out of funds from a bank. An overdraft is an act by reason of which the drawer and not the holder obtains money from the bank on his check. The holder therefore in the absence of fraud or express understanding for repayment, has no concern with the question whether the drawer has funds in the bank to meet the check. The bank is estopped, as against him, from claiming that by its acceptance an overdraft occurred. A mere mistake is not sufficient to enable it to recover from him. Banks cannot always guard against fraud, but can guard against mistakes.

> "It is therefore the general rule, sustained by almost universal authority, that a payment in the ordinary course of business of a check by a bank on which it is drawn under the mistaken belief that the drawer has funds in the bank subject to check is not such a payment under a mistake of fact as will permit the bank to recover the money so paid from the recipient of such payment. To permit the bank to repudiate the payment would destroy the certainty which must pertain to commercial transactions if they are to remain useful to the business public. Otherwise no one would ever know when he can safely receive payment of a check."

7 Zollman, The Law of Banks and Banking § 5062 (1936). See generally 3 Paton's Digest of Legal Opinions, Overdrafts § 4 (1944).

Virginia followed the same rule. Citizens Bank of Norfolk v. Schwarzchild & Sultzberger Co., 109 Va. 539, 64 S.E. 954, 23 L.R.A., N.S. 1092 (1901); Bank of Virginia v. Craig, 33 Va. (6 Leigh) 399, 431 (1835); see Va.Code Ann. § 8.3–417, Virginia Comment at 220 (1965 added vol.); Va.Code Ann. § 8.4–207, Virginia Comment at 271 (1965 added vol.)

Nevertheless, First & Merchants contends that under the terms of its deposit contract with Mrs. Kirby, the settlement was provisional and therefore subject to revocation whether or not the Neuse check was paid in cash on December 30.[6] It contends that in this regard the deposit contract changes the rule set forth in the Uniform Commercial Code. But in providing that "all items are credited subject to final payment", the contract recognizes that settlement for an item is provisional only until the item is finally paid. Since the deposit contract does not change the applicable rule as set forth in the Uniform Commercial Code, we do not decide whether a bank can provide by deposit contract that payment of a check in cash is provisional.

Even if the Bank's settlement for the Neuse check had been provisional, the Bank had the right to charge that item back to Mrs. Kirby's account only if it complied with U.C.C. §§ 4–212(3) and 4–301. Those sections authorize the revocation of a settlement if, before the "midnight deadline",[7] the bank

"(a) returns the item; or

"(b) sends written notice of dishonor or nonpayment if the item is held for protest or is otherwise unavailable for return". U.C.C. § 4–301.

6. The depositor's contract provides:

"Items received from deposit or collection are accepted on the following terms and conditions. *This bank acts only as depositor's collecting agent and assumes no responsibility beyond its exercise of due care. All items are credited subject to final payment and to receipt of proceeds of final payment in cash or solvent credits by this bank at its own office.* This bank may forward items to correspondents and shall not be liable for default or negligence of correspondents selected with due care nor for losses in transit, and each correspondent shall not be liable except for its own negligence. Items and their proceeds may be handled by any Federal Reserve bank in accordance with applicable Federal Reserve rules, and by this bank or any correspondent, in accordance with any common bank usage, with any practice or procedure that a Federal Reserve bank may use or permit another bank to use, or with any other lawful means. *This bank may charge back, at any time prior to midnight on its business day next following the day of receipt, any item drawn on this bank which is ascertained to be drawn against insufficient funds or otherwise not good or payable. An item received after this bank's regular afternoon closing hour shall be deemed received the next business day.*

"This bank reserves the right to post all deposits, including deposits of cash and of items drawn on it, not later than midnight of its next business day after their receipt at this office during regular banking hours, and shall not be liable for damages for nonpayment of any presented item resulting from the exercise of this right.

" * * * " (Italicized language is quoted in First & Merchants brief.)

7. "Midnight deadline" is defined in U.C.C. § 4–104(1)(h). See also the Bank's deposit contract, supra n. 6.

The Bank concedes that it neither sent written notice of dishonor nor returned the Neuse check before the "midnight deadline". So the Bank had no right to charge the item back to Mrs. Kirby's account.

For the reasons set forth, the trial court erred in entering judgment for First & Merchants against Mr. and Mrs. Kirby.

Reversed and final judgment.

HARRISON, JUSTICE (dissenting). I dissent from the holding of the majority that the check involved here was "cashed". It is apparent that the check of Neuse Engineering and Dredging Company was "deposited" in normal course by Mrs. Kirby, and received and accepted for deposit by the Princess Anne Plaza Branch of the First and Merchants National Bank. The same bank official, quoted by the majority, also testified:

Q. "Did Margaret Kirby or William Kirby bring you a check to deposit on December 29, 1966?

A. "Yes, sir, they did.

Q. "Tell what happened to this particular check.

A. "We received it for deposit on Friday night, the 29th. We deposited $2,300 and gave back cash, $200. . . ."

(Admittedly the correct date of the deposit was Friday, December 30, 1966.)

This witness, the only one who testified in the case, was Mr. Floyd E. Waterfield, Vice President of the bank. From his testimony we learn that late in the afternoon of December 30, 1966, Mrs. Kirby, a customer of the bank with an active checking account, came into the bank with the Neuse check. Apparently she desired $200 in cash. In making out the deposit slip, $2300 was erroneously written opposite the currency line instead of opposite the check line. However, indicated in writing on the face of the deposit slip is a notation that the deposit was evidenced by a check drawn on another of the bank's branches in the Norfolk-Virginia Beach area. Also on the face of the deposit slip is shown the manner in which Mrs. Kirby obtained the $200 she wanted, i.e. by deducting $200 from the $2500 check.

This was a perfectly normal and customary banking transaction. Mrs. Kirby, as a customer of that particular branch bank, presumably could have obtained $200 by writing her personal check, or by having the bank issue and she initial a debit memorandum or charge on her account, or by having the transaction reflected on the face of the deposit slip. She and the bank teller obviously pursued the latter course, and this was entirely in order. When the books of the bank were balanced for the day's operations, the bank had a $2500 check of Neuse, which was offset or balanced against a cash withdrawal of $200, plus a tentative or provisional credit of $2300 in the Kirby checking account.

There is nothing in this record from which it could possibly be deducted that Mrs. Kirby walked into the bank and cashed the Neuse check for $2500. That is, she presented the check and demanded and received $2500 in cash, and afterwards redeposited $2300 of it in currency. This simply did not occur, and the evidence does not reflect it. While the bank officer does refer to "cashing the check", the evidence and the records of the bank show that it was not cashed, but was accepted for deposit and clearance as any other check.

The fact that the bank permitted Mrs. Kirby to withdraw $200 is of no significance. She was a customer of the bank, with a checking account. Had the withdrawal, absent the Neuse deposit, caused an overdraft, this would not have been unusual for banks permit customers to overdraw from time to time in reasonable amounts. Furthermore, at that time neither Mrs. Kirby nor the bank had reason to anticipate that the Neuse check would be dishonored because of insufficient funds. . . .

NOTE

When "Final Payment" is "Final." As the court suggests in footnote 4, it has been argued that UCC 4–213(1) and 3–418 deal with the same question and that UCC 4–213(1) differs from UCC 3–418 in imposing no requirement of holding in due course or reliance. The argument then continues that UCC 4–213(1) is controlling in the case of a check because of UCC 4–102(1), which says that in the case of conflict the provisions of Article 4 govern those of Article 3. J. White & R. Summers, Handbook of the Law Under the Uniform Commercial Code § 16–2 (2d ed. 1980). This argument was accepted in Northwestern National Insurance Co. v. Midland National Bank, 96 Wis.2d 155, 292 N.W.2d 591 (1980). It was rejected in Demos v. Lyons, 151 N.J.Super. 489, 376 A.2d 1352 (1977), a decision that is praised in Leary & Schmitt, Some Good News and Some Bad News from Articles Three and Four, 43 Ohio St. L.J. 611, 621–24 (1982), and in National Savings & Trust Co. v. Park Corp., 722 F.2d 1303 (6th Cir.1983), a decision that notes that Professor White recanted in 1983.

Another reading of these two sections avoids any inconsistency. Under this reading, UCC 4–213(1) is concerned with when a check is paid while UCC 3–418 is concerned with the finality (or reversibility) of payment. Is it unreasonable to read UCC 3–418 to say "[final] payment [in the sense of UCC 4–213(1)] is final in favor" of the mentioned persons? Thus the Kirby case can be seen as involving two distinct questions. First, was the check *paid* on December 30 when the teller took the deposit slip from Mrs. Kirby and handed her $200 in cash? Second, if it was paid, was that act *final* as between the bank and the Kirbys? The first question is dealt with in UCC 4–213(1), which provides that a check "is finally paid . . . when the bank has . . . paid the item in cash." This question will be explored in detail in the following section.

Before the Code, the second question was analyzed in terms of the law applicable to a claim for restitution of money paid by mistake of fact. According to Restatement of Restitution § 33: "The holder of a check . . . who, having paid value in good faith therefor, receives payment from the drawee without reason to know that the drawee is mistaken, is under no duty of restitution to him although the drawee pays because of a mistaken belief that he has sufficient funds of the drawer . . .."

Note that under UCC 3–418, unless the Kirbys are prepared to show that they have "in good faith changed [their] position in reliance on the payment," they must show that they are holders in due course. Since most checks are not negotiated but are presented for payment by their payees, UCC 3–418 is most likely to be invoked by a payee, just as it was in the Kirby case. The scheme employed by the drafters of the Code in UCC 3–418 and 3–417, to replace the common law analysis based on restitution, makes it essential, therefore, that payees such as the Kirbys be able to qualify as holders in due course. UCC 3–302(2), which states that "A payee may be a holder in due course" is obviously intended to accomplish this. The Code, then, makes the concept of holder in due course do double duty: under UCC 3–305 it determines, as it always did, those who take free from claims and defenses; and under UCC 3–418, it plays an important part in determining, as it never did before, those in whose favor payment is final. In the next chapter, at page 212, we shall consider some of the difficulties raised by pressing this venerable concept into this additional service.

(B) WHAT AMOUNTS TO PAYMENT

Prefatory Note. In Kirby v. First & Merchants National Bank, p. 141 supra, the court concluded that the transaction at the counter on December 30 was "consistent with a cashing of the Neuse check" and that therefore "First & Merchants paid the Neuse check in cash on December 30 and . . . had no right thereafter to charge Mrs. Kirby's account with the amount of the check." As UCC 4–213(1) expresses it: "An item is finally paid by a payor bank when the bank has . . . paid the item in cash . . . . Upon a final payment . . . the payor bank shall be accountable for the amount of the item."[1]

Suppose, however, that the bank had not paid $200 in cash to Mrs. Kirby; that nothing had been entered on the deposit slip under "currency"; and that "$2,500" had been entered under "checks" and un-

---

1. In the Kirby case, the check was apparently drawn on a different branch of First & Merchants than the one to which Mrs. Kirby took it. (The dissenting opinion says it was deposited in the Princess Anne Plaza Branch. See footnote 1 to the court's opinion.) Does UCC 4–106 call into question the applicability of UCC 4–213(1)(a) in such a case? (Was the bank that paid cash the "payor bank" or a different bank under UCC 4–106?)

der "Total." Would the check then have been paid at the time that the teller took the check and the deposit slip at the counter or at some other time?

A leading pre-Code case on this point was White Brokerage Co. v. Cooperman, 207 Minn. 239, 290 N.W. 790 (1940), which held that a check presented over the counter was paid when the bank completed the transaction at its counter. This rule was not calculated to please banks whose tellers were too busy to look up each "on us" item as it came over the counter, nor perhaps the depositors who would be required to wait at the window while this was done. The simplest answer was a properly drafted clause in the deposit slip, making the settlement provisional, subject to revocation. Bank Collection Code § 3 made it provisional, even in the absence of such a clause at least until the end of the day of deposit. The Code deals with the problem in UCC 4–213(1).

Problem 10. Quaker and Empire both bank at Irving Trust. Empire's account has only $1,000 in it. Quaker deposits the Empire check along with the other checks in Irving Trust, using a deposit slip similar to that furnished by Philadelphia National. Later on the same day, when the check is put through the regular computer run, it is rejected as drawn on insufficient funds. What are Irving Trust's rights against Quaker? See UCC 4–212(3), 4–213, 4–301, 4–302; Douglas v. Citizens Bank of Jonesboro, infra.

DOUGLAS v. CITIZENS BANK OF JONESBORO

Supreme Court of Arkansas, 1968.
244 Ark. 168, 424 S.W.2d 532.

HARRIS, CHIEF JUSTICE. This litigation involves two separate causes of action, which however, by agreement, were set forth in one set of pleadings, and disposed of at one hearing. Appellants, Weldon Douglas, and Janie Chandler, each maintained a checking account in the Citizens Bank of Jonesboro. Rees Plumbing Company, Inc. (which is not presently a party to this proceeding), was a customer of the bank, and maintained checking accounts. On August 19, 1966, the plumbing company delivered its check in the amount of $1,000.00 to Douglas. On that same day Douglas presented the check to the bank for deposit to his own checking account; an employee at the teller's window prepared a deposit slip, dated as of that day, reflecting that the check was being deposited to Douglas' account. He was given a duplicate of the deposit slip, and an employee of the bank thereafter affixed to the back of the check a stamp in red ink, denoting the August 19th date, and stating, "Pay to any bank—P.E.G., Citizens Bank of Jonesboro, Jonesboro, Arkansas." Under date of August 20, 1966, the bank dishonored the check because of insufficient funds, and charged the amount back to the account of Douglas. This same statement of facts applies to Mrs. Chandler, except that the check she presented was originally made payable to a Richard R. Washburn (in the amount of $1,600.00) by the same Rees Company, and this check had been properly endorsed by Washburn before coming into the hands of Mrs. Chandler.[1]

Rees Plumbing Company filed an unverified complaint against the bank, alleging that it had issued the aforementioned checks to the parties, and that it had sufficient funds in the accounts to honor these checks. It was alleged that the checks were wrongfully dishonored, and Rees sought damages due to the alleged willful and wanton negligence of the bank in handling its checks. Subsequently, the complaint was amended to join appellants as parties plaintiff (together with another party which later took a non-suit). Thereafter, on motion of appellee, Rees Plumbing Company was stricken as a party plaintiff. After first demurring, and moving to make the complaint more definite and certain, the bank filed an answer setting out that the accounts of Rees were insufficient on August 19 to honor the checks, and further, that both were charged back to the accounts of the respective appellants on August 20, and the appellants so notified. The bank further denied that the endorsement stamp, heretofore mentioned, constituted an acceptance stamp. The bank asserted that the stamp was no more than a method of identification. Both appellants and the bank, appellee herein, filed verified motions for summary judgment. Appellants' motion was supported by the checks and the deposit slips, which had already been filed, and appellee's motion was supported by the affidavit of Major Griffin, Vice-President of the Citizens Bank, filed with the motion for summary judgment. The affidavit reflects that Griffin had been engaged in banking with the Citizens Bank for 20 years, and it asserted that he was familiar with the processing of items in the Citizens Bank, as well as the normal procedures of other banks, and particularly familiar with the stamps and symbols used by banks in the area. He then explained the procedure used by appellee, and stated that the stamp served only to identify the depository bank, and that the endorsement appeared on all checks received by appellee which are not received from other banking institutions. He then stated:

"Any item for any reason can be returned by the Citizens Bank or any other banking institution (except those cashed over the counter) if rejected before midnight of the next banking day following the banking day on which the item is received, and prior to the bank stamping its 'paid' stamp thereon and filing in the customer's file.

"I have examined the Citizens Bank records with reference to a $1,600.00 check drawn on Rees Plumbing Company, Inc. account number 810 657 payable to Richard R. Washburn and find that it was

---

1. The check presented to the bank by Mrs. Chandler was dated on August 18, instead of 19, and was drawn by Rees on another account, which it had in the Citizens Bank.

deposited to the account of Mrs. Janie Chandler, a customer of the Citizens Bank in account number 301 191 on August 19, 1966. This deposit was posted to the Citizens Bank Journal to the credit of Mrs. Janie Chandler's account on August 19, 1966, but the check was not posted to Citizens Bank Journal as a charge to the Rees Plumbing Company account on which it was drawn because there was no balance in the Rees Plumbing Company Account at close of business on the date of August 19, 1966. The account of Mrs. Janie Chandler was debited for the insufficiency under date of August 20, 1966, and was returned to Mrs. Chandler."

He stated that the same procedure was followed with the Douglas check. The court denied the motion of the appellants, but granted that of the bank.

Thereafter, appellants petitioned the court to reopen the case for the purpose of receiving additional evidence on the question of what weight, if any, might be given to a statement printed on the backs of the deposit slips which had been introduced into evidence by agreement. The language on the back of the deposit slips provides, *inter alia*, that "items drawn on this bank not good at close of business day on which they have been deposited may be charged back to depositor." Appellants desired to introduce evidence to show that they did not know of the language on the back of the slips. The court refused to reopen the case, but the trial judge did state that, in reaching his conclusions, he gave no consideration at all to this language; nor do we consider same in the present instance, it being immaterial to the disposition of the litigation. From the judgment denying the motion to reopen the case; denying the motion for summary judgment filed on behalf of appellants, and granting the motion for summary judgment on behalf of appellee, comes this appeal.

The principal question at issue is, "Did the bank, by stamping the endorsement upon the checks deposited by appellants, and by delivering to appellants the deposit slips, accept both of said checks for payment?" The answer is, "No," and it might be stated at the outset that cases decided prior to the passage of the Uniform Commercial Code are not controlling. This case is controlled by the following sections of the Code: Ark.Stat.Ann. § 85–4–212(3), § 85–4–213, and § 85–4–301(1) (Add.1961).

Subsection (3) of Section 85–4–212 reads as follows:

"A depositary bank which is also the payor may charge back the amount of an item to its customer's account or obtain refund in accordance with the section governing return of an item received by a payor bank for credit on its books (Section 4–301 [§ 85–4–301])."

Subsection (1) of Section 85–4–301 provides:

"Where an authorized settlement for a demand item (other than a documentary draft) received by a payor bank otherwise than for immediate payment over the counter has been made before midnight of the banking day [2] of receipt the payor bank may revoke the settlement and recover any payment if before it has made final payment (subsection (1) of Section 4–213 [§ 85–4–213]) and before its midnight deadline it

(a) returns the item; or

(b) sends written notice of dishonor or nonpayment if the item is held for protest or is otherwise unavailable for return."

Section 85–4–213 simply sets out the time that a payment becomes final, not applicable in this instance.

When we consider the statutes above referred to, it is clear that appellants cannot prevail.[3] Clark, Bailey and Young, in their American Law Institute pamphlet on bank deposits and collections under the Uniform Commercial Code (January, 1959), p. 2, comment as follows:

"If the buyer-drawer and the seller-payee have their accounts in the same bank, and if the seller-payee deposits the check to the credit of his account, his account will be credited provisionally with the amount of the check. In the absence of special arrangement with the bank, he may not draw against this credit until it becomes final, that is to say, until after the check has reached the bank's bookkeeper and, as a result of bookkeeping operations, has been charged to the account of the buyer-drawer. (The seller-payee could, of course, present the check at a teller's window and request immediate payment in cash, but that course is not usually followed.) If the buyer-drawer's account does not have a sufficient balance, or he has stopped payment on the check, or if for any other reason the bank does not pay the check, the provisional credit given in the account of the seller-payee is reversed. If the seller-payee had been permitted to draw against that provisional credit, the bank would recoup the amount of the drawing by debit to his account or by other means."

The comment of the commissioners is also enlightening. Comment 4, under Section 85–4–213, states:

"A primary example of a statutory right on the part of the payor bank to revoke a settlement is the right to revoke conferred by Section 4–301. The underlying theory and reason for deferred posting statutes (Section 4–301) is to require a settlement on the date of receipt of an item but to keep that settlement provisional with the right to revoke prior to the midnight deadline. In any case where Section 4–301 is applicable, any settlement by the payor bank is provisional

---

2. According to Section 85–4–104, " 'midnight deadline' with respect to a bank is midnight on its next banking day following the banking day on which it receives the relevant item or notice or from which the time for taking action commences to run, whichever is later."

3. An order denying a motion for summary judgment is merely interlocuto-

ry, leaving the case pending for trial, and is not appealable; however, in holding that the court did not err in granting the summary judgment to the bank, the question of whether appellants were entitled to summary judgment is necessarily answered in the negative.

solely by virtue of the statute, subsection (1)(b) of Section 4–213 does not operate and such provisional settlement does not constitute final payment of the item." . . .

Affirmed.

NOTES

(1) **Need for a Clause.** Did the court in the Douglas case read the Code correctly in deciding that it is now unnecessary for a bank to provide on its deposit slip that the credit given is provisional in order to avoid the rule of the White Brokerage case? Comment 3 to UCC 4–303 explains that "In this Section as in Section 4–213 reasoning such as appears in . . . White Brokerage Co. v. Cooperman, 207 Minn. 239, 290 N.W. 790 (1940) . . . is rejected." But what language in the Code rejects it?

Read with care UCC 4–301(1), on which the court relies. In view of the words "before it has made final payment," is the court in the Douglas case correct in its claim that UCC 4–213 "is not applicable in this instance"? Where does the Code say that, in the absence of appropriate language on the deposit slip, the transaction at the counter is one in which the bank has "made a provisional settlement for the item" under UCC 4–213(1)(d), rather than having "settled for the item without reserving a right to revoke the settlement and without having such right under statute, clearing house rule or agreement" under (1)(b)? See UCC 4–104(1)(j). Are UCC 4–213(1) and 4–301(1) circular in this respect? A portion of Comment 4 to UCC 4–213, following that quoted by the court, is revealing:

"An example of a reservation of a right to revoke a settlement is where the payor bank is also the depositary bank and has signed a receipt or duplicate deposit ticket or has made an entry in a passbook acknowledging receipt, for credit to the account of A, of a check drawn on it by B. If the receipt, deposit ticket, passbook or other agreement with A is to the effect that any credit so entered is provisional and may be revoked pending the time required by the payor bank to process the item to determine if it is in good form and there are funds to cover it, such reservation or agreement keeps the receipt or credit provisional and avoids it being either final settlement or final payment.

"In other ways the payor bank may keep settlements provisional: by general or special agreement with the presenting party or bank; by simple reservation at the time the settlement is made; or otherwise. Thus a payor bank (except in the case of statutory provisions) has control whether a settlement made by it is provisional or final, by participating in general agreements or clearing house rules or by special agreement or reservation. If it fails to keep a settlement provisional and if no applicable statute keeps the settlement provisional, its settlement is final and, unless the item had previously been paid by one of the other methods prescribed in subsection (1), such final settlement constitutes final payment. In this manner payor banks may without difficulty avoid the effect of such cases as . . . White Brokerage Co. v. Cooperman, 207 Minn. 239, 290 N.W. 790 (1940). . . .''

(2) The Process of Posting. Under UCC 4–213(1)(c), the Citizens Bank of Jonesboro would have paid the check if it had ''completed the process of posting.'' When would this have occurred? See UCC 4–109. The Comment to UCC 4–109 gives three helpful examples to illustrate what constitutes completion of the ''process of posting.''

''Completion of the 'process of posting' is one of the measuring points for determining when an item is finally paid (subsection (1)(c) of Section 4–213) and when knowledge, notice, stop order, legal process and set-off come too late to affect a payor bank's right or duty to pay an item (subsection (1)(d) of Section 4–303). This Section defines what is meant by the 'process of posting'. It is the 'usual procedure followed by a payor bank in determining to pay an item and in recording the payment . . .'. It involves the two basic elements of some decision to pay and some recording of the payment with a listing of some of the typical steps that might be involved. Procedures followed by banks in determining to pay an item and in recording the payment vary. Examples of some of these procedures will illustrate what is meant by completion of the 'process of posting'.

''Example 1. A payor bank receives an item through the clearing on Monday morning. It is sorted under the name of the customer on Monday and under deferred posting routines (Section 4–301) reaches the bookkeeper for that customer on Tuesday morning. The bookkeeper examines the signature, verifies there are sufficient funds and decides at 11 a.m. on Tuesday to pay the item. A debit entry for or including the amount of the item is entered in the customer's account at 12 noon on Tuesday. The process of posting is completed at 12 noon on Tuesday.

''Example 2. A payor bank with branches receives an item through the clearing on Monday morning. One branch does all the bookkeeping for itself and nine other branches. The item is sent to that branch and a provisional debit is entered to the customer's account for the amount of the item on Monday. After this entry is made the item is sent to the branch where the customer transacts business and at this branch a clerk verifies the signature on Tuesday, e.g. at 12 noon. If the clerk determines the signature is valid and makes a decision to pay, the process of posting is completed at 12 noon on Tuesday because there has been both a charge to the customer's account and a determination to pay. If, however, the clerk determines the signature is not valid or that the item should not be paid for some other reason, the item is then returned to the presenting bank through the clearing house and an offsetting credit entry is made in the customer's account by the bookkeeping branch. In this case there has been no determination to pay the item, no completion of the process of posting and no payment of the item.

"Example 3. A payor bank receives in the mail on Monday an item drawn upon it. The item is sorted and otherwise processed on Monday and during Monday night is provisionally recorded on tape by an electronic computer as charged to the customer's account. On Tuesday a clerk examines the signature on the item and makes other checks to determine finally whether the item should be paid. If the clerk determines the signature is valid and makes a decision to pay and all processing of this item is complete, e.g., at 12 noon on Tuesday, the 'process of posting' is completed at that time. If, however, the clerk determines the signature is not valid or that the item should not be paid for some other reason, the item is returned to the presenting bank and in the regular Tuesday night run of the computer the debit to the customer's account for the item is reversed or an offsetting credit entry is made. In this case, as in Example 2, there has been no determination to pay the item, no completion of the process of posting and no payment of the item."

(3) Split Deposits. What instructions should a bank issue to its tellers with respect to the common situation in which a customer wishes, as Kirby did, to make a "split deposit" of a check, i.e., to deposit only part of the amount of the check and to take the rest in cash?

(C) EFFECT OF THE MIDNIGHT DEADLINE

Prefatory Note. In Kirby v. First & Merchants National Bank, p. 141 supra, the court stated, as an alternative ground for its decision, that since the bank "neither sent written notice of dishonor nor returned the Neuse check before the 'midnight deadline,' . . . the Bank had no right to charge the item back to Mrs. Kirby's account." To understand the effect of a bank's midnight deadline on the question of payment, it is useful to know a little history.

History of Check Collections. For an appreciation of the forces and events that shaped the check collection process and led to the midnight deadline, we turn back to the late nineteenth and early twentieth centuries. The critical periods were those of bank failures.

Suppose that a Seller received in the mail a check from Buyer in a distant city in payment for goods. Seller would deposit the check for collection in his bank, Sellersville Bank. Most such nonlocal items were collected through correspondents. Thus Sellersville Bank might forward the check to Correspondent Bank in a nearby large city, which would undertake to present it to Buyersville Bank, the drawee. This system raised several questions.

First, what was the relationship of Sellersville Bank, the depositary bank, to Seller, the depositor? Did the bank become an owner of the check? Bankers, conscious of the risk of bank failure, feared that if the depositary bank took the check as owner it would bear the loss if the check were paid and the proceeds then lost due to the failure of a subsequent bank in the chain of collection. (There could be no recourse against the depositor on his indorsement because the check would not have been dishonored.) If, however, the bank were an agent, the loss would fall on its principal, the depositor. Therefore clauses were added to deposit slips to make it clear that a collecting bank was only an agent and not an owner of the check.

Second, assuming that Sellersville Bank, the depositary bank, was the agent of Seller, the depositor, what was the relationship between the depositor and subsequent collecting banks such as Correspondent Bank? There were two schools of thought. Under the "Massachusetts collection rule," such banks were regarded as sub-agents of the depositor, responsible directly to him; the authority of the depositary bank to employ such sub-agents was inferred from the deposit of the check for collection; the depositary bank discharged its duty to its principal if it selected sub-agents with care. Under the "New York collection rule," the depositary bank appointed its own agents and not those of the depositor; the deposit of the check did not authorize the depositary bank to appoint agents on behalf of its depositor; the depositary bank, rather than the subsequent bank, was liable to the depositor for the defaults of the subsequent bank. Where the depositor had been caused loss by the fault of a distant collecting bank, the Massachusetts rule often left the depositor with recourse only against that bank and not against the bank with which he had dealt.[1] Clauses were added to deposit slips invoking the Massachusetts rule.

A third question caused bankers more trouble than the first two. How was presentment of the check to be made? A simple way to present the check was by "direct routing," in which Correspondent

1. It is interesting that when drawee banks were faced with a similar inconvenience in the case of checks bearing forged indorsements, their situation was quickly ameliorated by the use of "prior indorsements guaranteed." See p. 268 infra.

When shippers of goods were in a somewhat analogous situation with respect to the liability of a connecting carrier for loss, their situation was ameliorated by enactment of the Carmack Amendment, now recodified in 49 U.S.C. § 11707(a)(1). The amendment allowed a shipper to hold the carrier that received the goods from the shipper, and that carrier could, if the loss had occurred while the goods were in the hands of a later carrier, recover over against the later carrier. Prior to the amendment, "the shipper could look only to the initial carrier for recompense for loss, damage or delay occurring on its part of the route. If such primary carrier was able to show a delivery to the rails of the next succeeding carrier, although the packages might and usually did continue the journey in the same car in which they had been originally loaded, the shipper must fail in his suit. He might, it is true, then bring his action against the carrier so shown to have next received the shipment. But here, in turn he might be met by proof of safe delivery to a third separate carrier." Atlantic Coast Line Railroad Co. v. Riverside Mills, 219 U.S. 186, 200, 31 S.Ct. 164, 168, 55 L.Ed. 167 (1911).

Bank mailed the check, along with any others drawn on Buyersville Bank, directly to that bank. Buyersville Bank would then make payment for all of these checks by mailing its remittance draft, its own check on yet another bank, to Correspondent Bank.

Before the First World War, however, there was a practical obstacle to direct routing. At that time many banks refused to remit at par, or face value, exacting an exchange charge when paying checks by remittance draft. They argued that their contract with the drawer called for no more than payment at par over the counter; for remitting to a distant point they should be allowed a fee. Because of the competition for accounts, depositary banks were reluctant to pass on such fees to the depositor of the check, and to avoid exchange charges the practice of circuitous routing developed. Banks made reciprocal agreements to remit at par, and checks were shunted about the country over devious routes, in order to take advantage of these agreements and avoid paying exchange fees.[2]

Aside from the obvious disadvantages of delay and expense, circuitous routing compounded another evil—paper reserves. It was then the practice of banks to give the depositor immediate credit, subject to drawing, for out of town checks. The depositary bank was frequently also given immediate credit when it forwarded the check to its correspondent, and this counted as part of its reserves. The dangers of this practice were demonstrated during the panic of 1907 when many checks were dishonored and banks were unable to realize on much of their paper reserves. The delay due to circuitous routing increased the amount of such reserves created by the "float" of items in the process of collection.

The Federal Reserve System, established by the Federal Reserve Act of 1913, undertook corrective action and in 1916 issued Regulation J requiring Federal Reserve banks to establish a clearing and collection system. Over 40% of all on-others items are now collected through the System. Among the objectives of the System was the elimination of three evils: (1) exchange charges; (2) paper reserves; and (3) circuitous routing. The attack on the first resulted in the stormy par clearance controversy, in which the System scored an incomplete victory. The second evil was substantially eliminated by setting up availability schedules using estimated times for collection based on the location of the bank. A bank using the collection facilities of the Federal Reserve System is not given absolute credit, subject to drawing, until the available date determined from the schedule.

2. In one notorious instance a check drawn on a Sag Harbor, Long Island bank was deposited in a bank in Hoboken, New Jersey, one hundred miles distant, and traveled 1,500 miles in eleven days, passing through banks in New York City, Boston, Tonawanda, Albany, Port Jefferson, Far Rockaway, New York City, Riverhead and Brooklyn before reaching Sag Harbor. Spahr, The Clearing and Collection of Checks 106 (1926).

The third evil, circuitous routing, was reduced by granting to member and certain other banks the privilege of forwarding out of town checks through the Federal Reserve bank in the depositary bank's district.[3] Thus a bank in Sacramento, California, which received from a depositor a check drawn upon a bank in Albany, New York, might mail it to the Federal Reserve Bank of San Francisco, which would forward it to the Federal Reserve Bank of New York, which would in turn mail it to the drawee bank in Albany.[4]

The practice of direct routing, however, posed legal problems. Suppose that Buyersville Bank delayed before sending its remittance draft and then became insolvent, so that its remittance draft, which would have been paid had there been no delay, was dishonored. Might not Seller hold Sellersville Bank for negligence? Mailing the check to the drawee, Buyersville Bank, placed Seller's check in the hands of an adversary in whose interest it would be to procrastinate. A bank is not a suitable agent to collect from itself. Had the check been presented by a proper third party and prompt payment demanded, even the use of a remittance draft would not have caused loss. So it was held in cases such as Minneapolis Sash & Door Co. v. Metropolitan Bank, 76 Minn. 136, 78 N.W. 980 (1899).

To avoid the result of such cases and encourage direct routing, the Federal Reserve Board included in its Regulation J a provision that banks using the System authorized Federal Reserve Banks to send checks directly to the drawee. But was this sufficient? Might not Seller, the depositor, hold Sellersville Bank, the depositary bank, for negligence since Seller had not consented to direct routing? This was clearly a problem under states that applied the New York collection rule. Even under the Massachusetts collection rule, was it due care for a depositary bank to select a Federal Reserve Bank if that bank was expected to mail the check to the drawee? To protect themselves, banks put clauses on their deposit slips granting themselves permission to use direct routing and invoking the Massachusetts collection rule. In 1918 the American Bankers Association proposed a statute authorizing direct routing and many states adopted

3. There are twelve numbered districts with Federal Reserve banks in (1) Boston, (2) New York City, (3) Philadelphia, (4) Cleveland, (5) Richmond, (6) Atlanta, (7) Chicago, (8) St. Louis, (9) Minneapolis, (10) Kansas City, (11) Dallas, and (12) San Francisco. Most of these banks have branches in the same district. The numerator (1–67) of the fraction on the check form, p. 96 supra, is the bank transit number of the drawee. The number 1 indicates New York City, and 67 is the number, in that city, of the Irving Trust Company. The denominator (210) is the routing symbol. The first digit, 2, indicates that the drawee is in District Number 2. The second digit, 1, indicates that the drawee is served by the Reserve bank head office rather than a branch. The third digit, 0, indicates that credit for the check will be available immediately upon its receipt by that office of the Reserve bank. If the digit is other than zero, the item is receivable for deferred credit. The bank transit number and the routing symbol also appear in the magnetized symbols in the lower left-hand corner of the check.

4. The Sacramento bank might have the privilege of "direct sending," in which case it could mail the check directly to the Federal Reserve Bank of New York.

this or a similar statute. Thus armed, the banks were ready for the next round.

That round was fought and lost by the banks in the Supreme Court of the United States in Federal Reserve Bank v. Malloy, 264 U.S. 160, 44 S.Ct. 296, 68 L.Ed. 617 (1924). That case involved the familiar situation of a remittance draft that had been dishonored because the drawer of the remittance draft (the drawee of the check) had become insolvent after issuing it. The payee of the check sued the Federal Reserve Bank that had presented it, alleging negligence in collection of the check. The Supreme Court affirmed a judgment for the plaintiff, holding that the Federal Reserve Bank was liable for its negligence in taking in payment a remittance draft instead of cash. The Court did not quarrel with the proposition that under Regulation J the Federal Reserve Bank was authorized to send the check directly to the drawee. But the Court pointed out that "a collecting agent is without authority to accept for the debt of his principal anything but 'that which the law declares to be a legal tender, or which is by common consent considered and treated as money, and passes as such at par.' . . . This regulation, while it contemplates the sending of checks for collection to the drawee banks, does not expressly permit the acceptance of payment other than in money." Nor would the Court read in that authority by implication or from custom.

However, it was simple enough to deprive the depositor of the right upheld in the Malloy case. Regulation J was amended to allow Federal Reserve banks to accept remittance drafts, and a new crop of clauses appeared on deposit slips permitting collecting banks to take remittance drafts.

Now that Seller, as depositor, was deprived of any right against either Sellersville Bank or Correspondent Bank, the collecting banks, it was important to ask whether Seller had any action on the check against Buyer, as drawer. Logically it followed from decisions like that in the Malloy case that the check had been paid and Buyer was no longer liable to Seller. For if Seller could still sue Buyer, Seller would have sustained no loss as the result of Correspondent Bank's taking a remittance draft. There was dictum to this effect in the Malloy opinion and it was borne out in other cases. The result was that the Seller's rights against the collecting banks were his sole recourse, and this recourse had been effectively cut off. It could be argued that when Regulation J and deposit slips were amended to avoid the result in the Malloy case, this had the incidental effect of imposing liability on the Buyer as drawer of the check. But most courts found it hard to see any reason why Buyer, as drawer, should be adversely affected by such a contract between Seller, as depositor, and the collecting banks. Therefore Buyer was still discharged because the check had been paid.

The erosion of Seller's rights as depositor was now nearly complete. Seller had lost the right to hold Sellersville Bank, the depositary bank, and was left to an action against a remote collecting bank when the banks invoked the Massachusetts collection rule. Seller had lost the right to hold even that bank for loss caused by direct routing when deposit slips and Federal Reserve Board Regulation J were amended and statutes were enacted to permit direct routing. Seller had lost the right to hold that bank for loss caused by accepting payment by remittance draft when there was a similar response to the Malloy case. Seller had, at least in most states, no recourse against Buyer, the drawer of the check, because the check had been paid. So Seller was left with what he had received in payment, a bank draft on which only Buyersville Bank, the drawee of the check, was liable, and that bank was insolvent. Seller would have to stand in line for the money with its general depositors.

There was one hope left for Seller as depositor of the check. If he could show that he came ahead of the general depositors of the insolvent bank, that he had a preferred claim, he stood a chance of being paid in full. This was the tack followed by ingenious counsel and in a number of states they succeeded. An example is People ex rel. Nelson v. Peoples Bank & Trust Co., 353 Ill. 479, 187 N.E. 522, 89 A.L.R. 1328 (1933), where the court concluded that the drawee of the check, the insolvent drawer of the remittance draft, was the agent of the depositor, that the agent bank's assets had been augmented by the transaction, that the depositor could trace the funds into the hands of the receiver, and that therefore the depositor had a preferred claim in the assets of the insolvent bank based on trust doctrines. Other courts rejected this argument and left the depositor to share with general depositors.

The Bank Collection Code. In 1929 the American Bankers Association proposed for adoption the Bank Collection Code. By 1932 eighteen states had adopted it. Because of the statute's origin, it is hardly surprising that it was bank-oriented. It made collecting banks agents rather than owners, adopted the Massachusetts collection rule, sanctioned direct routing, authorized the acceptance of remittance drafts, and gave the depositor a preferred claim.

For a discussion of the history of check collections up to this point, see Scott, The Risk Fixers, 91 Harv.L.Rev. 737 (1978).

The Code. The Code carries over many of the provisions of the Bank Collection Code the comparable provisions of the Code. The Code also makes banks agents rather than owners (UCC 4–201(1)), and adopts the Massachusetts collection rule (UCC 4–202(3)). The Code authorizes direct routing (UCC 4–204(2)(a)) and the acceptance of remittance drafts (UCC 4–211(1)(a)). And the Code gives a preferred claim on insolvency (UCC 4–214 and Comment 3). If a remittance draft is used, when is a check paid under the Code? See UCC 4–213(1).

The Federal Reserve System and Remittance Drafts. Member banks of the Federal Reserve System commonly rely on its facilities and thus avoid the use of remittance drafts. Settlement between member banks in the same district can be effected through the account that they are required to maintain in the Federal Reserve bank. Settlements between member banks in different districts are made through their respective Federal Reserve banks by means of the Interdistrict Settlement Fund in Washington, in which each Reserve bank has a share.

In 1972, the Federal Reserve Board amended Regulation J so that drawee banks no longer have the right to use remittance drafts to pay for checks presented by Federal Reserve Banks. Payment is instead to be by debit "to an account on the Reserve Bank's books." 12 C.F.R. § 210.9. The purpose is to reduce the "float" of checks in the process of collection. As the Board explained: "Until the mid-1960's many banks outside Federal Reserve cities paid for [checks presented by Reserve Banks] by drawing and dispatching a draft on the day of receipt of the checks. Remittance drafts were usually not received and collected until the following day, resulting in a deferment of payment. In recent years the use of modern accounting and communications systems has led to the payment of checks on the day of presentment. Roughly 80 percent of the total amount of payments by paying banks on checks presented by Reserve Banks is through direct charges to reserve accounts. Now it is feasible to make universal the practice of paying in immediately available funds on the day of presentment." 37 Fed.Reg. 6695 (1972).

When transmission of the proceeds between collecting banks is by means of bank credit, the collecting bank fulfills its function by giving a final credit to the bank from which it received the check. See UCC 4–213(2). Comment 8 to UCC 4–213 explains that to the extent that settlement between banks is either through a clearing house or by debits and credits in accounts between them, "when the item is finally paid by the payor bank under subsection (1) this final payment automatically without further action 'firms up' other provisional settlements made for it."[5]

The Federal Reserve System and the Midnight Deadline. In amending Regulation J in 1972, the Federal Reserve Board also tightened up on the midnight deadline. The history of the midnight deadline goes back to a problem that arose well before the advent of the Code.

5. In periods of bank failure, trouble came when one of the collecting banks failed. Suppose that Sellersville Bank, the depositary bank, failed after Buyersville Bank, the drawee, had paid Correspondent Bank, the presenting bank. It was to Seller's advantage to demand the proceeds directly from Correspondent Bank, rather than to allow Correspondent Bank to give a final credit in the amount of the check to the insolvent Sellersville Bank. It was to Correspondent Bank's advantage to resist this and to credit Sellersville Bank in the amount of the check, thereby reducing the debt that it was most probably owed by its insolvent correspondent and on which it would receive less than full payment. For the Code solution, see UCC 4–201, 4–211, 4–213, 4–214.

Before the Second World War banks generally exchanged checks at the clearing house by eleven in the morning and the return item clearing took place at two or three in the afternoon of the same day. The heavy workload, combined with the wartime labor shortage, put a severe strain on the system and banks began deferred posting. Clearing house rules were changed to allow until afternoon of the day following receipt of the item for the return of "not good" items. But bankers worried about Negotiable Instruments Law § 137, which provided that "where a drawee to whom a bill is delivered for acceptance . . . refuses within twenty-four hours . . . to return the bill," he was deemed to have accepted it. Could a drawee safely retain a check for more than twenty-four hours? The law on such a "constructive acceptance" was unclear.

To eliminate the risk that deferred posting might result in constructive acceptance, committees appointed by the Federal Reserve Banks and the American Bankers Association met and agreed upon a Model Deferred Posting Statute. In order to reduce the "float," the Federal Reserve Banks insisted that the privilege of making delayed returns be limited to banks that settled by giving credit on the day of receipt. Under the model statute, therefore, only if a drawee settled before midnight on the day of receipt, did it have until midnight of its next banking day to revoke the credit and refuse to pay the check. All states adopted deferred posting legislation, most of them substantially in the form recommended by the Association in 1948. Regulation J of the Board of Governors of the Federal Reserve System was amended, effective in 1949, to permit deferred posting.

The Code abolishes the constructive acceptance in UCC 3–410. In its place, UCC 3–419(1)(a) bases liability on conversion, but requires that the drawee "refuses on demand . . . to return it." The Code adopts deferred posting in UCC 4–301, 4–302, 4–104(1)(h).

Note that under UCC 4–302, if the drawee bank "is also the depositary bank," the drawee has until its midnight deadline—"midnight on its next banking day following the banking day on which it receives the relevant item" (UCC 4–104(1)(h))—to revoke any settlement if it has not already made final payment. See also UCC 4–301(1). Thus in Douglas v. Citizens Bank of Jonesboro, p. 149 supra, the bank would have been "accountable" for the checks under UCC 4–302 if it did not "pay or return the item or send notice of dishonor until after its midnight deadline." Since the checks were received by the bank on August 19, the bank's midnight deadline under UCC 4–104(1)(h) was midnight on the next banking day, August 20.[6] But because both checks "were charged back to the accounts of the respective [drawees] on August 20, and the [drawers] so notified," the bank act-

---

6. Purists may question whether a "banking day," as UCC 4–104(1)(c) defines that term, will commonly have a "midnight," as UCC 4–104(1)(h) suggests that it must. Would it be better if UCC 4–104(1)(h) said "midnight on the date of its next banking day"? See Mellinkoff, The Language of the Uniform Commercial Code, 77 Yale L.J. 185, 188 (1967).

ed before its midnight deadline and so did not become accountable under UCC 4–302.

Note, however, that under UCC 4–302, if the drawee bank "is not also the depositary bank," the drawee has until its midnight deadline only if "an authorized settlement . . . has been made before midnight of the banking day of receipt." See also UCC 4–301(1). This requirement is intended to reduce the "float" and, in effect, codifies the compromise reached between the Federal Reserve Banks and the American Bankers Association in the Model Deferred Posting Statute. See Comments 1 and 2 to UCC 4–301.

When the Federal Reserve Board amended Regulation J in 1972, it required that the "proceeds of any payment shall be available to the Reserve Bank by the close of the Reserve Bank's banking day on the banking day of receipt of the item by the paying bank." If the drawer bank does not do this, it loses the benefit of its midnight deadline and becomes accountable for the amount of the check "at the close of the paying bank's banking day" on which it received the item. 12 C.F.R. § 210.9; see also § 210.12. Thus the Board, in an effort further to reduce the "float," required that the drawee settle before the end of the banking day of receipt and not merely before midnight on the day of receipt as required by the Code.[7]

Problem 11. Empire's account has only $1,000 in it. On Wednesday, Irving Trust receives the check payable to Quaker directly from the Federal Reserve Bank in Phildelphia, to which Philadelphia National had sent it. Irving Trust mislays the check for two days and on Friday, when the check is put through the regular computer run, it is rejected as drawn on insufficient funds. What are Irving Trust's rights against Quaker? See UCC 4–213, 4–301, 4–302; First Wyoming Bank v. Cabinet Craft Distributors, infra. (How would it affect your answer if the check were presented through the Clearing House?) Would your answer be the same if the check had already been presented and dishonored by insufficient funds and was being represented when it was mislaid? See UCC 3–511(4); David Graubart v. Bank Leumi Trust Co., infra.

---

7. In Community Bank v. Federal Reserve Bank of San Francisco, 500 F.2d 282 (9th Cir.), cert. denied 419 U.S. 1089, 95 S.Ct. 680, 42 L.Ed.2d 681 (1974), a group of state banks that were neither members of nor affiliated with the Federal Reserve System challenged the amendments insofar as they affected such banks. The banks argued that they were not bound by the amendments because the amendments were inconsistent with the Uniform Commercial Code provisions on time of settlement. The court rejected this argument on the reasoning that UCC 4–103(2) gives Federal Reserve regulations the effect of agreements varying the provisions of Article 4 and that the banks' assent was shown by their use of the Federal Reserve routing number as part of the MICR numbers on their checks. However, in Kane v. American National Bank & Trust Co., 21 Ill.App.3d 1046, 316 N.E.2d 177 (1974), it was held that the amendment had no effect on checks collected outside of the System's check collection channels.

FIRST WYOMING BANK v. CABINET CRAFT DISTRIBUTORS, INC.

Supreme Court of Wyoming, 1981.
624 P.2d 227.

ROSE, CHIEF JUSTICE. The Uniform Commercial Code provides that except in certain circumstances a bank is liable for the amount of a check which it fails to timely dishonor. Section 34–21–451, W.S.1977 (U.C.C. § 4–302). In this case, the appellee presented a check payable to itself to the appellant bank. The payor had insufficient funds on deposit with the bank to cover the check. The bank dishonored the check but failed to do so within the time mandated by the Uniform Commercial Code.

Appellee then sued in district court for the face amount of the check, interest and costs. The district court agreed with the appellee that the bank was liable under the Code and gave judgment accordingly. The bank has appealed and argues that its "excuse" for failing to timely dishonor the check is sufficient under the Code to enable it to escape liability. Section 34–21–408(b), W.S.1977 (U.C.C. § 4–108(2)).   .   .   .   In arguing that the delay in dishonoring the check was excusable, appellant bank also relies on 12 Code of Federal Regulations 210.14 which provides:

"If, because of interruption of communication facilities, suspension of payments by another bank, war, emergency conditions or other circumstances beyond its control, any bank (including a Federal Reserve bank) shall be delayed beyond the time limits provided in this part or the operating letters of the Federal Reserve banks, or prescribed by the applicable law of any State in taking any action with respect to a cash item or a noncash item, including forwarding such item, presenting it or sending it for presentment and payment, paying or remitting for it, returning it or sending notice of dishonor or nonpayment or making or providing for any necessary protest, the time of such bank, as limited by this part or the operating letters of the Federal Reserve banks, or by the applicable law of any State, for taking or completing the action thereby delayed shall be extended for such time after the cause of the delay ceases to operate as shall be necessary to take or complete the action, provided the bank exercises such diligence as the circumstances require."

The bank points out that under § 34–21–403, W.S.1977 (U.C.C. § 4–103), if not under the supremacy clause of the Federal Constitution, the above regulation is controlling law in Wyoming. We agree that the regulation controls but fail to see how it adds anything to § 34–21–408(b) (U.C.C. § 4–108(2)), supra. In light of the stipulated facts to be presented immediately below, it appears that either under the statute or the regulation the bank must show that its delay in dishonoring the check was due to circumstances beyond its control and that the bank exercised such diligence as the circumstances required.   .   .   .

As we understand the facts, both parties to this suit have acted in good faith and the plaintiff-appellee has made no showing that it was prejudiced by the untimely dishonor of the check. The untimely dishonor of the check was due to delay in delivering checks from a computer center in Billings, Montana, to the bank in Sheridan. Normally, the same courier delivering the checks to the Montana computer center from Sheridan would have driven them back to Sheridan after the center had processed them. However, after the check in issue had been taken to Billings, the main road between Billings and Sheridan became flooded. Although the courier could have taken an alternate route back to Sheridan, the check was instead given to Western Airlines by the computer center to be placed on the next morning's flight to Sheridan. For unknown reasons Western Airlines failed to deliver the check to Sheridan although it made its usual flight. Western Airline's failure to deliver the check to Sheridan as planned caused the bank to miss its Uniform Commercial Code deadline for dishonoring the check.   .   .   .[1]

Liability Under U.C.C. § 4–302

Courts generally interpret U.C.C. § 4–302 (our § 34–21–451), supra, as imposing strict liability upon a bank which fails to dishonor a check in time unless the bank meets its burden of proving a valid defense. In Sun River Cattle Co., Inc. v. Miners Bank of Mont. N.A., 164 Mont. 237, 521 P.2d 679, 684 (1974), reh. den., the Montana Supreme Court spoke of U.C.C. § 4–302 as imposing a "standard of strict accountability" and cited the Official Code Comment for the proposition that the bank has the burden of proving an excuse under U.C.C. § 4–108(2) (our § 34–21–408(b)), supra. *Sun River Cattle Co.,* supra, 521 P.2d at 685 and also citing 3 Anderson, Uniform Commercial Code 191. The United States Tenth Circuit Court of Appeals has said that if it is shown that a check has not been dishonored within

---

1. The briefs on appeal reveal that the check was for $10,000 and was drawn by Quality Kitchens to the order of Cabinet Craft as partial payment for cabinets and related kitchenware. Cabinet Craft deposited the check in its account in the Security Bank of Billings, which sent it on for collection. On Saturday, May 20, 1978, the Federal Reserve Bank of Denver mailed the check to the First Wyoming Bank of Sheridan, which received it before three in the afternoon on Monday, May 22 and sent it at six that evening to a computer center in Billings run by Data Share, Inc. The computer center's printout showed "insufficient funds."

The checks that ordinarily would have been returned to the First Wyoming Bank late on Monday night were put on an early morning Western Airlines flight and arrived in Sheridan shortly after eight on Tuesday morning. Counsel for Cabinet Craft writes that, apparently because First Wyoming Bank did not meet the plane, the checks were not taken off the plane at Sheridan. On Thursday, the bank was notified by First Wyoming Bank in Casper that the checks had been received there. Counsel for First Wyoming Bank writes that the bank ultimately recovered from Western Airlines for negligence. (The facts in the court's opinion are taken from a brief stipulation entered into by the parties in order to reduce expenses.) [Ed.]

the Code time limit, a prima facie case is established for imposing liability on the bank and the bank has the obligation of proving an excuse for untimely dishonor under U.C.C. § 4–108(2) (our § 34–21–408(b)), supra. Port City State Bank v. American National Bank, Lawton, Okl., 10 Cir., 486 F.2d 196, 198 (1973). The United States Fifth Circuit Court of Appeals recently said, "Failure . . . to perform these duties within the time limits prescribed [by U.C.C. § 4–302] mandates the imposition of strict liability for the face amount of any late instrument. . . ." *Union Bank of Benton v. First Nat. Bank*, 5 Cir., 621 F.2d 790, 795 (1980). The Supreme Court of New Mexico has said, "The liability created by [U.C.C. § 4–302 (our § 34–21–451), supra] is independent of negligence and is an absolute or strict liability for the full amount of the items which it fails to return, . . ." Engine Parts v. Citizens Bank of Clovis, 92 N.M. 37, 582 P.2d 809, 815 (1978).

Both the Illinois Supreme Court and the Kentucky Court of Appeals have rejected arguments that a bank which fails to timely dishonor a check under U.C.C. § 4–302 (our § 34–21–451), supra, is only liable if the delay in the dishonoring of the check injured the check's payee. Rock Island Auction Sales v. Empire Packing Co., 32 Ill.2d 269, 204 N.E.2d 721, 723–724 (1965); and Farmers Coop. Livestock Mkt. v. Second Nat. Bank, Ky., 427 S.W.2d 247, 250 (1968).

Other cases which have come to similar conclusions concerning the relevant Code provision include: Pecos County State Bank v. El Paso Livestock, Tex.Civ.App., 586 S.W.2d 183, 187 (1979), reh. den.; and Templeton v. First Nat. Bank of Nashville, 47 Ill.App.3d 443, 5 Ill.Dec. 720, 362 N.E.2d 33, 37 (1977).

Thus, since there is no issue of bad faith, our examination of appellant bank's claim of a valid excuse under U.C.C. § 4–108(2) (our § 34–21–408(b)), supra, does not entail a consideration of the equities involved. Rather our task is simply to determine whether the record demonstrates a sufficient excuse under the above statute. . . .

Excuses Under U.C.C. § 4–108(2)

It is obvious that the flooded road between Billings and Sheridan which disrupted the normal procedure for delivery of the check was a "circumstance beyond the control of the bank" as contemplated by § 34–21–408(b) (U.C.C. § 4–108(2)), supra. Our inquiry is whether the bank used "such diligence as the circumstances required," in allowing the Montana computer center to give the check to Western Airlines for delivery and in not following up the failure of the airline to deliver the packet on schedule. In answering this question we must consider that the stipulated facts show that the bank had an alternative to using Western Airlines: its courier could have taken a different route. We are also somewhat handicapped by a lack of information. For example, although we know that the bank had previously used the airline's delivery service, we do not know what the airline's previous record for timely deliveries had been. We do not know if the computer center in turning the check over to the airline emphasized the need for a timely delivery. We do not know if the bank could have traced the checks which failed to arrive on the Western Airlines flight and gotten them sooner.

We have found no case involving a claimed U.C.C. § 4–108(2) (our § 34–21–408(b)), supra, excuse identical to the one involved here and only a few cases involving somewhat similar excuses. Surveying the area in 1977 the Kentucky Court of Appeals found "only two cases involving the application of U.C.C. § 4–108 to a payor bank's midnight deadline." Blake v. Woodford Bank & Trust Co., Ky.App., 555 S.W.2d 589, 594 (1977). The two cases found by the Kentucky court are *Sun River Cattle Co.,* supra, and *Port City State Bank,* supra. We have not been able to discover any cases in addition to the Kentucky, Montana and Tenth Circuit decisions.

The Montana case is, perhaps, most in point. A bank in Butte, Montana, had its checks processed at a computer center in Great Falls, Montana. In the usual course of business the Butte bank's checks were sent by armored car to Great Falls for processing. Ordinarily, the checks would leave Butte at 5:00 or 6:00 p.m. on the day of receipt, arrive at Great Falls about 10:30 p.m., be processed by 11:30 p.m., be loaded back onto the armored car headed for Butte at 4:00 a.m. and arrive back in Butte at 7:00 a.m. *Sun River Cattle Co.,* supra, 521 P.2d at 684.

Unfortunately for the Butte bank, it received some checks on May 11, 1970. That day the armored car broke down and did not reach Great Falls until 1:30 a.m., May 12. Moreover, the computer in Great Falls malfunctioned with the result that the checks were not returned to Butte until 2:30 p.m. on May 12, rather than at 7:00 a.m. on that date. The Butte bank's "midnight deadline" for dishonoring the checks was midnight of May 12. Id. and U.C.C. § 4–104(1)(h) (our § 34–21–404(a)(viii)), supra. Thus, even though the armored car and computer breakdowns threw the bank off its normal schedule, it would have been physically possible for the bank to have dishonored the checks by midnight of May 12. The bank was unable to offer an explanation for failing to dishonor the checks by midnight of May 12.

The Montana court said:

> "Under the exception of section 4–108(2) the bank must show: (1) A cause for the delay; (2) that the cause was beyond the control of the bank; and (3) that under the circumstances the bank exercised such diligence as required. *In the absence of any one of these showings, the excuse for the delay will not apply,* and the bank will be held liable under the provisions of section 4–302. . . ." (Emphasis added.) 521 P.2d at 686.

Along these lines our appellee urges that we note that there is no evidence in the record that the appellant bank made any efforts to trace the checks when they did not arrive in Sheridan aboard the

Western Airlines flight as scheduled. Perhaps a trace started on the missing checks that morning would have enabled the bank to obtain the checks that day and meet the midnight deadline for dishonoring the insufficient-funds check which is the focus of this appeal.

However, although the appellant does not discuss this case, there is a distinguishing feature about *Sun River Cattle* which favors the appellant's cause. In the Montana case the checks in question were drawn on a business greatly indebted to the Butte bank and in precarious financial shape. The Montana court stated that it was holding the Butte bank to a stricter standard of proof under U.C.C. § 4–108(2) (our § 34–21–408(b)), supra, than would ordinarily be required. *Sun River Cattle*, supra, 521 P.2d at 685.

Our appellant bank relies almost solely on the Tenth Circuit case. *Port City State Bank*, supra. In this case the defendant, American National Bank, failed to timely dishonor two checks submitted to it by Port City State Bank. It was stipulated that the midnight deadlines for the two checks were December 1, and December 3. On December 1, American National computerized its operations and the computer broke down on its inauguration day. Despite assurances from the manufacturer that it could be repaired quickly, the computer was not repaired until late at night. When it became apparent that the computer could not be rapidly repaired, American National decided to use an identical computer in a bank some two and a half hours away, under a previous backup arrangement. Processing of checks was begun at 11:30 p.m. on December 1 on the backup bank's computer. Work was proceeding nicely on the backup computer when American National was notified by the computer manufacturer that its own computer was ready. The American National employees returned to their own bank. American National's computer worked for awhile and then broke down on December 2 and was rendered inoperable until a replacement part was installed on December 4. Because of the second failure of its new computer, American National Bank was again forced to utilize its backup arrangement. However, because of the distance between the American Bank and its backup computer, and the need of American to work around the schedule of the bank which owned the backup computer, American got behind in its processing.

The district court held that the cause of the delay in dishonoring the checks was the computer breakdowns, and the Tenth Circuit, applying its usual appellate rules, concluded that the holding was "not clearly erroneous." *Port City State Bank*, supra, 486 F.2d at 199. The Tenth Circuit also found that American reasonably relied on the assurance of the computer manufacturer that the initial malfunction could be repaired quickly; thus, the Tenth Circuit held that the bank was justified in not using the backup computer earlier. Id. at 200. Also, the Tenth Circuit accepted the argument that the bank's duty when the emergency became apparent was to remain open and serve its customers as best it could. "To abandon the orderly day by day process of bookkeeping to adopt radical emergency measures would have likely prolonged the delay in returning the bank to normal operations," the court said. Id. at 200.

As pointed out earlier, the Tenth Circuit stated in this case that it was the defendant bank's burden to prove an excuse under U.C.C. § 4–108(2) (our § 34–21–408(b)), supra. We agree with our appellee in this case that the Tenth Circuit case is readily distinguishable from the case before us. The defendant bank in the Tenth Circuit case proved to the satisfaction of the trial court that it used the diligence required by the above statute and that its failure to timely dishonor the checks was due to circumstances beyond its control—computer breakdowns. The showing of diligence included proof of utilization of a backup system. In the case before us, there is no showing that defendant-appellant bank used any diligence when the packet of checks failed to arrive as scheduled on the flight from Montana.

The Kentucky case involved a failure to timely dishonor two checks. *Blake*, supra. The two checks in this case were presented for payment to the defendant bank on December 24, 1973, so that under the midnight-deadline rule the bank was responsible for dishonoring the checks by midnight of December 26, December 25, of course, being a bank holiday. *Blake*, supra, 555 S.W.2d at 591. Unfortunately for the bank, it did not send notice that it was dishonoring the checks until December 27. In the trial court the bank sought to justify the delay for several reasons. The bank presented evidence that while it normally processes only 4,200 to 4,600 checks a day, it had 6,995 to process on December 26. The bank had four posting machines but two broke down on December 26, one for two and a half hours and one for one and a half hours. Also, one of the four regular bookkeepers was absent on December 26 and had to be replaced by a less proficient substitute. The bank regularly employed a Purolator courier to pick up checks at 4:00 p.m. and take them to the Federal Reserve bank. Because of the above-described problems, the bank did not have the two checks in question processed on December 26 in time for the Purolator courier. Id. at 595–596.

The trial court found these excuses sufficient under U.C.C. § 4–108(2) (our § 34–21–408(b)), supra, to relieve the bank of liability under U.C.C. § 4–302 (our § 34–21–451), supra. The Kentucky appellate court reversed. The appellate court focused on additional facts. One of the bookkeepers had in fact discovered that there were insufficient funds to pay the two checks on December 26 after the Purolator courier left. However, because of "the lateness of the hour" there was no responsible bank official on the premises and the bookkeeper merely left the two checks on the desk of the bank official who was supposed to handle insufficient funds checks. Id. at 596. Thus, the bank did not send out notice that it was dishonoring the check until the next day.

The Kentucky appellate court concluded:

"Even though the bank missed returning the two checks by the Purolator courier, it was still possible for the bank to have returned the checks by its midnight deadline. Under U.C.C. § 4–301(4)(b) [footnote] an item is returned when it is 'sent' to the bank's transferor, in this case the Federal Reserve Bank. Under U.C.C. § 1–201(38) [footnote] an item is 'sent' when it is deposited in the mail. 1 R. Anderson, Uniform Commercial Code § 1–201 pp. 118–119 (2d ed. 1970). Thus, the bank could have returned the two checks before the midnight deadline by the simple procedure of depositing the two checks in the mail, properly addressed to the Cincinnati branch of the Federal Reserve Bank.

"This court concludes that circumstances beyond the control of the bank did not prevent it from returning the two checks in question before its midnight deadline on December 26. The circumstances causing the delay in the bookkeeping department were foreseeable. On December 26, the bank actually discovered that the checks were 'bad,' but the responsible employees and officers had left the bank without leaving any instructions to the bookkeepers. The circuit court erred in holding that the bank was excused under § 4–108 from meeting its midnight deadline. The facts found by the circuit court do not support its conclusion that the circumstances in the case were beyond the control of the bank." 555 S.W.2d 596–597.

The cases discussed above persuade us that the appellant bank has failed to prove an excuse sufficient under § 34–21–408(b) (U.C.C. § 4–108(2)), supra, to enable it to escape liability under § 34–21–451 (U.C.C. § 4–302), supra, for its failure to dishonor the check in question by the midnight deadline imposed by the U.C.C.

The judgment of the district court is affirmed.

NOTES

(1) **Federal Reserve Operating Letters.** A Federal Reserve operating circular requires that all paying and collecting banks wire advice of nonpayment of any dishonored item of $2,500 or over prior to the bank's midnight deadline. (For an earlier version of this provision, see the Wells Fargo Bank case, p. 132 supra.) Is a drawee bank accountable under UCC 4–302 for the amount of an item of $2,500 or over if it sends it to the presenting bank within the midnight deadline but fails to wire advice of nonpayment? See UCC 1–201(38). Courts that have examined this question have generally held that the drawee bank is not accountable under UCC 4–302 for the amount of the item but is merely liable under UCC 4–103(5) for any damages caused by its failure to wire advice. Yeiser v. Bank of Adamsville, 614 S.W.2d 338 (Tenn.1981).

(2) Branches and the Midnight Deadline. If a check drawn on one branch of a bank is deposited in another branch of the same bank, is the midnight deadline determined by the time that the check is received by the branch in which it is deposited or the branch on which it is drawn? See UCC 4–106. When was the check in the Kirby case, p. 141 supra, received by the payor bank for this purpose? See footnote 1, p. 148 supra.

(3) Automation and the Midnight Deadline. Suppose that a bank has a data processing center that serves all the bank's branches. Is the midnight deadline under UCC 4–302 determined by reference to the time when the check is received by the data processing center or by reference to the time when the check is subsequently received by the branch on which it is drawn?

In Idah-Best v. First Security Bank, 99 Idaho 517, 584 P.2d 1242 (1978), the court held that the latter time controlled. A check drawn on the Hailey branch of First Security Bank of Idaho [1] was deposited in a Twin Falls bank, which mailed it together with other checks drawn on First Security branches in southwestern Idaho to the Boise branch of First Security, where the Twin Falls bank had an account that was provisionally credited. The check was sorted and encoded by the Boise branch's data processing center and, during the nighttime, the encoded information was transmitted to First Security's computer in Salt Lake City, which contained all accounts in all First Security branches. The computer posted the amounts of checks to the appropriate accounts and adjusted the account balances between the Boise branch and other branches, giving the Boise branch provisional credits. Since the computer found insufficient funds for the check in question, the Boise branch partially completed a "return check notice" for the drawer. The check, along with the notice, was then sent the following day to the Hailey branch, where checks were proofed to determine the validity of the drawers' signatures. Insufficient funds checks were then circulated among tellers to see whether there had been a recent deposit to cover the check and, if there was none, among branch officers who could approve payment despite insufficient funds. Payment of the check in question was not approved and it was returned to the Twin Falls bank on the banking day after its receipt by the Hailey branch but two days after its receipt by the Boise branch.

The payee of the check "argued that because the Boise data processing center performs for [First Security] the bookkeeping functions required of a payor bank, the center is part of the Hailey branch." The Supreme Court of Idaho rejected this contention, explaining that though the "process of posting" had begun while the

1. The court noted that under the Idaho banking law, "checks . . . drawn against any banking corporation . . . operating branch banks . . . ., shall indicate the particular branch or office at which the same are to be presented for payment or acceptance."

check was in the hands of the Boise branch, the check had not yet been presented to the payor, the Hailey branch.

"An analysis of the operations of the Boise data processing center shows that its functions are limited to the sorting and indorsing process typical of a collecting bank and to the transmitting of information that allows the Salt Lake City computer to keep tentative customer accounts. . . . Nevertheless, the data processing center performs a function beyond those of a collecting bank. The center is the 'capture site' and transmission point for data used by First Security's Salt Lake City computer to update customer and interbranch accounts. In performing this function, the data processing center performs one of the steps employed by a payor bank in recording payment of a check. The heart of this appeal is the question of whether the performance of this step in some way indicates that the process of paying a check and recording payment—that is, the functions of a payor bank—have been initiated.

"The payor bank's duties begin when it receives presentment. 'Presentment is a demand for acceptance or payment made upon the maker, acceptor, drawee or other payor by or on behalf of the holder.' I.C. § 28–3–504. Presentment must be made to the payor or to one authorized to make or refuse acceptance or payment. I.C. § 28–3–504. . . . In the instant case, the Hailey office of First Security Bank is the branch named on respondent's check. In addition, no action on the part of Twin Falls Bank & Trust can be characterized as a presentment to either the Boise branch or the data processing center. Even if such a demand for payment were made on the processing center, it could not have been accepted. First, there is nothing in the record that might show the processing center has authority to receive presentment under I.C. § 28–4–204(3), which provides that presentment may be made by a presenting bank at any place, presumably including an off-premises data processing center, where the payor bank requests presentment be made. I.C. § 28–4–204, Comment 4 . . . .. Secondly, the processing center has no way to judge the genuineness of a check or the sufficiency of the customer's funds to pay it. . . . First Security's data processing system had been designed to allow the collecting bank to both determine the status of the drawer's account and debit the account *before the check reaches the payor bank for a decision on whether to pay it.* Thus when the data processing center advises a branch of an account's status, the report is merely tentative, particularly for branches far from the processing center. For this reason the data processing center is not permitted to decide to dishonor a check; only the branch may make that decision after checking for recent deposits."

The court also rested its decision on UCC 4–106, noting that Idaho (like a majority of states) has omitted the bracketed optional words "maintaining its own deposit ledgers." "The effect of this section, then, is to give a branch bank that is a payor bank its own midnight deadline for carrying out its duties as a payor, even if it keeps no 'deposit ledgers' or similar books." [2]

In Central Bank of Alabama v. Peoples National Bank, 401 So.2d 14 (Ala.1981), the Supreme Court of Alabama declined to apply Idah-Best to a case in which the data processing center was, according to the trial court's findings of fact, the drawee bank's "designated place of presentment." The opinion noted that Alabama had omitted from UCC 4–106 the bracketed optional words "maintaining its own deposit ledgers," but concluded that it made no difference that the branch on which the check was drawn "is a separate bank; the computer is still an integral part of it." [3] It rejected the drawee's contention "that a substantial and burdensome logistical problem will be created" if branches are required to return the check on the day after its receipt at the computer center, which serves forty branches, some located as far as 100 miles from the center. "To allow this reasoning to permit the midnight deadline to begin running from the time of receipt at the local branch would be to thwart the very purpose of the midnight deadline: to encourage prompt return of dishonored checks" and it "would have the effect of allowing the payor bank to unilaterally decide when the deadline would begin to run by the simple device of choosing the time to forward the check to the branch."

Can the conclusions of the Alabama and Idaho courts be reconciled? If not, which is preferable? For cases characterizing the conclusions as "inconsistent" and agreeing with the Alabama case whether or not the computer center is an independent contractor, see Chrysler Credit Corp. v. First National Bank & Trust Co., 746 F.2d 200 (3d Cir. 1984); South Sound National Bank v. First Interstate Bank, 65 Or.App. 553, 672 P.2d 1194 (1983); South Sound National Bank v. Citiziens Valley Bank, 65 Or.App. 562, 672 P.2d 1198 (1983).

(4) **Underencoded Checks.** Suppose that a depositary bank takes a $25,000 check and underencodes it as a $2,500 check. If the drawee bank treats it as a $2,500 check and pays it and if the mistake is not discovered until after the drawee's midnight deadline has passed, is the drawee liable to the payee under UCC 4–302 for $25,000? If so, has the drawee a claim against the depositary bank? Are more facts needed? What facts? See Georgia Railroad Bank & Trust Co. v. First National Bank & Trust Co., 139 Ga.App. 683, 229 S.E.2d 482 (1976), affirmed, 238 Ga. 693, 235 S.E.2d 1 (1977).

---

2. In a later opinion in the same case, the court held that UCC 4–302(a)'s requirement of a settlement was met when the data processing center in Boise transmitted to the computer in Salt Lake City a provisional credit to the Boise branch and a provisional debit to the Hailey branch, even though the Hailey branch had not physically received the check. The court rejected the argument "that it is imposible to 'settle' for a check which has not been presented and received." Idah-Best v. First Security Bank, 101 Idaho 402, 614 P.2d 425 (1980).

3. Although the check was drawn on a designated branch, as was the check in Idah-Best, the opinion noted that Alabama, unlike Idaho, has no statute like that quoted in footnote 1, supra. Should this make a difference in the result?

DAVID GRAUBART, INC. v. BANK LEUMI TRUST CO.

Court of Appeals of New York, 1979.
48 N.Y.2d 554, 423 N.Y.S.2d 899, 399 N.E.2d 930.

FUCHSBERG, JUDGE.   On this appeal, here on a question certified by the Appellate Division pursuant to CPLR 5602 (subd. [b], par. 1), we are called upon to determine the role played by article 4 of the Uniform Commercial Code in fixing rights and obligations arising out of a second presentment of a check previously returned for insufficient funds.   The heart issue is whether a payor bank is relieved of liability for retaining such an instrument beyond its "midnight deadline" (see Uniform Commercial Code, § 4–302) when it does so pursuant to an agreement concordant with a practice among banks for a payor to hold a previously dishonored item long enough to provide an opportunity for sufficient funds to be deposited by the drawer to meet the check.

The operative facts are uncomplicated.   Plaintiff David Graubart, Inc. (payee), was issued a check for $13,000 drawn by the Prins Diamond Company on the latter's account with the defendant Bank Leumi Trust Company (payor bank).   Graubart then deposited the check in its own account with the National Bank of North America (depositary bank), which, pursuing normal collection channels, routed it to the payor bank via the New York Clearing House.[1]   When the payor bank found that the Prins account had been overdrawn, it marked the item "insufficient funds" and promptly returned it to the depositary bank, again through clearing house channels.   Notified of the dishonor, the payee redeposited the check with its bank, which this time apparently chose to forward it directly to Leumi on a collection basis, thus bypassing the clearing house (see Uniform Commercial Code, § 4–204, subd. [2], par. [a]).   The item was accompanied by an "advice to customer" slip—a copy of which was also delivered to Graubart—indicating, as with collection items generally, that credit would only be given on payment.   In addition, in a space bearing the printed legend "Special Instruction: (Return immediately if not paid unless otherwise instructed)", the slip contained a typed direction that the payor bank was to "remit [its] cashiers' *[sic]* check when paid" (cf. Uniform Commercial Code, § 4–211, subd. [1], par. [b]).   But when, after no more than seven banking days, the drawer's account remained bare of funds to permit the check to clear, Leumi again returned the check to the depositary bank.   Sometime during the course of these transactions the drawer made an assignment for the benefit of creditors.

1. A clearing house, of course, is a facility for transferring checks and other items to and from depositary banks and payor banks and for settling the balances due among them as a result of such transactions (see 8 Michie, Banks and Banking, ch. 18, § 1, p. 331, and n. 1).

The gravamen of the fourth cause of action [2] in the suit the payee thereafter commenced against Leumi, as well as of its subsequent motion for summary judgment, was that the latter's failure to return the resubmitted check to the depositary bank before its "midnight deadline"—defined as midnight of the next banking day following that on which the item was received (Uniform Commercial Code, § 4–104, subd. [1], par. [h])—without more, rendered it liable to the payee for the face amount of the check under subdivision (a) of section 4–302 of the Uniform Commercial Code. This section, with seeming finality, provides, in pertinent part, that "if an item is presented on and received by a payor bank the bank is accountable [3] for the amount of . . . a demand item . . . if the bank . . . retains the item beyond midnight of the bank day of receipt without settling for it or . . . does not pay or return the item or send notice of dishonor until after its midnight deadline".

In opposition, and in support of its own cross motion, the payor bank submitted an affidavit by its assistant vice-president, who, after setting out his knowledge of banking practice, asserted that the "advice to customer" slip constituted a memorandum of an agreement requiring it to process the instrument in question in accordance with a common banking practice whereunder previously dishonored checks were to be held for such time as is reasonable under all the circumstances, even beyond the midnight deadline if necessary, to enable funds from which to pay them to come into the account. To this the payee's only reply was in the form of counsel's affirmation. Aside from a bald assertion, for which no foundation was supplied, challenging the existence of the custom, the affirmation merely interjected, for the first time, unsupported allegations of bad faith and collusion on Leumi's part. Though it stated that the drawer was indebted to Leumi at the time of the assignment for the benefit of creditors, it made no showing of any unfair conduct on the part of the payor bank whatsoever.

Special Term denied both motions, holding that triable issues existed, and the Appellate Division, over a vigorous dissent by Mr. Justice Joseph P. Sullivan, has since affirmed. In thereafter granting leave to appeal to this court, it posed the very broad question: "Was the order of the Supreme Court, as affirmed by this Court, properly made?" For the reasons that follow, we conclude a negative response is mandated.

The payor bank's assault on the conclusion of the courts below is grounded on the contention that there were no factual issues precluding summary judgment and that, on the undisputed facts, its actions

2. The other causes of action in the payee's complaint challenged the timeliness of the payor bank's action in processing the check upon its initial deposit. These claims have been dismissed and are not before us on this appeal.

3. (I.e., liable, Rock Is. Auction Sales v. Empire Packing Co., 32 Ill.2d 269, 204 N.E.2d 721; Sun Riv. Cattle Co. v. Miners Bank, 164 Mont. 237, 521 P.2d 679.)

were proper as a matter of law for two reasons: (1) on the authority of Leaderbrand v. Central State Bank, 202 Kan. 450, 450 P.2d 1, it need not have given the payee notice of dishonor upon representment of the previously dishonored item, and (2) its conduct in varying the code's midnight deadline pursuant to a valid agreement which accords with custom and usage in the banking community relieves it of the effect of the provisions of article 4 (citing, *inter alia*, Uniform Commercial Code, § 4–103).

The preliminary dispute as to the existence of unresolved questions of fact need not detain us. The date of the contested transactions and the nonadherence to the midnight deadline, if applicable, were conceded for the purposes of the motion. The payor bank's officer established the custom as to collection of previously dishonored checks, and the payee's own submission of the "advice to customer" slip confirmed that the agreement had been made in contemplation of the custom. And, since Graubart's counsel's affirmation was made without personal knowledge of the facts, it was not competent to defeat the motion for summary judgment (Rotuba Extruders v. Ceppos, 46 N.Y.2d 223, 229, n. 4, 413 N.Y.S.2d 141, 144, 385 N.E.2d 1068, 1071; Columbia Ribbon & Carbon Mfg. Co. v. A–1–A Corp., 42 N.Y.2d 496, 500, 398 N.Y.S.2d 1004, 1007, 369 N.E.2d 4, 7; CPLR 3212, subd. [b]; see, generally, Mallad Constr. Corp. v. County Fed. Sav. & Loan Assn., 32 N.Y.2d 285, 292–293, 344 N.Y.S.2d 925, 931–932, 298 N.E.2d 96, 100–101). Leumi's recitations therefore went undisputed.

Turning to the legal merits, we conclude first that Leumi's reliance on Leaderbrand v. Central State Bank, 202 Kan. 450, 450 P.2d 1, supra, which held that no notice of dishonor need be given as to an item previously returned for insufficient funds, is unavailing. The *Leaderbrand* court reasoned that subdivision (4) of section 3–511 of the code, in excusing further notice of dishonor with respect to "drafts" once dishonored by "nonacceptance", necessarily encompassed dishonor of "checks" by "nonpayment". But, while a check is a kind of draft (Uniform Commercial Code, § 3–104, subd. [2], par. [b]), "nonpayment" and "nonacceptance" are distinctly different concepts, the latter referring specifically to a payor's refusal to certify that it will honor a *time* instrument when later presented for payment (Uniform Commercial Code, § 3–410, subd. 1; see Wiley v. Peoples Bank & Trust Co., 438 F.2d 513, 516–517 (5th Cir.); Comment, 18 Kan.L.Rev. 679, 682–684, n. 48). Since it would be futile to present for payment a draft that has been dishonored by nonacceptance (when the obligation is conditioned on acceptance [see Uniform Commercial Code, § 3–501, subd. (1), par. (a)]), such presentment and further notice are excused as superfluous. In contrast, a *demand* item such as a check may eventually be paid if resubmitted at a time when the drawer's account has an adequate balance. This possibility makes it entirely reasonable to afford redeposited checks the full panoply of article 4 protections. (See, generally, Clark & Squillante, Law of Bank Deposits, Collections and Credit Cards [1970], pp. 71–72.)

Though its *Leaderbrand* point is, therefore, without merit, Leumi's argument that its retention of the check beyond its midnight deadline was consonant with its agreement with the depositary bank is another matter. In this connection, initially we note that section 4–301 of the code, which establishes the procedural rules enforced by section 4–302, nowhere suggests that the deadline does not apply to previously dishonored items. But, it is well recognized that the code's requirements can be modified by agreement to conform them with commercial usage, in or out of banking circles, so that parties may advantage themselves of the "wisdom born of accumulated experience" (Bankers Trust Co. v. Dowler & Co., 47 N.Y.2d 128, 134, 417 N.Y.S.2d 47, 50–51, 390 N.E.2d 766, 769).[4] [The court quoted UCC 4–103(1), (4).]

The concept of an "agreement" under the code is, as with contract law generally, broad enough to permit the written terms of a memorandum to be supplemented and clarified by reference to customs and usages in the commercial milieu in which it is to be performed (e.g., Uniform Commercial Code, § 1–201, subd. [3]; § 1–205; 3 Corbin, Contracts [1960 ed.], § 556; Walls v. Bailey, 49 N.Y. 464). But the bare fact that the payor bank acted in accordance with its agreement with the depositary bank does not, in and by itself, relieve the former of liability (Official Comment, McKinney's Cons. Laws of N.Y., Book 62½, part 2, Uniform Commercial Code, § 4–203, p. 555). Section 4–103 demands that every party sought to be bound—here the payee—have assented to the agreement's terms (Official Comment 2, op. cit., Uniform Commercial Code, § 4–103, pp. 519–520). However, we hold that here there was such consent.

Under section 4–201 of the code, a payee's presentment of an item to a depositary bank for collection creates a principal-agent relationship between the two, a status that persists until final settlement (see Official Comment 4, op. cit., Uniform Commercial Code, § 4–201, pp. 544–545). Graubart's voluntary establishment of its bank's authority constitutes an assent to the latter's dealing with the check in the manner customary in the banking industry (see Restatement, Agency 2d, § 36).[5] To the extent that a payee deems itself aggrieved by a depositary bank's ignoring of limitations on its authority, of which none are claimed here, the law provides recourse against it, but not

4. As the Official Comments explain: "In view of the technical complexity of the field of bank collections, the enormous number of items handled by banks, the certainty that there will be variations from the normal in each day's work in each bank, the certainty of changing conditions and the possibility of developing improved methods of collection to speed the process, it would be unwise to freeze present methods of operation by mandatory statutory rules" (Official Comment 1, McKinney's Cons. Laws of N.Y., Book 62½, part 2, Uniform Commercial Code, § 4–103, p. 519).

5. The payee's second presentment of the check for payment was with full knowledge that its previous rejection was for insufficiency of the drawer's balance.

against a third party who relies on the agent's apparent authority.
. . .

   As to good faith and ordinary care, neither of these is a serious
obstacle in the circumstances of this case. The payee's complaint alleges no bad faith or favoritism on the part of the payor bank, and
the mere fact that the drawer was indebted to Leumi when it assigned for the benefit of creditors does not permit us to presume collusion in the absence of specific evidence. Moreover, beyond the su-
perficial sense in which ordinary care is relevant to virtually every
step in the collection process (see Uniform Commercial Code, § 4–202,
subd. [1]), this standard was not intended to prohibit banking procedures that themselves are reasonable and carried out with care.
. . .

   Further, in this case the reasonableness of the suspension of the
midnight deadline is demonstrated by an examination of the underlying purpose of the rule. Far from merely encouraging banks to process deposited instruments promptly, the deadline plays the central
role in "firming up" the provisional credit received by each transferor
in the payee—depositary bank— intermediary bank[6] chain. Under
section 4–213 of the code, provisional credits become final as soon as
the payor bank settles for the item and the time for revocation under
the midnight deadline passes. This point is particularly critical for
banks that funnel hundreds or thousands of checks per day into the
collection stream because it enables them to assume that payment
has been effectuated after a certain period of time unless there is a
prompt return. (See, generally, Blake v. Woodford Bank & Trust
Co., 555 S.W.2d 589, 600–601 [Ky.App.]; Official Comments 7–11, op.
cit., Uniform Commercial Code, § 4–213, pp. 591–593.)

   These concerns, however, are irrelevant to any evaluation of the
custom followed under the agreement between the banks here. It
creates no provisional credits that must be firmed up, and the payee
can only collect when the payor bank remits its cashier's check, thus
signifying that the drawer's account received sufficient funds to cover the check. By its nature, the procedure singles out the item as an
exceptional one; no transferor will assume it has been paid until specific notice is received.

   Moreover, the concept of a midnight deadline is not compatible
with any approach under which the payor bank seeks to wait for the
deposit of funds in the drawer's account. The reasonableness of such
a banking custom must, therefore, be measured on its own terms.
We conclude that this criterion is met when a depositary bank takes a
possibly worthless instrument and directs the payor bank to adopt a
technique that may provide the only chance for collection.[7]

   6. In some collection transactions convenience dictates that checks pass
through so-called "intermediary banks"
in addition to or instead of a clearing
house before being forwarded to the pay-
or bank (see Uniform Commercial Code,
§ 4–105, subd. [c]).

   7. Other than that the payor bank,
permissibly, as we have demonstrated,

There is nothing unfair about this procedure. It is calculated to produce satisfied obligations in many instances where legal recourse, with all its attendant expense, inconvenience and uncertainty, would otherwise be necessary. Furthermore, the payee here cannot claim it was injured by its reliance on the payor bank's silence after receipt of the item; the prior dishonor provided adequate warning of the questionable safety of the instrument. In any event, the payee's right to sue the drawer on the underlying obligation was revived upon the first dishonor, and representment in no way cut short that prerogative (Uniform Commercial Code, § 3–802, subd. [1], par. [b]; § 4–301, subd. [3]; Blake v. Woodford Bank & Trust Co., supra, pp. 598–599).

We therefore hold that the payor bank's adherence to the depositary bank's instructions for processing the drawer's check does not render it liable to the payee under section 4–302. Accordingly, the certified question should be answered in the negative, the order of the Appellate Division reversed, and summary judgment granted in the defendant's favor on the fourth cause of action.

NOTES

(1) **Conflicting Views.** The Leaderbrand case, discussed and rejected in David Graubart, represents a minority view. For support of Leaderbrand and criticism of David Graubart, see Leary & Schmitt, Some Bad News and Some Good News from Articles Three and Four, 43 Ohio St. L.J. 611, 624–32 (1982).

UNPC 420 adds a special seven-day midnight deadline for resubmitted checks and other orders, on the theory that the only hope for payment is for the payor to hold the order for longer than the usual time.

(2) **Variation by Agreement.** In Idaho Forest Industries v. Minden Exchange Bank & Trust Co., 212 Neb. 820, 326 N.W.2d 176 (1982), the depositary bank represented checks by mailing them directly to the drawee bank with a transmittal letter that stated "Hold 10 days if necessary." The court followed the Graubart case on the ground that the midnight deadline had been varied by an agreement "that the checks were to be held for collection by the defendant for a reasonable time until funds became available."

Is there any limit on the power of banks to vary the midnight deadline by agreement? Is the power limited to the situation of representment? Could banks by a clearinghouse rule agree that checks could be returned after the midnight deadline? See UCC 4–302 and 4–103(1) and (2), and recall the history of the midnight deadline recounted at p. 161 supra. Cf. Catalina Yachts v. Old Colony Bank & Trust Co., 497 F.Supp. 1227 (D.Mass.1980) (agreement that "receipt" occurred when drawee bank had actual receipt of check and did not feel bound by the deadline, the payee pointed to no facts indicating that the check was held for an unreasonable length of time.

not when check was received by off-premises processing center was "mere definition of what action constitutes receipt").

Problem 12. Philadelphia National, after giving Quaker a provisional credit, negligently mislays the check and does not forward it for three days. It is dishonored because Empire has become insolvent during the delay. Philadelphia National returns the check to Quaker and revokes the credit. Quaker disputes Philadelphia National's right to do this, arguing that the Empire check would have been paid if Philadelphia National had used due care. Quaker draws checks against the disputed $2,178.50 credit which Philadelphia National marks "N.S.F." and dishonors. Quaker sues Philadelphia National for wrongful dishonor. What result? See UCC 4–103(5), 4–202, 4–212(4) and Comment 5.

Problem 13. Philadelphia National and Irving Trust use a system of electronic processing of checks in which the depositary bank "encodes" the amount of the check in a third "field" on the bottom right hand corner of the check, so that it can be "read" by a machine at the drawee bank. (Compare Forms 2 and 2B pp. 96, 98 supra.) Philadelphia National mistakenly encodes the Empire check as a $3,178.50 check, and it is paid in that amount by the Irving Trust. Shortly thereafter, Irving Trust dishonors several other checks drawn by Empire which would have been honored had the mistaken overpayment not been made. What are the rights of Empire and Irving Trust? See J. Clarke, H. Bailey and R. Young, Bank Deposits and Collections 147–49 (4th ed. 1972), where the authors state: "It would seem unlikely that the payor bank that had dishonored an over-encoded item, which if correctly encoded would have been paid, could recover damages arising out of the wrongful dishonor from the encoding bank in such circumstances, for presumably the payor bank would have had the 'last clear chance' to examine the item about to be returned and to discover the error." Does the doctrine of "last clear chance" apply to our problem? Could the banks involved allocate the risk by contract? See also H. Bailey, Brady on Bank Checks § 15.26 (5th ed. 1979).

Problem 14. A few hours after Irving Trust has paid the Empire check and before Philadelphia National has received any advice of credit, a $5,000 check drawn by Quaker is presented to Philadelphia National for payment. Quaker has in its account, exclusive of the $2,178.50 credit from the Empire check, only $4,000. Philadelphia National dishonors the $5,000 check and returns it to the payee with a return item ticket marked "uncollected funds." Can Quaker recover from Philadelphia National for wrongful dishonor? See UCC 4–213(4).[1]

---

1. Note that UCC 4–213(4)(a) gives the bank "a reasonable time to learn that the settlement is final" and that UCC 1–204(1) provides that whenever the Code "requires any action to be taken within a reasonable time, any time which is not manifestly unreasonable may be fixed by agreement." Could a bank effectively provide that the proceeds of checks drawn on other banks are not available to

the depositor for six business days in the case of local checks and fifteen business days in the case of nonlocal checks? Such a provision was upheld in Rapp v. Dime Savings Bank, 48 N.Y.2d 658, 421 N.Y.S.2d 347, 396 N.E.2d 740 (1979), affirming 64 A.D.2d 964, 408 N.Y.S.2d 540 (1978). For state legislation curtailing such provisions, see Cal.Fin.Code §§ 866–866.9; N.Y. Banking Law § 14–d.

The concerns of banks are dramatized by Northpark National Bank v. Bankers Trust Co., 572 F.Supp. 524 (S.D.N.Y. 1983), in which a malefactor put into the collection process a $62,500 check fraudulently printed with the name of a fictitious drawee, the "Bank of Detroit," and the MICR number of Bankers Trust in New York. The check was shunted around and the fraud was not discovered until the 14-day "hold" had expired and the malefactor had been allowed to withdraw most of the amount of the check.

Chapter 4

COUNTERMANDED CHECKS

Introduction. Some of the most troublesome problems concerning checks result from attempts by drawers to stop payment. Suppose, for example, that Buyer as drawer has issued a check to Seller as payee in payment for goods, and then discovers that Seller has breached a warranty and the goods are defective. As has already been observed, since a check is not of itself an assignment, Buyer as drawer retains the power to countermand the order to the drawee bank. But if the check is dishonored as a result of a stop order, Buyer will still be subject to suit as drawer of the instrument. Buyer may, however, set up by way of defense the breach of warranty that prompted the stop order. Should the check still be in the hands of Seller, the payee, this defense is, of course, good against Seller (UCC 3–306). Should the check have come into the hands of another, however, Buyer may be met with the claim that the instrument has been negotiated to a holder in due course against whom the defense is unavailable. The first section of this chapter takes up three aspects of this problem: first, when is there a negotiation; second, what are the requirements of holding in due course; and third, which are the real defenses, good even as against a holder in due course, and which the personal defenses, no good against a holder in due course? The second section considers the problems that arise when a bank mistakenly pays a check in violation of a stop order, including fixing the points in time at which a check has been paid and at which it is too late for the drawer to stop payment. The third section considers the assertion of an adverse claim as an alternative to stopping payment.

SECTION 1. LIABILITY OF DRAWER TO HOLDER
ON DISHONOR

(A) NEGOTIATION

Prefatory Note. The Code, in UCC 3–201, distinguishes between transfer and negotiation. Although the transferee acquires "such rights as the transferor has," a mere transferee cannot qualify as a holder in due course. According to UCC 3–202(1), "If the instrument is payable to order it is negotiated by delivery with any necessary indorsement; if payable to bearer it is negotiated by delivery." Most of the difficulties arise in connection with negotiation of order paper.

182

132/00 10-78

STOP PAYMENT ORDER

IRVING TRUST COMPANY
NEW YORK, N. Y.

DATE   January 18, 1984

A/C NO   26-965-143

GENTLEMEN:

   ☒ CHECK
   ☐ DRAFT
   ☐ NOTE
   ☐ ACCEPTANCE

PLEASE STOP PAYMENT ON

DESCRIBED BELOW WHICH HAS NOT BEEN RETURNED WITH STATEMENTS OF ACCOUNT:

NUMBER	DATE	TO THE ORDER OF	AMOUNT
109	1/16/84	Quaker Manufacturing Co.	$2,178.50

Empire Enterprises Co.

(TITLE OF ACCOUNT)

Stacey Smith

(AUTHORIZED SIGNATURE OF DEPOSITOR)

[D621]

DEPOSITOR PLEASE NOTE

THIS ORDER IS EFFECTIVE FOR ONLY SIX MONTHS AFTER ABOVE DATE
UNLESS RENEWED IN WRITING.

IF A NEW INSTRUMENT IS ISSUED. PLEASE DO NOT USE THE SAME DATE
AND NUMBER.

SHOULD THE ORIGINAL ITEM BE LOCATED AND DESTROYED BY YOU.
PLEASE INSTRUCT US TO CANCEL THIS STOP PAYMENT ORDER.

THIS ORDER IS INEFFECTIVE IF THE ITEM WAS NEGOTIATED THROUGH
THE USE OF A CHECK GUARANTEE CARD.

STOP ORDER

Problem 1. Instead of depositing the Empire check in its account for collection, Quaker asks Philadelphia National to "cash" it, and Philadelphia National pays Quaker $2,178.50 in cash. Quaker, however, neglects to indorse the check and the Philadelphia National does not notice this. The check is then dishonored by Irving Trust because Empire has stopped payment. Empire stopped payment on discovering that the cans are defective and on justifiably refusing to take and pay for them. Quaker is now insolvent. Can Philadelphia National recover the $2,178.50 from Empire? See UCC 3–201, 3–202, 4–205; Bowling Green v. State Street Bank and Trust, infra.

Problem 2. Instead of depositing the Empire check in its account for collection, Quaker asks Philadelphia National to "cash" it. Philadelphia National is willing to do so, but notices that Empire, evidently by an oversight, has made it payable to "Quaker Supply Co." How should Philadelphia National have Quaker indorse it if it cashes it? Does it take any risk if Quaker so indorses it? See UCC 3–203.

BOWLING GREEN, INC. v. STATE STREET BANK AND TRUST CO.

United States Court of Appeals, First Circuit, 1970.
425 F.2d 81.

COFFIN, CIRCUIT JUDGE. On September 26, 1966, plaintiff Bowling Green, Inc., the operator of a bowling alley, negotiated a United States government check for $15,306 to Bowl-Mor, Inc., a manufacturer of bowling alley equipment. The check, which plaintiff had acquired through a Small Business Administration loan, represented the first installment on a conditional sales contract for the purchase of candlepin setting machines. On the following day, September 27, a representative of Bowl-Mor deposited the check in defendant State Street Bank and Trust Co. The Bank immediately credited $5,024.85 of the check against an overdraft in Bowl-Mor's account. Later that day, when the Bank learned that Bowl-Mor had filed a petition for reorganization under Chapter X of the Bankruptcy Act, it transferred $233.61 of Bowl-Mor's funds to another account and applied the remaining $10,047.54 against debts which Bowl-Mor owed the Bank. Shortly thereafter, Bowl-Mor's petition for reorganization was dismissed and the firm was adjudicated a bankrupt. Plaintiff has never received the pin-setting machines for which it contracted. Its part payment remains in the hands of defendant Bank.

Plaintiff brought this diversity action to recover its payment from defendant Bank on the grounds that the Bank is constructive trustee of the funds deposited by Bowl-Mor. In the court below, plaintiff argued that Bowl-Mor knew it could not perform at the time it accepted payment, that the Bank was aware of this fraudulent conduct, and that the Bank therefore received Bowl-Mor's deposit impressed with a constructive trust in plaintiff's favor. The district court rejected plaintiff's view of the evidence, concluding instead that the Bank was a holder in due course within the meaning of Mass.Gen.Laws Ann. c. 106 §§ 4–209 and 3–302, and was therefore entitled to take the item in question free of all personal defenses. Bowling Green, Inc., etc. v. State Street Bank and Trust Co., 307 F.Supp. 648 (D.Mass.1969).

Plaintiff's appeal challenges the conclusion of the district court in three respects. First, plaintiff maintains that the Bank has not met its burden of establishing that it was "holder" of the item within the meaning of Mass.Gen.Laws Ann. c. 106 § 1–201(20), and thus cannot be a "holder in due course" within the meaning of § 4–209 and § 3–302. Second, plaintiff argues that the Bank's close working relation with Bowl-Mor prevented it from becoming a holder in good faith. Finally, plaintiff denies that defendant gave value within the meaning of § 4–209 for the $10,047.54 which it set off against Bowl-Mor's loan account.

Plaintiff's first objection arises from a technical failure of proof. The district court found that plaintiff had endorsed the item in question to Bowl–Mor, but there was no evidence that Bowl-Mor supplied its own endorsement before depositing the item in the Bank. Thus we cannot tell whether the Bank is a holder within the meaning of § 1–201(20), which defines holder as one who takes an instrument endorsed to him, or to bearer, or in blank. But, argues plaintiff, once it is shown that a defense to an instrument exists, the Bank has the burden of showing that it is in all respects a holder in due course. This failure of proof, in plaintiff's eyes, is fatal to the Bank's case.

We readily agree with plaintiff that the Bank has the burden of establishing its status in all respects. Mass.Gen.Laws Ann. c. 106 § 3–307(3), on which plaintiff relies to establish the defendant's burden, seems addressed primarily to cases in which a holder seeks to enforce an instrument, but Massachusetts courts have indicated that the policy of § 3–307(3) applies whenever a party invokes the rights of a holder in due course either offensively or defensively. Cf. Elbar Realty Inc. v. City Bank & Trust Co., 342 Mass. 262, 267–268, 173 N.E.2d 256 (1961). The issue, however, is not whether the Bank bears the burden of proof, but whether it must establish that it took the item in question by endorsement in order to meet its burden. We think not. The evidence in this case indicates that the Bank's transferor, Bowl-Mor, was a holder. Under Mass.Gen.Laws Ann. c. 106, § 3–201(1), transfer of an instrument vests in the transferee all the rights of the transferor. As the Official Comment to § 3–201 indicates, one who is not a holder must first establish the transaction by which he acquired the instrument before enforcing it, but the Bank has met this burden here.

We doubt, moreover, whether the concept of "holder" as defined in § 1–201(20) applies with full force to Article 4. Article 4 establishes a comprehensive scheme for simplifying and expediting bank collections. Its provisions govern the more general rules of Article 3 wherever inconsistent. Mass.Gen.Laws Ann. c. 106 § 4–102(1). As part of this expediting process, Article 4 recognizes the common bank practice of accepting unendorsed checks for deposit. *See* Funk, Banks and the UCC 133 (1964). § 4–201(1) provides that the lack of an endorsement shall not affect the bank's status as agent for collection, and § 4–205(1) authorizes the collecting bank to supply the missing endorsements as a matter of course.[1] In practice, banks comply with § 4–205 by stamping the item "deposited to the account of the named payee" or some similar formula. Funk, supra at 133. We doubt whether the bank's status should turn on proof of whether a clerk employed the appropriate stamp, and we hesitate to penalize a bank which accepted unendorsed checks for deposit in reliance on the Code, at least when, as here, the customer himself clearly satisfies the definition of "holder". Section 4–209 does provide that a bank must comply "with the requirements of section 3–302 on what constitutes a holder in due course," but we think this language refers to the enumerated requirements of good faith and lack of notice rather than to the status of holder, a status which § 3–302 assumes rather than requires. We therefore hold that a bank which takes an item for collection from a customer who was himself a holder need not establish that it took the item by negotiation in order to satisfy § 4–209.

[The rest of the opinion in this case, dealing with plaintiff's remaining two objections, is at p. 194 infra.]

NOTES

(1) **Criticism of Bowling Green Case.** Reaction to the Bowling Green case, on the indorsement issue, has been largely negative. With respect to the reading of UCC 4–205(1), one court wrote: "Nothing in this section or the comments indicates that a depository bank need not comply with endorsement requirements incident to the negotiation of 'order' paper if it seeks to be a holder. The purpose of the section is to permit the bank, in the interest of expediency . . . ., to supply what the bank could have required the customer to supply initially. Had § 4–205(1) been intended to eliminate the need for an endorsement . . . ., it would have been a simple matter for the drafters of the code to have [so] provided . . . ." United Overseas Bank v. Veneers, Inc., 375 F.Supp. 596 (D.Md.1973). See also Marine Midland Bank v. Price, Miller, Evans & Flowers, 57 N.Y.2d 220, 455 N.Y.S.2d 565, 441 N.E.2d 1083 (1982). With respect to the reading of UCC 3–201(1), another court wrote: "If the Bowling Green court in-

---

1. See also § 4–105(a), which defines "depositary bank" in terms of transfer rather than negotiation, and § 4–206, which speaks of transfer between banks. For the difference between transfer and negotiation, compare § 3–201 with § 3–202(1).

tended to say that a transfer by a holder without indorsement gives the transferee the status of a holder, that statement is irreconcilable with the language of section 3201 . . .." Security Pacific National Bank v. Chess, 58 Cal.App.3d 555, 129 Cal.Rptr. 852 (1976). For more criticism, see Note, 12 B.C.Ind. & Com.L.Rev. 282 (1970); Comment, 71 Colum.L.Rev. 302 (1971); Comment 59 Geo.L.J. 1379 (1971).

(2) Utility of Indorsements. In 1957 Parliament enacted the Cheques Act, which had as its principal objective elimination of the necessity for British banks to examine indorsements. It was found that over ninety-five per cent of the 800 million checks processed by British banks each year were deposited to the payees' accounts for collection through banking channels. Banks and commercial customers objected to the expense and inconvenience in indorsing and examining these checks. For a discussion of the British legislation see 71 Harv.L.Rev. 1374 (1958), and for its effect, see Perry, The Cheques Act 1957—The Experience of the Banks, 1967 J.Bus.Law 107.

In view of the decision in the Bowling Green case, why should the payee who deposits a check for collection in an American bank account have to take the trouble to indorse it, or the depositary bank to examine the indorsement? Would not payment to the payee's representative discharge the drawee whether the payee had indorsed or not? See UCC 3–603, 3–505. If the drawer wanted the payee's indorsement as a receipt, could not he indicate this on the check? Note also that the Code, in UCC 4–206, permits a substantial economy in indorsements between banks and sanctions the use of an identifying number or symbol in lieu of a full indorsement.

(3) Special Indorsement of Bearer Paper. The Code made a major change with respect to the effect of a special indorsement on bearer paper. The rule at common law was "once bearer paper always bearer paper." This rule was applied when a special indorsement was put on an instrument that was either (1) issued payable to bearer or (2) issued payable to order and later indorsed in blank. The subsequent special indorsement did not convert the instrument to an order instrument in either case.

It was commonly supposed that the Negotiable Instruments Law had the effect of changing the result in the second case but not the first case. In other words, a special indorsement still had no effect on an instrument issued payable to bearer.

The Code reverses the common law rule in both cases. Under UCC 3–204(1), "*Any* instrument specially indorsed becomes payable to the order of the special indorsee and may be further negotiated only by his indorsement."

(B) HOLDING IN DUE COURSE

Prefatory Note. In order to qualify as a holder in due course, a holder must satisfy the tests of UCC 3–302. The holder must have taken "in good faith," "without notice that it is overdue or has been dishonored or of any defense against or claim to it on the part of any person," and "for value." The following materials examine these requirements, in relation to checks.

Problem 3. If in Problem 1, p. 184 supra, Quaker indorses the check in such a way that Philadelphia National is a holder and has Philadelphia National cash it, can Philadelphia National recover the $2,178.50 from Empire? See UCC 3–302, 1–201(19). Would it make a difference if Empire can prove that it is highly unusual for banks in the Philadelphia area to cash a check for such a large amount? Would it make a difference if the assistant cashier of the Philadelphia National telephones a vice president of Irving Trust before cashing the Empire check and is assured that the check is "good" and that Irving Trust has had no problems with Empire's checks in the past? See Industrial National Commercial Bank v. Leo's Used Car Exchange, infra; Bowling Green v. State Street Bank & Trust, infra; McCook County National Bank v. Compton, 558 F.2d 871 (8th Cir.), cert. denied, 434 U.S. 905, 98 S.Ct. 302, 54 L.Ed.2d 191 (1977). Would it make a difference if the assistant cashier is told that Empire's balance in Irving Trust is too low to cover the check? See Vail National Bank v. J. Wheeler Construction Corp., 669 P.2d 1038 (Colo.App. 1983). Who has the burden of proof on the issue of "good faith"? See UCC 3–307, 1–201(8).

Problem 4. Assuming that the facts in the preceding problem are such that Philadelphia National takes in good faith, would it make any difference if Quaker does not have Philadelphia National cash the check until six weeks after its issue? See UCC 3–302, 3–304(3)(c).

INDUSTRIAL NATIONAL BANK v. LEO'S USED CAR EXCHANGE

Supreme Judicial Court of Massachusetts, 1973.
362 Mass. 797, 291 N.E.2d 603.

HENNESSEY, JUSTICE. This is an action in contract in which the plaintiff seeks to recover on two checks drawn by the defendant on the Security National Bank, one in the amount of $9,650 payable to Villa's Auto Sales, Inc., and the other in the amount of $5,500 payable to Villa's Auto Sales. The District Court judge found for the defendant, and the report to the Appellate Division was dismissed. The case is before us on appeal by the plaintiff.

We summarize the relevant evidence. On October 9, 1968, an agent of the defendant attended a car auction in the State of Connecticut, and purchased three cars from Frederick Villa, for which he gave the two checks described above. The defendant subsequently resold the cars at a profit.

Frederick Villa was a customer of the plaintiff bank and had a corporate account there under the name of Villa Auto Sales, Inc. The manager of the Centerville Branch of the plaintiff bank in Providence, Rhode Island, was personally acquainted with Frederick Villa. Corporate authority stating that Frederick Villa was the president and treasurer of Villa Auto Sales, Inc., and that he was authorized to sign or indorse any check held by the corporation, was on file with the bank.[1]

Frederick Villa presented both checks to the plaintiff bank on October 10, 1968, and as was his practice, asked the teller to cash them and give him the cash since he was going to another auction and needed it. The checks were cashed and sent through the bank collection process. Meanwhile, the defendant stopped payment on the checks at the Security National Bank in Springfield, Massachusetts, following a telephone call from an officer of the Rhode Island Hospital Trust Company which claimed to hold security interests in the cars he purchased. Consequently, the checks were not honored when presented, and were returned to the plaintiff bank.

There was also evidence of a rule at the plaintiff bank that any corporate checks drawn on another bank must be approved by the manager before being cashed by a teller. In this case, the teller did not obtain the manager's approval before he cashed both checks. However, the manager would cash a check for a corporation if he knew the person cashing the check and knew his business.

The plaintiff requested, among others, a ruling that there was no evidence that in cashing both checks it did not act in good faith.

---

1. The material provisions of this authority are as follows:

"Voted: That the President-Vice President-Treasurer or Secretary of this Corporation, signing singly and their successors in office, be and they hereby are authorized to sign, endorse or deposit on behalf of this Corporation, any and all checks drawn or held by this Corporation, and the use is hereby authorized of a rubber stamp endorsement on any check the proceeds of which are credited to any account of this Corporation with the Bank.

"Voted: That the Bank is hereby directed to pay or apply without limit as to amount, without inquiry and without regard to the application of the proceeds thereof, any or all checks of this Corporation when signed by the personnel set forth in the preceding vote and in the manner specified therein, including any such check drawn to the individual order of any person whose signature appears thereon or of any officer or officers, agent or agents, of this Corporation, which may be deposited with, or delivered or transferred to, the Bank, or any other individual, firm or corporation for the personal credit or account of any such person, officer or agent; and the Bank shall not be liable for any disposition which any such person, officer or agent shall make of all or any part of the proceeds of any such check, notwithstanding that such disposition may be for the personal account or benefit or in payment of the individual obligation to the Bank of any such person, officer or agent."

While the District Court judge found that the plaintiff met all the other requirements to qualify as a holder in due course, he denied this request and therefore found that the plaintiff was not a holder in due course of either check. The report to the Appellate Division was dismissed. The plaintiff claims an appeal on the basis that there was no evidence to support the District Court judge's finding of lack of good faith.

1. We first determine which State's law applies. The Appellate Division held that since the checks were negotiated in Rhode Island, its law should apply. See Restatement 2d: Conflict of Laws, § 216(2). This was erroneous. Conflict of law problems arising under the Uniform Commercial Code are resolved by the Code. The rule is stated in G.L. c. 106, § 1–105.[2] Since no special provision for Article three—Commercial Paper—is contained in paragraph (2) of § 1–105, paragraph (1) applies to this case. G.L. c. 106, § 3–102(4). Since there is no evidence that the parties agreed that a particular State's[3] law would apply, and since the transaction bears an appropriate relation to this State, Massachusetts law applies. G.L. c. 106, § 1–105(1).

2. A holder in due course is a holder who takes the instrument for value, in good faith, and without notice that it is overdue or has been dishonored or of any defense against or claim to it on the part of any person. G.L. c. 106, § 3–302(1). To the extent that a holder is a holder in due course he takes the instrument free from all claims to it on the part of any person, and all defences of any party to the instrument with whom the holder has not dealt (personal defences) except specifically enumerated "real defences," G.L. c. 106, § 3–305.

The District Court judge found that the plaintiff was a holder who took the checks for value, and without notice that they had been dishonored or of any defence against or claim to the checks on the part of any person. However, the judge found that the checks were not taken in good faith, and therefore the plaintiff was not a holder in due course. Since the judge also found that a defence existed, he found for the defendant. See G.L. c. 106, § 3–306. The only substantive issue before us is whether or not the evidence supports the finding of the judge that the plaintiff did not take the checks in good faith. If it is found that the plaintiff did take the checks in good faith, it is clear that it is entitled to judgment in its favor in the ab-

2. Section 1–105, inserted by St.1957, c. 765, § 1, reads in part: "(1) Except as provided hereafter in this section, when a transaction bears a reasonable relation to this state and also to another state or nation the parties may agree that the law either of this state or of such other state or nation shall govern their rights and duties. Failing such agreement this chapter applies to transactions bearing an appropriate relation to this state."

3. Since the parties could have selected any State to which the transaction bore a reasonable relation, Rhode Island, Connecticut or Massachusetts could have been eligible. G.L. c. 106, § 1–105(1). Since all three States have adopted the Uniform Commercial Code, § 3–302, any choice may have had little consequence. See G.L. (R.I.1956), § 6A–3–302, and Conn.Gen.Sts.Ann. § 42a–3–302 (1962).

sence of real defences.   G.L. c. 106, § 3–305.   No evidence of any real defence appears in the report.

The defendant argues that the plaintiff failed to exercise ordinary care in this transaction by violating the plaintiff's own rule of management when its teller cashed these checks without managerial approval.   The defendant points to this as evidence of lack of good faith, which would support the judge's finding.   Since there is no other evidence in the report which even arguably goes to the issue of good faith, we conclude that there was no evidence to support a finding of lack of good faith, and therefore both the District Court judge and the Appellate Division were in error.

"Good faith" as used in G.L. c. 106, § 3–302(1)(b), is defined in G.L. c. 106, § 1–201(19), as "honesty in fact in the conduct or transaction concerned."   G.L. c. 106, § 3–102(4).   Nothing in the definition suggests that in addition to being honest, the holder must exercise due care to be in good faith.   Where the Uniform Commercial Code has required more than "honesty in fact" it has explicitly so stated: as in the case of a payor in Article 3—Commercial Paper—who pays on an instrument which has been altered or has an unauthorized signature (good faith and in accordance with the reasonable commercial standards of his business) § 3–406; as in the case of a merchant in Article 2—Sales (honesty in fact and the observance of reasonable commercial standards of fair dealing in the trade) § 2–103(1)(b); as in the case of a bailee in Article 7—Documents of Title (good faith including observance of reasonable commercial standards) § 7–404; and as in the case of an agent or bailee in Article 8—Investment Securities (good faith, including observance of reasonable commercial standards if he is in the business of buying, selling or otherwise dealing with securities) § 8–318.   Each word of a statute is presumed to be necessary.   Hence, if good faith as defined by § 1–201(19) and applicable to § 3–302(1)(b) included the observance of due care or reasonable commercial standards, the additional words used in the articles cited above would be surplusage.

This conclusion which is so clear from the Uniform Commercial Code itself, is supported by the legislative history of § 3–302(1)(b).   Reference to "reasonable commercial standards" in the definition of a holder in due course of a negotiable instrument in the 1951 Final Text Edition [4] was deleted by the Editorial Board for the Uniform Commercial Code.   Section 3–302(1)(b) of the 1956 Recommendations and text [5] reads as follows: "in good faith [including observance of the reasonable commercial standards of any business in which the holder may be engaged]."   (P. 102)   As the comment states: "The omission [of the bracketed material] is intended to make clear that the doctrine of an objective standard of good faith, exemplified by the case of Gill v. Cubitt, 3 B. & C. 466 (1824), is not intended to be incorporated in

---

4. Am.Law Inst.Uniform Commercial Code, 1951 Final Text Edition.

5. Am.Law Inst.Uniform Commercial Code, 1956 Recommendations.

Article 3." (P. 103) Our conclusion is also supported by the pre-code case of Macklin v. Macklin, 315 Mass. 451, 455, 53 N.E.2d 86, 88, where we said, "The rights of a holder of a negotiable instrument are to be determined by the simple test of honesty and good faith, and not by a speculative issue as to his diligence or negligence."

This is not to say that negligence has no role in the determination of a holder's status as a holder in due course under § 3–302.[6] But negligence goes to the notice requirement of § 3–302(1)(c), as defined by § 3–304, and § 1–201(25). See also § 3–406. Since the District Court judge found that the plaintiff had no notice of dishonor, defence or claim, and the evidence supports this finding, the defendant's argument that the plaintiff failed to exercise due care is inapposite.

Since the evidence discloses no dishonesty, it does not support the District Court judge's finding that the plaintiff did not act in good faith. The order of the Appellate Division dismissing the report is reversed, the finding on each count for the defendant is vacated, and judgments are to be entered for the plaintiff.

So ordered.

NOTES

(1) **Burden of Proof.** Since the questions of good faith and lack of notice are usually for the trier of the facts, the burden of proof can be of controlling importance, a point that might well cause concern to an out-of-state bank if its case went to a jury. Where did that burden fall in the preceding case under UCC 3–307, 1–201(8)?

(2) **Check Kiting and the Requirements of Good Faith and Lack of Notice.** Interesting questions of good faith and lack of notice may arise as a result of check-kiting schemes. Check kiting is a type of fraud in which the kiter creates a continuous exchange of overdrafts between accounts in at least two banks. Kiting depends on the combination of two circumstances: first, the willingness of depositary banks to allow the kiter immediate credit when he deposits checks drawn on other banks and, second, the period of time between the deposit of those checks and their presentment to the drawees.

The simplest form of check kiting involves only two banks, preferably some distance apart. For example, the kiter opens accounts in X Bank and in Y Bank by depositing $1,000 in each. The kiter then draws on X Bank a $5,000 check in payment for goods or in exchange for cash. But before this overdraft is presented to X Bank, he covers it by depositing in X Bank a $5,000 check drawn on Y Bank. And before this second overdraft is presented to Y Bank, he covers it with a $5,000 check drawn on X Bank. The process is then repeated, escalating the amounts of which the banks have been defrauded.

---

6. Indeed, conduct which is outrageous may provide evidence relevant to the issue of honesty, and therefore, good faith.

In practice, kiting schemes are more complex than this and often involve several banks, for if one of the banks notices the pattern of deposits and withdrawals, the kite will be discovered. The bank that discovers the kite can maneuver to avoid loss by waiting for an opportune moment in the kite, presenting checks deposited in it, and then dishonoring at the last possible moment checks drawn on it.[1]

The questions with which we are concerned arise when a kiter exchanges a check drawn on a kited account for a check of an innocent drawer and then deposits the innocent drawer's check in a kited account. If the innocent drawer stops payment on his check, he can set up against the kiter the defenses of fraud and failure of performance. Is the bank in which the kiter has deposited the innocent drawer's check a holder in due course that takes free of these defenses? Or does its involvement in the kiting scheme prevent its taking in good faith and without notice?

In First State Bank & Trust Co. of Edinburg v. George, 519 S.W.2d 198 (Tex.Civ.App.1974), the court affirmed a judgment for the innocent drawer based on a jury verdict. The court held that the jury was justified in finding that the bank did not take in good faith because there was testimony that the bank should have known of the kite and that "by looking at the accounts involved, any banker could see that check kiting was going on." The jury was also justified in finding that the bank had notice since UCC 1–201(25) provides that a person has notice of a fact when "from all the facts and circumstances known to him at the time in question he had reason to know that it exists." Cf. Community Bank v. Ell, 278 Or. 417, 564 P.2d 685, rehearing denied, 279 Or. 245, 566 P.2d 903 (1977) (involving a defense in the nature of an offset).

(3) Status of Collecting Bank. As was pointed out earlier, a depositary bank that takes a check for collection acts as agent for the depositor and does not take the check as owner. See p. 156 supra. This rule reflects the banker's fear that if the bank were owner it would bear the loss if the check were paid and the proceeds then lost due to the insolvency of a subsequent bank in the chain of collection. But situations also arose where the banker found it advantageous to claim at least some of the attributes of an owner. Compare UCC 4–201 with 4–208 and 4–209.

Comment 1 to UCC 4–201 states: "The general approach of Article 4, similar to that of other articles, is to provide, within reasonable limits, rules or answers to major problems known to exist in the bank

---

1. It has been held that this is not a breach of any duty owed to other banks involved in the kite. Citizens National Bank v. First National Bank, 347 So.2d 964 (Miss.1977) ("these two banks were competitors in the banking field and ordinarily banks deal with each other at arm's length"); cf. Mid-Cal National Bank v. Federal Reserve Bank of San Francisco, 590 F.2d 761 (9th Cir.1979) ("if a bank in such a situation cannot be held liable for failing to notify even when it knows of kiting activity, a bank should not be called to account for failing to discover information that, in any event, it was not required to convey").

collection process without regard to questions of status and owner-ship but to keep general principles such as status and ownership available to cover residual areas not covered by specific rules." Comment 6 goes on to explain: "It is unrealistic . . . to base rights and duties on status of agent or owner. This Section 4–201 makes the pertinent provisions of Article 4 applicable to substantially all items handled by banks for presentment, payment or collection, recognizes the prima facie status of most banks as agents, and then seeks to state appropriate limits and some attributes to the general rules and presumptions so expressed."

———

BOWLING GREEN, INC. v. STATE STREET BANK AND TRUST CO.

United States Court of Appeals, First Circuit, 1970.
425 F.2d 81.

[The facts and the first part of the opinion in this case are at p. 184 supra. The court there rejected plaintiff's contention that the absence of an endorsement by Bowl-Mor was fatal to the Bank's case.]

COFFIN, CIRCUIT JUDGE. . . . Plaintiff's second objection arises from the intimate relationship between Bowl-Mor and the Bank, a relationship which plaintiff maintains precludes a finding of good faith. The record shows that the Bank was one of Bowl-Mor's three major creditors, and that it regularly provided short term financing for Bowl-Mor against the security of Bowl-Mor's inventory and unperformed contracts. The loan officer in charge of Bowl-Mor's account, Francis Haydock, was also a director of Bowl-Mor until August 1966. Haydock knew of Bowl-Mor's poor financial health and of its inability to satisfy all its creditors during 1966. In the five months before the transaction in question, the Bank charged $1,000,000 of Bowl-Mor's debt to the Bank's reserve for bad debts. However, the record also shows that the Bank continued to make loans to Bowl-Mor until September 12.

The Bank was also aware of the underlying transaction between Bowl-Mor and the plaintiff which led to the deposit on September 26. During the week prior to this transaction, Bowl-Mor had overdrawn its checking account with the Bank to meet a payroll. In order to persuade the Bank to honor the overdraft, officials of Bowl-Mor contacted Haydock and informed him that a check for $15,000 would be deposited as soon as plaintiff could obtain the funds from the Small Business Administration. The district court found, however, that the Bank was not aware that the directors of Bowl-Mor had authorized a Chapter X petition or that Bowl-Mor officials planned to file the petition on September 27.

On the basis of this record, the district court found that the Bank acted in good faith and without notice of any defense to the instru-

ment. The Code defines "good faith" as "honesty in fact", Mass.
Gen.Laws Ann. c. 106 § 1–201(19), an essentially subjective test
which focuses on the state of mind of the person in question. The
Code's definition of "notice", Mass.Gen.Laws Ann. c. 106 § 1–201(25),
while considerably more prolix, also focuses on the actual knowledge
of the individuals allegedly notified. Since the application of these
definitions turns so heavily on the facts of an individual case, rulings
of a district court under § 3–302(1)(b) and 3–302(1)(c) should never be
reversed unless clearly erroneous. In this case, the evidence indicated that Bowl-Mor had persevered in spite of long-term financial ill
health, and that the event which precipitated its demise was the withdrawal of financial support by another major creditor, Otis Elevator
Co., on the morning of September 27, after the deposit of plaintiff's
check. Thus, at the time of deposit, the Bank might reasonably have
expected Bowl-Mor to continue its shambling pace rather than cease
business immediately. The findings of the district court are not,
therefore, clearly erroneous.

Plaintiff, however, urges us to adopt the "objective" standard of
good faith promulgated in Jones v. Approved Bancredit Corp., 256
A.2d 739 (Del.Sup.Ct.1969), which held that a finance company could
not as a matter of law be a holder in due course of a consumer installment note which it discounted for a closely affiliated construction
company. We doubt whether *Approved Bancredit* represents the
law in Massachusetts. In a similar case, Universal C.I.T. Credit
Corp. v. Ingel, 347 Mass. 119, 196 N.E.2d 847 (1964), the consumer
sought to introduce evidence concerning the credit company's cooperation with the payee of the note in arranging financing and the company's knowledge of previous complaints concerning the payee's performance. The Supreme Judicial Court held that such evidence was
properly excluded because it did not establish that the credit company
had notice of the payee's fraud. 347 Mass. at 125, 196 N.E.2d 847.
While this decision is not squarely addressed to good faith, it indicates to us that Massachusetts continues to look to the facts of the
individual case rather than applying an "objective standard" based on
the general business dealings between the transferor and transferee
of an instrument.[1]

We note, moreover, that the balance of convenience on which the
Delaware Court relied in *Approved Bancredit* inclines in a different
direction when the instrument is a check rather than a consumer
note. A consumer who executes a note often has no way of investi-
gating the honesty of the person with whom he deals and his only
realistic remedy in the event of breach is to withhold payment. A
bank or finance company, on the other hand, will find it relatively
easy to check the honesty and competence of those who regularly
present consumer paper for discounting. When the instrument is a

1. Massachusetts has handled the
problem of consumer credit by legisla-
tively banning the use of negotiable instruments in installment sales of consumer goods. Mass.Gen.Laws Ann. c. 255
§ 12C (Supp.1969).

check, however, the equities are quite different. The check is the major method for transfer of funds in commercial practice. The maker, payee, and endorsers of a check naturally expect it will be rapidly negotiated and collected. Even companies which, like Bowl-Mor, are tottering on the brink of financial collapse will continue to deposit checks for collection during each business day. The wheels of commerce would grind to a halt if the bank became "constructive trustee" of these items at the first whiff of insolvency. We therefore see no sufficient reason not only to adopt the objective standard but also to extend it to a commercial bank accepting a check.

This brings us to plaintiff's final argument, that the Bank gave value only to the extent of the $5,024.85 overdraft, and thus cannot be a holder in due course with respect to the remaining $10,047.54 which the Bank credited against Bowl-Mor's loan account. Our consideration of this argument is confined by the narrow scope of the district court's findings. The Bank may well have given value under § 4–208(1)(a) when it credited the balance of Bowl-Mor's checking account against its outstanding indebtedness. See Banco Espanol de Credito v. State Street Bank & Trust Co., 409 F.2d 711 (1st Cir.1969). But by that time the Bank knew of Bowl-Mor's petition for reorganization, additional information which the district court did not consider in finding that the Bank acted in good faith and without notice at the time it received the item. We must therefore decide whether the Bank gave value for the additional $10,047.54 at the time the item was deposited.[2]

Resolution of this issue depends on the proper interpretation of § 4–209, which provides that a collecting bank has given value to the extent that it has acquired a "security interest" in an item. In plaintiff's view, a collecting bank can satisfy § 4–209 only by extending credit against an item in compliance with § 4–208(1).[3] The district

---

2. Defendant suggests that we can avoid the analytical problems of § 4–209 by simply holding that the Bank's inchoate right to set off Bowl-Mor's outstanding indebtedness against deposits, as they were made constituted a giving of value. See Wood v. Boylston National Bank, 129 Mass. 358 (1880). There are, however, some pitfalls in this theory. First, under prior law a secured creditor could not exercise its right of set-off without first showing that its security was inadequate. Forastiere v. Springfield Institution for Savings, 303 Mass. 101, 104, 20 N.E.2d 950 (1939). Second, although the Uniform Commercial Code forswears any intent to change a banker's right of set-off, § 4–201 does change the presumption that a bank owns items deposited with it. This presumption played a role under prior law in assessing the bank's rights against uncollected

commercial paper. Compare Wood v. Boylston National Bank, supra, with Boston-Continental National Bank v. Hub Fruit Co., 285 Mass. 187, 190, 189 N.E. 89 (1934) and American Barrel Co. v. Commissioner of Banks, 290 Mass. 174, 179–181, 195 N.E. 335 (1935). [This thought is pursued in the later case of Rockland Trust Co. v. South Shore National Bank, 314 N.E.2d 438 (Mass.1974). [Eds.]]

3. Mass.Gen.Laws Ann. c. 106, § 4–208.

"Security Interest of Collecting Bank in Items, Accompanying Documents and Proceeds. (1) A bank has a security interest in an item and any accompanying documents or the proceeds of either

(a) in case of an item deposited in an account to the extent to which credit given for the item has been withdrawn or applied;

court, on the other hand, adopted the view that a security interest is a security interest, however acquired. The court then found that defendant and Bowl-Mor had entered a security agreement which gave defendant a floating lien on Bowl-Mor's chattel paper. Since the item in question was part of the proceeds of a Bowl-Mor contract, the court concluded that defendant had given value for the full $15,306.00 at the time it received the deposit.

With this conclusion we agree. Section 1–201(37) defines "security interest" as an interest in personal property which secures payment or performance of an obligation. There is no indication in § 4–209 that the term is used in a more narrow or specialized sense. Moreover, as the official comment to § 4–209 observes, this provision is in accord with prior law and with § 3–303, both of which provide that a holder gives value when he accepts an instrument as security for an antecedent debt. Reynolds v. Park Trust Co., 245 Mass. 440, 444–445, 139 N.E. 785 (1923). Finally, we note that if one of the Bank's prior loans to Bowl-Mor had been made in the expectation that this particular instrument would be deposited, the terms of § 4–208(1)(c) would have been literally satisfied. We do not think the case is significantly different when the Bank advances credit on the strength of a continuing flow of items of this kind. We therefore conclude that the Bank gave value for the full $15,306.00 at the time it accepted the deposit.

We see no discrepancy between this result and the realities of commercial life. Each party, of course, chose to do business with an eventually irresponsible third party. The Bank, though perhaps unwise in prolonging its hopes for a prospering customer, nevertheless protected itself through security arrangements as far as possible without hobbling each deposit and withdrawal. Plaintiff, on the other hand, not only placed its initial faith in Bowl-Mor, but later became aware that Bowl-Mor was having difficulties in meeting its payroll. It seems not too unjust that this vestige of caveat emptor survives.

Affirmed.

NOTES

(1) **Stale Checks.** To be a holder in due course, a holder must take the instrument "without notice that it is overdue" (UCC 3–302(1)(c)). Although a check, as a demand instrument, has no due date, the rule grew up that after the passage of time a check became "stale" and should be treated as overdue. UCC 3–304(3)(c) provides that thirty days is presumed to be a reasonable time in the case of a domestic check. See also UCC 3–503(2). What is the difference between these two thirty-day provisions?

(b) in case of an item for which it has given credit available for withdrawal as of right, to the extent of the credit given whether or not the credit is drawn upon and whether or not there is a right of charge-back; or

(c) if it makes an advance on or against the item. . . ."

(2) Rights of Purchasers After Maturity and Other Holders Not in Due Course. Chafee, in Rights in Overdue Paper, 31 Harv.L.Rev. 1104, 1122 (1918), distinguished between "equitable defenses" and "equitable claims to ownership" and argued that one who took a negotiable instrument in good faith and for value after maturity should not be subject to the latter. "Maturity indicates nothing about them. Instead of being a red flag to give warning of all hidden dangers, it resembles more closely a printed placard calling attention to one special peril. A person approaching a grade-crossing and seeing the sign 'Stop, Look, and Listen' is bound to watch for trains, but he does not assume the risk of a savage bull-dog maintained on the railroad right of way to scare off track-walkers." The Code rejects Chafee's views in UCC 3–306. See Warren, Cutting Off Claims of Ownership Under the Uniform Commercial Code, 30 U.Chi.L.Rev. 469, 478–82 (1963).

But note that under UCC 3–201(1) a transferee from a holder in due course ordinarily has all the rights of the holder in due course. This preserves for a holder in due course the market for the instrument should knowledge of a defense or claim of ownership become widespread.

(3) Fiduciaries. The law relating to transfers by a fiduciary, except as it concerns negotiable instruments, is beyond the scope of this course. Generally, a bona fide purchaser for value of trust property from a trustee may retain the property and is under no liability to the beneficiary, even though the transfer may have been in breach of trust. But if the transferee has notice of the breach of trust the transfer will not cut off the beneficiary's interest and the transferee will take subject to the trust. This principle applies to transfers of negotiable instruments which are held in trust, where the paramount question is what amounts to notice of the breach of trust. Compare UCC 3–304(4)(e) with 3–304(2). To clarify the law in this area the Uniform Fiduciaries Act was proposed in 1922 and is now in effect in over twenty jurisdictions. It is not one of the acts specifically repealed by the Code (UCC 10–102).

Problem 5. In indorsing the Empire check, Quaker omits the words "For deposit only." A few hours after giving Quaker a provisional credit for the Empire check, Philadelphia National allows Quaker to draw upon that credit to the extent of $1,000. The check is then dishonored because Empire has stopped payment. Empire stopped payment on discovering that the cans are defective and on justifiably refusing to take and pay for them. Quaker is now insolvent. Can Philadelphia National recover any part of the $2,178.50 from Empire? (It may help to assume first that the Empire check was deposited by itself.) Does the answer depend on whether the other checks deposited at the same time are paid? (See the deposit slip at p. 99 supra.) See UCC 3–303, 4–208(1), 4–209; Citizen's National Bank of Englewood v. Fort Lee Savings and Loan Association, infra; Bowling Green v. State Street Bank and Trust, supra.

Problem 6. How can one tell whether a provisional credit has been "withdrawn or applied" under UCC 4–208(1)(a)? Assume that Quaker had a balance of $1,000 before making the deposit and that a few hours later the Philadelphia National allowed Quaker to withdraw $2,500 in cash and certified a check drawn by Quaker in the amount of $2,000. To what extent, if any, would the $2,178.50 provisional credit be "withdrawn or applied"? See UCC 4–208(2). Would it make any difference if Quaker deposited $5,000 in cash immediately after the $2,178.50 deposit and before the withdrawal and certification?

Problem 7. Assume that before Quaker deposited the Empire check, Quaker's account was overdrawn in the amount of $3,500, and that after the deposit the account showed a balance of $3,717.68. To what extent, if any, has Philadelphia National taken the check for value? Compare UCC 4–208 and 4–209 with UCC 3–303; and compare Bowling Green v. State Street Bank and Trust, supra, with Marine Midland Bank-New York v. Graybar Electric Co., 41 N.Y.2d 703, 395 N.Y.S.2d 403, 363 N.E.2d 1139 (1977), and with other cases discussed in Note, 1981 U.Ill.L.Rev. 395.[1]

CITIZENS NATIONAL BANK OF ENGLEWOOD v. FORT LEE SAVINGS AND LOAN ASSOCIATION

Superior Court of New Jersey, 1965.
89 N.J.Super. 43, 213 A.2d 315.

BOTTER, J.S.C.   Citizens National Bank of Englewood has moved for summary judgment to recover monies advanced against a check which was deposited with the bank for collection but was later dishonored. The issue is whether the bank should be protected for advances made to its depositor before the check cleared. The summary judgment is sought against the drawer and payee-indorser who stopped payment on the check.

On August 27, 1963, George P. Winter agreed to sell a house in Fort Lee, New Jersey to defendant Jean Amoroso and her husband. On the same day Amoroso requested her bank, Fort Lee Savings and Loan Association (Fort Lee Savings), to issue the bank's check to her order for $3,100 to be used as a deposit on the contract for sale. Fort Lee Savings complied by drawing the check against its account with the Fort Lee Trust Company. Later that day Amoroso indorsed and delivered the check to Winter, and he deposited the check in his account at the plaintiff bank. At that time he had a balance of $225.33. After the $3,100 check was deposited the bank cashed a $1,000 check for him against his account. In addition, on August 27 or August 28,

---

1. As to the depositary bank's power to affect the answer to this problem by a dragnet security clause in its agreement with its customer, see Rosenthal, Negotiability—Who Needs It?, 71 Colum.L.Rev. 375, 391–92 (1971).

the bank cleared and charged Winter's account with four other checks totaling $291.76.

The next day Amoroso discovered that Winter had previously sold the property to a third party by agreement which had been recorded in the Bergen County Clerk's Office. Amoroso immediately asked Winter to return her money. She claims that he admitted the fraud and agreed to return the deposit. But when Mrs. Amoroso and her husband reached Winter's office they learned that he had attempted suicide. He died shortly thereafter.

Upon making this discovery, in the afternoon of August 28, the Amorosos went to Fort Lee Savings to advise it of the fraud and request it to stop payment on the check. The bank issued a written stop payment order which was received by the Fort Lee Trust Company, the drawee, on the following day, August 29. In the meantime the $3,100 check was sent by plaintiff through the Bergen County Clearing House to the Fort Lee Trust Company. By then the stop payment order had been received. Notice of nonpayment was thereafter transmitted to plaintiff.

Plaintiff contends that, under the Uniform Commercial Code, N.J.S. 12A:1–101 et seq., N.J.S.A., it is a holder in due course to the extent of the advances made on Winter's account and is entitled to recover these moneys from the drawer and payee-indorser of the check. Plaintiff's claim against the drawee, Fort Lee Trust Company, was voluntarily dismissed by plaintiff at the pretrial conference.

The central issue is whether plaintiff bank is a holder in due course, since a holder in due course will prevail against those liable on the instrument in the absence of a real defense. Of course, it must first be determined that plaintiff is a "holder" if plaintiff is to be declared a holder in due course. Amoroso contends that plaintiff bank does not own the check because it is only an agent of its depositor Winter for collection purposes and, consequently, plaintiff is not a "holder." It is true that a collecting bank is presumed to be an agent of the owner of the item unless a contrary intention appears, or until final settlement. N.J.S. 12A:4–201(1), N.J.S.A. Assuming that the bank was at all times an agent in this case, it does not follow that the bank cannot also be a holder. On the contrary, a collecting bank may be a holder whether or not it owns the item. N.J.S. 12A:4–201(1) and 12A:3–301, N.J.S.A. Pazol v. Citizens Nat'l Bank of Sandy Springs, 110 Ga.App. 319, 138 S.E.2d 442 (Ct.App.1964); and see generally Bunn, "Bank Collections under the Uniform Commercial Code," Wis. L.Rev. 278 (1964). The definition of "holder" includes a person who is in possession of an instrument indorsed to his order or in blank. N.J.S. 12A:1–201(20), N.J.S.A. It is clear that the bank is a holder of the check notwithstanding that it may have taken the check solely for collection and with the right to charge back against the depositor's account in the event the check is later dishonored. Pazol v. Citizens

Nat'l Bank of Sandy Springs, supra; accord, Citizens Bank of Boone-ville v. Nat'l Bank of Commerce, 334 F.2d 257 (10 Cir.1964).

To be a holder in due course one must take a negotiable instrument for value, in good faith and without notice of any defect or defense. N.J.S. 12A:3–302(1), N.J.S.A. Amoroso contends that plaintiff did not act in good faith or is chargeable with notice because it allowed Winter to draw against uncollected funds at a time when his account was either very low or overdrawn. Winter's account was low in funds. However, this fact, or the fact that Winter's account was overdrawn, currently or in the past, if true, would not constitute notice to the collecting bank of an infirmity in the underlying transaction or instrument and is not evidence of bad faith chargeable to the bank at the time it allowed withdrawal against the deposited check. N.J.S. 12A:1–201(19) and (25); N.J.S. 12A:3–304, N.J.S.A. See United States Cold Storage Corp. v. First Nat'l Bank of Fort Worth, 350 S.W.2d 856 (Tex.Civ.App.1961), declaring the bank a holder in due course where it applied a deposited check against a large overdraft of its depositor, the court specifically holding that lack of good faith was not shown merely by the fact that the bank knew the depositor was considerably overdrawn in his account. . . . Moreover a depositary bank may properly charge an account by honoring a check drawn by a depositor even though it creates an overdraft. N.J.S. 12A:4–401(1), N.J.S.A. It would be anomalous for a bank to lose its status as a holder in due course merely because it has notice that the account of its depositor is overdrawn.

Lacking bad faith or notice of a defect or defense, plaintiff will be deemed a holder in due course if one additional element is satisfied, namely, the giving of value for the instrument. Prior to the adoption of the Uniform Commercial Code the general rule was that a bank does give value and is a holder in due course to the extent that it allows a depositor to draw against a check given for collection notwithstanding that the check is later dishonored. . . . The cases clearly hold that this rule applies even though the item is received for collection only under an agreement with the bank that gives the bank the right to charge back against the depositor's account the amount of any item which is not collected. It is sometimes said that the contract of conditional credit is changed when the bank honors the deposit by allowing a withdrawal, and the bank then becomes the owner of or holder of a lien on the item to the extent of value given. . . .

This result is continued by provisions of the Uniform Commercial Code which give plaintiff a security interest in the check and the monies represented by the check to the extent that credit given for the check has been withdrawn or applied. N.J.S. 12A:4–208 and 209, N.J.S.A. See also N.J.S. 12A:4–201, N.J.S.A. and U.C.C. Comment 5 thereunder. . . .

The New Jersey Study Comment under N.J.S. 12A:4–209, N.J.S.A., includes the following: "Because the bank is a holder of the item in most cases, it is possible for it to be a holder in due course if it otherwise qualifies by its good faith taking, prior to maturity, for value. See, U.C.C. sec. 3–302; NIL sec. 52 (N.J.S.A. 7:2–52). It is important for a bank to be a holder in due course when the depositor fails, for this status enables it to prevail over the obligor (drawer or maker) of the instrument even though the obligor has some personal defense against the payee (depositor)."

It would hinder commercial transactions if depositary banks refused to permit withdrawal prior to clearance of checks. Apparently banking practice is to the contrary. It is clear that the Uniform Commercial Code was intended to permit the continuation of this practice and to protect banks who have given credit on deposited items prior to notice of a stop payment order or other notice of dishonor. N.J.S. 12A:4–208 and 209, N.J.S.A., supra; Pazol v. Citizens Nat'l Bank of Sandy Springs, supra; Citizens Bank of Booneville v. Nat'l Bank of Commerce, supra; see also Universal C.I.T. Credit Corp. v. Guaranty Bank & Trust Co., 161 F.Supp. 790 (D.C.Mass.1958); Trumbull, "Bank Deposits and Collections in Illinois Under the Proposed Uniform Commercial Code," 55 Nw.U.L.Rev. 253, 270–272 (1960); Penney, "Uniform Commercial Code: Symposium—A Summary of Articles 3 and 4 and Their Impact in New York," 48 Cornell L.Q. 47, 58–59 (1962).

It is also contended that liability on the check is excused because N.J.S. 12A:4–403, N.J.S.A. gives Fort Lee Savings the right to order Fort Lee Trust Company to stop payment on the check. However, U.C.C. comment 8 under this section makes it clear that the stop payment order cannot avoid liability to a holder in due course. "The payment can be stopped but the drawer remains liable on the instrument to the holder in due course . . . ." See Carhart v. Second Nat'l Bank, 98 N.J.L. 373, 120 A. 636 (Sup.Ct.1923).

Finally, Amoroso attempts to raise the fraud perpetrated by Winter against Amoroso as a defense to plaintiff's claim. Plaintiff's status as a holder in due course insulates it from all personal defenses of any party to the instrument with whom it has not dealt, although real defenses may still be asserted. N.J.S. 12A:3–305, N.J.S.A. The defense raised here is fraud in inducing Amoroso to enter into the contract. There is no suggestion that either defendant signed the check without knowledge of "its character or its essential terms." N.J.S. 12A:3–305(2)(c), N.J.S.A. Therefore the fraud is a personal defense available only against Winter and cannot be asserted against plaintiff. See Bancredit, Inc. v. Bethea, 65 N.J.Super. 538, 168 A.2d 250 (App.Div.1961); Meadow Brook Nat'l Bank v. Rogers, 44 Misc.2d 250, 253 N.Y.S.2d 501 (D.Ct.1964).

Accordingly both Fort Lee Savings as drawer and Amoroso as indorser of the check are liable to plaintiff. N.J.S. 12A:3–413(2) and 12A:3–414(1), N.J.S.A., defining the liability of a drawer and indorser of a negotiable instrument to a holder in due course.

The motion for summary judgment will be granted in the sum of $1,066.43, plus interest. The amount of the judgment represents advances made on Winter's account before notice of dishonor, $1,291.76, less the existing balance of $225.33 in Winter's account. This opinion will not deal with the disposition of claims between Amoroso and Fort Lee Savings. By reason of the stop payment order Fort Lee Savings has on hand sufficient funds which were charged against Amoroso's account to meet plaintiff's judgment, and part of these funds, representing the difference between the potential judgment and the $3,100 retained, has been refunded to Amoroso pursuant to the pretrial order.

NOTES

(1) **Negotiability of Checks.** Dean Albert Rosenthal has pointed out that there is likely to be an increase in the number of instances in which withdrawals are permitted against unpaid checks, both because of the increased use of automation and the growing practice of banks to agree to let their customers overdraw subject to interest charges. He believes that the Code "sometimes gives a bank a windfall at the expense of drawers, who lose the right to assert legitimate defenses" under "a thoroughly irrational rule as applied in most check deposit situations." As an alternative, he suggests that "the right of a depositary bank, as a holder in due course, to cut off defenses of a drawer ought to be limited to cases in which the bank can prove that, in allowing withdrawals against the check before collection, it had relied at least in part on the credit of the drawer." Rosenthal, Negotiability—Who Needs It?, 71 Colum.L.Rev. 375, 381–94 (1971).

Would the practices of depositary banks be affected by such proposals? Consider the following: "With the high percentage of good checks, and the high cost of maintaining any record of the journeys of a particular check, obviously banks do not keep track on an individual item basis. The availability of deposited tentative credits to a depositing customer depends on two factors, the credit rating of the customer and schedules of normal availability. The accounts of customers with a high credit rating are not normally monitored for drawing against uncollected funds, as the chance of not having a balance against which to charge back a returned item is negligible. In the case of the monitored accounts, the availability schedules also reflect average times. Hence, there always will be cases in which checks will come back unpaid with no balance in the depositor's account to cover the charge-back. The holder in due course status of depositary banks in this situation gives the bank an added chance of recovery if the reason for the return is not the insolvency or permanent inability to pay of the drawer." Leary and Tarlow, reflections on Articles 3 and 4 for a Review Committee, 48 Temple L.Q. 919, 923 (1975).

The great majority of all checks are deposited by the payees for collection and never come into the hands of a holder in due course.

Would there be any serious adverse effects if checks were not negotiable instruments? Would there be any advantages? Compare the significance of negotiability of checks with that of the negotiability of credit instruments such as time drafts and notes.

(2) Uniform New Payments Code. The UNPC would make a dramatic change in the rights of depositary banks and others who claim to be holders in due course of checks. Under UNPC 103, the rights of a claimant on an order that is "drawn on a consumer account" are subject to claims and defenses arising out of the underlying transaction until the order is finally paid. After discussing the abolition of the holder-in-due-course doctrine in connection with promissory notes, the commentary concludes that the same "concerns also apply to checks and other orders drawn by consumers . . . If a bank takes a check from a payee, it is relying on that person's credit if it allows withdrawal against uncollected funds, not the credit standing of a drawer with whom it is unfamiliar. The bank in the case of checks, just as the merchant in the case of notes, is in a better position to appraise and take the risk of insolvency of the party with which it deals in the event the check is unpaid. If the 'purchaser' of the check can cut-off the defenses of the buyer-drawer, the drawer is remitted to a second action against the seller-payee, thus incurring litigation costs and current outlay of funds." The UNPC also gives the same protection to a non-consumer drawer whose order is marked "not entitled to due-course rights." (Does not UCC 3–805 give a drawer similar protection?) See Benfield, The New Payments Code and the Abolition of Holder in Due Course Status as to Consumer Checks, 40 Wash. & Lee L.Rev. 11 (1983).

RESTRICTIVE INDORSEMENTS

In the Citizens National Bank case, the court began its opinion by mentioning that the check "was deposited with the bank for collection." The holder of a check deposits it for collection by using the kind of restrictive indorsement described in UCC 3–205(c)—an indorsement that "includes the words 'for collection,' 'for deposit,' 'pay any bank,' or like terms signifying a purpose of deposit or collection." (The other kinds of restrictive indorsements listed in UCC 3–205 are not of great practical importance.)

In understanding the Code provisions on restrictive indorsements, it is helpful to realize that prior to the Code there was a substantial body of authority for the view that if a depositor restrictively indorsed a check, the depositary bank could not become a holder in due course of it. This was based on a restrictive reading of Negotiable Instruments Law §§ 37 and 47. Other courts rejected this view. All courts, however, agreed that if the depositary bank had not given value, no intermediary collecting bank could, by giving value itself, rise above the depositary bank and become a holder in due course of such a check.

Problem 8. Would it make any difference in Problem 5 if Quaker included the words "For deposit only" in its indorsement? See UCC 3–205, 3–206.

Problem 9. After the Empire check is indorsed "For deposit only, Quaker Manufacturing Co.," but before it is deposited in Philadephia National, it is stolen by a thief who deposits it in his account in Philadelphia National. Philadelphia National then sends the check to Citibank, which obtains payment from Irving Trust, and the $2,178.50 is ultimately withdrawn by the thief. What rights has Quaker against Philadelphia National, Citibank and Irving Trust? See UCC 3–206, 3–419(4). What advantages, if any, does this indorsement have over "Quaker Manufacturing Co."? Over "To Philadelphia National Bank, Quaker Manufacturing Co."? Would Quaker be better protected if it indorsed "For deposit in Philadelphia National Bank, Quaker Manufacturing Co."? See Rutherford v. Darwin, infra.

Problem 10. Why do the two banks add "Pay any bank" to their indorsements? Why does not Philadelphia National indorse the Empire check "To Citibank, The Philadelphia National Bank"? See UCC 4–201(2).

RUTHERFORD v. DARWIN

Court of Appeals of New Mexico, 1980.
95 N.M. 340, 622 P.2d 245.

ANDREWS, JUDGE. Tom Darwin was a general partner of both Rancho Village Partners and The Settlement, Ltd., which are New Mexico limited partnerships. He had full authority to manage the funds of both entities with his signature alone.

On May 17, 1977, Darwin made a $300,000 draw against a construction loan made by Albuquerque National Bank (ANB) to Rancho Village Partners. He received the money in the form of a money order payable to "Rancho Village Partnership, Ltd." He endorsed the money order with "Deposit to the account of Rancho Village Partners, Ltd.", and took it to the First National Bank in Albuquerque (FNBIA), where both Rancho Village Partners and The Settlement had accounts. Darwin gave the money order to the teller with a pre-printed deposit slip for the account of The Settlement, and the teller wrote out the account number of The Settlement on the reverse side of the money order, below the endorsement. The teller then deposited the money order to the account of The Settlement, notwithstanding the endorsement, which directed otherwise.

Darwin intended that the deposit be made into The Settlement account. He then withdrew the bulk of the $300,000 within two weeks of the deposit of the money order, and the account was almost entirely depleted before any of the other members of the Rancho Village partnership learned of the draw seven months later. The embezzlement of Darwin was not earlier discovered because the construction loan on which the draw was made was not monitored by monthly statements which would normally be sent in conjunction with monthly billings of interest. It was unusual for a loan of that size not to be so monitored and was a deviation from the usual ANB practice with regard to such loans. Rancho Village Partners acted promptly to notify FNBIA and to protect its interest after the other members of the partnership learned of Darwin's action.

Rancho Village Partners brought suit against Darwin, The Settlement, and FNBIA to recover the $300,000. A stipulated judgment was entered against Darwin and The Settlement, and the trial court entered summary judgment against the bank. FNBIA appeals from this summary judgment.

The words "Deposit to the account of Rancho Village Partnership, Ltd." clearly constitute a restrictive endorsement under § 55–3–205, N.M.S.A.1978. Section 55–3–206 imposes upon FNBIA the duty to pay consistently with the restrictive endorsement, and this duty gives rise to liability for the bank if it fails to do so. Underpinning & Foundation Constructors, Inc. v. Chase Manhattan, 46 N.Y.2d 459, 386 N.E.2d 1319, 414 N.Y.S.2d 298 (1979).

FNBIA contends that Darwin "waived" the restrictive endorsement, and thus released it from its duty to pay as directed by the endorsement. We conclude, however, that New Mexico does not recognize any doctrine of the waiver of restrictive endorsements, and thus we cannot accept FNBIA's theory.

There has never been a case recognizing a doctrine of waiver of restrictive endorsements in New Mexico, but several cases decided in other jurisdictions under the Uniform Negotiable Instruments Law (NIL) suggest that the doctrine was once generallly recognized. See, e.g., Glens Falls Indemnity Co. v. Palmetto Bank, 104 F.2d 671 (4th Cir.1939). We are aware of no cases decided since the Uniform Commercial Code (UCC) superseding the NIL as the law governing negotiable instruments which has recognized the doctrine, and thus the dispositive issue is whether the doctrine survives as part of the common law under the UCC.

The NIL was silent on the key issue of this case; both the bank's duty to pay as directed by a restrictive endorsement and the waiver exception to that rule were matters of common law under the NIL. With the adoption of the UCC, the rule as to the duty of the bank was codified in § 55–3–206.

Courts have frequently given effect to common law limitations and exceptions to newly codified common law rules. For example, many jurisdictions have held that a murderer may not take from the estate of his victim even where the general law of descent and distribution of the jurisdiction has been codified without the inclusion of that sensible and time honored common law limitation. See, e.g.,

Budwit v. Herr, 339 Mich. 265, 63 N.W.2d 841 (1954). However, the general rule is that:

> general and comprehensive legislation prescribing minutely a course of conduct to be pursued and the parties and things affected, and specifically describing limitations and exceptions, is indicative of a legislative intent that the statute should totally supersede and replace the common law dealing with the subject matter.

2A Sutherland, Statutory Construction § 50.05 (Rev.3d Ed.1972).

This idea was applied in Tietzel v. Southwestern Const. Co., 43 N.M. 435, 94 P.2d 972 (1939), where it was held that a statute empowering a trial judge to refer certain enumerated sorts of cases to a special master over the objection of the parties abrogated his common law power to do so in any other kind of case which sounded in equity.

We hold that the codification of the law of restrictive endorsements contained in the UCC is sufficiently comprehensive and detailed to exclude common law exceptions which are not mentioned. Section 55–3–206, which is entitled "Effect of restrictive endorsement", sets forth with particularity when and by whom restrictive endorsements must be observed; it must be inferred that if the legislature had intended that restrictive endorsements would become ineffective for some other reason, such a direction would have been included in this section or elsewhere in the UCC.

The official comment to this section, which is persuasive authority of the meaning of the section even though it is not binding on this Court, First State Bank v. Clark, 91 N.M. 117, 570 P.2d 1144 (1977), gives a further indication that the section was not to be encumbered with the common law accessories of the NIL. The comment describes the changes made by the new section as "completely revised" from the prior provision under the NIL. FNBIA argues that waiver of a restrictive endorsement as recognized prior to the UCC should be allowed because § 55–1–103 of the UCC provides for the continued effect of common law principles unless displaced by particular provisions of the UCC. However, as discussed above, we believe that § 55–3–206 displaces the preexisting law in the entire area of the effect of restrictive endorsements. Section 55–1–103 does not preserve common law principles in an area which is thoroughly covered by the UCC simply because they are not expressly excluded. Alaska Airlines, Inc. v. Lockheed Aircraft Corp., 430 F.Supp. 134 (D.Alaska 1977).

FNBIA further argues the endorser of an instrument should be allowed to waive the endorsement by analogy to § 55–3–208, which states that one who reacquires an instrument may cancel any endorsement which is not necessary to his title. While the presence of this section cuts against any notion of the "sanctity" of restrictive endorsements, it very specifically suggests that it was not the intention of its drafters to make such endorsements freely negatable. The section is not applicable because the instrument was not reacquired and because Darwin did not strike the restrictive endorsement.

This second distinction is particularly important. The presence of an uncancelled restrictive endorsement on a negotiable instrument creates the legitimate expectation that it was negotiated in accordance with the restriction, and thus it would, at least in some cases, tend to conceal embezzlement or misappropriation to allow such endorsements to be waived without being physically struck from the instrument.

FNBIA also argues that Rancho Village Partners is estopped from recovering from the bank for its wrongful disregard of the restrictive endorsement because it did not use ordinary care in structuring its affairs so that Darwin's actions should have been discovered sooner. In particular, FNBIA would have us rule that Rancho Village Partners should have arranged to receive a monthly statement showing any draws on the construction loan account at the Albuquerque National Bank, as would have been the usual practice with a loan of that size. [The court discussed and rejected this argument. E]ven if we were willing to impose upon the customer the obligation to structure his relationship with a third party so as to discover the improper payment the trial court would have had to believe FNBIA exercised ordinary care in its handling of the money order. The trial court did not so find.

The circumstances of the transaction cry out for attention on the part of the bank. We hold, as a matter of law, that the bank had a duty to refuse to deposit the money to the account of The Settlement. The money order was restrictively endorsed to the account of an entity entirely different from that named, on the accompanying deposit slip. The trial court observed that, particularly in light of the sum involved, the bank had an obligation to be sure that the money went into the proper account.

We adopt the reasoning of the New York Court of Appeals in Underpinning & Foundation Constructors, Inc. v. Chase Manhattan, supra:

> The presence of a restriction imposes upon the depository bank an obligation not to accept that item other than in accord with the restriction. By disregarding the restriction, it not only subjects itself to liability for any losses resulting from its actions, but it also passes up what may well be the best opportunity to prevent the fraud. The presentation of a check in violation of a restrictive endorsement is an obvious warning sign, and the depositary bank is required to investigate the situation rather than blindly accept the check. Based on such a failure to follow the mandates of due care and commercially reasonable behavior, it is appropriate to shift ultimate responsibility from the drawer to the depository bank.

46 N.Y.2d at 469, 386 N.E.2d at 1324, 414 N.Y.S.2d at 303.

FNBIA also suggests that the endorsement on the money order was not restrictive or that it was deposited in accord with the restriction. These arguments are entirely without merit.

The decision of the trial court is affirmed.

SUTIN, JUDGE (dissenting). . . . A waiver is the intentional relinquishment of a known right. The Bank had to establish (1) that Darwin knew of the restrictive endorsement on the money order— that which he himself wrote, and (2) that Darwin intended to give up the Rancho Village's right to the deposit of the money. These facts were established beyond dispute. Regardless of what endorsement he, himself, wrote on the ANB money order, Darwin had the exclusive right to change the endorsement at anytime before or at the time of deposit. When Darwin obtained the money order he wrote in the restrictive endorsement. He intended to deposit it to the account of Rancho Village. Thereafter, he wrote up a Settlement deposit slip, either to carry out the order of Rutherford or on his own, effect a transfer of the money order from Rancho Village to Settlement.

"No restrictive endorsement prevents further transfer or negotiation of the instrument." Section 55–3–206(1), N.M.S.A.1978. Darwin negotiated the restrictive endorsement to FNB. After any transfer or negotiation with the Bank, the Bank must act consistently with the type of endorsement that appears. Section 55–3–206(2). It logically follows that when the general partner of payee, Rancho Village, acts as endorser of the money order and presents the money order with The Settlement slip to the bank teller, and the bank teller writes The Settlement account number thereon, the deposit slip was equivalent to a line drawn through the restrictive endorsement. The restrictive endorsement was cancelled.

When FNB accepted the money order and deposited it to the account of Settlement, FNB became a holder in due course. It owed no duty of inquiry to Rancho Village, the payee. Handley v. Horak, 82 Misc.2d 692, 370 N.Y.S.2d 313 (1975). . . .

In Cooper v. Albuquerque National Bank, 75 N.M. 295, 404 P.2d 125 (1965), Peke was administrator of a trust fund and general manager of an association of contractors. He received checks payable to the trust fund. He stamped the endorsement of the trust fund and immediately followed it by another stamp endorsement in sum:

Pay to the Order of

Albuquerque National Bank
For Deposit Only
All prior endorsements guaranteed
Associated Contractors.

The trust fund sued the Bank to recover the amount of the trust fund checks paid by ANB on forged, unauthorized, unlawful, fraudulent, or irregular endorsements. The court held that since Peke had authority to make the deposits, there being no evidence that the Bank acted in bad faith, the Bank was not put upon inquiry as to the amount Peke was authorized to deposit.

In the instant case, Darwin acted under authority and there was no evidence of bad faith on the part of FNB. The only person to whom the FNB teller could inquire as to propriety and priority of the restrictive endorsement was Darwin. No duty existed to inquire of a general partner, who acted for the payee as endorser, whether he was violating his duty to Rancho Village. It would have been a useless gesture. The teller's duty was to deposit the money order to The Settlement account. She did. In good faith, she accepted the deposit slip and the money order and wrote The Settlement account number under the restrictive endorsement and credited The Settlement account. She knew the account numbers of both limited partnerships. A reasonable inference can be drawn that she may have known of Darwin's relationship with Rancho Village and Settlement. We can arrive at no other conclusion but that Darwin waived the Rancho Village restrictive endorsement as a matter of law. The "contradiction" in the two endorsements is irrelevant.

The majority opinion concluded that "New Mexico does not recognize any doctrine of the waiver of restrictive endorsements, and thus we cannot accept FNBIA's theory." This issue is a matter of first impression. . . . Section 55–1–103 reads in pertinent part:

> Unless displaced by the particular provisions of this act [this chapter], the principles of law and equity . . . shall supplement its provisions.

Inasmuch as there is nothing in the Code to take the place of "waiver" of restrictive covenants, "waiver" in its pre-code law is a supplement of the Uniform Commercial Code. . . .

Section 48 of the former Negotiable Instruments Law (Section 50–1–48, N.M.S.A.1953) repealed by the Uniform Commercial Code reads:

> The holder may at any time strike out any endorsement which is not necessary to his title. The endorser whose endorsement is struck out, and all endorsers subsequent to him are thereby relieved from liability on the instrument.

Under official Comment of § 55–3–208 it is stated with reference to § 48 of the Negotiable Instruments Law, "No change in the substance of the law is intended."

Glens Falls Indemnity Co. v. Palmetto Bank, 104 F.2d 671 (4th Cir. 1939), quoted at length in *Cooper*, supra, established the right of Darwin to waive a "for deposit" endorsement on the Rancho Village money order under § 48 of the Negotiable Instruments Law. The court said:

> . . . If he had authority to indorse the checks in the name of the mill and collect the cash on them, as is admitted, it necessarily follows that he had authority to waive the restrictive

character of a special indorsement which he himself had placed on them and to collect them as though they had been generally indorsed. . . .   [Id. 674.]

Glens Falls was not only followed in New Mexico, it was followed in other jurisdictions. . . .

New Mexico via *Glens Falls* does recognize the doctrine of waiver of restrictive endorsements. It is undisputed that Darwin waived the restrictive endorsement and absolved FNB of any liability.

[W]e turn to the case relied on in the majority opinion which held that a claim based upon an effective forged restrictive endorsement, stated a claim for relief. Underpinning, etc. v. Chase Manhattan, 46 N.Y.2d 459, 386 N.E.2d 1319, 414 N.Y.S.2d 298 (1979). The court was "called upon to determine when, if ever, the drawer of a check may sue a depositary bank which accepts the check and pays out the proceeds in violation of a forged restrictive endorsement." In this case, "[a]n employee of plaintiff . . . falsified invoices from plaintiff's suppliers, stole the checks written to pay these false invoices, *restrictively indorsed them to the named payees and then deposited them to his own or confederate's accounts*, maintained with, among others the defendant Bank of New York (BNY). When these checks were presented BNY, despite the restrictive indorsements, accepted them and applied the proceeds thereof to the credit of accounts other than those indicated in the indorsements." [Emphasis added.] None of the named payees kept accounts there, 403 N.Y.S.2d 501–2, 61 A.D.2d 628 (1978). The Court of Appeals affirmed the lower court. It held that the complaint stated a claim upon which relief could be granted. The court said:

> In summary, we hold today that a drawer may directly sue a depositary bank which has honored a check in violation of a forged restrictive indorsement in situations in which the forgery is effective . . . It is basic to the law of commercial paper that as between innocent parties any loss should ultimately be placed on the party which could most easily have prevented that loss . . . . [386 N.E.2d 1323, 414 N.Y.S.2d 302.]

Underpinning stands for the proposition that a depositary bank like FNB can be held liable if it and Rancho Village were innocent parties and FNB could most easily have prevented the loss. FNB was an innocent party. It cannot be said with impunity that Rancho Village was an innocent party. It put the conduct of its business solely in the hands of its general partner. Its general partner, acting within the scope of his authority, set this transaction in motion and directly caused the loss of Rancho Village. In effect, Rancho Village promoted the loss by making Darwin its general manager. The loss must fall on Rancho Village. Continental Bank v. Wa-Ho Truck Brokerage, 122 Ariz. 414, 595 P.2d 206 (1979).

NOTE

The Bank's Own Petard. Marine Midland Bank v. Price, Miller, Evans & Flowers, 57 N.Y.2d 220, 455 N.Y.S.2d 565, 441 N.E.2d 1083 (1982), involved two checks totalling $36,906.54, given to a building contractor as progress payments on a construction job. Marine Midland Bank, as it had done with several previous progress payments, cashed the checks, wired the amount to another bank, and then forwarded the checks for collection. Since the checks had not been indorsed, Marine Midland stamped them "credited to the account of the payee herein named," though the payee had no account at the bank. The building contractor defaulted on the construction contract, the drawer stopped payment, and Marine Midland sued the drawer claiming to be a holder in due course, free of the drawer's defenses. Marine Midland lost.

The court noted that under UCC 4–205(1), "a statement placed on the item by the depositary bank to the effect that the item was deposited by a customer or credited to his account is effective as the customer's indorsement." The court thought this provision applicable though the payee had no account capable of being credited.[1] However, the court went on to conclude that the bank's stamp had the effect of a restrictive indorsement, and, since "the bank did not comply with the conditions of the indorsement which it supplied, it cannot be said to have given value within the contemplation of the code and therefore was not a holder in due course."

PAYEE AS HOLDER IN DUE COURSE

We have already seen that the drafters of the Code made the notion of "holder in due course" do double duty, under UCC 3–418 as well as under UCC 3–305. See Note, p. 147 supra. For this reason, it was important to affirm in UCC 3–302(2) that a "payee may be a holder in due course," a proposition that had been unclear under prior law. But even a holder in due course only takes free of defenses of a party "with whom the holder *has not dealt*," and the payee has ordinarily "dealt" with the drawer. So the ordinary payee, even though a holder in due course, takes subject to the drawer's defenses.

Comment 2 to UCC 3–302, however, suggests some exceptional situations where this is not the case. But the drafters appear to have become confused by their own innovation, for the examples given under UCC 3–302 are illustrative of the words "has not dealt" in UCC 3–305. (Surely it was not necessary to find such elaborate examples

---

1. For more on the applicability of UCC 4–205(1), see Krump Construction Co. v. First National Bank of Nevada, 98 Nev. 570, 655 P.2d 524 (1982), holding that a bank had no power to supply the missing indorsement of a joint payee that had no account in it and had no contact with the bank. The court distinguished the situation from that in Marine Midland on the ground that the joint payee, "whose missing endorsement the bank supplied, did not initiate interaction with the bank by seeking its services in any manner."

of cases in which the payee was a holder in due course. Consider, for example, the Kirby case, p. 141 supra.)

Comment 2 to UCC 3–302 gives these examples along with others, of cases in which the payee is a holder in due course:

"a. A remitter, purchasing goods from P, obtains a bank draft payable to P and forwards it to P, who takes it for value, in good faith and without notice as required by this section.

"b. The remitter buys the bank draft payable to P, but it is forwarded by the bank directly to P, who takes it in good faith and without notice in payment of the remitter's obligation to him."

Evidently what is meant here is not merely that P is a holder in due course under UCC 3–302, but that P "has not dealt," as those words are used in UCC 3–305, with the bank that drew the draft. Therefore P takes free of defenses that the bank may have against the remitter, as where, for example, the remitter obtained the bank draft by fraud.

An illustrative case is Eldon's Super Fresh Stores v. Merrill Lynch, Pierce, Fenner & Smith, 296 Minn. 130, 207 N.W.2d 282 (1973). Merrill Lynch, a stock brokerage firm, took as payee a $4,150 check drawn by Eldon Prinzing as president of Eldon's Super Fresh Stores. The check was delivered to Merrill Lynch by William Drexler, who was lawyer for both Eldon's and Prinzing, in payment for stock that he had bought for himself. Drexler, who was later disbarred, claimed that the check was given to him in payment for legal services. Prinzing, however, claimed that the check was given to Drexler as agent for Eldon's to buy the stock for Eldon's.

The court decided that it was not necessary to resolve this dispute. Merrill Lynch, though a payee, was a holder in due course who had not dealt with Eldon's, so Merrill Lynch took the check free of any defenses that Eldon's might have against Drexler. As to whether Merrill Lynch had taken in good faith, the court noted that Drexler had an account at Merrill Lynch, but Eldon's did not. "Merrill Lynch was entitled to conclude that Drexler, known to be an attorney, had lawfully obtained and was delivering the instrument to discharge the debt incurred by his own stock purchase." [1]

---

1. Suppose that both Drexler and Eldon's had had accounts with Merrill Lynch. Or suppose that neither had had an account with Merrill Lynch. Would Merrill Lynch then have been "required to surmise that the check, rather than being a payment for Drexler's legal services, was being misused"? See Saka v. Sahara-Nevada Corp., 92 Nev. 703, 558 P.2d 535 (1976), rejecting the argument that a hotel had "a duty to make further inquiries" when it took as payee a third person's check in payment for a $3,046.03 hotel bill. But cf. Key Appliance v. National Bank of North America, 75 A.D.2d 92, 428 N.Y.S.2d 238 (1980), holding that a bank that cashed for the drawer's comptroller checks drawn on the bank and payable to its order "had a duty to inquire as to the disposition of the funds" since though "cashing checks in small amounts without inquiry may not be unusual, cashing 26 checks in odd and large amounts so as to total $363,489.50 is plainly not ordinary banking practice." And cf. footnote 5, p. 283 infra.

(C) REAL AND PERSONAL DEFENSES

Prefatory Note. Once a holder has established that he is a holder in due course of an instrument, he takes free from "all claims to it on the part of any person" and "from all defenses of any party to the instrument with whom the holder has not dealt except" a small number of defenses which are known as *real* defenses. See UCC 3–305. Those defenses which are cut off as against a holder in due course are commonly called *personal* defenses. These include such common defenses as want or failure of consideration, breach of warranty in the sale of goods, non-performance of a condition precedent, fraud in the inducement, nondelivery of the instrument or delivery for a special purpose, and most cases of illegality. See UCC 3–306.[1] Note that the list includes those defenses which are most commonly asserted in commercial transactions. Real defenses include such less common defenses as infancy and some other types of incapacity, some instances of duress and illegality, fraud in the execution, and discharge in insolvency proceedings.

The most common instances of illegality that render a party's obligation "a nullity" and thus come within UCC 3–305(2)(b) are violation of the gambling and usury laws, which expressly make contracts that violate them "void." In Farmers' State Bank v. Clayton National Bank, 31 N.M. 344, 245 P. 543, 46 A.L.R. 952 (1925), the court said: "The consideration of an instrument won at gambling may, of course, be said to be 'illegal,' but that is not all. The instrument itself is void. . . . Giving the term 'illegal consideration' the interpretation placed upon it at the common law, no change took place in the law of this state when we adopted . . . the Negotiable Instruments Law. If the Legislature did not change, nor intend to change even the law of negotiable instruments, it, of course, did not intend to change the gaming law."

Other kinds of illegality have generally not been held to be real defenses. Commercial bribery was held to be only a personal defense in Bankers Trust Co. v. Litton Systems, 599 F.2d 488 (2d Cir.1979). The court said: "Bribery which induces the making of a contract is much like a fraud which has the same result. The bribery of a contracting party's agent or employee is, in effect, a fraud on that party. . . . Inasmuch as the New York Uniform Commercial Code allows a holder in due course to enforce a contract induced by fraud, § 3–305(2), the same treatment should be given to a contract induced by bribery. The result ought not be changed by the additional fact that commercial bribery is a criminal offense in New York. Finally, it

---

1. Courts have disagreed over whether the word "defenses" in UCC 3–306(b) includes offsets. Compare Olsen-Frankman Livestock Marketing Service v. Citizens National Bank, 605 F.2d 1082 (8th Cir.1979), with Bank of Wyandotte v. Woodrow, 394 F.Supp. 550 (W.D.Mo. 1975). See Note, 1981 U.Ill.L.Rev. 869.

would be poor policy for courts to transform banks and other finance companies into policing agents charged with the responsibility of searching out commercial bribery committed by their assignors. We doubt that denying recovery to holders in due course would have an appreciable effect on the frequency of commercial bribery."

For what amounts to fraud in the execution under UCC 3–305(2) (c), see First National Bank of Odessa v. Fazzari, p. 62 supra. UCC 3–305 does not list unconscionability in violation of UCC 2–302 as a real defense. How strong an agrum&nt can be made that it is nevertheless a real defense? (Remember that fraud in the inducement is only a personal defense.)

Problem 11. Would it make any difference in Problem 5, p. 198 supra, if Empire discovered not only that the cans are defective, but also that Quaker had fraudulently misrepresented their quality before the contract was made? See UCC 3–305.

———

SECTION 2. DRAWEE'S RECOURSE AFTER PAYMENT BY MISTAKE

———

(A) BASIC RULES

———

Prefatory Note. What is the legal position of a bank that overlooks its depositor's stop order and pays the check by mistake? The case law in New York prior to the Code affords an interesting contrast with the law under the Code.

New York law began with the rule that the bank was not entitled to charge the amount of the check to its depositor's account as long as the depositor had not ratified the wrongful payment by, for example, taking and keeping goods for which the check had been given.[1] The bank, therefore, had to bear the loss, as against its depositor, even though the depositor may have issued the stop order without justification.

Banks counterattacked by putting on stop order forms clauses disclaiming any liability to the depositor for ignoring a stop order. Courts in some states had held such clauses invalid, sometimes on the ground of public policy and sometimes on the ground of lack of consideration. See Note 2, p. 220 infra. But the New York Court of Appeals, mindful of having already fastened liability on the bank without regard to the depositor's justification for stopping payment, sustained such a clause.[2]

1. American Defense Society v. Sherman National Bank, 225 N.Y. 506, 122 N.E. 695 (1919).

2. Gaita v. Windsor Bank, 251 N.Y. 152, 167 N.E. 203 (1929).

The use of such a clause generally gave the bank adequate protection by allowing it to charge the check to its depositor, whether justified or not in stopping payment. Could it, in the alternative, recover the amount paid by mistake from the payee to whom it had paid it? The Court of Appeals concluded that, in the usual case, the bank's recourse against its depositor was exclusive, so that "when a bank pays a check after and despite receiving a stop-payment order from its depositor it cannot recover on the check from the payee of the check." [3]

The Code deals with the problem in a very different way. UCC 3–418 generally makes the bank's payment final. But UCC 4–407 gives the bank rights of subrogation which may allow it to recover against either its depositor or the payee, depending on the facts relating to the transaction between the two of them.[4] This is in sharp contrast to the prior New York law under which "Our courts have never permitted a bank . . ., after breaching its depositor's instructions, to involve him against his will in litigation with a third party in order that the bank may recoup a potential loss resulting from its own error. The doctrine of subrogation . . . is not properly applicable under such circumstances." [5] If the bank has already charged the amount of the check to its depositor's account and refuses to recredit it, the depositor presumably has an action against the bank to the extent that its payment caused loss. Where is there an express provision to this effect? Can such a rule fairly be read into the Code by inference from UCC 4–403(3) or by analogy to UCC 4–407(b)? [6]

---

3. Rosenbaum v. First National City Bank, 11 N.Y.2d 845, 227 N.Y.S.2d 670, 182 N.E.2d 280 (1962). An exception was made, however, "if at the time of presentation and payment the payee has notice that payment has been stopped; then the payee has no right to retain the proceeds of the check mistakenly paid by the bank." National Boulevard Bank v. Schwartz, 175 F.Supp. 74 (S.D.N.Y.1959). See also Chase National Bank v. Battat, 105 N.Y.S.2d 13 (Sup.Ct.1951).

4. The reader who has not studied the concept of subrogation in another course may find the following description useful. "Where property of one person is used in discharging an obligation owed by another . . ., under such circumstances that the other would be unjustly enriched by the retention of the benefit thus conferred, the former is entitled to be subrogated to the position of the obligee . . . .." Restatement of Restitution § 162. Thus if A owes B $100, and C, believing that C owes this debt to B, pays B $100, then C is entitled to be subrogated to B's claim against A in the amount of $100.

5. Chase National Bank v. Battat, 297 N.Y. 185, 78 N.E.2d 465 (1948).

6. It is worthy of note at this point that in the 1952 edition of the Code a person who obtained payment or certification warranted that he had "no knowledge of any effective direction to stop payment" (UCC 3–417(1)(b) (1952 ed.); see also UCC 4–207(1)(d) (1952 ed.)). At the 1954 hearings on the Code in New York, the New York Clearing House Association objected to this rule. "The holder who is told that the drawer intends to stop payment who thereafter collect[s] the check takes the risk that, if it is paid over an effective order, he may have to repay the payor at some future time when he may have changed his position. It has been suggested that the holder should advise the payor bank of his information after which the payor bank may not, it is suggested, hold him on his warranty. This is not practical in most cases because any such notice would require that the item be given special handling; and it is unrealistic in all cases. The only practical alternative is to suggest that the holder disclaim the

Problem 12.   Before the Empire check has been presented to the Irving Trust, Empire offers to return the cans to Quaker and stops payment on the check, in the belief that they are defective and that it is entitled to refuse to pay for them.   The Irving Trust mislays the stop payment order, pays the check, and charges Empire's account.

(a) What are the rights of the Irving Trust, Empire and Quaker? Does it make any difference whether Empire is correct in its belief? See UCC 4–403, 4–407; Sunshine v. Bankers Trust Co., infra.

(b) Would it make any difference if the stop order contained the following clause:

Should you pay this check through inadvertence or oversight, it is expressly understood that you will in no way be held responsible.

(c) Suppose that Empire insists that the cans are defective and Quaker insists that they are not.   Before the Irving Trust has a chance to investigate, a second check drawn by Empire is presented to the Irving Trust for payment.   Empire's balance is insufficient to pay it, but would be sufficient if the amount of the $2,178.50 check had not been charged to Empire's account.   Advise the Irving Trust whether or not to pay the second check.   See the discussion at the end of this problem.

(d) Suppose that Empire is correct in its belief that it is entitled to refuse to pay for the cans.   Assume that Quaker had a balance of $1,000 before making the deposit and that on that afternoon the Philadelphia National allowed Quaker to withdraw $2,500 in cash and certified a check drawn by Quaker in the amount of $2,000.   What would be the rights of Empire, Quaker, the Philadelphia National and the Irving Trust?   Would it make any difference if Quaker had included the words "for deposit" in its indorsement?   Does the answer depend on whether the other checks deposited at the same time are paid? (See the deposit slip at p. 99 supra.)   See Problems 5 and 6, pp. 198–199 supra.

(e) Suppose that the facts are otherwise the same as in (d) but that the withdrawal from and certification by the Philadelphia National do not occur until after the Irving Trust has paid the check.

warranty in his indorsement.   But how many holders are sufficiently learned in the law to do so?   And if this is what the holder should do, why propose the rule at all?"   Record of Hearings on the Uniform Commercial Code (N.Y.Leg.Doc. (1954) No. 65) 445–46.

The warranty was dropped out of the 1957 edition of the Code.   The Editorial Board gave the following reason: "This warranty was consistent with some case law but has been extensively criticized and appears to be productive of more trouble than benefit.   Further, the protection afforded payors by this statutory warranty becomes less necessary in view of the provisions of Section 4–407.   However, deletion of the warranty evidences no intent to change the common law, insofar as there are common law decisions on the question."   1956 Recommendations of the Editorial Board for the Uniform Commercial Code 146.   What, then, is the rule under the Code in New York? See footnote 3, supra.

Will the result be the same? (Can a holder become a holder in due course of a check after it has been paid?)

(f) Suppose that the Irving Trust concludes that the Philadelphia National in (e) supra, is a holder in due course and that it is entitled to maintain the charge to Empire's account. If for this reason, it dishonors a second check drawn by Empire and returns it marked "insufficient funds," is it liable to Empire if a court later decides that the Philadelphia National was not a holder in due course? See the discussion at the end of this problem.

In connection with parts (c) and (f) of this Problem, it may be of interest that the 1952 edition of the Code contained a Comment 9 to UCC 4–403: "When a bank pays an item over a stop payment order, such payment automatically involves a charge to the customer's account. Subsection (3) imposes upon the customer the burden of establishing the fact and amount of loss resulting from the payment. Consequently until such burden is maintained either in a court action or to the satisfaction of the bank, the bank is not obligated to recredit the amount of the item to the customer's account and, therefore, is not liable for the dishonor of other items due to insufficient funds caused by the payment contrary to the stop payment order."

The Study of the Uniform Commercial Code made by the New York Law Revision Commission in 1955 had this to say about Comment 9: "Where the item upon which payment has been stopped has come into the hands of a holder in due course, the drawer or maker will be liable to the holder in due course, unless there is a 'real' defense, and under this section the bank is subrogated to the rights of the holder in due course. Where this situation arises, must the bank recredit the customer's account and sue the customer on the instrument, or can the bank let the charge to the customer's account remain and defend an action by the customer on the ground that the customer has suffered no loss since he is liable to the holder in due course whose rights the bank now holds? Subrogation to a right to enforce is not the same thing as a right to charge the customer's account. However, Section 4–403, providing for the right to stop-payment, provides that the burden is on the customer to establish the fact and amount of loss resulting from payment contrary to a binding stop-payment order, and Comment 9 to that section states that until such burden is maintained the bank is not obligated to recredit the customer's account. It is not clear that the rule indicated in this Comment 9 does result from the text of Section 4–403(3). In any event, however, there would be occasions of a dispute as to whether the stop-payment order was timely, or whether, if there had been a stipulation validly exonerating the bank from liability for a payment made without failure of 'ordinary care', the bank was liable at all for the payment. In any such case, the rights against the drawer or maker to which the bank is subrogated by Section 4–407 would be raised in the customer's action against the bank." N.Y.L.Rev.Comm. Study of UCC, Vol. 2, p. 339 (1955).

In 1955 the Code's Enlarged Editorial Board stated, "We . . . believe that Comment 9 is consistent with Section 4–403(3) and should stand. See discussion of this problem in Bailey & Clarke, ch. 8." Supplement November 1 to the 1952 Official Draft 145 (1955). The cited work explained that the rule in Comment 9 "would seem logically to result from the fact that the customer has the burden of proving loss; therefore, the charge made by the bank against the customer's account for payment of the stopped item would be valid until the customer meets that burden." J. Clarke and H. Bailey, Bank Deposits and Collections 124 (1955). The text of UCC 4–403(3) remained the same but when the revised Comments to the Code appeared early in 1958, Comment 9 had been dropped without explanation.[8]

NOTES

(1) **Validity of Stop Payment Orders and Automation.** The order, to be effective must, of course, sufficiently identify the check. At common law a stop order could be oral and in the absence of agreement was valid indefinitely. However, a majority of states enacted statutes limiting the period of effectiveness. Statutory periods ranged from 30 days to one year with similar variations as to renewals. Under UCC 4–403 an oral order is effective for fourteen days, a written order for six months.

In a computerized bank, stop orders may be handled by having the computer reject all checks of the amount of the stopped check until the stopped check is selected manually from among those rejected. Would the drawee bank be responsible if the computer failed to reject a stopped check for $4,999.99 because the stop order had incorrectly described it as a check for $4,999.98? Would the depositary bank be responsible if the computer failed to reject a stopped check for $4,999.99 because it had incorrectly encoded it as one for $4,999.98?

In FJS Electronics v. Fidelity Bank, 288 Pa.Super. 138, 431 A.2d 326 (1981), the court said that the drawee "made a choice when it elected to employ a technique which searched for stopped checks by amount alone. . . . A bank's decision to reduce operating costs by using a system which increases the risk that checks as to which there is an outstanding stop payment order will be paid invites liability when such items are paid. An error of fifty cents ['$1,844.48' for $1,844.98 check] in the amount of a stop payment order does not deprive the bank of a reasonable opportunity to act on the order." (In that case the bank's notice confirming the stop order said "PLEASE ENSURE AMOUNT IS CORRECT.")

8. UNPC 425(5), which is otherwise similar to UCC 4–303(3), adds that "such burden shall not affect the right of the drawer to have its account recredited."

Would it make a difference if the drawee bank were more specific in explaining to its customer the importance of the amount? Compare Delano v. Putnam Trust Co., 33 UCC Rep. 635 (Conn.Super.Ct.1981), with Poullier v. Nacua Motors, 108 Misc.2d 913, 439 N.Y.S.2d 85 (1981). A few states have non-uniform versions of UCC 4–403(1). See Capital Bank v. Schuler, 421 So.2d 633 (Fla.App.1982) (decided under version requiring that check be described with "certainty").

(2) Validity of Stipulations. Prior to the Code banks frequently printed on their stop order forms clauses such as:

> Should you pay this check through inadvertency or oversight, it is expressly understood that you will in no way be held responsible.

There was a conflict of authority on the validity of such clauses. Some courts held them invalid on the ground of public policy, at least in so far as they purported to relieve the bank of liability for its negligence. Other courts held them invalid on the basis of lack of consideration, since a bank was bound to observe a stop order and gave up nothing in exchange for the clause.

The Code, in UCC 4–103(1), prohibits disclaimer of the bank's responsibility for "failure to exercise ordinary care." Does this mean that an exculpatory clause on a stop order is of *no* effect under the Code? What would be the effect under the Code of a clause on the signature card requiring stop orders to be in writing and on a form provided by the bank? What risk inherent in an oral stop order might a bank seek to avoid by such a clause?

Even where it is against public policy for a bank to limit its liability for negligent payment, might it not be advantageous to a bank to put such a clause on its stop order form? Would the inclusion of such a clause come within Rule 1.2(d) of the American Bar Association's Model Rules of Professional Conduct (1983), which states: "A lawyer shall not counsel a client to engage, or assist a client, in conduct that the lawyer knows is criminal or fraudulent . . ."? The final draft of that rule contained additional language that was deleted: ". . . or in the preparation of a written instrument containing terms the lawyer knows are expressly prohibited by law.. . ." The following comment was also deleted: "Law in many jurisdictions expressly prohibits various provisions in contracts and other written instruments. Such proscriptions may include usury laws, statutes prohibiting provisions that purport to waive certain legally conferred rights and contract provisions that have been held to be prohibited as a matter of law in the controlling jurisdiction. A lawyer may not employ expressly prohibited terms. On the other hand, there are legal rules that simply make certain contractual provisions unenforceable, allowing one or both parties to avoid the obligation. Inclusion of the latter kind of provision in a contract may be unwise but it is not a violation of this Rule, nor is it improper to include a provision whose legality is subject to reasonable argument."

Can you draft a clause that would meet this standard under UCC 4–103(1)? Would the same reasoning apply to a clause which was unenforceable because of lack of consideration?

(3) **Death of a Customer.** Since a check operates as the drawer's order on the drawee bank and not as an assignment, in principle the drawer's death revokes his order just as would a stop payment order. This means that if the drawer has attempted to use a check in place of a will, and then dies before it is paid, the payee, as donee, not only has no right to payment against the drawee bank, but has none against the drawer's estate. Occasionally, however, a sympathetic court has allowed recovery against the estate. See Burks v. Burks, 222 Ark. 97, 257 S.W.2d 369, 38 A.L.R.2d 589 (1953). But see Burroughs v. Burroughs, 240 Mass. 485, 137 N.E. 923, 20 A.L.R. 174 (1922).

A more important consequence of the rule that death revokes the drawer's order, and one that is by no means limited to checks issued as gifts, is that it puts the bank in a precarious position if it pays after the drawer's death. Case law generally relieved the bank where it paid without knowledge of the death. In a few states special statutes were enacted permitting the drawee to pay a depositor's checks after death, even with knowledge.

For the Code provisions, see UCC 4–405. Comment 3 states that, "The purpose of the provision, as of the existing statutes, is to permit holders of checks drawn and issued shortly before death to cash them without the necessity of filing a claim in probate. The justification is that such checks normally are given in immediate payment of an obligation, that there is almost never any reason why they should not be paid, and that filing in probate is a useless formality, burdensome to the holder, the executor, the court and the bank. [What of other creditors if the estate has insufficient assets?] The section does not prevent an executor or administrator from recovering the payment from the holder of the check. It is not intended to affect the validity of any gift causa mortis or other transfer in contemplation of death, but merely to relieve the bank of liability for the payment." Under what circumstances would you advise a bank to pay checks after it knows that the drawer is dead?

(4) **Bankruptcy of a Customer.** A problem analogous to that posed by the drawer's death is posed by the drawer's bankruptcy. Suppose that a drawer issues a check and then files a voluntary petition in bankruptcy, but the bank subsequently pays the check in ignorance of the petition. Is the bank liable to the trustee in bankruptcy?

In Bank of Marin v. England, 385 U.S. 99, 87 S.Ct. 274, 17 L.Ed.2d 197 (1966), the Supreme Court read the old Bankruptcy Act to protect the bank. The new Bankruptcy Code § 542(c) codifies the rule of that case, protecting the bank if it pays "in good faith" and with "neither actual notice nor actual knowledge of the commencement of the case concerning the debtor." (However, the recipient of such a postpetition payment may not be protected. See § 549(b).)

SUNSHINE v. BANKERS TRUST CO.

Court of Appeals of New York, 1974.
34 N.Y.2d 404, 358 N.Y.S.2d 113, 314 N.E.2d 860.

WACHTLER, JUDGE.   On September 28, 1971, Oscar Sunshine, the ailing president of Modern Pillow, Inc. (Modern) gave his wife Elizabeth a signed check from Modern drawn on Bankers Trust Company (Bank).   He allegedly told her to fill in the check for whatever amount she needed.   That night Elizabeth inserted her name and the amount ($10,000), thus completing the check (see Uniform Commercial Code, § 3–115, subd. [1], Consol.Laws, c. 38).   Soon thereafter Oscar died.   On November 11, 1971, Elizabeth deposited the duly indorsed check in her special checking account at the Bank, the same branch on which the check was drawn.   The same day, Melvin Sunshine, who was now president of Modern, put a stop order on the check, claiming his stepmother, Elizabeth, had obtained the check by chicanery.   Initially, the Bank did nothing to withdraw the provisional credit given Elizabeth.   Two or three banking days after the Bank had credited her account and received the stop order from Melvin, the Bank debited Elizabeth's account.   Elizabeth commenced suit against the Bank to recover the $10,000 charge back.   The Bank impleaded Modern and issue was joined.

The trial court denied Elizabeth's motion for summary judgment but granted summary judgment in favor of Modern against the Bank. Elizabeth appealed the refusal of the trial court to grant summary judgment; however the Bank did not appeal the court's granting of summary judgment to Modern.   And the Bank's motion to have that unappealed judgment reopened at Special Term was denied.

The Appellate Division, First Department, 42 A.D.2d 544, 345 N.Y.S.2d 19, unanimously modified the order of the trial court and granted summary judgment to Elizabeth.   The Bank appeals from that decision and attempts as well to have its case against Modern reinstated by this court.

The Bank's initial contention is that this court should revive its cause of action against Modern (see CPLR 5015, subd. [a], par. 5, Consol.Laws, c. 8).   Since a determination of the issue relating to the unappealed judgment is crucial to our consideration of issues between the parties in this case, we would but point out that Special Term was correct as a matter of law in denying the Bank's attempt to reinstitute its action against Modern.   This is so since the judgment sought to be reopened was not "based" on the prior determination (5 Weinstein-Korn-Miller, N.Y.Civ.Prac., par. 5015.11).

The Bank's primary assault is on the summary judgment granted to Elizabeth by the Appellate Division. Although the pleadings are confusing, a close reading of all the papers before the trial court discloses that there are triable issues of fact.

Initially, it is important to note that the Bank in this case was both the depository and payor bank. The Bank asserts that payment was not final to Elizabeth based, *inter alia*, on subdivision (1) of section 4–212 of the Uniform Commercial Code. The "reasonable time" provision of that section applies to collecting banks. The mitigating circumstances in that section (see, also, § 4–108) are not available to the Bank in this case. The code specifically defines a collecting bank as any bank handling an item for collection except a payor bank (see § 4–105, subd. [d]). The Bank, therefore, cannot claim defenses available to a collecting bank relating to final payment or breach of presentment warranty (see § 4–207, subd. [2]) as it has attempted to do.

The pertinent code section to determine when the depository bank which is also the payor bank may charge back an account is subdivision (3) of section 4–212. That section allows a bank to obtain a refund for its provisional credit in accordance with subdivision (2) of section 4–301 provided the bank acts within the time limits prescribed by subdivision (1) of section 4–301. Subdivision (1) of section 4–301 states the bank must return the item or give written notice of dishonor "before it has made final payment (subsection (1) of Section 4–213) and before its midnight deadline" or it may not "revoke the settlement and recover any payment" pursuant to that section. The midnight deadline is the banking day following the banking day the bank receives the relevant item (see Uniform Commercial Code, § 4–104, subd. [1][h]). If the item is not returned or dishonored within that time limit, the item becomes available for withdrawal as of right "at the opening of the bank's second banking day following receipt of the item" (Uniform Commercial Code, § 4–213, subd. [4], par. [b]). In the case at bar, the bank did not send notice of dishonor until at least three banking days following receipt of the item. The item was therefore available for withdrawal as of right by Elizabeth.

The Bank asserts, *inter alia*, that it had the right to charge back Elizabeth's account pursuant to agreements between the Bank and the depositor which superseded the code provisions. The Bank specifically refers to the Regulations Governing Special Check Accounts which Elizabeth signed when she opened her checking accounts.

The agreement states: "If claim is made to the bank for the recovery of any part of any collected items (including any item cashed for depositor) after final payment thereof, on the ground that such item was altered or bore a forged endorsement or was otherwise not properly payable, the Bank may withhold the amount thereof from the account until final determination of such claim."

The deposit slip states: "All items are credited subject to final collection and receipt of proceeds in cash or by unconditional credit to and accepted by Bankers Trust Company." These agreements appear to refer to the Bank's role as depository or collecting bank and thus would attempt to alter its obligations under subdivision (3) of section 4–213 rather than under section 4–302.

To the extent that either of the agreements attempts to extend the period during which the Bank can charge back a depositor's account in a situation such as the one before us now, they are invalid.

Appellant cites subdivision (1) of section 4–103 of the code which states that "parties may by agreement determine the standards by which such responsibility is to be measured if such standards are not manifestly unreasonable". But appellant fails to cite the caveat in that provision which states "except that no agreement can disclaim a bank's responsibility for its own lack of good faith or failure to exercise ordinary care". The Official Comment to that code section states (McKinney's Cons.Laws of N.Y., Book 62½, Part 2, Uniform Commercial Code, p. 519): "In view of the technical complexity of the field of bank collections, the enormous number of items handled by banks, the certainty that there will be variations from the normal . . . in each bank, the certainty of changing conditions and the possibility of developing improved methods of collection to speed the process, it would be unwise to freeze present methods of operation by mandatory statutory rules". There is nothing in the comment that even hints at an intention to allow banks to alter code provisions in order to render themselves harmless from their own error. Whatever the validity of bank disclaimers to customers in general or attempts to render themselves harmless from the results of someone else's errors or disputes,[1] it is clear that here the Bank is attempting to disclaim its own responsibility for ordinary care.

The next issue presented is whether there is a triable issue of fact as to Elizabeth's alleged breach of warranty of presentment. Even if the bank has initially lost its right to charge back, it can hold the depositor accountable for an item if the depositor committed a breach of presentment warranty (see Uniform Commercial Code, § 4–302). We find however no facts alleged which would support a theory of breach presentment warranty.[2]

1. As would be the case if the "agreement" was interpreted as an attempt to alter the provisions of subdivision (3) of section 4–213 of the Uniform Commercial Code.

2. The "good title" warranty in section 4–207 (subd. [1], par. [a]) appears to apply mainly to forged indorsements and would not be applicable in this case. There is no allegation of a forged indorsement. We do not construe the warranty that the item has not been materially altered (subd. [1], par. [c]) as

covering a case where an item has allegedly been fraudulently obtained. Since there is no allegation that Elizabeth filled in an amount other than that authorized by her husband, this provision would not apply to the case at bar.

Section 4–207 (subd. [1], par. [b]), the warranty that Elizabeth had no knowledge that Oscar's signature was unauthorized is a bit more bothersome. The third-party counterclaim filed by Modern, and available for use by the Bank (see 622 West 113th St. Corp. v. Chemical

Another remedy appellant attempts to pursue is that of subrogation. Section 4–407 of the code states that: "If a payor bank has paid an item over the stop payment order of the drawer or maker or otherwise under circumstances giving a basis for objection by the drawer or maker, to prevent unjust enrichment and only to the extent necessary to prevent loss to the bank by reason of its payment of the item, the payor bank shall be subrogated to the rights . . . (c) of the drawer or maker against the payee . . . with respect to the transaction out of which the item arose." The papers before the trial court were replete with allegations of fraud, lack of authority, and other allegations that would give rise to a cause of action by Modern against Elizabeth. The Bank specifically claimed the right to be subrogated to Modern's claims against Elizabeth in the affidavit of its vice-president opposing the summary judgment motion.

Respondent does not deny that normally the Bank would be subrogated to Modern's rights, but claims such rights do not arise in this case for two reasons.

First, respondent points out that the Bank never debited Modern's account. Therefore, it is alleged, Modern suffered no loss to which the Bank can be subrogated. Technically respondent's argument is colorable. Section 4–407 allows subrogation "under circumstances giving a basis for objection by the drawer or maker".[3] The "drawer or maker", Modern, in this case had no basis for objection since its account was never debited. In addition the Official Comment to section 4–407 (subd. [c]) talks of the bank "reimburs[ing] the drawer for such payment". There was no reimbursement here since the account was never debited.

Bank, N.Y. Trust Co., 52 Misc.2d 444, 276 N.Y.S.2d 85) asserts lack of authority by Oscar to sign the check for Elizabeth's personal use (see Wen Kroy Realty Co. v. Public Nat. Bank & Trust Co. of N.Y., 260 N.Y. 84, 183 N.E. 73). However, paragraph (b) of subdivision (1) refers to the signature being unauthorized not the instrument being unauthorized. There is no doubt that Oscar's signature was authorized (i.e., he had authority as president of Modern to sign checks for Modern). Section 3–417 of the code is a parallel of section 4–207 (McKinney's Cons.Laws of N.Y., Book 62½, Part 2, Uniform Commercial Code, Clarke and Young, Practice Commentary, p. 564). The Official Comments to section 3–417 of the code support the assertion that "authorized signature" means only what it says and was not meant to include unauthorized purpose. Official Comment No. 4 talks of "parties accepting or paying instruments bearing unauthorized maker's or drawer's *signatures*" (emphasis added, p. 356). And further on, the comment talks of the "drawee who ac-

cepted without detecting the unauthorized signature" (p. 358). That phrase certainly appears to refer to an examination of the signature only and not the purpose for which the instrument was given. Therefore, we conclude that the Bank has not stated an affirmative defense under section 4–207.

3. If we were to read the phrase "giving a basis for objection by the drawer or maker" as modifying the phrase "otherwise under circumstances" only and not the phrase "over the stop payment order of the drawer or maker", there would be no need to require a basis for objection by the drawer or maker as a predicate to recovering under this section in this case. Inserting, in effect, a comma after the word "Maker" in the first sentence of section 4–407 would not be unreasonable, but our conclusion for policy reasons would come out the same even if we read "giving a basis for objection" as modifying everything that comes before it in the sentence (infra).

The policy arguments regarding the proof that the subrogor has some basis for objection compel a liberal rather than strict interpretation of the pertinent wording of section 4–407. When a stop-payment order has been timely given, the party issuing the order should not lose the use of its funds. Yet, if we were to accept respondent's argument, the bank would be compelled to debit the account of the party issuing the stop payment as a precondition for suing as a subrogee of that party. The "innocent" party who issued the timely stop-payment order would then lose the use of those funds for some time. Certainly the court should not compel a bank to, in effect, wrongfully convert a customer's fund in order to vindicate its subrogation rights.[4]

Moreover, if we were to compel a bank to debit Modern's account as a condition precedent to bringing suit, the transaction would merely be a sham directed by this court in order to enable form to triumph over substance. The "loss" which will serve as the predicate for the subrogation suit will really be an ersatz loss because a party issuing a timely stop order cannot suffer a legal loss by way of an account debit.

The second allegation raised by respondent concerning the subrogation issue is more bothersome. Respondent asserts that since the summary judgment granted Modern against the Bank is final and nonvacatable, Modern can never suffer any loss, and thus, the Bank has no rights to which it can be subrogated.

It cannot be gainsaid that the decision of the trial court in granting summary judgment to Modern appeared to be quite broad in its application. The court stated that since the stop-payment order was timely Modern "[could] in no way be liable to [the] Bank". There is no doubt that this wording would be broad enough to prevent a suit against Modern by the Bank should it lose its action against Elizabeth (but see § 4–407, subd. [b]).[5] The question is considerably more

4. In most cases, we realize, the Bank will inadvertently debit Modern's account until it realizes a timely stop order has been issued. We should not exacerbate that unfortunate situation by compelling a bank to debit the account even after it realizes a timely stop-payment order has been issued.

5. The questions of whether, absent the trial court's decision, the Bank could sue Modern under subdivision (b) of section 4–407 of the code is not before this court, and we therefore do not reach it. However, it should be pointed out that an implicit assertion underlying many of appellant's arguments is that a bank cannot be made to suffer a loss by paying over a timely stop order. Usually, the code provides the Bank with a means of recoup-

ing any loss it has suffered, but this is by no means always the case. The Official Comment to section 4–403 of the Code (McKinney's Cons.Laws on N.Y., Book 62½, Part 2, Uniform Commercial Code, p. 611) makes clear that a stop-payment order need not be supported by a sound legal basis; it is, instead, a service that must be provided by the banking industry: "2. The position taken by this section is that stopping payment is a service which depositors expect and are entitled to receive from banks notwithstanding its difficulty, inconvenience and expense. The inevitable occasional losses through failure to stop should be borne by the banks as a cost of the business of banking".

difficult when determining whether the trial court judgment forecloses the Bank's rights as subrogee of Modern.

Respondent asserts that the trial court decision forecloses the possibility of the Bank debiting Modern's account in the future to acquire the necessary prerequisite to bring suit as Modern's subrogee. The factual basis for this contention appears correct, but as we have noted above such a debit is not a condition precedent to a subrogation action.

We read the trial court decision as barring the possibility of the Bank ever recovering against Modern in a suit arising out of the underlying transaction or occurrence. However, it did not prevent the Bank from recovering against Elizabeth by asserting its own rights under the code or Modern's rights under the code subrogation provision.

In short, we read section 4–407 as conferring on the Bank the substantive rights of subrogation even if the technical mechanical requirements of common-law subrogation have not been met.[6]

Section 4–407 also contains a provision that allows a bank to recover only to the extent that the party the bank is moving against has been unjustly enriched. In the case at bar, we have held that Elizabeth should be awarded summary judgment on the charge back issue. Hence the money is now hers subject to recovery by the Bank qua subrogee of Modern. Her award, however, should be stayed pursuant to CPLR 3212 (subd. [e], par. 2) to make certain the money is still extant and collectible should the Bank later prevail on the subrogation issue.[7]

There is one last assertion by respondent that deserves the attention of this court. Banks are in the unique position of holding the

6. Although there appeared to have been no cases directly in point, in 1955 the Law Revision Commission stated that in a situation such as the one at bar, New York allowed the Bank to recover on a common-law restitution theory rather than a subrogation theory (see 1955 Report of N.Y.Law Rev.Comm., Study of the Uniform Commercial Code, vol. 2, pp. 1558–1559). Whatever the continued viability of a common-law restitution theory in connection with other parts of the code or on a different fact pattern, it appears that such a theory has been subsumed by section 4–407 of the code in this case. If we had required an account debit as a precondition to a section 4–407 suit, or if we had, in effect, read section 4–407 out of the code by prohibiting an account debit but requiring Modern to suffer some loss, then it is clear that the common-law right of restitution would not have merged into the code provision. But if we allow the Bank a separate cause of action for common-law restitution in the case at bar, we would be allowing it two bites of the same apple.

7. Whenever a bank is relying on a right of charge back and a subrogation right, it should always plead in the alternative. A court should always decide, and the parties should always litigate the charge back issue first. Then, in the event the bank loses on the charge back issue, the claimant will have been ("unjustly") enriched, and the bank will be able to proceed with its subrogation action. When a verdict is returned simultaneously on both the charge back and the subrogation issue, it will be assumed that the charge back issue was determined first. Such procedures are necessary because the bank can hardly claim an opposing party has been unjustly enriched when the bank is holding the funds in question under color of right.

very stakes for which they are contending. Respondent asserts that if we send this case back for trial, we would in effect, allow the Bank to be the arbiter of a dispute between two outside parties. We are not unmindful that banks may, perhaps even under a colorable claim of right, charge back a depositor's account even when no such right exists. The burden on a depositor of then going forward to bring a suit is a heavy one, and, indeed, an impossible one to bear where the amount involved is small. Our decision should not be interpreted to permit this result. Before payment becomes final, or the midnight deadline has passed, a bank may charge back an account when it has received a timely stop order precisely so the Bank can avoid taking part in the dispute at all. However, once the Bank loses its right to charge back, the item becomes comingled with the general funds of the depositor (see 622 West 113th St. Corp. v. Chemical Bank N.Y. Trust Co., 52 Misc.2d 444, 276 N.Y.S.2d 85). When the Bank is suing as subrogee, it may not at the same time make a preliminary determination of the merits of the case by charging back on the depositor's account (cf. Banking Law, Consol.Laws, c. 2, § 134, subd. 5). So that in this case the Bank has no more or less right to take away or freeze Elizabeth's account than would the Bank's subrogor, Modern.[8] When the Bank is acting as subrogee, it has the burden of going forward.

In sum then, we find that there are triable issues of fact relating to the allegations surrounding the underlying transactions raised by the Bank qua subrogee of Modern. Accordingly the case should be remanded to the trial court for a trial of these issues.

NOTES

(1) **Effect of Sunshine.** In Thomas v. Marine Midland Tinkers National Bank, 86 Misc.2d 284, 381 N.Y.S.2d 797 (1976), a buyer of rugs, who had given the seller a $2,500 check as a deposit, stopped payment on the check. When the drawee bank mistakenly paid the check, the buyer sued the bank. The bank "chose to try its case against the plaintiff alone without asserting any affirmative defense as to non loss, or adducing any evidence to negate the claimed loss at trial. No attempt was made to implead any other party from whom the defendant might acquire subrogated rights, to vouch any such party into the action, or to commence its own action against such party and thereafter move for a single consolidated trial. The defendant bank chose rather to maintain a position that plaintiff was required to come forward with evidence as to the underlying transaction to negate any inference of non loss or lesser loss in order to prove plaintiff's prima facie case."

The court awarded the buyer a $2,500 judgment against the bank. "The Court of Appeals in Sunshine clearly states that a defendant

8. This, of course, should in no way prevent a bank from obtaining an attachment of the funds or otherwise freezing them in any manner available to it under the law.

bank exercising its subrogation rights created by UCC § 4–407 has the burden of coming forward and presenting evidence which would show an absence of actual loss sustained by a plaintiff depositor suing it for damages arising from an improper payment over a stop payment order. In so stating, the Court of Appeals has not negated plaintiff's ultimate burden of proof upon the issue of loss if the defendant comes forward with proof. The Court of Appeals has thereby provided a means of harmoniously construing §§ 4–403(1), 4–403(3) and 4–407 of the Uniform Commercial Code to effectuate the statutory intent and design. This distinction between burden of proof and burden of coming forward is not uncommon. . . . [I]f the bank fails to meet its burden with legally sufficient proof of non loss, the customer has proven a prima facie case and is entitled to judgment. Where the burden of going forward is met by the bank, the customer must sustain the ultimate burden of proof on the issue of loss."

(2) **Another Analysis.** In Siegel v. New England Merchants National Bank, 386 Mass. 672, 437 N.E.2d 218 (1982), a case growing out of mistaken payment of a post-dated check, the Supreme Judicial Court of Massachusetts gave a different reading to UCC 4–401, 4–403, and 4–407. (Note that, unlike UCC 4–407, UCC 4–403 is limited to stopped checks and would apply to a post-dated check by analogy only.) The court began with UCC 4–401 and 4–407.

"The depositor has a claim against the bank for the amount improperly debited from its account, and the bank has a claim against the depositor based on subrogation to the rights of the payee and other holders. The bank may assert its subrogation rights defensively when its depositor brings an action for wrongful debit. . . . The rule of § 4–403(3), that a depositor must prove his loss, may at first seem at odds with our conclusion that § 4–401(1) provides the depositor with a claim against the bank in the amount of the check, leaving the bank with recourse through subrogation under § 4–407. . . . We believe, however, that § 4–403(3) was intended to operate within the process of credit and subrogation established by §§ 4–401(1) and 4–407. . . . Section 4–403(3) simply protects the bank against the need to prove events familiar to the depositor, and far removed from the bank, before it can realize its subrogation rights. The depositor, who participated in the initial transaction, knows whether the payee was entitled to eventual payment and whether any defenses arose. Therefore, § 4–403(3) requires that he, rather than the bank, prove these matters.

"This view of the three relevant sections of the code suggests a fair allocation of the burden of proof. The bank, which has departed from authorized bookkeeping, must acknowledge a credit to the depositor's account. It must then assert its subrogation rights, and in doing so must identify the status of the parties in whose place it claims. If the bank's subrogation claims are based on the check, this would entail proof that the third party subrogor was a holder, or perhaps a holder in due course. This responsibility falls reasonably upon the bank, because it has received the check from the most recent holder and is in at least as good a position as the depositor to trace its history.

"The depositor must then prove any facts that might demonstrate a loss. He must establish defenses good against a holder or holder in due course, as the case may be. See G.L. c. 106, § 3–305, 3–306. If the initial transaction is at issue, he must prove either that he did not incur a liability to the other party, or that he has a defense to liability. Thus the bank, if it asserts rights based on the transaction, need not make out a claim on the part of its subrogor against the depositor. Responsibility in this area rests entirely with the depositor, who participated in the transaction and is aware of its details. Further, the depositor must establish any consequential loss."

Among other cases, the court cited Thomas v. Marine Midland Tinkers National Bank, Note 1 supra, and said by way of comparison: "Although our analysis will often have the same result . . . it may in some cases give greater force to § 4–403(3)." Which is the better analysis?

As to the possibility that a drawee bank might have a claim against the person paid for restitution of money paid by mistake, as an alternative to its claim under UCC 4–407(c), see Bryan v. Citizens National Bank, 628 S.W.2d 761 (Tex.1982).

(3) Electronic Fund Transfers Act. The Electronic Fund Transfers Act and Regulation E deals with countermanding payment only in connection with preauthorized transfers. Under Regulation E:

> A consumer may stop payment of a preauthorized electronic fund transfer from the consumer's account by notifying the financial institution orally or in writing at any time up to three business days before the scheduled date of the transfer. The financial institution may require written confirmation of the stop-payment order to be made within 14 days of an oral notification if, when the oral notification is made, the requirement is disclosed to the consumer together with the address to which confirmation should be sent. If written confirmation has been required by the financial institution, the oral stop-payment order shall cease to be binding 14 days after it has been made.

12 C.F.R. § 205.10(c).

(4) Uniform New Payments Code. The Uniform New Payments Code would make a major change in the law on countermanding payment. UNPC 425 allows a drawer to stop payment. In addition, it gives a consumer drawer in some cases a right "to direct a payor account institution, orally or in writing, to reverse payment on an order in the amount of $50 or more until three (3) business days after that order has been finally paid." In the case of a check, the drawer has this right if the check has been truncated before collection but not if the check has been transmitted for payment to the drawee bank.[2]

The commentary explains: "The fundamental reason for providing this right is to protect the bargaining position of consumer drawers. At present, the right to stop payment is greatly limited in value [because] the time in which the consumer can exercise it is a function of the arbitrary time it takes to collect a check, see UCC 4–303, since the right is cut-off after the order is paid. This stop payment window may be appreciably shortened and ultimately eliminated, by check truncation or by use of on-line debit cards at the point-of-sale. . . . [T]his Section gives the consumer three days after final payment to reverse regardless of how quickly the order is transmitted and paid. . . . [However,] when a written draw order, e.g. paper check, is paid there is no reversal right. This exception does not apply to checks truncated before collection because they are not written draw orders when paid. Where paper checks are involved, the stop payment right gives the consumer a limited measure of protection. Moreover, the operational problems of reversing normal checks would be substantial."

(B) WHAT AMOUNTS TO PAYMENT

Introduction. If the drawee bank "has *paid* an item over the stop payment order of the drawer," the bank is subrogated as provided in UCC 4–407. However, until "final payment," under UCC 4–213(1), the bank is not yet "accountable for the amount of the item" to the holder and is free to honor its depositor's stop order. Thus the drawee's situation changes fundamentally at the moment that the check is paid. When, then, does "payment" occur?

We have already considered this question in the context of the check drawn on insufficient funds. See Chapter 3, Section 2(B). There we saw that a bank generally has until its midnight deadline to decide whether to dishonor a check for insufficient funds. During that time it can also make sure that the check has not been stopped.

The bank will usually take steps to pay the check well before its midnight deadline. In the context of the check on which payment has been stopped, a question may arise as to whether those steps amount to payment of the check. Suppose that the drawee bank has complet-

---

2. Even if the check has been truncated before collection, payment is not reversible if the check was for cash withdrawal of if the drawer has elected to have an account that is not reversible.

ed the first four steps described in (a) through (d) of UCC 4–109, but that the relevant clearing house or midnight deadline has not yet passed. If the drawer stops payment during this interval, can the bank properly refuse to pay the check? Or has it, by making "final payment" under UCC 4–213(1), already become "accountable" for the check? [1]

In one of the most controversial cases decided under Article 4 of the Code, the Supreme Court of Wisconsin held that a bank that had received a check through the clearing house had not made "final payment" because the clearing house deadline had not passed. The bank had therefore not become "accountable" for the check and was free to follow its depositor's stop order and refuse to pay it. West Side Bank v. Marine National Exchange Bank, 37 Wis.2d 661, 155 N.W.2d 587 (1968). The drawee bank contended that the process of posting is not completed until the end of the fifth step, that in UCC 4–109(e) ("correcting or reversing an entry or erroneous action with respect to the item"). The drawee bank argued that "so long as time remains in which entries can be reversed (until the clearing-house deadline), a check is not finally paid under the Code." The court agreed.[2]

Most of the comment on the West Side Bank case has been adverse, as the following case suggests. Although the Schultz case arose out of the drawer's bankruptcy, the reasoning also applies to a stop payment order.

Problem 13. Just after all of the steps recited at pages 103–104 have taken place, the Irving Trust receives a stop order from Empire. Advise the Irving Trust as to its legal position if it: (a) ignores the stop order and takes no further action with respect to the check; (b) promptly reverses the steps that it has just taken, stamps the check "cancelled in error" and returns it through the Clearing House to the First National City with a return item stamp like that on page 111 with "payment stopped" checked; (c) waits until Friday, January 20, and then takes the steps described in (b). Would your advice be different if the Irving Trust received the stop order when it had taken some but not all of the steps it has just taken? See UCC 4–213, 4–301, 4–302, 4–303, 4–109; H. Schultz & Sons v. Bank of Suffolk County, infra; Yandell v. White City Amusement Park, infra.

1. Can you see why, in the situation in which presentment is made through the clearing house or by a Federal Reserve Bank, this question of the time of payment does not normally arise in the context of the check drawn on insufficient funds? Recall that we are assuming that the drawee bank has already completed the step described in UCC 4–109(b) ("ascertaining that sufficient funds are available").

2. Why should it make a difference to Philadelphia National whether Irving Trust has paid the check or not? Would not Philadelphia National have a right against Empire to the extent of any withdrawals that it had allowed against the check? Might it make a difference if Philadelphia held a demand obligation of Quaker that it could offset against any proceeds realized by it on the Empire check?

H. SCHULTZ & SONS v. BANK OF SUFFOLK COUNTY

United States District Court, Eastern District of New York, 1977.
439 F.Supp. 1137.

GEORGE C. PRATT, DISTRICT JUDGE. Plaintiff H. Schultz & Sons, Inc. is incorporated and maintains its principal place of business in New Jersey. Defendant Suffolk County Bank is incorporated and maintains its principal place of business in New York. Plaintiff brought this diversity action to obtain the $40,000 face value of a check which was drawn to plaintiff by Unishops, Inc. on an account maintained by Unishops at the defendant bank, and which plaintiff alleges was wrongfully dishonored after the bank learned of Unishops' bankruptcy. Jurisdiction therefore lies under 28 U.S.C. § 1332.

Now before the court are cross-motions for summary judgment originally made in January, 1976. At the request of counsel, argument of the motions was deferred until April, 1977. For the reasons set forth below, plaintiff's motion is granted, and defendant's is denied.

FACTS

There is no dispute over the essential facts. For purposes of these motions the parties have agreed that the following facts are true:

1. The $40,000 check was dated November 26, 1973 and drawn by Unishops on its account at defendant's bank, payable to the order of plaintiff. Parties' 9(g) statement.

2. Plaintiff deposited the check for collection on November 27, 1973 in its account at Fidelity Union Trust Co. of Newark, New Jersey. Id.

3. Fidelity forwarded the check to the Federal Reserve Bank of New York, which in turn forwarded the check to defendant. Id.

4. Defendant received the check on November 29, 1973. Stipulated upon oral argument.

5. On the same day, November 29, 1973, the check was photographed, "proven", and debited to Unishops' account by defendant. Id.

6. Defendant learned of Unishops' bankruptcy on November 30, 1973 and on that same day gave telephone notice of dishonor of the check to the Federal Reserve Bank. Parties' 9(g) statements.

7. If defendant had not subsequently learned of Unishops' bankruptcy, no additional processing of the check would have taken place prior to the sending out of Unishops' monthly statement. Stipulated upon oral argument.

8. Defendant never honored the check. Id.

9. Plaintiff was never a depositor with defendant. Id.

CLAIMS

Initially, plaintiff sought judgment on two theories: (1) that since defendant failed to return the check by its "midnight deadline", it was obligated to pay the check to plaintiff, and (2) since defendant had "finally paid" the check it could not thereafter refuse payment based on its subsequent receipt of notice of Unishops' bankruptcy. Prior to and at the time of argument plaintiff withdrew the first ground for relief, urging only that final payment had been made so that subsequent notice of bankruptcy was ineffective to prevent plaintiff's recovery of the proceeds. Defendant seeks summary judgment on the ground that final payment had not occurred and could not occur until expiration of the maximum time permitted for return of the check, here, midnight on the day following receipt of the check or midnight of November 30, 1973.

As to most of the applicable law the parties are in agreement:

1. If under the circumstances of this case a "final payment" had been made, then defendant bank is accountable to plaintiff for the $40,000 proceeds of the check. NYUCC § 4-213(1).

2. Final payment did occur if the bank had "completed the process of posting" the check to Unishops' account. NYUCC § 4–213(1)(c).

3. If the bank had "completed the process of posting", the notice of Unishops' bankruptcy came too late to affect defendant's accountability to plaintiff. NYUCC § 4–303(1)(d).

The parties disagree on whether the bank's "process of posting" was completed here, and this squarely raises a question of law, the proper interpretation of § 4–109 of New York's Uniform Commercial Code. NYUCC § 4–109 defines the "Process of posting" as

> The usual procedure followed by a payor bank in determining to pay an item and in recording the payment including one or more of the following or other steps as determined by the bank;
>
> > (a) verification of any signature;
> >
> > (b) ascertaining that sufficient funds are available;
> >
> > (c) affixing a "paid" or other stamp;
> >
> > (d) entering a charge or entry to a customer's account;
> >
> > (e) *correcting or reversing an entry or erroneous action* with respect to the item. (Emphasis supplied)

The first four steps listed were completed by the defendant. As to the fifth step defendant argues that, because of the language of subparagraph (e) of § 4–109, it retained discretion, and indeed had the duty under the Bankruptcy Law, to reverse the entry, and it could properly do so anytime up until the "midnight deadline" even though all other steps in the process of posting had been completed.

The "midnight deadline" is defined as midnight on the next banking day on which the bank receives the relevant item. NYUCC § 4–104(1)(h). Under the deferred posting practice employed by defendant and authorized by NYUCC § 4–301 the latest possible time for defendant to have returned the subject check unpaid was the midnight deadline.

The Official Comments to this uniform act also aid in its interpretation, and their failure to support defendant's position argues strongly against its validity.

Under defendant's interpretation of the statute, however, the only time the process of posting could be completed would be upon expiration of the midnight deadline. This would mean that the draftsmen's specification of the other steps in the process of posting, aimed at the subjective decision of whether to pay the check and the mechanical process of recording the payment, become meaningless.

Plaintiff's interpretation of subparagraph (e) would permit the "correcting or reversing of an entry or erroneous action" only in the event that an error had been made, whether in decision making or in mechanical recording. It does not, according to plaintiff, authorize correcting or reversing an entry merely upon the receipt of additional information or notice which was not brought to the bank's attention prior to completion of the other elements in the process of posting.

DISCUSSION

The question presented here was considered by the Supreme Court of Wisconsin in West Side Bank v. Marine National Exchange Bank, 37 Wis.2d 661, 155 N.W.2d 587 (1968) and decided in favor of the bank. There, the Wisconsin court read the words "reversing an entry" in subsection (e) to authorize the bank to do precisely that—reverse an entry—without restriction as to the reason for the reversal. The court adopted what it viewed to be the plain meaning of the statute, even though it acknowledged that the legislature's intent was probably to the contrary.

The same problem has been reviewed in depth in a law review note entitled "Bank Procedures and the UCC—When is a Check Finally Paid?", 9 Boston College Industrial and Commercial L.Rev. 1957 (1968). The importance of the concept of "final payment" in the banking sections of the UCC is highlighted by the following paragraph from that article:

> The concept of final payment is central to the scheme of Article 4 because the time of final payment of a check or similar item is the starting point for determining the rights and obligations of a number of parties in relation to an item. When final payment occurs, the payor bank is deemed to be accountable to the presenting party for the amount of the item. At the same time the drawer of the instrument is relieved of

liability to the holder because the amount is deemed to have been paid. Also, if the payor bank becomes insolvent and suspends payment once final payment has occurred, the owner of an item will have a preferred claim against the payor bank for the amount. Final payment, furthermore, is one of the occurrences which can prevent the "four legals"—notice, stop-order, legal process and setoff—from being effective to prevent actual payment of the item. Provisional settlement, the credit given by the payor bank to the party presenting an item for collection, becomes final when final payment is made, as does credit for the item between the presenting bank, other collecting banks and the customer seeking payment for the item. Final payment, moreover, marks the end of the collection process and the beginning of the remitting process, whereby the amount of the item is returned to the party demanding payment.

Discussing the Wisconsin case, the author rejects the Wisconsin court's analysis, and suggests an alternative design to accommodate both the language of § 4–109 and the policies underlying its adoption: The author's suggestion would apply subsection (e) only to that part of the process of posting relating to the "recording the payment" and not to the second part relating to "determining to pay". While this reasoning has some appeal, it does not fully solve the problem since an error made in the "determining to pay" part of the process of posting should be just as capable of correction prior to the midnight deadline as would be a typographical or mechanical error in "recording the payment".

Sounder analysis seems to require that the legislature's intent be honored. As described in the excerpt from the law review article quoted above, the process of posting was viewed by the draftsmen as encompassing two parts, the mechanical steps of "recording the payment" and the judgmental steps of "determining to pay". Whatever elements a bank injects into those two parts, and, in whatever sequence they may be performed, once all steps have been taken the "process of posting" is then deemed by the statute to be complete. Moreover, the bank's right to return the check unpaid is subject to two conditions: (1) that it has not "made final payment", i.e. "completed the process of posting", and (2) that the midnight deadline has not passed. The failure of either condition would defeat the bank's right to return the check.

(a) Examples 1 and 2 of the Official Comment to UCC § 4–109 contemplate that the process of posting is completed when both the decision to pay has been made and the payment has been recorded, regardless of the order in which those events occur. No mention in those examples is made of an automatic, universal extension of time to the midnight deadline; on the contrary, discussion of the examples given would be unnecessary if, indeed, the draftsmen had intended to make the midnight deadline the only temporal measure of final payment.

(b) Paragraphs 3 and 5 of the Official Comment to UCC § 4–213 indicate the policies sought to be accomplished by the final payment concept. In neither is it suggested that all there is to final payment is the mere expiration of the midnight deadline.

Nor is the language of § 4–109(e) as plain and unambiguous as the Wisconsin court described. If the language as the Wisconsin court viewed it read merely "reversing an entry", there might be substance to the plain meaning argument for rejecting an otherwise clear legislative intent. However, the statute does not read "reversing an entry". Those words appear in a larger phrase: "correcting or reversing an entry or erroneous action". In the context of this larger phrase, the legislature could have contemplated several different meanings. Following a principle of parallel grammatical construction, it could have meant "correcting an entry or reversing an erroneous action", thereby permitting the first verb to operate on the first direct object, and the second verb to operate on the second direct object. Under this interpretation both phrases involve elements of righting an error. "Correcting an entry" would remedy mechanical or recording errors; "reversing an erroneous action" would permit correction of more complex actions such as judgments over a correct signature or determination of whether sufficient funds were available.

Another possible reading of subsection (e) would present four possible combinations of the two verbs and two direct objects: "correcting an entry", "correcting erroneous action", "reversing an entry", and "reversing erroneous action". Under this view of the language, three of the four involve concepts of "correcting" or "erroneous". Only one of them, "reversing an entry", omits any specific reference to a prior mistake. Thus, five out of these six possible readings of subsection (e) focus upon errors, either mechanical or judgmental.

Under these circumstances the statute cannot reasonably be read as having a plain meaning and unambiguously providing that "error" was not the determinative factor. When the underlying policies and intent of the bank collection sections of the UCC are so clearly demonstrated by its history, see Bank Procedures of the UCC—When is a Check Finally Paid?, supra, and by the Official Comments, the court should not adopt an aberrational interpretation of § 4–109(e) such as urged by the defendant here and adopted by the Wisconsin Supreme Court. This is particularly so when the interpretation urged by defendant would render meaningless the remaining four subsections of § 4–109. Furthermore, on a policy level, an enormous legislative effort would be required to substitute in the states' separate enactments of this uniform law language which would unambiguously state the clear legislative purpose.

The underlying policy being clear, the legislative intent being bolstered by the Official Comments, and the language of subsection (e) strongly implying merely a device to rectify mistakes, the court concludes that subsection (e) of § 4–109 does not permit a payor bank, without regard to its reason or purpose, to reverse an entry at anytime up to the midnight deadline. Instead, subsection (e) permits corrective action to be taken only in those cases where an error of some type has been made by the bank in completing its process of posting.

Applied to the facts of this case, defendant had made no error and it had, indeed, completed its process of posting. Thereafter, when notice of the bankruptcy was received, it was too late to reverse the entry. Once the process of posting was complete, payment was final, and defendant became accountable to plaintiff for the proceeds, unaffected by the notice of bankruptcy or any other knowledge, notice, stop order, or legal process thereafter received.

Accordingly, plaintiff's motion for summary judgment is granted and defendant's motion is denied.

NOTES

(1) **West Side Criticized.** The court's suggestion that "entry" be limited to "mechanical or recording errors" finds support in the history of UCC 4–109. That history is discussed in Note, 68 Colum.L.Rev. 349, 352–54 (1968).[3]

"The words 'completed the process of posting' are not defined in section 4–213. According to Comment 5 to that section, the phrase was chosen over 'simple "posting"' because under current machine operations posting is a process and something more than simply making entries on the customer's ledger.'

"Bankers, however, were dissatisfied with the words. They were afraid a court might find the process of posting completed by some mechanical step in the Magnetic Ink Character Recognition (MICR) check collecting system that was not equivalent to the recorded determination to pay reached by the old 'posting' rule. A payor bank employing the MICR system collects all the checks presented to it on the same day and runs them through a computer. The computer sorts the checks, and charges every check—including overdrafts—to its proper account. After subsequent human examination, checks which the payor decides to dishonor are sent back through the computer and charges to the various accounts are reversed. Thus simple 'posting' may be thought to occur automatically before a check has been examined; it was feared a court might hold that 'final payment' took place during this mechanical stage.

"Objections to the possible ambiguity of 'completed the process of posting' came largely from two important commercial states, Califor-

3. Reproduced with permission of the Columbia Law Review.

nia and New York. The California solution was to delete section 4–213(1)(c), thus clearly compelling the sort of result reached in the instant case. New York, however, took a different approach—defining the doubtful term. The UCC's Permanent Editorial Board, seeking to 'remove all doubt [that] subparagraph (c) is adequate to cover satisfactorily the "post first-verify later" practice,' opted for the New York definition of the process of posting and approved it as section 4–109 of the Official Text. . . .

"It was established in the instant case that the payor bank had performed steps (a) through (d); the court held, however, that the process of posting could not be completed within the meaning of section 4–213(1)(c) until the payor's clearing house deadline precluded it from 'reversing an entry' under step (e). This reading of section 4–109(e) renders section 4–213(1)(c) meaningless; the 'process of posting' will never, under the court's interpretation, be completed before the time described in section 4–213(1)(d). The interpretation also ignores the Comment to section 4–109, which recites as illustrations three situations in which the process of posting is completed prior to the payor's deadline for return of an item. And the instant case's approach necessarily creates a period of time when the payor is given complete discretion whether to act on any stop payment order, for the payor is not compelled to act if it 'has evidenced by examination of [the drawer's] account and by action its decision to pay the item.'

"These results can be avoided by a more sensitive approach to the text of section 4–109. The statute defines the process of posting in terms of the payor bank's usual procedure in 'determining to pay an item and in recording the payment.' Subparagraphs (a) to (e) of section 4–109 illustrate possible steps in the process. Subparagraph (e), in particular, can refer only to the reversal 'of an entry or erroneous action' before there has been a determination to pay.

"The court in the instant case did not accept this interpretation because it thought that 'reversing an entry' could not be construed to apply to erroneous entries only. However, examination of the MICR check collection process—which provided the impetus for enacting section 4–109—demonstrates that this construction is not compelled. When a payor deliberately makes 'entries' for all the checks it receives, knowing that some of the 'entries' will have to be reversed after examination, the 'entries' that require reversal are not properly described as 'erroneous.' Rather, section 4–109(e) seems to use 'entry' in an accounting sense, so as to include only those debits and credits made during the computer run. After the computer run is completed, the payor bank's conduct—such as cancelling the check and stamping it paid—appears to constitute 'action' of the payor bank within the meaning of section 4–109(e). An 'entry' may be reversed for any reason since there has never been a determination to pay the check, but an 'action' may be reversed only if erroneous because mistake in cancelling a check, for example, negates the existence of a determination to pay it."

The coverage of the Federal Deposit Insurance may also be relevant. As was pointed out earlier, the holder of an uncertified check is not insured. However, the "owner" of such a check is given an insured deposit in "a closed bank [that] has become obligated for the payment of items forwarded for collection." 12 C.F.R. § 330.12. Thus one effect of payment is to give the owner an insured deposit. If this is so, what is the effect of West Side?

(2) West Side Distinguished. In the West Side Bank case, the check was presented through the clearing house. As an alternative ground for its decision, the court gave a questionable reading to the clearing house rule as derogating from UCC 4–213(1)(c) and 4–109. The court then held that regardless of how the Code should be read, "the clearing house agreement supersedes any inconsistent portions of the Code, and in this instance additionally serves to expand the time in which entries may be reversed." 37 Wis.2d at 674, 155 N.W.2d at 594. (Since the check in the Schultz case was presented by a Federal Reserve Bank and not through a clearing house, that court did not face this problem.) Should banks be able to adopt a clearing house rule that would exclude completion of the process of posting as an indication of final payment? See UCC 4–103.

A surprising aspect of West Side is that the clearing house deadline in that case was *later* than the midnight deadline. Assuming that the answer to the preceding question is yes, should banks be able to adopt a clearing house deadline that is later than the midnight deadline? See pages 161–163 supra and Note 2, p. 179 supra.

"THE FOUR LEGALS"

UCC 4–303(1) deals with what are sometimes called "the four legals." "Bankers call the matters handled by section 4–303(1) 'the four legals' because four legal questions are answered by determining the exact point of time at which the drawer loses control of the funds against which he has drawn his checks: (1) If the drawee (payor) bank becomes insolvent, who takes the loss, the drawer of the check or its holder?; (2) At what point does the drawer lose his right to stop payment?; (3) For how long may creditors attach the funds against which a check is drawn?; and (4) For how long may the bank set off against the drawer's account the various claims it holds against him?" 1 W. Hawkland, A Transactional Guide to the Uniform Commercial Code 399 (1964).

While UCC 4–213(1) is concerned with the drawee's accountability to a holder of the check, UCC 4–303(1) is concerned with drawee's duty to the drawer, its customer.[1] UCC 4–303(1) provides, with less

1. For a different view of the relationship between UCC 4–213 and 4–303, see J. White & R. Summers, Handbook of the   Law Under the Uniform Commercial Code § 17–7 at 701–02 (2d ed. 1980), where it is argued "that 4–303 is an inde-

elegance of expression than might be desired, that a stop order "comes too late to . . . terminate [the drawee's] right or duty [to pay the check] if the . . . stop-order . . . is received . . . and a reasonable time for the bank to act thereon expires . . . after the bank has done any of" five things. One of those things is: "(d) completed the process of posting the item to the indicated account of the drawer . . . or otherwise has evidenced by examination of such indicated account and by action its decision to pay the item." Compare this with UCC 4–213(1)(c). Why the additional language in UCC 4–303(1)(d)?

Comment 3 to UCC 4–303 states: "This general 'omnibus' language is necessary to pick up other possible types of action impossible to specify particularly but where the bank has examined the account to see if there are sufficient funds and has taken some action indicating an intention to pay. An example is what has sometimes been called 'sight posting' where the bookkeeper examines the account and makes a decision to pay but postpones posting. The clause . . . is not intended to refer to various preliminary acts in no way close to a true decision of the bank to pay the item, such as receipt of the item over the counter for deposit, entry of a provisional credit in a passbook, or the making of a provisional settlement for the item through the clearing house, by entries in accounts, remittance or otherwise. All actions of this type are provisional and none of them evidences the bank's decision to pay the item. In this Section as in Section 4–213 reasoning such as appears in . . . White Brokerage Co. v. Cooperman, 207 Minn. 239, 290 N.W. 790 (1940) . . . is rejected."

The following case sheds light on UCC 4–303(1)(d). (For a discussion of when a bank has "evidenced . . . its decision to pay the item," see Citizens & Peoples National Bank v. United States, 570 F.2d 1279 (5th Cir.1978).)

YANDELL V. WHITE CITY AMUSEMENT PARK, 232 F.Supp. 582 (D.Mass.1964). "JULIAN, DISTRICT JUDGE. On August 1, 1960, at 2:15 p.m., the Commerce Bank and Trust Co. of Worcester, Massachusetts, was summoned as a trustee [1] in a suit commenced by W. A. Yandell and Jack Love against White City Amusement Park, Inc. On August 3, 1960, the alleged trustee answered under oath that it had on deposit in the name of White City Amusement Park, Inc., $246.60.

. . .

"The trustee bank was on a deferred posting basis, by which transactions would not be machine posted to the ledger cards until the day after their actual occurrence. This procedure was followed except for the last business day of the month when, except for 'outs'

pendent basis for liability of the payor bank to the holder."

1. Trustee Process in Massachusetts is similar to garnishment. [Ed.]

that could not be posted, all transactions for that day were machine posted on that same day to bring all accounts up to date where possible.

" 'Outs' were items (checks) that were not machine posted in the normal process by a bookkeeping machine operator but were set aside so that the head bookkeeper or an officer could make a decision to pay or not to pay. An item which became an 'out' late on the last business day of the month might not be posted on that day.

"Transactions not machine posted on the last business day were, in effect, made 'first business day of the month' transactions which would be posted on the second business day of the month as of the first business day. There was no posting on the first business day of the month to reflect the last business day of the month transactions.

. . .

"On July 29, 1960, [a Friday and the last business day of the month,] the trustee bank received four checks totaling $7,998.75 from the Federal Reserve Bank for payment, which were drawn on the White City regular account. These checks were not machine posted but were withdrawn from that process on that day and became 'outs'. An authorized officer of the bank examined the ledger card to determine if there were sufficient funds in it to pay those items. The officer made a penciled notation in the amount of $7,998.75 next to the then current balance, which notation indicated that that amount was committed to the payment of the four checks. Those checks were then hand-stamped by an authorized officer of the bank with a symbol consisting of three concentric circles, referred to as a 'bull's-eye,' and initialed by him, which, in accordance with procedure followed by the bank, manifested the bank's decision to pay the items on the date of the stamping, July 29, 1960. Since these actions came too late in the day, the machine posting of this transaction did not occur until August 2 in accordance with the bank's deferred posting procedure.

. . .

"By an examination of the ledger card of the White City regular account, by penciling the notation on the ledger card, and by stamping and initialing the 'bull's-eye' on each check supra the bank had evidenced its decision to pay the checks totaling $7,998.75 on July 29, 1960.

"Taking the plain meaning of Mass.G.L. c. 106, § 4–303(1)(d), it is clear that the trustee writ was served after the bank had made and manifested its decision to pay the checks. The trustee writ, therefore, was served too late to terminate or suspend the bank's right and duty to charge the amount of $7,998.75 to the White City regular account. . . .

"At the time of the service of the writ upon the trustee, it had in its possession credits of the defendant in the amount of $246.60, as stated in the trustee's answer. The trustee is therefore charged in that amount."

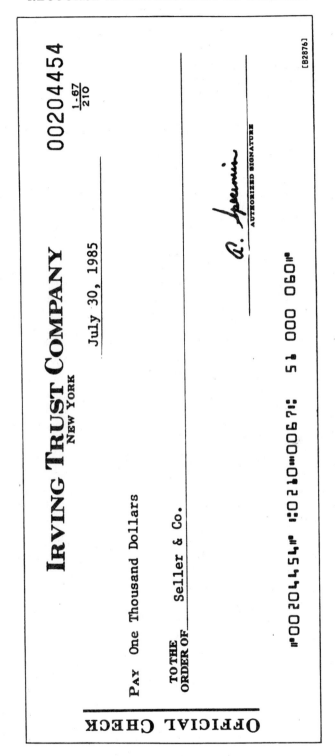

CASHIER'S OR OFFICIAL CHECK

NOTE

Period of Discretion. The writer quoted in Note 1, p. 238 supra, faulted West Side because it "necessarily creates a period of time when the payor is given complete discretion whether to act on any stop payment order, for the payor is not compelled to act if it has evidenced by examination of [the drawer's] account and by action its decision to pay the item?" Is there such a period of time under the Code? If so, how does West Side effect it?

Problem 14. In Problem 12(a), supra, suppose that Quaker takes the Empire check to the Irving Trust and asks for a cashier's check for $2,178.50 payable to Quaker's order, and that the Irving Trust, having mislaid Empire's stop payment order, issues such a cashier's check.[1] What are the rights of Quaker against the Irving Trust if it refuses to pay the cashier's check? See Travi Construction Corp. v. First Bristol County National Bank, infra.

TRAVI CONSTRUCTION CORP. v. FIRST BRISTOL COUNTY NATIONAL BANK

Court of Appeals of Massachusetts, 1980.
10 Mass.App.Ct. 32, 405 N.E.2d 666.

PERRETTA, JUSTICE. This appeal is from a summary judgment granted in favor of the plaintiff Travi Construction Corporation against the defendant First Bristol County National Bank. Mass.R. Civ.P. 56, 365 Mass. 824 (1974). In its action Travi sought to recover the sum of $7,500, representing the face amount of a cashier's check issued by the Bank to Travi as payee. The Bank stopped payment on this check because Travi purchased it with a personal check it had received from the third-party defendant Lesser. Lesser's check was drawn on the Bank, but he placed a stop-payment order on his check prior to Travi's presentment of it at the Bank in exchange of the cashier's check. Due to an error on its part, the Bank accepted Lesser's check and issued its cashier's check to Travi. When the cashier's check was subsequently presented to the Bank by Travi's bank, the Bank refused to honor it, and Travi brought suit. The Bank argues that it can refuse to honor its cashier's check for a failure of consideration when it is presented by a party to the instrument with whom the Bank has dealt. We agree, and we reverse the judgment.

There are two conflicting lines of authority on the question whether a bank can dishonor its cashier's check. Those jurisdictions which apply a flat prohibition against dishonor of a cashier's check by the

---

1. Where the issuing bank is a state chartered bank, which unlike a federally chartered bank does not have an officer known as a "cashier," the check may be called an "official check" rather than a "cashier's check."

issuing bank do so on the reasoning that a cashier's check is a bill of exchange or draft drawn by a bank upon itself and accepted in advance by the act of its issuance. Because a stop-payment order must be made prior to acceptance of the instrument, Uniform Commercial Code, § 4–303(a), a cashier's check cannot be dishonored.[1] Some jurisdictions refuse to recognize such an ironclad rule, and they allow a bank to dishonor its cashier's check in certain situations, primarily a failure of consideration. In such a case the bank may assert its own defenses against one who is not a holder in due course.[2]

This conflict among jurisdictions is treated by Brady on Bank Checks, wherein it is concluded, at § 20.12, at 20–30—20–31 (5th ed. 1979), "While courts have not set forth a clear rule on this matter, it would seem that courts which hold flatly that payment may not be stopped are in error . . . . In short, the rule that payment may not be stopped on a cashier's check should not be regarded as an immutable principle; under some situations, it would seem that the issuing bank ought to be able to resist payment." To each dispute Brady would apply the "finality of payment" rule found in § 3–418 of the Uniform Commercial Code.[3] Jurisdictions eschewing the flat-prohibition against dishonor take notice of the fact that the analysis of the question employed by conflicting courts depends upon the premise that a cashier's check is a draft. For example, in TPO, Inc. v. Federal Deposit Ins. Corp., 487 F.2d 131, 135–136 (3rd Cir.1973), the court observed that the "acceptance upon issuance" reasoning fails when § 3–118(a) of the Uniform Commercial Code is applied to a cashier's check. That section of the Code states: "Where there is doubt whether the instrument is a draft or a note the holder may treat it as

1. See Swiss Credit Bank v. Virginia Natl. Bank-Fairfax, 538 F.2d 587 (4th Cir. 1976); State v. Curtiss Natl. Bank, 427 F.2d 395 (5th Cir.1970); Munson v. American Natl. Bank & Trust Co., 484 F.2d 620 (7th Cir.1973); Texaco, Inc. v. Liberty Natl. Bank & Trust Co., 464 F.2d 389 (10th Cir.1972); Kaufman v. Chase Manhattan Bank Natl. Assn., 370 F.Supp. 276 (S.D.N.Y.1973); Able & Associates, Inc. v. Orchard Hill Farms, 77 Ill.App.3d 375, 32 Ill.Dec. 757, 395 N.E.2d 1138 (1979), overruling Bank of Niles v. American State Bank, 14 Ill.App.3d 729, 303 N.E.2d 186 (1973); Meador v. Ranchmart State Bank, 213 Kan. 372, 517 P.2d 123 (1973); State ex rel. Chan Siew Lai v. Powell, 536 S.W.2d 14 (Mo.1976); National Newark & Essex Bank v. Giordano, 111 N.J.Super. 347, 268 A.2d 327 (1970); Moon Over the Mountain, Ltd. v. Marine Midland Bank, 87 Misc.2d 918, 386 N.Y.S.2d 974 (N.Y. Civ.Ct.1976); Wertz v. Richardson Heights Bank & Trust, 495 S.W.2d 572 (Tex.1973).

2. See TPO, Inc. v. Federal Deposit Ins. Corp., 487 F.2d 131 (3rd Cir.1973);

Wilmington Trust Co. v. Delaware Auto Sales, 271 A.2d 41 (Del.1970); Tropicana Pools, Inc. v. First Natl. Bank, 206 So.2d 48 (Fla.App.1968); Wright v. Trust Co. of Georgia, 108 Ga.App. 783, 134 S.E.2d 457 (1963); State Bank v. American Natl. Bank, 266 N.W.2d 496 (Minn.1978); Dakota Transfer & Storage Co. v. Merchants Natl. Bank & Trust Co., 86 N.W.2d 639 (N.Dak.1957).

3. General Laws c. 106, § 3–418, inserted by St.1957, c. 765, § 1, provides: "Except for recovery of bank payments as provided in the Article on Bank Deposits and Collections (Article 4) and except for liability for breach of warranty on presentment under section 3–417, payment or acceptance of any instrument is final in favor of a holder in due course, or a person who has in good faith changed his position in reliance on the payment." Brady suggests that because in Rockland Trust Co. v. South Shore Natl. Bank, 366 Mass. 74, 78, 314 N.E.2d 438 (1976), the court hinted that the rule applied to certified checks, it would also be applicable to cashier's checks.

either. A draft drawn on the drawer is effective as a note." The observation that a cashier's check is a negotiable promissory note and not a draft is, however, by no means central to the rule that a bank may, in certain circumstances, dishonor its cashier's check. These cases turn on whether the holder of the check is a holder in due course because "whether a bank is considered to have accepted a cashier's check, as a draft, by the act of its issuance, or is considered to be the maker of a note, it is primarily obligated upon the instrument." Banco Ganadero y Agricola, S.A. Agua Prieta, Sonora, Mexico v. Society Natl. Bank, 418 F.Supp. 520, 523 (N.D.Ohio 1976). See also 6 E. Bender's Uniform Commercial Code Service, Reporter—Digest § 2–1194 (Willier and Hart, 1980) ("This difference alone would not alter the result, however, since the liability of an acceptor is precisely the same as that of a maker. See Section 3–413[1].").

We are persuaded that an issuing bank may refuse to honor its cashier's check because of a failure of consideration when the check is held by a party to the instrument with whom it has dealt. We do not look to either G.L. c. 106, § 3–118(a) or § 3–418, in reaching this conclusion. Instead, we rely upon the fact that in this limited situation the policy concerns which justify a rule against dishonor do not exist, and there is overwhelming reason for an exception to the rule. As stated in TPO Inc., 487 F.2d at 135, "There are no third parties, or customers of the Bank, or holders in due course whose rights are involved . . . Hence, the strong considerations of public policy favoring negotiability and reliability of cashier's checks are not germane." Compare Dziurak v. Chase Manhattan Bank, 58 App.Div.2d 103, 107, 396 N.Y.S.2d 414 (1977). Moreover, where the bank, and not its customer, stops payment on a cashier's check the bank's reputation and credit are not exposed to third party reprobation. See 6 Michie, Banks and Banking 371 (1975). Compare White & Summers, Uniform Commercial Code 579, n. 91 (1972) (concern for a bank's reputation and credit may be legitimate where a customer can demand that its bank stop payment on a cashier's check).

These policy concerns are not at issue in the present case. The Bank received Lesser's stop-payment order on March 30, 1978, at 5:15 P.M. Travi presented Lesser's check at the Bank's branch office on Friday, March 31, sometime between 12:00 P.M. and 1:00 P.M. The cashier's check was presented to the Bank for payment by Travi's bank on or about April 4. Lesser's account cannot be charged; the Bank admits his stop-payment order was timely made.[4] Travi has received no funds on account of the cashier's check which bears the stamped legend "Payment Stopped." The check cannot fall into the

4. Lesser's order, although timely under G.L. c. 106, § 4–303, was received by the Bank after the "cut-off" time of 4:30 P.M. for its computer center to process the work for that day. The order was then posted at the close of business on March 31. The Bank's mistake occurred when, for some reason not revealed on the record before us, Lesser's order was not manually brought forward on his account on the morning of March 31.

hands of an innocent third party. In this situation, we perceive no policy need for application of a stringent rule prohibiting the Bank's dishonor of its cashier's check.

The issue for resolution is whether the Bank has a defense which it can assert against Travi's presentment of the check for payment. Travi argues that it does not. It claims that the pleadings, the affidavits, and the Bank's responses to interrogatories demonstrate that there is no dispute that Travi took the cashier's check in good faith and without notice of the fact that Lesser had stopped payment on his check. We reject Travi's assessment of the affidavits,[5] but even were we to agree that Travi holds the check as a holder in due course, Travi would not be sheltered from the Bank's defense to payment.

The Bank received Lesser's order before it issued its check to Travi, and it has no right to charge Lesser's account with the amount of his check. "A complete failure of consideration for the [cashier's] check resulted and the bank had the right to refuse to honor it when presented by the payee." Wilmington Trust Co., supra, 271 A.2d at 42. While the defense of a failure of consideration cannot be asserted against a holder in due course, compare G.L. c. 106, § 3–305(2) with §§ 3–306 and 3–408, even a holder in due course takes an instrument subject to the defenses of any party to the instrument with whom the holder has dealt, G.L. c. 106, § 3–305(2). See Waltham Citizens Natl. Bank v. Flett, 353 Mass. 696, 699, 234 N.E.2d 739 (1968). See also Wilmington Trust, supra, 271 A.2d at 42; Brotherton v. McWaters, 438 P.2d 1, 4 (Okl.1968); Brady on Bank Checks, supra, at 9–7—9–8, 15–3; Quinn, UCC Commentary and Law Digest par. 3–305(A)(5) (1978).

The Bank had a right to refuse to honor its cashier's check because of a failure of consideration when the check was presented by Travi, a party to that instrument with whom the Bank had dealt. The foregoing analysis obviates the need to consider the Bank's remaining contention [6] because it establishes that summary judgment

5. Lesser alleged in his affidavit that he notified Travi's bookkeeper and president by telephone and "explained that I was stopping payment on my check" to Travi. Travi's bookkeeper and president denied any such notice from Lesser in their affidavits. Travi claims that a factual dispute as to its status as a holder in due course does not exist because the Bank's answers to interrogatories demonstrate that Lesser stopped payment on his check at 5:15 P.M. on March 30, after his alleged notice to Travi's employees. Travi concludes that even if Lesser's affidavit is accepted, it shows only a threat or indication that payment on his check might be stopped, and Travi could not have had knowledge of the order when it presented Lesser's check. Lesser's affidavit was sufficient to dispute Travi's status as a holder in due course on the elements of good faith and notice. G.L. c. 106, §§ 1–201(19) and (25). See Industrial Natl. Bank v. Leo's Used Car Exchange, Inc., 362 Mass. 797, 800–802, 291 N.E.2d 603 (1973). See also Bowling Green, Inc. v. State Street Bank & Trust Co., 425 F.2d 81, 85 (1st Cir. 1970).

6. The Bank also complains of the order denying its motion to amend its answer to include a compulsory counterclaim against Travi. Mass.R.Civ.P. 13(a), 365 Mass. 758 (1974). The basis for the counterclaim was that when Travi endorsed

against Travi is appropriate under Mass.R.Civ.P. 56(c), 365 Mass. 824 (1974).

The order allowing Travi's motion for summary judgment and the judgment are reversed. The Superior Court is to enter a new judgment dismissing the action.

NOTE

The "Iron-Clad Rule." A recent case recognizing what the Massachusetts court called the "iron-clad rule" that a bank cannot refuse to pay its cashier's check, even when the cashier's check is still in the payee's hands, is Able & Associates v. Orchard Hill Farms of Illinois, cited in the Massachusetts court's first footnote. There the Illinois court asserted that "policy considerations require a rule which prohibits a bank from refusing to honor its cashier's checks." But it concluded that the payee of the cashier's check would be "nonetheless liable to the bank on an offset claim . . . based on the underlying contract obligations for the purchase of the cashier's checks." The court remanded the case to permit the bank "to amend its answer to include as an affirmative defense its claim of a breach of the underlying contractual obligation." How does this "iron-clad rule" as applied by the Illinois court differ in practice from the rule laid down by the Massachusetts court?

Cases are collected in Lawrence, Making Cashier's Checks and Other Bank Checks Cost-Effective: A Plea for Revision of Articles 3 and 4 of the Uniform Commercial Code, 64 Minn.L.Rev. 275 (1980).

SECTION 3. ADVERSE CLAIM

Prefatory Note. Thus far we have considered the power to countermand only in the case of the drawer's personal uncertified check. Can the drawer ever countermand a certified check? UCC 4–303 (1) (a) answers this question in the negative, at least insofar as countermanding by means of a stop order is concerned. There is, however, another means by which the drawer might attempt to accomplish the same result—by assertion of an adverse claim to the property represented by the certified check, i.e., to the debt owed by the drawee bank on that check.

At common law, when ownership of a deposit in a bank was claimed by a person other than the depositor, the adverse claimant might, by giving the bank adequate notice of his claim, require it to

terclaim was that when Travi endorsed Lesser's check, it engaged that upon dishonor it would pay the instrument according to the tenor at the time of its endorsement. G.L. c. 106, § 3–414(1). See Community Natl. Bank v. Dawes, 369 Mass. 550, 561, 340 N.E.2d 877 (1976).

hold the deposit for a reasonable length of time to afford the claimant an opportunity to assert the claim in court. Thus if the drawer were to assert an adverse claim to the deposit represented by the certified check, the court might properly require the bank to refuse payment on the check, for at least a reasonable time. (What was a reasonable time in such a case was not entirely clear.) Note, however, that in order for there to be an adverse claim, there must be a claim of ownership of the deposit, as where it is asserted that the instrument representing the deposit was procured by theft or by fraud;[1] it is not enough to assert that there has been a want or failure of consideration for the instrument. Note too that the drawee must be given adequate notice of the facts in support of the claim to justify it in acting upon it; it is not enough for the drawer merely to countermand payment.

In order to afford banks some protection from the risk of adverse claims, over half of the states adopted adverse claim statutes usually in the form recommended by the American Bankers Association. These statutes provided that a notice of an adverse claim was not effective unless it was accompanied by a court order restraining payment of the deposit or a bond indemnifying the bank against loss. The Code's version of an adverse claim statute is set out in UCC 3–603, which requires a court order or indemnity in most cases of adverse claim to a deposit represented by a negotiable instrument.

When and how can the drawer of a certified check take advantage of the doctrine of adverse claim under the Code? What of the remitter of a cashier's check?

The discussion so far has centered on whether the adverse claimant can require the bank to recognize a claim. But suppose that the bank is willing to recognize it. Then the question arises whether the bank can set up the adverse claim when it is sued by the holder of the instrument. Whether a party to a negotiable instrument can set up in defense the *jus tertii*, a claim of ownership of a third party, has been the subject of considerable controversy. Although the Negotiable Instruments Law was not explicit on the matter, its implication was that a party to the instrument could set up a third party's claim of ownership, at least in defense against one who was not a holder in due course. Perhaps if, under the common law rules relating to adverse claims, voluntary payment made following notice of an adverse claim might have left the payor liable to the adverse claimant, it was only reasonable to allow the payor to set up the adverse claim against the holder, even in an action to which the adverse claimant is not a party. On the other hand, might not such a rule have made possible inconsistent findings of fact in separate actions, and consequent double liability or unjust enrichment?

1. Even where there has been fraud, so that the transaction is voidable, the adverse claimant may be required to rescind before the bank must recognize his claim. See Note, 21 U.Chi.L.Rev. 135, 141 (1953).

AFFIDAVIT AND INDEMNITY AGREEMENT
LOST PASSBOOK, OFFICIAL CHECK, CERTIFIED CHECK, OR MONEY ORDER

STATE OF NEW YORK } ss.
COUNTY OF

The undersigned, _____, being duly sworn, depose(s) and say(s):

1. The undersigned reside(s) at _____

and make(s) this affidavit and indemnity agreement for the benefit of _____
(herein called the "Bank").

On or about _____, the Bank issued to the order of _____

an ☐ Official Check, or a ☐ Money Order, No. _____ (herein called the "Instrument") for the sum

of $ _____. Instrument was endorsed as follows:

_____

2. On or about _____, the Instrument was { accidentally lost / stolen / destroyed } and cannot be found after diligent

search therefor. The Instrument is not in the possession of the undersigned and the undersigned do (does) not have knowledge of its whereabouts.

3. The undersigned is (are) the lawful owner(s) of the Instrument and is (are) entitled to possession thereof. The undersigned has (have) not sold, given, transferred, assigned, delivered, hypothecated or otherwise encumbered the Instrument or the funds or debt thereby represented, nor has (have) the undersigned given any authority to any person to deal in any way with the Instrument or the funds or debt thereby represented.

4. The undersigned request(s) the Bank not to pay any funds upon presentation to it of the Instrument and further request(s) the Bank to issue a duplicate of the Instrument to the undersigned without requiring the prior surrender of the Instrument.

5. In consideration of the Bank issuing a replacement for the Instrument to the undersigned as above requested, the undersigned (jointly and severally if more than one) agree(s) to return the Instrument, or cause the same to be returned, to the Bank for cancellation promptly upon the same being found and to indemnify and save the Bank harmless of and from any and all claims, damages, loss or expense (including attorneys' fees) which it may suffer or incur by reason thereof or by reason of any presentment of the Instrument and demand for payment of the funds or debt represented thereby or by reason of any other matter arising out of these premises.

6. This agreement shall be binding on the executors, administrators, successors and assigns of the undersigned jointly and severally, and shall be construed in accordance with the laws of the State of New York.

(Corporate Seal)

BY _____

STATE OF NEW YORK   } ss.:
COUNTY OF _____

On the _____ day of _____ in the year 19' _____, before me personally came

_____

to me known, who, being by me duly sworn, did depose and say that he resides at No. _____

in the _____ of _____ ; that he is the _____ President of the

_____ the corporation described in and which executed the above instrument; that he knows the seal of said corporation; that the seal affixed to said instrument is such corporate seal; that it was so affixed by order of the board of directors of said corporation, and that he signed his name thereto by like order.

Corporation

Notarial Stamp

[D622]

INDEMNITY AGREEMENT

The Code, in UCC 3–306(d), provides that with two exceptions, involving theft and restrictive indorsements, "The claim of any third person to the instrument is not . . . available as a defense to any party liable thereon unless the third person himself defends the action for such party." The exception as to theft "is based on the policy which refuses to aid a proved thief to recover unless the transferee is a holder in due course." Comment 5 to UCC 3–306. Would the greater certainty that is usually possible in establishing the fact of theft as opposed, for example, to the fact of fraud also help to justify this exception?

Problem 15. Seller fraudulently induced Buyer to give a certified check on X Bank in payment for worthless goods. Upon discovery of the fraud, Buyer rescinded the sale, tendered the goods back to Seller, notified X Bank of these circumstances, and instructed it not to pay the check.

(a) If X Bank refuses to pay, can it successfully resist an action brought by Seller by setting up the right of a third party (the *jus tertii*), the Buyer, even though the Buyer is not a party? If X Bank were to be allowed to set up Seller's fraud, but lost because of a finding of fact that there was no fraud, would X Bank then be protected against a subsequent recovery by Buyer?

(b) Could X Bank have safely paid Seller after having received notice of the fraud?

(c) What answers if Seller were instead a thief who had stolen from Buyer a certified check payable to the order of "Cash"?

See UCC 3–306, 3–603; Dziurak v. Chase Manhattan Bank, infra.

DZIURAK v. CHASE MANHATTAN BANK

Supreme Court of New York, Appellate Division, Second Department, 1977.
58 A.D.2d 103, 396 N.Y.S.2d 414.

COHALAN, JUSTICE PRESIDING. The sole question on this appeal is whether a bank depositor to whom an "official bank check" has been issued (and by him endorsed to the order of a third party), can legally stop payment thereon, in the absence of a court order or an indemnification bond. An official bank check is commonly referred to as a "cashier's check". Trial Term held it could be stopped. We disagree.

A recitation of the facts is necessary to place the problem in proper focus.

The plaintiff currently holds a judgment against the defendant Chase Manhattan Bank (Bank) in the amount of $17,000, plus interest and costs.

During the year 1973 Dziurak maintained a savings account with "Branch # 40" of the Bank in the sum of $18,000. He was cozened by an acquaintance named Staveris into a proposal whereby, for $22,000 cash, he could acquire a one-third interest in a corporation whose sole asset was a going restaurant. There was nothing in writing to bind the bargain. Dziurak paid Staveris $5,000 down. He then went to the Bank and, through the assistant manager, arranged for the proper withdrawal. He asked for a "check" to be drawn to the order of Staveris. Monaco, the assistant manager, advised him to have the check drawn to himself as payee. A further bit of advice by Monaco was for Dziurak to go to his attorney, who would instruct him how to endorse the check.

The $17,000 was transferred to the Bank's coffers and Dziurak's savings account was debited accordingly. A cashier's check was then issued to the order of "Francis A. Dziurak".

Plaintiff ignored the suggestion that he consult with his attorney. Instead he wrote on the back of the instrument "Francis Dziurak. Pay to order Mario Staveris" and delivered the item to Staveris. The latter, instead of depositing the check into the corporate restaurant account, deposited it in his own savings account.

Before he learned of Staveris' perfidy and before the cashier's check had cleared, Dziurak belatedly sought the advice of a local attorney. Very properly, the attorney advised him to try to stop payment on the cashier's check.

Back went Dziurak to the Bank. He saw Monaco and asked him if the check had cleared. It had not, but had arrived at the Bank that morning.

While plaintiff was with him, Monaco telephoned the Bank's attorneys and was advised that the check could not be stopped, absent a court order. He so advised the plaintiff and while Dziurak was still with him he telephoned the plaintiff's attorney to advise him to the same effect. The attorney said he was aware that a court order could effectively produce a stop of the payment.

This action was started against the Bank after judgment was first taken against Staveris, and after execution was returned unsatisfied.

As to the law, the controlling statutes are contained in several sections of the Uniform Commercial Code (hereafter UCC) which, in turn, are fleshed out in reported decisions of nisi prius and appellate courts.

We begin with subdivision (1) of section 4–403 of the UCC ("Customer's Right to Stop Payment; Burden of Proof of Loss"):

> "A customer may by order to his bank stop payment of *any item payable for his account* but the order must be received at such time and in such manner as to afford the bank a reasonable opportunity to act on it prior to any action by the bank with respect to the item described in Section 4–303" (emphasis supplied).

As to this section (4–403) we part company with Trial Term, which held that the $17,000 represented by the cashier's check was actually Dziurak's money and not that of the Bank. As noted in Wertz v. Richardson Hgts. Bank & Trust, 495 S.W.2d 572, 574 [Tex.]:

"A cashier's check is not one payable for the customer's account but rather for the bank's account. It is the bank which is obligated on the check".

The reference in section 4–403 more properly fits the situation where the depositor, as drawer, issues his own check on his own bank, as drawee. Such a check can be stopped if reasonable notice is given.

"A cashier's check is of a very different character. It is the primary obligation of the bank which issues it (citation omitted) and constitutes its written promise to pay upon demand (citation omitted). It has been said that a cashier's check is a bill of exchange drawn by a bank upon itself, accepted in advance by the very act of issuance" (Matter of Bank of United States [O'Neill], 243 App.Div. 287, 291, 277 N.Y.S. 96, 100).

This exposition of the law has been followed consistently. (See Garden Check Cashing Serv. v. First Nat. City Bank, 25 A.D.2d 137, 267 N.Y.S.2d 698; Rose Check Cashing Serv. v. Chemical Bank N.Y. Trust Co., 43 Misc.2d 679, 252 N.Y.S.2d 100; Tinker Nat. Bank v. Grassi, 57 Misc.2d 886, 889, 293 N.Y.S.2d 847, 850; Garden Check Cashing Serv. v. Chase Manhattan Bank, 46 Misc.2d 163, 165, 258 N.Y.S.2d 918, 920; Moon Over Mountain Bank v. Marine Midland Bank, 87 Misc.2d 918, 386 N.Y.S.2d 974).

No decisions holding to the contrary have been unearthed.

But to go on. Subdivision (1) of section 4–303 of the UCC ("When Items Subject to . . . Stop-Order") states, in part:

"Any . . . stop-order received by . . . a payor bank, whether or not effective under other rules of law to terminate . . . the bank's right or duty to pay an item . . . comes too late to so terminate . . . if the . . . stop-order . . . is received . . . and a reasonable time for the bank to act thereon expires . . . after the bank has done any one of the following:

"(a) accepted or certified the item".

The next section to consider is 3–410 ("Definition and Operation of Acceptance"):

"(1) Acceptance is the drawee's signed engagement to honor the draft as presented. It must be written on the draft, and may consist of his signature alone. It becomes operative when completed by delivery or notification."

At this point we can refer back to annotation 5 in the Official Comment under section 4–403 of the UCC (McKinney's Cons.Laws of N.Y., Book 62½, Part 2, p. 611):

"There is no right to stop payment after certification of a check or other acceptance of a draft, and this is true no matter who procures the certification. See Sections 3–411 and 4–303. The acceptance is the drawee's own engagement to pay, and he is not required to impair his credit by refusing payment for the convenience of the drawer."

Thus, the Bank's one signature on the instrument constitutes both a drawing and an acceptance and makes the Bank a drawer and a drawee. (See Matter of Bank of United States [O'Neill] supra).

In the recitation of the facts, mention was made that the local attorney for the plaintiff remarked to Monaco that he was aware that a court order (presumably one of a court of competent jurisdiction) could have acted as a "stop payment" order. The statute providing for such an order is section 3–603 of the UCC. It is headnoted "Payment or Satisfaction" and, pertinently, reads:

"(1) The liability of any party is discharged to the extent of his payments . . . to the holder even though it is made with knowledge of a claim of another person to the instrument unless prior to such payment . . . *the person making the claim either supplies indemnity deemed adequate by the party seeking the discharge* or enjoins payment or satisfaction by order of a court of competent jurisdiction in an action in which the adverse claimant and the holder are parties" (emphasis supplied).

The fact that the attorney for the plaintiff was aware that a court order could effect a stop payment presupposes that he also knew he could file an indemnity bond to protect the Bank, since both options are included in subdivision (1) of section 3–603 of the UCC.

Viewed in retrospect, the Bank, as a practical matter, could quite safely have stopped payment on its cashier's check and, by interpleader, have paid the money into court. Staveris could not have established himself as a holder in due course (see UCC, § 3–302). But, if the Legislature laid upon a bank the onus of questioning the reason for the issuance of all cashier's checks it would destroy the efficacy of such instruments, which, for all practical purposes, are treated as the equivalent of cash (Goshen Nat. Bank v. State of New York, 141 N.Y. 379, 387, 36 N.E. 316, 317).

To do justice to the Bank, it is only fair to observe the the entire brouhaha was occasioned by the intransigence of Dziurak. Had he followed the advice of Monaco to consult his own attorney, the situation in which the parties are now involved would have been averted. It was well said in National Safe Deposit, Sav. & Trust Co. v. Hibbs, 229 U.S. 391, 394, 33 S.Ct. 818, 57 L.Ed. 1241, wherein the doctrine of equitable estoppel was invoked for dismissing the complaint and cited with approval in Bunge Corp. v. Manufacturers Hanover Trust Co., 31 N.Y.2d 223, 228, 335 N.Y.S.2d 412, 415, 286 N.E.2d 903, 905:

> "That where one of two innocent persons must suffer by the acts of a third, he who has enabled such third person to occasion the loss must sustain it."

Dziurak provoked the issue; Dziurak should shoulder the blame.

There is a profusion of cases to the effect that a cashier's check, once issued and in the possession of a third party, cannot legally be stopped except as provided by statute (see UCC, § 3–603). One of the leading cases of recent vintage is Kaufman v. Chase Manhattan Bank, Nat. Ass'n, D.C., 370 F.Supp. 276.

There, in an opinion by Chief Judge Edelstein, plaintiff Kaufman was granted summary judgment. In that case the bank, at the request of a depositor, drew a cashier's check to plaintiff as payee. When it was presented for payment the bank refused to honor it. Chief Judge Edelstein wrote that (p. 278):

> "A cashier's check . . . is a check drawn by the bank upon itself, payable to another person, and issued by an authorized officer of the bank. The bank, therefore, becomes both the drawer and drawee; and the check becomes a promise by the bank to draw the amount of the check from its own resources and to pay the check upon demand. Thus, the issuance of the cashier's check constitutes an acceptance by the issuing bank; and the cashier's check becomes the primary obligation of the bank."

A reference to subdivision (1) of section 3–410 of the UCC was contained in a footnote to the opinion with respect to acceptance upon issuance.

Contrary to Trial Term's opinion, the statute makes no distinction between a cashier's check presented for payment by a payee or one presented by an endorsee of the payee. (See Moon Over Mountain Bank v. Marine Midland, 87 Misc.2d 918, 386 N.Y.S.2d 974, supra, and the cases therein cited.) It engages to pay on demand to the person who presents the check unless he falls within either of the categories listed in subdivision (1) of section 3–603 of the UCC (theft or restrictive endorsement).

From all that has been stated, and harsh as it may appear, it follows that the judgment must be reversed and the complaint dismissed, with costs.

Whether future remedies are available to persons situated as is the plaintiff at bar must be left to the discretion of the State Legislature.

Judgment of the Supreme Court, Kings County, entered September 24, 1976, reversed, on the law, with costs to appellant payable by respondent, and complaint dismissed.

DZIURAK v. CHASE MANHATTAN BANK

Court of Appeals of New York, 1978.
44 N.Y.2d 776, 406 N.Y.S.2d 30, 377 N.E.2d 474.

MEMORANDUM. The order of the Appellate Division should be affirmed, with costs.

A cashier's check is the primary obligation of the issuing bank which, acting as both drawer and drawee, accepts the check upon its issuance. (Matter of Bank of United States, 243 App.Div. 287, 291, 277 N.Y.S. 96, 100; Moon Over the Mountain v. Marine Midland Bank, 87 Misc.2d 918, 920, 386 N.Y.S.2d 974, 975.) As such, a cashier's check does not constitute an item payable for a customer's account within the meaning of subdivision 1 of section 4–403 of the Uniform Commercial Code. (White and Summers, Uniform Commercial Code, § 17–5, p. 579, n. 91.) Consequently, respondent was under no legal obligation to honor appellant's order to stop payment.

NOTE

Relation to "Iron-Clad Rule." Recall that the Massachusetts court in the Travi Construction case, page 244 supra, asks the reader to "Compare Dziurak . . . ." What do you make of this comparison? Would Dziurak's right to assert against Chase a claim adverse to Staveris's depend on whether the court followed the "iron-clad rule"?

Problem 16. Buyer bought a used car from Seller, giving Seller a teller's check drawn by Savings Bank on Commercial Bank. Almost immediately, Buyer discovered that the car is seriously defective. Advise Buyer. See UCC 3–306, 3–603; Fulton National Bank v. Delco, infra.

FULTON NATIONAL BANK v. DELCO CORP.

Court of Appeals of Georgia, 1973.
128 Ga.App. 16, 195 S.E.2d 455.

Delco Corporation sued the Fulton National Bank and Maslia jointly for $2,500 alleging the following: Maslia is indebted to the plaintiff in the sum of $2,500 for payment of a franchise fee, and delivered to plaintiff a check of the Fulton National Bank drawn on its account in a Federal Reserve Bank, showing Maslia as remitter; upon receipt of the check and in reliance thereof plaintiff expended money in setting Maslia up as a franchisee of the corporation; before the check was cashed, the bank stopped payment on it at Maslia's request, and is therefore liable on the instrument. Maslia undertook to defend on behalf of the bank. Delco then moved for summary judgment against the bank based on its liability as drawer, and Maslia in opposition submitted an affidavit stating in substance that the check was delivered to the plaintiff in the course of negotiation for a contemplated agreement which was never consummated; that in the negotiations it was understood that the proposed transaction was contingent on Maslia's ability to borrow the remainder of the money necessary for the franchise down payment, which he was unable to do; that plaintiff represented to him that he was at liberty to withdraw from the negotiations at any time and receive a refund in full of any money paid; that the down payment required before the contemplated contract could be consummated was an undetermined sum between $4,000 and $10,000, and that prior to the presentation of the bank check "affiant advised plaintiff that affiant had decided not to go through with the transaction, that affiant was unable to borrow additional money for the down payment, and requested the return of the check." The motion for summary judgment was granted and defendant appeals.

DEEN, JUDGE. 1. The instrument in question is a bank draft and does not operate as an assignment of funds, as does a certified check (Code Ann. §§ 109A–4–303(1)(a) and 109A–3–411(1), certification constituting a legal acceptance) or a cashier's check or bank money order, which are considered to be notes carrying unconditional promises to pay. 67 Columbia Law Review, Money Orders & Teller's Checks, pp. 524, 527. The plaintiff, being the named payee, is not a holder in due course. Under Code Ann. § 109A–4–403 any *customer* may by order to his bank stop payment on his check prior to action by the drawee, and specifically under Code Ann. § 109A–4–104(1)(e) a bank carrying an account with another bank is included as a customer. The defendant bank therefore had a right to stop payment on its check, which would, however, still leave it liable for the value of the item unless some legal and valid defense is available to it.

2. Code Ann. § 109A–3–306 provides: "Unless he has the rights of a holder in due course any person takes the instrument subject to (a) all valid claims to it on the part of any person" but "(d) The claim of any third person to the instrument is not otherwise available as a defense to any party liable thereon unless the third person himself defends the action for such party." The defendant bank has of course no defense against the check, having voluntarily stopped payment on it at Maslia's request and refunded Maslia's money to him, unless Maslia's own defense is both good and available to the bank. Maslia himself cannot defend on the instrument, not being a party to it, but he can, under the above quoted code section, defend in behalf of the bank provided he has a "valid claim." A "claim" is more than a mere "defense" as indicated by Code Ann. § 109A–3–305. The

word descends from the law merchant and indicates certain rights in the instrument on which the suit is based rather than mere reasons why the alleged debtor is not liable for the fund. It is, however, to some extent broader than the concept of legal title to the instrument. Note 2 of the Official Comment to UCC 3–306 states: " 'All valid claims to it on the part of any person' includes not only claims of legal title, but all liens, equities, or other claims of right against *the instrument or its proceeds. It includes claims to rescind a prior negotiation and to recover the instrument or its proceeds.*" (Emphasis supplied). The affidavit opposing the motion for summary judgment states that the underlying transaction consisted of a prior negotiation which was rescinded; that it was understood during such negotiations that Maslia was at liberty to withdraw at any time before they were concluded and receive a refund of any down payment, and that he has requested the return of the check. Since the bank, being the party opposing the motion for summary judgment, is entitled to all reasonable inference in its favor, we take this to mean a claim of ownership in the uncashed check as well as ownership of the fund represented by it, and it is therefore such a third party claim as is available to the defendant bank, the party prima facie liable, since Maslia is himself defending the action on its behalf. The validity of the claim is thus the only real issue in the case; it is controverted, and the bank's ultimate liability must depend upon its outcome. It was accordingly error to grant the motion for summary judgment.

Nothing in Wright v. Trust Co. of Ga., 108 Ga.App. 783, 134 S.E.2d 457, is contradictory of what is said here. The appellee further cites State of Pa. v. Curtiss Nat. Bank of Miami Springs, Fla., 5 Cir., 427 F.2d 395 involving a cashier's check and Krom v. Chemical Bank New York Trust Co., 329 N.Y.S.2d 91 involving a bank money order, both of which differ from a bank draft, as observed above, because they are considered unconditional promises to pay. This leaves two New York cases, Malphrus v. Home Savings Bank of City of Albany, 44 Misc.2d 705, 254 N.Y.S.2d 980 and Ruskin v. Central Fed. Savings & Loan Assn. of Nassau County, 3 UCC Rep.Serv. 150 (N.Y.Sup.Ct., 1966), which reached a conclusion that the bank would be unconditionally liable to the plaintiff and could seek reimbursement in a separate action against the remitter at whose request payment was stopped. These cases are not binding upon us and have been severely criticized in 67 Columbia Law Review p. 524, supra, and denominated erroneous in 71 Columbia Law Review, "Negotiability—Who Needs it?", pp. 375, 388. With all parties before the court, it is obviously the better procedure, where possible, to allow the issues to be tried out here, rather than require a possible second lawsuit by the bank against Maslia and a possible third lawsuit by Maslia against Delco.

Judgment reversed.

NOTES

(1) **Teller's Checks.** The Malphrus case, criticized by the court, involved the common situation in which a buyer, in order to pay for goods, makes a withdrawal from a savings bank, taking a "teller's check" [1] drawn by the savings bank on a commercial bank payable to the seller's order. If the buyer, after giving the seller the teller's check, claims fraud and induces the savings bank to stop payment on the check, what are the rights of the seller on the dishonored check against the savings bank? The Malphrus case apparently held, in an action to which the buyer was not a party, that the savings bank was liable to the seller regardless of whether the buyer had been defrauded. Consider the analysis of teller's checks that follows the next note. See also Note, 73 Mich.L.Rev. 424 (1974).

(2) **Personal Money Orders.** What is the legal position of the "remitter" of a personal money order who seeks to countermand payment? Is the "issuer" liable to the "remitter" if it ignores a stop order? See McLaughlin v. Franklin Society Federal Savings & Loan Ass'n., 6 UCC Rep. 1183 (N.Y.Civ.Ct.1969). Is the "issuer" liable to the holder if it obeys a stop order? See Berler v. Barclays Bank of New York, 82 A.D.2d 437, 442 N.Y.S.2d 54 (1981). See Note 1, p. 128, supra.

———

NOTE, PERSONAL MONEY ORDERS AND TELLERS CHECKS: MAVERICKS UNDER THE UCC, 67 Colum.L.Rev. 524, 542–48 (1967).[2] "Whether a bank which issues a teller's check has a right to stop payment presents a straightforward question of Code interpretation. Prior to the Code, there was considerable dispute over the right of a drawer bank to stop payment on its own draft. The majority view recognized the bank's right to stop, specifically including the right of a savings bank to stop payment on a teller's check at the purchaser's request; a minority of jurisdictions, including New York, considered the purchase of a bank draft to be an executed contract and not subject to rescission, or classified the draft with cashier's and certified checks. However, this dissension was conclusively settled by the Code. Under section 4–403, a customer may stop payment on any instrument payable for his account, and 'customer' is defined to include 'a bank carrying an account with another bank' by section 4–104(1)(e).

"It seems clear, then, that the bank which issues a teller's check has the right to stop payment. In most instances, however, it is the purchaser rather than the drawer bank which has an interest in stop-

1. A "teller's check" is one drawn by a savings bank or savings and loan institution on a commercial bank with which it maintains a checking account. It is used because banking restrictions prohib- it such savings institutions from issuing cashier's checks.

2. Reproduced with permission of the Columbia Law Review.

ping payment. The purchaser may attempt to persuade the drawer
to invoke its power; in many cases it will succeed, for the savings
bank will usually wish to please its depositor. If the purchaser fails
in this endeavor, however, he cannot assert a right to stop payment
under section 4–403; for he is not a 'customer' of the drawee bank,
which is charged with the payment of the item. Any power which
the purchaser may have to compel the stopping of payment must instead be derived from his assertion of an adverse claim to the instrument.

" 'Stopping Payment' Through the Assertion of an Adverse Claim

"1. *Adverse Claim and Jus Tertii at Common Law.* The ability or duty of a party who is obligated on an instrument to raise a
defense based upon the rights of a third person is rooted in the common law doctrines of *jus tertii* and adverse claim. Under the rules
of adverse claim, the third party—frequently, but not necessarily, a
former holder or legal owner of the instrument—could force the obligor to delay payment by asserting an equitable claim to the instrument or the funds on which it was drawn. Upon due notice to the
obligor, payment on the instrument could be restrained until the
claimant had a reasonable opportunity to secure judicial determination of his rights. The banks thus faced a dilemma: they had to decide the merits of adverse claims under the threat of double liability
if they paid an instrument over a valid claim, and of an action for
slander of credit if they refused to pay because of an invalid claim.
To relieve banks of this responsibility, many states enacted measures—perpetuated by the Code—requiring notice of adverse claims
to be accompanied by a court order restraining payment or a bond
indemnifying the bank against loss.

"Under the common law restrictions on *jus tertii* defenses, the
obligor on an instrument could not set up equities of third persons as
a defense to a holder's action on the instrument. There were a number of justifications for this doctrine. If the defendant obligor lost,
he might nevertheless be held liable to the third party in a second
action; and the successful plaintiff might also be subjected to suit by
the third party, necessitating another litigation of the same issues.
On the other hand, the obligor might escape liability altogether on the
instrument if he prevailed in a defense based on the rights of a third
party who did not thereafter lay claim to the instrument. Common
law authorities generally conceded, however, that the defense of *jus
tertii* was available to the obligor when the claimant was either a
party to the action, or would otherwise be bound by the result of the
proceeding against the obligor.

"2. *The Code Solution.* Although the issue was temporarily ob-
fuscated by the Negotiable Instruments Law, the Uniform Commercial Code in a large measure restored the common law approach to
jus tertii defenses. Under section 3–306(d), the obligor may raise the
defense that the instrument was acquired by theft, or was restrictive-

ly endorsed, but 'the claim of any third person to the instrument is not otherwise available as a defense to any party liable thereon unless the third person himself defends the action for such party.' Under section 3–603 the obligor is not liable for payment with knowledge of an adverse claim unless the claimant has either supplied indemnity deemed adequate by the obligor or has secured an order of a court of competent jurisdiction enjoining payment.

"The Code procedure protects drawee banks from the necessity of deciding the merits of a customer's adverse claim at the peril of double liability. By ensuring that the adverse claimant is a party to any suit in which his rights are determined, the Code also prevents the relitigation of identical issues in subsequent actions. Finally, the Code minimizes the possibility that the successful plaintiff might be unjustly enriched if no subsequent action were brought against him by the adverse claimant.

"3. *The Remitter as an Adverse Claimant.* The remitter might seek to prevent payment of the instrument by giving notice of his adverse claim—accompanied by the requisite indemnity or court order—to either the drawee or the drawer. No matter which bank is involved, however, the remitter's action raises difficult issues in the interpretation of section 3–603.

"Section 3–603 provides that 'the liability of any party is discharged' to the extent of its payment to the holder, unless the payor has received appropriate notice of the claim of another person to the instrument. A typical claim provided for in this section is that of a payee of a certified check who asserts that the instrument was obtained from him by fraud. In such a case, the drawee clearly has a pre-existing liability to the payee, which is discharged by payment in the absence of appropriate action by the payee. However, section 3–603 does not, by its terms, provide for the remitter's making of an adverse claim upon the drawee of a teller's check; even if the remitter's claim of ownership is valid, the drawee has no pre-existing liability to the remitter on the instrument. Nor does the language of section 3–603 literally encompass an adverse claim by the remitter on the drawer. A party's liability is discharged to the extent of 'his payment.' Yet, in the case of the teller's check, payment is made by the drawee rather than the drawer.

"It is apparent that the drafters of section 3–603 did not envision the possibility of adverse claims to a teller's check. But it seems clear that the section was intended as a general solution to the threat of double liability faced by the payor of an instrument. Since that danger exists in the case of the teller's check, section 3–603 should be interpreted to encompass the remitter's adverse claim despite the inaptness of the language employed by the drafters.

"The remitter's right to assert an adverse claim under section 3–603 would be an effective substitute for a right to stop payment in some but not all cases. By following the procedure set forth in that section, the remitter could be assured of a hearing on his claim. But he could do so only in those cases in which he claimed *title* to the instrument—as where it was obtained from him by fraud, theft or forgery. Where he wishes to raise only defenses to the underlying obligation which do not bring into question the payee's ownership of the check, he is not protected as he would be if he were empowered to stop payment.

"Jus Tertii Defenses of the Drawer Bank

"Where payment is in fact stopped—either voluntarily or through notice of adverse claim—the drawer faces the prospect of a suit on the instrument by the payee or holder. In the case of the payee who is not a holder in due course, the drawer may assert 'the *claim* of any third person to the instrument . . . as a defense' if that person defends the action for the drawer. The language of section 3–306(d) apparently encompasses only the assertion of the third person's claims of ownership, to the exclusion of mere contract defenses. That restriction prevailed at common law. Moreover, the comment to section 3–306(d) cites a number of examples, all of which involve claims of title. While the language of section 3–306(d) requires this result, restricting *jus tertii* to claims of ownership is unfortunate; there is an interest in avoiding a second litigation between parties who are before the court.

"Where the plaintiff in a suit on a teller's check is not the payee, he is likely to be someone who has given value for the instrument in good faith and without notice of any claim or defense, and will thus be a holder in due course. Where, however, the plaintiff is the payee, as in *Malphrus* . . ., he may not have acquired that privileged status. The Code provides that the payee may be a holder in due course, but to be so classified he must take the instrument 'for value,' and taking 'for value' includes performance of the 'agreed consideration.' It may be argued, therefore, that when there is a failure of consideration in the commercial transaction between the payee and the remitter, the payee has not taken 'for value' and is not a holder in due course.

"If the payee is a holder in due course, under section 3–305 he takes the instrument free from '(1) all claims to it on the part of any person and (2) all defenses of any party to the instrument with whom the holder has not dealt' except for certain 'real' defenses. Unlike section 3–306(d), this provision does not deal with the availability of third party claims. It is apparent, however, that *jus tertii* may not be asserted against the holder in due course. The purpose of section 3–305 is to insulate the holder in due course from all claims to recover the instrument. Should the holder in due course seek to enforce another party's liability on the instrument, however, that party is permitted to assert *defenses*, if he is a party with whom the holder has dealt. To permit an obligor who has not dealt with the holder (the drawer of a teller's check) to assert the defense of a party with whom the holder has dealt (the remitter) would elevate that defense to the status of an affirmative claim. Indeed, to do so would place the holder in due course in virtually the same position as one who does not hold in due course.

"The restrictions which the Code imposes on the range of *jus tertii* defenses available to the drawer bank severely limit the efficacy of stopping payment on a teller's check. Even if he can persuade or compel the drawer to stop payment, the remitter will be able to assert only his proprietary claims to the instrument, in defending the holder's action against the drawer. And he cannot assert even these, if the party suing on the instrument is a holder in due course. The restrictions compelled by the Code provisions seem somewhat incongruous; if the remitter had employed a personal money order or ordinary check, he would have been able to assert all available defenses against the payee, even if the payee was a holder in due course. Because the uses and users of teller's checks are typically similar to those of personal money orders, it might appear that the remitter's rights on the instrument should parallel the rights of a money order purchaser. Yet in one respect the remitter is in a better position: his liability on the underlying transaction is discharged when he uses a bank instrument. Inability to assert all his claims and defenses in the holder's action against the drawer is the price he pays in return."

Chapter 5

FORGERY AND ALTERATION

SECTION 1. BASIC RULES FOR ALLOCATION OF LOSS

Prefatory Note. Although forgery and alteration of negotiable instruments are far from common, they give rise to a surprisingly large number of litigated cases, and the risk of loss due to forgery and alteration is not to be ignored by one who deals in negotiable paper. This is particularly true since the wrongdoer is often not caught until after having disposed of part or all of the gains, with the consequence that one of several innocent parties must be selected to bear the loss. Which party should be selected? What remedies are available to shift the loss to that party? The materials which follow are directed to answering these questions.

Since nearly all of the bank's share of this loss, as well as some of the rest, is covered by insurance, no contemporary discussion of the allocation of risk of loss is complete without reference to available insurance. Three principal types of coverage are available: fidelity bonds, depositors' forgery bonds, and forgery insurance under bankers' blanket bonds.

The fidelity bond protects an employer against losses sustained through forgeries by employees who are covered by the bond. Such bonds were originally written on an individual basis by a bonding company as surety, on behalf of a named employee as principal, and in favor of a named employer. When the number of employees in a single concern made this cumbersome, surety companies drafted schedule bonds to cover two or more employees, who may be designated by name in a name schedule bond or by position in a position schedule bond. More recently, blanket fidelity bonds have been made available, covering all officers and employees collectively. Nevertheless, many businesses eligible for fidelity coverage carry none at all.

The depositor's forgery bond, which is available to all persons and commercial enterprises other than financial institutions, insures against loss due to forgery or alteration in connection with checks, drafts or notes made or purporting to have been made by the insured or its agent. In order to prevent litigation between the insured and its bank, the insured is permitted to include loss suffered by the depositary bank in its proof of loss. The bond covers only outgoing checks. An incoming check rider is also available to cover 75% of the insured's interest in checks received in payment for services or property, other than property sold on credit. Coverage under the depositor's forgery bond has not, however, become as popular as that under the fidelity bond.

Bankers' blanket bonds have been issued by domestic underwriters since 1916 and are carried by all banks. They cover losses due to such hazards as robbery, burglary, larceny, misplacement, employee dishonesty. Although forgery insurance is optional for commercial banks under such a bond, most banks have clause D, which covers forgery and alteration. In the case of commercial banks, premiums on clause D are computed on the basis of a standard rate which takes into account the size of the bank, as indicated by total deposits, the number of accounts, and the limit of liability. The blanket bond premium may be substantially reduced on the basis of the experience under the bond during the preceding five years. Where the experience has been unsatisfactory, the underwriter may review the insured's procedures, a deductible policy may be issued or a surcharge may be requested.

Is insurance available to the parties who must bear the risk of loss under the Code? To what extent do those parties in fact insure? Should the answers to these questions affect the allocation of the risk? For a discussion of these questions, see Farnsworth, Insurance Against Check Forgery, 60 Colum.L.Rev. 284 (1960). For a general survey of the field of forgery and alteration, see O'Malley, Common Check Frauds and the Uniform Commercial Code, 23 Rutgers L.Rev. 189 (1969).

Problem 1. Y Bank presented to X Bank a check which appeared to have been drawn on X Bank by A for $1,000 payable to the order of B, then indorsed by B to C, and then indorsed by C and deposited in Y Bank. Who bears the loss under the Code in each of the following situations, assuming that the forger cannot be held responsible and that none of the parties is at fault? Are the results in any way consistent?

(a) A's signature was forged by F, who gave it for value to B, who cashed it with C; X Bank discovered the forgery and refused to pay the check.

(b) Same as in (a), but X Bank did not discover the forgery and paid the check by mistake.

(c) S, A's secretary, who had been told to mail the check to B, stole it from A, forged B's indorsement and cashed it with C; A discovered the theft and notified X Bank, which refused to pay the check.

(d) Same as in (c), but A did not discover the theft and X Bank paid the check by mistake.

(e) B, to whom A had made out the check for $100, raised the amount to $1,000 and cashed it with C; X Bank discovered the alteration and refused to pay the check.

(f) Same as in (e), but X Bank did not discover the alteration and paid the check by mistake.

SOME BASIC RULES

Basic Situations.   Consider, at the outset, three basic situations. Suppose that an innocent party has purchased: (1) a check on which the drawer's signature has been forged (a "forged check"); (2) a check on which a necessary indorsement has been forged; (3) a check that has been altered by raising the amount. If the check is not paid, what recourse does that party have against prior parties? If the check is paid by mistake, what recourse does the drawee bank have, against either its depositor or the person whom it paid? (We shall assume, realistically, that recourse against the forger is not a practicable solution.)

Forged checks.   If a forged check is not paid, the innocent purchaser can turn to a prior party, if there is one other than the forger, for recourse. (Note that this recourse may be based on the warranty provided by UCC 3–417(2)(b) and 4–207(2)(b) and, in the case of a collecting bank, on the right of charge-back or refund provided by UCC 4–212(1).) If it is paid by mistake, the bank that pays it has no recourse, against either its depositor or the person whom it paid. That it has no recourse against its depositor is clear from UCC 3–404(1) and 4–401(1). That it has no recourse against the person whom it paid follows from the provision on finality of payment in UCC 3–418 coupled with the absence of any right to recover for breach of warranty under UCC 3–417(1)(b) and 4–207(1)(b) as long as the person whom it paid had "no *knowledge*" of the forgery. This rule denying the bank recovery against the person paid is popularly known as "the rule in Price v. Neal," after the great case of that name. Lord Mansfield there reasoned that "If there was no neglect in the [drawee], yet there is no reason to throw off the loss from one innocent man upon another innocent man; but in this case, if there was any fault or negligence in any one, it certainly was in the [drawee] and not in the [person paid]." Price v. Neal, 3 Burr. 1354, 97 Eng.Rep. 871 (K.B.1762).

Forged Indorsements.   If a check on which a necessary indorsement has been forged is not paid, the innocent purchaser can also turn to a prior party, if there is one other than the forger, for recourse. UCC 3–417(2)(a), 4–207(2)(a); see also UCC 4–212(1). Furthermore, as in the case of the forged check, if the drawee bank pays a check by mistake over a forged indorsement, it has no recourse against its depositor.[1] UCC 3–404(1), 4–401(1). (Remember that the

---

1. This general statement assumes that payment has in fact been made to the wrong person (or to the right person but in payment of the wrong debt). If, in

drawer's order is to pay only to "the order of " the payee.)   In contrast to the case of the forged check, however, the bank that pays a check by mistake on a forged indorsement can recover from the person paid, including a collecting bank, on the warranties of UCC 3–417(1)(a) and 4–207(1)(a).   In an early leading case, the court justified recovery on the "reason that the parties were equally innocent," and said, by way of disposing of the rule of Price v. Neal, that "it is sufficient to distinguish the case, that it goes on the superior negligence of the party paying."   Canal Bank v. Bank of Albany, 1 Hill 287 (N.Y.1841).

Prior to the adoption of the Code, the theory on which the drawee bank was generally allowed to recover was one of restitution of money paid by mistake of fact, rather than one of warranty.   Under that theory, however, it had been held that an agent collecting bank that had already paid over the proceeds to its principal was no longer liable to the drawee bank, since "an agent who has received money paid by mistake cannot be compelled to repay it where he has paid it over to his principal without notice."   National Park Bank v. Seaboard Bank, 114 N.Y. 28, 20 N.E. 632 (1889).   See also National Park Bank v. Eldred Bank, 90 Hun. 285, 35 N.Y.S. 752 (N.Y.1895), affirmed mem., 154 N.Y. 769, 49 N.E. 1101 (1897).   This meant that the drawee bank would often have to skip the presenting bank, which would usually be in its own jurisdiction, and proceed against a party with which it had no direct relationship and which might be inconveniently located.   To avoid this, banks voluntarily adopted the practice of adding the words "prior indorsements guaranteed" to their indorsement stamp, so that suit could be brought on this engagement.   Regulation J of the Federal Reserve Board provides that by sending a check for collection through the Federal Reserve System, "The sender shall be deemed to warrant to each Federal Reserve bank handling such item .   .   .   that it has good title to the item or is authorized to obtain payment on behalf of one who has good title, whether or not such warranty is evidenced by its express guaranty of prior endorsements on such item.   .   .   ."   12 Code Fed.Regs. § 210.5(b).

The Code changes the underlying theory of recovery from one of restitution to one of implied warranty under UCC 3–417(1) and 4–207(1).   Comment 2 to UCC 4–207 says that that section is "intended

spite of a forged indorsement or the lack of any indorsement, payment is in fact made as the drawer intended it, the drawee should be entitled to charge the drawer's account.   As one court put it, "The drawer is not damaged by the application of the rule, for no person not intended by him to take an interest has done so as a consequence of the forged indorsement .   .   .   ."   Gordon v. State Street Bank and Trust Co., 361 Mass. 258, 280 N.E.2d 152 (1972).   That case, like most in which this exception has been applied, involved a check made jointly to two payees, one of whom was intended to receive the proceeds to the exclusion of the other, although the indorsements of both were required for negotiation.   If the drawee bank pays the check to the payee intended to receive the proceeds, it can charge the drawer's account even though that payee has signed the other payee's indorsement without authorization, assuming, of course, that the drawer has not been otherwise adversely affected.

to give the effect presently obtained in bank collections by the words 'prior indorsements guaranteed' in collection transfers and present-ments between banks . . . . This section is also intended to make it clear that the so-called equitable defense of 'payment over' does not apply to a collecting bank. . . . Subsections (2) and (3) indicate that these results are intended notwithstanding the absence of in-dorsement or words of guarantee or warranty in a transfer or pre-sentment. Consequently, if for purposes of simplification or the speeding up of the bank collection process, banks desire to cut down the length or size of indorsements (Section 4–206), they may do so and the standard warranties and engagements to honor still apply."[2]

Altered checks. If a raised check is not paid, the innocent pur-chaser can, on establishing holder in due course status, enforce the instrument for its original amount even against the drawer. UCC 3–407(3). In addition, the purchaser can turn to a prior party, if there is one other than the forger, for recourse in the raised amount. UCC 3–417(2)(c), 4–207(2)(c); see also UCC 4–212(1). The bank that pays a raised check by mistake can charge its depositor's account for the original amount only, UCC 4–401(2)(a). The balance it can recover from the person paid, on the warranties of UCC 3–417(1)(c) and 4–207(1)(c).

Rationale. Suppose that a merchant cashes for the forger a check bearing a forged drawer's signature. If the drawee bank de-tects the forgery and refuses to pay the check, who bears the loss? If the drawee bank fails to detect the forgery and pays the check, who bears the loss? Why the difference in result? Although nearly all states recognized the rule of Price v. Neal under the Negotiable Instruments Law, there was no uniformity of reasoning. Is any of the following statements convincing?

(a) "The justification for the distinction between forgery of the signature of the drawer and forgery of an indorsement is that the drawee is in a position to verify the drawer's signature by comparison with one in his hands, but has ordinarily no opportunity to verify an indorsement." Comment 3 to UCC 3–417. But note that the rule stated in UCC 3–417(1)(b) and 4–207(1)(b) does not depend on the drawee's negligence.

(b) "The traditional justification for the result is that the drawee is in a superior position to detect a forgery because he has the mak-er's [sic] signature and is expected to know and compare it; a less fictional rationalization is that it is highly desirable to end the trans-action of an instrument when it is paid rather than reopen and upset

---

2. Note that UCC 4–302, which deals with a payor bank's responsibility for re-turn of a check after the midnight dead-line, applies only if there is no "valid de-fense such as breach of a presentment warranty," citing UCC 4–207(1). For a case holding that a delay of roughly eight weeks did not preclude a payor bank from returning as unpaid a check lacking the payor's indorsement, see Mill-er v. Federal Deposit Insurance Corp., 134 Ariz. 342, 656 P.2d 631 (App.1982).

a series of commercial transactions at a later date when the forgery is discovered." Comment 1 to UCC 3–418.

(c) "The rule stated in this Section [that of Price v. Neal] is in accord with mercantile convenience, supporting the finality of transactions with mercantile instruments in situations where ordinarily it is reasonably possible for the payor to ascertain the fraud. Furthermore, the payee has surrendered the instrument." Restatement, Restitution § 30, Comment a (1937).

(d) "Of the variety of justifications that have been advanced over the years, [two] are most convincing. The first is that the rule has a healthy cautionary effect on banks by encouraging care in the comparison of the signatures on 'on us' items against those on the signature cards that they have on file. Prompt detection of the forgery and return of the dishonored check will often prevent loss, especially where the check has been taken from the forger for collection only, and although a detailed examination of every check may not be practicable for a bank that may pay as many as several hundred thousand checks a day, the rule of Price v. Neal ensures that the bank has a lively interest not only in the rapid processing of checks but also in the detection of forgery and the reduction of forgery losses. Although this risk is covered by Clause D of the bankers blanket bond, experience rating retains the cautionary effect of the rule. The second justification is that this very opportunity of the drawee to insure and to distribute the cost among its customers who use checks makes the drawee an ideal party to spread the risk through insurance. This argument, to be sure, is junior to the rule, since forgery insurance is a century and a half younger than Price v. Neal. Nevertheless, there is no question today that forgery bonds are adequate to cover loss due to the mistaken payment of forged checks." Farnsworth, Insurance Against Check Forgery, 60 Colum.L.Rev. 284, 302–03 (1960).[3]

What is the position under the Code of a holder who takes a check in due course and then discovers that the drawer's signature has been forged? If the holder says nothing and is paid by the drawee, can the drawee recover the payment? Which answer accords with the reason behind the rule of Price v. Neal? Comment 4 to UCC 3–417 explains that "the warranty of subsection (1)(b) is pertinent in the case of a holder in due course only in the relatively few cases where he acquires knowledge of the forgery after the taking but before the presentment. In this situation the holder in due course must continue to act in good faith to be exempted from the basic warranty." How is it possible for the holder to act in good faith with knowledge of the forgery? See Mellinkoff, The Language of the Uniform Commercial Code, 77 Yale L.J. 185, 219 (1967).

Uniform New Payments Code. In a major departure from present law, UNPC 204 provides: "Each customer, transmitting account

3. Reproduced with permission of the Columbia Law Review.

institution or transferor of an unauthorized draw order is liable to all parties to whom the draw order is subsequently transmitted and who pay, accept or give value in exchange for the order in good faith, if it has transmitted an unauthorized order. . . ." The commentary gives the following explanation:

"[This provision] marks the death knell for Lord Mansfield's famous opinion in Price v. Neal . . . , which held that no warranty of the genuineness of a forged drawer's signature is given to the payor bank by a person transmitting a check for collection. . . .

"The rationale for the rule is not convincing. First, the traditional justification that the drawee is in a superior position to detect the forgery seems dubious today. Given the computerized payment of checks, necessitated by the high volume of items submitted for payment, it is uneconomical for an account institution to check the validity of all signatures. This is reflected by the reality that banks do not check signatures under a certain dollar amount even though they will be liable. It is cheaper to bear the liability than to avoid it . . . .

"The second rationale for the rule is finality—the need for repose on transactions . . . . It must be recognized, however, that there is no such repose in cases of forged endorsements where warranties are now given to the payor bank . . . .

"Not only is the rationale for the rule questionable, but the rule can be thought of as not giving adequate incentives to payees to check on the bona fides of people drawing checks to them. Under existing law, a merchant cashing a check need not be concerned with whether a person paying by check is actually the owner of the account on which the check is drawn. If Price v. Neal is abolished such incentives would exist. Check cashing outside the banking system is much less computerized thus allowing better opportunities for verifying the identity of a check casher . . . . Absent Price v. Neal . . . , loss would ultimately lie with the payee, the taker from the thief . . . . Account institutions should generally support abolishing Price v. Neal because risks now borne by them could be shifted to their customers.

"In addition, application of Price v. Neal makes no sense in cases of check truncation, where the drawer's signature is not available for inspection by the payor account institution—assuming technology could not capture the signature at a reasonable cost. Since, on balance, the rule has no convincing justification and some significant costs in today's high speed check processing environment, it is abolished. The Code rejects the possibility of allowing the collector of a check to avoid liability by showing that the payor account institution was negligent, e.g., failed to detect an obvious forgery on a $1 million check. While such a rule might be justified in theory, importing the issue of negligence into liabilities among account institutions would probably cause more confusion for operations personnel and litigation than it is worth . . . ."[1]

Personal Money Order. How do the rules relating to forged checks apply to personal money orders? What is the legal position of the bank if a person, claiming to be the "remitter," asks for a refund on an unsigned personal money order?

Problem 2. Perini Corporation used a facsimile signature machine for writing checks. It authorized the banks in which it had accounts

> to honor and charge Perini Corporation for all such checks . . . regardless of by whom or by what means the actual or purported facsimile signature thereon may have been affixed thereto, if such facsimile signature resembles the facsimile specimen from time to time filed with said banks.

Someone either gained access to the machine or developed a perfect copy of the facsimile and drew over a million dollars worth of checks payable either to "Quisenberry Contracting Co." or "Southern Contracting Co." These checks were deposited in the Habersham bank by a man calling himself "Jesse D. Quisenberry," who had already opened accounts in that bank in the names of the payees. The man did not, however, put authorized indorsements of the payees on the checks that he deposited, indorsing them simply "Jesse D. Quisenberry" with no indication that he was acting for the payee. The checks were paid by the drawees and the proceeds credited to the accounts in the Habersham bank, from which the man withdrew them. Has Perini any claim against the Habersham bank or the drawees? Do the rules on forged checks or those on checks bearing forged indorsements apply? See Perini Corp. v. First National Bank of Habersham County, 553 F.2d 398 (5th Cir.1977); Baker, The *Perini* Case: Double Forgery Revisited (pts. 1 & 2), 10 U.C.C.L.J. 309, 11 U.C.C.L.J. 41 (1978).

COMPARATIVE NOTE

Geneva Convention. The solution of civil law countries to the problem of forged indorsements offers an interesting comparison with our own. Under the Geneva Convention on Cheques, which was promulgated in 1931 and has been adopted in much of the civil law world, a person acquiring a check in good faith and without gross negligence by an interrupted series of indorsements has good title even if the instrument was stolen from the true owner and his in-

---

1. The New York Clearing House has criticized the proposal to abolish the doctrine of Price v. Neal on the ground that it may reduce the willingness of merchants to take checks instead of cash. "Currently, merchants do bear a relatively short-term risk that a check may not be paid during the process of collection. Under the revised rule, however, they would remain liable for the length of the applicable statute of limitations, under UCC § 4–406 now one year." Statement of the New York Clearing House on the Proposed Uniform New Payments Code 13–14 (1983).

dorsement forged. Similarly, a drawee bank that pays a check need only examine the apparent regularity of the chain of indorsements and is discharged if it pays in good faith to a person who takes by virtue of an apparently regular chain. See Kessler, Forged Indorsements, 47 Yale L.J. 863, 863–64 (1938).

Consider the situation illustrated by Problem 1(d), p. 266 supra, in which a thief steals a check before it is received by the payee, forges the payee's indorsement, and cashes it with an innocent merchant. The merchant deposits the check in his bank, which presents it to the drawee bank and obtains payment. In this situation the Code puts the loss on the merchant who, having taken the check from the forger, is left to pursue the forger.

The Geneva Convention, however, puts the loss on the drawer. Since the indorsements appeared on their face to be regular, the drawee can charge the drawer's account in spite of the forged indorsement.

Under the Geneva Convention, however, the drawer can, by crossing the check, protect himself from the risk that the check will be stolen. Two types of crossing are possible, general and special. A general crossing is made by drawing two parallel lines across the face of the instrument. A special crossing is made in the same way, but the name of the payee's bank is added between the lines. Any bank that fails to observe the crossing is liable for any loss caused by its failure. A bank may not take a crossed check except from its customer or from another bank, and such a check is payable only to a bank or a customer of the drawee. Thus a general crossing in the example above would have prevented the thief from presenting the check directly to the drawee but not from cashing it with a merchant or from depositing it in his own bank for collection. If the crossing is special, however, the drawee may pay it only to the bank named in the crossing or, if it is the named bank, to a customer.[1] Thus a special crossing in the example above would not only have prevented the thief from presenting the check directly to the drawee but also from cashing it with a merchant or depositing it in a bank for collection.[2]

Obviously this system will not work unless the drawer has an incentive to cross checks—unless the drawer has an appreciable risk that can be avoided by crossing them. Furthermore, since only a special crossing affords substantial protection, the system will not work unless most payees have bank accounts and most drawees know

1. In order to prevent the thief from opening a bank account for the purpose of collecting crossed checks bearing forged indorsements, courts have generally required an "anterior and permanent" relationship between customer and bank.

2. A payee who has received a check may also cross it or may convert a general crossing into a special crossing adding the name of the payee's bank. If an uncrossed check is stolen and paid over the payee's forged indorsement, the payee must bear the loss since the amount will be charged to the drawer, who cannot be required to issue a second check to the payee. By crossing the check, the payee will have a right against the drawer or depositary bank if it has acted inconsistently with the crossing.

where their payees bank.[3] See Farnsworth, The Check in France and the United States, 36 Tul.L.Rev. 245, 266–68 (1962).

UNCITRAL Draft. The United Nations Commission on International Trade Law is working on an international convention to govern a special category of checks that would bear the designation "international cheque" on their face. See p. 13 supra. This project is of special interest because it attempts to achieve a compromise among the various national solutions to the forged indorsement problem. For a discussion of this aspect of the draft convention, see Note, 21 Colum.J.Trans.L. 585 (1983).

Problem 3.   A drew a $1,000 check on the X Bank, which B the payee raised to $10,000. B negotiated it to C, a holder in due course, who procured its certification and then negotiated it to D, a holder in due course. Must the X Bank pay D $10,000? If it does, has it any recourse against A or C? What answers if the certification were "payable only as originally drawn"? See UCC 3–413, 3–417, 3–418, 4–207. Compare carefully UCC 3–413(1) with 3–417(1)(c)(iii) and 4–207(1)(c)(iii), and see UCC 1–102(3).

Problem 4. Suppose that in Problem 3 D had presented the check to X Bank and had been paid $10,000. Could X Bank recover any part of that sum from D? Would it make any difference if D had discovered the alteration between the time that D took the check and the time that D obtained payment from X Bank?

THE CERTIFICATION PUZZLE

The convoluted provisions of UCC 3–413(1), 3–417(1)(c) and 4–207(1)(c) deal with a puzzling problem as to which the law before the Code was both uncertain and unsatisfactory. The problem, stated simply, was: How should the loss be allocated when a check that was raised *before* certification was taken by a holder in due course *after* certification? The holder in due course could, of course, proceed against a prior indorser, if there was one other than the forger, but this would not give the holder the supposed security of a certified check. Could the holder hold the certifying bank on its certification for the *raised* amount of the check? Common sense said that the holder should be able to, if certification was to be meaningful. The Negotiable Instruments Law was ambiguous. Courts disagreed, with decisions in California and Illinois holding the bank liable for the raised amount. See Wells Fargo Bank & Union Trust Co. v. Bank of Italy, 214 Cal. 156, 4 P.2d 781 (1931). In practice, however, it made little difference what courts decided. Banks found a sufficient answer by including on their certification stamps some such phrase as "payable only as originally drawn," which resolved the issue in their

----

3. This information is often given on letterheads, bills, and invoices.

favor by making certification less meaningful. (Did they run any risk in refusing certification absent such a qualification? See Refusal to Certify as a Dishonor, p. 139, supra.)

Here is a perceptive analysis of the situation. "At the core of the banker's present discomfiture, insofar as certification matters trouble him at all, is the action of the Illinois and California courts in putting all loss upon the bank where altered paper is certified. To those who see negotiable instruments questions only through the eyes of a bona fide purchaser, without counting costs, those decisions should be codified without qualification. If the bank must take a dead loss, since recourse against the forger is not promising, it can of course insure. Why not? The court in the Wells Fargo case, in fact, went out of its way to deny the bank any other recourse by saying that the holder makes no warranties to the drawee. . . . But while there is reason apparent for charging the drawee with responsibility for the regularity of its drawer's signature and for the adequacy of his account—both matters peculiarly within the bank's knowledge—the same cannot be said for alterations in the body of the paper. On generally accepted risk analysis principles it is the person who takes the paper from the forger, often at a substantial discount, often with more than a suspicion of the fraud, who should take this risk.

"The first suggestion, therefore, is to provide that the person who presents a check for certification warrants to the bank not only that he has title to the item but that it has not been materially altered. The purchaser *after* certification, however, should be deemed to make no warranty to the drawee, either by indorsement or presentment for payment, except of course that his title to the item *as certified* is good. This suggestion proceeds upon the theory that upon certification for the holder, the check is in effect paid . . . and the bank is put in much the same position as if it had taken up the check and issued its cashier's check instead, as is often done. The bank in so doing runs only the usual business risks involved in paying items generally. The purchaser in good faith of the certified item, on his part, takes the instrument in confidence and at its face value. There would thus be no need for the banker either to abandon the practice of certifying checks for the holder or to qualify his undertaking so scrupulously." Steffen and Starr, A Blueprint for the Certified Check, 13 N.C.L.Rev. 450, 477–79 (1935).[4]

Such a complete solution, affecting the rights and duties of several parties, had to await legislative intervention. (Compare the situation involving mistaken payment over a stop order, in which bank disclaimers were followed by Code revision. See Prefatory Note, p. 215, supra.) To the drafters of the Code, the solution suggested was an attractive one in view of their adoption of a theory of liability in warranty to replace that of liability in restitution. It is implemented in

4. Reproduced with permission of The North Carolina Law Review.

UCC 3–413(1), 3–417(1)(c) and 4–207(1)(c). Furthermore, once the certifying bank was given recourse for breach of warranty by the person who presented the check for certification, there was scant justification in allowing it to qualify its certification, and UCC 3–417(1)(c) (iii) and 4–207(1)(c)(iii) purport to deprive such phrases as "payable as originally drawn" of their effectiveness. Was it an oversight to have omitted such a provision from UCC 3–413(1)?

SECTION 2. RIGHTS OF ONE WHOSE INDORSEMENT HAS BEEN FORGED

Prefatory Note. As the preceding materials showed, if a check is stolen from the *drawer* and paid on a forged indorsement, the rights of the parties are reasonably clear under the Code. If, however, the check is stolen from the *payee* and paid on a forged indorsement, the rights of the parties are far from clear. Prior to the Code, most courts held that the payee could recover from the drawee bank in conversion. "It is the conversion by the bank of the payee's property, the check, which gives rise to the action." State v. First National Bank of Albuquerque, 38 N.M. 225, 30 P.2d 728 (1934). At least the Code makes it clear that the drawee is liable on this theory. UCC 3–419(1)(c), (2). (It is not, of course, liable to the payee in contract because of UCC 3–409.)

The payee whose check has been paid on a forged indorsement will, however, usually find it more convenient to ask the drawer for a second check to replace the first than to demand payment from the drawee bank, ordinarily a stranger to it. Is the drawer liable to the payee if it does not comply with such a request? There was authority, before the Code, that it was not, a logical view if the drawee was liable to the payee in conversion. "Under these same circumstances, the liability of the drawer of the check upon the original account, to pay which the check is drawn, should be held discharged, having regard to the general rules of law governing the correlated duties and rights of the parties and to commercial usage and custom." McFadden v. Follrath, 114 Minn. 85, 130 N.W. 542 (1911). The same result can be justified under the Code. (Since the drawee's liability in conversion is for the face amount of the check under UCC 3–419(2), does this not compel the conclusion that the conversion consisted of the destruction of the payee's claim against the drawer in that amount, and not merely the misappropriation of a piece of paper?) On the other hand, it is possible to argue that the payee has an action against the drawer on the check under UCC 3–804 and on the underlying obligation under UCC 3–802. (Does either of these sections appear to have been drafted with this problem in mind?) See White, Some Petty Complaints About Article Three, 65 Mich.L.Rev. 1315, 1333–38 (1967). Of course, the practical importance of the question is lessened since the drawee on paying the check a second time, this time to the payee, will presumably have the right to charge the drawer's account once. Cf. UCC 4–401(1).

Unanswered questions multiply if one considers the possibility of suit by either the drawer or the payee against the depositary or other collecting banks. Some of these questions are dealt with in the opinions that follow. For a general discussion, see Dugan, Stolen Checks—The Payee's Predicament, 53 B.U.L.Rev. 955 (1973).

Problem 5. A thief steals Empire's check from Quaker after it has been received in the mail, forges Quaker's indorsement, and obtains payment directly from the Irving Trust. Quaker asks Empire for another check to replace the stolen one. Advise Empire of its legal position if it refuses to give Quaker a second check. Advise Empire of its legal position if it gives Quaker a second check. Compare this situation with that in Problem 1(d), p. 266 supra. See UCC 3–419.

Problem 6. A thief steals Empire's check from Empire before it has been mailed to Quaker, forges Quaker's indorsement, and deposits it in the Penn Bank, which forwards it to the Irving Trust, which pays it. The thief then withdraws the amount of the check from the Penn Bank. Advise Empire of its legal position with respect to Quaker, the Irving Trust, and the Penn Bank. See UCC 3–419; Stone & Webster Engineering v. First National Bank, infra.

Problem 7. A thief steals Empire's check from Quaker after it has been received in the mail, forges Quaker's indorsement, and deposits it in the Penn Bank, which forwards it to the Irving Trust, which pays it. The thief then withdraws the amount of the check from the Penn Bank. Advise Quaker of its legal position with respect to Empire, the Irving Trust, and the Penn Bank. See UCC 3–419; Knesz v. Central Jersey Bank & Trust Co., infra. Would it make a difference if the thief had cashed the check at the Penn Bank?

STONE & WEBSTER ENGINEERING CORP. v. FIRST NATIONAL BANK & TRUST CO.

Supreme Judicial Court of Massachusetts, 1962.
345 Mass. 1, 184 N.E.2d 358, 99 A.L.R.2d 628.

WILKINS, CHIEF JUSTICE. In this action of contract or tort in four counts for the same cause of action a demurrer to the declaration was sustained, and the plaintiff, described in the writ as having a usual place of business in Boston, appealed. G.L.(Ter.Ed.) c. 231, § 96. The questions argued concern the rights of the drawer against a collecting bank which "cashed" checks for an individual who had forged the payee's indorsement on the checks, which were never delivered to the payee.

In the first count, which is in contract, the plaintiff alleges that between January 1, 1960, and May 15, 1960, it was indebted at various times to Westinghouse Electric Corporation (Westinghouse) for goods and services furnished to it by Westinghouse; that in order to pay the indebtedness the plaintiff drew three checks within that period on its checking account in The First National Bank of Boston (First National) payable to Westinghouse in the total amount of $64,755.44; that before delivery of the checks to Westinghouse an employee of the plaintiff in possession of the checks forged the indorsement of Westinghouse and presented the checks to the defendant; that the defendant "cashed" the checks and delivered the proceeds to the plaintiff's employee who devoted the proceeds to his own use; that the defendant forwarded the checks to First National and received from First National the full amounts thereof; and that First National charged the account of the plaintiff with the full amounts of the checks and has refused to recredit the plaintiff's checking account; wherefore the defendant owes the plaintiff $64,755.44 with interest.

By order, copies of the three checks were filed in court. The checks are respectively dated at Rowe in this Commonwealth on January 5, March 8, and May 9, 1960. Their respective amounts are $36,982.86, $10,416.58, and $17,355. They are payable to the order of "Westinghouse Electric Corporation, 10 High Street, Boston." The first two checks are indorsed in typewriting, "for Deposit Only: Westinghouse Electric Corporation By: Mr. O.D. Costine, Treasury Representative" followed by an ink signature "O.D. Costine." The third check is indorsed in typewriting, "Westinghouse Electric Corporation By: [Sgd.] O.D. Costine Treasury Representative." All three checks also bear the indorsement by rubber stamp, "Pay to the order of any bank, banker or trust co. prior indorsements guaranteed . . . [date][1] The First National Bank & Trust Co. Greenfield, Mass."

The demurrer, in so far as it has been argued, is to each count for failure to state a cause of action. . . .

1.   Count 1, the plaintiff contends, is for money had and received. We shall so regard it. "An action for money had and received lies to recover money which should not in justice be retained by the defendant, and which in equity and good conscience should be paid to the plaintiff." . . .

The defendant has no money in its hands which belongs to the plaintiff. The latter had no right in the proceeds of its own check payable to Westinghouse. Not being a holder or an agent for a holder, it could not have presented the check to the drawee for payment. Uniform Commercial Code, enacted by St.1957, c. 765, § 1, G.L. c.

---

1. The respective dates are January 13, March 9, and May 11, 1960. Each check bears the stamped indorsement of the Federal Reserve Bank of Boston and on its face the paid stamp of The First National Bank of Boston.

106, §§ 3–504(1), 1–201(20). See Am.Law Inst. Uniform Commercial Code, 1958 Official Text with comments, § 3–419, comment 2: "A negotiable instrument is the property of the holder." See also Restatement 2d: Torts, Tent. draft no. 3, 1958, § 241A. The plaintiff contends that "First National paid or credited the proceeds of the checks to the defendant and charged the account of the plaintiff, and consequently, the plaintiff was deprived of a credit, and the defendant received funds or a credit which 'in equity and good conscience' belonged to the plaintiff."

In our opinion this argument is a non sequitur. The plaintiff as a depositor in First National was merely in a contractual relationship of creditor and debtor. Forastiere v. Springfield Inst. for Sav., 303 Mass. 101, 103, 20 N.E.2d 950; Krinsky v. Pilgrim Trust Co., 337 Mass. 401, 405, 149 N.E.2d 665. The amounts the defendant received from First National to cover the checks "cashed" were the bank's funds and not the plaintiff's. The Uniform Commercial Code does not purport to change the relationship. See G.L. c. 106, §§ 1–103, 4–401 to 4–407. Section 3–409(1) provides: "A check or other draft does not of itself operate as an assignment of any funds in the hands of the drawee available for its payment, and the drawee is not liable on the instrument until he accepts it." This is the same as our prior law, which the Code repealed. See, formerly, G.L. c. 107, §§ 150, 212. Whether the plaintiff was rightfully deprived of a credit is a matter between it and the drawee, First National.

If we treat the first count as seeking to base a cause of action for money had and received upon a waiver of the tort of conversion—a matter which it is not clear is argued—the result will be the same. In this aspect the question presented is whether a drawer has a right of action for conversion against a collecting bank which handles its checks in the bank collection process. Unless there be such a right, there is no tort which can be waived.

The plaintiff relies upon the Uniform Commercial Code, G.L. c. 106, § 3–419, which provides, "(1) An instrument is converted when . . . (c) it is paid on a forged indorsement." This, however, could not apply to the defendant, which is not a "payor bank," defined in the Code, § 4–105(b), as "a bank by which an item is payable as drawn or accepted." See Am.Law Inst. Uniform Commercial Code, 1958 Official Text with comments, § 4–105, comments 1–3; G.L. c. 106, §§ 4–401, 4–213, 3–102(b).

A conversion provision of the Uniform Commercial Code which might have some bearing on this case is § 3–419(3). This section implicitly recognizes that, subject to defences, including the one stated in it, a collecting bank, defined in the Code, § 4–105(d), may be liable in conversion. In the case at bar the forged indorsements were "wholly inoperative" as the signatures of the payee, Code §§ 3–404(1), 1–201(43), and equally so both as to the restrictive indorsements for deposits, see § 3–205(c), and as to the indorsement in

blank, see § 3–204(2). When the forger transferred the checks to the
collecting bank, no negotiation under § 3–202(1) occurred, because
there was lacking the necessary indorsement of the payee. For the
same reason, the collecting bank could not become a "holder" as defined in § 1–201(20), and so could not become a holder in due course
under § 3–302(1). Accordingly, we assume that the collecting bank
may be liable in conversion to a proper party, subject to defences,
including that in § 3–419(3). See A. Blum Jr.'s Sons v. Whipple, 194
Mass. 253, 255, 80 N.E. 501, 13 L.R.A.,N.S., 211. But there is no
explicit provision in the Code purporting to determine to whom the
collecting bank may be liable, and consequently, the drawer's right to
enforce such a liability must be found elsewhere. Therefore, we conclude that the case must be decided on our own law, which, on the
issue we are discussing, has been left untouched by the Uniform
Commercial Code in any specific section.

In this Commonwealth there are two cases (decided in 1913 and
1914) the results in which embrace a ruling that there was a conversion, but in neither was the question discussed and, for aught that
appears, in each the ruling seems to have been assumed without conscious appreciation of the issue here considered. Franklin Sav. Bank
v. International Trust Co., 215 Mass. 231, 102 N.E. 363; Quincy Mut.
Fire Ins. Co. v. International Trust Co., 217 Mass. 370, 140 N.E. 845,
L.R.A.1915B, 725. . . . The Franklin Sav. Bank case cannot be
distinguished on the ground of the limited powers of a city treasurer.
That issue was important as charging the bank with notice of the
treasurer's lack of authority to indorse but, that fact established
there was this further question as to whether there was a remedy in
tort for conversion.

The authorities are hopelessly divided. We think that the preferable view is that there is no right of action. . . . We state what
appears to us to be the proper analysis. Had the checks been delivered to the payee Westinghouse, the defendant might have been liable for conversion to the payee. The checks, if delivered, in the
hands of the payee would have been valuable property which could
have been transferred for value or presented for payment; and, had a
check been dishonored, the payee would have had a right of recourse
against the drawer on the instrument under § 3–413(2). Here the
plaintiff drawer of the checks, which were never delivered to the payee (see Gallup v. Barton, 313 Mass. 379, 381, 47 N.E.2d 921), had no
valuable rights in them. Since, as we have seen, it did not have the
right of a payee or subsequent holder to present them to the drawee
for payment, the value of its rights was limited to the physical paper
on which they were written, and was not measured by their payable
amounts.

The enactment of the Uniform Commercial Code opens the road
for the adoption of what seems the preferable view. An action by
the drawer against the collecting bank might have some theoretical

appeal as avoiding circuity of action. See Home Indem. Co. v. State Bank, 233 Iowa 103, 135–140, 8 N.W.2d 757. Compare 36 Harv.L. Rev. 879. It would have been in the interest of speedy and complete justice had the case been tried with the action by the drawer against the drawee and with an action by the drawee against the collecting bank. See Nichols v. Somerville Sav. Bank, 333 Mass. 488, 490, 132 N.E.2d 158. So one might ask: If the drawee is liable to the drawer and the collecting bank is liable to the drawee, why not let the drawer sue the collecting bank direct? We believe that the answer lies in the applicable defences set up in the Code.[2]

The drawer can insist that the drawee recredit his account with the amount of any unauthorized payment. Such was our common law. . . . This is, in effect, retained by the Code §§ 4–401(1), 4–406(4). But the drawee has defences based upon the drawer's substantial negligence, if "contributing," or upon his duty to discover and report unauthorized signatures and alterations. §§ 3–406, 4–406. As to unauthorized indorsements, see § 4–406(4). Then, if the drawee has a valid defence which it waives or fails upon request to assert, the drawee may not assert against the collecting bank or other prior party presenting or transferring the check a claim which is based on the forged indorsement. § 4–406(5). See Am.Law Inst. Uniform Commercial Code, Official Text with comments, § 4–406, comment 6, which shows that there was no intent to change the prior law as to negligence of a customer. . . . If the drawee recredits the drawer's account and is not precluded by § 4–406(5), it may claim against the presenting bank on the relevant warranties in §§ 3–417 and 4–207, and each transferee has rights against his transferor under those sections.

If the drawer's rights are limited to requiring the drawee to recredit his account, the drawee will have the defences noted above and perhaps others; and the collecting bank or banks will have the defences in § 4–207(4) and § 4–406(5), and perhaps others. If the drawer is allowed in the present case to sue the collecting bank, the assertion of the defences, for all practical purposes, would be difficult. The possibilities of such a result would tend to compel resort to litigation in every case involving a forgery of commercial paper. It is a result to be avoided.

The demurrer to count 1 was rightly sustained. [The court's discussion of the remaining three counts is omitted.]

Order sustaining demurrer affirmed.

NOTE

(1) Conflicting Authority. The Massachusetts court noted that allowing recovery "by the drawer against the collecting bank might

---

2. Cases where a payee has acquired rights in an instrument may stand on a different footing.

have some theoretical appeal as avoiding circuity of action." In Sun 'n Sand, Inc. v. United California Bank, 21 Cal.3d 671, 148 Cal.Rptr. 329, 582 P.2d 920 (1978), the Supreme Court of California found appeal in such reasoning. Eloise Morales, an employee of Sun 'n Sand, made out nine checks for small amounts payable to United California Bank (UCB), had them signed by her employer, raised the amount of each check by several thousand dollars, and deposited them in her account with UCB. They were paid by the drawee, Union Bank, which charged them to Sun 'n Sand. Sun 'n Sand sued both Union Bank and UCB. The trial court sustained a demurrer by UCB and ordered the case against it dismissed, and Sun 'n Sand appealed. The Supreme Court of California reversed, holding that Sun 'n Sand had stated a cause of action against UCB for breach of its warranties against material alteration under UCC 3–417(1)(c) and 4–207(1)(c).

"Section 4207, subdivision (1), provides that its warranties extend to 'the payor bank or other payor who in good faith pays or accepts the item.' To receive the benefit of these warranties, then, the drawer of a check must qualify as an 'other payor who . . . pays.' At least one court has held, although without offering any explanatory rationale, that a drawer whose account was debited by his bank is a payor entitled to claim the benefit of these warranties. (Insurance Company of No. Amer. v. Atlas Supply Co. (1970) 121 Ga.App. 1, 172 S.E.2d 632, 636.) We find this broad construction of the payor concept justified by inferences that can be drawn from the structure of section 4207 and language in the official comments to the UCC.[3]

"The warranties provided for in subdivisions (1)(b) and (1)(c) of section 4207 are expressly made subject to certain exceptions which operate in favor of a holder in due course who acts in good faith. These warranties are not extended to a number of parties, including a drawer 'whether or not the drawer is also the drawee.' (§ 4207, subds. (1)(b)(ii) & (1)(c)(ii).) By negative implication, the warranties are given by a collecting bank to a drawer who is not also the drawee (payor) bank—at least when the collecting bank is not a holder in due course or does not act in good faith. Section 4207 is quite clear in excepting drawers under subdivisions (1)(b)(ii) and (1)(c)(ii); accordingly, we may infer that drawers are among those to whom the warranty of section 4207, subdivision (1)(a), extends, as no comparable exceptions are there made.

"The inferences thus compelled by the structure of section 4207 indicate the Code contemplates that the drawer of a check is an 'other payor' for purposes of that section who may, unless specifically excepted, claim the benefits of the warranties therein created. Although the term 'payor' is more commonly used in reference to the drawee than the drawer, it is not defined anywhere in the Code and

3. The court noted that UCC 4–207 applied because, though UCB was the payee of the checks, it "treated the checks as though it was merely a nominal payee, named as such to facilitate collection." [Ed.]

hence should not be regarded as a term of art used in a narrow, technical sense; when a check is negotiated, it is the drawer who ultimately 'pays' when his account is charged in the amount of the check. This is implicitly recognized in the official comments to the UCC: 'Similarly, under subparagraph (ii) a drawer of a draft is presumed to know his own signature and if he fails to detect a forgery of his signature and *pays a draft* he may not recover that payment from a holder in due course acting in good faith.' (Italics added.) (UCC, § 3417, com. 4.)

"We therefore hold that the drawer of a check whose account is charged is a payor within the meaning of section 4207 and may maintain an action against a collecting bank based on that section's warranties. For the foregoing reasons, we further hold that the drawer of a check is 'a person who in good faith pays' within the meaning of section 3417 and may maintain an action against the payee of a check based on the section 3417 warranties.[4]

"Courts in other jurisdictions that have denied to drawers a direct right of action have apparently been concerned that collecting banks would not always be able to assert defenses available to drawee banks. They have assumed that direct suits by drawers would not merely avoid circuity of action, but would alter substantive rights. (See, e.g., Stone & Webster Eng. Corp. v. First National B. & T. Co. (1962) 345 Mass. 1, 184 N.E.2d 358, 362–363. . . .) We find nothing to prevent collecting banks (and payees) from asserting the same defenses as drawee banks." The court went on to explain that the most important of these defenses were those under UCC 3–406 and 4–406 (discussed in Section 3, infra) and asserted that both were available to a collecting bank in a direct suit by the drawer.[5]

The court also held that Sun 'n Sand had stated a "cause of action on a theory of negligence, asserting that UCB breached its duty of care in permitting checks on which the bank was named payee to be deposited in the personal account of Sun 'n Sand's employee."

In Insurance Company of North America v. Purdue National Bank, __ Ind.App. __, 401 N.E.2d 708 (1980), a drawer sued a collecting bank for breach of its warranties as to title on checks bearing forged indorsements. The court adopted the reasoning in Sun 'n

4. The language of subdivisions 1(a), 1(b), and 1(c) of section 3417 are identical in all relevant respects to the corresponding subdivisions of section 4207, thus giving rise to the same negative implication that direct suit by a drawer is permitted.

5. In the court's view, UCB would not have broken the warranties against material alteration if it were "a holder in due course acting in good faith" because Sun 'n Sand was "the drawer of a draft" under UCC 3–417(1)(c)(ii) and 4–207(1)(c)(ii).

The court thought, however, that even if it were assumed that UCB had given value, Sun 'n Sand "alleged facts that create serious doubt as to whether UCB is sufficiently 'without notice' to qualify as a holder in due course" because it alleged that the checks "were drawn to the order of UCB as payee but were nonetheless negotiated by a Sun 'n Sand employee (fiduciary) for her own benefit." Cf. footnote 1, p. 213 supra.

Sand, but held that the drawer's negligence gave the collecting bank a defense under UCC 3–406.

Since the drawee is likely to be closer to the drawer than is any collecting bank, why would a drawer want to litigate the question of a collecting bank's liability?

(2) Indemnification. Suppose that a payee loses a check and requests that the drawer send a substitute check. The drawer who does so risks having to pay twice if the first check had already been indorsed by the payee and comes into the hands of a holder in due course. To protect against this risk, the drawer may under UCC 3–804 require that the payee supply security indemnifying the drawer "against loss by reason of further claims on the instrument." Santos v. First National State Bank of New Jersey, 186 N.J.Super. 52, 451 A.2d 401 (1982), arose out of such a demand for security in the case of a lost cashier's check.

In 1978, Santos, who was preparing to return to Puerto Rico, withdrew the entire balance of $15,514.46 from his savings account and took a cashier's check payable to his own order, which he then mailed to his father in Puerto Rico. Eleven days later, he told the bank that the check had been lost in the mail and asked for a substitute check. The bank insisted on security under UCC 3–804, but Santos could not, even with the bank's assistance, get a bond because he was unemployed and had no other assets.

In 1980, Santos sued the bank to compel it: (1) to issue a duplicate check or credit him with $15,514.46 without security; or (2) to establish an interest-bearing account in trust, paying him interest periodically, with the principal to be paid six years from the date the check was issued or at another date fixed by the court.

The court concluded that under UCC 3–122 the six-year statute of limitations began to run when the check was issued and that, though it was "highly improbable" that the check would reappear during that time, "to require payment now without security for indemnification would expose defendant to a risk of loss through no fault of its own." The court therefore ordered the bank "to issue at this time a certificate of deposit in plaintiff's name for $15,514.46 bearing the highest prevailing interest rate for such an instrument." Subject to any further order of the court, the bank was to hold the certificate as security for its obligation until the six-year statute ran in 1984, unless the check sooner reappeared, and during this period was to pay Santos quarterly interest.

KNESZ v. CENTRAL JERSEY BANK & TRUST CO.

Superior Court of New Jersey, 1982.
188 N.J.Super. 391, 457 A.2d 1162.

PRESSLER, J.A.D. The issue raised by this appeal, unaddressed in this State since its adoption of the Uniform Commercial Code, N.J. S.A. 12A:1–101 et seq., is whether the payee of a check whose indorsement has been forged had a cause of action in conversion against the depositary-collecting bank which has paid on the forged indorsement. We hold that N.J.S.A. 12A:3–419(3), relied on by defendant bank, does not immunize it from a conversion action by the payee and hence that the Code does not deprive the payee of the common-law conversion action theretofore available to him. Accordingly, we reverse the summary judgment entered in defendant bank's favor and remand for trial.

The facts giving rise to this action are basically undisputed insofar as they implicate the viability of plaintiff-payee's cause of action in conversion against defendant, the depositary and collecting bank. Plaintiff Steve Knesz was the nonoccupant owner of a cooperative apartment in New York City. He employed a New York attorney, Thomas G. Moringiello, who has since been disbarred, to act as his rental agent. It appears that Moringiello did not regularly transmit rental proceeds to plaintiff since the amount of the rent did not exceed the disbursements required to be made for taxes, mortgage amortization and maintenance expenses. In any event, in March 1979 Moringiello, without plaintiff's knowledge or authority, sold the apartment to Lois Gartlir. She paid the purchase price by way of five checks drawn on three different banks and totaling $32,651. Four of these checks, three drawn on Morgan Guaranty Trust Company of New York and one drawn on Bankers Trust, were payable to the order of Gartlir who, in turn, endorsed them under the legend "pay to the order of Steve Knesz." The fifth was a bank check of Citibank, N.A., payable to plaintiff's order. Moringiello forged plaintiff's indorsement on all five instruments. He apparently deposited three of the checks payable to Gartlir to his own account in Citibank, N.A., which ultimately repaid plaintiff.

Thus, the controversy involves only two instruments, a check drawn on Morgan Guaranty payable to Gartlir in the amount of $5,000 and the Citibank check payable to plaintiff in the amount of $16,974.24. These two checks were delivered by Moringiello to a New Jersey attorney, James E. Collins, under the following circumstances. Moringiello at the time of this transaction was representing other clients in connection with their sale of a residence in Staten Island. Collins fortuitously represented the same people in connection with their purchase of a residence in Monmouth County, New Jersey. The proceeds of the Staten Island sale were intended to be applied to the New Jersey purchase and, in accordance with this plan, Moringiello sent Collins a check drawn on his "special attorney account" in the amount of $24,000 purportedly representing the sales proceeds. Collins deposited this check into the trust account maintained by his firm, Cerrato, O'Connor, Mehr & Saker (firm) in the Central Jersey Bank and Trust Co. of Freehold (Central Jersey). Moringiello's attorney's check was returned for insufficient funds, and Collins made demand upon Moringiello for the immediate replacement of his bad check. Moringiello obliged by turning over to Collins the two checks on which he had forged Knesz's indorsement, placing his own indorsement immediately below Knesz's forged signature. He added to these another check drawn by him on his attorney's account making up the difference between Knesz's $21,974.24 and the required $24,000. Collins indorsed all three instruments and deposited them in the firm's account in Central Jersey. The collection process proceeded and was completed in due course.

Some nine months later, in January 1980, plaintiff first learned of the unauthorized sale of the apartment. He apparently chose to ratify the sale and seek recovery of the proceeds. With the gratuitous assistance of yet another bank, he finally obtained the necessary information regarding the five instruments, and in August, 1980 he executed affidavits of forgery as to each. As noted, Citibank paid him the amount of the three checks Moringiello had deposited to his account there. Central Jersey refused to pay, however, on the two checks as to which it was both depositary and collecting bank. Plaintiff consequently brought this action against the bank, which filed a third-party complaint against the firm.

Both plaintiff and the bank moved for summary judgment. Plaintiff took the position that the bank, having paid on a forged instrument, was absolutely liable to him in conversion. The bank crossmoved for summary judgment. Its theories of defense included the claims that the bank was not liable in conversion pursuant to the terms of N.J.S.A. 12A:3–419(3); that plaintiff had been negligent and hence was foreclosed from recovery by N.J.S.A. 12A:3–406, and finally, that in ratifying Moringiello's sale of the apartment, plaintiff also necessarily ratified Moringiello's disposition of the proceeds thereof. It was on the basis of N.J.S.A. 12A:3–419(3) that plaintiff's motion was denied and the bank's motion granted. We agree with plaintiff that the trial judge erred in his construction of this section.

N.J.S.A. 12A:3–419(1)(c) states with unmistakable clarity that "an instrument is converted when . . . it is paid on a forged indorsement." N.J.S.A. 12A:3–419(3), which poses the constructional problem here, provides in full as follows:

> Subject to the provisions of this Act concerning restrictive indorsements a representative, including a depositary or collecting bank, who has in good faith and in accordance with the reasonable commercial standards applicable to the business of such representative dealt with an instrument or its proceeds on

behalf of one who was not the true owner is not liable in conversion or otherwise to the true owner beyond the amount of
any proceeds remaining in his hands.

Thus, the question is whether a depositary or collecting bank, when it
engages in the customary business of accepting checks for cash payment or ordinary collection, is entitled to the statutory immunity
from conversion liability afforded by § 3–419(3).

We note preliminarily that this is a question which has generated
substantial controversy among those courts and commentators who
have addressed it and who apparently are unanimous in their conclusion that there is neither commercial nor practical nor rational justification for construing it as applicable to depositary and collecting
banks engaging in normal check collection business. Consequently,
the section has either been ignored altogether, applied reluctantly, or
held inapplicable on a variety of theories. For the reasons hereafter
stated we agree with those courts which have concluded that the section does not apply in this situation but we reach that conclusion on
grounds somewhat different from those heretofore articulated.

Our beginning point is pre-Code common law, which virtually universally recognized the right of the payee whose indorsement was
forged to recover on theories of conversion, contract or money had
and received directly against the depositary-collecting bank which
paid on the forged indorsement. . . .

The common law right of action by the payee against the depositary-collecting bank rests, of course, upon sound and established principles dependent upon the legal fact that neither the forger of the indorsement nor those taking through him have title to the instrument
and hence that the payee or last genuine indorser remains its owner.
The check owner's right of direct action against the depositary-collecting bank is also recognized as resting upon sound considerations
of public policy as well. First, the loss is appropriately placed upon
the depositary bank since it has dealt most immediately with the
forged instrument and consequently has the best as well as the last
opportunity to have avoided the loss. Second, since the depositary
bank is the most immediately connected with the transaction involving the forged instrument, it is, in most situations, in the best position to raise the traditional defenses of negligence, estoppel and ratification. Finally, it is the depositary bank upon which, as a
consequence of the normal operation of the collection system the loss
will in any event be ultimately placed since, as a consequence of their
respective indorsement warranties, each bank in the collection chain,
from drawee to depositary, has a right to look to its own transferor
for recovery.[1] See e.g., Cooper v. Union Bank, 9 Cal.3d 371, 107 Cal.
Rptr. 1, 507 P.2d 609, 616–617 (Sup.Ct.1973); . . . .

1. This right over has been codified
by the Code, N.J.S.A. 12A:4–207, which
specifies the warranties undertaken by
each customer or collecting bank obtaining payment or acceptance of an
item. Among them is the warranty of

If N.J.S.A. 12A:3–419(3) is construed as applying to the normal and customary check collection business of a depositary and collecting bank, then by the terms of that provision its liability in "conversion or otherwise" to the payee of the check whose indorsement has been forged will be limited to those situations in which the bank has acted either in bad faith or contrary to a reasonable commercial standard, and to those situations in which it still has the proceeds of the check available to it because of the pendency of the collection process. Unless one of these liability-triggering elements is available to the payee, he will be unable to proceed directly against the depositary-collecting bank. Rather, his remedy will be against the drawer of the check or the drawee bank. The drawer will then look to the drawee and the drawee, as noted, will have the right to recover successively against its transferor, who in turn will look to its transferor until ultimately, the loss will be borne by the depositary bank. The effect of N.J.S.A. 12A:3–419(3), therefore, would be in no way to immunize the depositary bank from the consequences of its payment on a forged indorsement. It undertakes that liability by the mere act of sending the check through for collection. All that such a construction of N.J.S.A. 12A:3–419(3) would therefore accomplish would be the replacement of a single direct action by a circuity of action. If the depositary bank and the payee are in the same jurisdiction and the drawee-payor bank is in another jurisdiction as is typical, that construction of N.J.S.A. 12A:3–419(3) would also have the effect of prejudicing the recovery opportunity of the payee, who would be forced to go elsewhere to sue. Furthermore, the raising and litigating of defenses based on the payee's culpability are ordinarily most effectively accomplished by the bank closest to the transaction, and customarily this is the depositary rather than the drawee bank.[2]

The question, then, is whether the framers of the Code and the New Jersey Legislature intended by enactment of § 3:419(3) to abrogate a common law principle which is legally sound, commercially practical and judicially expeditious, and to replace it, not by altering the allocation of ultimate liability, but only by limiting the remedy of the wronged party in a manner which is inevitably circuitous, cumbersome, burdensome and impractical. We conclude that this was neither the legislative intention nor the legislative prescription.

As we have noted, the apparent anomaly of § 3–419(3) in this context is by now a well-recognized phenomenon. As early as 1964 it was held to be inapplicable to the normal check collection activities of

good title. N.J.S.A. 12A:4–207(1)(a) and (2)(a).

2. Cf. Western Union Tel. Co. v. Peoples Nat'l Bk., Lakewood, 169 N.J.Super. 272, 404 A.2d 1178 (App.Div.1979), a case dealing with the right of action of a drawer rather than a payee. There the drawer was denied the right of direct action against the depositary-payor on the ground that the proximate cause of its loss was the drawee's improper handling of its account. Despite the circuity of action thus created, the court noted that the drawee is in the best position to raise Code defenses against the drawer based upon the drawer's own negligence and failure to inspect its statements.

banks. Ervin v. Dauphin Deposit Trust Co., 38 Pa.D. & C.2d 473
(C.P.1964). The court in *Ervin* relied, first, on legislative history,
noting that the Official Comment on this section (Comment 5 on § 3–
419) does not evince an intention to abrogate the common law. That
Comment reads in full as follows:

> Subsection (3), which is new, is intended to adopt the rule of
> decisions which has held that a representative, such as a bro-
> ker or depositary bank, who deals with a negotiable instrument
> for his principal in good faith is not liable to the true owner for
> conversion of the instrument or otherwise, except that he may
> be compelled to turn over to the true owner the instrument it-
> self or any proceeds of the instrument remaining in his hands.
> The provisions of subsection (3) are, however, subject to the
> provisions of this Act concerning restrictive indorsements (Sec-
> tions 3–205, 3–206 and related sections.)

The court in *Ervin* concluded that the operative term "representative," by expressly including a "broker," was not intended in its reference to a depositary or collecting bank as a possible representative,
to include such a bank acting simply as the acceptor of a check for
collection or as the payor of a check to be transmitted by it for collection. Alternatively, *Ervin* held that since the bank there had cashed
the check for the customer, it had used its own funds, and the "proceeds" of the check received by it through the collection process remained thereafter in its hands, available to the payee by the explicit
terms of § 3–419(3). Both of these theories were thereafter elaborat-
ed upon by the California Supreme Court in Cooper v. Union Bank,
supra, 107 Cal.Rptr. 1, 507 P.2d 609, which also rejected the applicability of § 3–419(3) to depositary banks acting in a check-collection
function. Noting the unlikelihood that the Code's framers would
have intended to so radically depart from the common law without
making some comment either acknowledging or explaining that departure,[3] the California court reasoned that for purposes of § 3–
419(3), whether the depositary bank has cashed the forged check or
has merely accepted it for collection, it never actually pays over the
"proceeds" within the intendment of that section if it pays on a
forged indorsement to one who is not entitled thereto. *Cooper* further relied on the conclusion, reinforced by its own state's study comments on the Code, that "representative," as used by § 3–419(3), was
intended only to protect investment brokers, those acting as investment brokers, and other "true agents." 107 Cal.Rptr. at 10, 507 P.2d
at 618.

3. Of singular interest in this regard
is the apparent contemporaneous perception of at least one leading commentator
that § 3–419(3) did not alter the common
law rule. Thus, in 2 Anderson, Uniform
Commercial Code (1971), the author, after a perfunctory reference to the section
at 1033, makes this observation: "Where
the name of the indorsee is forged, a
bank which collects the check bearing
such forgery and credits the proceeds to
the account of the forger commits conversion and is liable to the person who
was the lawful holder prior to the forged
indorsement." Id. at 1037.

Ervin and *Cooper* generated considerable commentator response, the consensus of which was that there was little justification, if any, for generally immunizing a depositary bank from direct liability to the owner of a check which was paid by it on a forged indorsement; that the Code apparently did not intend such a result, but that the reasoning of both *Ervin* and *Cooper* was nevertheless strained. See, e.g. Note, "Cooper v. Union Bank: California Protects the True Owner Against a Forged Indorsement Despite Uniform Commercial Code Section 3–419(3)," 25 Hastings L.J. 715 (1974); Note, "Depositary Bank Liability under § 3–419(3) of the Uniform Commercial Code," 31 Wash. & Lee L.Rev. 676 (1974); Note, "Payee v. Depositary Bank: What is the UCC Defense to Handling Checks Bearing Forged Indorsements?" 45 U.Colo.L.Rev. 281 (1974); Recent Developments, "Section 3–419(3) of the U.C.C. Does Not Limit the Liability of a Depositary Bank to the True Owner of a Check Paid on a Forged Indorsement," 74 Colum.L.Rev. 104 (1974).

The judicial response to *Ervin* and *Cooper* is even more instructive. Virtually all courts which have had to address § 3–419(3), whether or not they have finally opted to apply that section to a depositary bank which has paid on a forged check indorsement, have expressly failed to find any policy justification for such an immunity. Among the most thoughtful and carefully analytical of the opinions which have nevertheless accorded the section a broad immunity construction are Jackson Vitrified China v. People's American, 388 So.2d 1059 (Fla.D.Ct.App.1980), and Denn v. First State Bank of Spring Lake Park, supra, 316 N.W.2d 532 (Minn.Sup.Ct.1982). Both did so reluctantly. The Florida court, in Jackson Vitrified China v. People's American, supra, pertinently observed:

> Why the common law was abrogated in subsection (3) is not clear. The doctrine of a collector's ultimate responsibility to a true payee for payment on a forged endorsement was an element of the laws of commerce from as early as 1607. [388 So. 2d at 1062–1063, n. 1; citations omitted]

It had this to say as well:

> We believe that the laws of commerce would benefit by the absence of § 673.419(3), Fla.Stat. (1980), UCC § 3–419(3) (1962). Certainly, Florida payees would so benefit, since collecting banks are nearly always accessible in state courts: By direct action, a single and convenient determination of rights could be effected. The impact of the provision is to create the need for as many actions as there are drawers or drawee banks, many of which may be foreign, especially where a payee's business is interstate in nature. Moreover, to the extent such drawees do not absorb their losses or negotiate a settlement with the collecting bank, they may well have to undertake distant litigation (here) against the collecting bank. Presumably, even a recalcitrant collecting bank would often prefer

a single adjudication of liability than defend several suits for parts of the whole. The only possible advantage to subsection (3) is that it allows the banking community to conduct whatever customary resolution of accounts it has evolved for the spreading of risks. Absent a showing to the Legislature that such customary resolution results in a net state societal gain, via benefit to the banking community, over the known disadvantages—mainly, high costs of collection—to payees and drawers, we perceive the statutory provision to have been ill-conceived, as engendering a landslide of litigation inconsistent with the basic thrust of the Code toward simplification of commercial practice and remedy. [388 So.2d at 1063]

The Minnesota court noted that

There are strong policy arguments in Denn's favor. It is judicially efficient to allow the true payee to proceed directly against a collecting bank. The collecting bank will bear the ultimate loss in most cases. If the payee must sue the drawee bank, the drawee bank will sue the collecting bank on the warranties of Minn.Stat. § 336.4–207 as Northfield did in this case. Therefore, "a suit by the owner-payee against the depositary bank avoids an additional suit and thus resolves the entire dispute in a more economical manner." J. White & R. Summers, Uniform Commercial Code 590 (2d ed. 1980). Collecting banks are also more convenient defendants. While the forged checks may be drawn on several different banks, the forger often cashes or deposits them all at the same bank, or at banks in the same geographical area. Both the payee and the judicial system suffer when the payee is required to sue the drawee banks in a number of jurisdictions to recover on a forged indorsement. The Michigan Court of Appeals relied on this policy consideration when it held that "3–419(3) provides no defense for the collecting bank in a suit by the true owner of the instrument in this type of fact situation." Sheriff-Goslin Co. v. Cawood, 91 Mich.App. 204, 210, 283 N.W.2d 691, 694 (1979). The court was concerned about the number of suits that would result if it did not allow a payee's direct action against a depositary bank. [Denn v. First State Bank of Spring Lake Park, supra, 316 N.W.2d at 537]

Nevertheless, both courts concluded that the reasoning of *Ervin* and *Cooper* constituted an inadequate basis for overcoming the apparent plain meaning of the section.

Other courts, however, have been willing to conclude, whether or not they accept the *Ervin-Cooper* rationales, that in view of the common law precedents and the strong public policy arguments against immunity, the immunity intent of the Code is simply too improbable to warrant judicial enforcement. They have accordingly refused to apply the section to depositary and collecting banks paying on forged indorsements.   See, e.g., Tubin v. Rabin, 389 F.Supp. 787 (N.D.Tex. 1974), aff'd 533 F.2d 255 (5 Cir. 1976); Sherriff-Goslin Co. v. Cawood, supra, 91 Mich.App. 204, 283 N.W.2d 691 (Ct.App.1979).   Still other courts have avoided the immunity consequence by a strict construction of the exception based on failure to comply with a reasonable commercial standard.   See, e.g., Salsman v. National Community Bank of Rutherford, supra, 102 N.J.Super. 482, 246 A.2d 162; . . .. And, finally, despite the adoption of the Code by their states, some courts have applied the common law rule and accorded a right direct action against the depositary-collecting bank under § 3–419(1)(c) without any reference at all to § 3–419(3).   . . .

New Jersey courts have not yet had to face this problem.   The question of general applicability of § 3–419(3) was not addressed in Salsman v. National Community Bank of Rutherford, supra, 102 N.J. Super. 482, 246 A.2d 162, since the depositary bank there was held not to have conformed to a reasonable commercial standard and hence would not in any event have been entitled to any immunity from a payee's suit afforded by the section.   Here, we agree with the trial judge that the conduct of the bank was *prima facie* in accord with a reasonable commercial standard and that plaintiff made no showing which might raise a question of fact with respect thereto. We are satisfied that the bank was perfectly justified in accepting the checks with its own depositor's indorsement.   While it is true that Moringiello himself was one of the prior indorsers and that the bank constructively knew that Moringiello had drawn a previous check payable to its customer on insufficient funds, we do not conclude that the bank was obligated by that circumstance to inquire into every subsequent instrument presented to it which was indorsed by Moringiello, particularly since that indorsement and all prior indorsements were effectively guaranteed to it by virtue of its customer's own and final indorsement.   Having concluded that there was no question of fact impugning the bank's adherence to the required reasonable commercial standard, we are perforce constrained to address the question of the general applicability of § 3–419(3).

In concluding that that section does not apply to depositary or collecting banks engaging in customary check payment and collection activities, we are in full accord, for the reasons we have already stated, with both the judicial and commentator expressions of the public policy concerns militating against immunity.   We recognize however, that our view of salutary public policy may not override or contravene the Legislature's expressed view and that if the Legislature had indeed expressly elected to abrogate the common law, we would be obliged to enforce that election.   It is, however, our conviction, based both on legislative history and textual considerations, that our Legislature did not so intend.

With respect to legislative history, we agree with the perception of the California court in Cooper v. Union Bank, supra, that the Code drafters would have been unlikely to have substantially effected a change in well-settled common law without comment. More to the point, however, is the New Jersey Study Comment on the section. That Comment states, in its entirety, that § 3–419(3) and § 3–419(4) "are new provisions on which no New Jersey law has been found." As we have noted, New Jersey law, for over a century, has accorded the payee a direct right of action in conversion against a depositary-collecting bank which has paid a check on a forged indorsement. It is, therefore, evident that in its review of this section of the Code, the framers of the study comment could not have concluded that it was this principle which was being affected thereby. They must be assumed, therefore, to have believed that the section impacted upon some other legal principle or problem which had not been theretofore addressed in this jurisdiction.

There is, moreover, convincing evidence to believe that the sole problem which was apparently being addressed by § 3–419(3) and the problem which the New Jersey Commission to Study and Report Upon the Uniform Commercial Code [4] believed was being addressed was that of the liability of persons acting as brokers in negotiating the sale of securities. A comprehensive review of the legislative history of this section of the Code, starting with the 1948 Draft, undertaken by the author of the Colorado Law Review Note, supra at 308–311, traces the broker problem as the real concern of this section and concludes that

> . . . the intent of the drafters from the outset was to re-solve a particular problem area of the law as to whether persons acting as brokers in negotiating the sale of securities should be liable under the ordinary rules of conversion if they had no knowledge that the securities were stolen. The drafters evidently decided to adopt cases which held that "agents" or "representatives" who act as mere go-betweens as to seller and buyer should not have to face conversion liability on these noncash items. On the one hand, negotiability of such items does not depend upon indorsement so that the risk of taking stolen securities is much greater than on checks. On the other hand, such agents are already under a higher duty of care to act as trustee for any proceeds of sale of these items and to turn such proceeds over to the principal.

> As bankers themselves were "doubtless at work in the drafting of Section 3–419(3)," they probably inserted "including a depositary or collecting bank" after "representative" in order to insure that such banks would not be held liable when acting similarly in the capacity of broker. Unfortunately, the drafters of the Code did not leave this provision in a separate sec-

4. See, as to the organization and mandate of the Commission, its Second Report to the Governor, Senate and Assembly, N.J.S.A. 12A:1–101 et seq., at XIII. Nothing in this abbreviated discussion on Article III in this report suggests that it contained any substantial deviation from then existing law.

tion where it belongs. When it was incorporated as a subsection under Section 3–419, its meaning was inevitably intermingled with the notion of handling checks bearing forged indorsements. It is probably that the drafters never foresaw the way in which its meaning would get expanded. [Id. at 310–311; footnotes omitted]

Other commentators are in agreement with both this historical perspective and its import. See, e.g., Note, Wash. & Lee L.Rev., supra at 680–682. And see Cooper v. Union Bank, supra, 107 Cal.Rptr. at 10, 507 P.2d at 618, suggesting a similar understanding and concern by the California Study Commission.

In view of this historical perspective and its focus on the broker-securities situation, the intended meaning of the Official Comment on § 3–419(3) becomes clear. That Comment, quoted in full supra, begins with the statement that the section "is intended to adopt the rule of decisions which has held that a representative, such as a broker or depositary bank, who deals with a negotiable instrument for his principal in good faith is not liable to the true owner for conversion or otherwise . . . ." There was never, however, as heretofore discussed, a "rule of decisions" absolving the depositary bank from liability to the owner of a check which has been paid by the bank on a forged indorsement. To the contrary, the "rule of decisions" expressly and virtually uniformly imposed that liability on depositary banks in that situation, the question of their good faith notwithstanding. In the light of the section's history, it becomes evident then that the "rule of decisions" to which the official Comment referred was, rather, a well established pre-Code common law exception to the general principle that an agent is liable in conversion in respect of property which his principal has no authority to dispose of. The exception was intended to protect an agent who acts in good faith in transferring, on his principal's account, cash or securities which by their nature require only delivery for passage of good title, typically, bearer instruments. This exception has been codified by 1 Restatement, Torts 2d, § 233(4) at 454 (1965), as follows:

The statement in Subsection (1) [general rule of agent liability] is not applicable to an agent or servant who disposes of current money, or a document negotiable by common law or by statute, pursuant to a transaction by which the transferee becomes a holder in due course of such money or document, unless the agent or servant knows or had reason to know that his principal or master does not have authority so to dispose of it.

And see Comment e. on § 233(4), id. at 456. This exception is also recognized by 2 Restatement, Agency 2d, § 349 at 116 (1958). That section restates the general rule of agent liability for conversion of property to which the principal is not entitled to possession, but Comment g. at 119 explains that the agent is nevertheless protected when he deals in good faith with commercial paper to which title is transferable by delivery alone.

We do not address, since it is not before us, the question as to the extent, if any, of the applicability of § 3–419(3) to dealings in nonbearer commercial paper. See Hastings L.J., supra at 724–725. The point is that the immunity was not intended to apply to the routine check collection activities of banks, and the protected "representative" category was not intended to include an agency relationship having no independent existence but which is based, if at all, on a statutory presumption arising exclusively from the collection and handling of checks.

Assuming from all of these indicia that § 3–419(3) was intended only to preserve the common law exception protecting brokers dealing in bearer instruments and was not intended to abrogate the common law in respect of a depositary bank's well settled conversion liability to a payee of a check, we return to the text of § 3–419(3) in order to determine whether it nevertheless compels a construction expanding the immunity to check-collecting depositary banks.

At the outset, we reject the *Cooper* analysis of what is meant by "proceeds." While that analysis may be logically supportable and is certainly creative, we are nevertheless of the view that it is contrary to the common sense, design and import of the check-collection system. Rather, we find § 3–419(3) inapplicable in this situation because we conclude that a depositary bank functioning within the check collection system is not a "representative" encompassed by that section. First, as heretofore discussed, it was not, as a matter of legislative history, intended to be so encompassed. Nor is it required to be so encompassed by any textual imperatives.

The term "representative" is defined by the Code, N.J.S.A. 12:1–201(35), as "as agent, an officer of a corporation or association, or a trustee, executor or administrator or an estate, or any other person empowered to act for another." The argument for inclusion of a depositary or collecting bank within this definition customarily relies on Article 4 of the Code dealing with bank deposits and collections, and more particularly on § 4–201, which provides in pertinent part that

> Unless a contrary intent clearly appears and prior to the time that a settlement given by a collecting bank for an item is or becomes final . . . the bank is an agent or sub-agent of the owner of the item and any settlement given for the item is provisional.

The theory, then, is that by the act of accepting a check for collection, the bank constitutes itself an agent, hence a "representative," and hence is entitled to the benefit of § 3–419(3). Indeed, it is this statutorily-created agency status that has led one commentator at least to the conclusion that when a bank accepts a check for collection it is an agent entitled to rely on § 3–419(3), but when it cashes the check "over the counter," it is not within the agency definition of

§ 4–201 since it would then be a purchaser of the check and would consequently not be entitled to rely on § 3–419(3). See Farnsworth and Leary, "UCC Brief No. 10: Forgery and Alteration of Checks," 14 Prac.Law. No. 3, at 75, 79 (1968). We regard this distinction as sophistical in terms both of the text of § 4–201 and the common sense of the transaction. First, there is no practical justification from the perspective of either the payee or the bank for liability to be made to depend on the fortuity of whether the check is cashed or a credit given by the depositary bank. Moreover, typically the forged indorsement is not discovered until after final settlement when the bank's agency status in respect of that instrument has in any case already terminated. More significantly, however, this distinction is contrary to the text of § 4–201.

As we view it, the key concept of § 4–201 is acceptance by the bank of a check for collection *from the owner*. It is perfectly clear that if an instrument requires indorsement in order for its title to be transferred, title cannot have passed on the basis of a forged indorsement. Therefore, a person tendering such an instrument cannot be deemed to be its owner. As to such an instrument, consequently, the bank is not an agent for the owner when it accepts it for collection from a person who is not the owner. In this context we note that had an agency status been intended by the Code in respect of a forged check, other terminology would easily have accomplished that result, such as use of the word "customer," defined by § 4–104(e) to include any person for whom a bank has agreed to collect an item. It is, moreover, clear that the statutory agency presumption of § 4–201 was intended only to make uniform and to clarify the consequences of bank insolvency during the collection process. See New Jersey Study Comment 1 to N.J.S.A. 12A:4–201. It does not appear that there was any intent to transport that statutory agency presumption into the general definition of "representative" for purposes of either § 1–201(35) or § 3–419(3).

We are able to discern no basis, other than § 4–201, for concluding that a depositary bank, in accepting a forged instrument for collection, is acting as an agent. Since § 4–201 predicates agency status on acceptance from an owner, we are persuaded that, in respect of the forged instrument, the bank is not an agent, hence not a representative, and hence beyond the protection of § 3–419(3).

This conclusion explains other apparent anomalies in § 3–419(3). In conferring the immunity from conversion liability, the section speaks in terms of liability to the "true owner." We regard the "true owner" as singular terminology since ordinarily one is either the owner or not the owner. Why, then, the qualification that it is the true owner to whom the representative is not liable in conversion? If § 3–419(3) is understood as intended to codify the common law broker-bearer instrument exception to agent liability, the answer is obvious. Where indorsement of an instrument is not necessary for transfer of title, a *bona fide* transferee of the instrument obtains good title thereto, even if the transfer was not authorized by the prior actual owner—the true owner. It is thus only in the context of such instruments, as to which there can simultaneously be two "owners," that the concept of "true owner" as distinguished from "owner" has relevance. That concept is inapposite to forged checks since a check can only have one owner at a time.

Furthermore, by immunizing an agent dealing with bearer instruments, § 3–419(3) effectively affords real immunity from liability since ordinarily the agent would be liable only to the true owner. Extension of that immunity to a bank accepting an instrument with a forged indorsement does not similarly immunize the bank from ultimate liability since it is always in any case responsible to its transferee by reason of its statutory warranties. The immunity would, therefore, not affect liability but only the remedy of the wronged party and would deprive him of a remedy well recognized at common law with no apparent off-setting legitimate advantage to the commercial establishment. This result in our view is aberrational, was not intended, and is not dictated by any policy or provision of the Code.

The summary judgment in favor of defendant is reversed and the matter remanded to the trial court for further proceedings with respect to the Bank's defenses and for prosecution of its third-party complaint.

NOTES

(1) Conversion. For practical reasons the true owner may well prefer recourse against the merchant or bank that has taken the check to recourse against the drawee. In Sales Promotion Executives Association v. Schlinger & Weiss, Inc., 234 N.Y.S.2d 785 (City Civ.Ct.1962), an employee of the payee had forged the payee's indorsement on 49 checks over a nine-month period and cashed them at a supermarket. To recover from the drawees, the payee would have had to sue 49 different banks scattered throughout the country on checks ranging from $20 to $85. By suing the supermarket in conversion, the payee recovered the entire $1,760 in a single action.

If you were asked to redraft UCC 3–419 to provide an ideal solution, what would that solution be? Is it possible to read the existing language of UCC 3–419 in such a way as to arrive at that solution? The reasoning behind the drafting of UCC 3–419(3) is discussed in Leary & Schmitt, Some Bad News and Some Good News from Articles Three and Four, 43 Ohio St.L.J. 611, 632–38 (1982).

(2) Legislative History. In Jackson Vitrified China Co. v. People's American Bank, 388 So.2d 1059 (Fla.App.1980), cited in the Knesz case, the court relied on the history of UCC 3–419(3) in holding that it did not impose liability on a collecting bank.

"The one point of universal agreement with regard to subsection (3) is that it is one of the most ambiguous provisions in the Code. Thus, the most believable argument against its application to the facts sub judice does not consist in definitional hair-splitting; rather, it is arguable that subsection (3) was intended to apply to an entirely separate situation, and that it was drawn more broadly than was intended.

"The earliest ancestor of subsection (3) appeared in the May 1949 Draft of Article 3:

A representative who in good faith has dealt with an instrument or its proceeds is not liable for conversion even though his principal was not the owner of the instrument.

ALI & National Conference of Commissioners on Uniform State Laws, Uniform Commercial Code § 3–427 (May 1949 Draft). The purpose of the section was avowed to be adoption of

the rule of decisions which have held that a broker who sells a negotiable instrument for his principal in good faith, and in good faith turns over the proceeds to the principal, is not liable for conversion of the instrument. Its negotiable character protects him as it protects the purchaser in due course.

Id., and Official Comment.

"The November 1951 Draft contained the changes which comprise the present subsection (3). Thus, it was at that juncture that a provision protecting brokers of negotiable securities from liability to the true owners of those securities was grafted onto the provisions relating to payment on forged endorsements, with the inclusion of the phrase 'including a depositary or collecting bank.' At that juncture, the Official Comment relating to the provision read much as it does today (Comment 5):

Subsection (3), which is new, is intended to adopt the rule of decisions which has held that a representative, such as a broker or depositary bank, who deals with a negotiable instrument for his prinicipal in good faith is not liable to the true owner for conversion of the instrument or otherwise, except that he may be compelled to turn over to the true owner the instrument itself or any proceeds of the instrument remaining in his hands.

"It appears that, at that time, subsection (3) was still intended to apply solely to brokers, including banks acting as brokers, of negotiable securities. This is seen from the language which purports to derive the provision from the 'rule of decisions': The common law created a clear remedy for a payee against a collecting bank which paid a check on a forged endorsement, . . . so whatever subsection (3) applied to, it was not banks acting in their normal banking capacity.

"Thus, the dispositive question: Was the inclusion of subsection (3), as it appeared in the Final 1962 Draft (from which our statute is derived), intended to change the common law by removal of a remedy of the payee in instances of good faith, commercially responsible banking activity?

"We must answer in the affirmative, because of the language of Comment 6 to § 673.419, UCC § 3–419:

> The provisions of this section are not intended to eliminate any liability on warranties of presentment and transfer (Section 3–417). Thus a collecting bank might be liable to a drawee bank which had been subject to liability under this section, even though the collecting bank might not be liable directly to the owner of the instrument.

"Faced with the reasonably clear intention of the drafters of the Code, [1] our sole remaining task is the choice between following what appears to be bad law, or 'adapting' that law to what we perceive to be commercial reality, as some other states' courts have done.

"Our role commands adherence to lawful legislative decree. A judicial assay into lawmaking is inappropriate; moreover, the false assumption of power to do so diminishes public respect for our lawful authority, which is essential to a government of laws."

SECTION 3. EFFECT OF DRAWER'S FAULT

Prefatory Note. Under the usual rules seen thus far the drawer is free from the risk of loss due to forged and altered checks and checks bearing forged indorsements. A purchaser cannot shift the loss to the drawer in the event that the check is dishonored, and the drawee cannot shift the loss to the drawer in the event that the check is paid by mistake. The usual rules, however, are subject to exceptions, the most important of which are considered in this section. Cases under the Code are discussed in Hinchey, An Analysis of Bank Defenses to Check Forgery and Alteration Claims under Uniform Commercial Code Articles 3 and 4: Claimants' Negligence and Failure to Give Notice, 10 Pepperdine L.Rev. 1 (1982). See also Phillips, The Commercial Culpability Scale, 92 Yale L.J. 228, 236–43 (1982).

1. Why the common law was abrogated in subsection (3) is not clear. The doctrine of a collector's ultimate responsibility to a true payee for payment on a forged endorsement was an element of the laws of commerce from as early as 1607. Pragmatica III de Litteris Cambii, Nov. 8, 1607, art. 14. European Continental adoption of the 1931 and 1932 Geneva Uniform Codes on Bills of Exchange and Checks effected a general divergence between the Continental and Anglo-American laws mercantile on this point. The Geneva Codes' absolvance from liability of bona fide endorsees was itself derived from the German law. Preussisches Landrecht of 1794, II 8 §§ 835, 1156, 1169; Allgemeine Deutsche Wechselordnung of 1848, arts. 36, 74, 76. Whether subsection (3) defenses reflect the influence of the Geneva Codes, or whether they merely suggest that bankers were "doubtless at work in the drafting of Section 3–419(3) . . .", J. White & R. Summers, Handbook on the Law Under the Uniform Commercial Code 505 (1972), is an open question.

The seminal case is Young v. Grote, 4 Bing. 253, 130 Eng.Rep. 764 (1827). Young, a depositor, contested the right of Grote, his banker, to charge a check to his account in the amount of £350.2s. During his absence, Young left five signed blank checks with his wife, who was not conversant with business. She gave one to Worcester, Young's clerk, who filled it up for £50.2s. and showed it to her. The word "fifty", as written, began in the middle of the line, and Worcester later added before it the words "Three hundred and," inserted the digit 3, and obtained payment for £350.2s. from Grote. The court held that Young must bear the loss. Best, C.J., first stated the general rule that "a banker who pays a forged check, is in general bound to pay the amount again to his customer, because, in the first instance, he pays without authority." He went on to say that, "In the present case, was it not the fault of Young that Grote and Co. paid 350*l*. instead of 50*l*.? . . . It is urged, indeed, that the business of merchants requires them to sign checks in blank, and leave them to be filled up by agents. If that be so, the person selected for the care of such a check ought at least to be a person conversant with business as well as trustworthy. . . . [Such a person] would have guarded against fraud in the mode of filling it up; he would have placed the word fifty at the beginning of the second line; and would have commenced it with a capital letter, so that it could not have had the appearance of following properly after a preceding word; he would also have placed the figure 5 so near to the printed £ as to prevent the possibility of interpolation. It was by the neglect of these ordinary precautions that Grote and Co. were induced to pay." The Code counterpart of the rule in Young v. Grote is contained in UCC 3–406.

Problem 8. Empire uses a check embossing machine to print the amount of the checks that it draws in the center of each check. The rest of the check, including the amount on the upper right-hand side is typed and it is then signed by hand. The clerk who prepares the checks for signature keeps the machine in an unlocked desk drawer, because it would be inconvenient to lock it in the safe at night. Does this subject Empire to any risk if the machine is stolen? See UCC 3–406; compare Commercial Credit Equipment Corp. v. First Alabama Bank, 636 F.2d 1051 (5th Cir. 1981), with Fred Meyer, Inc. v. Temco Metal Products Co., 267 Or. 230, 516 P.2d 80 (1973).

Problem 9. A drew a check for $29 on X Bank, payable to B, leaving blanks to make it easy to raise it to $2,900. A had it certified by X Bank, raised it to $2,900, and gave it to B, who delivered to A goods worth $2,900. Can B recover $2,900 from X Bank? Compare Brower v. Franklin National Bank, 311 F.Supp. 675 (S.D.N.Y.1970), with Wallach Sons v. Bankers Trust Co., 62 Misc.2d 19, 307 N.Y.S.2d 297 (1970). Should a certifying bank include the amount of the check in its certification? See Sam Goody, Inc. v. Franklin National Bank, 57 Misc.2d 193, 291 N.Y.S.2d 429 (1968).

THOMPSON MAPLE PRODUCTS v. CITIZENS NATIONAL BANK OF CORRY

Pennsylvania Superior Court, 1967.
211 Pa.Super. 42, 234 A.2d 32.

HOFFMAN, J. In this assumpsit action, the plaintiff, Thompson Maple Products, Inc., seeks to recover more than $100,000 paid out on a series of its checks by defendant bank, as drawee. The payee's signature on each of the checks was forged by one Emery Albers, who then cashed the checks or deposited them to his account with the defendant.

The case was tried to the court below sitting without a jury. That court entered judgment in favor of the plaintiff in the amount of $1258.51, the face amount of three checks which the defendant had paid without any endorsement whatever. It dismissed the remainder of the claim, and this appeal followed.

The plaintiff is a small, closely-held corporation, principally engaged in the manufacture of bowling pin "blanks" from maple logs. Some knowledge of its operations from 1959 to 1962 is essential to an understanding of this litigation.

The plaintiff purchased logs from timber owners in the vicinity of its mill. Since these timber owners rarely had facilities for hauling logs, such transportation was furnished by a few local truckers, including Emery Albers.

At the mill site, newly delivered logs were "scaled" by mill personnel, to determine their quantity and grade. The employee on duty noted this information, together with the name of the owner of the logs, as furnished by the hauler, on duplicate "scaling slips."

In theory, the copy of the scaling slip was to be given to the hauler, and the original was to be retained by the mill employee until transmitted by him directly to the company's bookkeeper. This ideal procedure, however, was rarely followed. Instead, in a great many instances, the mill employee simply gave both slips to the hauler for delivery to the company office. Office personnel then prepared checks in payment for the logs, naming as payee the owner indicated on the scaling slips. Blank sets of slips were readily accessible on the company premises.

Sometime prior to February, 1959, Emery Albers conceived the scheme which led to the forgeries at issue here. Albers was an independent log hauler who for many years had transported logs to the company mill. For a brief period in 1952, he had been employed by the plaintiff, and he was a trusted friend of the Thompson family. After procuring blank sets of scaling slips, Albers filled them in to show substantial, wholly fictitious deliveries of logs, together with the names of local timber owners as suppliers. He then delivered the slips to the company bookkeeper, who prepared checks payable to the purported owners. Finally, he volunteered to deliver the checks to the owners. The bookkeeper customarily entrusted the checks to him for that purpose.

Albers then forged the payee's signature and either cashed the checks or deposited them to his account at the defendant bank, where he was well known. Although he pursued this scheme for an undetermined period of time, only checks paid out over a three-year period prior to this litigation are here in controversy. See Uniform Commercial Code, Act of April 6, 1953, PL 3, as amended, § 4–406, 12A PS § 4–406.

In 1963, when the forgeries were uncovered, Albers confessed and was imprisoned. The plaintiff then instituted this suit against the drawee bank, asserting that the bank had breached its contract of deposit by paying the checks over forged endorsements. See UCC § 3–404, 12A PS § 3–404.

The trial court determined that the plaintiff's own negligent activities had materially contributed to the unauthorized endorsements, and it therefore dismissed the substantial part of plaintiff's claim. We affirm the action of the trial court.

Both parties agree that, as between the payor bank and its customer, ordinarily the bank must bear the loss occasioned by the forgery of a payee's endorsement. Philadelphia Title Insurance Company v. Fidelity-Philadelphia Trust Company, 419 Pa. 78, 212 A.2d 222 [2 UCC Rep. 1011] (1965); UCC § 3–404, 12A PS § 3–404.

The trial court concluded, however, that the plaintiff-drawer, by virtue of its conduct, could not avail itself of that rule, citing § 3–406 of the Code: "Any person who by his negligence substantially contributes to . . . the making of an unauthorized signature is precluded from asserting the . . . lack of authority against . . . a drawee or other payor who pays the instrument in good faith and in accordance with the reasonable commercial standards of the drawee's or payor's business." 12A PS § 3–406.

Before this court, the plaintiff Company argues strenuously that this language is a mere restatement of pre-Code law in Pennsylvania. Under those earlier cases, it is argued, the term "precluded" is equivalent to "estopped," and negligence which will work an estoppel is only such as "directly and proximately affects the conduct of the bank in passing the forgery. . . ." See, e.g., Coffin v. Fidelity-Philadelphia Trust Company, 374 Pa. 378, 393, 97 A.2d 857, 39 A.L.R.2d 625 (1953); Land Title Bank and Trust Company v. Cheltenham National Bank, 362 Pa. 30, 66 A.2d 768 (1949). The plaintiff further asserts that those decisions hold that "negligence in the conduct of the drawer's business," such as appears on this record, cannot serve to work an estoppel.

Even if that was the law in this Commonwealth prior to the passage of the Commercial Code, it is not the law today. The language of the new Act is determinative in all cases arising after its passage. This controversy must be decided, therefore, by construction of the statute and application of the negligence doctrine as it appears in § 3–406 of the Code. Philadelphia Title Insurance Company v. Fidelity-Philadelphia Trust Company, supra, 419 Pa. at 84, 212 A.2d 222.

Had the legislature intended simply to continue the strict estoppel doctrine of the pre-Code cases, it could have employed the term "precluded," without qualification, as in § 23 of the old Negotiable Instruments Law, 56 P.S. § 28 (repealed).[1] However, it chose to modify that doctrine in § 3–406, by specifying that negligence which *"substantially contributes to . . . the making of an unauthorized signature. . . ."* will preclude the drawer from asserting a forgery. [emphasis supplied]. The Code has thus abandoned the language of the older cases (negligence which "directly and proximately affects the bank in passing the forgery") and shortened the chain of causation which the defendant bank must establish. "[N]o attempt is made," according to the Official Comment to § 3–406, "to specify what is negligence, and the question is one for the court or jury on the facts of the particular case."

In the instant case, the trial court could readily have concluded that plaintiff's business affairs were conducted in so negligent a fashion as to have "substantially contributed" to the Albers forgeries, within the meaning of § 3–406.

Thus, the record shows that pads of plaintiff's blank logging slips were left in areas near the mill which were readily accessible to any of the haulers. Moreover, on at least two occasions, Albers was given whole pads of these blank logging slips to use as he chose. Mrs. Vinora Curtis, an employee of the plaintiff, testified:

"Q. Did you ever give any of these logging slips to Mr. Albers or any pads of these slips to Mr. Albers?

"A. Yes.

. . .

"Q. What was the reason for giving [a pad of the slips] to him, Mrs. Curtis?

"A. Well, he came up and said he needed it for [scaling] the logs, so I gave it to him."

Mrs. Amy Thompson, who also served as a bookkeeper for the plaintiff, testified:

"Q. As a matter of fact, you gave Mr. Albers the pack of your logging slips, did you not?

"A. Yes, I did once.

---

1. Thus, the Pennsylvania Bar Association Note on § 3–404 observes: "The . . . phrase 'or is otherwise precluded' [in this section] continues the prior law as to estoppel, laches, and other grounds which prevent a person whose signature is forged from recovering. This is so because the same word 'precluded' was used in NIL § 23, 56 PS § 28 (repealed). . . ."

"Q.   Do you remember what you gave them to him for?

"A.   I don't right offhand, but it seems to me he said he was going out to look for some logs or timber or something and he needed them to mark some figures on. . . .

"Q.   Well, if he was going to use them for scratch pads, why didn't you give him a scratch pad that you had in the office?

"A.   That's what I should have done."

In addition, the plaintiff's printed scaling slips were not consecutively numbered. Unauthorized use of the slips, therefore, could easily go undetected. Thus, Mr. Nelson Thompson testified:

"Q.   Mr. Thompson, were your slips you gave these haulers numbered?

"A.   No, they were not.

"Q.   They are now, aren't they?

"A.   Yes.

"Q.   Had you used numbered logging slips, this would have prevented anybody getting logging slips out of the ordinary channel of business and using it to defraud you?

"A.   Yes."

Moreover, in 1960, when the company became concerned about the possible unauthorized use of its scaling slips, it required its own personnel to initial the slips when a new shipment of logs was scaled. However, this protective measure was largely ignored in practice. Mrs. Amy Thompson testified:

"Q.   And later on in the course of your business, if you remember Mr. Thompson said he wanted the logging slips initialed by one of the so-called authorized people?

"A.   Yes.

"Q.   [D]idn't you really not pay too much attention to them at all?

"A.   Well, I know we didn't send them back to be sure they were initialed. We might have noticed it but we didn't send them back to the mill.

"Q.   In other words, if they came to you uninitialed, you might have noticed it but didn't do anything about it.

"A.   Didn't do anything about it."

The principal default of the plaintiff, however, was its failure to use reasonable diligence in insuring honesty from its log haulers, including Emery Albers. For many years, the haulers were permitted to deliver both the original and the duplicate of the scaling slip to the company office, and the company tolerated this practice. These slips supplied the bookkeeper with the payees' names for the checks she was to draw in payment for log deliveries. Only by having the company at all times retain possession of the original slip could the plaintiff have assured that no disbursements were made except for logs received, and that the proper amounts were paid to the proper persons. The practice tolerated by the plaintiff effectively removed the only immediate safeguard in the entire procedure against dishonesty on the part of the haulers. [2]

Finally, of course, the company regularly entrusted the completed checks to the haulers for delivery to the named payees, without any explicit authorization from the latter to do so.

While none of these practices, in isolation, might be sufficient to charge the plaintiff with negligence within the meaning of § 3–406, the company's course of conduct, viewed in its entirety, is surely sufficient to support the trial judge's determination that it substantially contributed to the making of the unauthorized signatures. [3] In his words, that conduct was "no different than had the plaintiff simply given Albers a series of checks signed in blank for his unlimited, unrestricted use." Cf. Gresham State Bank v. O & K Construction Company, 231 Ore. 106, 370 P.2d 726, 372 P.2d 187, 100 A.L.R.2d 654 (1962); Park State Bank v. Arena Auto Auctions, Inc., 59 Ill.App.2d 235, 207 N.E.2d 158 (1965).

Finally, the plaintiff argues that the defendant bank cannot rely on § 3–406 because it did not pay the checks in accordance with "reasonable commercial standards" as required by that section. All the checks were regular on their face and bore the purported endorsement of the named payee. It is asserted, however, that the defendant bank was required, as a matter of law, to obtain the second endorsement of Albers before accepting the checks for deposit to his account.

The short answer to that contention is that the trial court did not find, nor does the record show, that obtaining such a second endorsement is a reasonable, or even a general, commercial practice, where the depositor is well-known to the bank and where his identity can later be ascertained from code markings on the check itself.

Furthermore, under the Code, the bank did not have an unqualified right to a second endorsement. A check endorsed in blank is bearer paper. It is negotiable by delivery alone, without further endorsement. See UCC §§ 3–201, 3–204, 12A PS §§ 3–201, 3–204.

---

2. We note that this procedure placed Albers in a position comparable to that of a trusted agent or employee, whose similar activities would have precluded his principal from asserting the forgeries, under § 3–405(1)(c). That section provides: "(1) An endorsement by any person in the name of a named payee is effective if . . . (c) an agent or employee of the drawer has supplied him with the name of the payee intending the latter to have no such interest." The trial court's opinion characterizes Albers as an "agent" of the plaintiff, but makes no findings with reference to this section. We decline the invitation to do so now, since the decision must be affirmed on other grounds.

3. In this connection, the trial court also noted that the plaintiff at all times prior to the commencement of this litigation failed to keep an accurate inventory account. It could not therefore verify, at any given point in time, that it actually possessed the logs which it had paid for.

To the extent that banks do obtain such endorsements, they apparently do so for their own protection, over and above that provided by the warranties arising on presentment and transfer. Cf. UCC § 3–414, 12A PS § 3–414 (Contract of Indorser), with UCC § 3–417, 12A PS § 3–417 (Warranties). In short, the practice is not designed for the protection of the drawer. [4] We are reluctant to hold that the plaintiff may shift the loss to the defendant bank, in this case, merely because the bank failed to exercise an excess of caution on its own behalf.

Judgment affirmed.

NOTE

Negligence. The question of the relevance to this case of the fictitious payee and imposter rules of UCC 3–405 can be deferred until the next section in this chapter. As to the argument that Albers' indorsement should have been required, see Note 2, p. 187 supra. Suppose that Albers had cashed some of the checks with businesses or other banks, which had required his indorsement. Would they have been protected by UCC 3–406 if the checks had been dishonored? Could such a taker be a "holder in due course" against whom Thompson Maple Products would have been precluded from asserting the forged indorsement. Is UCC 3–406 circular in this respect?

In Commonwealth of Pennsylvania v. National Bank & Trust Co., 469 Pa. 188, 364 A.2d 1331 (1976), the Supreme Court of Pennsylvania noted that "Thompson posits that § 3–406 lessened the burden on a defending bank in showing a drawer's negligence. Under this formulation, the substantial contribution standard would include negligent conduct of a drawer which might previously have been considered too remote in the chain of causation to constitute 'proximate cause.'" Although the Supreme Court of Pennsylvania accepted this formulation arguendo, it remarked that the "weight of the authority suggests that the Thompson rationale should be rejected and that § 3–406 in fact did not bring about a change in the pre-Code law regarding the drawer's negligence," and found this the "more persuasive reasoning." More recently, however, Thompson was cited in support of the proposition that UCC 3–406 is not "a mere restatement of pre-Code Law" in Insurance Company of North America v. Purdue National Bank, ___ Ind.App. ___, 401 N.E.2d 708 (1980).

Prefatory Note. Critten employed a clerk named Davis, whose duty it was to fill out checks for Critten's signature and give them, together with the relevant bills, to Critten, who signed them, put them in envelopes, and placed them in the mailing drawer. Over a

---

4. In any event, a second endorsement could not have protected *this* drawer, since the record shows that it was not plaintiff's practice to examine the backs of its checks when they were returned by the bank.

two-year period, Davis took twenty-four checks from the drawer, obliterated with acid the names of the payee and the amount, and made them payable to cash in a raised amount. He paid the bills himself and kept the excess. Since Davis was also entrusted with the verification of the bank balance, his peculations went unnoticed, although he usually failed to alter the check stubs to conceal them, until another clerk verified the balance when Davis was absent from work. Critten then sued the drawee for the excess it had paid on the checks. The court concluded that

> the depositor owes his bank the duty of a reasonable verification of the returned checks. . . . The practice of taking checks from check books and entering on the stubs left in the book the date, amount and name of the payee of the check issued has become general, not only with large commercial houses but with almost all classes of depositors in banks. The skill of the criminal has kept pace with the advance in honest arts and a forgery may be made so skillfully as to deceive not only the bank, but the drawer of the check as to the genuineness of his own signature. But when a depositor has in his possession a record of the checks he has given, with dates, payees, and amounts, a comparison of the returned checks with that record will necessarily expose forgeries or alterations. It is true that it will give no information as to the genuine character of the indorsements, and because the depositor has no greater knowledge on that subject than the bank, it owes the bank no duty in regard thereto. . . . It is also true that verification of the returned checks would not prevent a loss by the bank in the case of the payment of a single forged check, and probably not in many cases enable the bank to obtain a restitution of its lost money. It would, however, prevent the successful commission of continuous frauds by exposing the first forgeries. . . . While we hold that this duty rests upon the depositor, we are not disposed to accept the doctrine asserted in some of the cases that by negligence in its discharge or by failure to discover and notify the bank, the depositor either adopts the checks as genuine and ratifies their payment or estops himself from asserting that they are forgeries. . . . If the depositor has by his negligence in failing to detect forgeries in his checks and give notice thereof caused loss to his bank, either by enabling the forger to repeat his fraud or by depriving the bank of an opportunity to obtain restitution, he should be responsible for the damage caused by his default, but beyond this his liability should not extend.

Therefore, although a comparison of returned checks with unaltered stubs would have thwarted subsequent alterations, Critten was not precluded from recovering for the first and second checks, which were returned together; comparison would have come too late to have prevented their payment. But comparison of the first and second checks with the stubs would have prevented payment of the third, fourth and fifth checks, and Critten was accountable for these. The sixth check, however, had been so mutilated by Davis that the bank was itself negligent in paying it, and the bank was therefore liable for that and subsequent checks. Furthermore, Davis had presented one of the checks for which Critten would have been accountable through a collecting bank, rather than directly to the drawee. As to that check, the drawee had recourse against the collecting bank and could not hold Critten. Critten v. Chemical National Bank, 171 N.Y. 219, 63 N.E. 969 (1902). In 1904, shortly after this decision, New York enacted a statute precluding a drawer from contesting payment of a forged or altered check, regardless of his exercise of reasonable care, unless he had notified the drawee within one year after return of the cancelled check. In 1911 a similar statute was enacted providing for a two-year period for checks bearing forged indorsements.

Observe how closely UCC 4–406 tracks the Critten case and subsequent legislation. Subsections (1) and (2) deal with the duty of the depositor "to examine the statement and items." Subsection (3) deals with the effect of the bank's lack of care.[1] Subsection (5) resolves the controversy between drawer and collecting bank. Subsection (4) contains the counterparts of the statutory periods. Would UCC 4–406 change the result in the Critten case in any respect?

Would a check bearing only one of two required signatures be a check bearing an "unauthorized signature" under UCC 4–406(4)? See Rascar, Inc. v. Bank of Oregon, 87 Wis.2d 446, 275 N.W.2d 108 (App.1978). Would a check bearing both a forged drawer's signature and a forged indorsement be governed by the one-year or the three-year period under UCC 4–406(4)? See Winkie, Inc. v. Heritage Bank of Whitefish Bay, 99 Wis.2d 616, 299 N.W.2d 829 (1981).

Problem 10. Empire asks whether there is a specific period of time within which it must examine Irving Trust's statement (Form 6, p. 102 supra) and its returned checks. If there is, Empire would like to know the consequences of any delay. Empire would also like to know, since it is a small company, if it runs any risk by having the same employee prepare checks for signature, enter them in the checkbook, and reconcile the statements and returned checks with the checkbook. Advise Empire. See UCC 4–406; K & K Manufacturing, Inc. v. Union Bank, infra.

---

1. Would a regime of comparative negligence apply under UCC 4–406 in jurisdiction where comparative negligence has generally displaced contributory negligence? See Sun 'n Sand v. United California Bank, discussed at page 282 supra, 21 Cal.3d at 699–700, 148 Cal.Rptr. at 348–49, 582 P.2d at 939–40.

K & K MANUFACTURING, INC. v. UNION BANK

Court of Appeals of Arizona, 1981.
129 Ariz. 7, 628 P.2d 44.

HATHAWAY, CHIEF JUDGE.   In this case we must apply articles three and four of the Uniform Commercial Code to determine who should bear the risk of loss when a dishonest employee forges her employer's name as drawer on a number of checks on his business and personal checking accounts, then appropriates the proceeds for her personal use.

Appellant Bill J. Knight is the president and majority stockholder of both K & K Manufacturing, Inc. and Knight Foundry & Manufacturing, Inc.   Knight Foundry employed about 80 people at the time of trial, while K & K Manufacturing, which was formed to accomplish the contracting, buying and selling for the foundry business, employed only two persons when the events which form the basis of this action occurred.   These two employees were Knight and a bookkeeper, Eleanor Garza.   The bookkeeper's duties at K & K Manufacturing were very broad, including picking up the company mail and Knight's personal mail from a common post office box, preparing checks for Knight's signature to pay both company and personal bills, and making entries in a cash disbursement journal reflecting the expenses for which the checks were written.   Most importantly, it was her responsibility to reconcile the monthly statements prepared and sent by appellee Union Bank, where Knight kept both his business and personal checking and savings accounts.   No one shared these duties with Miss Garza.

Between March 1977 and January 1978, Miss Garza forged Knight's signature on some 66 separate checks drawn on his personal or business accounts at Union Bank.   The majority of these checks were made payable to her.   The total amount of the forgeries on the K & K Manufacturing account was $49,859.31.   The total on Knight's personal account was $11,350.   The bank paid each such check and Miss Garza received or was credited with the proceeds.

We need not concentrate on the details of the fraud, except to comment that it proved to be effective for nearly one year.   Miss Garza assured that the disbursement journal balanced by overstating legitimate expenditures, forging checks to herself for the difference, and later showing the forged check as "void."   Upon receipt of appellee's monthly statement and cancelled checks, she removed and concealed the bad checks.   The proceeds from most of the forgeries were deposited directly into her personal account rather than taken in cash.   She usually presented the bad checks to the bank tellers with numerous authorized checks, and spread her banking transactions among several tellers so that no one teller knew the extent of her business.

Eventually, an in-house audit showed the discrepancies in the 1977 disbursements.   Appellants brought this action against appellee for breach of contract, seeking repayment of the funds the bank paid out on checks with unauthorized signatures. After a court trial, judgment was entered in favor of appellant Knight for $5,500, representing the amount paid out of his personal account on forged checks from March 28 to May 20, 1977. This figure included eight forged checks paid by the bank prior to the mailing of its monthly statement containing a record of the payments and the checks themselves to Knight on May 6, plus a 14-day period. Since no forged checks on the K & K Manufacturing account were paid prior to May 20, judgment was entered for appellee against it. In addition, the trial court made findings of fact and conclusions of law. Both Knight and K & K Manufacturing have appealed.

Appellants contend that findings 13, 14 and 15 are not supported by the evidence. They argue the record shows their actions were not negligent and that the bank's practices and procedures were negligent as a matter of law. The disputed findings are as follows:

"13. Defendant bank [appellee] paid all the checks in good faith and in accordance with reasonable commercial standards.

14. Defendant bank did not fail to exercise ordinary care in paying the checks.

15. The plaintiffs [appellants] did not exercise reasonable care and promptness to examine the bank statements and cancelled checks in order to discover the forgeries."

Our duty begins and ends with the inquiry of whether the trial court had before it evidence which reasonably supports its actions, viewed in a light most favorable to sustaining its findings. United Bank v. Mesa N.O. Nelson Co., 121 Ariz. 438, 590 P.2d 1384 (1979). We will not weigh conflicting evidence or set aside the trial court's findings unless they are clearly erroneous. Id. The determination of which actions are commercially reasonable and what constitutes ordinary care on the part of the bank, as well as reasonable care and promptness on the part of the depositor, are questions of fact for the trier of fact. See West Penn Administration, Inc. v. Union National Bank, 233 Pa.Super. 311, 335 A.2d 725 (1975).

The concept of which party bears the loss in a forgery situation such as the one presented here is addressed in articles three and four of the Uniform Commercial Code, covering commercial paper and bank deposits and collections. [The court quoted UCC 3–406 and 4–406.]

These provisions impose a duty on the depositor to check his monthly statement for unauthorized signatures or alterations on checks. If the depositor fails to do so, after the first forged check and statement relating thereto is sent to him, plus a reasonable period not exceeding 14 days, he is precluded from asserting the unauthorized signature or alteration against the bank. U.C.C. Sec. 4–406, comment 3. The burden of proof of depositor's negligence is on the bank. Even if the bank succeeds in establishing the depositor's negligence, if the customer establishes that the bank failed to exercise ordinary care in paying the bad checks, the preclusion rule of [UCC 4–406(2)] does not apply. U.C.C. Sec. 4–406, comment 4.

We first address the issue of whether appellee met its burden of proof of showing that appellants "substantially contributed" to the forgeries or failed to exercise "reasonable care and promptness" in examining the monthly statements. The record shows that appellants trusted Miss Garza completely with both writing checks and reconciling the monthly statements. No spot checks were made by Knight or the controller at Knight Foundry, both of whom had access to the banking records. Knight was informed by a bank officer that his personal account was overdrawn on 12 occasions in 1977, yet did nothing to discover the reasons therefor. Knight testified he was aware Miss Garza's work was often inaccurate as well as tardy in 1977 and 1978.

Appellants argue they were not negligent in relying on a previously honest employee, citing Jackson v. First National Bank, 55 Tenn. App. 545, 403 S.W.2d 109 (1966). We decline to follow *Jackson,* which held, contrary to the bulk of authority, that since a defalcating financial secretary had been a longtime faithful and trusted member of the church he cheated, the church could not be found negligent. Misplaced confidence in an employee will not excuse a depositor from the duty of notifying the bank of alterations on items paid from the depositor's account. . . . We adopt the majority view that the depositor is chargeable with the knowledge of all facts a reasonable and prudent examination of his bank statement would have disclosed if made by an honest employee. . . . The trial court's finding number 15 is amply supported by the evidence.

Secondly, we turn to the question of whether appellants met their burden of proof of demonstrating appellee did not exercise ordinary care in paying the bad checks, and did not act in good faith and in accordance wth reasonable commercial standards. There appears to be no dispute regarding the good faith of appellee in paying the forgeries. The issue is whether its method of ascertaining unauthorized signatures on its depositor's checks met the standard of care under the circumstances.

Implied in the debtor/creditor relationship between a bank and its checking account depositor is the contractual undertaking on the part of the bank that it will only discharge its obligations to the depositor upon his authorized signature. . . . The mere fact that the bank has paid a forged check does not mean the bank has breached its duty of ordinary care, however. . . .

At trial, an operations officer for appellee testified as to the methods employed during the period the forgeries occurred to discover unauthorized signatures on depositor's checks. She testified that checks were organized so that a bundle from the same account could be compared with the authorized signature on the bank's signature card. A staff of five filing clerks handled an average of approximately 1,000 checks each per hour in this manner. She testified it was common for a file clerk to become familiar with the drawer's signature in large accounts such as appellants'. An official of a large Arizona bank testified that tellers and file clerks are not trained to be handwriting experts. He testified that in his opinion, because most large banks have completely abandoned physical comparison of checks with the signature card, the system employed by appellee was better than the norm of the banking community in Southern Arizona.

In view of this and other evidence, we conclude that there was sufficient evidence to support findings 13 and 14 and the judgment entered below. Similar methods of comparing drawer's signatures have been upheld as constituting ordinary care and being within reasonable commercial standards across the country. . . . Appellant Knight and his controller admitted the forgeries were quite good. Appellants also argue that because the bank tellers recognized Miss Garza was cashing large checks made to herself and her boyfriend and that she was driving an expensive sports car, they had a further duty to check the validity of the drawer's signature. This evidence was balanced by testimony that Miss Garza thoroughly explained the reasons for the large checks as increased salary, bonuses, and payment of Knight's expenses while he was out of town. Knight and Miss Garza were in the bank together on a regular basis and the tellers knew Miss Garza was authorized to handle large amounts of Knight's money. See Cooper v. Union Bank, 9 Cal.3d 123, 371, 507 P.2d 609, 107 Cal.Rptr. 1 (1973).

Finally, there was evidence that some K & K Manufacturing checks were forged with a rubber stamp facsimile of Knight's signature, which was only authorized for use with the Knight foundry account. Appellants argue appellee fell below the standard of ordinary care in honoring these checks. The trial court personally examined appellee's expert witness on this subject. There was testimony that if facsimile signatures appear "all of a sudden" on the checks, the depositor may be contacted, but there was sufficient evidence that the piecemeal use of the stamp here, which was at times authorized by appellants, was not such that appellee should be held to bring it to their attention. The finding of fact that appellee's acts, including those regarding the facsimile signature, did not fall below ordinary care or reasonable commercial standards was not clearly erroneous.

Affirmed.

NOTE

Validity of Stipulations. Would it be possible for a bank, by contract with its depositor, to shorten the statutory periods of UCC 4–406? See UCC 4–103, 1–102. Is UCC 2–302 applicable? See David v. Manufacturers Hanover Trust Co., 59 Misc.2d 248, 298 N.Y.S.2d

847 (1969). Where should the bank put such a clause? On the statement returned to the customer? On the signature card? See Note 2, p. 220 supra.

Problem 11. A gave B a $1,000 check on the X Bank, so negligently drawn that B easily raised it to $10,000, indorsed it "B," and deposited it in his account in the Y Bank. The Y Bank forwarded it, it was paid in the raised amount by the X Bank, and B absconded with the proceeds. A discovered the alteration upon return to him of the paid check and demanded that the X Bank recredit his account in the amount of $9,000. Must X Bank do so? May X Bank do so and then recover the $9,000 from Y Bank? Compare UCC 3–406 with 4–406(5). What does the difference suggest?

Is the following history of UCC 4–406 relevant? In 1946 it had been held in New York that the drawee bank which paid over a forged indorsement could waive its rights against its depositor under N.Y.N.I.L. Section 43, recredit the depositor's account, and recover from the presenting bank on its guarantee of prior indorsements. National Surety Corp. v. Federal Reserve Bank, 188 Misc. 207, 70 N.Y.S.2d 636 (1946), affirmed, 188 Misc. 213, 70 N.Y.S.2d 642. Fifteen years earlier it had been held that the drawee bank which paid an altered check could similarly waive its rights against its depositor arising out of the depositor's negligence in drawing his checks. Fallick v. Amalgamated Bank of New York, 232 App.Div. 127, 249 N.Y.S. 238 (1931). In the 1952 edition of the Code both UCC 3–406 and 4–406 were silent on the problem of waiver.

During the New York Law Revision Commission's hearings on the Code, a New York Clearing House subcommittee on Article 4 made this criticism in its report on that article: "Both the present N.Y. law and Section 4–406 put the drawee bank in the position of determining whether the loss shall fall upon the drawer or the presenting bank. Under present law the drawee has the right to be arbitrary in making such a decision, which can be, and is, an embarrassing position. Presumably, the same would be true under Section 4–406." Report of the N.Y. Law Revision Commission for 1954, N.Y.Leg.Doc. (1954) No. 65, p. 299.

A tentative redraft of the Code in 1955 added the following subsection to UCC 4–207: "(5) A payor bank or other payor and a collecting bank may not assert a claim under this section or under indorsement obligations against a prior party who acts in good faith with respect to an item in any case in which the payor bank, payor or collecting bank has waived or has failed upon request to assert a valid defense available to it against liability on the item." The reason stated was to "reject the holding of National Surety Co. v. Federal Reserve Bank of New York." Supplement No. 1 to the 1952 Official Draft of Text and Comments of the Uniform Commercial Code, p. 31 (1955). Note that this subsection would have applied to defenses under UCC 3–406 as well as under 4–406.

The present language of UCC 4–406(5) was introduced in the 1956 Recommendations of the Editorial Board for the Uniform Commercial Code with the comments that "The new subsection (5) replaces subsection (5) of 4–207 as appearing in Supplement No. 1," and "The new subsection (5) appearing in Supplement No. 1 has been transferred in slightly revised form to Section 4–406. The New York Law Revision Commission approved the principle of subsection (5) but expressed concern as to the possible extent of its application. The relocation of the subsection to Section 4–406 and the changes in language are designed to prescribe more specifically the area of application of the subsection."

What then is the explanation for the difference between UCC 3–406 and 4–406? What was the intention of the drafters? Of the legislature? What answer to the Problem? Do you agree with Comment 7 to UCC 4–406 which cites both the Fallick and National Surety cases and says that "Subsection (5) is intended to reject the holding of these and like cases. Although the principle of subsection (5) might well be applied to other types of claims of customers against banks and defenses to these claims, the rule of the subsection is limited to defenses of a payor bank under this section. No present need is known to give the rule wider effect." Does this comment make sense in the light of the Fallick case, which would have involved UCC 3–406?

Compare First National Bank of Arizona v. Plymouth-Home National Bank, 553 F.Supp. 448 (D.Mass.1982), affirmed mem., 705 F.2d 439 (1st Cir. 1983), with Canadian Imperial Bank of Commerce v. Federal Reserve Bank, 64 Misc.2d 959, 316 N.Y.S.2d 507 (1970).[1] See also Stone & Webster Engineering v. First National Bank, supra.

UNAUTHORIZED ORDERS AND AUTOMATION

The Problem. Automation of the check collection process has called into question the assumption that a drawee bank should not be entitled to charge its customer's account on a forged check. The drawee bank's computer can easily determine, with the aid of the information encoded on the check, whether the check is drawn on sufficient funds and whether payment has been stopped. Verifying the drawer's signature, however, must be done manually. On small checks, banks no longer verify drawers' signatures, since the cost of verification exceeds its benefit to the bank in terms of avoidance of the loss resulting from forged checks. Furthermore, under a system

---

1. For an interesting opinion, suggesting that if X Bank can recover from Y Bank, then Y Bank has a cause of action at common law against A for negligence, see Girard Bank v. Mount Holly State Bank, 474 F.Supp. 1225 (D.N.J.1979). The court acknowledged that the Y Bank could not invoke UCC 3–406, but cited UCC 1–103 and stated that such "a cause of action would further the Code policy favoring deterrence of the actor best able to prevent the fraud" and that it would extend the principles of Articles 3 and 4 "to a situation not specifically foreseen by the drafters."

of check truncation at the depositary bank, verification of the drawer's signature is no longer feasible, even for large checks.

It might still be concluded that the drawee bank should not be entitled to charge its customer's account on a forged check. Banks would then have to offset their losses on forged checks against their savings from increased automation. The advent of other kinds of payment systems, however, suggests a different conclusion. In these systems the user generally has a device, commonly a plastic card, that gives the user access to the system, and the user assumes some responsibility for retaining that device within his control in order to prevent other persons from making unauthorized transfers. If the numbered and encoded blank checks were regarded as analogous to the plastic card, it might be concluded that the drawee bank should be entitled to charge its customer's account on a forged check, in at least some circumstances, if the forgery was the result of the customer's failure to keep his blank checks within his control. [1]

Credit Cards. The law of bank credit cards offers an obvious analogy. Much of the early credit card litigation concerned the responsibility for the unathorized use of lost or stolen cards. In 1970, Congress pre-empted the field, by legislation now found in the Consumer Credit Protection Act, 15 U.S.C. § 1643, implemented by Federal Reserve Board Regulation Z, 12 C.F.R. § 226.12.

That legislation limits to $50 the cardholder's liability for use of a card by a person "who does not have actual, implied or apparent authority for such use and from which the cardholder receives no benefit." 15 U.S.C. § 1602(o), implemented by 12 C.F.R. § 226.2. For the consumer to be liable for even the $50, a number of conditions have to be met. One of the most important of these is that the card must be an "accepted credit card," one "which the cardholder has requested and received or has signed or has used, or authorized another to use." 15 U.S.C. § 1602(1), implemented by 12 C.F.R. § 226.2(a). Another important condition was that the unauthorized use must have occurred prior to notification to the issuer that the card has been lost or stolen. Lack of fault on the part of the cardholder is not a condition.

Does the federal credit card legislation strike a fair balance between issuers and cardholders? Should fault play a role in the allocation of loss?

Electronic Fund Transfer Act. "One of the most hotly debated topics during consideration of federal EFT legislation was the allocation of liability for unauthorized fraudulent transfers. Industry groups, believing that much of the fraudulent activity arose as a re-

---

1. French law reaches just this conclusion. "The drawer who by his own fault loses a check form is responsible if his signature is subsequently forged on it unless he has notified the bank in time to prevent payment. The drawer has been held where checks were stolen from a desk in his place of business, from an unlocked drawer in a workroom, and from his briefcase in his hotel room." Farnsworth, The Check in France and the United States, 36 Tul.L.Rev. 245, 264 (1962).

sult of consumers writing their PIN numbers on or near their EFT cards, argued that a negligence standard should be adopted. Under such a standard, the consumer would bear none of the loss unless his negligence substantially contributed to the unauthorized use; if it did, he would bear the entire loss. While this arrangement would encourage care in the handling and storing of EFT cards and PINs, consumer groups argued that it was unduly harsh on consumers and would enable financial institutions possessing greater legal resources to shift more than a fair share of the liability burden to consumers. They advocated a flat $50 limitation on liability like that applicable to credit cards under the Truth in Lending Act. These concerns ultimately carried the day, and although a pure $50 limit was rejected in favor of a compromise rule, the liability-allocation rule that was finally adopted will place strict limits upon consumer liability regardless of the consumer's negligence in safeguarding the account access devices.

"Under the EFT Act, an unauthorized transfer is defined as a transfer initiated by someone other than the consumer or a person to whom the consumer has given actual authority to initiate the transfer, and from which the consumer receives no benefit. Any transfer initiated by someone to whom the consumer furnishes his EFT card and PIN, however, is not to be considered unauthorized unless the consumer has notified the institution that transfers by that person are no longer permitted.

"As an initial matter, the amount of a consumer's liability for an unauthorized electronic transfer or related series of transfers will not exceed $50 or the amount of unauthorized transfers that occur before notice is given to the financial institution, whichever is less. Thus, the basic limitation on consumer liability is similar to the flat dollar-amount limitation of the Truth in Lending Act. There are two significant exceptions, however, that may escalate the initial $50 limitation on consumer liability.

"First, if the consumer fails to notify the financial institution within two business days after he discovers the loss or theft of an EFT card or PIN, the consumer may be liable for up to $500 of unauthorized use. This second tier of liability is intended to encourage prompt reporting of lost and stolen cards once the consumer becomes aware of the loss or theft. This scheme is designed to hold total system losses to a reasonable minimum, while protecting consumers from unlimited liability for indiscretions in safegarding their EFT cards and PINs, or for slight delays in reporting a loss or theft.

"Second, there is no ceiling on consumer liability for subsequent unauthorized transfers that occur because the consumer has failed to report within 60 days of the transmittal of a periodic statement any unauthorized transfer that appears on the statement. This is intended to provide an incentive for consumers to read and verify their periodic statements, and thus thwart fraudulent users who might otherwise drain the account over a lengthy period of time. It also provides necessary encouragement for consumers to report in a reasonably prompt fashion suspected unauthorized transfers which do not arise out of any loss or theft of the access devices." Brandel & Olliff, The Electronic Fund Transfer Act: A Primer, 40 Ohio St.L.J. 531, 555–57 (1979). [2]

What is the role of fault—on the part of the consumer or the financial institution—under the scheme just described? The scheme, along with some further qualifications, can be seen from the following excerpts from Regulation E (12 C.F.R. Part 205).

§ 205.2 Definitions and rules of construction.

For the purposes of this regulation, the following definitions apply, unless the context indicates otherwise:

(a)(1) "Access device" means a card, code, or other means of access to a consumer's account, or any combination thereof, that may be used by the consumer for the purpose of initiating electronic fund transfers.

(2) An access device becomes an "accepted access device" when the consumer to whom the access device was issued;

(i) Requests and receives, or signs, or uses, or authorizes another to use, the access device for the purpose of transferring money between accounts or obtaining money, property, labor or services;

(ii) Requests validation of an access device issued on an unsolicited basis; or

(iii) Receives an access device issued in renewal of, or in substitution for, an accepted access device, whether such access device is issued by the initial financial institution or a successor.

. . .

(l) "Unauthorized electronic fund transfer" means an electronic fund transfer from a consumer's account initiated by a person other than the consumer without actual authority to initiate the transfer and from which the consumer receives no benefit. The term does not include any electronic fund transfer (1) initiated by a person who was furnished with the access device to the consumer's account by the consumer, unless the consumer has notified the financial institution involved that transfers by that person are no longer authorized, (2) initiated with fraudulent intent by the consumer or any person acting in concert with the consumer, or (3) that is initiated by the financial institution or its employee.

2. Reproduced with permission of the Ohio State Law Journal.

. . .

§ 205.6   Liability of consumer for unauthorized transfers.

(a) *General rule.* A consumer is liable, within the limitations described in paragraph (b) of this section, for unauthorized electronic fund transfers involving the consumer's account only if:

(1) The access device used for the unauthorized transfers is an accepted access device;

(2) The financial institution has provided a means (such as by signature, photograph, fingerprint, or electronic or mechanical confirmation) to identify the consumer to whom the access device was issued; and

(3) The financial institution has provided the following information, in writing, to the consumer:

(i) A summary of the consumer's liability under this section, or under other applicable law or agreement, for unauthorized electronic fund transfers and, at the financial institution's option, notice of the advisability of promptly reporting loss or theft of the access device or unauthorized transfers.

(ii) The telephone number and address of the person or office to be notified in the event the consumer believes that an unauthorized electronic fund transfer has been or may be made.

(iii) The financial institution's business days, as determined under § 205.2(d), unless applicable State law or an agreement between the consumer and the financial institution sets a liability limit not greater than $50.

(b) *Limitations on amount of liability.* The amount of a consumer's liability for an unauthorized electronic fund transfer or a series of related unauthorized transfers shall not exceed $50 or the amount of unauthorized transfers that occur before notice to the financial institution under paragraph (c) of this section, whichever is less, unless one or both of the following exceptions apply:

(1) If the consumer fails to notify the financial institution within 2 business days after learning of the loss or theft of the access device, the consumer's liability shall not exceed the lesser of $500 or the sum of

(i) $50 or the amount of unauthorized electronic fund transfers that occur before the close of the 2 business days, whichever is less, and

(ii) the amount of unauthorized electronic fund transfers that the financial institution establishes would not have occurred but for the failure of the consumer to notify the institution within 2 business days after the consumer learns of the loss or theft of the access device, and that occur after the close of 2 business days and before notice to the financial institution.

(2) If the consumer fails to report within 60 days of transmittal of the periodic statement any unauthorized electronic fund transfer that appears on the statement, the consumer's liability shall not exceed the sum of

(i) The lesser of $50 or the amount of unauthorized electronic fund transfers that appear on the periodic statement or that occur during the 60-day period, and

(ii) The amount of unauthorized electronic fund transfers that occur after the close of the 60 days and before notice to the financial institution and that the financial institution establishes would not have occurred but for the failure of the consumer to notify the financial institution within that time.

(3) Paragraphs (b)(1) and (2) of this section may both apply in some circumstances. Paragraph (b)(1) shall determine the consumer's liability for any unauthorized transfers that appear on the periodic statement and occur before the close of the 60-day period, and paragraph (b)(2)(ii) shall determine liability for transfers that occur after the close of the 60-day period.

(4) If a delay in notifying the financial institution was due to extenuating circumstances, such as extended travel or hospitalization, the time period specified above shall be extended to a reasonable time.

(5) If applicable State law or an agreement between the consumer and financial institution imposes lesser liability than that provided in paragraph (b) of this section, the consumer's liability shall not exceed that imposed under that law or agreement.

(c) *Notice to financial institution.* For purposes of this section, notice to a financial institution is given when a consumer takes such steps as are reasonably necessary to provide the financial institution with the pertinent information, whether or not any particular officer, employee, or agent of the financial institution does in fact receive the information. Notice in writing is considered given at the time the consumer deposits the notice in the mail or delivers the notice for transmission by any other usual means to the financial institution. Notice in writing is considered given at the time of receipt or, whether or not received, at the expiration of the time ordinarily required for transmission, whichever is earlier. Notice is also considered given when the financial institution becomes aware of circumstances that lead to the reasonable belief that an unauthorized electronic fund transfer involving the consumer's account has been or may be made.

Regulation E is discussed in Connors, The Implementation of the Electronic Fund Transfer Act: An Update on Regulation E, 17 Wake Forest L.Rev. 329 (1981).

Suppose that a customer contests the right of her bank to charge her account for $800 that the bank claims were withdrawn at an ATM at a precise time by either the customer or someone authorized by her. The customer produces evidence that she was at work at the time in question and testifies that her card was never out of her possession and that she never told anyone her PIN and never even wrote it down. The bank produces evidence that the withdrawal could only have been made by someone using the customer's card together with her PIN. What result under the EFT Act and Regulation E? See Judd v. Citibank, 107 Misc.2d 526, 435 N.Y.S.2d 210 (1980) (not citing either the EFT Act or Regulation E[3]).

Uniform New Payments Code. The Uniform New Payments Code proposes a single set of rules for all unauthorized orders regardless of the type of payment system involved. It would therefore apply to payment by check, by credit card, or by EFT. Like the EFT Act, the UNPC relies on the concept of an "accepted access device," but it broadens the definition of "access device" to include checks as well as cards. See UNPC 50(18), 201, 202, 203.

SECTION 4.   FICTITIOUS PAYEES AND IMPOSTORS

Prefatory Note. This section is concerned with two rules that have been developed for two particular types of check fraud: the fictitious payee rule and the impostor rule.

The fictitious payee rule originated in the failure of several English commercial houses in the late eighteenth century. Lenders of credit had drawn or accepted bills of exchange payable to the order of imaginary firms, and given them to the houses which had indorsed them in the names of the imaginary firms and sold them to purchasers. The houses failed, and the lenders of credit, when sued by the purchasers of the drafts, claimed that the indorsements were forged. They lost in a number of suits and on a variety of theories. See Tatlock v. Harris, 3 T.R. 174, 100 Eng.Rep. 517 (1789); Minet v. Gibson, 3 T.R. 481, 100 Eng.Rep. 689 (1789), affirmed, 1 H.Bl. 569, 126

---

3. Under § 1693g(b) of the Act: "In any action which involves a consumer's liability for an unauthorized electronic fund transfer, the burden of proof is upon the financial institution to show that the electronic fund transfer was authorized or, if the electronic fund transfer was unauthorized, then the burden of proof is upon the financial institution to establish that the conditions of liability set forth in subsection (a) . . . have been met, and . . . that the disclosures required to be made to the consumer . . . were in fact made. . . ." (Regulation E does not contain a comparable provision.) Was this provision relevant to the Judd case? See Regulation E, § 205.2(a)(2)(i) supra.

Eng.Rep. 326 (H.L.1791).   During the next century the rule grew up that a bill payable to a fictitious person is payable to bearer as against all parties who knew that the payee was a fictitious person. When the Bills of Exchange Act was enacted in 1882, it provided, in Section 7(3), "Where the payee is a fictitious or nonexisting person the bill may be treated as payable to bearer."   In Bank of England v. Vagliano Brothers, [1891] A.C. 107, reversing 23 Q.B.D. 243 (1889), the House of Lords decided that this changed prior law and lack of knowledge of the fictitious character of the payee was immaterial.

In 1896 the Commissioners on Uniform State Laws approved Section 9(3) of the Negotiable Instruments Law which rejects the rule in Vagliano's case: "The instrument is payable to bearer . . . . When it is payable to the order of a fictitious or nonexisting person, and such fact was known to the person making it so payable." Courts read "fictitious" to include a living person not intended by the maker or drawer to take any interest in the instrument.   The prototype situation to which the rule applied was that where the treasurer of a corporation, authorized to sign its checks, drew its check payable to a payee who was a living person but one whom the treasurer had fraudulently added to the payroll with no intention that he receive the check.   The treasurer then forged the payee's indorsement.   The fictitious payee rule protected anyone who cashed the check as well as the drawee bank that paid it, for, since the check was payable to bearer, no indorsement was necessary and the forgery was for these purposes, immaterial.

But it was held that NIL 9(3) did not apply to the situation where an employee of the corporation, not authorized to sign its checks, fraudulently prepared the padded payroll containing the name of the payee, and the check was then signed by the innocent treasurer, and the indorsement of the payee forged by the employee.   Since the fictitious character of the payee was not known to the treasurer, "the person making it so payable," the check was not payable to bearer, no person who cashed it took as a holder, and the drawee bank that paid it could not charge the drawer's account.   Cf. Security First National Bank v. Bank of America, 22 Cal.2d 154, 137 P.2d 452 (1943). Banks objected to the injustice of this result, which placed on the drawee a risk that they felt should properly be borne by the corporation.   The American Bankers Association recommended a Fictitious Payee Act, which amended NIL 9(3) to cover situations in which "such fact was known to the person making it so payable, or known to his employee or other agent who supplies the name of such payee." About half of the states adopted this amendment.

The Code's version of the fictitious payee rule is found in UCC 3–405(1)(b), (c).   Note that it does not use the word "fictitious."   Comments 3 and 4 give a helpful explanation of the rule.   Note that it does not make the instrument payable to bearer, as the Negotiable Instruments Law did, but provides that "An indorsement by any person in the name of a named payee is effective." Is this change of much practical importance? See generally Comment, 47 Fordham L.Rev. 1083 (1979).

Problem 12. Kim Kaller, Empire's treasurer (see Form 5, p. 101 supra), drew a $5,000 check to the order of Quaker for a nonexistent delivery of goods. Kaller indorsed it in Quaker's name, and the Irving Trust paid it and charged it to Empire's account. Kaller has absconded with the proceeds. Does Empire have a claim against the Irving Trust? See UCC 3–405.

Problem 13. Merideth Hussler, one of Empire's clerks, furnished Kim Kaller, Empire's treasurer, with a forged invoice from Quaker for a non-existent delivery of goods. Kaller drew a $5,000 check to the order of Quaker in payment of the invoice. Hussler stole the check before it was mailed to Quaker, indorsed it in Quaker's name, and the Irving Trust paid it and charged it to Empire's account. Hussler has absconded with the proceeds. Does Empire have a claim against the Irving Trust? Would it make a difference if the invoice was a genuine one, as long as Hussler had it in mind to steal the check when furnishing the invoice to Kaller? See UCC 3–405; Danje Fabrics Division v. Morgan Guaranty Trust Co., infra.

DANJE FABRICS DIVISION v. MORGAN GUARANTY TRUST CO.

Supreme Court of New York, New York County, 1978.
96 Misc.2d 746, 409 N.Y.S.2d 565.

Louis Grossman, Justice. This is a motion by defendant Citibank, N.A., sued herein as "First National City Bank" ("Citibank") for summary judgment under CPLR 3212 dismissing this action as against defendant Morgan Guaranty Trust Company ("Morgan"), and a cross-motion by plaintiff Danje Fabrics Division of Kingspoint International Corp. ("Danje") for summary judgment against defendant Morgan.

The facts in this case are essentially undisputed by the parties. In November 1974, plaintiff Danje, a family owned company that converted yarn into fabric, hired one Raymond Caulder ("Caulder") as its Accounts Payable Bookkeeper. Specialty Dyers ("Dyers") located in North Carolina, is in the business of dying fabrics, a service which Dyers has performed for Danje for several years and for which Danje has paid Dyers regularly, amounting to millions of dollars.

Dyers would submit invoices to Danje to secure payment for the services it had performed. These invoices were first reviewed in Danje's production department. The invoices would then be sent to Caulder who would record them in the accounts payable ledger and file the invoices by due date. When the due date came, Caulder, at time with the help of another employee, would manually prepare the necessary checks and write in the name of the payee. The checks were then submitted by Caulder to Ernest J. Michel ("Michel"), president of Danje, or to his son Stanley, for signature. Along with the checks given to Ernest or Stanley Michel for signature, the original invoices supporting each check and adding machine tapes of the invoices, if more than one, were submitted to the signatory.

On May 28, 1975, Caulder's employment was terminated by Danje for appearing for work drunk, unshaven and unruly. Shortly thereafter, it was discovered that between April 23, 1975 and May 21, 1975, Caulder had taken twenty-seven checks totalling $49,645.82, made out to Dyers in payment of bona fide invoices for services actually performed and for which payments were actually due, after they had been signed, and diverted them into an account he or he and an accomplice had opened at Citibank in the name of Specialty Dyers. A private investigator hired by Danje to locate Caulder and obtain the return of the proceeds of the diverted checks reported to Danje that Caulder's true name was Raymond Flate. Caulder has not been found, nor has the money been retrieved. There is presently a balance of $6,435.29 in the Specialty Dyers account opened by Caulder at Citibank.

Thereafter, Danje commenced this action against Morgan as the payor or drawee bank and against Citibank as the collecting bank. Danje's complaint set forth three causes of action. The first was against defendant Morgan only for wrongfully debiting plaintiff's account for the twenty-seven checks which plaintiff alleged contained forged payee's endorsements. The second and third causes of action were against defendant Citibank only and alleged negligence on its part in permitting a fraudulent account to be opened by the forger. Citibank moved to dismiss the complaint as to itself for failure to state a cause of action, which was granted. The order dismissing the complaint as to Citibank was served with notice of entry. No appeal was ever taken from the said order and the time for plaintiff to appeal has expired. Thus, the only cause of action remaining is the one against Morgan as drawee bank. However, Citibank is still in the action since Morgan has cross-claimed against Citibank on its prior endorsements as the collecting bank. Citibank recognizes and concedes that if plaintiff has judgment against Morgan, then Morgan is entitled to judgment over against Citibank in like amount and has therefore brought this motion in which Morgan has joined.

Citibank contends that Morgan has a complete defense to the claim set forth by Danje in its complaint by reason of the provisions of § 3–405 of the Uniform Commercial Code.

This section provides in pertinent part:

"§ 3–405.   *Imposters; Signature in Name of Payee*

(1) An endorsement by any person in the name of a named payee is effective if . . . (c) an agent or employee of the

maker or drawer has supplied him with the name of the payee
intending the latter to have no such interest."

Since it was Caulder who was responsible for the preparation of
checks based upon invoices given to him by plaintiff Danje's production department and who presented such checks to the individual who
was authorized to sign them, Citibank argues, and Morgan agrees,
that, based upon the facts as herein set forth, Caulder "supplied" the
plaintiff with the name of the payee intending the latter to have no
such interest and therefore the endorsements in question are effective. Danje's position is that, since the twenty-seven checks in question were prepared as a result of bona fide business transactions between Dyers, the named payee, and Danje, Caulder did not "supply"
plaintiff with the name of the payee but simply converted the checks
to his own use, and that therefore § 3–405(1)(c) of the Uniform Commercial Code has no application to the instant case.

Therefore, the issue to be decided in this case is what scope the
word "supplied", as used in § 3–405(1)(c) of the Uniform Commercial
Code was intended to have. Was it the legislature's intent for it to
cover all instances where an employee presents an instrument to the
maker for signature or must a line be drawn to distinguish between
those instances where the instrument is based upon a fraudulent
transaction and those where the instrument is based upon a bona fide
transaction occurring in the regular course of business.

There are extremely few cases in any jurisdiction dealing with
§ 3–405(1)(c) of the Uniform Commercial Code and the court has
found only three cases which bear any relation to the specific question raised herein. One is a New York case, Board of Higher Education v. Banker's Trust Co., 86 Misc.2d 560, 383 N.Y.S.2d 508, factually
similar to the present case, which discusses the point in question but
does not go into it in detail since the defendant did not seriously contest the applicability of the overall section. Another is a New Jersey
case, Snug Harbor Realty Co. v. First National Bank of Toms River,
N.J., 105 Super. 572, 253 A.2d 581, aff'd 54 N.J. 95, 253 A.2d 545,
which presents a very similar fact pattern to the instant case and
deals directly with the point in question. The third is a Federal Court
of Appeals case in the Third Circuit applying Pennsylvania law, New
Amsterdam Casualty Co. v. First Pennsylvania Banking & Trust Co.
(3rd Cir.) 451 F.2d 892, which also presents similar facts with one distinction upon which the court rests its decision, and which sets forth a
definition of the word "supplied" as used in § 3–405(1)(c) of the Uniform Commercial Code.

The law as set forth in § 3–405(1)(c) of the Uniform Commercial
Code reads exactly the same in all of the three states in which the
above-mentioned cases were decided. According to the official comment accompanying § 3–405(1)(c) of the Uniform Commercial Code as
set forth in the official statutes of all three states:

"Paragraph (c) is new. It extends the rule of the original subsection 9(3) to include the padded payroll cases, where the drawer's agent or employee prepares the check for signature or otherwise furnishes the signing officer with the name of the payee. The principle followed is that the loss should fall upon the employer as a risk of his business enterprise rather than upon the subsequent holder or drawee. The reasons are that the employer is normally in a better position to prevent such forgeries by reasonable care in the selection or supervision of his employees, or, if he is not, is at least in a better position to cover the loss by fidelity insurance; and that the cost of such insurance is properly an expense of his business rather than of the business of the holder or drawee."

Although the Official Comment quoted above, makes mention only of "padded payroll" cases, it is clear that the provisions of the Code extend beyond these to other "padded" cases where the operative facts are present, i.e., where the drawer's agent or employee prepares the checks, presumably drawn for payroll or other valid purposes, for signature or otherwise furnishes the signing officer with the name of the payee.

The Official Comment also provides two examples which illustrate situations in which § 3–405(1)(c) of the Uniform Commercial Code is applicable. Both examples use a fact pattern where an employee of a corporation prepares a padded payroll for the treasurer. In one instance, the employee adds a fictitious payee to the payroll without the knowledge of the treasurer, while in the other, the payee exists and the employee knows it but adds a check to the payroll intending the payee to have no interest in it. In both instances, any person could effectively endorse the payee's name and the loss would fall on the corporation rather than a subsequent holder or the drawee. The above illustrative situations are straightforward and clear. The problem with applying said illustrative situations to the instant case results from the fact that both of said situations are based on a payroll where an unauthorized check in each case has been added to it rather than a totally legitimate check. While it is clear that § 3–405(1)(c) of the Uniform Commercial Code applies to fraudulent checks, its application to a situation involving bona fide checks is not discussed in those examples.

In our present case, the checks stolen by Caulder were legitimate and bona fide payments due and owing to Dyers. The checks themselves involved in our case were not fraudulent in any respect and the facts herein indicate that proper and careful business procedures were followed in the drawing and making of said checks. The undisputed facts herein further show that it was only the criminal conduct of Caulder in appropriating, stealing and falsely endorsing said checks, which constituted legitimate payments to the named payee, that resulted in the loss herein incurred by Danje.

In Board of Higher Education v. Banker's Trust Co., supra, an employee of the plaintiff had as her duty the responsibility of preparing requisitions for checks to be issued by plaintiff for scholarships and other payments to students, to prepare the checks, to have them signed by the authorized personnel, and to send the checks to their recipients. On a number of occasions, the employee prepared duplicate requisitions and checks, which she retained after they had been signed. Also, in some instances, she retained checks which had been properly requisitioned instead of sending them. She then forged the endorsements of the named payees on these checks and cashed them. In arguing that these checks should not be debited against its accounts, plaintiff did not seriously contest the applicability of § 3–405(1)(c) of the Uniform Commercial Code to the facts of the case, but argued that the banks were estopped from relying on its provisions because of their gross negligence in allowing the forger to cash the checks. As a result, the court simply stated its conclusion that the forged endorsements were effective, lumping all of the checks together without distinguishing between the duplicate and the genuine checks, and proceeded to discuss the merits of the other arguments which were the main thrust of plaintiff's case.

In Snug Harbor Realty Co. v. First National Bank of Toms River, N.J., supra, plaintiff maintained a system under which parties asserting claims against it would submit invoices which were then given to its superintendent for verification. Upon verifying that the claims were valid, he would initial the invoices and forward them to the bookkeeper who would verify the contractual obligation and prepare the necessary checks. After the checks were signed by the company's authorized official, the superintendent would pick them up for delivery to the respective payees. Instead of delivering the checks, he proceeded to forge the endorsements of the named payees and cash the checks for his own personal use. The trial court found that the provisions of Section 3–405(1)(c) of the Uniform Commercial Code were "dispositive" and therefore the endorsements were effective and the bank not liable to the plaintiff. The appellate court reversed, stating:

> ". . . [the] unfaithful employee of the construction company did not supply to his employer 'the name of the payee intending the latter to have no such interest'. To the contrary, the payees were bona fide creditors of the company who had respectively submitted their invoices for work performed or materials furnished." *(Snug Harbor Realty Co.,* supra, 105 N.J.Super. at 574, 253 A.2d at 582).

Therefore, the creditors themselves "supplied" the plaintiff with the names of the payees, and the employee, in essence, stole the checks, thereby making his forged endorsements ineffective.

This Appellate Court decision in the *Snug Harbor* case, supra, appears to be on all fours with our instant case. In both situations, we are dealing with legitimate payments which were misappropriated and stolen by an employee instead of having them delivered or sent to the intended payee.

In New Amsterdam Casualty Co. v. First Pennsylvania Banking & Trust Co., supra, plaintiff was a stockbroker's insurer who had paid losses sustained by the stockbroker whose employee had forged endorsements on its checks and whose account had been debited by the drawee bank. The employee had submitted fraudulent sell orders to the trading room of the broker, thereby initiating the normal business procedure involved in the sale of items from various client's portfolios. The employee would then obtain the necessary confirmation slips, normally sent to the customer, by saying that he would deliver them personally. When the employee knew that the checks pursuant to the sale were ready, he would obtain them from the broker's cashier, stating that the customer had authorized his receipt of the checks. Instead of delivering the checks to the customer, he would then forge the endorsements of the named payees and cash the checks. The court decided that the endorsements were effective, relieving the drawee bank of liability. However, in explaining its decision, the court stated:

> "In the interest of business and bank stability, it is important that a reasonably clear line be drawn. Our decision places the burden on the drawer who, in the words of the official comment, is 'in a better position to cover the loss by fidelity insurance . . . ,' U.C.C. Section 3–405, comment 4.
>
> . . .
>
> "For the purpose of giving meaning to the word 'supplied' in section 3–405(1)(c), we can find no viable place to draw the line within the business enterprise of the drawer. Accordingly, in the context of the facts here, the only rational distinction lies between bona fide and fraudulent transactions because it is only in the case of a bona fide transaction that anyone other than the faithless employee may be said to have supplied the name of the payee to the company." (*New Amsterdam Cas. Co.*, supra, at 897, 898)

Thus, although the court decided that Section 3–405(1)(c) of the Uniform Commercial Code was applicable to the facts of that case as presented to it, the court clearly stated that this was only because a fraudulent transaction had been involved. If a bona fide business transaction had been the basis for the issuance of the checks in question, the court indicated that it would have found differently.

This court believes that if the plaintiff in Board of Higher Education v. Banker's Trust Co., supra, had seriously contested the applicability of Section 3–405(1)(c) of the Uniform Commercial Code to the facts of that case, the New York Court would have been forced to distinguish between the genuine checks retained by the employee and the duplicate checks which she caused to be issued.

In our instant case, the checks involved were based upon bona fide transactions and obligations of the plaintiff which arose out of the normal business relationship with the payee named on said checks. In such instance, it cannot be claimed that the employee, Caulder, supplied his employer, Danje, with the name of the payee, Dyers, as said checks were legitimately based upon open invoices due and owing to the payee, Dyers.

Accordingly, on the basis of the fact pattern existing in our instant case considered along with the cases herein discussed and the manner in which those respective courts arrived at their conclusions, defendant's motion for summary judgment is denied and plaintiff's cross-motion for summary judgment against defendant, Morgan, is granted.

Morgan's cross claim against Citibank based upon Citibank's prior endorsements, as the collecting bank, of the checks in question and Citibank's admitted liability under its warranties as set forth in Section 4–207 of the Uniform Commercial Code is also granted.

NOTE

Negligence and Fictitious Payees. Might a different result have been reached on the reasoning of the Thompson Maple Products case? Could the result in the Thompson Maple Products case have been reached under UCC 3–405(1)(c)? See footnote 2, p. 305 supra.

Should a drawer who would otherwise have to bear the loss under UCC 3–405 be able to shift that loss to the drawee bank by showing that it failed to use due care? For an answer in the negative, see Western Casualty & Surety Co. v. Citizens Bank of Las Cruces, 676 F.2d 1344 (10th Cir. 1982); Merrill Lynch, Pierce, Fenner & Smith v. Chemical Bank, 57 N.Y.2d 439, 456 N.Y.S.2d 742, 442 N.E.2d 1253 (1982). For an answer in the affirmative, see Comment, 27 U.C.L.A. L.Rev. 147 (1979).

What would your answer be if the drawer showed "a course of dealing so irregular in nature that the bank is shown to have violated its own policies and to have failed to act according to the standard of honesty-in-fact? See Kraftsman Container Corp. v. United Counties Trust Co., 169 N.J.Super. 488, 404 A.2d 1288 (1979). [1]

Should a drawer who would otherwise have to bear the loss under UCC 3–405 be able to shift that loss to the depositary bank by showing that it failed to use due care? That it did not act in good faith?

1. According to the commentary to UNPC 202, "while failure to observe reasonable standards on the part of the account institution operates as a counter-preclusion where the drawer is negligent, it does not operate where the drawer is strictly precluded. This reflects the notion that acts triggering strict drawer preclusion are more culpable. The result in Kraftsman Container Corp. v. United Counties Trust Co. . . . . is rejected."

For an answer in the affirmative, see E.F. Hutton & Co. v. City National Bank, 149 Cal.App.3d 60, 196 Cal.Rptr. 614 (1983).

UNDERPINNING & FOUNDATION CONSTRUCTORS, INC. v. CHASE MANHATTAN BANK, 46 N.Y.2d 459, 414 N.Y.S.2d 298, 386 N.E.2d 1319 (1979). Walker worked in Underpinning's accounting department, examining and verifying bills and invoices received by Underpinning, preparing checks to pay them, and submitting the verified invoices and prepared checks to the appropriate officers for signature. During a year and a half, Walker embezzled over a million dollars from Underpinning. He would make false invoices from firms with which Underpinning did business, prepare checks payable to them, obtain the signatures of the appropriate officers, and forge the payees' indorsements using stamps similar to those used by the payees. Though the stamps contained restrictive indorsements, such as "for deposit only," they were taken by banks for deposit in savings accounts that Walker had opened in names other than those of the payees—in complete disregard of the restrictive indorsements. The checks were paid by the drawee and charged to Underpinning's account. When Underpinning learned of the embezzlement, it sued the depositary banks. One of them, Bank of New York, which had taken ten checks totalling $452,979.27, moved to dismiss the complaint on the ground that the drawer of a check may never sue a depositary bank but is instead limited to whatever claims it has against the drawee bank. From denial of this motion, the Bank of New York appealed.

GABRIELLI, J. . . . Whether the drawer of a check has any cause of action against a depositary bank which wrongfully pays on the check is a question which has long divided the courts. . . . Prior to the enactment of the Uniform Commercial Code, the rule in this State apparently was that the drawer had no cause of action against the depositary bank, and could only seek to recover from the drawee bank. . . . The code itself contains nothing which directly or specifically changed this rule, but certain provisions thereof have required a re-examination of the prior rule in light of other changes made by the code. Unfortunately for the concept of uniformity in commercial law, the decisions in other States which have reconsidered the situation in light of the code have been far from unanimous in either result or rationale. Thus, in Massachusetts and New Jersey it is still the law that in no situation will a drawer be able to sue a depositary bank (Stone & Webster Eng. Corp. v. First Nat. Bank & Trust Co., 345 Mass. 1, 184 N.E.2d 358; Life Ins. Co. of Va. v. Snyder, 141 N.J.Super. 539, 358 A.2d 859). In California and Georgia, on the other hand, the opposite result has been reached by extending the definition of the term "payor" so as to include the drawer, who is thus given the benefit of the various warranties running to the payor (Sun 'N Sand v. United California Bank, 21 Cal.3d 671, 148 Cal.Rptr. 329, 582 P.2d 920; Insurance Co. of North Amer. v. Atlas Supply Co.,

121 Ga.App. 1, 172 S.E.2d 632). Whatever the ultimate validity of these various rationales, we need not, and accordingly we do not, reach them today. Rather, our examination of the reasons for precluding a drawer from proceeding against the depositary bank in the normal case, convinces us that such a bar should not apply in those situations in which the indorsement, although forged, is effective.

Simply stated, the reason why a drawer is normally held to have no cause of action against a depositary bank which wrongfully paid over a forged indorsement, is that the depositary bank is not deemed to have dealt with any valuable property of the drawer. In those cases in which the forgery is effective, however, this is not true. There are at least three theoretical grounds upon which the depositary bank could be deemed liable to the drawer: (1) conversion of proceeds of the check; (2) liability for money had and received to the extent of such proceeds; and (3) conversion of the instrument itself. Possibly there are others: plaintiff alleges liability based on "gross negligence amounting to bad faith". Each theory, however, requires that the depositary bank have dealt with property of the drawer, be that property the check itself or the proceeds thereof. In the typical forged indorsement case, the indorsement will be ineffective, and thus the check will not authorize the drawee bank to pay it from the drawer's account. Absent such authority, the drawee may not charge the drawer's account—and any payment made on the check is deemed to have been made solely from the property of the drawee, not the drawer. The drawer's property is thus not converted, and indeed no damages suffered, until the drawee refuses to honor a subsequent authorized draft upon the drawer's account which is deemed to have remained untouched by the prior payment. Since the money received by the depositary bank from the drawee is the property not of the drawer, but rather of the drawee alone, nothing the depositary bank does with those funds can be considered a conversion of the drawer's property. Similarly, insofar as the proceeds are the property of the drawee rather than the drawer, the depositary bank has not had and received any money of the drawer. With respect to the possibility of conversion of the check itself, since the drawer is not a holder, and could not present the check for payment, the drawer is normally considered as having no interest in the check. Moreover, since the check cannot be paid over a forged indorsement, the drawer is viewed as having no valuable interest in whatever right the check might otherwise be seen as transferring to the payee and to subsequent holders, for the simple reason that there exists no such right. [1]

. . .

---

1. Insofar as the drawer is deemed to have no interest in the check since he is not a holder, this rationale is suspect in situations such as this in which the payee has no interest in the check and the only person with any beneficial interest in the check at the time of its acceptance by the depositary bank was the drawer. Insofar as the instrument is deemed valueless because it does not serve to authorize payment from the drawer's account, this particular criticism of the traditional rule would be inapplicable.

Whatever the intrinsic validity of these arguments in the typical forged indorsement case in which the forged indorsement is "wholly inoperative" (Uniform Commercial Code, § 3–404), the applicable considerations change when the indorsement, although forged, is yet effective. In such cases, the check is both a valuable instrument and a valid instruction to the drawee to honor the check and debit the drawer's account accordingly. Since the result of valid payment on the check is the cancellation of a debt otherwise owed the drawer and the payment of funds otherwise claimable by the drawer, the drawer obviously does have an interest in the funds paid on the check. Where the indorsement is ineffective, the drawee is deemed to be paying out its own money because it cannot charge the drawer's account without authorization. Where, however, the indorsement is deemed effective, then the drawee is in fact paying out funds in which the drawer does have an interest and which may serve as the basis for an action against a depositary bank which has wrongfully obtained that money. Naturally, in such a case, since the indorsement is effective, no action would lie against the depositary bank for payment over the forged indorsement. Moreover, if the check was tainted in some other way which would put the drawee on notice, and which would make its payment unauthorized and subject it to suit, then the above rationale would not apply, since the payment would once again be from the drawee's funds rather than the drawer's account, and thus no action would lie against the depositary bank in favor of the drawer. Hence, it is only in those comparatively rare instances in which the depositary bank has acted wrongfully and yet the drawee has acted properly that the drawer will be able to proceed directly against the depositary bank.

Applying these principles to this case, we conclude that plaintiff has stated a cause of action against defendant Bank of New York sufficient to withstand a motion to dismiss for failure to state a cause of action. The allegations in the complaint indicate that the forgery involved in the case falls within the ambit of section 3–405 (subd. [1], par. [c]) of the Uniform Commercial Code, which provides as follows: "An indorsement by any person in the name of a named payee is effective if . . . (c) an agent or employee of the maker or drawer has supplied him with the name of the payee intending the latter to have no such interest." Thus, assuming as we must that these allegations are true, the indorsement was effective, and hence the traditional reasons for refusing to allow a drawer to sue a depositary bank directly in a forged indorsement situation are inapplicable, as the money paid to the depositary bank by the drawee was property in which the drawer had a very real interest.

In summary, we hold today that a drawer may directly sue a depositary bank which has honored a check in violation of a forged restrictive indorsement in situations in which the forgery is effective.

This result is not only theoretically viable, but is in accord with principles of equity and sound public policy. It is basic to the law of commercial paper that as between innocent parties any loss should ultimately be placed on the party which could most easily have prevented that loss. Hence, in most forged indorsement cases, the party who first took the check from the forger will ultimately be liable, assuming of course that there is no solvent forger available. This is so because it is the party who takes from the forger who is in the best position to verify the indorsement. This is not always true, however, and if the forgery is the result of some other interested party's negligence, the burden may ultimately be placed on that party (see Uniform Commercial Code § 3–406). In certain instances in which it is clear that the loss could have been most readily prevented by the drawer, the code may place the loss upon the drawer as a matter of law (Uniform Commercial Code, § 3–405). One such situation might be that alleged to be present in this case, in which the indorsement of a named payee has been forged by "an agent or employee of the maker or drawer [who] has supplied him with the name of the payee intending the latter to have no such interest" (Uniform Commercial Code, § 3–405, subd. [1] par. [c]). In such cases, the indorsement is deemed to be effective and the drawer is thus precluded from recovering solely on the basis of the forgery from banks which honor the check. The reason for this rule is that it is believed that as a practical matter the drawer is in a better position to prevent the fraud by utilizing proper accounting methods, than is even the first party to take from the forger. Although this presumption is not free from criticism, and may in some instances be less than sound, the language of the code makes it applicable.

Had the forger in this case not forged a check with a restrictive indorsement, it would appear that the loss might properly be placed upon the drawer alone. A restrictive indorsement, however, imposes a new and separate duty upon a transferee to pay the check only in accord with the restriction. In this case, the restrictive indorsements required that the checks be deposited only in the accounts of the respective restrictive indorsers, the named payees. This was not done and the failure to do so serves as a basis for liability independent of any liability which might be created by payment over a forged indorsement alone.[2]

It has been suggested that it is illogical to reach a different result dependent only on whether the forger adds a restriction to the indorsement or not. Although superficially attractive, this argument could as readily serve as a challenge to the soundness of the code provisions imposing a liability upon the drawer where the forger has

---

2. In an omitted part of the opinion, the court noted that it was not presented with the question whether the depositary bank might have a defense if the drawer had failed to use due care in examining its bank statements and returned checks. [Ed.]

chosen to act in one way rather than another (see Uniform Commercial Code, § 3–405). The obvious flaw in the argument made is that it ignores the prime function of all these rules and distinctions: to impose liability on the party which could most readily have prevented the fraud. Where the only defect is the forgery itself and the forgery could and should have been prevented by the drawer, liability is imposed on the drawer. Where, however, as here, the indorsement is not only forged, but is also restrictive, and the check is presented in what appears on its face to be an obvious violation of that restriction, then the situation is different, and the balance of obligations and potential liabilities shifts. That an indorsement is forged does not serve to justify a failure to apply normal commercial standards with respect to any restrictions imposed by the indorsement. The presence of a restriction imposes upon the depositary bank an obligation not to accept that item other than in accord with the restriction. By disregarding the restriction, it not only subjects itself to liability for any losses resulting from its actions, but it also passes up what may well be the best opportunity to prevent the fraud. The presentation of a check in violation of a restrictive indorsement for deposit in the account of someone other than the restrictive indorser is an obvious warning sign, and the depositary bank is required to investigate the situation rather than blindly accept the check. Based on such a failure to follow the mandates of due care and commercially reasonable behavior, it is appropriate to shift ultimate liability from the drawer to the depositary bank.

[Affirmed.]

NOTES

(1) **Underpinning Distinguished.** In Spielman v. Manufacturers Hanover Trust Co., 60 N.Y.2d 221, 456 N.E.2d 1192 (1983), the Court of Appeals distinguished Underpinning. A union welfare fund drew a check on Manufacturers Hanover payable to Pitney, Hardin & Kipp, a New Jersey law firm, at the direction of the fund's attorney, Robert Weisswasser, who was to use it to settle a lawsuit. Instead, Weisswasser forged the payee's indorsement, deposited the check in his account in Chemical Bank, withdrew the proceeds, absconded, and was later found dead from a bullet wound in the head. The fund was unsuccessful in a suit against Manufacturers, it being held that Weisswasser's indorsement was effective under UCC 3–405(1)(c). The fund recovered against Chemical Bank, however, under the Underpinning case, and the bank appealed. The Court of Appeals reversed, holding that Underpinning did not apply because Weisswasser had indorsed the check:

Pay to Special Account

012–043478

s/Pitney, Hardin & Kipp

For Deposit Only

Special Account 012–043478

The account number was Weisswasser's. Do you agree that the cases are distinguishable?

(2) Subrogation of Insurer. "It would be natural to assume upon a determination first of the allocation of loss among the parties in the absence of insurance, and then of the coverage of that loss by forgery or fidelity insurance, that the problem of the ultimate allocation of the loss among all the parties including insurers would be finally resolved. But this is not so because of the further question of subrogation of the insurer to the insured's rights against innocent third parties. Clearly both forgery and fidelity bonds, as forms of indemnity insurance, insure against the original loss, regardless of whether the insured may have the right to recover from the wrongdoer or from an innocent third party. Thus, for example, an insured drawer may recover from his insurer under a depositor's forgery or a fidelity bond on forged checks written by an employee, even though he could have recovered from either the employee or the drawee bank. To be sure, as soon as the loss occurs, the insurer stands in the position of a surety with the wrongdoer as principal, and upon payment of that loss the insurer is subrogated to the insured's rights against the wrongdoer. Since this is usually a remedy of no great promise, the insurer will turn to the insured's claim against the drawee bank. The right of the insurer to enforce this claim has most frequently been viewed as that of a surety to be subrogated to the creditor's (the drawer's) rights against an innocent third party (the bank)." Farnsworth, Insurance Against Check Forgery, 60 Colum.L.Rev. 284, 316 (1960). [1] Some cases have denied subrogation on the ground that the surety, having been paid by the drawer, is a "compensated surety." They are discussed and criticized in the cited article.

————

Prefatory Note. The following materials on impersonation in the law of commercial paper raise issues similar to those raised by impersonation in connection with the sale of goods. See Cundy v. Lindsay, p. 25 supra. How similar are the issues? How similar are the solutions? Compare UCC 2–403(1)(a) with 3–405(1)(a).

Problem 14. Cecil Conn approached Kim Kaller, Empire's treasurer, impersonating J.J. Sterling, a reputable merchant. Kaller drew a $5,000 check payable to Sterling as an advance payment for goods that Conn, as Sterling, promised to furnish to Empire. Conn indorsed it in Sterling's name, and the Irving Trust paid it and charged it to Empire's account. Conn absconded with the proceeds. Does Empire have a claim against the Irving Trust? See UCC 3–405; Philadelphia Title-Insurance v. Fidelity-Philadelphia Trust, infra.

---

1. Reproduced with permission of the Columbia Law Review.

Would it make a difference if Kaller had drawn the check payable to "Sterling Industries, Inc." rather than to Sterling?

PHILADELPHIA TITLE INSURANCE CO. v. FIDELITY-PHILADELPHIA TRUST CO.

Supreme Court of Pennsylvania, 1965.
419 Pa. 78, 212 A.2d 222.

COHEN, JUSTICE. This is an appeal in an action in assumpsit brought by plaintiff-appellant, Philadelphia Title Insurance Company, against defendant-appellee, Fidelity-Philadelphia Trust Company, to recover the sum of $15,640.82 which was charged against the Title Company's account with Fidelity in payment of a check drawn by the Title Company on Fidelity. The complaint alleged that the endorsement of one of the payees had been forged and that, therefore, Fidelity should not have paid the check. Fidelity joined the Philadelphia National Bank as an additional defendant claiming that if Fidelity were liable to plaintiff, PNB was liable over to Fidelity for having guaranteed the endorsements. PNB joined the Penn's Grove National Bank and Trust Company as a second additional defendant claiming that if PNB were liable to Fidelity, Penn's Grove was liable to PNB for having cashed the check and guaranteed the endorsements. By way of defense all of the banks asserted that none of them were liable because the issuance of the check by the Title Company was induced by an impostor and delivered by the Title Company to a confederate of the impostor thereby making the forged endorsement effective.

The case was tried before the lower court sitting without a jury. The trial judge found in favor of the Title Company. Exceptions to said finding were sustained unanimously by the court en banc and judgment was entered against the Title Company and in favor of the banks. The judgment must be affirmed.

The pertinent facts are stated by the lower court:

"Edmund Jezemski and Paula Jezemski were husband and wife, estranged and living apart. Edmund Jezemski was administrator and sole heir of his deceased mother's estate, one of the assets of which was premises 1130 North Fortieth Street, Philadelphia. Mrs. Jezemski, without her husband's knowledge, arranged for a mortgage to be placed on this real estate. This mortgage was obtained for Mrs. Jezemski through John M. McAllister, a member of the Philadelphia Bar, and Anthony DiBenedetto, a real estate dealer, and was to be insured by Philadelphia Title Insurance Company, the plaintiff. Shortly before the date set for settlement at the office of the title company, Mrs. Jezemski represented to McAllister and DiBenedetto that her husband would be unable to attend the settlement. She came to McAllister's office in advance of the settlement date, accompanied by a man whom she introduced to McAllister and DiBenedetto as her husband. She and this man, in the presence of McAllister and DiBenedetto, executed a deed conveying the real estate from the estate to Edmund Jezemski and Paula Jezemski as tenants by the entireties and also executed the mortgage, bond and warrant which had been prepared. McAllister and DiBenedetto, accompanied by Mrs. Jezemski, met at the office of the title company on the date appointed for settlement, the signed deed and mortgage were produced, the mortgagee handed over the amount of the mortgage, and the title company delivered its check to Mrs. Jezemski for the net proceeds of $15,640.82, made payable, as we have already mentioned, to Mr. and Mrs. Jezemski individually and Mr. Jezemski as administrator of his mother's estate."

. . .

"[The Title Company's] settlement clerk, in the absence of Edmund Jezemski at the settlement, accepted the word of McAllister and DiBenedetto that the deed and mortgage had been signed by Jezemski; he himself, though he had not seen the signatures affixed, signed as a witness to the signatures on the mortgage; he also signed as a witness to the deed, and in his capacity as a notary public he acknowledged its execution."

. . .

". . . Paula Jezemski, one of the payees, . . . presented [the check], with purported endorsements of all the payees, at the Penns Grove National Bank and Trust Company in Penns Grove, New Jersey, for cash. Edmund Jezemski received none of the proceeds, either individually or as administrator of the estate of Sofia Jezemski; and it is conceded that the endorsements purporting to be his were forged. The Penns Grove bank negotiated the check through the Philadelphia National Bank, and it was eventually paid by Fidelity-Philadelphia Trust Company, which charged the amount of the check against the deposit account of plaintiff."

. . .

"There is no question that the man whom Mrs. Jezemski introduced to McAllister and DiBenedetto was not Edmund Jezemski, her husband. It was sometime later that Edmund Jezemski, when he tried to convey the real estate, discovered the existence of the mortgage. When he did so he instituted an action in equity which resulted in the setting aside of the deed and mortgage and the repayment of the fund advanced by the mortgagee."

The parties do not dispute the proposition that as between the payor bank [1] (Fidelity-Philadelphia) and its customer [2] (Title Company), ordinarily, the former must bear the loss occasioned by the for-

---

1. " 'Payor bank' means a bank by which an item is payable as drawn or accepted." Uniform Commercial Code—

Bank Deposits and Collections, Act of April 6, 1953, P.L. 3, § 4–105(b), 12A P.S. § 4–105.

gery of a payee's endorsement (Edmund Jezemski) upon a check drawn by its customer and paid by it. . . . Uniform Commercial Code—Commercial Paper, Act of April 6, 1953, P.L. 3, § 3–404, as amended, 12A P.S. § 3–404. . . .

However, the banks argue that this case falls within an exception to the above rule, making the forged indorsement of Edmund Jezemski's name effective so that Fidelity-Philadelphia was entitled to charge the account of its customer, the Title Company, who was the drawer of the check. The exception asserted by the banks is found in § 3–405(1)(a) of the Uniform Commercial Code—Commercial Paper which provides:

"An indorsement by any person in the name of a named payee is effective if (a) an impostor by use of the mails or otherwise has induced the maker or drawer to issue the instrument to him or his confederate in the name of the payee; . . . .."

The lower court found and the Title Company does not dispute that an impostor appeared before McAllister and DiBenedetto, impersonated Mr. Jezemski, and, in their presence, signed Mr. Jezemski's name to the deed, bond and mortgage; that Mrs. Jezemski was a confederate of the impostor; that the drawer, Title Company, issued the check to Mrs. Jezemski naming her and Mr. Jezemski as payees; and that some person other than Mr. Jezemski indorsed his name on the check. In effect, the only argument made by the Title Company to prevent the applicability of Section 3–405(1)(a) is that the impostor, who admittedly played a part in the swindle, *did not "by the mails or otherwise" induce the Title Company* to issue the check within the meaning of Section 3–405(1)(a). The argument must fail.

Outside the Uniform Commercial Code, the impostor doctrine has taken many forms and been based on numerous theories, see Annotation 81 A.L.R.2d 1365 (1962), all of which, when applicable, place the loss on the "innocent" duped drawer of the check rather than the "innocent" duped drawee or payor. Although one form of the doctrine had existed in Pennsylvania for at least fifty-three years before the adoption of the Commercial Code, see Land Title and Trust Company v. Northwestern National Bank, 196 Pa. 230, 46 A. 420 (1900), no case has been found which decided whether or not the pre-Code doctrine would have applied to the instant factual situation—when the impostor, rather than communicating directly with the drawer, brings his impersonation to bear upon the drawer through the medium of the representations of third persons upon whom the drawer relies, in part, in issuing the check. But, regardless of the pre-Code form of the impostor doctrine and its applicability to the instant factual situation, the matter must be decided by statutory construction

2.   " 'Customer' means any person having an account with a bank . . . ." Id., § 4–104(e).

and application of the impostor doctrine as it now appears in Section 3–405(1)(a) of the Code.

Both the words of Section 3–405(1)(a) and the official Comment thereto leave no doubt that the impostor can induce the drawer to issue him or his confederate a check within the meaning of the section even though he does not carry out his impersonation before the very eyes of the drawer. Section 3–405(1)(a) says the inducement might be by "the mails or otherwise." The Comment elaborates:

"2. Subsection (1)(a) is new. It rejects decisions which distinguish between fact-to-face imposture and imposture by mail and hold that where the parties deal by mail the dominant intent of the drawer is to deal with the name rather than with the person so that the resulting instrument may be negotiated only by indorsement of the payee whose name has been taken in vain. The result of the distinction has been under some prior law, to throw the loss in the mail imposture forward to a subsequent holder or to the drawee. Since the drawer believes the two to be one and the same, the two intentions cannot be separated, and the 'dominant intent' is a fiction. The position here taken is that the loss, regardless of the type of fraud which the particular impostor has committed, should fall upon the drawer."

Moreover, the Legislature's use of the word "otherwise" and the Comment, which suggests that results should not turn upon "the type of fraud which the particular impostor committed," indicates that the Legislature did not intend to limit the applicability of the section to cases where the impostor deals directly with the drawer (face-to-face, mails, telephone, etc.). Naturally, the Legislature could not have predicted and expressly included all the ingenious schemes designed and carried out by impostors for the purpose of defrauding the makers or drawers of negotiable instruments. Something had to be left for the courts by way of statutory construction. For purposes of imposing the loss on one of two "innocent" parties, either the drawer who was defrauded or the drawee bank which payed out on a forged endorsement, we see no reason for distinguishing between the drawer who is duped by an impersonator communicating directly with him through the mails and a drawer who is duped by an impersonator communicating indirectly with him through third persons.[3] Thus,

3. The only judicial construction of the impostor provision of the Uniform Commercial Code that has come to our attention is that set forth by the dissenting minority in First State Bank of Wichita Falls v. Oak Cliff Savings & Loan Association, 387 S.W.2d 369 (Tex.1965). There the impostor did his impersonation before the officers of one bank upon which another bank relied when issuing its check to the impostor. There was no direct communication between the impostor and the drawer. The majority held that the case was not within the Texas version of the impostor doctrine. The majority's reason was that the maker had no intention "to pay the flesh and blood person who stood in [the first bank] and whom no official or employee of [the drawer] had ever seen . . . ." Id., p. 375. The Uniform Commercial Code was not adopted in Texas when the case was decided, and the majority made no mention of it. However, it is clear from the structure of § 3–405 and comment 2, quoted in the text, that the Code has rejected the rationale relied upon by the majority. Although not adopted by Tex-

both the language of the Code and common sense dictates that the drawer must suffer the loss in both instances.

The parties have argued at length respecting the effect that should be given to the "negligence" of the Title Company's settlement clerk. While ascertaining the negligence in each case used to play a significant role in the application of the impostor doctrine, see Annotation, 81 A.L.R.2d 1365, 1371–1372 (1962), Abel, The Impostor Payee, or Rhode Island Was Right, 1940 Wis.L.Rev. 362 (1940), such an approach is no longer warranted under the Uniform Commercial Code's version of the impostor doctrine. See Leary, Commercial Paper: Some Aspects of Article 3 of the Uniform Commercial Code, 48 Ky.L.J. 199, 222, fn. 54 (1960); Annotation, 81 A.L.R.2d 1365, 1372 (1962). On the other hand, the Code does include a separate provision, § 3–406, wherein the drawer's or maker's negligence is quite material to his right to recover. However, it is unnecessary to decide whether that section applies here to defeat the Title Company's recovery since recovery is precluded by reason of the applicability of § 3–405.

Judgment affirmed.

NOTE

Negligence and Impostors. Could the result in the Philadelphia Title Insurance case have been reached on the rationale of the Thompson Maple Products case, p. 301 supra? Could the result in the Thompson Maple Products case have been reached on the rationale of the Philadelphia Title Insurance case? Comment 2 to UCC 3–405 explains: " 'Impostor' refers to impersonation, and does not extend to a false representation that the party is the authorized agent of the payee. The maker or drawer who takes the precaution of making the instrument payable to the principal is entitled to have his indorsement." Why single out impersonation as opposed to other kinds of fraud? See Harbus, The Great Pretender—A Look at the Impostor Provision of The Uniform Commercial Code, 47 U.Cin.L.Rev. 385 (1978).

as, the minority would have applied the rule enunciated in the Code and in doing so would have construed it as we have here.

Part III

OTHER USES OF COMMERCIAL PAPER

Chapter 6

THE DRAFT IN THE DOCUMENTARY EXCHANGE

SECTION 1. THE BASIC TRANSACTION

Prefatory Note. This chapter deals with the use of the draft to facilitate the sale of goods. Many of the following cases raise issues that are similar to those already considered in connection with checks. However, the resolution of those issues is not always the same, because in large part of differences in the nature of the transactions involved. This chapter emphasizes the importance of a familiarity with the transaction as a prerequisite to an understanding of the law.

Most domestic sales, both to industrial buyers and ordinary consumers, are on open credit: the seller delivers to the buyer on faith that the buyer will pay later, say in 30, 60 or 90 days. The tremendous volume of domestic commercial credit is encouraged by the stability and size of most businesses, the highly organized channels for credit information, and the efficiency of shipment on open billing, which saves the trouble and expense in arranging a simultaneous exchange of goods for money; credit, of course, is attractive to buyers for their capital is enhanced by the possession and use of goods prior to payment.

Occasionally the seller will lack knowledge of or faith in the buyer's credit. In that event the seller may refuse to grant credit and insist upon an exchange of the goods for the price. It is the purpose of this introduction to explain how this is accomplished. For most modern commercial transactions are a far cry from the primitive but simple sale in which the buyer hands the bag of coins to the seller with one hand, grasping the purchase with the other. A specialized modern economy contemplates trade between parties physically remote from each other. Steel from Gary or Pittsburgh, tires from Akron, ball bearings from Philadelphia and commodities from a thousand other centers converge in a modern manufacturing operation.

340

Thereafter, the finished product moves from the manufacturing centers to points of distribution and use throughout the nation and in foreign countries. Where seller lacks trust, or information, with respect to buyer's credit, an equivalent to the primitive "cash on barrelhead" transaction can be arranged through the cooperation of both banks and carriers. These arrangements center around the handling of two important documents, drafts and bills of lading.

Bills of Lading. A bill of lading (originally, bill of "loading") is a document of title that a railroad or other carrier issues when goods are delivered to it for shipment. See UCC 1–201(6), (15). The Code rules governing it, like those governing its cousin, the warehouse receipt, are collected in Article 7—Warehouse Receipts, Bills of Lading and other Documents of Title. Some of these rules were considered in Part I of this book. It is important to realize, however, that bills of lading in exports and interstate shipments are still governed by the Federal Bills of Lading or Pomerene Act and not by the Code. See p. 4 supra. For our purposes, however, the differences will not often be crucial.

The bill of lading, in part, embodies a contract between the carrier and the shipper (often termed the *consignor*). In addition, control of the bill of lading can be used to control delivery of goods. This latter function makes it necessary to distinguish between the non-negotiable (or straight) and the negotiable bill of lading (see UCC 7–104). Under the non-negotiable bill of lading the carrier undertakes to deliver the goods to a stated person, e.g., "to Buyer & Co." Under the negotiable bill of lading, the carrier agrees to deliver to the order of a stated person, e.g., to "the order of Seller & Co." or occasionally to the bearer. The person to receive the goods may be someone other than Seller, to whom Seller may indorse and deliver the bill of lading.

One of the important practical consequences of shipping under a negotiable bill of lading is that the carrier will deliver the goods only to one who surrenders the bill of lading (see UCC 7–403, 7–404; Chapter 2, Section 3(A), supra.[1] See the provision on the front of the negotiable bill, p. 348 infra: "The surrender of this Original ORDER Bill of Lading properly indorsed shall be required before the delivery of the property." If the bill of lading runs to the order of Seller and Seller indorses in blank, the goods are then deliverable to the bearer of the document (see UCC 7–501), and control over delivery is exercised by possession of the bill of lading. Possession of a non-negotiable bill of lading naming Buyer as consignee does not control delivery of the goods. Under a non-negotiable bill the railroad promises to deliver to Buyer & Co. The railroad can perform that contract by delivering to the named person; Buyer need not present the bill of lading.

---

1. If a buyer represents to the railroad that the order bill of lading has been lost or temporarily delayed, the railroad will deliver the goods on the receipt of indemnity, by cash or a bond, protecting the railroad against the risk of liability to the seller or to some third person who might purchase the bill of lading.

If Seller wants to be sure of being paid before Buyer gets the goods, Seller may use a negotiable bill of lading, consign the shipment to the order of Seller, and keep control of the goods by holding the bill of lading until Buyer pays the cash; when Buyer hands Seller's agent the money, Seller's agent will indorse and deliver the bill of lading to Buyer. At that point Buyer can take the bill of lading to the railroad and get the goods.

Drafts. Instead of taking the bill of lading personally to Buyer, it will usually be more convenient for Seller to arrange through his local bank to send it to a bank in Buyer's city that will act for Seller in holding it until Buyer pays. To aid and channel the flow of money the parties will employ a draft. Seller draws the draft on Buyer for the amount due Seller. See the form on page 346 infra.

The function of the draft can readily be grasped by comparing it to a check since a check is, after all, a form of draft (see UCC 3–104). While the check is drawn on a bank, the draft in sales transactions is ordinarily drawn on the buyer. The seller who draws a draft on a buyer corresponds to the depositor who draws the check. The bank owes the depositor as the result of deposits in his account; the buyer owes the seller because of the purchase of goods. The check authorizes the bank to satisfy its debt to the depositor by paying some third person; the seller's draft authorizes the buyer to discharge his debt for the goods by paying a bank which represents the seller in presenting the shipping documents.

In the usual documentary transaction, Seller will order Buyer to pay "on sight"; Buyer is asked to pay when the draft is presented to him (UCC 3–108). The situation in which a bank acting for Seller holds an order bill of lading until Buyer pays a sight draft is the transaction often referred to as "sight draft against order bill of lading."

The Transaction. Assume a sale by Seller & Co. of Sellersville, New York, to Buyer & Co. of Buyersville, California under terms including payment by "sight draft against order bill of lading." Seller places the goods in the hands of the carrier and receives the original of a negotiable bill of lading made out to his order. Seller indorses the bill in blank and gives it to his bank, Sellersville Bank, attached to a sight draft, drawn by Seller on Buyer. The draft may be payable to the order of Sellersville Bank, or to the order of Seller and indorsed to Sellersville Bank. Seller will also usually attach a letter with instructions, an invoice, and such other documents as an insurance policy or an inspection certificate when required by his contract with Buyer.

Sellersville Bank will usually take the draft for collection as Seller's agent. It may make a small charge for this service. Sellersville Bank will then send the draft, with documents attached, to a bank in Buyersville, using much the same routing as for a check. The process is described in the following excerpt. The cases in the next two sections show the consequences of departures from this standard transaction.

————

FARNSWORTH, DOCUMENTARY DRAFTS, UNDER THE UNIFORM COMMERCIAL CODE, 22 Bus.Law. 479, 482–84 (1967).[2] "The bank, known as a 'collecting bank' (UCC 4–105(d)) and more specifically as the 'depositary bank' (UCC 4–105(a)), is required to 'present or send the draft and accompanying documents for presentment' (UCC 4–501), which it will normally do by forwarding them through 'customary banking channels' (UCC 2–308(c), 2–503(5)(b)). Most important, it will treat the draft as a 'collection' item rather than a 'cash' item. Checks, the most common items handled by banks, are dealt with in bulk as 'cash' items on the assumption that they will be honored in the overwhelming majority of cases; provisional credits are entered immediately for a check at all stages of the collection process and automatically become final without further action upon payment by the drawee bank (UCC 4–213(2)). Documentary drafts, on the other hand, are handled as 'collection' items and dealt with individually, rather than in bulk, and since no assumption is made that they will be honored, no credits, not even provisional credits, are given until the item has been paid by the buyer. Ultimately the draft will reach the 'presenting' bank (UCC 4–105(e)), which will undertake to present the documentary draft to the buyer.

"The presenting bank will know the identity and location of the buyer, who will be indicated on the bill of lading as the person to be notified of the arrival of the goods (cf. UCC 7–501(6)) as well as on the draft as the drawee. Unless otherwise instructed, the bank may make presentment to the buyer by sending him a written notice that it holds the item (UCC 4–210(1); see also UCC 2–503(1), (5) and Comment 3 to UCC 2–308). In the event that the buyer does not honor the draft before the close of business on the third banking day after the notice was sent, the bank may treat it as dishonored (UCC 4–210(2)). The buyer may, however, within this time require exhibition of the draft and documents by the bank so that he can determine whether it is properly payable (UCC 4–210, 3–505(1)(a), 3–506(2)). If direct presentment is made to the buyer, instead of presentment by notice, it must be made at the place specified in the draft, or if there be none at his place of business or residence (UCC 3–504(2)(c)), and he then has until the close of business on that day to pay (UCC 3–506(2)). Absent contrary instructions, a collecting bank may have an additional day 'in a good faith effort to secure payment'; it may also be excused for delay caused by circumstances beyond its control (UCC 4–108) . . .

"Since the draft under discussion is a sight draft, the buyer is called upon to pay, rather than to accept it, before he gets the docu-

2. Copyright 1967 by The Business
Lawyer and reproduced with permission.

ments. Only when the draft is payable more than three days after presentment may the presenting bank release the documents against the buyer's acceptance rather than his payment (UCC 2–514, 4–503(a)). Payment may be easily effected if the buyer offers cash or if the presenting bank happens to be one in which the buyer has an account. Short of this, the Code permits the presenting bank to take a cashier's check (a check drawn by a bank on itself), a certified check (a check accepted by the bank on which it has been drawn), or other bank check or obligation. Should the buyer tender his personal check on another bank, the presenting bank may hold the documents while it gets the check certified. Should it release the documents against his personal check, it will be liable to the seller for any loss caused by the dishonor of the check. The proceeds received from the buyer are then remitted by the presenting bank through banking channels.

"When the buyer honors the draft, he receives the bill of lading. When the goods arrive, he is notified by the carrier and surrenders the bill of lading in return for the goods. At this point the buyer will be able to inspect the goods. Should he find them to be defective, his only recourse will ordinarily be to journey to the seller's jurisdiction and there litigate the issues of breach and damages. Other possible remedies will be discussed presently.

"If the buyer does not pay the draft as outlined earlier, the presenting bank must treat it as dishonored. In this event the presenting bank 'must use diligence and good faith to ascertain the reason for dishonor, must notify its transferor of the dishonor and of the results of its effort to ascertain the reasons therefor and must request instructions' (UCC 4–503(b)). It need not, however, return the draft and documents unless so instructed (UCC 4–202(1)(b)). When the notice gets back to the depositary bank, which first took the draft for collection, it must 'seasonably notify its customer' of the dishonor (UCC 4–501). [The presenting bank] 'is under no obligation with respect to goods represented by the documents except to follow any reasonable instructions seasonably received; it has a right to re- imbursement for any expense incurred in following instructions and to payment of or indemnity for such expenses' (UCC 4–503). If it has seasonably requested instructions after dishonor but has not received them in a reasonable time, it may 'store, sell or otherwise deal with the goods in any reasonable manner' (UCC 4–504(1)), and has a lien, or security interest, on the goods or their proceeds for reasonable expenses incurred in doing so (UCC 4–504(2)). If, for example, it was commercially reasonable to put the goods in storage pending receipt of requested instructions, the presenting bank would be protected if it did so even though the requested instructions were later received (Comment to UCC 4–504). The Code seems, however, to make a re- quest for instructions and a failure to receive them within a reasona- ble time prerequisites to the exercise of initiative by the presenting bank in dealing with the goods."

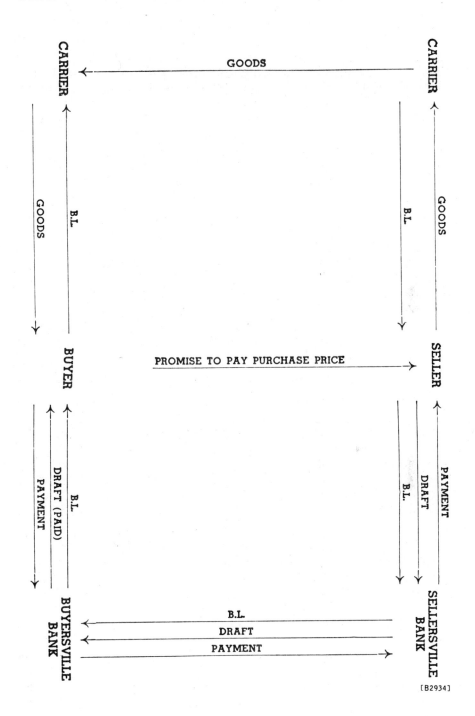

[B2934]

$5,000.00

January 15   19 85

At Sight

Pay to the

Order of   Seller & Co.

Five Thousand and 00/100 - - - - - - - - - - - - - - - - - - Dollars

Value Received and charge same to account of

To   Buyer & Co.

Address   1 Church Street

       Byersville, Cal.

SELLER & CO.

S. L. Seller
Pres.

809/00 (12-54)

NO PROTEST
Take this off before Presenting

[B2882]

SIGHT DRAFT

Maker or Drawee

BUYER & COMPANY

Please quote our number **218 - 39009**

Amount	$5,000.00
Other Charges	
ITC Charges	
Net Amount	

Documents

O/B/L

Customer's Number | Customer's Date | Due

SIGHT

We enclose for: ⊗ Acceptance and/or collection   ◯ Acceptance (Instructions covering this item are marked with an "X") and return

Date Sent 1/15

Advise Dishonor (give reasons) by

Protest for: ◯ Non-Payment ◯ Non-Acceptance   No protest for ◯ Non-Payment ◯ Non-Acceptance

◯ Remit by prime bankers check on N.Y.   ◯ Remit by telegraphic transfer

◯ Wire   ◯ Air Mail

◯ Hold for arrival if requested   ◯ All charges for A/C of drawee   ◯ Waive Charges

⊗ Protest for Non-Payment

Special Instructions

Mail To

BUYERSVILLE BANK
BUYERSVILLE, CALIFORNIA

Domestic Collection Dept.

Irving Trust Company
One Wall Street
New York, N.Y. 10015

Irving Trust

▲ Please address all correspondence to

This collection is subject to the uniform rules for collections
International Chamber of Commerce Publication No. 322.

COLLECTION LETTER

Conditions Under Which The Within Described Item Is Handled

For the purpose of presenting and/or collecting any item, we may forward the same to any agent of our own selection who may collect the item through one or more sub-agents selected by it or by any sub-agents; and our liability is limited to due diligence in selecting those to whom the items are forwarded by us. We may, however, without liability on our part, forward any item for presentation and/or collection directly to the bank where it is payable; and we, or any collecting agent or sub-agent, may accept a bank draft in payment of any item. We shall not be responsible for loss of any kind due to the acts or negligence of any such agents or sub-agents, or for loss in or through the mails, or for any failure to present, demand or collect, or protest or give notice of protest or dishonor of any item; and we are authorized to charge back the amount of any items (whether or not the items themselves can be returned) for which payment in cash has not actually been received by us.

[D625]

FD 2534 R4 1-76
PRINTED IN USA

(Uniform Domestic Order Bill of Lading, adopted by Carriers in Official, Southern, Western and Illinois Classification territories, March 15, 1922, as amended August 1, 1930, June 15, 1941, September 21, 1944, January 9, 1945, and July 14, 1949.)

UNIFORM ORDER BILL OF LADING — ORIGINAL

RECEIVED, subject to the classifications and tariffs in effect on the date of the issue of this Bill of Lading, the property described below, in apparent good order, except as noted (contents and condition of contents of packages unknown), marked, consigned, and destined as indicated below, which said company (the word company being understood throughout this contract as meaning any person or corporation in possession of the property under the contract) agrees to carry to its usual place of delivery at said destination, if on its own road or its own water line, otherwise to deliver to another carrier on the route to said destination. It is mutually agreed, as to each carrier of all or any of said property over all or any portion of said route to destination, and as to each party at any time interested in all or any of said property, that every service to be performed hereunder shall be subject to all the conditions not prohibited by law, whether printed or written, herein contained, including the conditions on back hereof, which are hereby agreed to by the shipper and accepted for himself and his assigns.
The surrender of this Original ORDER Bill of Lading properly indorsed shall be required before the delivery of the property. Inspection of property covered by this bill of lading will not be permitted unless provided by law or unless permission is indorsed on this original bill of lading or given in writing by the shipper.

190 CONSOLIDATED RAIL CORPORATION 190

BILL OF LADING DATE	BILL OF LADING NO.	INVOICE NO.	CUSTOMER NO.
2/6/85	102	A - 21	32 - B

CONSIGNED TO Seller & Co.

ORDER OF

NOTIFY	DESTINATION	STATE OF	COUNTY OF
	Buyersville, California		

WHEN SHIPPER IN THE UNITED STATES EXECUTES NO-RECOURSE CLAUSE OF SECT. 7 OF BILL OF LADING →

YES CHECK (x) [ ]

RECEIVED $_____
TO APPLY AS PREPAY-
MENT OF CHARGES ON
THE PROPERTY DE-
SCRIBED HEREON

SHIPPER _____

FULL NAME OF SHIPPER _____ Seller & Co.

ORIGIN	STATE	WEIGHED AT
		GROSS
		TARE
		ALLOWANCE

CAR INITIAL	CAR NUMBER	TRAILER INITIALS	TRAILER NUMBER	L/E	LEN	TY	L/E	LEN	TY	TRAILER INITIALS	TRAILER NUMBER	LENGTH/CAPACITY OF CAR ORDERED	FURNISHED	WEIGHT IN TONS GROSS	TARE	WAYBILL DATE	WAYBILL NO.

STOP THIS CAR

CONSIGNEE AND ADDRESS AT STOP

AT _____ FOR _____

AT _____ FOR _____

AT _____ FOR _____

1

AT

STATE OF   COUNTY OF

1 Church St., Buyersville, California

ROUTE (FOR SHIPPER'S USE ONLY)   DELIVERY CARRIER

PC – C&NW – UP – SP   SP

AGENT OR CASHIER

NET

PER

IF CHARGES ARE TO BE PREPAID WRITE OR STAMP HERE:

"TO BE PREPAID"

Subject to Section 7 of Conditions, if the shipment is to be delivered to the consignee without recourse on the consignor, the consignor shall sign the following statement: The carrier shall not make delivery of this shipment without payment of freight and all other lawful charges.

Signature of Consignor

(THE SIGNATURE HERE ACKNOWLEDGES ONLY THE AMOUNT PREPAID)

Note—Where the rate is dependent upon value, shippers are required to state specifically in writing the agreed or declared value of the property. The agreed or declared value of the property is hereby specifically stated by the shipper to be not exceeding   PER

CHARGES ADVANCED

$

"If the shipment moves between two ports by a carrier by water, the law requires that the bill of lading shall state whether it is "carrier's or shipper's weight."

SHIPPER'S SPECIAL INSTRUCTIONS (INCLUDE ICING, VENTILATION, HEATING, MILLING, WEIGHING, ETC.)

NO. PKGS.	DESCRIPTION OF ARTICLES, SPECIAL MARKS AND EXCEPTIONS	COMMODITY CODE NO.	*)	WEIGHT (SUBJECT TO COR.)	RATE	FREIGHT	ADVANCES	PREPAID
50 ctns.	Bags, paper			1,000 lbs.	$4.60	$46.00		$46.00

SHIPPER   Seller & Co.   PER AGENT

PERMANENT POST OFFICE ADDRESS OF SHIPPER   1 Main Street, Sellersville, N.Y.   PER

[D626]

NEGOTIABLE BILL OF LADING
[Printed on yellow paper; front]

ENDORSEMENTS

CONTRACT TERMS AND CONDITIONS

Sec. 1. (a) The carrier or party in possession of any of the property herein described shall be liable as at common law for any loss thereof or damage thereto, except as hereinafter provided.

NEGOTIABLE BILL OF LADING
[*Reverse*]

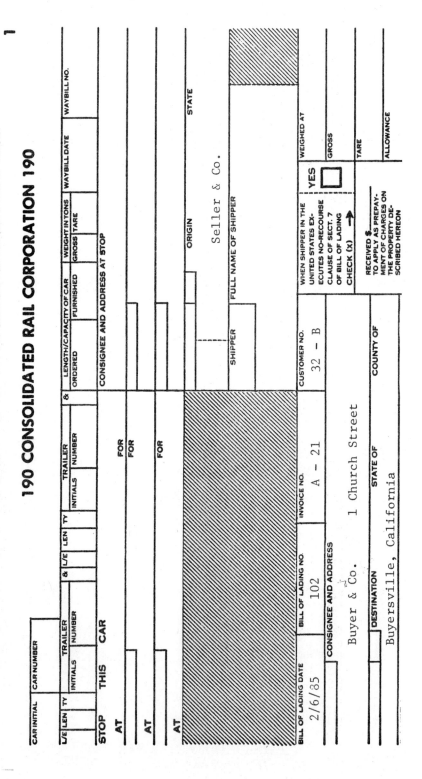

ROUTE (FOR SHIPPER'S USE ONLY)

PC – C&NW – UP – SP

DELIVERY CARRIER

SP

Subject to Section 7 of Conditions, if the shipment is to be delivered to the consignee without recourse on the consignor, the consignor shall sign the following statement. The carrier shall not make delivery of this shipment without payment of freight and all other lawful charges.

Signature of Consignor

Note—Where the rate is dependent upon value, shippers are required to state specifically in writing the agreed or declared value of the property. The agreed or declared value of the property is hereby specifically stated by the shipper to be not exceeding

PER

"If the shipment moves between two ports by a carrier by water, the law requires that the bill of lading shall state whether it is "carrier's or shipper's weight."

SHIPPERS SPECIAL INSTRUCTIONS (INCLUDE ICING, VENTILATION, HEATING, MILLING, WEIGHING, ETC.)

AGENT OR CASHIER

PER

(THE SIGNATURE HERE ACKNOWLEDGES ONLY THE AMOUNT PREPAID)

CHARGES ADVANCED

$

NET

IF CHARGES ARE TO BE PREPAID WRITE OR STAMP HERE:

"TO BE PREPAID"

NO. PKGS.	DESCRIPTION OF ARTICLES, SPECIAL MARKS AND EXCEPTIONS	COMMODITY CODE NO	*	WEIGHT (SUBJECT TO COR)	RATE	FREIGHT	ADVANCES	PREPAID
50 ctns.	Bags, paper			1,000 lbs.	$4.60	$46.00		$46.00

THIS IS TO CERTIFY THAT THE ABOVE NAMED MATERIALS ARE PROPERLY CLASSIFIED, DESCRIBED, PACKAGED, MARKED AND LABELED, AND ARE IN PROPER CONDITION FOR TRANSPORTATION, ACCORDING TO THE APPLICABLE REGULATIONS OF THE DEPARTMENT OF TRANSPORTATION.

SIGNED

PER AGENT

SHIPPER Seller & Co.   PER AGENT   PER

PERMANENT POST OFFICE ADDRESS OF SHIPPER 1 Main Street, Sellersville, N.Y.

NON–NEGOTIABLE BILL OF LADING
[Printed on white paper; front]

CONTRACT TERMS AND CONDITIONS

Sec. 1. (a) The carrier or party in possession of any of the property herein described shall be liable as at common law for any loss thereof or damage thereto, except as hereinafter provided.

(b) No carrier or party in possession of all or any of the property herein described shall be liable for any loss thereof or damage thereto or delay caused by the act of God, the public enemy, the authority of law, or the act or default of the shipper or owner, or for natural shrinkage. The carrier's liability shall be that of warehouseman, only, for loss, damage, or delay caused by fire occurring after the expiration of the free time allowed by tariffs lawfully on file (such free time to be computed as herein provided) after notice of the arrival of the property at destination or at the port of export (if intended for export) has been duly sent or given, and after placement of the property for delivery at destination, or tender of delivery of the property to the party entitled to receive it, has been made. Except in case of negligence of the carrier or party in possession (and the burden to prove freedom from such negligence shall be on the carrier or party in possession), the carrier or party in possession shall not be liable for loss, damage, or delay occurring while the property is stopped and held in transit upon the request of the shipper, owner, or party entitled to make such request, or resulting from a defect or vice in the property, or for country damage to cotton, or from riots or strikes.

(c) In case of quarantine the property may be discharged at risk and expense of owners into quarantine depot or elsewhere, as required by quarantine regulations or authorities, or for the carrier's dispatch at nearest available point in carrier's judgment, and in any such case carrier's responsibility shall cease when property is so discharged, or property may be returned by carrier at owner's expense to shipping point, earning freight both ways. Quarantine expense of whatever nature or kind upon or in respect to property shall be borne by the owner of the property or by the lien thereon. The carrier shall not be liable for loss or damage occasioned by fumigation or disinfection or other acts required or done by quarantine regulations or authorities even though the same may have been done by carrier's officers, agents, or employees, nor for detention, loss, or damage of any kind occasioned by quarantine or the enforcement thereof. No carrier shall be liable, except in case of negligence, for any mistake or inaccuracy in any information furnished by the carrier, its agents, or officers, as to quarantine laws or regulations. The shipper shall hold the carriers harmless from any expense they may incur, or damages they may be required to pay, by reason of the introduction of the property covered by this contract into any place against the quarantine laws or regulations in effect at such place.

Sec. 2. (a) No carrier is bound to transport said property by any particular train or vessel, or in time for any particular market or otherwise than with reasonable dispatch. Every carrier shall have the right in case of physical necessity to forward said property by any carrier or route between the point of shipment and the point of destination. In all cases not prohibited by law, where a lower value than actual value has been represented in writing by the shipper or has been agreed upon in writing as the released value of the property as determined by the classification or tariffs upon which the rate is based, such lower value plus freight charges if paid shall be the maximum amount to be recovered, whether or not such loss or damage occurs from negligence.

(b) As a condition precedent to recovery, claims must be filed in writing with the receiving or delivering carrier, or carrier issuing this bill of lading, or carrier on whose line the loss, damage, injury, or delay occurred, within nine months after delivery of the property (or, in case of export traffic, within nine months after delivery at port of export), or in case of failure to make delivery, then within nine months after a reasonable time for delivery has elapsed; and suits shall be instituted against any carrier only within two years and one day from the day when notice in writing is given by the carrier to the claimant that the carrier has disallowed the claim or any part or parts thereof specified in the notice. Where claims are not filed or suits are not instituted thereon in accordance with the foregoing provisions, no carrier hereunder shall be liable, and such claims will not be paid.

(c) Any carrier or party liable on account of loss of or damage to any of said property shall have the full benefit of any insurance that may have been effected upon or on account of said property, so far as this shall not avoid the policies or contracts of insurance: *Provided,* That the carrier reimburse the claimant for the premium paid thereon.

Sec. 3. Except where such service is required as the result of carrier's negligence, all property shall be subject to necessary cooperage and baling at owner's cost. Each carrier over whose route cotton or cotton linters is to be transported hereunder shall have the privilege, at its own cost and risk, of compressing the same for greater convenience in handling or forwarding, and shall not be held responsible for deviation or unavoidable delays in procuring such compression. Grain in bulk consigned to a point where there is a railroad, public or licensed elevator, may (unless otherwise expressly noted herein, and then if it is not promptly unloaded) be there delivered and placed with other grain of the same kind and grade without respect to ownership (and prompt notice thereof shall be given to the consignor), and if so delivered shall be subject to a lien for elevator charges in addition to all other charges hereunder.

Sec. 4. (a) Property not removed by the party entitled to receive it within the free time allowed by tariffs, lawfully on file (such free time to be computed as therein provided), after notice of the arrival of the property at destination or at the port of export (if intended for export) has been duly sent or given, and after placement of the property for delivery at destination, has been made, may be kept in vessel, car, depot, warehouse or place of delivery of the carrier, subject to the tariff charge for storage and to carrier's responsibility as warehouseman, only, or at the option of the carrier, may be removed to and stored in a public or licensed warehouse at the place of delivery or other available place, at the cost of the owner, and there held without liability on the part of the carrier, and subject to a lien for all freight and other lawful charges, including a reasonable charge for storage.

(b) Where nonperishable property, which has been transported to destination hereunder is refused by consignee or the party entitled to receive it, or said consignee or party entitled to receive it fails to receive it within 15 days after notice of arrival shall have been duly sent or given, the carrier may sell the same at public auction to the highest bidder, at such place as may be designated by the carrier: *Provided,* That the carrier shall have first mailed, sent, or given to the consignor notice that the property has been refused or remains unclaimed, as the case may be, and that it will be subject to sale under the terms of the bill of lading if disposition be not arranged for, and shall have published notice containing a description of the property, the name of the party to whom consigned, or, if shipped order notify, the name of the party to be notified, and the time and place of sale; such publication to be once a week for two successive weeks, in a newspaper of general circulation at the place of sale or nearest place where such newspaper is published: *Provided,* That 30 days shall have elapsed before publication of notice of sale after said notice that the property was refused or remains unclaimed was mailed, sent, or given.

(c) Where perishable property, which has been transported hereunder to destination is refused by consignee or party entitled to receive it, or said consignee or party entitled to receive it shall fail to receive it promptly, the carrier may, in its discretion, to prevent deterioration or further deterioration, sell the same to the best advantage at private or public sale: *Provided,* That if time serves for notification to the consignor or owner of the refusal of the property or the failure to receive it and request for disposition of the property, such notification shall be given, in such manner as the exercise of due diligence requires, before the property is sold.

(d) Where the procedure provided for in the two paragraphs last preceding is not possible, it is agreed that nothing contained in said paragraphs shall be construed to abridge the right of the carrier at its option to sell the property under such circumstances and in such manner as may be authorized by law.

(e) The proceeds of any sale made under this section shall be applied by the carrier to the payment of freight, demurrage, storage, and any other lawful charges and the expense of notice, advertisement, sale, and other necessary expense and of caring for and maintaining the property, if proper care of the same requires special expense, and should there be a balance it shall be paid to the owner of the property sold hereunder.

(f) Property destined to or taken from a station, wharf, or landing at which there is no regularly appointed freight agent shall be entirely at risk of owner after unloaded from cars or vessels or until loaded into cars or vessels, and, except in case of carrier's negligence, when received from or delivered to such stations, wharves, or landings shall be at owner's risk until the cars are attached to and after they are detached from locomotive or train or until loaded into and after unloaded from vessels.

Sec. 5. No carrier hereunder will carry or be liable in any way for any documents, specie, or for any articles of extraordinary value not specifically rated in the published classifications or tariffs unless a special agreement to do so and a stipulated value of the articles are indorsed hereon.

Sec. 6. Every party, whether principal or agent, shipping explosives or dangerous goods, without previous full written disclosure to the carrier of their nature, shall be liable for and indemnify the carrier against all loss or damage caused by such goods, and such goods may be warehoused at owner's risk and expense or destroyed without compensation.

Sec. 7. The owner or consignee shall pay the freight and average, if any, and all other lawful charges accruing on said property; but, except in those instances where it may lawfully be authorized to do so, no carrier by railroad shall deliver or relinquish possession at destination of the property covered by this bill of lading until all tariff rates and charges thereon have been paid. The consignor shall be liable for the freight and all other lawful charges, except that if the consignor stipulates, by signature, in the space provided for that purpose on the face of this bill of lading that the carrier shall not make delivery without requiring payment of such charges and the carrier, contrary to such stipulation, shall make delivery without requiring such payment, the consignor (except as hereinafter provided) shall not be liable for such charges. **Provided**, that, where the carrier has been instructed by the shipper or consignor to deliver said property to a consignee other than the shipper or consignor, such consignee shall not be legally liable for transportation charges in respect of the transportation of said property (beyond those billed against him at the time of delivery for which he is otherwise liable) which may be found to be due after the property has been delivered to him, if the consignee (a) is an agent only and has no beneficial title in said property, and (b) prior to delivery of said property has notified the delivering carrier in writing of the fact of such agency and absence of beneficial title, and, in the case of a shipment reconsigned or diverted to a point other than that specified in the original bill of lading, has also notified the delivering carrier in writing of the name and address of the beneficial owner of said property; and, in such cases the shipper or consignor, or, in the case of a shipment so reconsigned or diverted, the beneficial owner, shall be liable for such additional charges. If the consignee has given to the carrier erroneous information as to who the beneficial owner is, such consignee shall himself be liable for such additional charges. On shipments reconsigned or diverted by an agent who has furnished the carrier in the reconsignment or diversion order with a notice of agency and the proper name and address of the beneficial owner, and where such shipments are refused or abandoned at ultimate destination, the said beneficial owner shall be liable for all legally applicable charges in connection therewith. If the reconsignor or diverter has given to the carrier erroneous information as to who the beneficial owner is, such reconsignor or diverter shall himself be liable for all such charges.

If a shipper or consignor of a shipment of property (other than a prepaid shipment) is also the consignee named in the bill of lading and, prior to the time of delivery, notifies, in writing, a delivering carrier by railroad (a) to deliver such property at destination to another party, (b) that such party is the beneficial owner of such property, and (c) that delivery is to be made to such party only upon payment of all transportation charges in respect of the transportation of such property, and delivery is made by the carrier to such party without such payment, such shipper or consignor shall not be liable (as shipper, consignor, consignee, or otherwise) for such transportation charges but the party to whom delivery is so made shall in any event be liable for transportation charges billed against the property at the time of such delivery, and also for any additional charges which may be found to be due after delivery of the property, except that if such party prior to such delivery has notified in writing the delivering carrier that he is not the beneficial owner of the property, and has given in writing to such delivering carrier the name and address of such beneficial owner, such party shall not be liable for any additional charges which may be found to be due after delivery of the property; but if the party to whom delivery is made has given to the carrier erroneous information as to the beneficial owner, such party shall nevertheless be liable for such additional charges. If the shipper or consignor has given to the delivering carrier erroneous information as to who the beneficial owner is, such shipper or consignor shall himself be liable for such transportation charges, notwithstanding the foregoing provisions of this paragraph and irrespective of any provisions to the contrary in the bill of lading or in the contract of transportation under which the shipment was made. The term "delivering carrier" means the line-haul carrier making ultimate delivery.

Nothing herein shall limit the right of the carrier to require at time of shipment the prepayment or guarantee of the charges. If upon inspection it is ascertained that the articles shipped are not those described in this bill of lading, the freight charges must be paid upon the articles actually shipped.

Where delivery is made by a common carrier by water the foregoing provisions of this section shall apply, except as may be inconsistent with Part III of the Interstate Commerce Act.

Sec. 8. If this bill of lading is issued on the order of the shipper, or his agent, in exchange or in substitution for another bill of lading, the shipper's signature to the prior bill of lading as to the statement of value or otherwise, or election of common law or bill of lading liability, in or in connection with such prior bill of lading, shall be considered a part of this bill of lading as fully as if the same were written or made in or in connection with this bill of lading.

Sec. 9. (a) If all or any part of said property is carried by water over any part of said route, and loss, damage or injury to said property occurs while the same is in the custody of a carrier by water the liability of such carrier shall be determined by the bill of lading of the carrier by water (this bill of lading being such bill of lading if the property is transported by such water carrier thereunder) and by and under the laws and regulations applicable to transportation by water. Such water carriage shall be performed subject to all the terms and provisions of, and all the exemptions from liability contained in the Act of the Congress of the United States, approved on February 13, 1893, and entitled "An act relating to the navigation of vessels, etc.," and of other statutes of the United States according carriers by water the protection of limited liability, as well as the following subdivisions of this section; and to the conditions contained in this bill of lading not inconsistent with this section, when this bill of lading becomes the bill of lading of the carrier by water.

(b) No such carrier by water shall be liable for any loss or damage resulting from any fire happening to or on board the vessel, or from explosion, bursting of boilers or breakage of shafts, unless caused by the design or neglect of such carrier.

(c) If the owner shall have exercised due diligence in making the vessel in all respects seaworthy and properly manned, equipped, and supplied, no such carrier shall be liable for any loss or damage resulting from the perils of the lakes, seas, or other waters, or from latent defects in hull, machinery, or appurtenances whether existing prior to, at the time of, or after sailing, or from collision, stranding, or other accidents of navigation, or from prolongation of the voyage. And, when for any reason it is necessary, any vessel carrying any or all of the property herein described shall be at liberty to call at any port or ports, in or out of the customary route, to tow and be towed, to transfer, trans-ship, or lighter, to load and discharge goods at any time, to assist vessels in distress, to deviate for the purpose of saving life or property, and for docking and repairs. Except in case of negligence such carrier shall not be responsible for any loss or damage to property if it be necessary or is usual to carry the same upon deck.

(d) General Average shall be payable according to the York-Antwerp Rules of 1924, Sections 1 to 15, inclusive, and Sections 17 to 22, inclusive, and as to matters not covered thereby according to the laws and usages of the Port of New York. If the owners shall have exercised due diligence to make the vessel in all respects seaworthy and properly manned, equipped and supplied, it is hereby agreed that in case of danger, damage or disaster resulting from faults or errors in navigation, or in the management of the vessel, or from any latent or other defects in the vessel, her machinery or appurtenances, or from unseaworthiness, whether existing at the time of shipment or at the beginning of the voyage (provided the latent or other defects or the unseaworthiness was not discoverable by the exercise of due diligence), the shippers, consignees and/or owners of the cargo shall nevertheless pay salvage and any special charges incurred in respect of the cargo, and shall contribute with the shipowner in general average to the payment of any sacrifices, losses or expenses of a general average nature that may be made or incurred for the common benefit or to relieve the adventure from any common peril.

(e) If the property is being carried under a tariff which provides that any carrier or carriers party thereto shall be liable for loss from perils of the sea, then as to such carrier or carriers the provisions of this section shall be modified in accordance with the tariff provisions, which shall be regarded as incorporated into the conditions of this bill of lading.

(f) The term "water carriage" in this section shall not be construed as including lighterage in or across rivers, harbors, or lakes, when performed by or on behalf of rail carriers.

Sec. 10. Any alteration, addition, or erasure in this bill of lading which shall be made without the special notation hereon of the agent of the carrier issuing this bill of lading, shall be without effect, and this bill of lading shall be enforceable according to its original tenor.

EFFECTIVE JUNE 15, 1941 [D627]

NON-NEGOTIABLE BILL OF LADING
[Reverse]

SECTION 2. PROTECTION OF THE SELLER

Prefatory Note. The materials in this Section are intended to give an appreciation of the legal protection afforded the seller through the use of a documentary exchange. Consider particularly the legal consequences of a failure by any of the parties involved in the transaction to follow the usual procedure described above.

Problem 1. Seller & Co. sold goods to Buyer & Co. under terms including payment by "sight draft against order bill of lading." Seller & Co. placed the goods in the hands of the carrier, received a negotiable bill of lading "to the order of Seller & Co.," indorsed it in blank, and forwarded the bill, with a sight draft on Buyer & Co. attached, through Sellersville Bank to Buyer & Co.

(a) What rights has Seller & Co. if Buyer & Co. refuses to pay the draft when it is presented, and therefore does not obtain the bill of lading, but gets possession of the goods from the carrier without surrendering the bill of lading to it? See UCC 2–507, 7–403; Refrigerated Transport Co. v. Hernando Packing Co., infra.

(b) What rights has Seller & Co. if Buyersville Bank, the presenting bank, surrenders the bill of lading to Buyer & Co. on receipt of the personal uncertified check of Buyer & Co. on Tradesman's Bank and Buyer & Co. stops payment on the check but takes possession of the goods? See UCC 4–103(5), 4–202, 4–211(1); Note 3, p. 361 infra.

(c) What rights has Seller & Co. if Buyersville Bank surrenders the bill of lading on receipt of the personal check of Buyer & Co. on Tradesman's Bank certified by that bank, and Buyer & Co. then makes an adverse claim to that check pursuant to UCC 3–603?

Problem 2. Seller & Co. asks whether it would not be simpler for it in such a transaction to obtain a negotiable bill of lading to the order of Buyer & Co., which it would not have to indorse. What answer would you give?

Problem 3. A seller may also control delivery of goods by shipping under a straight bill of lading that names seller as consignee. Under this bill of lading the railroad will deliver to a third person only if the seller thereafter so instructs the railroad. Consequently, seller can ship to buyer's city under a straight bill of lading that names seller as consignee; when buyer pays, seller can instruct the railroad to deliver to buyer. Seller & Co. asks whether it would not be desirable to use this method of control. What answer would you give?

Could Buyer & Co. object to this method? Would Buyer & Co. be assured of delivery when it paid? See UCC 2–507(1).

REFRIGERATED TRANSPORT CO v. HERNANDO PACKING CO.

Supreme Court of Tennessee, 1976.
544 S.W.2d 613.

OPINION

HENRY, JUSTICE.

This controversy between a consignor and a common carrier of property involves the carrier's liability for misdelivery of cargo transported under a straight bill of lading. The trial court found the issues against the carrier and we conclude that he reached the correct conclusion.

I.

On January 3, 1975, Hernando Packing Company, Inc. of Memphis, shipped via Refrigerated Transport Company, Inc., a truck load of frozen meat consigned as follows:

[T]o BROWARD COLD STORAGE (acct. of J&A Trading Co.) 3220 S.W. 2nd Avenue . . . Fort Lauderdale, Florida.

Broward is a public warehouse.

Prior to making this shipment Hernando had received a call from an individual who identified himself as *Al Hark* and held himself out to be a representative of J&A Trading Company. In point of fact he had no connection with J&A Trading Company and that company had gone out of business. Hernando had never done business with Al Hark, but on one prior occasion, had shipped to J&A Trading Company pursuant to a transaction with *Joseph Hark*, its then representative and owner, and father of Al Hark.

It is fairly inferable from the record that this unfamiliarity with Al Hark prompted the precaution of making the shipment to Broward, a public warehouse, for the account of J&A. However, the record is not specific in this regard and the shipment may have been made thusly as a matter of custom in the business or trade.

On January 6, 1975, upon the arrival of Refrigerated's truck in Fort Lauderdale, it was met *across the street from Broward* by Al Hark, but within sight of Broward's manager. Without the knowledge of Hernando or reconsignment or assent of Broward, and after representing himself to Refrigerated's driver as being a representative of J&A, Al Hark caused 84 boxes, or 5,040 pounds of boneless beef to be delivered to another address. Refrigerated's driver did not contact Broward and, insofar as the record shows, delivery was made solely on the basis of the verbal representations of Al Hark.

The next morning Refrigerated's truck came to Broward's dock and was again met by Al Hark. In the sight and presence of the

Broward manager, Hark directed that a part of the remaining meat be reloaded on another truck and that the balance be stored with Broward to the account of J&A. Al Hark again represented himself to be a representative of J&A. The record does not show when, to whom, or if the driver surrendered the bill of lading.

By these maneuvers, Al Hark acquired possession of 246 boxes, or 9,520 pounds of meat ranging from ribeyes to oxtails and having a stipulated value of $5,880.86.

On January 7, 1976 [1975], Joseph Hark was informed of the arrival of the meat, whereupon he called Hernando and advised that J&A was out of business; that it had placed no order; and that this was not the first time his son, Al Hark, had placed such orders in the name of J&A. Hernando called Broward to direct that the meat not be delivered to Al Hark but was informed that delivery had already been made and without any reconsignment from Broward.

The trial judge, on this set of facts found and decreed:

That the consignee on the Straight Bill of Lading herein was Broward Cold Storage at 3220 S.W. Second Avenue, Ft. Lauderdale, Florida, and that the Defendant had an absolute duty to deliver the frozen meat involved herein to said consignee and to no other.

II.

This controversy pivots upon the precise provisions of the bill of lading, viz: the consignment to "Broward Cold Storage (account of J&A Trading Co.)." Refrigerated earnestly insists that this, in effect, was a consignment to "J&A Trading Co., care of Broward Cold Storage." While this position is plausible, when consideration is given to the nature and purpose of bills of lading, the duties and obligations arising thereunder, and to the plain terms of the consignment, we cannot embrace this theory of the case.

At the very outset we point out' that we are dealing with a "straight" bill of lading which is "[a] bill in which it is stated that the goods are consigned or destined to a specified person", 49 U.S.C. Sec. 82, which is not negotiable and must be so marked (it was in this case), 49 U.S.C. Sec. 86, as opposed to an "order" bill, 49 U.S.C. Sec. 83.[1]

Delivery under a straight bill of lading may only be made to "[a] person lawfully entitled to the possession of the goods, or (b) the consignee named" therein. 49 U.S.C. Sec. 89.

While there are various areas of potential disagreement inherent in this controversy they all boil down to a single question: Who was the consignee under the bill of lading?

---

1. "Bills of lading issued by any common carrier for the transportation of goods. . . . from a place in one State to a place in another State", among others, are governed by the Federal Bills of Lading Act, 49 U.S.C. Sections 81–124.

In our view, there is no ambiguity. The consignment was to Broward. The parenthetical matter inserted simply advised the warehouse as to the identity of the ultimate receiver of the goods upon Broward's reconsignment. The only address inserted was that of Broward. Al Hark's name does not appear on the bill. It is fairly inferable that the consignment was to Broward as a precautionary measure against an unknown purchaser. Such would have been reasonable and prudent. But we need not speculate since the language was clear. There is no way that this delivery could have been properly made except to Broward and at Broward's address. Most assuredly a street corner delivery to a stranger not named in the bill and not shown by the record to have presented any credentials or authority cannot constitute valid delivery. All the driver ever had to do was to present his bill of lading to an authorized representative of Broward. The failure to do so was a breach of the contract of carriage.

To constitute a valid delivery, absent special circumstances, it is imperative that delivery be made to the right person, at the proper time and place and in a proper manner. This is implicit in the Contract of Carriage.

It is stated in Volume 13, American Jurisprudence, 2nd, Carriers § 416 that "a carrier who delivers to an alleged agent of the consignee does so at its own peril with respect to his status as such." Cited in support of this assertion is our own case of Dean v. Vaccaro & Co., 39 Tenn. 488 (1859), which is fully supportive.

Pertinent to the issue is the North Carolina case of Griggs v. Stoker Service Co., 229 N.C. 572, 50 S.E.2d 914 (1948), wherein the Court said:

> The duty of a common carrier is not merely to carry safely the goods entrusted to him, but also to deliver them to the party designated by the terms of the shipment, or to his order, at the place of destination. 50 S.E.2d at 919.

Another case involving misdelivery of cargo, is Dickman v. Daniels Motor Freight, 185 Pa.Super. 374, 138 A.2d 165 (1958), wherein the delivery was made to a business establishment having a similar name and under circumstances suggestive of fraudulent conduct by a "swindler" who placed the order. The bill of lading was directed to a definite company at a definite address. The Court said:

> A common carrier is under an absolute duty to deliver goods to the person designated in the instructions of the shipper. If it fails to follow the express instructions of the shipper in making delivery, it acts at its peril and assumes the risk of wrong delivery. 138 A.2d at 167.

We hold that Refrigerated breached its duty to deliver the cargo to Broward, the party designated in the bill of lading; that delivery to Al Hark was at Refrigerated's peril; that the burden of validating this delivery by establishing Al Hark's ownership and right to possession was upon Refrigerated and that it failed to carry that burden.

While we make this holding within the context of our view that Broward was the consignee, had we adopted Refrigerated's view that J&A Trading Company was the consignee, with the goods being shipped "in care of" Broward, the result would be the same. This necessarily follows from the facts that J&A was not in existence; that Al Hark had no connection with J&A; and that delivery was made to him without proper inquiry and without notice to Broward, or J&A. Had such inquiry been made and such notice given the driver would have discovered that he was dealing with an imposter.

[Affirmed as to the misdelivered cargo.]

NOTES

(1) **The Case of the Ambivalent Bill.** In Rountree v. Lydick-Barmann, 150 S.W.2d 173 (Tex.Civ.App.1941), Crone Co. bought goods from Lydick-Barmann, which expected payment before delivery. Lydick-Barmann delivered the goods in Fort Worth to Rountree's trucking company. The bill of lading stated that the goods were "consigned to Lydick-Barmann Co." at an address in Little Rock County, Arkansas, "Notify Crone Company." The bill was yellow, the color required for an order bill, rather than white, the color for a straight bill. Lydick-Barmann had no place of business in Little Rock; the address there seemed to be that of Crone Co. The trucking company delivered the goods to Crone Co. at that address.

Lydick-Barmann sued Rountree for misdelivery of the goods. Judgment for the plaintiff was affirmed. It did not make a difference whether the bill was an order or a straight bill. If it were an order bill, the carrier would be liable for delivering it to someone who did not have the bill. If it were a straight bill, the carrier would be liable for delivering it to someone other than the consignee. The instruction to "Notify Crone Co." was not equivalent to "in care of Crone Co." The fact that the consignee did not have an office in Little Rock did not justify delivery to Crone Co.; when the trucking company found that it could not deliver to the consignee at the address given, it should have notified Lydick-Barmann in Fort Worth.

(2) **Trucking Problems.** Trucking concerns have found it awkward to accept goods under an order bill of lading. The problem is most acute when the trucker lacks terminal facilities at the point of destination: if the order bill of lading has not been surrendered to buyer, trucks are tied up which need to keep rolling.

In another case involving shipment by truck, the seller shipped aluminum sheets to the buyer by Mid-States truck lines, taking a straight bill of lading with the seller as consignee and a notation to "notify" the buyer. The seller sent the bill of lading and a draft to a correspondent bank. On arrival of the truck, the buyer was given delivery of the aluminum without payment of the draft or surrender of the bill of lading. Thereafter, the buyer sent the seller a check for $200 in part payment. The seller cashed the check. The buyer then went into receivership. The seller filed a claim for the balance of the price, and then brought action against Mid-States for improper delivery. Judgment for defendant affirmed. The seller had "ratified" the unauthorized delivery. What should the seller have done? Kesselman v. Mid-States Freight Lines, 78 R.I. 518, 82 A.2d 881 (1951).

(3) **Liability of Presenting Bank.** A leading case on the liability of the presenting bank in the documentary exchange is Bunge v. First National Bank of Mount Holly Springs, 118 F.2d 427 (3d Cir. 1941). The seller shipped wood pulp, consigned to himself, under an order bill of lading, which he indorsed in blank and sent along with a sight draft on the buyer for the price. The presenting bank took the buyer's uncertified personal check on another bank and released the bill of lading to the buyer, who obtained the pulp from the railroad. The check turned out to be drawn on insufficient funds, and the seller sued the presenting bank. The court held for the seller. The documentary exchange "has made it possible for parties to have the equivalent of a cash sale even though buyer and seller are hundreds of miles apart." To allow the presenting bank to take an uncertified personal check with impunity and "change that kind of arrangement from a cash transaction to what is a credit transaction would be to destroy what has come to be an accepted and useful commercial device." The presenting bank "became liable for the amount of the draft when it received something other than money in payment, cancelled the draft and delivered it to the drawee." Is the situation in the Bunge case distinguishable from that in Federal Reserve Bank of Richmond v. Malloy, p. 159 supra? What differences in the nature of the transactions would justify such a distinction? If Buyer does not have an account with the presenting bank, common practice is to release the documents only on Buyer's certified check. Buyersville Bank may hold the documents until it has had Buyer's check certified. See UCC 4–204(2)(c), 4–210, 4–211(1)(d).

SECTION 3.   PROTECTION OF THE BUYER

Prefatory Note. The preceding cases have been concerned with Buyer's default. Suppose instead that Buyer pays the draft and then discovers that Seller has breached by shipping defective goods. Certainly Buyer may journey to Seller's jurisdiction and there litigate the issues of breach and damages. Buyer would prefer, however, to bring an action at home. Buyer's state may have enacted a "long-arm" statute giving the courts of Buyer's state jurisdiction over Seller. But recourse to such an action can, at most, lead to a judgment;

successful realization on the judgment depends on finding assets of the Seller. Even if Seller is solvent its assets may be encumbered by effective security interests held by banks or other creditors; and Seller's financial position may deteriorate before the end of the long process of waiting for trial—which in some courts may take years—and defending a victory from appeal. Can funds held on Seller's behalf in Buyer's jurisdiction provide both (1) a basis for jurisdiction in an action against the seller *quasi in rem* and (2) assurance that a judgment for the Buyer will be paid? The following materials deal with the interplay between the substantive rules of law and these important procedural problems.

Problem 4. Seller & Co., located in the State of Euphoria, contracted to sell whiskey to Buyer & Co., located in the State of Depression, terms including "F.O.B. Happy Landing, Euphoria" and "payment of $100,000 price to be against sight draft with order bill of lading attached." Because of a delay in the mails, the whiskey and the documents arrived on the same day, a Monday. The presenting bank was the Buyersville Bank, to which Seller's bank, the Sellersville Bank, has forwarded the documents. Buyer gave the Buyersville Bank a check for $100,000, drawn on and certified by the Depression National Bank. Buyer immediately obtained the bill of lading, which described the goods as "barrels said to contain whiskey . . . contents . . . unknown" from the Nearly Insolvent Railroad and obtained the whiskey. On prompt inspection, Buyer discovered that the barrels contained a worthless colored liquid with alcoholic content under 2%. It is still Monday.

(a) What are Buyer's rights against Seller, the three banks, and the railroad? See UCC 2–314, 3–417, 4–207, 4–503, 7–301, 7–507, 7–508; Chesapeake & Ohio Railway Co. v. State National Bank, infra.

(b) Are there any steps that Buyer can take to enforce rights in the courts of the State of Depression (which has no "long-arm" statute giving personal jurisdiction over either Seller or Sellersville Bank)? See UCC 3–603, 4–201, 4–208, 7–301; Vickers v. Machinery Warehouse & Sales, infra.

Problem 5. Seller & Co. contracted to sell Buyer & Co. $100,000 worth of whiskey under a documentary exchange. Seller obtained an order bill of lading from the Nearly Insolvent Railroad for "100 barrels said to contain whiskey," bearing the notation "shippers load and count." The Sellersville Bank discounted the draft. Buyer refused to pay and the Sellersville Bank discovered that no whiskey was delivered by Seller to the railroad. What are Sellersville Bank's rights against the railroad? Would it make any difference if a straight bill of lading had been used? See UCC 7–301, 7–102(1)(g); Chesapeake & Ohio Railway Co. v. State National Bank, infra.

CHESAPEAKE & OHIO RAILWAY CO. v.
STATE NATIONAL BANK

Court of Appeals of Kentucky, 1939.
280 Ky. 444, 133 S.W.2d 511.

FULTON, JUSTICE. The appellant, Chesapeake and Ohio Railway Company, is appealing from a judgment for $2,359.38 in favor of the appellee, State National Bank of Maysville, Kentucky. The appeal presents a pure question of law, since all material facts were stipulated by the parties.

The Star Produce Company, located at Maysville, for a long time prior to July 6, 1935 had been a shipper of poultry over the line of the Railway Company, and shipments were ordinarily carried by an eastbound freight train known as No. 92, leaving Maysville at 3 o'clock in the morning. The freight depot of the Railway Company closed at 4:30 P.M., but the custom had long existed for the Railway Company to spot empty cars on the produce company's spur track for the purpose of being loaded with poultry and to issue bills of lading on cars the loading of which had been started and possibly on cars on which no loading had been done, with the understanding that the cars would be loaded after the bills of lading were issued and placed in train No. 92. When these bills of lading were issued the Railway Company knew that the loading of the cars had not been completed, but did not know to what extent the loading had been accomplished. The agent made no examination of any of the cars spotted or their contents before issuing bills of lading.

On July 6, 1935, pursuant to this custom, the Railway Company spotted a car on the Produce Company's spur track and, not knowing whether the car was loaded in whole or in part, issued a uniform straight bill of lading to the Produce Company for a car of live poultry of the weight of 14,000 pounds with the notation "shipper's load and count" on the bill. As a matter of fact, at the time of the issuance of the bill of lading on this car only 3,010 pounds of poultry were loaded on it and no more was ever loaded thereon and the agent was told that the loading would be completed that night in time for the car to go out on train No. 92.

On July 11, five days after the issuance of the first bill of lading, and at a time when the Railway Company knew that the car above mentioned had not been completely loaded and was still standing on the spur track, the Railway Company spotted another car for loading. Not only was the car of July 6 not loaded, but still a third car spotted for poultry (not involved in this litigation) for which a bill of lading had been issued on July 9 remained unloaded. After this second car had been spotted for the Produce Company, on July 11 a straight bill of lading on this second car similar in all respects to the first bill of lading, except that no notation of "shipper's load and count" appeared thereon, was issued to the Produce Company pursuant to the custom above mentioned, covering 14,000 pounds of live poultry. As a matter of fact, no poultry was ever loaded into this last mentioned car. Both cars, of July 6 and July 11, were recited in the bills of lading to be consigned to Julius Kastein, Inc., of New York.

On the date of the respective bills of lading the Produce Company drew a draft upon the consignee named in the bills of lading for the sum of $1,800 each and discounted the drafts with the bank. If the cars had been loaded with 14,000 pounds of live poultry, this cargo would have been the value of $1,800 for each car. The Bank, before discounting the sight drafts, received a guarantee signed by the Lawyers County Trust Company of New York, pursuant to instructions from Julius Kastein, that the drafts would be paid on condition that the cars of live poultry were received in New York within one week from the date of the bill of lading. The drafts with the respective bills of lading attached were forwarded for collection, but the consignee refused to pay them and they were returned to the Bank. At the time the drafts were returned, the Produce Company had on deposit with the bank $1,240.62, which was credited against the $3,600 advanced on the two drafts, leaving a balance of $2,359.38, the amount for which judgment was rendered in favor of the Bank against the Railway Company.

At the time the Bank discounted the drafts, it had no knowledge that the loading of the cars had not been completed and in discounting the drafts it was pursuing a course of conduct similar to that had between the Bank and the Produce Company theretofore. The loading of the cars was not completed because the Produce Company became insolvent and unable to comply with its agreement to load or complete the loading.

The rights of the parties in any action upon bills of lading issued by a common carrier for the transportation of goods in inter-state commerce are governed by the Federal Bill of Lading Act, 49 U.S. C.A. §§ 81 to 124. The Act itself, Section 1, so provides.

Prior to the enactment of the Federal Bill of Lading Act, bills of lading had not attained the exact status of negotiability although they were regarded as symbolic representations of the goods and title to the goods was passed by transfer of the bills with intention to transfer title. Consequently, it was definitely established in the Federal Courts and in most other jurisdictions that no liability was imposed on a carrier by reason of the issuance of a bill of lading when no goods had been in fact received, even in favor of an innocent purchaser for value of such a bill. . . . The basis of the rule was that it was not within the apparent scope of authority of a carrier's agent to issue a bill of lading for goods when none had been received and that therefore the carrier was not estopped to deny receipt of the goods.

Primary purposes of the bill of lading act, apparently, were to confer complete negotiability on certain types of bills (order bills) and to change the rule referred to, in so far as it applied to order bills. Negotiability was not conferred on order bills in express terms but the implication of negotiability is obvious when the entire act is considered.

By section 2 of the act a straight bill of lading is defined as "a bill in which it is stated that the goods are consigned or destined to a specified person." Section 3 of the act defines an order bill as a "bill in which it is stated that the goods are consigned or destined to the order of any person named in such bill." Section 29 of the act provides in part that: "A straight bill can not be negotiated free from existing equities, and the indorsement of such a bill gives the transferee no additional right."

While the act does not confer negotiability on straight bills, it recognizes the status of transferability and section 32 defines the rights of a transferee thereof in part as follows: "A person to whom a bill has been transferred, but not negotiated, acquires thereby as against the transferor the title to the goods, subject to the terms of any agreement with the transferor. If the bill is a straight bill such person also acquires the right to notify the carrier of the transfer to him of such bill and thereby to become the direct obligee of whatever obligations the carrier owed to the transferor of the bill immediately before the notification."

The section of the act changing the rule of non-liability for issuance of a bill covering goods which had not been received is section 22, which provides: "If a bill of lading has been issued by a carrier or on his behalf by an agent or employee the scope of whose actual or apparent authority includes the receiving of goods and issuing bills of lading therefor for transportation in commerce among the several States and with foreign nations, the carrier shall be liable to (a) the owner of goods covered by a straight bill subject to existing right of stoppage in transitu or (b) the holder of an order bill, who has given value in good faith, relying upon the description therein of the goods, for damages caused by the nonreceipt by the carrier of all or part of the goods or their failure to correspond with the description thereof in the bill at the time of its issue."

It will be observed that the last mentioned section changed the rule referred to only as to order bills and, in view of the rule existing when the act was passed, the situation is exactly the same as if the act had declared in express terms that as to the straight bills issued on goods not received no liability could be imposed on the carrier.

By virtue of section 29, there could be no liability on the part of the carrier in the instant case in an action on the bills by a holder or transferee, since an "existing equity" of the carrier was a right on its part to deny receipt of the goods as to the shipper, and a transfer of these straight bills created no additional rights.

By virtue of section 32, defining the rights of a transferee of a straight bill, the transferee acquires only the right to become "the direct obligee of whatever obligations the carrier owed to the trans-feror" and the carrier owed the transferor no obligation since no goods were received.

Again, since the status of straight bills was not changed by sec-tion 22, imposing liability on a carrier for issuing an order bill cover-ing goods not received, the holder or transferee of the bills has no cause of action thereon against the carrier.

So plain and unambiguous is the act and so obvious are the conclu-sions we have enunciated, that counsel for appellee frankly concede that if appellee were a transferee or holder of the bills, suing on the bills, there would be no right of action. To avoid the application of the bill of lading act, or rather in an attempt to short circuit the act and give it, in slang parlance, "the run around", counsel take the po-sition that the Bank is not a transferee or assignee of the bills and that the action is one based, not on the bills, but on the reckless or negligent use of language falsely certifying the receipt of loaded cars for shipment.

The position that the action is not on the bills but is based on the reckless or negligent use of language amounts to nothing more or less than a contention that the carrier is estopped to deny liability because it issued a bill certifying the receipt of goods when none had, in fact, been received. In short, we are urged to ignore the existence of the act and hold the carrier liable under the doctrine of estoppel. This we may not do since the bills were issued for the transportation of goods in inter-state commerce and by the terms of section 1 of the act all rights and liabilities under such bills must be governed by the act.

Were we to ignore the act, we would still be confronted by the rule previously mentioned, established by the overwhelming weight of authority, that estoppel cannot be invoked against the carrier to establish liability in these circumstances. . . .

In any event, and independent of other considerations, we are of the opinion that as the bills were issued for the transportation of goods in inter-state commerce, liability of the carrier must be deter-mined under the bill of lading act and that any action in connection with this issue is necessarily on the bills. Nor does the fact that the cars were not loaded or received for shipment militate against this conclusion since section 1 of the act refers to "bills of lading issued . . . for the transportation of goods" and the operation of the act is not predicated on actual loading. . . .

Great reliance is placed by appellee on Chicago & N.W.R. Co. v. Stephens Nat. Bank of Fremont, 8 Cir., 75 F.2d 398, in which the facts were the same as in the instant case except that neither car had anything loaded on it and the bills were "order notify" bills, contain-ing the notation "shipper's load and count". The carrier was held liable, the court seeming to have reached this conclusion largely by applying the doctrine of estoppel.

It appears to us that that court reached the right conclusion but used the wrong approach in doing so. It was unnecessary to invoke the doctrine of estoppel, which had no application because of the rule previously mentioned, and recognized in the opinion, that prior to the enactment of the bill of lading act no liability could be imposed on the carrier by reason of the issuance of a bill covering goods not received. Liability of the carrier could have been demonstrated by reference to sections 21 and 22 of the act, as was done by the Illinois court in a case where the exact question was involved. Mid-City Trust & Sav. Bank v. Chicago, Milwaukee & St. Paul Ry. Co., 192 Ill. App. 225, cited with approval in the Stephens Bank case. Section 22 of the act provides that, with certain limitations with which the court was not concerned, the carrier shall be liable to a purchaser for value of an *order* bill for damages caused by the nonreceipt of the carrier of all or part of the goods. But as the bills in the Stephens Bank case contained the notation "shipper's load and count", it was necessary to refer to section 21 of the act, which limits the liability imposed by section 22 by declaring that "The carrier may also by inserting in the bill of lading the words 'Shipper's weight, load, and count,' or other words of like purport indicate that the goods were loaded by the shipper and the description of them made by him; *and if such statement be true,* the carrier shall not be liable for damages caused by the improper loading or by the nonreceipt or by the misdescription of the goods described in the bill of lading."

By this section the limitation (or non-existence) of the carrier's liability is predicated on the truthfulness of the words in the bill indicating that the goods were loaded by the shipper. Since no goods were loaded, and the cars never received for shipment, the notation "shipper's load and count" was necessarily untrue and could not operate in the carrier's behalf to avoid liability. Since nothing was loaded on the cars, there was no load and no count, either by the shipper or the carrier and the carrier was bound to know it. The bills being order bills were negotiable and created additional rights in the transferee which were not created by the transfer of the straight bills in the instant case. The court in that case, in commenting on section 22 of the act, said: "It enlarged the agent's implied authority by imposing a new liability on the principal for the agent's act in issuing the bill, even though the merchandise was not received." That court, however, failed to point out that this new liability, imposed on the carrier was imposed only in favor of the holder of an *order* bill, which, in justice to that court, we might add it was not essential to point out as order bills and not straight bills were involved. We are in accord with the conclusion reached in that case but are of the opinion that it is applicable only to order bills. . . .

In view of our conclusions that the Bank was a transferee of the bills, suing on the bills, and that no liability attaches to the carrier under the bill of lading act which must control, it follows that the trial court was in error in rendering judgment against the appellant.

Judgment reversed, with directions to enter a judgment dismissing the petition.

NOTES

(1) **The Code and Interstate Shipments.** Would the Code govern the liability of the railroad if the case arose today? See the discussion of the Federal Bills of Lading or Pomerene Act at p. 341 supra. International shipments must take into account any inconsistent provisions of the Carriage of Goods by Sea Act, 1936, 46 U.S.C. §§ 1300–1315 and of international treaties such as the Warsaw Convention of 1929 on international air shipments.

(2) **Rights Based on Transfer or Negotiation.** The Code's basic rule on the rights of the transferee of a non-negotiable bill of lading appears in UCC 7–504. For rights based on a negotiable bill see the strong language in UCC 7–502(1). Compare the discussion of warehouse receipts in Chapter 1, Section 3. See generally Stubbs, Documents of Title Under the Uniform Commercial Code—Article Seven, 43 Neb.L.Rev. 773 (1964); Note, Article 7: Documents of Title, 29 Albany L.Rev. 36 (1965).

How satisfying is the court's handling of the "Shipper's Load and Count" notation? Should the loading of one small chicken make a large difference in the result? Note the phrase "any part or all" in UCC 7–301(1). Should the concluding qualification "if such indication be true" change the result where the shipper has loaded nothing? How should this language be read? Is the stamped notation false when the bill is issued before loading? Cf. Chicago & North Western Railway v. Stephens National Bank, 75 F.2d 398 (8th Cir.1935), cert. denied 295 U.S. 738, 55 S.Ct. 650, 79 L.Ed. 1685; R. Riegert & R. Braucher, 35–38 (3d ed. 1978).

VICKERS v. MACHINERY WAREHOUSE & SALES CO.

Supreme Court of Washington, 1920.
111 Wash. 576, 191 P. 869.

BRIDGES, J. In January, 1918, the defendant Machinery Warehouse & Sales Company, which we will hereafter speak of as the "machinery company," doing business in the state of Illinois, sold to Vickers & Sons Company, respondent and cross-complainant, of Seattle, Wash., often spoken of herein as the purchaser, a 15-ton crane for the sum of $8,800. The machinery company made certain warranties of the crane and, among the rest, one that it would pass Seattle inspection. The purchaser was to pay down before shipment $2,800, and thereafter within due course the crane was to be shipped to the purchaser at Seattle, and at the time of shipment the machinery company was to make a sight draft on the purchaser for the balance of the purchase price, to wit, $6,000. In compliance with this contract the purchaser paid $2,800 in cash to the machinery company. This sum was paid by sending a Seattle draft to the machinery company through the Continental & Commercial National Bank of Chicago. Shortly after the receipt of the first payment the machinery company loaded and shipped the crane to the purchaser at Seattle. It drew a sight draft against the purchaser, payable to the order of the Continental & Commercial National Bank of Chicago, of which it was a regular customer, for the balance of $6,000. The bill of lading was attached to the draft. This draft, with the bill of lading attached, was taken to the Chicago bank, and the latter, following its custom, deposited to the credit of the machinery company the whole of the $6,000, which deposit was at all times subject to the private check of the machinery company. The Chicago bank then indorsed the draft to the National Bank of Commerce, in Seattle, the appellant, as follows:

"Pay to the order of National Bank of Commerce without recourse on this bank, either as principal or agent, as to the quantity, quality or delivery of any goods covered by this draft, bill or bills of lading of other documents attached hereto, or herein referred to. Continental & Commercial National Bank of Chicago. W.W. Lampert, Cashier."

The draft so indorsed, together with the attached bill of lading, was immediately sent on to the appellant for collection. When the crane reached Seattle the respondent examined it while it was still on the car, and found that it would not pass Seattle inspection because of certain defects. Notwithstanding the information thus obtained, the respondent paid the draft of $6,000 to the appellant, and took up the bill of lading. Before the appellant had remitted the $6,000 to the Chicago bank, respondent brought suit in the superior court of King county, Wash., against the machinery company to recover $2,500 damages on account of the breach of warranty that the crane would pass Seattle inspection. At the same time it caused to be issued out of the superior court of King county writs of garnishment and attachment, and served the same upon the appellant while it had in its hands the identical $6,000 which the respondent had so recently paid to it. Thereafter respondent found certain additional defects in the crane, and amended its complaint against the machinery company, alleging additional breaches of warranty, and seeking to recover damages in the sum of $5,000. Additional attachments and garnishments were issued on this amended complaint, and served upon appellant while it still had the $6,000 paid to it in exchange for the draft and bill of lading. Very soon after the commencement of this suit both the Chicago bank and the machinery company were notified thereof. Respondent took judgment against the machinery company in the sum of $5,000, and now seeks to hold sufficient of the $6,000 paid appellant to satisfy that judgment. The appellant answered the writs of garnishment and attachment to the effect that it was not indebted to the machinery company in any sum, and that it did not have in its possession or under its control any personal property or effects belonging to it. The assistant cashier of the Chicago bank testified that, at the time the bank took the draft and bill of lading, there was no agreement or conversation between the machinery company and the bank concerning the terms or conditions upon which the latter should take the draft; that, following its custom, it discounted the draft, paying the full face thereof, and put the money to the credit of the account of the machinery company subject to its private check. He further testified that the bank bought the draft and became the owner of it; that had the draft or any portion of it not been paid, the bank, in accordance with universal custom, had and would have exercised the right to charge back the amount to the machinery company or look to that company for reimbursement. At the time the Chicago bank received notice that the $6,000 had been garnished, the machinery company had on deposit with it $3,000. It does not appear whether this balance of $3,000 was a part of the $6,000 which the bank had previously paid for the draft. The Chicago bank did not at any time charge any portion of the $6,000 back to the machinery company. The Chicago bank intended to charge back to the machinery company an amount equal to the interest on the $6,000 deposited to its credit for such period as might elapse between the time of such deposit and the payment of the draft. The trial court made findings substantially as we have set them out, but in addition thereto found that the Chicago bank extended a conditional credit to the machinery company in the full amount of the draft, with the understanding that the bank would act as agent for the machinery company in the collection of the draft, and that it received the draft, not to be treated as cash, but merely as collateral, and that at no time did the bank or the machinery company have any intention that the bank would become the purchaser or owner of the draft. The court's conclusion was that $3,000 of the $6,000 in the hands of the appellant were subject to the garnishment, and judgment was thereafter entered in accordance with such conclusions. From this judgment the garnished defendant has appealed. The respondent has cross-appealed.

The question involved in both the appeal and the cross-appeal is: How much, if any, of the $6,000 in the hands of the appellant was subject to garnishment, and properly applicable on respondent's judgment against the machinery company? A correct answer to this question depends upon the answer to another question: To whom did the money belong at the time of the service of the writ of garnishment?

There is a maze and tangle of authorities on this question. Much has been said in the briefs concerning the fact that the bill of lading was attached to the draft. We have come to the conclusion that the bill of lading does not, and cannot, in any way, affect the decision of the case. The custom of attaching bills of lading to drafts, and thus passing the drafts along for collection, has become so universal that the court must take judicial notice of the procedure. A bank has power to purchase a draft, but ordinarily it has not power to purchase machinery, and the purchase of a bill of lading would be the purchase of the machinery represented by it. Nor is a bank, even if it had the power, engaged in the business of purchasing machinery or other property the title to which is represented by a bill of lading. After all is said and done, the bill of lading is nothing more nor less than a bill of sale, and is attached to the draft purely as a matter of convenience in the transaction of business, and in order that the bill of lading, which is the evidence of the title, will not be delivered before the draft is paid. . . . The fact that a bill of lading was attached to the draft cannot alter the legal relationship between the Chicago bank and the machinery company, concerning their rights or privileges in the draft.

When a bank takes a draft drawn on a person who resides at a distance, it becomes one of three things: (1) A simple collector or agent of the drawer; (2) an absolute purchaser and owner of the draft, or (3) a conditional owner thereof. When the bank acts only as agent of the drawer, it becomes a collector and nothing else. The maker of the draft is its unconditional owner till it is paid. When it is paid the bank becomes the owner of the proceeds, and the debtor of the maker of the draft. If, however, the bank takes the draft and discounts it, and pays to the drawee the amount thereof, then and under those circumstances it is manifest that the bank has become something more than a collector or agent, and has either a qualified or absolute ownership of the draft. When we speak of one being the qualified owner, we mean any interest less than that of complete ownership, which would include the idea of a lien on the draft, or holding it as security for moneys advanced.

Generally speaking, whether a bank becomes a simple agent for collection, an absolute owner, or a qualified owner, will depend on the circumstances surrounding the deal and the agreement between, and the intention of, the parties. Much the greater number and weight of authorities is to the effect that, where one brings a check or draft to his bank, and such check or draft is made payable to the bank, or is unrestrictedly indorsed to it, and requests that the amount thereof be put to his credit subject to his private check and the bank complies therewith, and nothing else is said or done, it will be conclusively presumed that the bank has become the unqualified and absolute purchaser and owner of the check or draft, and consequently the absolute and unqualified owner of any proceeds to be derived therefrom. We think the theory is sound. It agrees with the idea and view generally accepted by business; it is the natural and unstrained construction of the action of the parties, and has the additional virtue of definitely fixing and at once defining the legal relationships of the parties in many check and draft transactions. Of course, this rule would not apply where the bank pays or advances an amount materially less than the face of the check or draft, and it is understood that the bank is to pay an additional sum when it has made collection. . . .

It has been argued that the fact that the Chicago bank took this draft, considering that it had the right to charge the same back to the machinery company if it were not paid, shows that the bank did not become the absolute owner of the draft; that it could not maintain the dual position of being the absolute owner and at the same time reserve the right to charge back if the draft were not paid. . . .

In the case of Noble v. Doughten [72 Kan. 336, 83 P. 1048, 3 L.R.A.,N.S., 1167], the court, in a case where the facts were very similar to those here, held that the bank became the absolute owner of the draft, and, commenting on the argument that the power to charge back would change the character of the ownership, said:

"It may be conceded that if, after due and legal effort to collect the check, it should be dishonored, the bank would have the right to charge the amount of it to the depositor's account. Whether this right may be said to rest merely on the custom of banks, or whether the custom has been crystallized into a rule, and the right now may be said to be an implied condition attaching to the transfer of the paper, makes no difference. It is nevertheless, in strictness, the right of an indorsee against an indorser, and hence is not in any sense inconsistent with ownership."

The fact that the bank intended to collect from the machinery company an amount equal to interest on the sum advanced by the bank to the machinery company, during the period from such advancement until the payment of the draft, could not have the effect of making the bank a collector or conditional owner of the draft. The bank paid the machinery company the full amount of the draft. If it had deducted a reasonable sum for the use of the money, instead of waiting until the draft was paid, it could not be argued that such would have had the effect of lessening the bank's ownership of the draft. That the bank did not take out this discount when it bought the draft was for the convenience of the parties, for the reason that at the time no one could tell how long it would be before the draft would be paid.

We frankly concede that the conclusion to which we have come and the reasons for such conclusions are opposed to the theory and reasoning of some of the earlier decisions of this court. . . .

Having decided that the Chicago bank became the unqualified owner of the draft, it must follow that the money which was paid to its agent and correspondent, the appellant herein, to take up the draft, was the property and money of the Chicago bank, and that the machinery company had no interest therein, and that the attempted garnishment was futile. We have not overlooked the fact that the trial court found that the Chicago bank received the draft simply for collection, and that it did not become the purchaser thereof. That so-called finding was a conclusion. While we always pay great deference to the findings made by the lower court based upon the evidence, it is the duty of this court to draw its own conclusions. We think the learned trial court erred.

But had we followed the reasoning of our earlier cases on this subject the ultimate result in this particular case must have been its reversal. If it be conceded that the Chicago bank did not become the owner of the draft, then it must be held that the transaction amounted to an equitable assignment to it of such portion of the proceeds of the draft as was necessary to repay it the amount it had advanced to the machinery company, which, indeed, was the full face of the draft and the total amount it had collected. The bank would have been the conditional owner of the draft, and the machinery company the conditional owner of the money which had been paid to its credit in that bank. Till the draft was paid the bank would have had the right to charge back to the machinery company the amount it had advanced, and the machinery company would have had the right to recall the draft. But this conditional relationship would have terminated when the draft was paid. At that time the bank would become the absolute owner of the proceeds of the draft and the machinery company its unconditional creditor. After the payment of the draft the bank would have had no right to charge back anything to the machinery company. The loan or advancement the bank had made would have been paid when the draft was paid. But it is argued that when the Chicago bank learned of this litigation, the machinery company had on deposit with it the sum of $3,000, and that it was the duty of the bank at that time to charge back that sum. But the bank had no right so to do, because the machinery company was not at that time indebted to the bank in any sum, the draft money having paid any indebtedness which it theretofore owed. Fourth National Bank v. Mayer, 89 Ga. 108, 14 S.E. 891; Central Mercantile Co. v. State Bank, 83 Kan. 504, 112 P. 114, 33 L.R.A.,N.S., 954.

Suppose that after the draft was paid the Chicago bank had undertaken to charge back to the machinery company, the latter could rightfully have answered that it owed the bank nothing, and that the loan or advancement made by the bank had been paid by the very money which it then had in its hands. When this garnishment was served, neither the appellant nor the Chicago bank was indebted to the machinery company, or had any money in its hands in which the machinery company had any interest.

The judgment is reversed, and the cause remanded, with instructions to dismiss the appellant out of the case.

NOTES

(1) **Inspection.** Why would Vickers pay the draft if it knew of the defects? (It will be seen in the next section that normally, under a documentary exchange, the carrier will not allow the buyer to inspect the goods and the buyer has, as against the seller, no right to do so.)

(2) **The Code.** What result under the Code? See UCC 4–201, 4–208(1)(b). Reread the quotation from Gilmore in Note 3, p. 56 supra. The author goes on to say: "Eventually, however, the drafting staff's proposals were accepted so far as bank credit was concerned, on the theory that bank credit is functionally different (as it is) from non-bank credit. Although the code's 'value' treatment is not unified as the drafting staff had hoped to make it, it is an improvement over the earlier Acts without being more complex." Gilmore, The Uniform Commercial Code: A Reply to Professor Beutel, 61 Yale L.J. 364, 369 (1952). But see Comment 3 to UCC 3–303.

(3) **Liability of Collecting Bank.** If the depositary bank has discounted the draft, with the bill of lading attached, is it not arguable that it assumes the warranties made by the seller as to the goods? Prior to the Code, there was some support for the proposition that the discounting bank did become responsible to the buyer for performance of the underlying contract of sale, but this notion was discussed and rejected in the leading case of Hawkins v. Alfalfa Products Co., 152 Ky. 152, 153 S.W. 201 (1913). Nevertheless, the rubber stamp which many banks use to indorse documentary drafts contains "Pay any bank or banker," "Prior indorsement guaranteed," and also a clause to the effect that the indorsing bank "does not warrant and will not be responsible for the existence, quantity, quality, condition or delivery of goods purporting to be covered by any accompanying documents nor the genuineness of such documents." Such a clause may also appear on the "Paid" stamp of the presenting bank.

The general rule of contract law applicable to such situations is stated in Restatement (Second) of Contracts § 328: "(1) Unless the language or the circumstances indicate the contrary, as in an assignment for security, an assignment of 'the contract' or of 'all my rights under the contract' or an assignment in similar general terms is an assignment of the assignor's rights and a delegation of his unperformed duties under the contract. (2) Unless the language or the circumstances indicate the contrary, the acceptance by an assignee of such an assignment operates as a promise to the assignor to perform the assignor's unperformed duties, and the obligor of the assigned rights is an intended beneficiary of the promise. . . ."

What is the rule under the Code? See UCC 7–507, 7–508.

(4) **Forged Bill of Lading.** Suppose that the seller forges a bill of lading, attaches it to a draft on the buyer, and sends it through banking channels to the buyer, who pays the draft. The seller then withdraws the proceeds from the depositary bank and absconds. What recourse has the buyer against the seller? Against the presenting bank? Against the depositary bank? Considering that both the buyer and the depositary bank dealt directly with the forger, on which of the two should this risk properly fall? Does the Code

support your answer?   See UCC 3–417, 3–418, 4–207; cf. Springs v. Hanover National Bank, 209 N.Y. 224, 103 N.E. 156 (1913).

SECTION 4.   INSPECTION AND PAYMENT

Prefatory Note.   Generally, "where goods are tendered or delivered or identified to the contract for sale, the buyer has a right before payment or acceptance to inspect them at any reasonable place and time and in any reasonable manner.   When the seller is required or authorized to send the goods to the buyer, the inspection may be after their arrival." UCC 2–513(1). (Inspection in this context must be distinguished from inspection before making the contract which, as will be seen later, may affect the scope of the seller's warranties.) This is not ordinarily true, however, for the documentary exchange.

"As already pointed out, under the face-to-face transaction, which the documentary exchange is designed to supplant, the buyer had the right to inspect the goods before paying for them (UCC 2–513(1)). Since the goods will normally travel much more slowly than the documents, they will not ordinarily be available for inspection at the time that the buyer is required to pay under the rules just discussed. Therefore, absent agreement to the contrary, the buyer has no right to inspect the goods before he pays when the contract provides for payment against documents of title, except in the case, to be discussed later, where payment is due only after the goods are to become available for inspection (UCC 2–513(3)(b); see also UCC 2–310(b)).   Indeed, the negotiable railway bill of lading typically bears the legend: 'Inspection of property covered by this bill of lading will not be permitted unless provided by law or unless permission is indorsed on this original bill of lading or given in writing by the shipper.'   The Code goes on to provide that where, as in the transaction under discussion, the contract calls for payment before inspection, even the non-conformity of the goods does not, with rare exceptions, excuse the buyer from paying (UCC 2–512(1)).[1]   But it makes it clear that such payment does not amount to an acceptance of the goods by the buyer and that the buyer retains his right to inspect the goods upon delivery and all of his remedies against the seller for breach of contract (UCC 2–512(2)).   He merely loses the opportunity of inspection before payment, an opportunity that gave him advantage of refusing to pay, rather than the disadvantage of having to sue to recover his payment, in the event of a non-conformity."   Farnsworth,

---

1. The Code is not clear on what remedy, if any, the seller would have for the buyer's breach of this duty in the event that the goods were in fact non-conforming.   It is of course a rare case in which the buyer learns of the nonconformity when he has no right to inspect.

Documentary Drafts Under the Uniform Commercial Code, 22 Bus. Law. 479, 482–83 (1967).[2]

Problem 6. Buyer wrote Seller "Send me lathe No. 3X." Seller replied "Sending lathe tomorrow." The next day, Seller shipped the lathe by rail and obtained an order bill of lading, attached it to a sight draft on the buyer for the price, and forwarded the draft and bill of lading through banking channels.

(a) Will the railroad let the buyer inspect the lathe before paying for it? What would you advise Buyer to do when the draft is presented? See UCC 2–503, 2–504, 2–505, 2–507, 2–511(1), 2–513, 2–601. Would your advice be different if Buyer's letter had added "f.o.b. Sellersville" ?

(b) Would it be possible for Seller to use a draft with order bill of lading attached without running the risk of being in breach of contract? How? See UCC 2–310(b) and Comment 2.

(c) Would your advice to Buyer be different if the sale were "c.i.f. Buyersville"? See UCC 2–320(4).

NOTES

(1) **"On Arrival" Draft.** "[U]nder the documentary exchange, [the buyer must] finance the transaction for [the] period of time between his payment of the draft and his receipt of the goods, a period that will, of course, depend upon the relative speed at which the documents and the goods are sent. One way for the buyer to shift this burden to the seller, or to a discounting bank, is to contract for payment against documents 'on arrival' of the goods. Under such a term seller's draft may be drawn payable 'on arrival.' Since the Code requires that a negotiable instrument be payable 'on demand or at a definite time' (UCC 3–104(1)(c)) and an 'on arrival' draft is neither (UCC 3–108, 3–109), such a draft can not be negotiable, but this is of little consequence if the draft is held by the seller or is at most discounted with the depositary bank which has recourse against the seller in any event. Any difficulty may be avoided by using a sight draft with instructions to present when the goods arrive. In either case, 'the collecting bank need not present until in its judgment a reasonable time for arrival of goods has expired. Refusal to pay or accept because the goods have not arrived is not dishonor; the bank must notify its transferor of such refusal but need not present the draft again until it is instructed to do so or learns of the arrival of goods' (UCC 4–502). Another incident of the use of an 'on arrival' term relates to the buyer's right of inspection. In the ordinary documentary exchange the buyer, as has been pointed out earlier, loses his right to inspect the goods before paying for them, under the rationale that

2. Copyright 1967 by The Business Lawyer and reproduced with permission.

the goods will not usually be available for inspection when the buyer is required to pay. This reason does not hold where payment is due only 'on arrival' of the goods, and the Code specifically provides for an exception to the rule denying inspection 'where such payment is due only after the goods are to become available for inspection' (UCC 2–513(3)(b)). Under such a term the seller is required to indorse permission for the buyer to inspect on the bill of lading itself or give written notice of permission to the carrier." Farnsworth, Documentary Drafts Under the Uniform Commercial Code, 22 Bus.Law. 479, 487–88 (1967).[1] But does not UCC 2–310(b) dispense with the necessity of inserting an express "on arrival" term in the contract?

(2) Inspection in Overseas Sales. Overseas sellers sometimes sharply resist buyers' attempts to inspect the goods on arrival but before payment. (Why should sellers be nervous in this setting?)

The House of Lords dealt with the problem in the leading case of E. Clemens Horst Co. v. Biddle Bros., [1912] A.C. 18. A contract called for the shipment of 100 bales of hops from San Francisco to an English port. The terms were "net cash" with the price quoted "90 shillings sterling per 112 lbs. C.I.F. to London, Liverpool or Hull." (As we shall see later in more detail, "C.I.F." stands for "Cost, Insurance, Freight" and means that for the stated price seller agrees not only to supply the goods ("cost") but also to pay for insurance and freight to the specified destination.) The seller offered to tender in England a negotiable bill of lading, insurance certificates, and certificates of quality of the Merchants' Exchange, San Francisco, or other evidence of quality by independent inspectors. The buyer refused to pay in exchange for documents, and proposed to pay only on inspection of the goods after arrival. The seller refused to ship under these circumstances, and both parties claimed for damages.

The House of Lords held that the buyer was wrong in insisting on inspecting the goods at the delivery-point before paying for them. The opinions emphasized the practice in c.i.f. sales of sending the documents to the buyer, calling for payment by the buyer, in advance of the arrival of the goods. The present contract was silent as to the time for payment, but the ambiguity should be resolved in the light of this practice. (At the time of the Clemens Horst case, documents sent by rail from San Francisco to New York, and on by fast steamer to England, would arrive long in advance of the ocean freight. Ocean freight is now faster than it was then, but documents now arrive even more rapidly by air mail.) The credit strain placed on the buyer by payment in advance of arrival can be offset by reselling the documents or by pledging the documents to a bank to secure a low-interest loan.

1. Copyright 1967 by The Business Lawyer and reproduced with permission.

$5,000.00

January 15,   1985

On Arrival of Goods

Pay to the

Order of Seller & Co.

Five Thousand and 00/100- - - - - - - - - - - - - - Dollars

Value Received and charge same to account of

To Buyer & Co.

Address   1 Church Street

Buyersville, Cal.

SELLER & CO.

S. S. Seller, Pres.

309/00 (12-84)

[B29563]

- -

Take this off before Presenting

NO PROTEST

ON ARRIVAL DRAFT

The Code takes as a starting point the same general rule. UCC 2–320 provides: "(4) Under the term C.I.F. or C. & F. unless otherwise agreed the buyer must make payment *against tender of the required documents* . . . ." This provision is subject to qualification in UCC 2–321: "Under a contract containing a term C.I.F. or C. & F. . . . (3) Unless otherwise agreed where the contract provides for payment on or after arrival of the goods the seller must before payment allow such preliminary inspection as is feasible. . . ." Cf. UCC 2–513(3)(b).

From this setting there arises this basic question: Is the rule concerning payment before arrival really a result of the form of price quotation (C.I.F. as contrasted with F.O.B. or F.A.S.)? Or does it flow from other factors such as the time to be consumed by ocean freight shipment and other practical considerations and practices in the particular trade? The problem arises where the price is quoted on some basis other than "C.I.F." or "C. & F." and the agreement is silent concerning the precise date for payment and does not use some verbal formula like "payment against documents." See UCC 2–513. In resolving a dispute over inspection in such cases, what relative weight to be given to: (1) an argument derived from the language of the Code; (2) the underlying nature of the transaction, such as the time consumed in ocean freight shipment, the drastic effect of rejection on inspection in a falling market, and the opportunity of a buyer-dealer to resell the documents before the goods arrive; (3) the way the seller and buyer have handled payment on earlier shipments (UCC 1–205(1)); (4) the way similar transactions have been handled by other traders (UCC 1–205(2))?

As we shall see shortly, the problem of inspection at destination becomes moot in the usual letter of credit transaction, for the buyer (through his confirming bank) has paid for the goods upon their shipment. Of course, the buyer may look at the goods when they arrive, but only with regret if they are defective, for he has long since paid cash for them. The burden then rests on him to press a claim against the seller for his loss.

(3) Inspection by Third Party. The fact that the carrier issues a bill of lading evidencing a shipment of "1 Lathe" or "100 bags sugar" or "100 crated refrigerators" gives the buyer no protection with respect to the quality of the goods. See e.g., the language of the bills of lading, supra: "contents and condition of contents of packages unknown." Moreover, as the Chesapeake & Ohio case, p. 363 supra, suggests, the seller often loads the car and supplies the carrier with the information which the carrier uses in making out the bill of lading; if the carrier (as is customary) then stamps on the bill of lading "Shipper's Load and Count" the buyer may have no recourse against the carrier even if there is little or nothing in the car.

Thus a buyer who pays in exchange for documents runs a risk—especially if the seller is at a distance or is of doubtful responsibility.

On the other hand, a seller may run a risk if inspection by buyer occurs after expensive shipment or in a locale where it would be expensive or awkward for the seller to redispose of the goods; and a buyer who is a sharp trader may take advantage of seller's awkward position by rejecting on trivial (or imaginary) grounds in order to bargain for a price concession or to escape from a contract that has gone sour because of a drop in the price.

A practice which may reduce the hazards of inspection by buyer at point of receipt is inspection at the point of shipment by an independent third party. The results of this inspection may be reflected in a certificate of quality which must be tendered with the bill of lading.

There has been some controversy over whether the inspection (a) serves only as prima facie evidence of quality which buyer is entitled to receive before he proceeds to accept and pay for the goods, subject to later recovery if the goods are defective, or (b) conclusively binds the parties. See Henderson v. Berce, 142 Me. 242, 50 A.2d 45 (1946) (buyer bought "Earlaine" seed potatoes which were certified according to state statute; only 30% turned out to be "Earlaine" when planted), noted in 31 Minn.L.Rev. 502 (1947); Smith v. Great Atlantic & Pacific Tea Co., 170 F.2d 474 (8th Cir.1948) (buyer purchased spinach shipped according to contract with inspection certificates from United States Dept. of Agriculture attached to bill of lading; spinach infested with plant lice). In what situations would you counsel reliance upon government inspection?

Practice in the fresh fruit and vegetable trade is reflected in "Trade Terms and Definitions" promulgated by the Secretary of Agriculture under the Perishable Agricultural Commodities Act, 7 U.S.C. §§ 499a–499s. The Secretary's regulations in part provide (7 Code Fed.Regs. § 46.43):

"§ 46.43. *Terms construed.* The following terms and definitions, when used in any contract or communication involving any transaction coming within the scope of the Act shall be construed as follows: . . . .

"(x) 'Shipping-point inspection' means that the seller is required to obtain Federal or Federal-State inspection, or such private inspection as has been mutually agreed upon, to show the compliance of the lot sold with the quality, condition, and grade specifications of the contract, and that the seller assumes the risk incident to incorrect certification.

"(y) 'Shipping-point inspection final,' or 'inspection final' following the name of the State or point, as 'California inspection final,' means that the seller is required to obtain Federal or Federal-State inspection, or such private inspection as has been mutually agreed upon, to show the compliance of the lot sold with the quality, condition, and grade specifications of the contract, and that the buyer assumes the risk incident to incorrect certification and is without recourse against the seller on account of quality, condition, and grade.

"(z) 'Subject approval Government inspection' means that the seller is required to obtain Federal or Federal-State inspection, or such private inspection as has been mutually agreed upon, and to correctly communicate, by wire or other agreed means, the statements on the certificate as to quality, condition and grade, and other essential information, whereupon the buyer, upon approval thereof, will be deemed to have accepted the produce without recourse against the seller on account of quality, condition, and grade."

(4) Documentary Exchanges and Fast Freight. The rapid carriage of goods by air has required the invention of new devices for the exchange of goods for money. Air freight which leaves New York in the morning can be in California or London the same day. Taking a bill of lading ("airbill") at the point of shipment and transmitting it through banks to the destination for exchange for price may be too slow.

One solution is for the carrier to be the collecting agent. Another proposed under the Code is the use of bills of lading issued by the carrier at destination. See UCC 7–305. The Comment to this section of the Code describes the operation as follows:

"Financing of shipments under this plan would be handled as follows: seller at San Francisco delivers the goods to an airline with instructions to issue a bill in New York to a named bank. Seller receives a receipt embodying this undertaking to issue a destination bill. Airline wires its New York freight agent to issue the bill as instructed by the seller. Seller wires the New York bank a draft on buyer. New York bank indorses the bill to buyer when he honors the draft. Normally seller would act through his own bank in San Francisco, which would extend him credit in reliance on the airline's contract to deliver a bill to the order of its New York correspondent."

In international trade the possibility that the cargo may arrive before the bill of lading has posed significant problems, as the following excerpt suggests.

"Multi-million dollar oil cargoes are frequently released against indemnities to recipients without proof of title. This unsatisfactory situation is encouraging efforts to find modern alternatives to the traditional bill of lading system.

"The problem arises because the key document buyer's need, the bill of lading, is often unavailable when the ship arrives at its destination. It may be held up with a bank financing the deal or mislaid in a long chain of buyers and sellers. Sometimes the carrying vessel travels faster than the mail.

"An oil cargo may change hands as many as 20 times in the 45 days or less that it takes to transport it from the Gulf to the Caribbean. The documents may take as long as 95 days to travel the same distance, even if each party holds them for just one day.

Farnsworth Cs. Com'l Paper 3rd Ed. UCB—14

"Legally, the carrier or shipowner can insist on receiving the bill of lading—which is a negotiable document of title as well as evidence of the contract of carriage—before delivering. If he fails to do so, and makes delivery to the wrong party, a bank or buyer holding the bill of lading can sue him for its loss. Should he sit tight, however, demurrage and interest charges build up, and in a buyer's market where carrying capacity exceeds demand, the commercial pressures to release are considerable.

"If the ship is chartered—as it normally is in the oil trade—the charterer may threaten to put the vessel 'off hire' if the shipowner insists on waiting for the receiver to produce the necessary documentation. Charter-parties sometimes contain clauses requiring the owner to discharge in this situation.

"Often the owner delivers against an indemnity given by the receiver. Unless the latter is an internationally-known company with a solid reputation, one of the oil majors for example, he will request that the buyer back up his indemnity with a bank guarantee. This request is frequently resisted, as a guarantee will tie up the buyer's credit lines and involve him in commission payments.

"Use of a non-negotiable waybill—which does not have to be produced at destination—eliminates the problem of non-production, although waybills may not be suitable if the cargo is to be negotiated during the voyage.

"Research is being made into ways of minimizing the delay. Computerization of trade documentation and the establishment of a registry for bills of lading are two possibilities." Rowe, Bills of Lading Must Move Fast, Int.Fin.L.Rev. 32 (April 1983).[1]

(5) Use of Draft for Credit. Buyer will not always be willing to pay before he gets the goods. Of course if Seller is willing to accept Buyer's unsecured promise, no documentary exchange is necessary. But Seller may want Buyer's promise in such form that he can easily raise money on it. Instead of ordering Buyer to pay on sight, Seller's draft may be payable, for example, 30 days after sight. Buyer will then be required to accept it before receiving the documents (see UCC 2–514, 4–503). The draft, when returned to Seller, is "two party paper," with Buyer liable as acceptor and Seller as drawer, and can be readily discounted by Seller. If Seller had sold on open credit it would not have been as easy to borrow against his own promissory note secured by an assignment of the open book account resulting from the sale.

Just prior to the First World War the Federal Reserve Board together with businessmen's organizations began an attempt to revive the trade acceptance, which had been popular in the United States before the Civil War. "Trade acceptance" was the name given to a

1. Copyright 1983 by the International Financial Law Review and reproduced with permission.

time draft drawn by a seller on a buyer for the purchase price of goods, and accepted by the buyer. Its proponents felt that its use in place of open credit would strengthen the economy by facilitating the financing of sales by banks and other discounting agencies. Because it arose in a current sales transaction between merchants, it was easier to raise money on it than on an ordinary accepted time draft which might stem from a stale debt of a less commercial nature. It was also suggested that this device would encourage buyers to meet their obligations more promptly than they would under open credit, and that buyers would be less likely to overextend their credit.

When used in the documentary exchange the trade acceptance, together with the documents, is forwarded to Buyer by Sellersville Bank, acting as Seller's agent. After acceptance, Sellersville Bank may itself discount the instrument or may return it to Seller for discount elsewhere. The willingness of financing institutions to discount such paper will depend, in part, upon their opportunity to rediscount it at a favorable rate. In order to encourage dealing in such paper the Federal Reserve Act of 1913, Section 13, authorized Federal Reserve banks to rediscount acceptances under certain conditions. The Federal Reserve Board required that, to be eligible for rediscount with a Federal Reserve bank at the rate to be established for trade acceptances, "A trade acceptance must bear on its face, or be accompanied by, evidence in form satisfactory to the Federal Reserve Bank, that it was drawn by the seller of the goods on the purchaser of such goods. Such evidence may consist of a certificate on or accompanying the acceptance to the following effect: 'The obligation of the acceptor of this bill arises out of the purchase of goods from the drawer.'" Federal Reserve Board Regulation P, July 15, 1915.

Although the trade acceptance is a common commercial instrument, it did not achieve the wide usage that its proponents had hoped it would largely because businessmen and bankers found other, more attractive, means of borrowing and lending. For a discussion of the negotiability of a trade acceptance, see State Trading Corp. v. Toepfert, 304 Mass. 473, 23 N.E.2d 1008 (1939).

It is customary for the buyer to accept "payable at" a named bank at which he has an account. The Code makes it clear that a draft that has been accepted "payable at" a domestic bank must be presented at that bank and that such an acceptance does not vary the draft. See UCC 3–504(4), 3–412(2).

SECTION 5. INTERNATIONAL SALES AND THE LETTER OF CREDIT

(A) PROTOTYPE AND PROBLEMS

Introduction to the Prototype Export Transaction. Grappling with cases on international sales runs some of the hazards of navigating among icebergs: many of the critical facts are invisible. Seldom do appellate opinions give the full setting from which the controversy arises and lawyers are often in no position to round out the picture. To help understand the cases which follow and to prepare for counselling in this area, this Section opens with a prototype export transaction which follows an international sale, step by step, through its most important stages. To be sure, infinite variations are possible in foreign trade as in other branches of sales; but one fairly typical transaction may provide a helpful point of departure for constructive legal work in this increasingly important field.

At the end of the prototype transaction appears a series of introductory problems which are designed to assist in understanding the transaction. It would be efficient to read the transaction quickly, and then to examine it more carefully in the light of the problems.

BALL BEARINGS FOR BRAZIL: A PROTOTYPE EXPORT TRANSACTION [1]

SKF Industries, Inc., is a Philadelphia manufacturer of ball and roller bearings. On December 4, 1983, SKF receives a letter from Companhia Importadora Brasileira, a distributor of bearings in Rio de Janeiro, Brazil (hereafter called "Brasileira"), requesting a price quotation for 1200 ball bearings (catalogue number 187B) and 2400 roller bearings (catalogue number 839R). On December 15 SKF replies by letter (FORM 1) explaining the quotation as set forth in the enclosed proforma invoice (FORM 2).

[1] Mr. B.A. Tassone, Director of International Marketing, and Mr. H.J. Gupfinger, Manager of Material Flow, SKF Industries, Inc., were exceedingly helpful in explaining their practices and in preparing the sample forms. Thanks are also owing to Mr. Robert S. Adamson, Assistant Vice President, Philadelphia National Bank, for preparing the letter of credit. Of course, any errors in presenting the transaction are my own responsibility.

SKF INDUSTRIES, INC.
INTERNATIONAL MARKETING/BEARINGS GROUP

December 15, 1983

Companhia Importadora Brasileira
Caixa Postal 10
Rio de Janeiro, Brazil

Re: <u>CIB - 43H2</u>

Gentlemen:

We are very pleased to acknowledge receipt of your above inquiry
dated December 4 requesting our quotation on a total quantity of
3,600 ball and roller bearings.

We are attaching hereto our proforma invoice in quadruplicate
showing the net price for each size, along with the total f.a.s.
Philadelphia or New York City value. For your convenience, we
have also estimated the insurance charges, ocean freight and
handling charges as well as the consular fees. We have, therefore, arrived at a total estimated c.i.f. Rio de Janeiro value.
We wish to call your attention specifically to the fact that our
quotation is an f.a.s. Philadelphia or New York City quotation
and the total c.i.f. value shown is simply as an estimated value
which we have included for your convenience in obtaining your
Import License and opening the Letter of Credit. The shipping
and handling charges will be for your account and we will invoice
the exact charges whether they are higher or lower than those
estimated.

We have been able to quote a January delivery for both sizes, but
have to point out that this promise is valid only if your firm
order will be received by return air mail. Even though the delivery
has been promised for January, we suggest that your Letter of Credit
be valid until February 28, 1984, so that there will be no necessity
to request an extension unless some unforeseen difficulties should
arise. Needless to say, the Letter of Credit should be for a minimum
of 10,950 United States dollars. As all of the bearings which you
require are available for shipment in January, we have estimated
shipping expenses for only one shipment. Therefore, it is not
necessary to allow for partial shipments in the Letter of Credit.

We appreciate very much this opportunity of quoting and will look
forward to the early receipt of your firm order.

Very truly yours,

C. L. Derry

E. L. Derry
General Supervisor

FORM 1

LETTER TRANSMITTING QUOTATION   [D626]

CABLE ADDRESS
"SKAYEF" – PHILADELPHIA

TELEX 83-4539

SKF INDUSTRIES, INC.

FRONT STREET AND ERIE AVENUE

PHILADELPHIA, PA. 19132

REFER CORRESPONDENCE TO
EXPORT SALES DEPT.
P.O. BOX NO. 6731
PHILADELPHIA, PENNA. 19132

Companhia Importadora Brasileira

Caixa Postal 10

Rio de Janeiro, Brazil

OUR PROFORMA INVOICE
NUMBER: LA/100
DATE: 12/15/83

YOUR INQUIRY
NUMBER: CIB-43H2
DATE: 12/4/83

ITEM NO.	MANUFACTURER'S PART NUMBER	MATERIAL SPECIFICATIONS SIZE DESCRIPTION	QUANTITY	PRICE UNIT	PRICE TOTAL	AVAILABILITY STOCK	WEIGHT IN LBS.
1	187 B		1200	2.15	2,580.00	January	
2	839 R		2400	3.37	8,088.00	January	

Os precos acima indicados sao os correntes no mercado de
exportacao para qualquer pais.

Nao ha comissao.

Nao sao publicados catalogos e/ou lista de preco para o material acima indicado.

Est. total net weight - 4520 lbs. - 2050 kilos
Est. total gross weight - 5010 lbs. - 2272 kilos

Schedule B Commodity Code - 7197010

TOTAL MAT'L. VALUE F.A.S. VESSEL PHILA. OR N.Y.C.	$10,668.00
ESTIMATED FREIGHT FORWARDER'S CHARGES	19.00
ESTIMATED CONSULAR CHARGES	58.00
ESTIMATED F.O.B. VESSEL	
ESTIMATED INSURANCE CHARGES	48.50
ESTIMATED TRANSPORTATION CHARGES	156.50
ESTIMATED C.I.F.	10,950.00

TERMS:

DELIVERY - FAS VESSEL PHILADELPHIA/NEW YORK CITY

PAYMENT   LETTER OF CREDIT

CONDITIONS: Prices shown are those in effect at time of quotation. Prices in effect at time of shipment will prevail.

PH-3718-F

THIS OFFER SUBMITTED SUBJECT TO PRIOR SALE AND CONFIRMATION OF TERMS AND PRICES AT TIME OF RECEIPT OF ORDER.

INDUSTRIES, INC.

[B28901]

FORM 2
PROFORMA INVOICE

TERMS AND CONDITIONS

Any order resulting from this quotation will be subject to the following conditions:

1. Delivery dates are approximate. Seller shall not be liable for any delay in, or inability to complete delivery because of any of the following causes: Acts of God; suspension or requisition of any kind; strikes or other stoppages of labor or shortage in the supply thereof; inability to obtain fuel, material or parts; fire, casualties or accidents; failure of shipping facilities; riot; or any cause, whether the same or a different character, beyond Seller's control.

2. Prices indicated are based on the prices in effect as of the date hereof. They are subject to change in accordance with the prices in effect as of the date of shipment.

3. Products are not returnable for credit or replacement, unless authorized in writing by Seller.

4. If, for any reason whatsoever, this order or any part thereof, is terminated by the Buyer, such termination shall be effected with the understanding that termination charges may result therefrom.

5. Orders for special products are subject to shipment of any overrun or underrun not to exceed 10%. The Buyer will pay, in full, for such overshipment, and in the event of an undershipment the Buyer will consider the order completed with such undershipment.

[B2891]

6.   Goods manufactured by Seller shall conform to the description, shall be fit for the ordinary purposes for which such goods are used, and shall be free of defects in material and workmanship at time of shipment. THERE ARE NO WARRANTIES OF MERCHANTABILITY OR OTHERWISE, EXCEPT OF TITLE, WHICH EXTENDS BEYOND THAT STATED ABOVE.

7.   Seller's liability and Buyer's remedy for breach of warranty or otherwise is expressly limited to the replacement of any products sold hereunder which Seller determines, by laboratory examination is non-conforming, provided said non-conforming products are returned F.O.B. Seller's warehouse within twelve (12) months of shipment hereunder. Seller retains the right to render credit for the purchase price in lieu of furnishing a replacement product.

8.   IN NO EVENT SHALL SELLER BE LIABLE HEREUNDER OR OTHERWISE FOR LOSS OF PROFITS, SPECIAL, INCIDENTAL, OR CONSEQUENTIAL DAMAGES OF ANY KIND.

9.   Shipments hereunder shall be at all times subject to the approval of Seller's Credit Department.

10.   The terms and conditions on the face and reverse side hereof constitute the entire agreement between Buyer and Seller. No reference herein to Buyer's inquiry or order shall in any way incorporate different or additional terms or conditions which are hereby objected to. No modification hereto shall be binding upon Seller unless made in writing by Seller's authorized representative. Receipt of this acknowledgment by Buyer without prompt written objection thereto shall constitute an acceptance of these terms and conditions by Buyer.

[*Reverse*]

PROFORMA INVOICE

FORM 2

Examination of the proforma invoice will show that it contains all the particulars for the proposed shipment which are then known to SKF. (It will be useful to consider whether this communication constitutes an offer which, on acceptance, would create a binding contract. Compare the letter with the printed language in the bottom right-hand corner of the proforma invoice.)[2]

The Price Quotation: F.A.S. and C.I.F. One will note that the proforma invoice in the bottom left-hand corner has a blank after "TERMS: DELIVERY" and that SKF inserted the following: "F.A.S. PHILA/NEW YORK CITY". "F.A.S." stands for "Free Along Side"; this means that the seller will be responsible for the cost and risks of bringing the goods "Along Side" an overseas vessel at the stated location: the buyer bears the costs and risks from that point.[3] Therefore, under this quotation the Brazilian buyer will understand that his total costs will include not only the quoted F.A.S. price of $10,668, but also freight charges from Philadelphia to Brazil, the cost of insurance and any other expenses of bringing the goods into Brazil.

It is necessary to pause in the description of this transaction to note that instead of quoting a price "F.A.S. Philadelphia," the price might have been quoted "C.I.F. Rio de Janeiro." The initials "C.I.F." stand for "Cost, Insurance, and Freight" and mean, among other things, that in exchange for this stated price the seller undertakes not only to supply the goods ("cost") but also to obtain and pay for insurance and bear the freight charges to the stated point.[4] In spite of the widespread use of C.I.F. quotations in foreign trade, sellers in the position of SKF often prefer to quote on a F.A.S. basis since this relieves them of the burdens and hazards of variations and fluctuations in freight and insurance costs for shipments to widely scattered points. This preference is reflected in the "F.A.S." quotation in the transaction which we are following. (Note the explanation in the second paragraph of the letter in FORM 1.)

Buyer's Purchase Order. In response to SKF's letter of December 15, on January 5, Brasileira sent SKF the Buyer's Purchase Order that follows (FORM 3).

The Letter of Credit. The proforma invoice (FORM 2), which SKF enclosed with its letter of December 15, under "TERMS . . . PAYMENT" contained the notation "Letter of Credit". Letters of credit play a central role in most exporting transactions and deserve careful attention. In following the domestic documentary transaction between Sellersville, New York and Buyersville, California, p. 342 su-

---

2. If the seller were a middleman purchasing goods for export could he safely leave the transaction open at this point?

3. See International Chamber of Commerce's INCOTERMS (1980) F.A.S.; UCC 2–319(2).

4. See International Chamber of Commerce's INCOTERMS (1980) C.I.F.; UCC 2–320. From the fact that the contract price includes the freight, do not leap to any conclusion about who has the risk of loss.

pra, we saw that one way for a seller to be assured of payment is to ship goods under a negotiable bill of lading and arrange for a bank in buyer's city to hold the bill of lading until the buyer pays the draft. In the usual foreign sale (and in some domestic sales) this arrangement for securing payment of the price is not adequate. For example, in our current SKF export it probably will not be advisable for SKF to allow payment to be delayed until the bearings reach Brazil. Under such an arrangement Brasileira might reject the bearings in Rio de Janeiro; at this point substantial shipping costs would have been incurred and the bearings would be at a location where it might be awkward and expensive for the seller to arrange for redisposition. Of course, the seller would have a claim against the buyer for this loss, but litigation is always hazardous and in a foreign country the hazards multiply. Moreover, in dealing with the many countries which control foreign exchange, it may be difficult to get the local money converted into usable dollars.

In some situations, sellers may need assurance of payment even before the time for shipment. This problem arises in contracts (either foreign or domestic) which call for the manufacture of goods to the buyer's specifications (electric generators; locomotives; steel girders to be cut in non-standard lengths). In these contracts the seller will need firm assurance of payment before he starts to manufacture.

Strong protection against these hazards can be created if the contract provides that, at a specified point in the transaction before the seller incurs costs he cannot readily recoup, the buyer must establish an irrevocable letter of credit. By such a letter of credit, a bank promises to honor the seller's draft for the price; in our export transaction the bank's promise will be conditioned upon seller's presenting specified documents, one of which will be a negotiable bill of lading evidencing shipment of the goods.

Although the proforma invoice did not so specify, SKF will expect the letter of credit to be "confirmed" by a local bank in the United States. (Cf. UCC 2–325.) It is easy to see why SKF wants the undertaking by a bank of known solvency and responsibility. But why does the local bank only "confirm", rather than "issue", the letter of credit? The answer arises from this practical consideration: the bank that issues a letter of credit needs assurance that it will be reimbursed by the buyer, on whose behalf it pays the seller. The Philadelphia bank will probably not know the Brazilian buyer, and cannot be sure of reimbursement. But the buyer's own bank (Banco do Brasil) can take steps to minimize or remove these hazards. As we shall see, it will receive the negotiable bill of lading controlling the goods which will provide security for the customer's obligation to reimburse the bank; in addition, the buyer's own bank can judge in the light of its knowledge of his financial standing whether added security is needed and can insist on such security before it issues the letter of credit.

COMPANHIA IMPORTADORA BRASILEIRA

Caixa Postal, 10   Fone 2-1881   End. Teleg. ROLESFER

RIO DE JANEIRO, BRAZIL

EXPORT SALES
DATE REC'D
DISTRIBUTORES DIRETOS
JAN 10 1900 REGLAMENTOS

Pedido No. ___42___
(Order)

Fornecedor: ___S K F Industries, Inc.___
(Supplier)

Endereço: ___P.O. Box 6731 - Philadelphia 32, Pa. USA___
(Address)

Data: ___5/1/84___
(Date)

Condições Pagamento: ___Irrevocable Letter of Credit___
(Payment Terms)

Banco: ___Advise___
(Bank)

Embarque: ___Ship to Rio de Janeiro___
(Shipment)

Marca: ___C.I.B.___
(Shipping Mark) Rio de Janeiro

Embarcador: ___Pierce-Byron, Inc., 325 Chestnut St., Phila., PA___
(Forwarder)

Declaração Consular: ___Rolamento de esfera, rolete cone ou agulhas para mancal___
(Consular Declaration)

Licença de Importação No. ___DG-59/10000___   Valôr: ___$10,950.00___
(Import License)   (Value)

Validade: ___2/28/84___
(Validity)

Seguro: ___Against all usual risks including theft and___
(Insurance) ___marine up to clients warehouse.___

Embalagem: ___Packing export___
(Packing) ___in wood cases___

[B2913]

Item No.	Quant.	DESIGNAÇÃO (Part No.)	DENOMINAÇÃO (Description)	Desconto (Discount)	Preço Unitário (Unit Price)	Imp. Total (Amount)
01	1,200	187-B	Bearings	US $ NETTO	2.15	2,580.00
02	2,400	839-R	Bearings	"	3.37	8,088.00
					F.A.S.	10,668.00
			Insurance Fee			48.50
			Documentation & Expenses			19.00
			Consular Fee on Invoice			52.00
			Consular Fee on Bill of Lading			6.00
			Ocean Freight			156.50
					Total C.I.F.	10,950.00

COMPANHIA IMPORTADORA BRASILEIRA

Juan Cordova Hernandez
Director Comercial

[B2914]

FORM 3
BUYER'S PURCHASE ORDER

By this process, a rather remarkable thing happens: large hazards inherent in a transaction between a seller and a remote buyer can be reduced almost to the vanishing point by breaking the transaction into steps, and by assigning each step to a party who is in a position to avoid mishap. Thus, the seller is assured of payment by the engagement of the confirming Philadelphia bank; the Philadelphia bank is assured of reimbursement by the undertaking of the issuing Brazilian bank; this Brazilian bank can take steps to assure reimbursement by its local customer. Unhappily, as will soon be seen, not every risk can be removed. But the success of these arrangements is shown by their widespread use by sellers and by the minimal rates charged by banks for the risks which remain.[5]

To meet SKF's letter of credit requirements, Brasileira requests its local bank, Banco do Brasil, to arrange for the issuance of a letter of credit which will comply with the terms of the proforma invoice. Brasileira will sign a detailed Application and Agreement for Commercial Credit prepared by the bank.[6] Banco do Brasil, after approving Brasileira's credit standing, transmits a letter of credit by cable to the Philadelphia confirming bank. The Philadelphia bank then delivers to SKF a document (FORM 4) advising SKF that Banco do Brasil has opened a described letter of credit in favor of SKF and adding the Philadelphia bank's confirmation. (See the end of FORM 4.)

By this arrangement, SKF, the beneficiary of the credit, is assured of payment of its sight drafts drawn on the local Philadelphia bank in the amount of the total cost of the sale, provided it presents the documents called for in the letter of credit. An examination of this letter of credit also reveals that the bill of lading is to be consigned to the "order of Banco do Brasil," thereby giving this bank control over the goods, with the consequent security for its claim against the buyer which has already been discussed.

5. In domestic or import letters of credit, an American bank might typically charge an opening commission of $20 and, for negotiations, $1/4$% (minimum of $10 for clean drafts and $30 for documentary drafts). A typical commission for accepting an export letter of credit would be $1\frac{1}{2}$% (rate varying with risk; minimum $50), and for confirming a foreign letter of credit $1/10$% (minimum $50). For paying under an export letter of credit, the charge might be $1/10$% ($35 minimum).

6. A typical American bank's Application and Agreement for Commercial Letter of Credit calls for the buyer to specify which documents should be required by the Letter of Credit, and other essential information such as the amount and expiration date of the credit. The form of agreement then contains two or more closely-printed pages of provisions most of which are designed to assure the bank of reimbursement from its customer for the bank's outlays under the credit in spite of various mishaps. The form also may provide that, except for points covered by the agreement, the operation of the credit will be governed by the Uniform Customs and Practice for Commercial Documentary Credits (1974 Revision in force from 1 October 1975).

This Application, of course, governs only the relationship between the bank and its customer requesting the credit (Brasileira). The obligation of the bank to the beneficiary (SKF) will be governed by the terms of the Letter of Credit which the bank thereafter issues.

Acceptance; Shipment. On receipt of the confirmed letter of credit, SKF sends Brasileira its Order Acknowledgment (FORM 5). This document repeats the description and price of the goods which had also appeared on the proforma invoice and states the number and expiration date of the letter of credit. Note the provision in the lower right hand corner that the buyer's order is accepted, "Subject To The Conditions Listed On The Reverse Side Of This Acknowledgment." (Note especially the conditions dealing with the effect of contingencies beyond the seller's control, fluctuations in the price of the goods, and liability for defective merchandise.)

The arrival of the letter of credit is the "go ahead" signal for SKF to make the shipment. SKF then prepares the Commercial Invoice (FORM 6) which provides a complete record of the transaction and is an important source of information to such interested parties as a bank discounting a draft or an underwriter extending insurance. Note that all data on the commercial invoice conforms to that found in the other shipping documents. By scanning it, one should be able to form a complete picture of the nature of the packing (number of packages, weights, etc.), the commodities being shipped, and the value of the shipment.

As the time for actual shipment of the bearings approaches, SKF contacts Pierce-Byron Inc., the forwarder who will act as the agent of the shipper in attending to the details of shipment and further documentation. Since SKF is located in a port city there are no problems regarding inland transportation to the port of export. SKF sends shipping instructions to Pierce-Byron that inform the forwarder that to comply with the requirements of the letter of credit, the bill of lading must be drawn to the "order of Banco do Brasil." In addition to these shipping instructions, SKF also sends its forwarder copies of the commercial invoice, a packing list and a Shipper's Export Declaration (a Department of Commerce form designed to give the government data from which foreign trade statistics can be compiled). When the forwarder receives these documents, he takes over all further documentation as the agent of the shipper; the latter merely has to dispatch the goods from the factory in accordance with the forwarder's instructions.

In shipments to many countries one of the documents specified in the letter of credit will be a "Consular Invoice", which is required by the buyer's government for foreign customs and statistical purposes. In the case of Brazil, such a separate invoice is not necessary. Instead, a notarized statement is set forth at the end of the Commercial Invoice (FORM 6, supra) and this document is visaed by the Brazilian consul in Philadelphia.

PNB **Philadelphia National Bank** [X] To be collected at negotiation.
INTERNATIONAL DIVISION
P O Box 13866, Phila , PA 19101
[ ] We have debited your Account/ H. O. Account
CABLE ADDRESS: **PHILABANK** TELEX: 845-355

L/C Advisiong Comm.		ACCOUNT NUMBER
$ 30.00		
Confirmation commission		AMOUNT
$ 50.00	$ 80.00	

IRREVOCABLE DOCUMENTARY CREDIT

OUR CREDIT NO.	CR NO—CORRESPONDENT	DATE	EXPIRY DATE	LETTER OF CREDIT AMOUNT
E 4450	164	JAN.11,1984	FEB.28,1984	US$10,950.00

BENEFICIARY

SKF INDUSTRIES, INC.
PHILADELPHIA, PA.

CORRESPONDENT

BANCO do BRAZIL S.A.
RIO de JANEIRO, BRAZIL

Gentlemen:

We are instructed by the above correspondent to advise you that they have opened their irrevocable credit in your favor for account of <u>COMPANHIA IMPORTADORA BRASILEIRA, CAIXA POSTAL 10, RIO de JANEIRO, BRAZIL</u> available by your drafts on THE PHILADELPHIA NATIONAL BANK AT SIGHT accompanied by the following documents:

1. FULL SET OF CLEAN ON BOARD OCEAN BILLS OF LADING STATING "FREIGHT PREPAID" MADE OUT TO ORDER OF BANCO do BRAZIL S.A.
2. INSURANCE POLICY OR CERTIFICATE COVERING MARINE AND WAR RISK.
3. PACKING LIST.
4. COMMERCIAL INVOICE IN SEXTUPLICATE OF WHICH THREE COPIES MUST BE LEGALIZED BY THE BRAZILIAN CONSUL AND VISAED BY THE LOCAL CHAMBER OF COMMERCE.

<u>COVERING:</u> 1200 BALL BEARING NO. 187-B AND 2400 ROLLER BEARINGS NO. 839-R.
            TOTAL VALUE $10,950.00 CIF RIO de JANEIRO
            IMPORT LICENSE DC-59/10000 EXPIRES 2/28/84

<u>SPECIAL INSTRUCTIONS:</u>

A. ALL DRAFTS SO DRAWN MUST BE MARKED "DRAWN UNDER ADVICE NO. E 4450/164".

<u>SHIPMENT FROM:</u> PHILADELPHIA   <u>TO</u>: RIO de JANEIRO

<u>PARTIAL SHIPMENTS:</u>ARE NOT PERMITTED   <u>TRANSHIPMENTS:</u>ARE NOT PERMITTED

THE ABOVE CORRESPONDENT ENGAGES WITH YOU THAT ALL DRAFTS DRAWN UNDER AND IN COMPLIANCE WITH THE TERMS OF THIS CREDIT WILL BE HONORED ON DELIVERY OF DOCUMENTS AS SPECIFIED IF PRESENTED AT THIS OFFICE ON OR BEFORE THE EXPIRATION DATE SHOWN ABOVE.

IF DESIRED, DRAFTS AND DOCUMENTS MAY BE PRESENTED AT PHILADELPHIA INTERNATIONAL BANK, 55 BROAD STREET, NEW YORK, N.Y. 10004.

[D629]

PNB Philadelphia National Bank
INTERNATIONAL DIVISION
P.O. Box 13866, Phila., PA 19101

☐ To be collected at negotiation.

☐ We have debited your Account/ H. O. Account

L/C Advisiong Comm.	ACCOUNT NUMBER
$	
Confirmation commission	AMOUNT
$	$

CABLE ADDRESS: PHILABANK TELEX: 845-355

IRREVOCABLE DOCUMENTARY CREDIT

ATTACHED TO AND FORMING PART OF DOCUMENTARY CREDIT NO. E4450 DATE: JANUARY 11,1984
CR. NO. CORRESPONDENT 164

MAIL TO·

DOCUMENTS MUST CONFORM STRICTLY WITH THE TERMS OF THIS CREDIT, IF YOU ARE UNABLE TO COMPLY WITH ITS TERMS, PLEASE COMMUNICATE WITH YOUR CUSTOMER PROMPTLY WITH A VIEW TO HAVING THE CONDITIONS CHANGED. THIS WILL ELIMINATE DIFFICULTIES AND DELAY WHEN YOUR DOCUMENTS ARE PRESENTED FOR NEGOTIATION.

X WE CONFIRM THIS CREDIT AND THEREBY UNDERTAKE THAT ALL DRAFTS DRAWN IN ACCORDANCE WITH TERMS THEREOF WILL BE DULY HONORED ON PRESENTATION.

ALL DRAFTS AND DOCUMENTS MUST INDICATE THE REFERENCE NUMBER OF THE CORRESPONDENT BANK AND THE REFERENCE NUMBER OF THE PHILADELPHIA NATIONAL BANK.

Carrie Cash
AUTHORIZED SIGNATURE

EXCEPT SO FAR AS OTHERWISE EXPRESSLY STATED, THIS DOCUMENTARY CREDIT IS SUBJECT TO THE "UNIFORM CUSTOMS AND PRACTICE FOR DOCUMENTARY CREDITS: (1974 REVISION), INTERNATIONAL CHAMBER OF COMMERCE, PUBLICATION NO. 290.

[D630]

FORM 4

LETTER OF CREDIT

CUSTOMER
Companhia Importadora Brasileira

ADDRESS
Caixa Postal 10
Rio de Janeiro, Brazil

SOLD TO • Companhia Importadora Brasileira

TERMS • Letter of Credit

IMPORT LICENSE • DG-59/10000 expires 2/28/84

CUSTOMER ORDER NO. CIB-43H2 •

CUSTOMER ORDER DATE 1/5/84   **CUSTOMER NO.** 88831

TERRITORY NO. 824   **IND. NO.** X4   100

OF Caixa Postal 10
Rio de Janeiro, Brazil

EXPORT LICENSE G-DEST

LETTER OF CREDIT • NO. E 4450/164 expires 2/28/84

SKF ORDER NO. W-77   **SHPT. NO.** 1

DATE 1/12/84

MARKS AND CASE NUMBERS	QUANTITIES		DESCRIPTION OF GOODS	SELLING PRICE	
	ORDERED	SHIPPED		UNIT	TOTAL
187-B	1,200	1,200	Bearings	2.15	2,580.00
839-R	2,400	2,400	Bearings	3.37	8,088.00
					10,668.00

CUSTOMER'S DELIVERY REQUIREMENTS:

January 1984

EXPORT TERMS:
SHIPPING F.A.S. PHILADELPHIA PA.
OR NEW YORK, N. Y.

PAYMENT: SEE ABOVE

SKF DELIVERY PROMISES:

January 1984

GENTLEMEN:
WE THANK YOU FOR THE ORDER LISTED ABOVE, WHICH WE
ACCEPT SUBJECT TO THE CONDITIONS LISTED ON THE
REVERSE SIDE OF THIS ACKNOWLEDGMENT.

SKF INDUSTRIES, INC.
PHILADELPHIA, PA. 19132

[B2893]

FORM 5

ORDER ACKNOWLEDGEMENT

[The reverse side of this form is the same as the reverse side of
Form 2]

SKF INDUSTRIES, INC.
FRONT STREET AND ERIE AVE.
PHILADELPHIA, PA. 19132
P. O. BOX 6731

CUSTOMER ORDER NO. NUMERO DE PEDIDO DEL CLIENTE	SKF ORDER NO. NUMERO DE PEDIDO DE SKF	SHPT. NO. DESPACHO
CIB-43H2	W-77	1

EXPORT SALES DEPT.
CABLE ADDRESS   "SKAYEF"

SKF INVOICE DATE
FECHA DE LA FATURA   1/12/84

SOLD TO
VENDIDO A   Companhia Importadora Brasileira
OF / DE   Caixa Postal 10
Rio de Janeiro, Brazil

TERMS
PLAZOS   Letter of Credit
FAS/   Philadelphia

IMPORT LICENSE
LICENCIA DE IMPORTACION   DG-59/10000 expires 2/28/84

LETTER OF CREDIT
CARTA DE CREDITO   No. E 4450/164 expires 2/28/84

"ROLAMENTOS COMPLETOS DE ESFERAS"

MARKS AND CASE NUMBERS MARCAS Y NUMEROS DE CAJA	QUANTITY SHIPPED CANTIDAD EMBARCADA	DESCRIPTION OF GOODS DESCRIPCION DEL MATERIAL		SELLING PRICE PRECIO DE VENTA	
				UNIT UNIDADES	TOTAL TOTAL
				US$	US$
C.I.B. RIO DE JANEIRO #1/25	1,200	187-B	Bearings	2.15	2,580.00
	2,400	839-R	Bearings	3.37	8,088.00
					10,688.00
			Consular Fees		58.00
			Freight Forwarders Chrgs.		19.00
			Insurance Charge		48.50
			Transportation Charge		156.50
			TOTAL C.I.F.		10,950.00

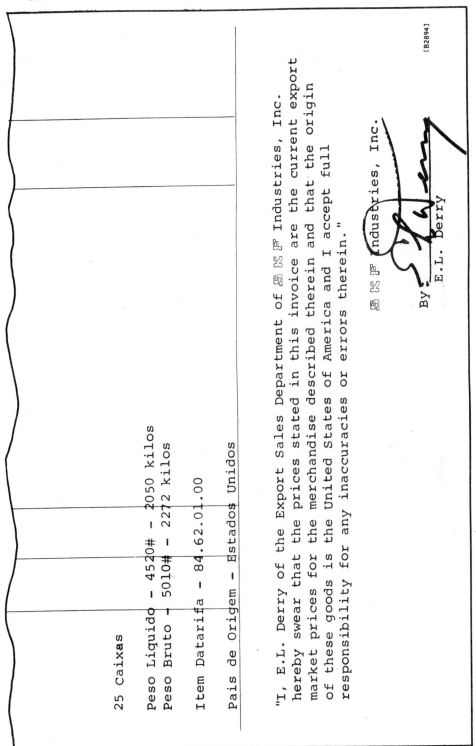

25 Caixas

Peso Liquido - 4520# - 2050 kilos
Peso Bruto - 5010# - 2272 kilos

Item Datarifa - 84.62.01.00

Pais de Origem - Estados Unidos

"I, E.L. Derry of the Export Sales Department of SKF Industries, Inc. hereby swear that the prices stated in this invoice are the current export market prices for the merchandise described therein and that the origin of these goods is the United States of America and I accept full responsibility for any inaccuracies or errors therein."

[B28941]

SKF Industries, Inc.

By E.L. Derry

FORM 6
COMMERCIAL INVOICE

SKF then sends the cases of bearings by truck to the pier where they are delivered to the ocean carrier's receiving clerk who signs a dock receipt. The dock receipt is a form supplied by the ocean carrier which contains information relevant to the shipping of the bearings such as the number of the pier, and (if known) the name of the ship. The dock receipt is non-negotiable; as its name suggests, when signed by the receiving clerk, the dock receipt serves as a temporary receipt for the goods until they are loaded on board.

The S.S. Mormacoak is soon ready to receive cargo. When the bearings are loaded on board, the steamship line issues a Bill of Lading (FORM 7) which, to comply with the letter of credit, is "CONSIGNED TO ORDER OF *Banco do Brasil*". The bill of lading is initially prepared by the forwarder on a form supplied by the ocean carrier; it sets forth the markings and numbers of the packages, a description of the goods, and the number and weight of the packages. The reverse side of the bill of lading states that the goods are "Received for Shipment," but a statement "FREIGHT PREPAID *ON BOARD*" is initialed by a representative of the steamship line after loading. (Note carefully this indorsement; the distinction between a "Received for Shipment" and an "on board" bill of lading may be important. See infra.) The forwarder delivers the bill of lading and the commercial invoice to SKF.

Insurance. It was noted above that in this transaction the price was quoted "F.A.S. Philadelphia", whereas in many overseas transactions the price is quoted as "C.I.F.". One of the important differences between these two forms of quotation relates to the handling of insurance. Under the C.I.F. quotation the seller is obliged to obtain and pay for insurance on the shipment. Receiving this insurance coverage is, of course, important to the buyer; to assure this the letter of credit under C.I.F. transaction would require the seller to present an appropriate insurance policy covering the shipment, along with the shipping and other documents, when seller presents his draft to the bank for payment.

The present F.A.S. transaction of itself imposes no such obligation. However, one will note that the letter of credit (FORM 4) requires SKF to present "Insurance Policy or Certificate covering marine and war risk." If there were no letter of credit, the buyer might arrange independently for insurance. But a bank issuing a letter of credit needs insurance to protect its interest in the goods as security for the buyer's obligation to reimburse the bank for its payments under the credit. As the first step towards complying with this requirement, you may have noted that on the proforma invoice SKF computed an "estimated value—C.I.F. which included an item for "estimated insurance charges" of $48.50.

SKF, like most sellers who ship goods abroad, has an "open" policy of insurance which covers all goods in transit from warehouse to warehouse plus 30 days; the premiums depend on the volume of shipments reported to the insurer and covered by the policy. SKF fills out a Marine Insurance Policy (FORM 8) stating the necessary details of the specific shipment. Since the insurance policy will pass through various hands which may need its protection, the policy provides that it "does insure SKF Industries, Inc., For account of whom it may concern . . . Loss, if any, payable to assured *or order.*" The policy will be countersigned by the insurance company to provide evidence to third persons of its obligation under the policy.

Payment; the Draft. The Philadelphia bank stated in their letter that the estimated C.I.F. price of $10,950 would be "available by your drafts on us at sight" when accompanied by the listed documents. SKF accordingly draws a sight draft for $10,950 on the Philadelphia bank (FORM 9). The sight draft together with the commercial invoice (in sextuplicate), insurance certificate (original and duplicate), full set of ocean bills of lading (three originals) and the packing list (original and duplicate) are presented to the Philadelphia bank. When the bank receives these documents it issues its bank draft to SKF's order for $10,950 and transmits the documents by air mail to Banco do Brasil, which will reimburse the Philadelphia bank.

The documents, sent by air mail, will reach the Brazilian bank well ahead of the ocean shipment. The time for the release of the documents to buyer and his reimbursement to the bank will depend upon the arrangement which was made between the bank and buyer when the letter of credit was initially established. If the buyer plans to resell the bearings, he may not be able to reimburse the bank until the goods arrive and he resells the goods. In this event, the Brazilian bank may need to take further steps to secure its claim against the buyer. Happily, such added complications need not concern us now.

MOORE McCORMACK LINES, Incorporated

COMBINED TRANSPORT
PORT TO PORT
BILL OF LADING

NOT NEGOTIABLE UNLESS
CONSIGNED "TO ORDER"

SHIPPER/EXPORTER

SKF INDUSTRIES, INC
1100 FIRST AVENUE
KING OF PRUSSIA, PA 19406

DOCUMENT NO.

EXPORT REFERENCES

EXPORT DEC. NO.

CONSIGNEE
ORDER OF

BANCO DO BRAZIL, S.A.
RIO DE JANEIRO, BRAZIL

FORWARDING AGENT - REFERENCES

PIERCE BYRON, INC.
325 CHESTNUT ST. PHILA., PA

MMC NO.

POINT AND COUNTRY OF ORIGIN

NOTIFY PARTY

COMPANHIA IMPORTADORA BRASILEIRA
CAIXA POSTAL 10
RIO DE JANEIRO, BRAZIL

DOMESTIC ROUTING/EXPORT INSTRUCTIONS

DELIVERY TO STEAMER
BY DELAIR TRUCKING CO.

PRECARRIAGE BY

PACKER AVENUE

PLACE OF RECEIPT

EXPORTING CARRIER (SHIP)   USA FLAG

S/S MORMACOAK   AM

PORT OF LOADING

PHILA., PA

PORT OF DISCHARGE

RIO DE JANEIRO

PLACE OF DELIVERY

ONWARD INLAND ROUTING

PARTICULARS FURNISHED BY SHIPPER OF GOODS

MARKS AND NUMBERS	NO. OF PKGS.	SHIPPERS DESCRIPTION OF PACKAGES AND GOODS	GROSS WEIGHT		MEASUREMENT
			KILOS	POUNDS	
C.I.B. RIO DE JANEIRO #1/25	25	(TWENTY-FIVE) CASES OF: STEEL AND ROLLER BEARINGS "IMPORT LICENSE DG-59/10000 EXPIRES FEBRUARY 28, 1984" LETTER OF CREDIT NO E4450/164 "EVIDENCING SHIPMENT OF 1200 BALL BEARINGS NO 187-B AND 2400 ROLLER BEARINGS NO 839-R" FREIGHT PREPAID "ON BOARD" JANUARY 12, 1984 "O R I G I N A L"	2272 KGS	5010 LBS	

* Notice: All rates apply from ships tackle at port of loading to end of ships tackle at port of discharge, unless otherwise mentioned.

FREIGHT TO BE PREPAID IN U.S.A.

ITEM	WEIGHT (2)	CUBIC FEET (3)	@ RATE	FREIGHT CHARGES	TYPE/RATE	TYPE BRKGE	TYPE CARGO	COMMODITY NO.	P P or COLL.	COLLECT PORT	ACCOUNT CODE
	5010 LBS.		$70.00	$ 156. 50							
		(per 2240 LBS)	$								
			$								
			$								
	TERMINAL CHARGE		$	10. 00							
			$								
			$								
			$								
			$								

EXCESS VALUATION (See reverse side)

Freight to be COLLECTED $	Freight to be PREPAID $	$166.50

'N WITNESS whereof THREE (3) original Bills of Lading (unless otherwise stated above) have been signed, one of which being accomplished, the others shall be void.

MOORE McCORMACK LINES, Incorporated

By

IN ACCEPTING THIS BILL OF LADING, the Merchant expressly accepts and agrees to be bound by all its terms, conditions, exceptions, limitations, exemptions and liberties, whether printed, typed, stamped, endorsed or written, or otherwise incorporated, either on the front or back hereof.

JANUARY	12	1984
MONTH	DAY	YEAR

5

[D631]

FORM 7

OCEAN BILL OF LADING

[Front]

SHORT FORM BILL OF LADING

Received the Goods, or containers, vans, trailers, vehicles, transportable tanks, flats, palletized units, skids, platforms, frames, cradles, sling-loads or other packages said to contain the Goods herein mentioned in apparent external good order and condition, except as otherwise indicated herein, to be transported to the port of discharge named herein and/or such port or place as authorized or permitted hereby or so near thereunto as the vessel can get, lie and leave, always in safety and afloat under all conditions of tide, water and weather and there to be delivered to the Merchant or on-Carrier on payment of all charges due thereon.

This short form Bill of Lading issued for the Merchant's convenience and at its request instead of the Carrier's regular long form Bill of Lading, shall have effect subject to the provisions of the United States Carriage of Goods by Sea Act approved April 16, 1936 or, if this Bill of Lading is issued in any other locality where there is in force a compulsorily applicable Carriage of Goods by Sea Act, Ordinance or Statute of a nature similar to the International Convention for the Unification of Certain Rules Relating to Bills of Lading, dated at Brussels, August 25, 1924, it shall be subject to the provisions of said Act, Ordinance or Statute and rules thereto annexed.

All the terms and conditions of the Carrier's regular long form Bill of Lading, including any clauses presently being printed, typed, stamped, endorsed or written thereon, are incorporated herein by reference with the same force and effect as if they were written at length herein, and all such terms and conditions so incorporated by reference are agreed by Merchant to be binding and to govern the relations, whatever they may be, between all who are or may become parties or holders of this Bill of Lading or owners of the Goods, or containers or other packages covered thereby, as fully as if this Bill of Lading had been prepared on the Carrier's regular long form Bill of Lading.

At all times when the Goods, or containers or other packages are in the care, custody or control of a participating Carrier, such Carrier shall be entitled to all the rights, privileges, liens, limitations of and exonerations from liability, granted or permitted to such participating Carrier under its Bill(s) of Lading, tariff(s) and law compulsorily applicable, and nothing contained in this Bill of Lading shall be deemed a surrender thereof by such participating Carrier.

Each Carrier shall, subject to the terms and conditions of this Bill of Lading and the applicable tariffs, laws, rules and regulations, be responsible for any loss or damage to the Goods, or containers or other packages only during the time the Goods, or containers or other packages are in its actual care, custody and control, except as otherwise expressly provided herein.

In making any arrangements for transportation by participating Carriers of the Goods, or containers or other packages carried hereunder, either before or after ocean carriage, it is understood and agreed that the ocean Carrier acts solely as agent of the Merchant, without any other responsibility whatsoever as Carrier for such transportation.

The Merchant's attention is directed to the fact that the Carrier's regular long form Bill of Lading contains a number of provisions giving the Carrier and participating Carriers certain rights and privileges and certain exemptions and immunities from and limitations of liability additional to those provided by the said United States Carriage of Goods by Sea Act, 1936 and/or Convention and/or such other Act, Ordinance or Statute as may be applicable and, in addition, extends the benefit of its provisions to-stevedores and other independent contractors. The Carrier's regular long form Bill of Lading is on file with the Federal Maritime Commission and Interstate Commerce Commission in Washington, D.C. and copies can be obtained from the Carrier or from the Federal Maritime Commission or, if covering Intermodal Transporation, from the Interstate Commerce Commission if applicable.

In case of any loss or damage to or in connection with Goods exceeding in actual value the equivalent of $500 lawful money of the United States, per package, or in case of Goods not shipped in packages, per shipping unit, the value of the Goods shall be deemed to be $500 per package or per shipping unit. The Carrier's liability, if any, shall be determined on the basis of a value of $500 per package or per shipping unit or pro rata in case of partial loss or damage, unless the nature of the Goods and a valuation higher than $500 per package or per shipping unit shall have been declared in writing by the shipper before shipment and inserted in this Bill of Lading, and extra freight or charge paid. In such case, if the actual value of the Goods per package or per shipping unit shall exceed such declared value, the value shall nevertheless be deemed to be declared value and the Carrier's liability, if any, shall not exceed the declared value and any partial loss or damage shall be adjusted pro rata on the basis of such declared value.

The words "shipping unit" shall mean and include physical unit or piece of cargo not shipped in a package, including articles or things of any description whatsoever, except Goods shipped in bulk, and irrespective of weight or measurement unit employed in calculating freight charges.

Where containers, vans, trailers, vehicles, transportable tanks, flats, palletized units, skids, platforms, frames, cradles, sling-loads and other such packages are not packed by the Carrier, each individual such container, van, trailer, vehicle, transportable tank, palletized unit, skid, platform, frame, cradle, sling-load and other such package, including in each instance its contents, shall be deemed a single package and Carrier's liability limited to $500 with respect to each such package.

A signed original Bill of Lading, duly endorsed, must be surrendered to the Carrier on delivery of the Goods, or container or other packages.

All agreements with respect to the Goods, or containers or other packages carried hereunder are superseded hereby and none of the terms hereof shall be deemed waived or surrendered unless in writing and signed by a duly authorized agent of the Carrier.   [D632]

FORM 7

OCEAN BILL OF LADING

[*Reverse*]

A STOCK COMPANY

MARINE INDEMNITY INSURANCE COMPANY OF AMERICA
Wm. H. McGEE & CO., Inc., Managers, 4 World Trade Center, New York, N. Y. 10048

SPECIAL CARGO POLICY

R-32251 OC 970788

In correspondence refer to those letters and numbers

SUM INSURED	ASSURED'S REFERENCE	PLACE AND DATE
$ 10,950.00	CIB-43H2	KING OF PRUSSIA, PA 19406 JANUARY 12, 1984

This Company, in consideration of an agreed premium and subject to the terms and conditions below and on the reverse hereof or stamped or endorsed hereon, does insure

_ _ _ SKF INDUSTRIES, INC. _

in the sum of_ _ _ TEN THOUSAND NINE HUNDRED FIFTY AND _ _ _ _ _ _ _ _ _ _ _ _ _ _ _ _ _ 00/100 US _ _ _ _ _ _ _ _ _ _ _ _ Dollars

on _ _ TWENTY-FIVE (25) CASES CONTAINING: STEEL BALL AND ROLLER _ _   **MARKS AND NUMBERS**

_ _ _ BEARINGS GROSS WT: 5010 LBS _   C.I.B.

valued at sum insured, to be shipped subject to an "Under Deck" Bill of Lading unless otherwise specified hereon,   RIO DE JANEIRO #1/25

by _ _ S.S MORMACOAK _ _ _ _ _ _ _ _ _ _ _ _ _ or other vessel, and connecting conveyances B/L date JANUARY 12, 1984   IMPORT LICENSE DG-59/10000

at and from _ _ PHILADELPHIA, PA USA _ _ _ _ _ via_ _ _ _ _ _ _ _ _ _ _ _ _ _ _ _   EXPIRES FEBRUARY 28, 1984

to _ _ RIO DE JANEIRO, BRAZIL _   L/C NO E 4450/164

Loss, if any, payable to the order of the Assured.

────────────── SPECIAL TERMS AND CONDITIONS ──────────────

SHIPMENTS ON DECK, AIR CARGO and MAIL or PARCEL POST SHIPMENTS, when insured under this Policy are subject to average terms and conditions specified in clauses 18, 19 and 20 hereof. SHIPMENTS SUBJECT TO AN "UNDER DECK" BILL OF LADING AND SHIPMENTS IN CONTAINERS SUBJECT TO AN "UNDER DECK" BILL OF LADING OR A BILL OF LADING WHICH DOES NOT DISCLOSE THE NATURE OF STOWAGE ARE INSURED:—

Machinery, Tools, Ball Bearing Parts, Factory Instruments, Steel and Raw Materials incidental to the business of the Assured are insured:—

To cover against all risks of physical loss or damage from any external cause or spontaneous combustion (excepting such risks as are excluded by the F. C. & S. Warranty and S. R. & C. C. Warranty in this policy) irrespective of percentage.

This Insurance is also subject to the following American Institute Clauses current on the date of issuance of this policy:—			When goods are so destined this insurance is subject to:—
MARINE EXTENSION CLAUSES	S. R. & C. C. ENDORSEMENT	WAR RISK INSURANCE	SOUTH AMERICAN 60 DAY CLAUSE

ORIGINAL — DUPLICATE UNPAID

This Policy not transferable unless countersigned by an authorized representative of this Company or the Assured

SKF Industries, Inc.

Countersigned

IN WITNESS WHEREOF, this Company has executed and attested these presents.

Secretary   *President*

[D833]

FORM 8
MARINE INSURANCE POLICY

This insurance is against the perils of the seas, fire, assailing thieves, jettisons, barratry of the master and mariners, and all other like perils, losses or misfortunes that have or shall come to the hurt, detriment or damage of the property insured hereunder or any part thereof except as otherwise provided for herein.

TERMS AND CONDITIONS REFERRED TO ON THE FACE OF THIS POLICY

AMERICAN INSTITUTE CARGO CLAUSES (February, 1949)
(F. C. & S. Warranty October, 1948)

1. **WAREHOUSE TO WAREHOUSE CLAUSE:** This insurance attaches from the time the goods leave the Warehouse and/or Store at the place named in the Policy for the commencement of the transit and continues during the ordinary course of transit, including customary transhipment, if any, until the goods are discharged overside from the overseas vessel at the final port. Thereafter the insurance continues while the goods are in transit and/or until delivered to final destination to which the goods are insured is outside the limits of the port) whichever shall first occur. The time limits referred to above to be reckoned from midnight of the day on which the discharge overside of the goods hereby insured from the overseas vessel is completed. Held covered at a premium to be arranged in the event of transhipment, if any, other than as above and/or in the event of delay in excess of the above time limits arising from circumstances beyond the control of the Assured.
If it be necessary for the Assured to give prompt notice to these Assurers when they become aware of an event for which they are "held covered" under this Policy and the right to such cover is dependent on compliance with this obligation.

2. **CRAFT, &c. CLAUSE:** Including transit by craft and/or lighter to and from the vessel. Each craft and/or lighter to be deemed a separate insurance. The Assured are not to be prejudiced by any agreement exempting lightermen from liability.

3. **DEVIATION CLAUSE:** This insurance shall not be vitiated by any unintentional error in description of vessel, voyage or interest, or by deviation, over-carriage, change of voyage, transhipment or any other error or omission, over which the Assured have no control. It is agreed, however, that said such error or deviation be disclosed, and additional premium paid if required.

4. **F. P. A. CLAUSE:** Warranted free from Particular Average unless the vessel or craft be stranded, sunk, or burnt; but notwithstanding this warranty these Assurers are to pay any loss of or damage to the interest insured which may reasonably be attributed to fire, collision or contact of the vessel and/or craft and/or conveyance with any external substance (ice included) other than water, or to discharge of cargo at port of distress. The foregoing warranty, however, shall not apply where broader terms of Average are provided for herein or endorsed hereon.

5. **WAREHOUSING & FORWARDING CHARGES, PACKAGES TOTALLY LOST LOADING, ETC.** Notwithstanding any average warranty contained herein, these Assurers agree to pay any loss, warehousing, forwarding and special charges for which this Policy in the absence of such warranty would be liable, also to pay the landing, warehousing and value of any package or packages which may be totally lost in loading, transhipment or discharge.

6. **LABELS CLAUSE:** In case of damage affecting labels, capsules or wrappers, these Assurers, if liable therefor under the terms of this Policy, shall not be liable for more than an amount sufficient to pay the cost of new labels, capsules or wrappers, and the cost of reconditioning the goods, but in no event shall these Assurers be liable for more than the insured value of the damaged merchandise.

7. **MACHINERY CLAUSE:** In the event the property insured under this Policy includes a machine consisting when complete for sale or use, of several parts, then in case of loss or damage covered by this insurance to any part of such machine, these Assurers shall be liable only for the proportion of the insured value of the part lost or damaged, or at the Assured's option, for the cost and expense, including labor and forwarding charges, of replacing or repairing the lost or damaged part; but in no event shall these Assurers be liable for more than the insured value of the complete machine.

8. **G/A CLAUSE:** General Average and Salvage Charges payable according to United States laws and usage and/or as per Foreign Statement and/or as per York-Antwerp Rules (as prescribed in whole or in part) if in accordance with the Contract of Affreightment.

9. **EXPLOSION CLAUSE:** Including the risk of explosion, howsoever or wheresoever occurring during the currency of this insurance, unless excluded by the F. C. & S. Warranty or the S. R. & C. C. Warranty.

10. **SHORE CLAUSE:** Where this insurance by its terms covers while on docks, wharves or elsewhere on shore, and/or during land transportation, it shall include the risks of collision, derailment, overturning or other accident to the conveyance, fire, lightning, sprinkler leakage, cyclone, hurricane, earthquake, floods (meaning the rising of navigable waters) and/or collapse or subsidence of docks or wharves, even though the insurance be otherwise F. P. A.

11. **BILL OF LADING, &c. CLAUSE:** The Assured are not to be prejudiced by the presence of the negligence clause in the Bill of Lading and/or Charter Party, and/or the seaworthiness of the vessel as between the Assured and these Assurers is hereby admitted and the wrongful act or misconduct of the shipowner or his servants causing a loss is not to defeat the recovery by an innocent Assured if the loss in the absence of such wrongful act or misconduct would have been a loss recoverable on the Policy. With leave to sail with or without pilots, and to tow and ...

12. **INCHMAREE CLAUSE:** This insur...

OTHER TERMS AND CONDITIONS OF THIS POLICY

18. **SHIPMENTS ON DECK:** Goods shipped on deck (which must be so declared to this Company and specified hereon) are insured:—F.P.A. as per American Institute Cargo Clauses omitting this Policy, but including the risks of jettison and/or washing overboard irrespective of percentage.
Notwithstanding the above, goods shipped subject to an "Under Deck" Bill of Lading when stowed on deck without the knowledge and consent of the Assured and/or shipper shall be treated and insured as shipments "Under Deck", provided such occurrence be reported to this Company as soon as known to the Assured.

19. **AIR CARGO:** When this Policy covers goods shipped by air freight or air express and/or meeting conveyances, such shipments are insured:—Against all risks of physical loss or damage from any external cause (excepting such risks as are excluded by the F. C. & S. Warranty in this Policy) irrespective of percentage.
Note:—Wherever the words "ship", "vessel", "seaworthiness", "ship or vessel", "aircraft", "airworthiness", this Policy, they are deemed to include also the words "aircraft", "airworthiness".

20. **MAIL AND PARCEL POST SHIPMENTS:** When this Policy covers goods shipped by Registered and/or Unregistered Mail and Registered Mail and/or Ordinary Parcel Post, including Air Mail or Air Parcel Post, such shipments are insured:—Against all risks of physical loss or damage from any external cause (excepting such risks as are excluded by the F. C. & S. Warranty and S. R. & C. C. Warranty in this Policy) irrespective of percentage.
Attaching from time of delivery to postal authorities and covering until delivered at address. Warranted by the Assured that all packages insured will be shipped in strict accordance with Postal Regulations of the Country to or from which they are mailed.
No claim shall in such for any unexplained shortage or for any shortage in goods claimed to have been forwarded in each package, when the package is received by the consignee in apparent good order with seals unbroken.

21. **G/A CONTRIBUTORY CLAUSE:** This Company shall be liable for only such proportion of General Average and Salvage Charges as the sum hereby insured (less Particular Average, if any, for which this Company is liable hereunder) bears to the contributory value of the property hereby insured.

22. **GROUNDING IN CANALS, HARBORS, ETC.:** Grounding in canals, harbors or tidal rivers not to be deemed a stranding, but this Company shall be liable for any damage or loss which may be proved to have resulted therefrom and which would be recoverable if caused by stranding.

23. **FUMIGATION CLAUSE:** This Company will indemnify the Assured for loss or damage to the insured property directly resulting from fumigation of the vessel.

24. **GRAIN LOADING WARRANTY:** Warranted by the Assured that any Vessel to be loaded at any United States port with grain in excess of the Vessel's gross registered tonnage is to be loaded under the inspection of a surveyor appointed by National Cargo Bureau, Inc. or of a surveyor appointed by the Assurers, and that a certificate of such surveyor shall be issued before the sailing of such Vessel, stating that the loading was in accordance with the regulations of the United States Coast Guard, or the insurance under this Policy shall be void.

25. **OTHER INSURANCE:** If an interest insured hereunder is covered by other ocean marine insurance, has, if any, shall be collected from the several policies in the order of their attachment. Insurance attaching on the same date to be deemed simultaneous and contribute pro rata.
If at the time of loss or damage there is available to a named or unnamed Assured or any other interested party any other insurance, excepting ocean marine insurance, which would apply in the absence of this Policy, the insurance under this Policy shall apply only as excess insurance over such other insurance.

26. **SUE AND LABOR:** In case of any loss or misfortune, it shall be lawful and necessary to and for the Assured, his or their factors, servants and assigns to sue, labor and travel for, in and about the defense, safeguard and recovery of the property insured hereunder, or any part thereof, without prejudice to this insurance nor shall the acts of the Assured or the Company in recovering, saving and preserving the property insured, in case of disaster, be considered a waiver or an acceptance of abandonment; the expenses so incurred shall be borne by the Assured and the Company in proportion as the sum hereby insured bears to the whole sum at risk.

27. **PARTIAL LOSS:** In case of partial loss or damage caused by a peril insured against, the proportion of loss shall be determined by a separation of the damaged portion of the insured property from the sound and by agreed estimate (by survey) of the percentage of damage of such portion, or, when practicable, by public sale of such damaged portion for the account of the owner of the property and by comparison of the amount so realised with the sound market value on the day of sale.

28. **NOTICE OF LOSS:** In case of loss or damage ...

[B3311J]

the insured hereunder ... the bursting of boilers, breakage of shafts or any latent defect in the hull or machinery, hull or from faults or errors in the navigation and/or management of the vessel by the master, mariners, engineers or pilots ...

13. **DELAY CLAUSE:** Warranted free of claim for loss of market or for loss, damage or deterioration arising from delay, whether caused by a peril insured against or otherwise, unless expressly assumed in writing hereon.

14. **BOTH "BOTH to Blame Collision" Clause:** Where goods are shipped under a Bill of Lading containing the so-called "Both to Blame Collision" Clause, these Assurers agree to indemnify the Insurance, to indemnify the Assured for this Policy's proportion of any amount (not exceeding the amount insured) which the Assured may be legally bound to pay to the shipowners under such clause. In the event that such liability is asserted the Assured agree to notify these Assurers who shall have the right, at their own cost and expense to defend the Assured against such claim.

15. **CONSTRUCTIVE TOTAL LOSS:** No recovery for a Constructive Total Loss shall be had hereunder unless the property insured is reasonably abandoned from actual total loss without an appearing to be unavoidable or because it cannot be preserved from actual total loss without an expenditure which would exceed its value when the expenditure shall have been incurred.

16. **CARRIER CLAUSE:** Warranted that the insurance shall not inure, directly or indirectly, to the benefit of any carrier or bailee.

17. **The following Warranties shall be paramount and shall not be modified or superseded by any other provision included herein o: stamped or endorsed hereon unless such other provision refers specifically to the risks excluded by these Warranties and expressly assumes the said risks:—**

(A) **F. C. & S. WARRANTY.** *Notwithstanding anything herein contained to the contrary, this insurance is warranted free from capture, seizure, arrest, restraint, detainment, confiscation, preemption, requisition or nationalization, and the consequences thereof or any attempt thereat; whether in time of peace or war and whether lawful or otherwise; also warranted free, whether in time of peace or war, from all loss, damage or expense caused by any weapon of war employing atomic or nuclear fission and/or fusion or other reaction, or radioactive force or matter or by any mine or torpedo, also warranted free from all consequences of hostilities or warlike operations (whether there be a declaration of war or not), but this warranty shall not exclude collision or contact with aircraft, rockets or similar missiles or with any fixed or floating object (other than a mine or torpedo), stranding, heavy weather, fire or explosion unless caused directly (and independently of the nature or proximate cause of the voyage or therein, which the vessel concerned or, in the case of a collision, any other vessel involved posts of this warranty "power" includes the act by or against a belligerent power, and for the purposes in association with a power.*

Further warranted free from the consequences of civil war, revolution, rebellion, insurrection, or civil strife arising therefrom, or piracy.

(B) **S. R. & C. C. WARRANTY:** *Warranted free of loss or damage caused by or resulting from strikes, lockouts, labor disturbances, riots, civil commotions or the acts of any person or persons taking part in any such occurrence or disorder.*

claim under this ... shall be given, proof and adjustment of loss, ... to the ... may ... this Company; proof and adjustment of loss and proof of interest shall be filed with this Company or its authorized Settling Agent as soon as practicable thereafter. Failure to report loss or damage promptly and to file such proof of loss as herein provided shall invalidate any claim under this Policy.

29. **CLAIMS AGAINST THIRD PARTIES:** In the event of any loss of or damage to the property covered hereunder the Assured shall immediately make claim in writing against the carrier(s), bailee(s) or others involved.

30. **PROOF OF LOSS:** Proofs of loss to be authenticated by an approved Claims Agent of this Company, or if there be one at or near the place where such proofs are taken, or if there be none in the vicinity, by a Correspondent of the American Institute of Marine Underwriters, or Lloyd's Agent and such agent or correspondent must be represented on all surveys. It is agreed that Claims are only to intervene for the purpose of ascertaining the nature, cause and extent of the loss or damage and that they shall not be cited in any legal proceedings.

31. **COMPANY'S RIGHTS OF SUBROGATION AND RECOVERY:** It is a condition of this insurance that upon payment of any loss this Company shall be subrogated to all rights and claims against third parties arising out of such loss. It is a further condition of this insurance that if the Assured or their assigns (1) have entered or shall enter into any special agreement whereby any carrier or bailee is released from its common law or statutory liability for any loss, or (2) waive, compromise, settle, or otherwise impair any right of claim against a third party, to which this Company would be subrogated upon payment of a loss then, and in that event, this Company shall be free from liability with respect to such loss, but its right to retain or recover the premium shall not be affected.

32. **COMPANY OPTION:** It is expressly agreed that in the event of claim under this Policy the Company, at its election, may either (1) make payment against delivery of instruments securing the Company's right of subrogation, or (2) make an advance on loan, without interest and repayable only out of net recoveries from third parties, in respect of said claim, against delivery of such loan agreement as may be required by the Company. A loan or advance shall not be construed as an admission of liability hereunder or a waiver of any terms or conditions hereof. Upon receipt of an advance or loan the recipient shall use all reasonable means to recover such loss from third parties, and, at the Company's request and expense, shall aid in such recovery and under its exclusive direction and control make claim upon and institute legal proceedings against any party which the Company believes is liable for the loss, cooperating fully in the prosecution of such legal proceeding.

33. **SETTLEMENT OF LOSS:** Losses property claimed for hereunder shall be paid or made good in thirty (30) days after satisfactory proofs and adjustment of loss and proofs of interest are filed with the Company.

34. **SUIT OR ACTION AGAINST THE COMPANY:** No suit, action or proceeding against this Company for the recovery of any claim shall be sustainable unless commenced within one year from the date of the happening of the accident out of which the claim arises, provided that such limitation is invalid by the laws of the state within which this Policy issued then such action or proceeding shall be barred unless commenced within the shortest limit of time permitted by the laws of such state.

Warranted that no action will be taken by the Assured or their assigns to enforce payment of any claim under this Policy except before the tribunals of the United States, Canada or England.

INSTRUCTIONS TO CLAIMANTS

In case of loss or damage which may become a claim under this Policy follow these instructions to protect your insurance claim and facilitate adjustment thereof:

PROMPTLY REPORT LOSS OR DAMAGE to the Company's nearest Agent (see list on the reverse side) and request him to conduct a survey. Invite Carrier's representative to attend survey. If loss is discovered on dock, have survey held there without delay.

TAKE PROPER EXCEPTIONS on the delivery receipt when any loss or damage is apparent at time of taking delivery.

FILE CLAIM IN WRITING against the delivering carrier holding him responsible as soon as loss or damage is discovered even though the full extent thereof is not apparent; details can be furnished later. Such action will not prejudice your insurance claim.

COLLECT COMPLETE DOCUMENTS in support of your insurance claim, consisting of:

☐ Original or Duplicate of this Special Cargo Policy properly endorsed by the payee.

☐ Claims Agent's Certificate or Survey Report.

☐ Certificate of Condition, when issued, by Customs, Port or Terminal Authority or Carrier.

☐ Copies of delivery receipts with proper exceptions of loss or damage noted thereon.

☐ Copy of written claim against Carrier or other parties with their reply when available.

☐ Original or certified copy of shipper's invoice(s) covering the entire shipment insured.

☐ Original or certified copy of bill(s) of lading covering the entire shipment insured, including transshipment bill(s) of lading, freight note(s) and/or way-bill(s) when applicable.

☐ Bills of repairs, reconditioning or other expenditures and such other proofs of loss as may be required in each specific case.

HAVE CLAIMS AGENT AUTHENTICATE all proofs of loss and forward the complete documents without delay to the Company or its nearest Settling Agent.

FORM 8

MARINE INSURANCE POLICY

[Reverse]

$ 10,950.00

PHILADELPHIA, JANUARY 12   1984

AT SIGHT

SKF INDUSTRIES, INC.

PAY TO THE ORDER OF

TEN THOUSAND NINE HUNDRED FIFTY-----------------------00/100 DOLLARS

SKF INDUSTRIES, INC.

THE PHILADELPHIA NATIONAL BANK
DRAWN UNDER ADVICE NO. E 4450/164

To FOR THE ACCOUNT OF: COMPANHIA
IMPORTADORA BRASILEIRA, CAIXA
POSTAL 10, RIO DE JANEIRO
BRAZIL

FORM 86 1/70

[D634]

FORM 9

DRAFT

PROBLEMS UNDER THE PROTOTYPE

The following problems should be solved on the basis of a careful examination of the prototype transaction.

Problem 7. Why was not SKF content to deliver under a documentary transaction like that between Buyersville and Sellersville described at p. 342 supra? What risk does SKF avoid by requiring a letter of credit? How do the parties expect that claims for defects in the goods will be handled?

Problem 8. In the letter of credit (FORM 4), what is the scope of the Philadelphia Bank's commitment in the first paragraph? Where is its liability stated? If the Brazilian Bank failed, who would bear the loss? Are there other risks that SKF avoids by having an American bank confirm the letter of credit?

Problem 9. Is SKF expressly entitled under the contract to have the letter of credit confirmed by a local bank? Can the obligation be implied? See UCC 2–325. What change in the forms would avoid any question?

Problem 10. After establishment of the letter of credit but before shipment by SKF, suppose that ocean freight rates rise. Who bears the added expense, and how should the payment be handled?

Problem 11. Under an F.A.S. quotation, is the seller obliged to take out an insurance policy covering the shipment? Compare UCC 2–319 with 2–320. Was such an obligation imposed in this case?

Problem 12. Could SKF effectively tender a "Received for Shipment" bill of lading? See UCC 5–114; Voest-Alpine International Corp. v. Chase Manhattan Bank, infra; Dixon, Irmaos & Cia. v. Chase National Bank, infra. Which provision of the bill of lading (FORM 7) shows its conformity to the letter of credit in this regard? What is the importance of such a requirement in a letter of credit?

(B) RESPONSIBILITY OF BANKS

Prefatory Note. Classic teaching concerning letters of credit is that there are three separate and distinct contracts in the case of an unconfirmed credit: (1) that between buyer and seller; (2) that between buyer (customer) and issuing bank; and (3) that between seller (beneficiary) and issuing bank. The leading American case, before the Code, was Maurice O'Meara Co. v. National Park Bank, 239 N.Y. 386, 146 N.E. 636 (1925).

The National Park Bank had issued a letter of credit in favor of Ronconi & Millar to cover payment for 1,322⅔ tons of newsprint paper purchased by the Sun-Herald Corporation. The letter of credit described the paper as "to test 11–12, 32 lbs.," but the only documents required were "Commercial invoice in triplicate. Weight returns. Negotiable dock delivery order. . . ." The bank refused to pay, writing the seller:

> There has arisen a reasonable doubt regarding the quality of the newsprint paper. . . . Until such time as we can have a test made by an impartial and unprejudiced expert we shall be obliged to defer payment.

The seller claimed from the bank damages including the amount of loss on its resale of the paper due to a fall in the market price. The court held for the seller.

"[T]he contract for the purchase and sale of the paper . . . was a contract between buyer and seller, which in no way concerned the bank. The bank's obligation was to pay sight drafts when presented if accompanied by genuine documents specified in the letters of credit. If the paper when delivered did not correspond to what had been purchased . . ., then the purchaser had his remedy against the seller for damages. . . . All that the letter of credit provided was that documents be presented which described the paper shipped as of a certain size, weight and tensile strength. To hold otherwise is to read into the letter of credit something which is not there, and [which] would impose upon a bank a duty which in many cases would defeat the primary purpose of such letters of credit."

Judge Cardozo dissented. "I cannot accept the statement of the majority opinion that the bank was not concerned with any question as to the character of the paper. If that is so, the bales tendered might have been rags instead of paper, and still the bank would have been helpless, though it had knowledge of the truth, if the documents tendered by the seller were sufficient on their face."

The principle of the O'Meara case has been followed and reaffirmed in more recent decisions. See, e.g., Dulien Steel Products, Inc. v. Bankers Trust Co., 298 F.2d 836 (2d Cir.1962), approved in 26 Modern L.Rev. 713 (1963). In the O'Meara case, would the position of the issuing bank be improved by taking an assignment of the buyer's claim against the seller?

The ICC Uniform Customs and the Code. Of large importance to both the law and practice concerning letters of credit is a set of uniform customs developed by committees of bankers under the aegis of the International Chamber of Commerce. Originating in 1929 and revised in 1933, 1951, 1962, 1974, and 1983, the current revision is in force from 1 October 1984. Uniform Customs and Practice for Commercial Documentary Credits (ICC Brochure No. 400), cited as "ICC Uniform Customs."

New York Exclusion of Article 5 in Favor of the Uniform Customs. In 1963, New York amended Section 5–102, which defines the scope of Article 5, by adding the following subsection (N.Y.Sess.Laws 1963, ch. 327):

(4) Unless otherwise agreed, this Article 5 does not apply to a letter of credit or a credit if by its terms or by agreement, course of dealing or usage of trade such letter of credit or credit is subject in whole or in part to the Uniform Customs and Practice for Commercial Documentary Credits fixed by the Thirteenth or by any subsequent Congress of the International Chamber of Commerce.

In view of the importance of the Uniform Customs, and of New York as a center of international finance, this amendment sharply restricts the impact of Article 5, and produced a vigorous reaction from the sponsors of the Code. Report No. 2 of the Permanent Editorial Board for the Uniform Commercial Code (1964) at 95–100 gave its reasons for rejecting this New York amendment. The Board's statement is as follows:

PERMANENT EDITORIAL BOARD COMMENT

Reasons for Rejection. The New York Clearing House Association (NYCHA) in its report of December 1, 1961 recommended the entire elimination of Article 5 on letters of credit. The above variation in Section 5–102(1), as the Code was enacted in New York, represents a continuation of the views of the NYCHA. Article 5 is still printed as a part of the Code but the variation as enacted provides that "Article 5 does not apply to a letter of credit or a credit if by its terms or by agreement, course of dealing or usage of trade such letter of credit or credit is subject in whole or in part to the Uniform Customs and Practice for Commercial Documentary Credits fixed by the Thirteenth or by any subsequent Congress of the International Chamber of Commerce" (Uniform Customs). This point of view and the action in New York constitutes a sufficiently fundamental departure from the Code that it needs to be dealt with on fundamental lines.

1. The underlying and basic concept behind the NYCHA position is that there should be no legislation in the letter of credit field. The reasoning is that it is better for banks, if not for all interested parties, to have the determination of rights and duties of parties under letters of credit left to the present combination of case law, Uniform Customs, agreements, practices and customs in the field.

This underlying point of view is contrary to the fixed policy of the sponsoring organizations of the Uniform Commercial Code, long considered and carefully determined. The Editorial Board sees no good reason to reverse this policy. . . .

2. A second basic position taken by the NYCHA is that most letters of credit finance international shipments of merchandise and are, therefore, international in character, with the result that there should

be no unilateral legislation on the subject in the United States. Conversely, the NYCHA appears to contend that the only controlling rules governing letters of credit should be international rules. The NYCHA further contends that if one or more American states sees fit to enact statutory legislation in this field, other countries may do likewise to the detriment of the United States.

The Editorial Board considers this view to be totally unrealistic. Carried to its logical conclusion, under this view no court in the United States should render a decision in a letter of credit case because such a decision, which clearly creates law in the United States, is unilateral. An equally logical extension of the same argument is that there should be neither statutory law nor case law in the United States in any international field because such law is necessarily unilateral.

Assuming that letters of credit are used preponderantly to finance international shipments of goods, in the absence of a world order and world courts, the problems of society and commerce can only be solved by the various instrumentalities of law available in the several sovereign nations. The great preponderance of what law there is today controlling international transactions is exactly "unilateral" law, established either by courts or legislatures, in independent, sovereign nations. Recognizing the imperfections in this process, the conflict of laws questions arising from it, and the uncertainties and confusion involved in it, this process has done fairly well to establish rules of law and, in any event, absent a world order and world courts, it is all that society has except for a very limited number of treaties. . . .

3. The third basic position taken by the NYCHA is that, recognizing the need of some rules as to "international" letters of credit, the Uniform Customs which are now in existence, and have been for twenty or more years, fill all needs and work well.

The Editorial Board approves of the effort to provide rules governing letters of credit by way of the drafting and promulgation of the Uniform Customs. The Editorial Board considers that the Uniform Customs contribute materially to the aggregate body of rules making more definite and certain letter of credit operations. However, the Board does not agree that the Uniform Customs constitute the only set of rules and guide lines that are available and needed.

Of paramount importance is that the Uniform Customs do not have the status of "law". Not being law they are subject to all of the weaknesses and vicissitudes of what they purport to be, namely, "customs". Have they been accepted by, are they binding upon, all interested parties? . . .

4. A fourth basic position advanced by the NYCHA is that the Uniform Customs have preempted the field of rules dealing with letters of credit and, consequently, no state legislation can or should be enacted in this field. The argument is that New York and the other

several states must have either the Uniform Customs or Article 5; they cannot have both.

The Editorial Board cannot agree with this reasoning. A fundamental concept of the Code as a whole is that there can be a set of statutory rules (with varying degress of completeness of coverage) in the fields of the different articles but there is also room and need for customs, course of dealing, usages of trade, agreement of parties and business practices. See Sections 1–102(2)(b), 1–205, 4–103 and 5–102(3). The Code also recognizes the need of supplementary principles of law other than the specific terms of the Code itself. See Sections 1–103, 9–104 and 9–203(2). . . .

5. The Editorial Board considers that the attempt, through the New York variation in Section 5–102(4), to find a compromise between the Code position on Article 5 and that of the NYCHA, is highly confusing, unwise and potentially productive of substantial litigation. Of first importance, the New York variation adopts the mutually exclusive concept that if the Uniform Customs in any way apply, then Article 5 is totally inapplicable. Aside from the general wisdom of any state legislature's enacting comprehensive and serious legislation, all of which can be rendered completely nugatory by the election of individual persons, the Board considers that the determination of when a credit is "by agreement, course of dealing or usage of trade . . . subject in whole or in part to the Uniform Customs . . ." will be a matter of great difficulty. The added New York language is almost a direct invitation to litigation. If Article 5 and the Uniform Customs overlap only to the extent of, let us say, 25% of their respective provisions and, of such overlapping, the rules of Article 5 and the Uniform Customs are, in substance, the same, with inconsistency occurring in only two instances, the Board entirely fails to see why, whether there is a large or trifling application of the Uniform Customs, Article 5 should be rendered totally inapplicable. The Board considers the New York variation both unacceptable and unsound.

NOTE

Revocability. The doctrine that a promisor can revoke a promise that is not supported by consideration led to interesting academic speculation on the power of a bank to revoke its promise embodied in a letter of credit that it has promised not to revoke. These speculations were laid to rest by UCC 5–105, which provides: "No consideration is necessary to establish a credit or to enlarge or otherwise modify its terms."

There remains this question: Has the bank promised not to revoke the letter of credit? A letter of credit used in an international sales transaction usually states that it is "irrevocable" and that the bank's promise is good until a stated expiration date (see FORM 4). However, ambiguous documents occasionally appear.

The assurance usually needed from a letter of credit is illusory if the bank may revoke the credit at its pleasure, and the Sales article of the Code provides (UCC 2–325): "(3) Unless otherwise agreed the term 'letter of credit' or 'banker's credit' in a contract for sale means an irrevocable credit . . . ." This rule resolves ambiguity in the *contract for sale*; but how should one construe a *letter of credit* which does not state whether it is revocable or irrevocable? The ICC Uniform Customs provide in Article 1: "All credits, therefore, should clearly indicate whether they are revocable or irrevocable. In the absence of such indication the credit shall be deemed to be revocable." Until 1957, the Code followed this rule. UCC (1952) 5–103(1)(a), 5–105. This provision came under heavy attack; since 1957 the Code has been silent on the question. See Comment 1 to UCC 5–103; 3 N.Y.L.Rev.Comm., Study of UCC 1607–12 (1955).

One moral for anyone needing protection under a letter of credit is obvious: he must make sure that the credit is clearly designated as "irrevocable." If a seller relies on a document which is ambiguous and the bank attempts to revoke, his lawyer will have an interesting case on his hands. If, as is probable, the letter of credit refers to the ICC Uniform Customs, supra, should the seller's lawyer conclude that all is lost?

VOEST–ALPINE INTERNATIONAL CORP. v. CHASE MANHATTAN BANK

United States Court of Appeals, Second Circuit, 1983.
707 F.2d 680.

CARDAMONE, CIRCUIT JUDGE. This appeal involves an interpretation of the law applied to commercial letters of credit. When analyzing that law the unique characteristics of a letter of credit must be kept firmly in mind. Otherwise, a court may unknowingly paint broadly over the letter of credit's salient features and compromise its reliability and fluidity.

BACKGROUND

Originally devised to function in international trade, a letter of credit reduced the risk of nonpayment in cases where credit was extended to strangers in distant places. Interposing a known and solvent institution's (usually a bank's) credit for that of a foreign buyer in a sale of goods transaction accomplished this objective. See Joseph, Letters of Credit: The Developing Concepts and Financing Functions, 94 Banking L.J. 816, 816–17 (1977) (Letters of Credit: Developing Concepts). A typical letter of credit transaction, as the case before us illustrates, involves three separate and independent relationships—an underlying sale of goods contract between buyer and seller, an agreement between a bank and its customer (buyer) in which the bank undertakes to issue a letter of credit, and the bank's resulting engagement to pay the beneficiary (seller) providing that certain documents presented to the bank conform with the terms and conditions of the credit issued on its customer's behalf. Significantly, the bank's payment obligation to the beneficiary is primary, direct and completely independent of any claims which may arise in the underlying sale of goods transaction.

Several distinct features characterize letters of credit. By conditioning payment solely upon the terms set forth in the letter of credit, the justifications for an issuing bank's refusal to honor the credit are severely restricted, thereby assuring the reliability of letters of credit as a payment mechanism. Banks readily issue these instruments because they are simple in form. Hence, they are convenient and economical for a customer (buyer) to obtain. Further, employing concepts which underlie letters of credit in non-sale of goods transactions enables these devices to serve a financing function, see Letters of Credit: Developing Concepts at 818–19. And it is this flexibility that makes letters of credit adaptable to a broad range of commercial uses. See id. at 820–51; Note, Judicial Development of Letters of Credit Law: A Reappraisal, 66 Cornell L.Rev. 144, 146–47 (1980) (Judicial Development of Letters of Credit Law).

Letters of credit evolved as a mercantile specialty entirely separate from common law contract concepts and they must still be viewed as entities unto themselves. Completely absorbed into the English common law by the 1700s along with the Law Merchant—of which it had become an integral part by the year 1200—2 W. Holdsworth, A History of English Law 570–72 (1922), letter of credit law found its way into American jurisprudence where it flourishes today. Its origins may be traced even more deeply into history. There is evidence letters of credit were used by bankers in Renaissance Europe, Imperial Rome, ancient Greece, Phoenicia and even early Egypt. See Trimble, The Law Merchant and The Letter of Credit, 61 Harv.L.Rev. 981, 982–85 (1948). These simple instruments survived despite their nearly 3000-year-old lineage because of their inherent reliability, convenience, economy and flexibility.

Since the great utility of letters of credit arises from the independent obligation of the issuing bank, attempts to avoid payment premised on extrinsic considerations—contrary to the instruments' formal documentary nature—tend to compromise their chief virtue of predictable reliability as a payment mechanism. See Judicial Development of Letters of Credit Law at 160; Justice, Letters of Credit: Expectations and Frustrations—Part 2, 94 Banking L.J. 493, 505–06 (1977). Viewed in this light it becomes clear that the doctrine of strict compliance with the terms of the letter of credit functions to protect the bank which carries the absolute obligation to pay the beneficiary. Adherence to this rule ensures that banks, dealing only in documents, will be able to act quickly, enhancing the letter of credit's fluidity. Literal compliance with the credit therefore is also essential so as not to impose an obligation upon the bank that it did not undertake and so as not to jeopardize the bank's right to indemnity from its customer. Documents nearly the same as those required are not good enough. See H. Harfield, Letters of Credit 51 (1979). See generally Marino Industries v. Chase Manhattan Bank, N.A., 686 F.2d 112, 114–15 (2d Cir.1982); Venizelos, S.A. v. Chase Manhattan Bank, 425 F.2d 461, 464–65 (2d Cir.1970).

We note that there is a distinction between rights obtained and obligations assumed under letter of credit concepts. While a party may not unilaterally alter its obligations, nothing in the purpose or function of letters of credit forecloses the party from giving up its rights.

FACTS

Metal Scrap Trading Corporation (MSTC) is an agency of the Indian government that had contracted to buy 7000 tons of scrap steel from Voest-Alpine International Corporation (Voest), a trading subsidiary of an Austrian company. In late 1980 MSTC asked the Bank of Baroda to issue two letters of credit in the total amount of $1,415,550—one for $810,600 and the other $604,950—to Voest to assure payment for the sale. The credits were expressly made subject to the Uniform Customs and Practice for Documentary Credits.

The parties originally contemplated that Chase Manhattan Bank, N.A. (Chase or Bank) would serve as an advising bank in the transaction. As such, Chase was to review documents submitted by Voest in connection with its drafts for payment. Amendments to the letters of credit increased Chase's responsibilities and changed its status to that of a confirming bank, independently obligated on the credit to the extent of its confirmation.

The contract between MSTC and Voest provided that Voest, as seller, would ship the scrap metal no later than January 31, 1981. The terms and conditions of the credits required proof of shipment, evidenced by clean-on-board bills of lading; certificates of inspection indicating date of shipment; and weight certificates issued by an independent inspector. Sometime between February 2 and February 6 (beyond the January 31 deadline), the cargo was partially loaded aboard the M.V. ATRA at New Haven. Unfortunately, the ATRA never set sail for India. A mutiny by the ship's crew disabled the ship and rendered it unseaworthy. The scrap steel was later sold to another buyer for slightly over a half million dollars, nearly a million dollars less than the original contract price.

On February 13, two days before the expiration date of the credits, Voest presented three drafts with the required documentation to Chase. The documents contained what the district court termed "irreconcilable" inconsistencies. The bills of lading indicating receipt on board of the scrap metal were signed and dated January 31 by the captain of the ATRA. The weight and inspection certificates accompanying the drafts revealed, however, that the cargo was loaded aboard the ATRA sometime between February 2 and February 6.

Despite this glaring discrepancy Chase advised the Bank of Baroda on February 25 that the drafts and documents presented to it by Voest conformed to the terms and conditions set forth in the letters of credit. At Voest's request (Chase having provided Voest with an advance copy of the advice it planned to forward to the Bank of Baroda), Chase added the following language: "PAYMENT OF ABOVE–MENTIONED DRAFT . . . WILL BE MADE AT MATURITY ON JULY 30, 1981, TO VOEST . . . ." The Bank of Baroda apparently looked at the documents with more care than Chase. It promptly advised Chase that the documents did not comply with the requirements of the letters of credit, that it would therefore not honor the drafts, and that it would hold the documents at Chase's disposal. When Voest presented the drafts for payment on July 30 Chase refused to honor them.

Voest thereupon instituted the present suit. It asserted that Chase waived the right to demand strict compliance with the terms of the credits and therefore wrongfully dishonored the drafts. Voest further alleged that regardless of whether the documents conformed to the letters of credit Chase was liable on the drafts because it accepted them. Chase, in turn, served a third-party complaint on the Bank of Baroda, alleging that were Chase to be held liable for wrongfully dishonoring the drafts, the Bank of Baroda should be liable to Chase in the same amount. In granting summary judgment against Voest the United States District Court for the Southern District of New York (Duffy, J.), 545 F.Supp. 301, found that Chase had not waived compliance with the terms and conditions of the letters of credit and that the drafts had not been wrongfully dishonored. The district court also rejected Chase's affirmative defense that Voest committed fraud in presenting documents which contained such obvious discrepancies. Voest has appealed from the order insofar as it granted summary judgment against it and Chase has cross-appealed from that part of the order which dismissed its third-party complaint against the Bank of Baroda.

DISCUSSION

I. *Waiver*

Voest urges that summary judgment was inappropriate because there were disputed factual issues as to whether Chase accepted the documents submitted and, if so, thereby waived any deficiencies in them. Chase contends that a waiver analysis is inappropriate because the defects in Voest's documentation were "incurable." In urging that such defects preclude any waiver on its part, Chase relies upon Flagship Cruises Ltd. v. New England Merchants National Bank of Boston, 569 F.2d 699 (1st Cir.1978) and American Employers

Insurance Co. v. Pioneer Bank and Trust Co., 538 F.Supp. 1354 (N.D.Ill.1981). These cases afford the Bank little comfort. In neither case was there any indication that the issuing or confirming bank accepted defective or untimely documents.

Two other cases including a decision of this Court have indicated that the terms and conditions of a letter of credit may be waived. In Marino Industries Corp. v. Chase Manhattan Bank, N.A., 686 F.2d at 117, one of the questions raised was whether an official of Chase, with apparent authority to act, had waived the expiration date of a letter of credit. Since that issue had not been resolved by the trial court the case was remanded for further consideration. By remanding on the waiver issue, the *Marino* court impliedly approved a waiver analysis even though it reaffirmed its adherence to the rule of strict compliance expressed in *Venizelos, S.A.*, 425 F.2d at 465. Moreover, the Court apparently recognized that a confirming bank may waive the requirements contained in the credit without approval of either the issuing bank or its customer who originally established the credit. Id. In the instant case Chase could have waived the right to demand strict compliance without approval from either the Bank of Baroda or MSTC.

In Chase Manhattan Bank v. Equibank, 550 F.2d 882 (3d Cir.1977), Chase, as beneficiary of a letter of credit, contended that its untimely presentation of documents resulted from an agreement with the issuing bank (Equibank) to extend the time beyond that specified in the credit. The Third Circuit held that the possibility of a waiver of the time requirement by Equibank existed. The court stated that in such instances the "beneficiary bases his claim on the letter of credit as modified by the bank and acceptable to him." *Equibank*, 550 F.2d at 886. The court noted that such a waiver merely jeopardizes a bank's right to reimbursement from its customer, in the case of an issuing bank, see Courtaulds North American, Inc. v. North Carolina National Bank, 528 F.2d 802, 806 (4th Cir.1975), or from the issuing bank, in the case of a confirming bank. Id. at 886–87 & n. 6.

Chase argues that *Equibank* is distinguishable because in that case the defects were arguably curable while in the present case they are not. Chase contends that incurability of defect defeats any possibility of waiver. We reject this argument because it is totally at odds with the concept of waiver, which is defined as the intentional relinquishment of a known right. Whether or not a defect can be cured is irrelevant, for it is the right to demand an absence of defects that the party is deemed to have relinquished.

Since a waiver by Chase of the inconsistencies in the documents is possible, we must determine whether Voest presented sufficient evidence which, if believed, could establish a waiver. As proof of waiver Voest relies most heavily on deposition testimony by the Chase official who inspected the documents that he "must have noticed" the discrepancy between the dates in the documents. Other evidence of waiver included: an initialed approval of the documents by a Chase official on the Voest letter which accompanied the presentation of the documents; a letter from Voest to Bank of Baroda, allegedly co-authored by a Chase official, stating that the documents had been accepted; the statement which appeared at the bottom of Chase's advice to Bank of Baroda that payment of the draft would occur on July 30; and a deposition by a Voest official in which he quotes an unknown Chase employee as stating that Chase had accepted the drafts and that payment would definitely be forthcoming.

All parties seem to agree that New York law governs. To establish waiver under New York law one must show that the party charged with waiver relinquished a right with both knowledge of the existence of the right and an intention to relinquish it. . . . There is little doubt that Voest sufficiently established Chase's knowledge of an existing right. Chase clearly had the right to demand strict compliance with the specifications required by the letters of credit, and since it is an established commercial bank we may assume that it had constructive, if not actual, knowledge of that right . . . . The remaining question is whether that right had been intentionally relinquished.

The intention to relinquish a right may be established either as a matter of law or fact. Examples of the former include instances of express declarations by a party or situations where the party's undisputed acts or language are "so inconsistent with his purpose to stand upon his rights as to leave no opportunity for a reasonable inference to the contrary." Alsens American Portland Cement Works v. Degnon Contracting Co., 222 N.Y. 34, 37, 118 N.E. 210 (1917). More commonly, intention is proved through declarations, acts and nonfeasance which permit different inferences to be drawn and "do not directly, unmistakably or unequivocally establish it." Id. In these instances intent is properly left to the trier of fact. . . .

Claims by a beneficiary of a letter of credit that a bank has waived strict compliance with the terms of the credit should generally be viewed with a somewhat wary eye. As noted earlier, if equitable waiver claims are treated too hospitably by courts, letters of credit may become less useful payment devices because of the increased risk of forfeiting the right to reinbursement from their customers which banks would soon face. Nonetheless, because Voest offered evidence which, if believed by the trier of fact, could establish the requisite intentional relinquishment of Chase's right to insist on strict compliance, summary judgment was inappropriately granted to Chase in this case.

II.   *Acceptance*

Having discussed Voest's claim that Chase waived strict compliance, we turn to Voest's contention that Chase "accepted" the drafts drawn under the letters of credit. The issue is specifically addressed by Uniform Commercial Code (U.C.C.) § 3–410. This section states that acceptance is the drawee's signed engagement to honor the draft as presented and that it "must be written on the draft." The official comment acknowledges that § 3–410 was intended to eliminate "virtual" acceptances by written promise to accept a draft still to be drawn and "collateral" acceptances proved by separate writing. By requiring written acceptance on the draft the U.C.C. impliedly eliminated oral acceptances as well. Id. The present record is silent as to whether Chase actually accepted the drafts by proper notation on them. Since this issue was not ruled on by the district court, it should be remanded for futher consideration.

III. Fraud

Presentation of fraudulent documents to a bank by a beneficiary subverts not only the purposes which letters of credit are designed to serve in general, but also the entire transaction at hand in particular. Falsified documents are the same as no documents at all. . . . We are not persuaded upon the present record, as was the trial court, that Voest did not intend to deceive Chase when it submitted deliberately back-dated documents falsely indicating compliance with the terms of the credits in order to have the documents accepted. Since Chase has raised a sufficient question of fact regarding fraud, a trial of this issue is mandated. If it is found that fraud on the part of Voest caused Chase to act, then Voest would be estopped from claiming any benefit accruing to it from its misconduct.

IV. Chase's Cross-Appeal

Finally, we affirm the judgment in favor of the Bank of Baroda. All parties have acknowledged that the documents tendered Chase did not conform to the established terms and conditions of the letters of credit. The Bank of Barona, as the issuing bank, was entitled to strict compliance and there is no claim that it waived that right. Further, Chase itself has acknowledged that its cross-appeal has been rendered academic in light of Voest's admission regarding the nonconformity of the documents.

CONCLUSION

This case must be remanded to determine the factual issues raised by the claims of waiver, acceptance and fraud. The order appealed from is thus affirmed in part, reversed in part and remanded for further proceedings in accordance with this opinion.

NOTES

(1) **Beneficiary's Knowledge of Defects.** In Philadelphia Gear Corp. v. Central Bank, 717 F.2d 230 (5th Cir. 1983), Philadelphia Gear, the beneficiary under a letter of credit governed by the ICC's Cus-

toms and Practice, presented a series of drafts with documents attached through Provident Bank to Central Bank, the issuing bank. Central Bank refused to pay the drafts, returning them "due to their non-compliance with the terms of the relevant credit." It neither returned the documents nor stated that they were held at Provident's disposal. When asked for a more definite statement of its reasons, Central responded that "reasons for dishonor are as previously stated." In a suit by Philadelphia Gear against Central Bank, the trial court found that in each instance there were curable defects, some of which were known to Philadelphia Gear. (For example, in six instances drafts were accompanied by photocopies of "shipping evidences" or "shipping notices" rather than the required inland bills of lading.)

Under the ICC's Customs and Practice, an issuing bank "must state that the documents are being held at the disposal of [the remitting] bank or are being returned thereto." The trial court held that Central Bank was estopped to assert the defects in the documents because its failure to comply with this rule thwarted any attempt to cure the drafts.

The Court of Appeals reversed, holding that as to the documents that Philadelphia knew to be defective, Central Bank's notice was not deficient. The court relied on both the general requirement of good faith in UCC 1–203 and on the beneficiary's warranty in UCC 5–111. It concluded: "It would be a strange rule indeed under which a party could tender drafts containing defects of which it knew and yet attain recovery on the ground that it was not advised of them. . . . We do not hold today that a beneficiary may never prevail where its supporting documentation fails to meet the credit's requirements, but only that, upon the present facts, the beneficiary has failed so abysmally in meeting its contractual obligations that no inquiry beyond that failure is required." A dissenting opinion argued that the decision "injects into the otherwise mechanical and simple inquiry that most subjective issue of the knowledge of the beneficiary."

(2) Bills of Lading: "Clean" and "Foul." Letters of credit usually call for "clean" bills of lading (see Form 4, p. 396 supra); in any event, such a requirement may be implied. British Imex Industries Limited v. Midland Bank Limited, [1958] 1 Q.B. 542. If a carrier receives a shipment in torn or leaky cartons, he will note that fact on the bill of lading to protect himself from the claim that he damaged the goods. A bill of lading with such a notation is not "clean," and a bank need not pay under a letter of credit when such bills of lading are tendered.

Article 34 of the ICC Uniform Customs deals with this question as follows:

"A clean transport document is one which bears no superimposed clause or notation which expressly declares a defective condition of the goods and/or the packaging.

"Banks will refuse transport documents bearing such clauses or notations unless the credit expressly states the clauses or notations which may be accepted. . . ."

Suppose that a bill of lading covering a shipment of oil well casing and tubing is tendered under a letter of credit. In the bill of lading the phrase "in apparent good order and condition" has been deleted and the following inserted: "Ship not responsible for kind and condition of merchandise." The bill also bears the stamped notation, "Ship not responsible for rust." If the ICC Uniform Customs are applicable, may the bank decline to pay under the letter of credit? See Liberty National Bank & Trust Co. v. Bank of America National Trust & Savings Association, 218 F.2d 831 (10th Cir. 1955), affirming 116 F.Supp. 233 (W.D.Okl.1953).[1]

(3) "Back-to-Back" Credits; Assignability. Assume that Buyer agrees to buy a large shipment of goods from Seller, and establishes a letter of credit covering the purchase with Seller as beneficiary. Seller will buy goods to fill this contract from Distributor. Distributor requires cash for the goods and Seller lacks sufficient cash until he delivers to Buyer. Can the assurance of payment under the letter of credit give Seller the credit he needs to make the purchase? (Distributor may face the same credit problem in arranging a purchase from Manufacturer. Indeed, in some cases a long string of transactions needs to be financed on the strength of the letter of credit established by the ultimate buyer.)

A dilemma appears. The initial letter of credit from Buyer to Seller needs to be utilized as a source of credit before Seller gets the goods; on the other hand, tender of these goods is a condition of the bank's obligation to pay. Ingenious attempts to answer this problem have produced the so-called "back-to-back" credits. The bank which has issued the initial credit to Seller issues a second letter of credit to Distributor, contingent on Distributor's presenting documents which either satisfy the initial letter of credit or which can readily be made to satisfy the letter of credit, as by getting a new bill of lading evidencing shipment from Seller to Buyer. Distributor is thus assured of payment; and credit strain on Seller and the bank are avoided since Distributor will not be paid until (a) Seller's right to obtain funds under the credit, and (b) the bank's right to reimbursement from Buyer have both been established.

Added flexibility may be achieved if the rights under a letter of credit may be assigned. In this area, as in others, there is possible conflict between the Code and the ICC Uniform Customs if the latter's language is given its full, literal sweep. Article 54 of the Uniform Customs provides: "A credit can be transferred only if it is ex-

1. See Draper, What is a "Clean" Bill of Lading, 37 Corn.L.Q. 56 (1951); Davis, Recent Developments in the Law of Commercial Credits, 1959 J.Bus.L. 323, 328; Minett, Certain Aspects of Bills of Lading and Documentary Credits, 74 J.Inst. of Bankers 110 (1953); Miller, Problems and Patterns of the Letter of Credit, 1959 U.Ill.L.F. 162, 174.

pressly designated as 'transferable' by the issuing bank." UCC 5–116(1) establishes a similar rule as to "the right *to draw* under a credit." But subsection (2) states: "Even though the credit specifically states that it is nontransferable or nonassignable the beneficiary may before performance of the conditions of the credit assign his *right to proceeds.*" The balance of the subsection contains interesting rules regulating such assignments. Compare UCC 2–210(2) and 9–318(4) which similarly invalidate "restraints on alienation" of the right to receive cash proceeds.

(4) **Banker's Acceptances and Letters of Credit.** If the buyer in the letter of credit transaction does not wish to pay upon presentment, a slightly different transaction may be arranged. The seller will draw a time draft rather than a sight draft on the issuing bank, which will accept it, return it to the seller, and release the documents to the buyer on open credit or perhaps against trust receipts. The buyer has his goods; the seller has a "banker's acceptance" which can easily be discounted; the issuer has lent its credit but has paid no money. Before the maturity date of the draft, the buyer will place the necessary funds in the hands of the issuing bank.

The banker's acceptance is defined by Federal Reserve regulations as "a draft or bill of exchange, whether payable in the United States or abroad and whether payable in dollars or some other money, accepted by a bank or trust company or a firm, person, company, or corporation engaged generally in the business of granting bankers' acceptance credits." 12 Code Fed.Regs. § 201.3(c), fn. 7 (1963). It is more versatile and more widely used than the trade acceptance because it is not limited to domestic transactions.

"A money market is a center where the demand for short-term funds meets the supply. The leading international money market has been established in New York City. The facilities there attract and redistribute funds from all over the nation and the world. This general market comprises many different clearly defined markets, each of which deals in a different type of credit.

"The bankers' acceptance is an attractive instrument for the short-term investor in that it is one of the few instruments in a varied market that relies on the name of prime commercial banks. The bankers' acceptance market has been active since the 1920s although there was a decline during the depression and World War II. Because the market trades in 'eligible' acceptances and is therefore limited to the existence of specific underlying transactions, bankers' acceptances cannot compete by supplying the volume of instruments such as U.S. Treasury Bills. The skills needed for marketing bankers' acceptances are the same as those needed for marketing other short-term obligations. Dealers who handle bankers' acceptances generally do so as a part of their active market in the wide range of government paper—federal, state, and municipal.

"The bankers' acceptance market, like any other market, has a product that must be created, merchandised, and consumed. This instrument is merchandised by a group of dealers who create the open market, and the demand for it comes from as many sources as the transactions financed. The bankers' acceptance is an attractive short-term investment since its rates, while usually moving in concert with those of U.S. Treasury bills, offer a slightly higher yield. In normal circumstances, most investors will find that the higher yield more than compensates for what is not, in many judgments, a significantly higher risk.

"In most banks the international department handles acceptance financing even when the transaction is entirely domestic. That is natural, since most of the bills created arise from international transactions." P. Oppenheim, International Banking 195–96 (4th ed. 1983).[2]

DIXON, IRMAOS & CIA. v. CHASE NATIONAL BANK

United States Circuit Court of Appeals, Second Circuit, 1944.
144 F.2d 759. Cert. denied 324 U.S. 850, 65 S.Ct. 687, 89 L.Ed. 1410 (1945).

Action by Dixon, Irmaos & Cia. Ltda. against the Chase National Bank of the City of New York for breach of contract by refusing to honor drafts drawn against letters of credit issued by defendant. From a judgment dismissing the complaint on the merits after trial to the court without a jury, 53 F.Supp. 933, plaintiff appeals. . . .

SWAN, CIRCUIT JUDGE. This appeal raises interesting and important questions as to letters of credit covering C.I.F. shipments abroad. The plaintiff, an exporter of cotton in Sao Paulo, Brazil, contracted to sell cotton to a purchaser in Belgium. A Belgian bank requested the Chase Bank to issue in favor of the plaintiff two irrevocable letters of credit for $7,000 and $3,500 respectively to finance such sales. Chase Bank did so and mailed them to Sao Paulo, where they were received by the plaintiff on May 2, 1940. They bound Chase Bank to honor 90 day drafts drawn under the credits, if presented at its office on or before May 15, 1940 and accompanied by specified documents, including a "full set of bills of lading" evidencing shipment of a stated quantity and quality of cotton "C.I.F. Ghent/Antwerp." One of the letters of credit (both being the same in form) is set out in the Margin.[4] The plaintiff duly shipped the cotton to its

---

2. Reproduced with permission of the American Bankers Association.

4. "The Chase National Bank
of The City of New York
"April 8, 1940.
"Confirmed Irrevocable Straight Credit
"Dixon Irmaos and Cia. Ltda.,
"Sao Paulo, Brazil

"Gentlemen:

"We are instructed by Banque de Bruxelles, S.A., Brussels, Belgium to advise you that they have opened their irrevocable credit in your favor for account of by order of Georgie Alost under their credit Number 40466 for a sum or sums not exceeding a total of About $7000.00

Belgian customer in two lots, receiving for each shipment two originals of the bills of lading. Instead of prepaying freight the plaintiff shipped the goods freight collect and deducted the freight charges from the invoice price. Through the Guaranty Trust Company of New York, the plaintiff's representative, drafts and documents were presented to Chase Bank on May 15, 1940, but only one of the set of two bills of lading was delivered. In lieu of the other, which was in the mail and not yet arrived in New York, an indemnity agreement or guaranty against loss resulting from its absence was tendered by the Guaranty Trust Company.[5] Chase Bank had no objection to the form of the guaranty or to the responsibility of the guarantor, but it refused the drafts on two grounds: (1) Absence of a full set of the bills of lading and (2) failure to prepay the freight. The plaintiff then brought the present action to recover the amount of its drafts, $5,587.15 under the larger letter of credit and $2,757.49 under the smaller. The case was tried without a jury. At the conclusion of the evidence each side moved for judgment. Decision being reserved, the district judge thereafter rendered an opinion and filed findings of fact and law. He gave judgment for the defendant on the ground that the tender of less than a full set of bills of lading did not comply with the terms of the letters of credit.

Assuming for the moment that a C.I.F. shipment does not require the shipper to prepay freight if the freight charges are credited against the invoice price, the Guaranty Trust Company's tender to

(Seven Thousand Dollars) U.S. Currency available by your drafts on us at 90 days sight, in duplicate to be accompanied by

"Commercial invoice in triplicate, or invoice copy

"Insurance certificate which must cover land and sea risks into the mills, and showing merchandise covered on board the steamer named and/or other steamer or steamers.

"Full set bills of lading. Port or custody bills of lading acceptable evidencing shipment of 22 tons Bresilian Sao Paulo Cotton type MINI shipped during April 1940, CIF Ghent/Antwerp

"All documents in name of La Georgie.

"All drafts so drawn must be marked 'Drawn under Chase National Bank Credit No. E71582'

"The above mentioned correspondent engages with you that all drafts drawn under and in compliance with the terms of this credit will be duly honored on delivery of documents as specified if presented at this office on or before May 15, 1940; we confirm the credit and thereby undertake that all drafts drawn and presented as above specified will be duly honored by us.

"Unless otherwise expressly stated, this credit is subject to the uniform customs and practice for commercial documentary credits fixed by the Seventh Congress of the International Chamber of Commerce and certain guiding provisions.

"Yours very truly,

"C.F. Wellman
Assistant Manager
"F.N. Powelson
Assistant Cashier"

5. The Guaranty Trust Company's indemnity agreement stated:

"In consideration of your accepting the above described draft, we hereby agree to hold you harmless from any and all consequences which might arise due to the following discrepancy:

"Only 1 copy presented out of a set of 2 bills of lading issued.

"It is understood that this guarantee will remain in force until such time as you may obtain a release from your clients.

"We shall thank you to take the necessary steps to obtain this release as soon as possible and inform us promptly when it has been obtained."

Chase Bank of drafts and documents fully met the requirements of the letters of credit, except for the fact that one original bill of lading out of each set of two was missing. The plaintiff contends that this fact did not defeat the adequacy of its tender because the evidence established the existence of a custom among New York banks issuing letters of credit to finance a shipment from outside the United States and calling for a "full set of bills of lading", to accept in lieu of a missing part of the set a guaranty by a responsible New York bank against any loss resulting from the absence of the missing part. On this subject the trial judge made the following findings of fact:

"12. The letters of guaranty of the Guaranty Trust Company tendered to the defendant are in the usual form of guaranties tendered by and accepted by leading New York Banks issuing commercial credits, when less than all bills of lading are presented under credits calling for a full set of bills of lading.

"12A. The Guaranty Trust Company was and is a prime and leading New York bank with sound financial standing.

"12B. The defendant raised no objection to the form of the guaranties tendered by the Guaranty Trust Company nor with the financial responsibility of the Guaranty Trust Company.

"13. On May 15, 1940, and for some time prior thereto, there existed a general and uniform custom among New York banks, exporters and importers to the effect that in lieu of a missing bill or missing bills of lading presented under credits calling for a full set of bills of lading, that the bank issuing the credits would accept in lieu of the missing bill or bills of lading, a guaranty of a leading New York bank, if it determined the guaranty to be satisfactory in form and if it was satisfied as to the responsibility of the bank issuing the guaranty. The bank issuing the credit was, however, free to exercise its own discretion and make its own determination as to whether it would accept a guaranty in lieu of a missing bill of lading."

We are not entirely clear as to the meaning of the final sentence of finding 13. If it means that the issuer of credit is free to reject the tendered guaranty if doubts are entertained regarding the guarantor's financial responsibility or the sufficiency of the form of the document, it is not inconsistent with the custom stated in the first sentence and may be disregarded; in these respects Chase Bank was satisfied with the guaranty tendered by Guaranty Trust Company. But if it means that even when so satisfied the bank issuing the credit may reject the tendered guaranty and refuse to accept the draft, it is inconsistent with the stated custom and is unsupported by the evidence. Numerous witnesses, experts in the fields of banking and of commerce, testified to the existence of the custom; not one testified to a single instance where a tender such as was here made had been rejected and the draft dishonored solely on the ground that the set of bills of lading was incomplete. Indeed, it is clear that the Chase Bank would in this very case have honored the drafts, had they been presented before the German invasion of Belgium. One of its witnesses naively said that before May 15, 1940 it was the custom to accept such a guaranty as was tendered, but not on that date or thereafter—as though the determining moment were not at the latest when the plaintiff acted upon the letters of credit. In short, the existence of the custom was established beyond dispute.

It is true, as the defendant argues, that the law requires strict compliance with the terms of a letter of credit. International Banking Corp. v. Irving Nat. Bank, 2 Cir., 283 F. 103. It is likewise true that numerous cases, several of which are cited by the defendant, declare that evidence of a custom is not admissible to contradict the unambiguous terms of a written contract. . . . But it is also well settled "that parties who contract on a subject-matter concerning which known usages prevail, incorporate such usages by implication into their agreements, if nothing is said to the contrary." . . . In our opinion the custom under consideration explains the meaning of the technical phrase "full set of bills of lading" and is incorporated by implication into the terms of the defendant's letters of credit. No authority on the precise point has come to our attention. The statement of Bankes, L.J. in Scott & Co., Ltd. v. Barclay's Bank, Ltd., [1923] 2 K.B. 1, 11, upon which the defendant relies, is inapposite because no custom such as the court found here was there proved or attempted to be proved. Finally, the defendant urges that the reference in the concluding paragraph of the letters of credit to the uniform customs and practice for commercial documentary credits fixed by the Seventh Congress of the International Chamber of Commerce excludes incorporation into the contracts of any other custom. We do not think so. Those customs do not deal with the meaning of a "full set of bills of lading." Hence the problem whether the New York custom gives meaning to those words is unaffected by the reference to those other customs. The reasonableness and utility of the local New York custom is obvious. It is absolutely essential to the expeditious doing of business in overseas transactions in these days when one part of the bill of lading goes by air and another by water. Unless an indemnity can be substituted for the delayed part, not only does quick clearance of such transactions become impossible but also the universal practice of issuing bills of lading in sets and sending the different parts by separate mails loses much of its purpose. We conclude therefore that the defendant's first ground for dishonor of the drafts was not a valid reason.

The second ground for dishonor, was that while the credits specified a C.I.F. shipment, the plaintiff deducted freight charges from the invoices and shipped the goods freight collect. On this subject the court made the following findings:

"15. The ordinary and accepted meaning of a c.i.f. contract is that the contract price includes the cost of the goods, the cost of insurance and the cost of freight to the point of destination. The term does not imply the time when or the place where the freight is to be paid and there was no uniform practice in New York on May 15, 1940 or prior thereto of prepaying freight to the point of destination under a c.i.f. shipment. The practice was that it was sometimes prepaid and sometimes deducted from the invoice.

"16. The 'American Foreign Trade Definitions' are incorporated by reference in the letters of credit and such definitions, including the definition of a c.i.f. contract, is a part of the credit. Under the definition of a c.i.f. contract as defined in 'American and Foreign Trade Definitions' there is no requirement that a shipper must prepay freight.

"18. The tender of documents showing a deduction of freight from the invoices was not a deviation from the requirement of defendant's credits calling for C.I.F. shipment."

We agree with this conclusion. In the case of a sight draft, it is wholly immaterial to the buyer whether freight is prepaid or credit given on the invoice price. In the case of a time draft, it is true that the buyer may be deprived of the credit period as to part of the purchase price, that is, so much of it as the freight amounts to. In the case at bar the freight was $1359.14. The measure of any possible loss to the buyer is the interest upon this sum for the period between arrival of the goods and the date the drafts would fall due and the possible inconvenience of being called upon for early payment in cash of this portion of the price. The bills of lading were endorsed "on board" on May 5th and, if we assume the voyage would take 30 days, the buyer would not be called upon for the freight until June 5th. The draft if accepted on May 15th would have been due 90 days later, that is, the buyer would have had to pay freight about 70 days earlier than he would otherwise have paid such sum. Interest at 6% would amount to about $17. On a transaction involving about $9,700 such a sum is insignificant. The law has not cut so fine. The point of possible inconvenience is taken care of by ancient usage. The seller has so long had the option of shipping either freight collect or freight prepaid that the cases recognize the option as part of the standard meaning of the term C.I.F., making no distinction between prepayment or shipping freight collect and crediting it on the invoice irrespective of whether the draft be time or sight. . . . As the court pointed out in finding 16 the American and Foreign Trade definitions provide that under a C.I.F. contract the seller must pay the freight but make no mention of prepayment. Furthermore, if the buyer sells the documents before arrival of the goods, as frequently happens in C.I.F. transactions, whether freight was prepaid will be wholly immaterial to him.

The judgment for the defendant is reversed and judgment directed in favor of the plaintiff.

NOTES

(1) Dixon and the Code. The practice of issuing bills of lading in a set of parts grew up in overseas transportation in an era when the transmission of such a document across the ocean was more hazardous than it is today. Bills of lading in a set are governed by UCC 7–304, which limits their issue. What risk would a bank run if it honored a letter of credit against less than a full set of parts? Was that risk a factor in the bank's decision in the Dixon case?

For buyer's obligation to accept indemnities in lieu of missing documents see UCC 2–323. In the final version of the Code, no position is taken with respect to whether banks are subject to a similar obligation. See UCC 2–323, Comment 2; cf. UCC 5–113. Is the Dixon result possible under the Code? See UCC 1–205(3) and Comment 1.

The Dixon case was sharply criticized by Dana Backus and Henry Harfield in their article Custom and Letters of Credit: the Dixon, Irmaos Case, 52 Colum.L.Rev. 589 (1952). The authors conclude that the court's use of custom overrides the plain meaning of the contract and threatens freedom of contract and sound banking practice. But see Honnold, Letters of Credit, Custom, Missing Documents and the Dixon Case: A Reply to Backus and Harfield, 53 Colum.L.Rev. 504 (1953).

(2) The Form of Indemnity. Must an indemnity tendered by seller assume the risk of *all* losses to the bank issuing the letter of credit or only "those consequences which may arise from" the specified discrepancies? Should seller undertake to reimburse the issuing bank from loss by reason of buyer's insolvency or currency restrictions in buyer's country? Note that if seller's bank must pay under an indemnity, seller will be obliged to reimburse his bank. See Editorial, Removing "Booby Traps" from Commercial Letters of Credit, Export Trade & Shipper, August 21, 1950, p. 9; Committee on Uniformity in Documents & Practices of the Bankers Association for Foreign Trade, Eighth Interim Report (Oct. 5, 1945); UCC 5–113(2)(a).

Apparently sellers who have made a defective shipment which would be reflected on the bill of lading (e.g., "torn cartons," "leaky bags," "rusted barrels") sometimes give the carrier an indemnity against liability to induce the carrier to issue a "clean" bill of lading omitting the offensive notation. See Miller, Problems and Patterns of the Letter of Credit, 1959 U.Ill.L.F. 162, 178–79. Is such a practice comparable to that discussed in the Dixon case?

(3) Problems of Proof. Attorneys planning to rely on usage will encounter thorny problems, combining evidence and substantive law, to which they should give careful thought prior to trial. Is it enough to offer testimony by traders that *they* customarily handle the problem in a specified fashion, or must there also be evidence that traders *generally* act in this fashion?

Must there also be testimony that traders regard themselves as *obliged* so to act? On this problem, should it make a difference whether the issue is the commercial meaning of a specified term, such as "dibutyl phthalate"[6] or whether the issue relates to trade custom at variance with a statutory rule on which the contract is silent? Is it necessary to show that *all* traders follow the practice, or will occasional "sharp" practice on which most merchants frown break the custom? (Note the testimony in the Dixon case that the "practice" changed when war made reimbursement on letters of credit hazardous.) Are written rules or customs of a commodity exchange barred by the hearsay rule? See Wigmore, Evidence, §§ 1954, 2053, 2440, 2580 (1940). Patterson, Jurisprudence 226–30 (1953). The law in this area seems as yet surprisingly undeveloped. Could the reason be that attorneys have not been sufficiently alerted to the force of usage?

In an arbitration what reception is likely to be given to evidence of usage?

Problem 13. Seller, in London, agreed to sell "Coromandel groundnuts" to a Danish buyer. Pursuant to the contract Bank opened a letter of credit in Seller's favor. Seller tendered documents to Bank which conformed to the letter of credit except that the bill of lading described the goods as "machine shelled groundnut kernels" instead of "Coromandel groundnuts." The invoice described the goods in the manner called for in the letter of credit. The war intervened, and Bank refused to honor Seller's draft because of the discrepancy between the bill of lading and the letter of credit. In action by Seller against the Bank, Seller proved that in the London produce market the two terms referred interchangeably to the same commodity. What result? See Rayner & Co. v. Hambros Bank, [1942] 2 All E.R. 694 (C.A.). Compare UCC 5–109(1) (preamble) with paragraph (1)(c) of that section.

The ICC Uniform Customs provide in Article 41: "The description of the goods in the commercial invoice must correspond with the description in the credit. In all other documents the goods may be described in general terms not inconsistent with the description of the goods in the credit". In the above case, were the goods described in "general terms" in the bill of lading? Will the distinction drawn by the Uniform Customs, Art. 41 be binding under the Code? See UCC 5–109.

Problem 14. A contract for the sale of 3000 tons of Brazilian groundnuts called for shipment from Brazil for Genoa between February 1 and April 30, at the option of the sellers. The contract further provided: "Payment: By opening of a confirmed, irrevocable, divisible, transmissible and transferable credit opened in favour of the sellers and utilisable by them against delivery of the following docu-

---

6. See Heede, Inc. v. Roberts, 303 N.Y. 385, 103 N.E.2d 419 (1952).

ments." The buyer established a letter of credit on April 22. The seller had already resold the goods on the ground that the credit was established too late in the light of the seller's privilege to ship in February or March. Seller sued the buyer for damages. What evidence of custom and what arguments concerning seller's need for the letter of credit would be relevant? See Pavia & Co. v. Thurmann-Nielsen, [1952] 1 All Eng.L.R. 492 (C.A.).

If the buyer has the obligation to arrange for shipping and has the privilege of selecting the date for shipment within a designated period, may the buyer delay establishing the letter of credit until the end of the period? What would be the effect of a showing by seller that it was customary in this trade to use the letter of credit in order to raise funds to pay the seller's supplier? See Ian Stach, Limited v. Baker Bosly, Limited, [1958] 1 All E.R. 542 (interesting and instructive opinion by Diplock, J., on the practical problems presented by using the ultimate buyer's letter of credit to finance "a string of merchants' contracts between the manufacturer or stockist and the ultimate user"); 108 L.J. 388 (1958).

Problem 15. What would you advise Philadelphia National Bank to do if Brasileira notified it that the goods were defective and instructed it not to pay? Are there any circumstances in which Brasileira could prevent payment on the ground of defects in the goods? See United Bank Limited v. Cambridge Sporting Goods Corp., infra.

UNITED BANK LIMITED v. CAMBRIDGE SPORTING GOODS CORP.

Court of Appeals of New York, 1976.
41 N.Y.2d 254, 392 N.Y.S.2d 265, 360 N.E.2d 943.

GABRIELLI, JUSTICE. On this appeal, we must decide whether fraud on the part of a seller-beneficiary of an irrevocable letter of credit may be successfully asserted as a defense against holders of drafts drawn by the seller pursuant to the credit. If we conclude that this defense may be interposed by the buyer who procured the letter of credit, we must also determine whether the courts below improperly imposed upon appellant buyer the burden of proving that respondent banks to whom the drafts were made payable by the seller-beneficiary of the letter of credit, were not holders in due course. The issues presented raise important questions concerning the application of the law of letters of credit and the rules governing proof of holder in due course status set forth in article 3 of the Uniform Commercial Code. In addition, we are called upon to determine whether it was proper for the trial court to permit respondents to introduce as direct evidence their responses to interrogatories served by appellant, as part of respondents' case-in-chief.

In April, 1971 appellant Cambridge Sporting Goods Corporation (Cambridge) entered into a contract for the manufacture and sale of boxing gloves with Duke Sports (Duke), a Pakistani corporation. Duke committed itself to the manufacture of 27,936 pairs of boxing gloves at a sale price of $42,576.80; and arranged with its Pakistani bankers, United Bank Limited (United) and The Muslim Commercial Bank (Muslim), for the financing of the sale. Cambridge was requested by these banks to cover payment of the purchase price by opening an irrevocable letter of credit with its bank in New York, Manufacturers Hanover Trust Company (Manufacturers). Manufacturers issued an irrevocable letter of credit obligating it, upon the receipt of certain documents indicating shipment of the merchandise pursuant to the contract, to accept and pay 90 days after acceptance, drafts drawn upon Manufacturers for the purchase price of the gloves.

Following confirmation of the opening of the letter of credit, Duke informed Cambridge that it would be impossible to manufacture and deliver the merchandise within the time period required by the contract, and sought an extension of time for performance until September 15, 1971 and a continuation of the letter of credit, which was due to expire on August 11. Cambridge replied on June 18 that it would not agree to a postponement of the manufacture and delivery of the gloves because of its resale commitments and, hence, it promptly advised Duke that the contract was canceled and the letter of credit should be returned. Cambridge simultaneously notified United of the contract cancellation.

Despite the cancellation of the contract, Cambridge was informed on July 17, 1971 that documents had been received at Manufacturers from United purporting to evidence a shipment of the boxing gloves under the terms of the canceled contract. The documents were accompanied by a draft, dated July 16, 1971, drawn by Duke upon Manufacturers and made payable to United, for the amount of $21,288.40, one half of the contract price of the boxing gloves. A second set of documents was received by Manufacturers from Muslim, also accompanied by a draft, dated August 20, and drawn upon Manufacturers by Duke for the remaining amount of the contract price.

An inspection of the shipments upon their arrival revealed that Duke had shipped old, unpadded, ripped, and mildewed gloves rather than the new gloves to be manufactured as agreed upon. Cambridge then commenced an action against Duke in Supreme Court, New York County, joining Manufacturers as a party, and obtained a preliminary injunction prohibiting the latter from paying drafts drawn under the letter of credit; subsequently, in November, 1971 Cambridge levied on the funds subject to the letter of credit and the draft, which were delivered by Manufacturers to the Sheriff in compliance therewith. Duke ultimately defaulted in the action and judgment against it was entered in the amount of the drafts, in March, 1972.

The present proceeding was instituted by the Pakistani banks to vacate the levy made by Cambridge and to obtain payment of the drafts on the letter of credit. The banks asserted that they were holders in due course of the drafts which had been made payable to them by Duke and, thus, were entitled to the proceeds thereof irrespective of any defenses which Cambridge had established against their transferor, Duke, in the prior action which had terminated in a default judgment. The banks' motion for summary judgment on this claim was denied and the request by Cambridge for a jury trial was granted. Cambridge sought to depose the petitioning banks, but its request was denied and, as an alternative, written interrogatories were served on the Pakistani banks to learn the circumstances surrounding the transfer of the drafts to them. At trial, the banks introduced no evidence other than answers to several of the written interrogatories which were received over objection by Cambridge to the effect that the answers were conclusory, self-serving and otherwise inadmissible. Cambridge presented evidence of its dealings with Duke including the cancellation of the contract and uncontested proof of the subsequent shipment of essentially worthless merchandise.

The trial court concluded that the burden of proving that the banks were not holders in due course lay with Cambridge, and directed a verdict in favor of the banks on the ground that Cambridge had not met that burden; the court stated that Cambridge failed to demonstrate that the banks themselves had participated in the seller's acts of fraud, proof of which was concededly present in the record. The Appellate Division affirmed, agreeing that while there was proof tending to establish the defenses against the seller, Cambridge had not shown that the seller's acts were "connected to the petitioners [banks] in any manner." The Appellate Division also held that CPLR 3117 "seemingly" authorized the introduction of the challenged interrogatories into evidence.

We reverse and hold that it was improper to direct a verdict in favor of the petitioning Pakistani banks. We conclude that the defense of fraud in the transaction was established and in that circumstance the burden shifted to petitioners to prove that they were holders in due course and took the drafts for value, in good faith and without notice of any fraud on the part of Duke (Uniform Commercial Code, § 3–302). Additionally, we think it was improper for the trial court to permit petitioners to introduce into evidence answers to Cambridge's interrogatories to demonstrate their holder in due course status.

This case does not come before us in the typical posture of a lawsuit between the bank issuing the letter of credit and presenters of drafts drawn under the credit seeking payment (see, generally, White and Summers, Uniform Commercial Code, § 18–6, pp. 619–628). Because Cambridge obtained an injunction against payment of the drafts and has levied against the proceeds of the drafts, it stands in the same position as the issuer, and, thus, the law of letters of credit governs the liability of Cambridge to the Pakistani banks.[1] Article 5 of the Uniform Commercial Code, dealing with letters of credit, and the Uniform Customs and Practice for Documentary Credits promulgated by the International Chamber of Commerce set forth the duties and obligations of the issuer of a letter of credit.[2] A letter of credit is a commitment on the part of the issuing bank that it will pay a draft presented to it under the terms of the credit, and if it is a documentary draft, upon presentation of the required documents of title (see Uniform Commercial Code, § 5–103). Banks issuing letters of credit deal in documents and not in goods and are not responsible for any breach of warranty or nonconformity of the goods involved in the underlying sales contract (see Uniform Commercial Code, § 5–114, subd. [1]; Uniform Customs and Practice, General Provisions and Definitions [c] and article 9; O'Meara Co. v. National Park Bank of N.Y., 239 N.Y. 386, 146 N.E. 636; . . . 1955 Report of N.Y. Law Rev.Comm., vol. 3, Study of Uniform Commercial Code, pp. 1654–1655). Subdivision (2) of section 5–114, however indicates certain limited circumstances in which an issuer *may* properly refuse to honor a draft drawn under a letter of credit or a customer may enjoin an issuer from honoring such a draft.[3] Thus, where "fraud in the transac-

1. Cambridge has no direct liability on the drafts because it is not a party to the *drafts* which were drawn on Manufacturers by Duke as drawer; its liability derives from the letter of credit which authorizes the drafts to be drawn on the issuing banks. Since Manufacturers has paid the proceeds of the drafts to the Sheriff pursuant to the levy obtained in the prior proceeding, it has discharged its obligation under the credit and is not involved in this proceeding.

2. It should be noted that the Uniform Customs and Practice controls, in lieu of article 5 of the code, where, unless otherwise agreed by the parties, a letter of credit is made subject to the provisions of the Uniform Customs and Practice by its terms or by agreement, course of dealing or usage of trade (Uniform Commercial Code, § 5–102, subd. [4]). No proof was offered that there was an agreement that the Uniform Customs and Practice should apply, nor does the credit so state (cf. Oriental Pacific [U.S.A.] v. Toronto Dominion Bank, 78 Misc.2d 819, 357 N.Y.S.2d 957). Neither do the parties otherwise contend that their rights should be resolved under the Uniform Customs and Practice. However, even if the Uniform Customs and Practice were deemed applicable to this case, it would not, in the absence of a conflict, abrogate the precode case law (now codified in Uniform Commercial Code, § 5–114) and that authority continues to govern even where article 5 is not controlling (see White and Summers, *op. cit.*, pp. 613–614, 624–625). Moreover, the Uniform Customs and Practice provisions are not in conflict nor do they treat with the subject matter of section 5–114 which is dispositive of the issues presented on this appeal (see Banco Tornquist, S.A. v. American Bank & Trust Co., 71 Misc.2d 874, 875, 337 N.Y.S.2d 489; Intraworld Ind. v. Girard Trust Bank, 461 Pa. 343, 336 A.2d 316, 322; Harfield, Practice Commentary, McKinney's Cons. Laws of N.Y., Book 62½, Uniform Commercial Code, § 5–114, p. 686). Thus, we are of the opinion that the Uniform Customs and Practice, where applicable does not bar the relief provided for in section 5–114 of the code.

3. Subdivision (2) of section 5–114 of the Uniform Commercial Code provides that,

"[u]nless otherwise agreed when documents appear on their face to comply with the terms of a credit but . . . there is fraud in the transaction (a) the issuer must honor the draft or demand for payment if honor is demanded by a . . . holder of the draft . . . which has taken the draft . . . under the credit and under circumstances which would make it a holder in due course (Section 3–302) . . . ; and

tion" has been shown and the holder has not taken the draft in circumstances that would make it a holder in due course, the customer may apply to enjoin the issuer from paying drafts drawn under the letter of credit (see 1955 Report of N.Y. Law Rev.Comm., vol. 3, pp. 1654–1659). This rule represents a codification of precode case law most eminently articulated in the landmark case of Sztejn v. Schroder Banking Corp., 177 Misc. 719, 31 N.Y.S.2d 631, Shientag, J., where it was held that the shipment of cowhair in place of bristles amounted to more than mere breach of warranty but fraud sufficient to constitute grounds for enjoining payment of drafts to one not a holder in due course. . . . Even prior to the *Sztejn* case, forged or fraudulently procured documents were proper grounds for avoidance of payment of drafts drawn under a letter of credit . . . and cases decided after the enactment of the code have cited *Sztejn* with approval. . . .

The history of the dispute between the various parties involved in this case reveals that Cambridge had in a prior, separate proceeding successfully enjoined Manufacturers from paying the drafts and has attached the proceeds of the drafts. It should be noted that the question of the availability and the propriety of this relief is not before us on this appeal.[4] The petitioning banks do not dispute the validity of the prior injunction nor do they dispute the delivery of worthless merchandise. Rather, on this appeal they contend that as holders in due course they are entitled to the proceeds of the drafts irrespective of any fraud on the part of Duke (see Uniform Commercial Code, § 5–114, subd. [2], par. [b]). Although precisely speaking there was no specific finding of fraud in the transaction by either of the courts below, their determinations were based on that assumption. The evidentiary facts are not disputed and we hold upon the facts as established, that the shipment of old, unpadded, ripped and mildewed gloves rather than the new boxing gloves as ordered by Cambridge, constituted fraud in the transaction within the meaning of subdivision (2) of section 5–114. It should be noted that the drafters of section 5–114, in their attempt to codify the *Sztejn* case and in utilizing the term "fraud in the transaction", have eschewed a dogmatic approach and adopted a flexible standard to be applied as the circumstances of a particular situation mandate.[5] It can be difficult to draw a precise line between cases involving breach of warranty (or a difference of opinion as to the quality of goods) and outright fraudulent practice on the part of the seller. To the extent, however, that Cambridge established that Duke was guilty of *fraud* in shipping, not merely noncon-

"(b) in all other cases as against its customer, an issuer acting in good faith may honor the draft . . . despite notification from the customer of fraud, forgery or other defect not apparent on the face of the documents but a court of appropriate jurisdiction may enjoin such honor."

4. It is not necessary, therefore, for us to reach the difficult question whether the Pakistani banks were indispensible parties in the first action. . . .

5. In its original version section 5–114 contained the language "fraud in a required document" (see 1955 Report of N.Y. Law Rev.Comm., pp. 1655–1658).

forming merchandise, but worthless fragments of boxing gloves, this case is similar to *Sztejn*.

If the petitioning banks are holders in due course they are entitled to recover the proceeds of the drafts but if such status cannot be demonstrated their petition must fail.[6] The parties are in agreement that section 3–307 of the code governs the pleading and proof of holder in due course status and that section provides:

"(1) Unless specifically denied in the pleadings each signature on an instrument is admitted. When the effectiveness of a signature is put in issue

"(a) the burden of establishing it is on the party claiming under the signature; but

"(b) the signature is presumed to be genuine or authorized except where the action is to enforce the obligation of a purported signer who has died or become incompetent before proof is required.

"(2) When signatures are admitted or established, production of the instrument entitles a holder to recover on it unless the defendant establishes a defense.

"(3) After it is shown that a defense exists a person claiming the rights of a holder in due course has the burden of establishing that he or some person under whom he claims is in all respects a holder in due course."

Even though section 3–307 is contained in article 3 of the code dealing with negotiable instruments rather than letters of credit, we agree that its provisions should control in the instant case. Section 5–114 (subd. [2], par. [a]) utilizes the holder in due course criteria of section 3–302 of the code to determine whether a presenter may recover on drafts despite fraud in the sale of goods transaction. It is logical, therefore, to apply the pleading and practice rules of section 3–307 in the situation where a presenter of drafts under a letter of credit claims to be a holder in due course. In the context of section 5–114 and the law of letters of credit, however, the "defense" referred to in section 3–307 should be deemed to include only those defenses available under subdivision (2) of section 5–114, i.e., noncompliance of required documents, forged or fraudulent documents or fraud in the transaction. In the context of a letter of credit transaction and, specifically subdivision (2) of section 5–114, it is these defenses which

---

6. Although several commentators have expressed a contrary view, the weight of authority supports the proposition that fraud on the part of the seller-beneficiary may not be interposed as a defense to payment against a holder in due course to whom a draft has been negotiated (see Finkelstein, op. cit., p. 246; Ward and Harfield, Bank Credits and Acceptances, pp. 94–98; 1955 Report of N.Y. Law Rev.Comm., pp. 1662–1663, and authorities cited therein). This approach represents the better view that as against two innocent parties (the buyer and the holder in due course) the former, having chosen to deal with the fraudulent seller, should bear the risk of loss (see Harfield, Practice Commentary, McKinney's Cons. Laws of N.Y., Book 62½, Uniform Commercial Code, § 5–114, pp. 686–687).

operate to shift the burden of proof of holder in due course status upon one asserting such status. . . . Thus, a presenter of drafts drawn under a letter of credit must prove that it took the drafts for value, in good faith and without notice of the underlying fraud in the transaction (Uniform Commercial Code, § 3–302).

Turning to the rules of section 3–307 as they apply to this case, Cambridge failed to deny the effectiveness of the signatures on the draft in its answer and, thus, these are deemed admitted and their effectiveness is not an issue in the case. However, this does not entitle the banks as holders to payment of the drafts since Cambridge has established "fraud in the transaction". The courts below erroneously concluded that Cambridge was required to show that the banks had participated in or were themselves guilty of the seller's fraud in order to establish a defense to payment. But, it was not necessary that Cambridge prove that United and Muslim actually participated in the fraud, since merely notice of the fraud would have deprived the Pakistani banks of holder in due course status.

In order to qualify as a holder in due course, a holder must have taken the instrument, "without notice . . . of any defense against . . . it on the part of any person" (Uniform Commercial Code, § 3–302, subd. [1], par. [c]). Pursuant to subdivision (2) of section 5–114 fraud in the transaction is a valid defense to payment of drafts drawn under a letter of credit. Since the defense of fraud in the transaction was shown, the burden shifted to the banks by operation of subdivision (3) of section 3–307 to prove that they were holders in due course and took the drafts without notice of Duke's alleged fraud. As indicated in the Official Comment to that subdivision, when it is shown that a defense exists, one seeking to cut off the defense by claiming the rights of a holder in due course "has the full burden of proof by a preponderance of the total evidence" on this issue. This burden must be sustained by "affirmative proof" of the requisites of holder in due course status (see Official Comment, Mc-Kinney's Cons. Laws of N.Y., Book 62½, Uniform Commercial Code, § 3–307, p. 212). It was error for the trial court to direct a verdict in favor of the Pakistani banks because this determination rested upon a misallocation of the burden of proof; and we conclude that the banks have not satisfied the burden of proving that they qualified in all respects as holders in due course, by any affirmative proof. The only evidence introduced by the banks consisted of conclusory answers to the interrogatories which were improperly admitted by the Trial Judge (see discussion, infra). The failure of the banks to meet their burden is fatal to their claim for recovery of the proceeds of the drafts and their petition must therefore be dismissed. . . .

Accordingly, the order of the Appellate Division should be reversed, with costs, and the petition dismissed.

NOTES

(1) The Letter of Credit in a Wider Setting. The documentary letter of credit, illustrated in the prototype transaction, is but one example of the many uses of this device. A traditional example is the letter of credit carried by travellers, usually a handsome document in which a bank promises to pay drafts drawn by the beneficiary of the letter up to a specified total, provided that the sums so drawn are noted on the document. (For rules governing such "notation credits," see UCC 5–108.) Such a letter of credit differs from the one in the prototype in that the beneficiary of the letter need not accompany the draft with documents such as an invoice, bill of lading, and insurance policy. In banking circles, it is called a "clean" credit, in contrast to a "documentary" credit.

One of the most important uses of the letter of credit occurs in domestic commerce to facilitate the delivery of new automobiles to dealers. Banks financing car dealers often promise the car manufacturer to pay drafts covering the price of new cars shipped to the dealers. The document accompanying the draft which entitles the manufacturer to payment is normally the manufacturer's invoice identifying the cars shipped to dealers by trailer-truck.

(2) Standby (or Guaranty) Letters of Credit. In recent years the letter of credit has been put to an important new use. Suppose that a builder contracts to build a building for an owner of land and is required to furnish a guaranty of performance. The traditional practice has been to provide a performance bond issued by a surety company. Commercial banks are not generally authorized to act as sureties. A bank can, however, issue a standby (or guaranty) letter of credit under which the bank agrees to pay on presentation of a certificate, perhaps by the owner or perhaps by the architect, that the builder is in default. This practice appeals to banks because it allows them to participate in a type of activity that would otherwise be prohibited. It appeals to builders because the cost of such a letter of credit is likely to be less than that of a performance bond. However, the practice raises some serious questions. Consider the following analysis.

"A traditional letter of credit does . . . provide the bank with some additional protection when it honors the letter of credit. When it pays the beneficiary, the bank receives documents of title to goods in which it has an immediate security interest of some value. If it finds that its customer is insolvent, the bank may obtain some redress by liquidating its security interest. It is thus one of the important features of the traditional letter of credit that when the bank pays it has in its hands security in the form of title to the goods. Its relationship to its customer (the buyer) then becomes a regular banking relationship, the consequences of which appear on its balance sheet. The bank can debit the buyer's account, thereby reducing its deposit liabilities, or it can extend him credit, replacing the cash paid out to the seller with a receivable from the buyer. But in all events the bank's letter of credit issued for its customer is, in function, a secured loan, and the bank's lending risks should be measured in light of that fact. As will be discussed next, guaranty letters of credit occur in an unrelated business context, and, thus, present entirely different problems." Verkuil, Bank Solvency and Guaranty Letters of Credit, 25 Stan.L.Rev. 716, 721 (1973).

Note that in the traditional letter of credit transaction the bank expects, in the normal course of events, to pay and be reimbursed by its customer, with the additional security just mentioned. Under a standby letter of credit, however, the bank is called upon to pay only when the transaction goes awry. Note also that since a letter of credit is regarded as independent of the underlying transaction, if the documents conform the bank must honor the letter of credit and the customer must reimburse the bank, and the burden is then on the customer to pursue the beneficiary if the documents do not correctly reflect the underlying transaction. Under a surety bond, however, the surety's liability is only that of its principal on the underlying transaction. If the purpose of prohibiting banks from making surety-ship contracts is to reduce the risk of bank insolvency, is any of these differences significant in determining when and on what conditions banks should be allowed to issue standby letters of credit? See 12 C.F.R. § 7.1160(a), (b).

Standby letters of credit are used in sales transactions. But whereas it is the seller who is the beneficiary of the ordinary documentary letter of credit, it is the buyer who is the beneficiary of the standby letter of credit. The standby letter may be given to secure performance by the seller and, if the buyer has paid something in advance, to secure the buyer's advance.

In 1978, at the time of the Iranian Revolution, American firms were contingently liable for millions of dollars secured by standby letters of credit payable to the Government of Iran. The American firms, fearful that the disruption of performance of their contracts would provoke unwarranted calls on their letters of credit by the new government of Iran and conscious of the practical impossibility of suit in the Iranian courts, sought to enjoin payment of the letters under principles analogous to those invoked in the United Bank Limited v. Cambridge Sporting Goods Corp. For the various results arrived at in the Iranian cases, see KMW International v. Chase Manhattan Bank, 606 F.2d 10 (2d Cir.1979); Itek Corp. v. First National Bank, 566 F.Supp. 1210 (D.Mass.1983); American Bell International, Inc. v. Islamic Republic of Iran, 474 F.Supp. 420 (S.D.N.Y.1979). The cases are discussed in Weisz & Blackman, Standby Letters of Credit after Iran: Remedies of the Account Party, 1982 U.Ill.L.Rev. 355; Note, 93 Harv.L.Rev. 992 (1980).

(3) General References. The leading text on letters of credit is H. Harfield, Bank Credits and Acceptances (5th ed. 1974). For a shorter treatment, see H. Harfield, Letters of Credit (1979). For a comparative work, see B. Kozolchyk, Commercial Letters of Credit in the Americas (1966).

Chapter 7

ACCOMMODATION PARTIES

Introduction. This chapter is concerned with the use of the obligation of a third party to secure the obligation of a party to commercial paper. Most commonly this occurs in connection with a loan, evidenced by the borrower's note and secured by the obligation of a third party known as an accommodation party and perhaps by collateral as well. Although the obligation of the third party who acts as a surety is not "collateral" (UCC 9–105) subject to a "security interest" (UCC 1–201(37)), such an obligation is nevertheless classified within the general category of "security" by the Restatement of Security. "Suretyship is included in the general field of Security because the obligation of a surety is an additional assurance to the one entitled to the performance of an act that the act will be performed." Restatement of Security, Scope Note to Division II (1941). Professor, now Justice, Peters has outlined some of the advantages of this kind of security in the following excerpt.

"A borrower in search of credit may encounter resistance from the money market if all that he is prepared to offer is his own unsupported promise to repay. Today, one alternative for such a borrower is to tender a security interest in any or all of his property, present and future. The Uniform Commercial Code in Article 9 makes such a secured transaction easy to arrange, but it does not necessarily make it advisable. A borrower may well have misgivings both about the notoriety and about the controls which a secured transaction is likely to entail. The Code minimizes these drawbacks, but it cannot eliminate them: a secured creditor must still perfect, in order to prevail over competing third parties, and perfection will ordinarily take the form of a financing statement placed on a public record; a secured creditor must still police for maximum protection in the event of his debtor's bankruptcy, and policing must, despite the comforting repeal of Benedict v. Ratner, encompass at least the proceeds from collateral and perhaps even the acquisition of collateral. No well advised secured creditor will be likely to forego these protective maneuvers, and their execution involves real costs to the borrower. Not only must he bear the expenses of administration inherent in a secured transaction, but he must also run the risk that the filing of a financing statement may impede the flow of unsecured credit from independent suppliers and servicers. . . .

"Any secured transaction which focuses on collateral, then, has potential drawbacks from the borrower's point of view, drawbacks which may persuade him to investigate other sources of support for his loan application. His most likely alternative is the suretyship contract, which offers security to the creditor in the financial responsibility of the surety rather than in the property and business operations of the debtor. Suretyship can take a variety of forms, from the commercial bond of a professional surety company, complete with painstaking elaboration of terms and conditions, to a signature—with or without qualifying legend—on a negotiable instrument, to an informal assumption of responsibility for the debts of another.

"Interestingly, the institution of suretyship has so far escaped the elaborate statutory regulation which has attended collateral security devices. The Uniform Commercial Code goes further toward setting operative guidelines than has ever been done before, but even the Code's regulation is remarkably skeletonic." Peters, Suretyship Under Article 3 of the Uniform Commercial Code, 77 Yale L.J. 833–35 (1968).[1] Because of the "skeletonic" character of the Code's treatment of suretyship problems arising out of commercial paper, a nodding acquaintance of the elements of suretyship is a useful introduction to a consideration of those problems.

SECTION 1. ELEMENTS OF SURETYSHIP

Fortunately it is unnecessary to attempt here a hair-splitting definition of "surety" or "suretyship" since the following cases are not in the penumbra of suretyship law. The Restatement of Security § 82 gives the following, which may be taken as a working definition: "Suretyship is the relation which exists where one person has undertaken an obligation and another person is also under an obligation or other duty to the obligee, who is entitled to but one performance, and as between the two who are bound, one rather than the other should perform." The Restatement uses *guaranty* as a synonym for suretyship. Considerable confusion surrounds the scope of these two terms, and if there is any sense in attempting to dispel it, the task is best left for an advanced course.

As a simple example, suppose that P wishes to borrow $5,000 from C. In order to induce C to make the loan, P has S join with him in promising to repay. As further security, P pledges $3,000 worth of corporate bonds to C. Both P and S are under obligation to C; C is entitled to but one performance; and as between P and S, P rather than S should perform. The relationship thus fits the Restatement definition of suretyship. P is the *principal,* S is the *surety,* and C is the *creditor.* If S engages in the business of executing surety contracts for a premium determined by a computation of risks spread over a large number of transactions, he is a *compensated surety* under Restatement terminology, and may not be discharged from liability as readily as an uncompensated surety.

The creditor's rights against the principal are governed basically by contract law and need little attention at this point. Absent peculiar circumstances (e.g., C's fraud upon P, P's infancy) C will have the right to enforce the obligation against P.

In the alternative, the creditor may proceed against the surety. If P defaults, generally C need not attempt to collect from P nor to satisfy the debt from the corporate bonds before enforcing S's liability. Immediate recourse against S upon P's default was one of the advantages which C expected from S's suretyship contract. Even if C's lack of diligence in pursuing P causes loss, S is not discharged.[2] In about twenty states this rule is subject to an exception under which the creditor's failure to sue the principal at the surety's request discharges the surety.[3] Compare the engagement of secondary parties to negotiable paper under UCC 3–413(2), 3–414.

The surety, who is thus subject to action by the creditor should the principal default, has in turn three major remedies against the principal: exoneration, subrogation and reimbursement. The surety's right of exoneration is an equitable one. Its qualifications and exceptions need not be considered here. Basically it allows S, upon P's default, to compel P in a suit in equity to pay C. It is reasoned that without this remedy S might undergo considerable hardship in raising the money to pay C, even though he could afterwards recover over from P. However, the right to exoneration is not commonly asserted, and the surety will usually pay the creditor himself and then

---

2. It is, of course, possible for the surety to limit his engagement to a guaranty of *collection* of the principal's obligation. Such a *guarantor of collection* is, by the nature of his undertaking, discharged to the extent of any loss caused by the creditor's lack of diligence in proceeding against the principal. See Restatement, Security § 130(2).

3. The exception was laid down in Pain v. Packard, 13 Johns (N.Y.) 174 (1816). In that case the surety, when sued by the creditor, pleaded that he had requested the creditor to proceed immediately to collect from the principal; that the creditor had not done so; and that although the principal could have then been compelled to pay, he later became insolvent and absconded. The court held that his plea stated a good defense for,

since the defendant was known to be a surety, the principal was "bound to use due diligence against the principal in order to exonerate the surety." A number of other states have adopted some form of the rule in Pain v. Packard, in most instances by statute. It has been rejected by the Restatement of Security § 130 and by the great majority of courts that have faced the issue without statutory guidance. The reason given by the Restatement is that, "Since the surety may pay the claim of the creditor and himself proceed against the principal for exoneration in advance of payment . . ., the creditor's non-action generally affords no equitable basis for a claim of discharge by the surety." Pain v. Packard was overruled by statute in New York in 1968. N.Y.Gen.Obl.L. § 15–701.

attempt to recover from the principal under his right to subrogation or reimbursement.

When the surety pays in full the principal's debt to the creditor, he is subrogated to the rights of the creditor. See Restatement, Security § 141. Subrogation may be viewed as equitable assignment. S would therefore succeed, as by assignment, to C's rights against P as pledgee of the corporate bonds. Since the right is an equitable one, it is subject to equitable limitations.[4] An important qualification is that if the debt has not been paid in full, the surety ordinarily has no right of subrogation. Thus in the usual case if S should pay C only $4,000, leaving a balance of $1,000 due, he would not thereby be entitled to any part of C's security interest in the bonds.

S would, however, have the right to reimbursement (sometimes called indemnification) from P to the extent of $4,000. See Restatement, Security § 104. Since S became bound as surety at the request of P, S's right to reimbursement can be spelled out from P's implied request to S to pay the debt at maturity if P does not and from P's implied promise to reimburse S for such payment. It is, of course, only a right *in personam* against P and may be, for this reason, less satisfactory to S than subrogation, particularly if S must compete with other creditors of P.

Exoneration, subrogation and reimbursement, then, are the three principal remedies of S against P. An elementary understanding of them is necessary to answer the next question: In what circumstances will agreement between C and P to modify P's obligation to C operate to discharge S from his obligation as surety?[5] Suppose that C and P should modify their original agreement so as to increase the interest rate from four to five per cent. S would be discharged. The modification has increased the burden on P and made it more likely that he will default. However, should the modification decrease the interest rate from four to three per cent, it is difficult to justify discharge of the surety on the basis of prejudice to him. Nevertheless, there is authority for the proposition that since the surety's contract is *strictissimi juris*, he will be discharged whether the modification increases or decreases the burden of the principal's performance. Under the Restatement of Security § 128, however, the surety is not discharged if "the modification is of a sort that can only be beneficial to the surety." Under either view, since the compensated surety has not only been paid for his undertaking but has usually, in addition, supplied the form setting forth its express terms, he is less likely to be discharged because of modification. See Restatement, Security § 128(b).

4. This is particularly true where the surety attempts to enforce a right which the creditor would have had against a third party.

5. In this discussion of discharge of a surety it is assumed that the creditor has knowledge of the suretyship relation. See Restatement, Security § 114.

Two more frequent kinds of modification, release of the principal and extension of time for the principal to perform, are particularly significant because of the related provisions of UCC 3–606 concerning discharge of parties secondarily liable on negotiable instruments. It is hardly surprising that release of the principal generally discharges the surety. Two reasons suggest themselves. One rests upon concern for the surety, for if C released P, C would have no rights to which S could be subrogated should he be required to pay. The other rests upon concern for the principal, for should S be required to pay C, he would still be entitled to reimbursement from P, thus accomplishing indirectly the enforcement of P's debt to C, contrary to P's expectations upon discharge.

Two exceptions to the general rule discharging the surety upon release of the principal involve consent of the surety and reservation of rights by the creditor against the surety. Suppose that a fourth party, upon P's default, agrees to make good $3,000 of P's debt to C in consideration for P's release. If C releases P but obtains S's consent to remain bound, S's liability to pay C the balance of $2,000 will be unaffected by the release. S has consented to the loss of his remedy of subrogation and is deemed to have relinquished his right to reimbursement. He has, in effect, become principal debtor.

More startling is the doctrine that C, without obtaining S's consent, can preserve his liability merely by reserving his rights against S at the time of P's release. The reasoning runs as follows. Concern for S does not require his discharge for S has not lost his remedy of subrogation. The release of P with reservation of rights against S is construed as a covenant by C not to sue P. It does not deprive C of the power to enforce P's liability, although it places him under a duty not to do so. Concern for P does not require the discharge of S because when P accepted his release with the reservation, he assumed the risk that the liability might be enforced against him by S. But has not the release of P made it almost inevitable that S will now be called upon to perform? Does this not unfairly increase his burden? It may be an answer to say that S's expectation that P will pay and discharge the obligation is a matter solely between S and P, and of no concern to C. Certainly it would seem that S's remedy of exoneration would be unaffected. Perhaps a more satisfactory answer is one suggested by the Restatement of Security § 122, that it may encourage compositions. The Restatement suggests that should P propose a composition to creditors, C could accept the composition, releasing P but reserving rights against S. If S pays C, he has a right of reimbursement against P.

A binding agreement between the creditor and the principal extending the time for the principal's performance will also discharge the surety. See Restatement, Security § 129. It is reasoned that S would be precluded by the extension from paying C at maturity and proceeding against P.[6] Here, too, exceptions are made where the surety consents and where the creditor reserves his rights against the surety. If C has reserved his rights against S, S may avoid any prejudicial effect of the extension by paying at maturity and proceeding against P in spite of the extension.

Finally, if the creditor releases security which he holds for the principal's performance, the general rule is that the surety is discharged to the extent of the value released. See Restatement, Security § 132. Discharge is based on the impairment of the surety's right of subrogation to enforce the security. Thus if C should release the $3,000 worth of bonds to P, S would be discharged to the extent of $3,000. Note that UCC 3–606 deals expressly with the release of security.

This has been, of course, only the barest introduction to a complicated subject. For further discussion, see Restatement, Security (1941), Simpson, Suretyship (1950), 10 Williston, Contracts §§ 1211–84A (3rd ed. 1967). For a general discussion of problems under the Code, see Peters, Suretyship Under Article 3 of the Uniform Commercial Code, 77 Yale L.J. 833 (1968). See also Martin, Some Suggestions for Nonurgent Reforms in the UCC's Treatment of Accommodation Parties, 6 U.Mich.J.L.Ref. 596 (1973); Murray, Accommodation Parties: A Potpourri of Problems, 22 U.Miami L.Rev. 814 (1968); Wladis, U.C.C. Article 3 Suretyship and the Holder in Due Course: Requiem for the Good Samaritan, 70 Geo.L.J. 975 (1982).

SECTION 2. THE ACCOMMODATION PARTY'S CONTRACT

Prefatory Note. If C required P to give a negotiable promissory note, the transaction might take several forms. Probably the note would be made payable to C's order. P might sign as maker with S adding his indorsement on the back of the instrument. In this case C could be expected to require that S sign a waiver of due presentment and notice of dishonor. See p. 49 supra. Or S might sign as maker with P as indorser, waiving presentment and notice. Or P and S might sign as co-makers. In any of these situations, S would be an accommodation party within the meaning of UCC 3–415(1).

---

6. The rule is not without its critics. "How many would hold that a surety is released, irrespective of resulting damage, if by agreement between principal and creditor the time of payment of the debt is extended for a single day?" Cardozo, A Ministry of Justice, 35 Harv.L. Rev. 113, 117 (1921).

In A/C Electric Co. v. Aetna Insurance Co., 251 Md. 410, 247 A.2d 708 (1968), the court refused to apply the rule in favor of a compensated surety, a surety company that had been paid a fee for undertaking its obligation. "Although we are mindful of the division which exists among the reported cases, . . . we think that the modern and correct view is that adopted by Restatement, Security (1941) § 129," under which: "Where the surety is a compensated surety he is discharged only to the extent that he is harmed by the extension."

Problem 1. A made a promissory note payable to the X Bank in consideration for a loan to him. B later indorsed the note for the accommodation of A. Is B liable to the X Bank on A's default? See UCC 3–408, 3–415; Franklin National Bank v. Eurez Construction Corp., infra. Would the result be the same if B, instead of indorsing A's note, had made his own note payable to the X Bank and given it to X Bank as security for the original note? Would it be the same if B had made his own note payable to A, who had indorsed it to the X Bank as security for the original note? Should the form of the transaction be controlling?

FRANKLIN NATIONAL BANK v. EUREZ CONSTRUCTION CORP.

New York Supreme Court, Special Term, Nassau County, 1969.
60 Misc.2d 499, 301 N.Y.S.2d 845.

BERNARD S. MEYER, JUSTICE. In this action, tried without a jury, plaintiff bank seeks in its first cause of action to require defendant Eurez Construction Corporation to endorse a promissory note of J.J. White Ready Mix Concrete Corp. payable to Eurez and negotiated to the bank by an officer of Eurez; in the second cause of action seeks to recover from Eurez the $20,000 which it received from the bank as a result of such negotiation; in the third cause of action seeks to recover from Eurez, J.J. White Ready Mix Concrete Corp. and John J. White, as indorser, on the note, it having been dishonored when due; and in the fourth cause of action seeks to recover from defendants Rezendi, Euzebio and Salonia, as guarantors of the obligations of Eurez Construction Corp.

Though defendants Rezendi and Euzebio denied execution of guarantees, they failed to appear and testify and the authenticity of their signatures was established by the signature cards filed with the bank for the Eurez account and for a savings account of defendant Euzebio. Each guarantee includes a waiver of "protest, presentment, demand for payment, notice of default or nonpayment, and notice of dishonor," and provides that it is "an absolute and unconditional guarantee of payment, without regard to the validity, regularity, or enforceability of any obligation or purported obligation . . .." The note in suit was delivered to the bank on May 13, 1968 by the defendant Salonia, an officer of Eurez, and though it was not indorsed on behalf of Eurez, the proceeds of the note were credited to the Eurez account on that day and thereafter were drawn against by that corporation. The fact that the bank had no corporate resolution authorizing Salonia to deal with the bank does not, under those circumstances, avail either Eurez or the individual guarantors, Bank of North America v. Shapiro, 31 A.D.2d 465, 466, 298 N.Y.S.2d 399, 400.

Plaintiff is, therefore, entitled to judgment as demanded in the complaint on the second and fourth causes of action.

The transfer of the note for value to plaintiff gives it "the specifically enforceable right to have the unqualified indorsement of the transferor," U.C.C. § 3–201(3). Thus, plaintiff is also entitled to judgment on the first cause of action. Its right to recover against defendants J.J. White Ready Mix Concrete Corp. and John J. White on the third cause of action is less clear, however. Section 3–201(3) provides that "Negotiation takes effect only when the indorsement is made . . . ". As to any defense of which the transferee of an instrument payable to order has notice prior to the time "indorsement is made", the transferee is not a holder in due course, U.C.C. §§ 1–201(20); 3–202(1); 3–302(1)(c). Defendants J.J. White Ready Mix Concrete Corp. and John J. White urge as a complete defense to the third cause of action that the note was made by the corporate defendant and indorsed by the individual defendant an an accommodation to Eurez and without consideration. They urge that under U.C.C. §§ 3–306(c) and 3–408 want of consideration is a defense against one who is not a holder in due course. Plaintiff, relying on U.C.C. § 3–415(1) and (2), argues that absence of consideration is not available as a defense to an accommodation maker or indorser when the instrument is taken for value before it is due. Though the court finds that defendant J.J. White Ready Mix Concrete Corp. made, and defendant John J. White indorsed, the note in suit as an accommodation to defendant Eurez and without consideration, it holds plaintiff's interpretation of the Uniform Commercial Code to be correct and, therefore, awards plaintiff judgment against them as well as defendant Eurez on the third cause of action.

As Professor Peters states "While Section 3–415(2) seems to opt for liability in this situation, the outcome is by no means clear," Peters, Suretyship Under Article 3 of the Uniform Commercial Code, 77 Yale L.J. 833, 848. The problem arises because U.C.C. § 3–408 states that "Want or failure of consideration is a defense as against any person not having the rights of a holder in due course (Section 3–305), except that no consideration is necessary for an instrument or obligation thereon given in payment of or as security for an antecedent obligation of any kind", but fails to except cases in which an accommodation party signs without consideration. Under well known rules of construction that omission would lead to the conclusion that want of consideration to the accommodation maker and indorser is a defense available to them, were it not for the provisions of section 3–415(1) and (2).

Section 3–415(1) provides that "An accommodation party is one who signs the instrument in any capacity for the purpose of lending his name to another party to it" and subdivision (2) states that "When the instrument has been taken for value before it is due the accommodation party is liable in the capacity in which he has signed even though the taker knows of the accommodation." Nothing in subdivision (1) suggests that consideration running to an accommodation maker is a *sine qua non* of his liability; indeed Official Comment 2 to U.C.C. § 3–415 makes clear that its definition includes both gratuitous and paid sureties. Furthermore, nothing in subdivision (2) requires that the accommodation party have received value. Ostensibly its purpose is to protect the taker when the instrument has been taken for value and before maturity. In light of the phrase "before it is due" it seems unreasonable to construe the Code to require that value have been given at the time of issuance in order to hold an accommodation maker, but see Peters, op. cit. supra, 77 Yale L.J. at 845. Nor can the concluding clause ("even though the taker knows of the accommodation") be seized upon as limiting the effect of the subdivision to the negation of knowledge of accommodation status as a defense, for that construction would either make § 3–304(4)(c) superfluous or in view of the provisions of that section and § 3–302 would make meaningless the reference in § 3–415(2) to taking for value and before maturity. If § 3–415(2) was not intended to give status to a taker for value before maturity different from the status he would have as a holder in due course, the section should have referred not to a "taker" but to a "holder who when he takes" (compare § 3–302(1) which uses the phrase "holder who takes"), especially since "holder" is expressly defined in § 1–201(20) whereas the Code nowhere defines "taker", and since the predecessor to U.C.C. § 3–415(2), Section 55 of the Negotiable Instruments Law (U.N.I.L. § 29), used the phrase "holder for value". Some significance must also be accorded the fact that though Professor Brannan pressed for amendment of the Negotiable Instruments Law provisions to substitute in place of "holder for value" the words "one who is in other respects a holder in due course," Brannan, Some Necessary Amendments of the Negotiable Instruments Law, 26 Harv.L.R. 493, the draftsmen of the Uniform Commercial Code (who, it may be presumed, were aware of the Brannan article), while modifying the Negotiable Instruments Law concept to include not only taking "for value" (which was the sole N.I.L. criterion) but also taking "before it [the instrument] is due," and to drop the former § 52 (U.N.I.L. § 26) definition of "holder for value" as "erroneous and misleading, since a holder who does not himself give value cannot qualify as a holder in due course in his own right merely because value has previously been given for the instrument," Official Comment 1 to U.C.C. § 3–303, nevertheless did not incorporate in § 3–415 all of the holder in due course criteria and substituted for the word "holder" previously used the word "taker". It seems fair to argue from this that the draftsmen did not intend to require that a taker for value before maturity have holder in due course status in order to hold an accommodation party liable. The difficulty with the argument is that it proves too much, for to paraphrase Professor Brannan, op. cit. supra at p. 498, if the argument is sound, a taker of accommodation paper occupies a position superior to that of any other purchaser of negotiable paper, since there are no other requirements for his recovery except that he be a taker for value and before maturity, see also 1955 Report Law Rev.Comm. (Leg.Doc. [1955] No. 65), Vol. 2, pp. 918–919. It is not now necessary to determine to what extent defenses other than want of consideration are available against a taker for value before maturity who is not a holder in due course, cf. U.C.C. §§ 3–306(c) and 3–408. It is sufficient to note that Official Comment 3 to § 3–415 states that: "The obligation of the accommodation party is supported by any consideration for which the instrument is taken before it is due" and to hold on the basis of that Comment and the history and wording of the section, that there is no want of consideration within the meaning of § 3–408 when consideration moves before maturity to the party accommodated, even though the accommodation maker receives no consideration for executing the instrument.

The conclusion thus reached, while it reads into § 3–408 an exception which the draftsmen of the Code have not articulated, can be supported by a number of additional arguments. "Consideration" is distinguished from "value" throughout Article 3 of the Code, Official Comment 1 to § 3–408; Official Comment 2 to § 3–303. "Consideration" refers to what the obligor has received for his obligation and is important only on the question whether the obligation can be enforced against him, ibid. "Value" on the other hand refers to what the holder or taker has given up and is important only on the question whether the holder "qualifies as a particular kind of holder", Official Comment 2 to § 3–303. The fact that in § 3–424 of the May 1949 Draft of the Uniform Commercial Code, the sentence which became § 3–415(2) of the Code in its final form began "When the instrument has been taken for *consideration* before it is due . . ." (emphasis supplied) and that the word "consideration" was changed to "value" in the Spring 1950 draft, when read together with Official Comment 3 to § 3–415 ("The obligation of the accommodation party is supported by any consideration [sic] *for which the instrument is taken* before it is due", [emphasis supplied]), suggests that the draftsmen intended the taker's right to enforce an instrument against an accommodation party to turn on whether the taker had given value, rather than whether the accommodation party had received consideration.

Secondly, U.C.C. § 1–103 provides that : "Unless displaced by the particular provisions of this Act, the principles of law and equity, including the law merchant . . . shall supplement its provisions." The rule of law prior to the Code was that one who receives before maturity a note signed by the maker for the accommodation of another is not affected by the mere fact that it was made without consideration, Chester v. Dorr, 41 N.Y. 279, 284; Grocers' Bank v. Penfield, 69 N.Y. 502; see McGoldrick v. Family Finance Corp., 287 N.Y. 535, 538, 41 N.E.2d 86, 88, 141 A.L.R. 909; Packard v. Windholz, 88 App. Div. 365, 84 N.Y.S. 666, affd. 180 N.Y. 549, 73 N.E. 1129; Welbilt

Concrete Construction Corp. v. Kornicki, 26 A.D.2d 661, 272 N.Y.S.2d 422. The omission from U.C.C. § 3–408 of any exception covering the situation suggests an intention on the part of the draftsmen to change the rule; the fact that gratuitous accommodation is covered by U.C.C. § 3–415, the specific language of § 3–415(2) and the absence of any logical basis for change suggest an intention to preserve the prior rule. If the latter reasons be an insufficient basis for concluding that the prior rule continues, it is likewise impossible to view the omission from § 3–408 as a displacement "by the particular provisions of this Act" of the prior rule. Absent such displacement, the prior rule continues.

Thirdly, Section 1–102(2)(c) of the Code directs that it be liberally construed to promote its purposes and policies, one of which is "to make uniform the law among the various jurisdictions". Though based on somewhat different reasoning, there are cases in other jurisdictions holding that one who is not a holder in due course but who takes accommodation paper for value before it is due may, under § 3–415(2), enforce it against the accommodation maker, James Talcott, Inc. v. Fred Ratowsky Associates, Inc., 84 Dauphin 258, 38 Pa.Dist. & Co.R.2d 624; see, A.J. Armstrong Inc. v. Janburt Embroidery Corp., 97 N.J.Super. 246, 234 A.2d 737, and that want of consideration is no defense to an accommodation maker, Seaboard Finance Co. of Connecticut, Inc. v. Dorman, 4 Conn.Cir. 154, 227 A.2d 441.

Brief mention must also be made of a few additional points. While defendants J.J. White Ready Mix Concrete Corp. and John J. White were accommodation parties, plaintiff bank did not know that fact when it took the note. That it did not does not, however, change the result in light of the wording of § 3–415(2). Defendant White's testimony was that when he gave the note to Alfredo Rezendi he told him it was not to be used unless Eurez needed it to make its payroll. Defendants presented no proof that when the note was discounted by Eurez no part of its proceeds was required by Eurez to make its payroll, but in any event, the court finds that plaintiff took the note without notice of that restriction and may, therefore, enforce it even if the note was in fact used in violation of the restriction, Davis v. Sisti, 3 Misc.2d 132, 148 N.Y.S.2d 76; see Rheinstein v. Case, 23 Misc.2d 41, 197 N.Y.S.2d 41. Finally, the court finds that defendant White directed his bank not to honor the note and, therefore, that neither he nor his corporation was entitled to notice of protest, U.C.C. § 3–511(2)(b).

The foregoing constitutes the decision of the court pursuant to CPLR 4213(b) and all motions on which decision was reserved are decided accordingly. While plaintiff is entitled to judgment against defendant Eurez on the theory of either the second or the third cause of action, the same moneys are involved in both, and plaintiff is, therefore, entitled to but one judgment on both causes of action against defendant Eurez.

NOTES

(1) **Consideration.** The Eurez Construction case is discussed in Steffen and Johns, The After-Acquired Surety: Commercial Paper, 59 Calif.L.Rev. 1459, 1461–62 (1971). The authors point out that "there was an abundance of consideration in the usual sense, and the case might well have been put on that ground. But the defendants appear to have urged a quibble—that they were due a personal consideration. In any case, the court expressly found that the accommodation parties had signed 'the note in suit as an accommodation to defendant Eurez and *without consideration.* . . . ' Perhaps the court meant 'without consideration' in the *paid surety* sense, but it did not say so. Judgment for plaintiff was given on the sole stated ground that, under section 3–415(1) and (2), 'absence of consideration is not available as a defense to an accommodation maker or indorser when the instrument is taken for value before it is due.' The court may have felt bound to put the case on that ground, since the bank, as a 'taker' without endorsement, could not qualify as a 'holder' in due course." The authors go on to argue that if UCC 3–415(2) had been inteded to have the effect given it by the court, it would have been drafted as follows:

> When the instrument has been taken for value before it is due *an* accommodation party *then on the instrument or who signs at any later time* is liable in the capacity in which he has signed. . . .

They point out that to the extent that Comment 3 to UCC 3–415 suggests that the "occasional decisions" referred to were in a minority, it is misleading, and that "comments were never to be a *crutch* for faulty draftsmanship." As for UCC 3–408, they conclude that the Code would "be improved appreciably by deleting altogether the 26 words comprising the 'except' clause." [1]

(2) **Protection of Cosigners in Consumer Transactions.** A Federal Trade Commission Rule on Credit Practices protects natural persons who cosign in consumer transactions. The rule makes it a deceptive act or practice "for a lender or retail installment seller, directly or indirectly, to misrepresent the nature or extent of cosigner liability to any person," or "directly or indirectly to obligate a cosigner unless the cosigner is informed prior to becoming obligated . . . of the nature of his or her liability as cosigner." To avoid such a practice, "a disclosure consisting of a separate document that shall

---

1. See also Martin, Some Suggestions for Nonurgent Reforms in the UCC's Treatment of Accommodation Parties, 6 U.Mich.J.L.Ref. 596, 601 (1973) ("[T]here was consideration: the loan made to the accommodated party . . . . Section 3–408 is inapplicable here, not because, as the *Eurez* court thought, it is superseded in the case of accommodation parties by the more specific language of Subsection 3–415(2), but because by its own terms it deals with a factual premise (lack of consideration) not present in the *Eurez* case.").

contain the following statement and no other, shall be given to the cosigner prior to becoming obligated . . .:

Notice to Cosigner

You are being asked to guarantee this debt. Think carefully before you do. If the borrower doesn't pay the debt, you will have to. Be sure you can afford to pay if you have to, and that you want to accept this responsibility.

You may have to pay up to the full amount of the debt if the borrower does not pay. You may also have to pay late fees or collection costs, which increase this amount.

The creditor can collect this debt from you without first trying to collect from the borrower. The creditor can use the same collection methods against you that can be used against the borrower, such as suing you, garnishing your wages, etc. If this debt is ever in default, that fact may become a part of *your* credit record.

This notice is not the contract that makes you liable for the debt.

16 C.F.R. § 444.3.

The Commission noted that some cosigners "believe that they are merely acting as a reference. Legal Aid attorneys estimate that only 20 percent of cosigners understand the nature of their obligation." There are, however, occasional exceptions (e.g., "I generally tell any cosigner that a cosigner is a damn fool with a pencil.").

Prefatory Note. To what extent does the capacity in which a surety signs a negotiable instrument affect his rights as surety? The maker of a note is not a "secondary party" under UCC 3–102(1) (d), although the indorser of a note is. Does this mean that an accommodation maker's rights as surety differ from those of an accommodation indorser? And what of the anomalous or irregular indorser, who signs the instrument without appearing in the chain of title? Is a person who signs in this way bound as an indorser, as a surety, or in some other capacity? UCC 3–202(4) helps to clear this up by providing that even words of guaranty accompanying an indorsement do not affect its character as an indorsement. But assuming that the anomalous or irregular indorser *is* an indorser, to whom is he liable and who is liable to him?

Problem 2. A made a promissory note payable to B in payment of a debt. B discounted the note with the X Bank. A defaulted on the note, and B took it up and paid the X Bank. Can B recover from I, an accommodation indorser whose indorsement appears above that of B on the note? If I had taken it up and paid the X Bank, could I recover from B? How can I establish that he is an *accommodation* indorser? How can he establish for *whose* accommodation he indorsed?   See UCC 3–415, 3–603; Fithian v. Jamar, infra; T.W. Sommer Co. v. Modern Door and Lumber Co., infra.

FITHIAN v. JAMAR

Court of Appeals of Maryland, 1979.
286 Md. 161, 410 A.2d 569.

COLE, JUDGE. The dispute in this case involves the rights and liabilities of co-makers of a note in a suit among themselves, where none of the disputants is a holder of the note. We granted certiorari to consider two questions, which simply stated are:

1.   Whether a co-maker of a note was also an accommodation maker of the note and thus not liable to the party accommodated;

2.   Whether the agreement of one co-maker to assume another co-maker's obligation on a note constitutes a defense to the latter when sued for contribution by the former.

In 1967 Walter Fithian (Walter) and Richard Jamar (Richard), who were employed as printers at Baltimore Business Forms, decided to form a partnership to carry on their own printing business. They applied to the People's Bank of Chestertown, Maryland (Bank) for an $11,000 business loan to enable them to purchase some equipment. The Bank agreed to lend the money to Walter and Richard only if Walter's wife, Connie, Richard's wife, Janet, and Walter's parents, Walter William (Bill) and Mildred Fithian would co-sign the note. The Executive Vice-President of the Bank explained that the additional signatures were required to make the Bank more secure.   The note, which authorized confession of judgment in the event of default, was signed on its face in the bottom righthand corner by these six parties.   The monies loaned were deposited in Walter and Richard's business checking account and were used to purchase printing equipment.

By 1969, Walter and Richard were encountering business problems. They spoke with Frank Hogans (Hogans) and Gerald Bos (Bos) (who were interested in joining the business) about forming a corporation to be called J–F Printing Co., Inc. and refinancing the note so that it (the note) could become a corporate rather than an individual obligation. The business continued to falter and on March 23, 1972 Walter, Richard, Hogans and Bos met and entered into a written agreement in their individual capacities whereby Richard was to take over management and ownership of the business in exchange for his assumption of liability for the company's outstanding obligations, one of which was the note in question in this case.   The agreement also provided that should Richard default in the performance of those obligations, Walter, Hogans, and Bos would have the right to terminate the agreement and resume ownership of the business.

Pursuant to the agreement Richard assumed control of the business but was unable to make any further payments on the note. Consequently, the Executive Vice-President of the Bank requested that Bill and Mildred Fithian pay the note in full. They did and the Bank assigned the note to them for whatever disposition they might choose. Bill demanded that Richard indemnify him for the total amount Bill paid on the note.

Receiving no satisfaction from Richard, Bill and Mildred sought judicial relief. On November 10, 1976, a confessed judgment against Richard and Janet of $8,953.95, the balance on the note paid by Bill and Mildred, with interest from January 18, 1974, court costs, and attorney's fees of $472.70, was entered in the Circuit Court for Kent County. Richard and Janet filed a motion to vacate the judgment, which the circuit court granted and ordered a hearing on the merits. Prior to trial, Richard and Janet filed a third party claim against Walter and Connie averring that as co-makers of the note, Walter and Connie were liable to Richard and Janet for any judgment that Bill and Mildred might recover against Richard and Janet. Walter and Connie counterclaimed contending that the agreement barred Richard's recovery.

The matter was brought to trial on August 25, 1977 before the circuit court, sitting without a jury. The court found that the J–F Printing Company, Inc. was never a de jure corporation and that those who attempted to act under that name were merely acting in their individual capacities; that the March 23, 1972 agreement was not material to the determination of the case; that Bill and Mildred were accommodation makers for Richard, Janet, Walter and Connie and were entitled to collect from any one of the four.

Final judgment was entered on September 6, 1977 for Bill and Mildred against Richard and Janet in the amount of $8,953.95, the principal sum due, plus $2,288.95, representing interest from January 18, 1974 to August 25, 1977. The court denied Bill and Mildred's claim for collection fees specified in the note and also entered a judgment for Richard and Janet on Walter and Connie's counterclaim. In the third party claim of Richard and Janet against Walter and Connie, judgment was entered for Richard and Janet in the amount of $5,621.45, fifty percent of the total judgment. The costs of the case were to be divided equally between Richard and Janet and Walter and Connie.

Bill and Mildred Fithian filed a timely appeal to the Court of Special Appeals, complaining of the circuit court's adverse ruling as to the collection fees. Walter and Connie took their own appeal, challenging the lower court's findings concerning both Connie's status in relation to the note and the materiality of the March, 1972 agreement. These appeals were consolidated for oral argument in that court.

In an unreported per curiam decision filed on April 7, 1978, Fithian v. Jamar, No. 946, Sept. Term, 1977, the Court of Special Appeals affirmed the circuit court in part and reversed in part. The Court of Special Appeals reversed on the issue of collection fees, ruling that there was a "valid and enforceable contract right of Bill and Mildred to the payment of collection costs . . . .."; the Court of Special Appeals affirmed the circuit court's finding that Connie Fithian was a co-maker of the note, and not an accommodation party. The Court of Special Appeals also affirmed the trial court's finding that the March, 1972 agreement was not material to the case because it was "a private agreement between only two (2) of the six (6) makers of the note."

Walter and Connie (appellants) requested review of these rulings in this Court, and we granted their petition for certiorari on June 21, 1978 to consider the two questions presented: whether Connie Fithian was an accommodation maker of the note and thus not liable to the party accommodated; and whether the March, 1972 agreement constitutes a defense to Richard and Janet's (appellees) third party claim against Walter and Connie.

Our disposition of the questioned rulings requires us to reverse and remand. The error which occurred in the court below was caused in part by a failure to fully analyze the individual rights and obligations of Connie, Walter, Janet and Richard. Therefore, in the discussion which follows, in addition to examining the two questions presented, we will clarify the resulting rights and obligations of these parties.

Richard v. Connie

Since there is no dispute that Connie signed the note, the answer to the first question depends on her purpose in doing so. This is made clear by Maryland Code (1975), § 3–415(1) of the Commercial Law Article which provides that an accommodation party is "one who signs the instrument in any capacity for the purpose of lending his name to another party to it." The undisputed evidence as presented by the Executive Vice-President of the Bank was to the effect that the wives' signatures were required before the Bank would make the loan to Walter and Richard. Such practices are common among lending institutions which recognize that

> [o]ne with money to lend, goods to sell or services to render may have doubts about a prospective debtor's ability to pay. In such cases he is likely to demand more assurance than the debtor's bare promise of payment. The prospective creditor can reduce his risk by requiring some sort of security. One form of security is the Article 9 security interest in the debtor's goods. Another type of security takes the form of joining a third person on the debtor's obligation. [J. White and R. Summers, Uniform Commercial Code § 13–12, at 425 (1972)].

It is readily apparent, therefore, that Connie lent her name to facilitate the loan transaction. As such she lent her name to two parties to the instrument, Richard and Walter, to enable them to receive a *joint* loan for the purchase of equipment for their printing business, thereby giving the Bank the added assurance of having another party to the obligation. Connie signed as an accommodation party as to both Walter and Richard.

Nor is there any merit in the argument advanced by Richard that Connie must be either be a co-maker or an accommodation party, that she cannot be both. The actual language of § 3–415(1) indicates that an accommodation party also signs in a particular capacity, as maker, acceptor or indorser of an instrument. The Official Comment 1 to § 3–415 explains that

> [s]ubsection (1) recognizes that an accommodation party is always a surety (which includes a guarantor), and it is his only distinguishing feature. He differs from other sureties only in that his liability is on the instrument and he is a surety for another party to it. His obligation is therefore determined by the capacity in which he signs. An accommodation maker or acceptor is bound on the instrument without any resort to his principal, while an accommodation indorser may be liable only after presentment, notice of dishonor and protest.

Moreover, § 3–415(2) refers specifically to the liability of an accommodation party "in the capacity in which he has signed." It follows, therefore, that the fact that Connie was a co-maker of the note does not preclude her from also being an accommodation party.

Section 3–415(5) of the Commercial Law Article states that "[a]n accommodation party is not liable to the party accommodated"; thus, Connie is not liable to Richard. Our predecessors, prior to Maryland's adoption of the Uniform Commercial Code, explained the reasons for this proposition in Crothers v. National Bank, 158 Md. 587, 593, 149 A. 270, 273 (1930):

> Since the accommodating party lends his credit by request to the party accommodated upon the assumption that the latter will discharge the debt when due, it is an implied term of this agreement that the party accommodated cannot acquire any right of action against the accommodating party.

Richard contends, however, that Connie intended to accommodate only her husband, Walter. Even if there were evidence to this effect (and there is none), the subjective intent of a co-maker of a note is of little weight when objective facts and circumstances unambiguously demonstrate the capacity in which the note was signed. . . . It is clear to us that the signatures of both wives were required to effect this joint business venture and thus Connie's signature was as much an accommodation to Richard as it was to Walter. We hold that Connie was an accommodation maker and that she cannot be liable to

Richard, the party accommodated. The Court of Special Appeals erroneously held to the contrary.

Janet v. Connie

The preceding discussion of Connie's status demonstrates that each of the four parties, Walter, Connie, Richard, and Janet, has certain rights and obligations with respect to this note which are not affected by his or her marital status. The court below erred in not fully analyzing these separate rights and obligations. It follows that our finding that Connie has no liability to Richard in no way changes any obligation she may have to Janet. Janet, as well as Connie, is a co-accommodation maker on this note.

The question is therefore whether one co-accommodation maker who pays more than her proportionate share of the debt has a right of contribution against another co-accommodation maker. The Uniform Commercial Code contains no provision expressly dealing with the right of an accommodation party to contribution from another accommodation party. However, the Code does provide that the principles of the common law remain applicable "[u]nless displaced by the particular provisions" of the Code. Maryland Code (1975), § 1–103 of the Commercial Law Article.

That an accommodation maker has a right of contribution from a co-accommodation maker is a settled principle of the law. The Restatement of Security provides

A surety who in the performance of his own obligation discharges more than his proportionate share of the principal's duty is entitled to contribution from a co-surety. [Restatement of Security § 149 (1941)].

. . .

Maryland has followed this rule. Jackson v. Cupples, 239 Md. 637, 212 A.2d 273 (1965). *Jackson* was decided after the effective date of the U.C.C. in Maryland, but the note in question had been executed prior to that date. The Court held that a co-surety who pays a debt has a right of contribution from his co-sureties.

This Court has not addressed this question in regard to a note controlled by the U.C.C. Our research revealed only one case which directly confronted the effect of the U.C.C. on the common law rule. The court stated that the U.C.C. does not change the rule of suretyship law permitting contribution by one surety from a co-surety. McLochlin v. Miller, 139 Ind.App. 443, 217 N.E.2d 50 (1966).

Accordingly Janet has a right of contribution against Connie. But this right to contribution is an inchoate claim which does not ripen into being unless and until Janet pays more than her proportionate share to Bill and Mildred. . . . Judgment can be entered on behalf of Janet against Connie, but it must be fashioned so that it may not be enforced until Janet proves she actually paid more than her proportionate share to Bill and Mildred.[1]   .   .   .

Richard v. Walter

We now turn to the second question as to whether the March, 1972 agreement by which Richard assumed full liability on the note constitutes a defense to Richard and Janet's third party claim that Walter and Connie reimburse them for fifty percent of the primary judgment granted to Bill and Mildred against Richard and Janet.   In the circuit court Bill and Mildred Fithian, having paid the instrument to the Bank, successfully exercised their right of recourse on the note under § 3–415(5) of the Commercial Law Article which provides that "[a]n accommodation party is not liable to the party accommodated, and if he pays the instrument has a right of recourse on the instrument against such party."   In discussing this general principle of suretyship law Professors White and Summers explain that

> [a]s between the surety and the debtor, it is clear that the debtor has the primary obligation to pay the debt.   Since the creditor is entitled to only one performance and the debtor receives the benefit of the transaction, the surety's obligation is undertaken with the expectation that the debtor will meet his commitment to the creditor.   Thus, if the surety is made to pay his principal's debt, he has the right to recover from the principal.   [J. White and R. Summers, Uniform Commercial Code, § 13–12, at 426 (1972) (footnote omitted)].

This Court has adhered to the principle that if an accommodation party pays the note to the holder, he has a right of recourse against the party accommodated.   .   .   .   Other courts have also adopted this viewpoint.   .   .   .

Similarly, it is axiomatic that one joint obligor may ordinarily claim contribution from a co-obligor after having discharged their mutual obligation.   Jackson v. Cupples, supra, ...   However, this principle is not controlling in the instant case.   While the courts below ruled that Walter and Connie must reimburse Richard and Janet for one-half the judgment against them and discounted the significance of the 1972 agreement on this question, we believe that under both statutory and common law principles the 1972 agreement is material to the decision of this case and plays a substantial role in our determination of whether Walter was properly required to pay contribution to Richard.   Because neither Connie nor Janet were parties to the agreement, their rights and obligations are not affected.

---

1.   A surety who is called upon to pay more than his proportionate share of the debt has a right of contribution from his co-sureties in an amount not to exceed each co-surety's proportionate share of the debt.   See Schindel v. Danzer, 161 Md. 384, 157 A. 283 (1931); 72 C.J.S. Principal and Surety § 369 (1951).   Here the note was signed by four sureties (Bill, Mildred, Connie and Janet); Janet's proportionate share of indebtedness to her co-sureties is 25% of the debt.

In the first place, § 3–601(2) of the Commercial Law Article and the Official Comments thereto specifically recognize the possibility of discharge by act or agreement of a party who is otherwise liable on an instrument. Section 3–601(2) reads: "Any party is also discharged from his liability on an instrument to another party by any other act or agreement with such party which would discharge his simple contract for the payment of money." Official Comment 2 to § 3–601 reads in pertinent part that

> [s]o far as the discharge of any one party is concerned a negotiable instrument differs from any other contract only in the special rules arising out of its character to which paragraphs (a) to (i) of subsection (1) are an index, and in the effect of the discharge against a subsequent holder in due course (Section 3–602). *Subsection (2) therefore retains from the original Section 119(4) the provision for discharge by "any other act which will discharge a simple contract for the payment of money," and specifically recognizes the possibility of a discharge by agreement.*
>
> *The discharge of any party is a defense available to that party as provided in sections on rights of those who are and are not holders* in due course (Sections 3–305 and 3–306). He has the burden of establishing the defense (Section 3–307). [emphasis supplied].

While this Court has not addressed this precise issue under § 3–601(2), two recent decisions of other jurisdictions do acknowledge that under § 30–601, liability of a party on a negotiable instrument may be discharged by a written agreement. . . . Several other courts have endorsed the proposition that co-makers of an instrument may vary their obligations between themselves. . . . Still other courts have held that parol evidence of a special agreement between co-obligors is admissible where liability to a payee is not at issue. . . .

Applying these principles to the present case, we believe that the 1972 agreement operated to modify the liabilities of Richard and Walter on the note between themselves. We accept the trial court's finding based on the record before it that the partnership between Richard and Walter never was converted into a duly constituted corporation and that the parties conducted the business in their individual capacities rather than as directors of a corporation.[2] Thus, the agreement expressed the intentions of these individuals as between themselves, and as such reflects the transfer of all of the assets and liabilities of the business to Richard in return for his promise to keep the other interested parties, Walter, Hogans and Bos, free from any responsibility for payment of any and all of the business debts, in-

---

2. In any event, assuming a corporation had been duly formed, it would not change the result we reach under the facts of this case since the corporation was not a party to the agreement and had assumed no obligation to pay the note.

cluding the note in question. The only safety valve for the transferring individuals was their right upon their own decision to terminate
the agreement if Richard demonstrated an inability or unwillingness
to keep his promise. Richard and Janet in their briefs concede that
the evidence of this agreement is "arguably material" but contend
that it is "not highly probative." We disagree. The language of the
agreement shows that Richard specifically consented to take responsibility for the obligations of the printing business, including the
$11,000 note to the Bank:

> 1.   Richard F. Jamar, party of the first part, agrees to take
> over the operation of J–F Printing Company, Inc., *and to be*
> *responsible for the payment of the accounts payable and ob-*
> *ligations of said corporation now existing and to be in-*
> *curred henceforth in the operation of said business.*

> 2.   The parties of the second part do agree to turn over to
> Richard F. Jamar, party of the first part, full responsibility for
> the complete operation of said business as of the full execution
> and date of this agreement, *conditioned upon said party of*
> *the first part proceeding to* operate said business full time
> and in a businesslike manner, and proceeding to *methodically*
> *reduce the outstanding obligations of said corporation, in-*
> *cluding but not limited to: Two monthly payment notes*
> *payable to The People's Bank of Chestertown,* . . ..

> . . .

> 4.   Parties of the second part do hereby agree that upon
> party of the first part either paying off all obligations of the
> corporation, or upon making arrangements with all creditors to
> release parties of the second part from any and all liability for
> the payment of any indebtedness of the corporation, past, pres-
> ent or incurred in the future, that parties of the second part
> will forthwith formally assign unto party of the first part all of
> their right, title and interest in and to said corporation and the
> assets thereof . . ..

> . . .

> 7.   Party of the first part agrees not to pledge the credit of
> any of the parties of the second part, and agrees to hold harm-
> less parties of the second part as to the payment of any bills
> incurred in his operation of said business during the term of
> his agreement. [emphasis supplied].

By this agreement, which was not terminated when Richard defaulted on payment of the loan in subsequent years, Walter and Richard
agreed that Richard alone was to henceforth bear responsibility for
the note. Thus the document's operative effect was to discharge
Walter from any obligation on the note as to Richard. Thus the trial
court should have entered judgment for Walter on his counterclaim
against Richard for indemnification. In other words, by the agree-

ment, Richard gave up his right to claim contribution from his joint obligor, Walter. Therefore, the Court of Special Appeals below erred in affirming judgment for Richard against Walter.

Janet v. Walter

That the 1972 agreement serves as a defense by Walter against Richard in no way serves to insulate Walter against Janet. Janet's status as an accommodation maker is unaffected by the agreement. As an accommodation maker, Janet has a right to look to any principal, including Walter for any amounts she actually pays. Maryland Code (1975), § 3–415 of the Commercial Law Article. Janet's status as Richard's wife does not affect her status as an accommodation maker. She is entitled to judgment from either principal when she actually pays any amount of the debt.

In summary, Richard is not entitled to judgment against Walter because of the agreement. Rather, Walter is entitled to indemnification from Richard for any amount Walter is forced to pay. Richard is not entitled to judgment against Connie because an accommodation party is not liable to the party accommodated. Janet is entitled to contribution from her co-surety, Connie, the judgment being unenforceable unless and until Janet proves she actually has paid more than her proportionate share of the debt to Bill and Mildred. Similarly, Janet as a surety is entitled to judgment against Walter as a principal for any amount of the debt for which Janet proves payment.[3]

NOTE

Applicability of Code. In dealing with Janet's right to contribution from Connie, the court noted that the Code "contains no provision expressly dealing with the right of an accommodation party to contribution from another accommodation party." But in dealing with Richard's right to contribution from Walter, the court relied on UCC 3–601(2). Does that provision apply between comakers, whether accommodation parties or not? Was Walter's liability to Richard a "liability on an instrument"? Should this affect the result?

T.W. Sommer Co. v. Modern Door and Lumber Co., 293 Minn. 264, 198 N.W.2d 278 (1972). Prettyman was an officer of Modern Door, a corporation engaged in wood fabricating and owned largely by his father and himself. In 1967 Modern Door sustained heavy losses due to a fire and began liquidating its inventory under the supervision of James Talcott, Inc., a finance company that had substantial notes and liens against the inventory. Modern Door also owed money to two companies owned by Sommer, a friend of Prettyman.

---

3. Whether Bill and Mildred were entitled to judgment in the full amount of the debt against Janet we do not decide because Janet did not appeal from that judgment. [What *were* their rights against Janet? Ed.]

On September 3, 1968, Prettyman and Sommer went to the Liberty State Bank, where new notes for $36,000 covering this indebtedness were prepared by the bank, payable to the companies. They were signed by Prettyman as an officer of Modern Door, signed by him personally on the back as guarantor, and indorsed by the two companies to the bank as security for a loan to Sommer. On dishonor of the notes, the two companies took them up and sued Prettyman.

"KNUTSON, CHIEF JUSTICE . . . . The question involved here is whether Prettyman as guarantor is personally liable on these notes or whether he signed as an accommodation party for the payees and is therefore not liable to the person accommodated. The trial court found that Modern Door was liable on the notes but that Prettyman individually was not. . . . There is no claim that plaintiffs are holders in due course. Whether the court's finding that Prettyman signed the guaranty as an accommodation for the payees of these two notes is sustained by the evidence depends almost wholly on whether the testimony of Sommer or that of Prettyman is accepted. We think the court, as the trier of facts, had the right to rely on the testimony of Prettyman.

"There are several things that would support Prettyman's testimony. At the time the guaranty was signed, Modern Door was in the process of liquidation. It did very little business after the fire in 1967. The liquidation was under the control of James Talcott, Inc., and it would be somewhat doubtful whether Prettyman under these circumstances would assume liability of the notes to the payees. His testimony is that he guaranteed the notes to enable Sommer to obtain a loan from the bank for his own personal use and not otherwise. The trial court accepted that version of the transaction, and we are compelled to accept the evidence most favorable to this finding. From this it follow that the court's findings are amply sustained by the evidence. . . .

"We are therefore convinced that the evidence sustains the court's findings that Prettyman individually signed the guaranty on the back of the two notes for the accommodation of the payees, and as such he is not liable to the payees. There is no question that the corporate defendant Modern Door is liable to the payees and that, had suit been brought on the guaranty by the bank as holder of the notes as collateral to a loan to Sommer, Prettyman would be liable to the bank. . . ."

Affirmed.

NOTE

Right of Recourse. Prior to the Code it had been held that the anomalous accommodation indorser, on paying and taking up the instrument, could not recover on it from the party accommodated. This startling result is reversed in UCC 3–415(5) and 3–603(2). Comment 5 to UCC 3–415 explains that "Subsection (5) is intended to change the result of such decisions as Quimby v. Varnum, 190 Mass. 211, 76 N.E. 671 (1906) which held that an accommodation indorser who paid the instrument could not maintain an action on it against the accommodated party. . . . Under ordinary principles of suretyship the accommodation party who pays is subrogated to the rights of the holder paid, and should have his recourse on the instrument." See also Comment 4 to UCC 3–603.

SECTION 3.   AVAILABILITY OF SURETYSHIP DEFENSES

Prefatory Note. Prior to the Code there was uncertainty with regard to the availability to sureties on negotiable instruments of suretyship defenses based on impairment of recourse or of collateral. UCC 3–606 is intended, as Comment 1 explains, to make it clear that "The suretyship defenses here prior provided are not limited to parties who are 'secondarily liable,' but are available to any party who is in the position of a surety, having a right of recourse either on the instrument or dehors it, including an accommodation maker or acceptor known to the holder to be so."   On the scope of UCC 3–606, see Noble, The "Surety" and Article 3: A New Identity for an Old Friend?, 19 Duq.L.Rev. 245 (1981).

Problem 3. A made a promissory note payable to the X Bank in consideration of a loan to A. B signed the note as a co-maker for A's accommodation at the time of the loan. Before the loan came due, A asked for and the X Bank granted a one-month extension. If A defaults at the end of the month, is B liable to X Bank? See Lee Federal Credit Union v. Gussie, infra. Would it affect the result if the extension were not binding? Might the terms of either the note or the extension affect the result?

LEE FEDERAL CREDIT UNION v. GUSSIE

United States Court of Appeals, Fourth Circuit, 1976.
542 F.2d 887.

WIDENER, CIRCUIT JUDGE. This is an appeal from an order dismissing the complaint of Lee Federal Credit Union (Credit) against Warnetta Gussie, the accommodation co-maker of a promissory note. Since it held Gussie not liable, it follows there is no liability on Gussie's third party complaint, and it should be noted Rowe had no liability as an accommodation co-maker.

Credit instituted this action against Warnetta Gussie, a co-maker on a promissory note. Gussie thereafter filed a third party complaint against Ernest Lee, Susan Lee,[1] James Lee and Kwang Rowe, the remaining co-makers on the note. The case was tried before a judge sitting without a jury who, at the close of plaintiff-Credit's evidence entered judgment for the defendants. Upon a review of the record and the opinion of the trial judge, we affirm.

The controversy in this case arose out of a loan in the amount of $30,000 which was secured by a promissory note. Ernest Lee initially applied for the loan for the purpose of purchasing a restaurant. Before approving his application, however, Credit requested that Ernest Lee provide additional co-makers as security. James Lee, Warnetta Gussie and Kwang Rowe, having submitted co-makers applications, signed the note as co-makers. As mentioned Susan Lee, wife of Ernest, also signed as a co-maker. The loan was subsequently granted on September 1, 1971. It became delinquent at the latest on June 3, 1972, the last payment having been received from Ernest Lee on April 9 of that year. No attempt was made at that time to collect the note nor was any effort made to inform the co-makers of the delinquency. It was not until some months later, on August 8, 1972, that Ernest Lee finally stopped by at a dinner meeting of the board of directors of Credit and gave them a check for $4,900 which would have brought the note up to date through October of 1972. That check was not made payable until October. When Credit inquired as to the post-dated check it was assured by Ernest that there would be funds to cover the check when it became payable.

Based upon this assurance, Credit did nothing further until October when it deposited the check. It was returned due to insufficient funds and Credit thereupon made repeated, unsuccessful attempts to contact Ernest Lee and collect the monies owed. Again, however, Credit failed to give the co-makers notice regarding either its acceptance of the post-dated check or the delinquency of the note. It was not until August 28, 1973, after Credit learned that Ernest Lee had filed a petition in bankruptcy,[2] that Gussie was finally notified of the delinquency and turned to for satisfaction.

It is clear from the evidence that both Gussie and Rowe signed the note in question "for the purpose of lending [their] name[s] to another party to it," namely Ernest Lee. As such, they were accommodation parties within the meaning of § 8.3–415(1) of the Virginia Code. Credit contends that the oral evidence as to the accommodation status of the co-makers should have been excluded since the face of the note reveals that they signed it as makers without any reservation of rights. Therefore, according to Credit, they are liable in the same manner and to the same extent as Ernest Lee. Section 8.3–415(3) provides to the contrary, however. It reads:

---

1. Susan Lee was the wife of Ernest Lee, the principal maker on the note.

2. Credit also learned at about this time that James Lee had also filed a petition in bankruptcy.

"As against a holder in due course and without notice of the accommodation oral proof of the accommodation is not admissible to give the accommodation party the benefit of discharges dependent on his character as such. In other cases the accommodation character may be shown by oral proof."

While Credit may have been a holder in due course, the district court found as a fact, which is not clearly erroneous, that Credit knew that the co-makers on the note were in fact accommodation parties, so Credit could not have been a holder in due course "without notice of the accommodation." This is one of the "other cases" mentioned in § 8.3–415(3) in which "the accommodation character may be shown by oral proof." Thus, the oral evidence as to the status of the parties was properly admitted.

The question then becomes whether the actions of Credit in relation to the note were sufficient to discharge Rowe and Gussie from any further liability. We are of opinion they were. Section 8.3–606 of the Virginia Code provides that:

"(1) The holder discharges any party to the instrument to the extent that without such party's consent the holder

(a) without express reservation of rights releases or agrees not to sue any person against whom the party has to the knowledge of the holder a right of recourse or agrees to suspend the right to enforce against such person the instrument or collateral or otherwise discharges such person, except that failure or delay in effecting any required presentment, protest or notice of dishonor with respect to any such person does not discharge any party as to whom presentment, protest or notice of dishonor is effective or unnecessary . . ."

In the instant case, Credit accepted Ernest Lee's post-dated check and, without notice or reservation of rights, extended the time of payment from the date the note had become delinquent until October when the check became payable. Such extension of time was granted without the consent of the accommodation parties and they were thus relieved of further liability upon the note. Credit, by its extension of time, at the very least, had "agree[d] to suspend the right to enforce against" Ernest Lee. § 8.3–606(1)(a).

We recognize it is at least arguable that the agreed extension of time may not have been binding upon Credit and that it may have been able to institute proceedings against Lee prior to the date the check became payable. Yet, under the UCC in Virginia, it is the agreement which is controlling and not whether that agreement is necessarily binding. This represents a change from earlier Virginia law as is pointed out by the Virginia Comments to § 8.3–606. There, it states:

"Under the NIL [Negotiable Instruments Law] an agreement to extend the time of payment in order to have the effect of discharging parties secondarily liable had to be 'binding upon the holder.' The UCC, in accordance with its general definition of an agreement as being a bargain in fact, as distinguished from a contract, which is the effect given by law to an agreement, eliminates the requirement that the agreement be binding."

Compare, e.g., Cawley v. Hanes, 173 Va. 381, 389, 4 S.E.2d 376 (1939); Cape Charles Bank, Inc. v. Farmers Mutual Exchange, 120 Va. 771, 92 S.E. 918 (1917) dealing with the requirements under the NIL. The evidence clearly indicates that Credit agreed to extend additional time for payment on the note to Ernest Lee in exchange for the post-dated check which he tendered in August. This agreement, having been reached without the consent of either Rowe or Gussie, was sufficient to relieve them from further liability.[3]

The judgment of the district court is accordingly affirmed.

NOTES

(1) **Consent to Extension.** Under UCC 3–606, an extension of time does not discharge an accommodation party who consents to the extension. Comment 2 explains: "Consent may be given in advance, and is commonly incorporated in the instrument; or it may be given afterward. It requires no consideration, and operates as a waiver of the consenting party's right to claim his own discharge."

A promissory note may contain a clause by which indorsers consent in advance to extension. See the promissory note at p. 49 supra. Does such a clause give authorization to more than one extension? See UCC 3–118(f). Comment 7 to that section states that the provision "has reference to such clauses as 'The makers and indorsers of this note consent that it may be extended without notice to them.' Such terms usually are inserted to obtain the consent of the indorser and any accommodation maker to extension which might otherwise discharge them under Section 3–606 dealing with impairment of recourse or collateral. An extension in accord with these terms binds secondary parties." See also UCC 3—109(1)(d).

(2) **Reservation of Rights.** UCC 3–606 makes an exception when there is an "express reservation of rights" by the holder against the party claiming discharge. The requirement that the reservation be "express" is an important one, as is suggested by a leading pre-Code case, National Park Bank v. Koehler, 204 N.Y. 174, 97 N.E. 468 (1912).

The National Park Bank was the holder of a note made by Para Recovery Company and indorsed by Koehler for Para's accommodation. Before maturity of the note, Para asked the bank for an exten-

---

3. Susan Lee has entered no appearance in this appeal. No judgment in this case has been entered against her.

sion of time and the bank agreed to take a series of new notes providing for delayed payment in installments if they too were indorsed by Koehler. Because Koehler was out of the country for several months, Para suggested "that you hold the old note with Mr. Koehler's indorsement as collateral until the new notes are paid, as a way out of the difficulty." On Para's default on the new notes, the bank sued Koehler as accommodation indorser on the original note. Koehler successfully defended on the ground that he had been discharged by an extension of time. The court pointed out that if "the new notes had been given as collateral to secure the payment of the old note, a different question would be presented. . . . What could have been the purpose of giving new notes . . . except that it was intended to procure a definite extension of time?" It dismissed the bank's argument that it had reserved its rights against Koehler. "[W]e must hold that the agreement of the parties did not distinctly, nor impliedly, reserve the right of the bank to proceed by immediate action against the defendant. . . . If the parties actually had in mind a reservation of the right of action against the defendant, . . . it would have been easy to have said so."

In Stanley v. Ames, 378 Mass. 364, 391 N.E.2d 908 (1979), the payees of a note agreed to accept late payment under a new "Agreement and Note." The accommodation maker on the original note never signed or consented to this Agreement and Note. However, the Agreement and Note provided: "The Promisors agree that the Promisee's forbearance . . . does not waive nor forbear any of the terms of the original Note, and that all rights set forth therein . . . are binding in all respects." The court held that this was a reservation of rights and that therefore the extension did not discharge the accommodation maker. UCC 3–606 "does not create any formal requirements for an effective reservation of rights" and "does not require actual notice to the accommodation party of the reservation of rights." [1]

Problem 4. A made a promissory note payable to the X Bank in consideration of a loan to A. B signed the note as co-maker for A's accommodation at the time of the loan. The note was secured by a security interest on A's equipment, but the X Bank failed to file a financing statement as required to protect that interest under UCC 9–302. Some of A's equipment subject to the security interest was attached and sold by a judgment creditor of A. If A defaults, is B liable to X Bank? See Langeveld v. L.R.Z.H. Corporation, infra. Might the terms of the note affect the result?

---

1. In justifying the reservation-of-rights exception, the court explained that "where the extension is accompanied by an express reservation of rights, the surety is not prejudiced, because he can immediately pay the instrument and exercise his right of recourse against the principal debtor." (See p. 449 supra.) But how can the surety do this unless informed of the extension?

LANGEVELD v. L.R.Z.H. CORP.

Supreme Court of New Jersey, 1977.
74 N.J. 45, 376 A.2d 931.

MOUNTAIN, J. This case presents an important question of commercial law requiring the interpretation of N.J.S.A. 12A:3–606, a section of the Uniform Commercial Code which we have not hitherto been called upon to consider.

In the trial court, summary judgment in the amount of $57,500, together with interest, was entered against defendant Higgins,[1] 130 N.J.Super. 486, 327 A.2d 683 (Ch.Div.1974). The Appellate Division affirmed, substantially for the reasons expressed by the court below. 137 N.J.Super. 557, 350 A.2d 76 (App.Div.1975). We granted defendant's petition for certification. 70 N.J. 511, 361 A.2d 526 (1976).

On March 10, 1972, defendant, L.R.Z.H. Corporation, made and delivered to plaintiff, Langeveld, its promissory note in the sum of $57,500. The indebtedness evidenced by the note was secured by a mortgage in like amount on land in Montvale in Bergen County owned by the defendant corporation. This mortgage was junior in lien to a first mortgage in the sum of $825,000 held by The Howard Savings Institution and to a second mortgage in the approximate amount of $58,000 held by persons named Castellane. The latter mortgage covered only a portion of the whole tract upon which The Howard Savings and Langeveld mortgages were liens. By an instrument of guaranty set forth at the foot of the note, defendant, together with certain other persons not here involved, undertook to become individually obligated for the payment of the debt. The note matured February 15, 1973 and was not paid.

It was then for the first time discovered, apparently by defendant, that the Langeveld mortgage had never been recorded. Upon this being brought to plaintiff's attention, the instrument was forthwith recorded on March 1, 1973. It then developed that between the execution and delivery of the Langeveld mortgage on March 10, 1972 and the recording of the instrument on March 1, 1973, the following lien claims had become a matter of record:

1. Mortgage by L.R.Z.H. Corporation to James E. Hanson and Company in the amount of $100,000.

2. Mechanic's Notices of Intention filed by Reed Electric Corporation in the total sum of $111,825.48.

3. Mechanic's Notice of Intention filed by Samuel Braen and Company in the sum of $12,804.56.

On March 8, 1973 plaintiff instituted this suit on the guaranty. In defense of the claim thus asserted against him, defendant pointed out that there existed here the tripartite arrangement typical of a surety-

---

1. The term "defendant," as used hereafter in this opinion will, unless otherwise indicated, refer to defendant Higgins.

ship relationship.[2] L.R.Z.H. Corporation was principal debtor. Plaintiff was its creditor; defendant stood in the position of a guarantor or surety. He further called attention to the fact that plaintiff, as such creditor, held the mortgage from L.R.Z.H. Corporation as collateral security for the corporate obligation and that it owed a duty to him, as surety for the same debt, to protect this security and allow nothing to occur to impair its value and worth that reasonable effort and foresight on plaintiff's part could prevent or avoid. Failure to record the mortgage for about a year, predictably followed by the intervention of recorded liens in substantial amounts, constituted, he argued, a failure on plaintiff's part to fulfill this duty. Accordingly, concluded defendant, he should be released from all liability on his guaranty. Particular attention was drawn to a section of the Uniform Commercial Code, which in pertinent part reads,

Impairment of Recourse or of Collateral.

(1) The holder discharges any party to the instrument to the extent that without such party's consent the holder

. . .

(b) unjustifiably impairs any collateral for the instrument given by or on behalf of the party or any person against whom he has a right of recourse. [N.J.S.A. 12A:3–606]

Doctrines and rules taken from the common law of suretyship have been incorporated within various provisions of the Uniform Commercial Code. It has been said that "[s]ection 3–606 is probably the most important provision in the Code to the surety." Clark, Suretyship in the Uniform Commercial Code, supra, 46 Tex.L.Rev. at 457. "Perhaps the most significant provision of the UCC affecting suretyship is section 3–606." Note, Suretyship in Article 3 of the Uniform Commercial Code, 17 West. Reserve L.Rev. 318 (1965).

It is a well-recognized principle of the law of suretyship that a release of collateral held by a creditor, or its impairment by improper action or inaction on his part, will extinguish the obligation of the surety, at least to the extent of the value of the security released or impaired. This rule has come to be accepted as the law of our State. . . . The section of the Uniform Commercial Code we are considering is essentially a restatement of this rule, as the courts that have examined it have consistently held. . . .

The doctrine is an equitable one, designed to protect the surety's right of subrogation. Upon paying the debt, the surety is, as a matter of law, subrogated to all the creditor's rights against the principal debtor and is entitled to all benefits derivable from any security of the principal debtor that may be in the creditor's hands. The rule

2. Suretyship is invariably a tripartite relationship in which the obligation of the surety is intended to supplement an obligation of the principal (also described as the debtor or obligor) owed to the creditor (also described as the obligee). [Clark, Suretyship in the Uniform Commercial Code, 46 Tex.L.Rev. 453 (1968)]

forbidding impairment of collateral has as its chief aim the protection of these potential benefits made available through subrogation.

Defendant has made out a prima facie case to support his contention that he comes within the favor of the rule. Relating his contentions to the language of the act clearly demonstrates that this is so. Thus we see that plaintiff is the "holder" of collateral, as the word is used in the statute. Defendant is a "party to the instrument"[3] in his capacity as guarantor. A failure to record a mortgage held as collateral security—absent waiver, estoppel or the like—seems clearly to be an instance of unjustifiable impairment. Common law authorities so held, almost without exception. . . . The mortgage is "collateral for the instrument" (note) "given by [a] person (L.R.Z.H. Corporation) against whom he (Higgins) has a right of recourse."

Plaintiff essentially disputes defendant's position on two grounds. He urges, first, that the guaranty is unconditional in form and that this being so, the alleged impairment of collateral in no way affects the obligation to which the guaranty gives rise. In the second place he contends that there has in fact been no impairment of collateral, or at least none that has caused defendant to suffer loss.

The form of guaranty appears below.[4] The provisions dispensing with presentment, notice of dishonor and protest add nothing not already provided by the Code.

> When words of guaranty are used presentment, notice of dishonor and protest are not necessary to charge the user. [N.J.S.A. 12A:3–416(5)]

The language assuring continued liability on the part of the guarantor in the event of the obligor's insolvency was likewise superfluous.

3. Since the guaranty is appended at the foot of the note, we are not called upon to decide whether any different result might ensue were the guaranty to take the form of a separate document. Supporting the view that the result should be the same, see Murray, Secured Transactions—Defenses of Impairment and Improper Care of Collateral, 79 Com.L.Jour. 265, 267 (1974) (collecting authorities).

4. To induce the said JOHN P. LANGEVELD to accept the above note, the undersigned hereby guaranty performance of all obligations of the obligors under the note and under the mortgage securing the indebtedness described in the note. The said undersigned guarantors agree to be principally liable on the indebtedness jointly and severally and further agree to their obligation jointly and severally without the necessity of presentment, demand or notice of dishonor.

The undersigned guarantors agree to pay the tenor of this instrument notwithstanding that L.R.Z.H. CORPORATION may effectuate an assignment for the benefit of creditors, be declared a bankrupt, be discharged from Bankruptcy, or otherwise be excused, except by payment, of the debt.

/s/ Joseph A. Higgins, Sr.   L.S.
JOSEPH A. HIGGINS, SR.
/s/ Albin H. Rothe   L.S.
ALBIN H. ROTHE
/s/ Louis J. Zoghby   L.S.
LOUIS J. ZOGHBY

In addition to the guaranty itself, the following paragraph of the note should be considered,

The undersigned and all other parties who at any time may be liable hereon in any capacity, jointly and severally waive presentment, demand for payment, protest and notice of protest of this note, and authorize the holder hereof, without notice to grant extensions in the time of payment and reductions in the rate of interest on any moneys owing on this note.

Such liability would continue in the face of this eventuality whether explicitly so stated or not.

The only expression which may be said at all to support plaintiff's contention is found in the words, "[t]he said undersigned guarantors agree to be *principally* liable on the indebtedness. . . ." (emphasis added). Plaintiff argues that this language justified him in treating Higgins as if he were in every sense a principal. This contention must be carefully examined. To accept plaintiff's argument literally would be to deprive defendant of all right of recourse against the true principal, or at the very least render the right of recourse of uncertain value by permitting the impairment of collateral. This result should be permitted only where the instrument of guaranty specifically frees the creditor from liability for such impairment.

> If the destruction or impairment of such a right [subrogation to unimpaired collateral] is to be waived by a guarantor, it should only be by the most unequivocal language in the guaranty agreement. The right does not originate in contract, and it cannot lightly be destroyed by contract. [D.W. Jaquays & Co. v. First Security Bank, 101 Ariz. 301, 419 P.2d 85, 89 (1966)]

Here there has been no unequivocal waiver. We think the wording of this guaranty may fairly be equated with language purporting to make a person in defendant's position an "unconditional guarantor." Such language is normally held to permit the creditor to move against the guarantor without first proceeding either against the principal debtor or the collateral. It is not customarily interpreted as providing a creditor with any further rights. As one commentator has put it,

> It is one thing to say that a creditor need not pursue the collateral as a condition precedent to pursuing the guarantor of payment and quite another to say that because of this condition precedent the creditor can by misfeasance or nonfeasance prevent the guarantor of payment from ever recovering from the collateral. [Murray, Secured Transactions—Defenses of Impairment and Improper Care of Collateral, supra, 79 Com.L. Jour. at 278]

Recent case law expressly sustains the position that terms of absolute or unconditional guaranty should be so limited. . . .

The point to be made and emphasized is that absent express agreement, waiver or renunciation, a surety's right of subrogation to *unimpaired* collateral will be protected. We do not find this right to have been waived or relinquished by anything contained in this guaranty.

Plaintiff's second contention is that the collateral has not as a matter of fact been impaired, or at least not to an extent that it has caused defendant any loss.

On March 9 and 20, 1973, James E. Hanson and Company and The Howard Savings Institution commenced separate actions to foreclose their respective mortgages. On July 3, 1973 an order was entered consolidating the two foreclosure suits. On August 26, 1974, at sheriff's sale, Higgins, acting through a corporation, purchased the property for $1,080,000. By this time the amounts due on The Howard Savings and Castellane mortgages had substantially increased. The sum received at sheriff's sale was sufficient only to satisfy the amount due on the first mortgage and to apply about $20,000 in reduction of the second. The trial judge took the position that the amount received at sheriff's sale represented the fair market value of the premises. Since it was insufficient to satisfy the two mortgages admittedly senior to plaintiff's mortgage, this demonstrated that plaintiff's mortgage was without value. Therefore, although he found that plaintiff's failure to record his mortgage was "unjustifiable," the trial judge concluded that this had not harmed Higgins because the Langeveld mortgage had now been shown to be valueless. Accordingly, plaintiff's motion for summary judgment was granted. We find this disposition of the case to have been error.

In the first place, and most importantly, the factual situation and the respective rights and obligations of the parties should have been assessed and determined not at the time of the sheriff's sale, in August, 1974, but rather at the time the obligation matured, in February, 1973. It was then that defendant was entitled to exercise his rights as surety. Had he paid plaintiff the amount then due— $57,500, together with interest at the rate of 10% from October 15, 1970—he would have stood in plaintiff's shoes as holder of the note and mortgage. Had the mortgage originally been promptly recorded, as it should have been, there would then have been available to him a variety of options, the relative merits of which we are in no position to evaluate at this time and on this record. For instance, as holder of a junior lien (the Langeveld mortgage) he would have had a right to redeem either or both The Howard Savings and Castellane mortgages. Osborne, Law of Mortgages, 628–29. He could have foreclosed any mortgage acquired. Other possibilities suggest themselves. The point is that defendant appears to have been deprived of the opportunity effectively to exploit his right of subrogation to unimpaired collateral by the failure of plaintiff to record the mortgage given him by L.R.Z.H. Corporation.

The Hanson mortgage as well as various mechanics' notices of intention had intervened before the Langeveld mortgage was recorded. Although the Hanson mortgage is said to contain a clause subordinating it to the lien of the Langeveld mortgage, Hanson has nevertheless filed various contentious pleadings apparently attacking the alleged priority of plaintiff's lien. Reed Electric Company claims to have been junior in lien only to The Howard Savings Institution and complains that the relative priority of its claim has *never* been adjudicated. These points of contention and others as well should have been resolved at trial. The facts so found should have then been assayed to determine their effect, if any, with respect to the alleged impairment of collateral. The case was in no way ripe for the entry of summary judgment.

The parties express sharply differing views as to the extent to which an impairment of collateral should be held to discharge one secondarily liable. Defendant suggests that the Code has adopted the rule, sometimes referred to as that of *strictissimi juris*, that a surety is completely discharged by any impairment of collateral, whether or not he has sustained loss or prejudice. Plaintiff, on the other hand, contends that the surety should only be released from liability to the extent that actual, calculable monetary loss can be shown to have occurred.

We think the statute should be read as adopting a rule somewhere between these extremes. If the impairment of collateral can be measured in monetary terms, then the calculated amount of the impairment will ordinarily measure the extent of the surety's discharge. But there are factual situations—this may or may not be one of them—where a surety may be able to establish that he has sustained prejudice, but be unable to measure the extent of the prejudice in terms of monetary loss. Where such a situation is presented the surety will normally be completely discharged.[5]

To recapitulate briefly, at the plenary hearing which must follow our order of remand, the Chancery Division judge will determine from all of the evidence presented, to what extent, if at all, plaintiff's failure seasonably to record his mortgage impaired the collateral given by L.R.Z.H. Corporation to plaintiff as security for the indebtedness. The effect of the impairment upon one secondarily liable may or may not be translatable into dollars. There may be clear prejudice without precisely calculable loss. This will normally result in the discharge of the surety. To the extent that such impairment is found, defendant, Higgins will stand discharged of his obligation as guarantor.

---

5. Our dissenting colleague argues that this Court should enter judgment for the defendant rather than direct a remand to the trial court. In so doing he places reliance upon language found in Bell v. Martin, 18 N.J.L. 167 (Sup.Ct. 1840). That case involved the question as to whether a binding agreement between the creditor and the principal debtor to extend the time of payment would discharge one who was secondarily liable. The case held, in accordance with well settled authority, that such an extension agreement *did* result in the discharge of a surety. This rule was later embodied in the Negotiable Instruments Law, N.J. S.A. 7:2–120. This statute was expressly repealed by the Uniform Commercial Code, N.J.S.A. 12A:10–105, but the subject matter of the earlier act was carried forward into N.J.S.A. 12A:3–606(1)(a). The discussion of "prejudice" in *Bell* was clearly unnecessary to the decision. Where a surety seeks to be discharged because of a binding agreement to extend time, neither loss nor prejudice need be shown. "Although application of the rule to cases where the extension of time appears to have caused little or no actual injury to the surety has been criticized, it is nevertheless firmly settled." Simpson, Law of Suretyship 352. Where the surety, however, seeks to be discharged because of an alleged impairment of collateral as is here the case, a quite different situation is presented.

The judgment of the Appellate Division is reversed and the case is remanded to the Chancery Division for further proceedings not inconsistent with what has been said above.

CONFORD, P.J.A.D., Temporarily Assigned, concurring in part and dissenting in part.

I am in agreement with the Court's determination that summary judgment should not have been entered for plaintiff. I take issue, however, with the Court's failure to direct the entry of summary judgment in favor of defendant on the ground of impairment by plaintiff of the collateral for defendant's obligation as surety on the note in suit.

There is some support in the history of the adoption of Section 3.606 of the Uniform Commercial Code for defendant's contention that its intent was to entitle a surety to discharge upon impairment of recourse or of collateral without having to demonstrate either prejudice or actual loss. Prior to the promulgation of the official version of the Code in 1958 (later adopted in New Jersey) the New York Law Revision Commission made a full study of the 1952 draft code. It is generally believed that certain alterations of the draft code were attributable to recommendations of the New York Commission.[1] See Uniform Commercial Code in Uniform Laws Annotated (Master edition 1968) Explanation, p. iii. The New York Commission concluded that Section 3–601(1) of the code adopted the strict rule of suretyship, not requiring a showing of prejudice to the surety. 2 New York Law Revision Commission Report, op. cit. supra, at 1179. Also adverting to the study and conclusion of the New York Commission in this regard was the Supreme Court of Oregon in Philco Finance Co. v. Patton, 248 Or. 310, 432 P.2d 686, 689, n. 7 (1967).

Notwithstanding the foregoing legislative history, I agree with the Court's view that as a matter of sound policy we should not adopt the principle of *strictissimi juris* in this regard but that a surety should be entitled to relief if he is "able to establish that he has sustained prejudice", even if the prejudice cannot be measured "in terms of monetary loss". P. 937. But apparently the Court and I do not share a common understanding of the meaning of the word "prejudice" in this respect since I view the record on the motion for summary judgment as conclusively establishing prejudice to defendant in plaintiff's failure to have promptly recorded the Langeveld mortgage while the Court holds that a plenary hearing is necessary to establish prejudice. In this regard, the legislative history aforementioned at least militates against an approach which would unduly circumscribe the surety in establishing prejudice by an impairment of collateral.

1. For example, the Commission recommended deletion of a Comment to Section 3–606(1) declaring there would be a *pro tanto* discharge of the surety upon partial release or impairment of security. See 2 New York Law Revision Report, 1189–1190 (1955). The official draft adopted that recommendation.

I am in full accord with the Court's assertion that the question of prejudice must be assessed as of the time the note matured, in February 1973. It cannot be left to the hindsight of events as they later unfolded and as they apparently stood in August 1974, when the sheriff's sale took place. P. 936. What must be appraised and compared, in order to determine whether defendant was prejudiced, are the hypothetical situation which defendant would have faced on the maturity date had the Langeveld mortgage been timely recorded, on the one hand, and the actual situation which in fact confronted him on that date, on the other hand. That actual situation consisted of the fact that the mortgage had not been recorded, and three new liens had been recorded in the interim, apparently assuming priority to the Langeveld mortgage, to which defendant was subrogated as a surety.

As of the maturity date, had plaintiff's mortgage been a good and subsisting mortgage ahead of any other liens except the first two mortgages (which it was not, because it had not been recorded until March 1, 1973), defendant as surety would have been entitled to pay off the Langeveld mortgage and assume a position of priority to the later intervening liens, i.e., the Hanson mortgage of $100,000, the Reed Electric Corporation mechanic's notice of $111,000 and the Samuel Braen mechanic's notice of $12,000. He could then have paid or refinanced the first two mortgages at the amount due in March 1973. He would not have had to wait until completion of the foreclosure of The Howard Savings mortgage, necessary, as it turned out, because of the contending claims for priority of the other lienors, and he would have been able to save the additional interest which accrued on the first (Howard Savings) mortgage between February 15, 1973 (maturity of Langeveld note) and August 26, 1974 (sheriff's sale).

As well stated in the Court's opinion, "defendant appears to have been deprived of the opportunity effectively to exploit his right of subrogation to unimpaired collateral by the failure of plaintiff to record the mortgage given him by L.R.Z.H. Corporation." P. 936.

"Prejudice" is adequately established, in my view, by the substantial possibility of a worsened position of the surety due to the impairment of the collateral by the creditor. The surety does not have to show the certainty of loss from the impairment in order to demonstrate prejudice. Frequently, as in this case, the course of events makes it impossible to establish actual loss to a certainty or even a reasonable probability thereof. It should be enough that it is reasonably possible that the surety has been disadvantaged. Comparable views were articulated as long ago as 1840 in Bell v. Martin, 18 N.J.L. 167 (Sup.Ct.), holding that, in order to discharge an endorser because of a creditor's agreement to extend time to the debtor, such extension need only be to the "prejudice" of the endorser. The court said: "But this does not mean to his *actual, ascertained loss or injury:* but to his prejudice, in contemplation of law; by depriving him of his right to take up the note, and sue the prior indorsers, or the maker, until after the expiration of the extended credit, given by the holder." (Id. at 170; emphasis in original). The court goes on to explain that any other rule would "subvert the very foundations, upon which the whole system of commercial paper has been erected". (Id. at 170–171).

Since it is impossible to rerun the course of events and discover to a certainty what defendant, as surety, would have done at maturity of the note if the Langeveld mortgage had been recorded immediately upon execution, rather than delayed to a date letting in other encumbrances ahead of it, it seems to me that prejudice must be assumed on these facts, as a matter of law, on the basis of what defendant would have had the right to do at that time in protection of his interests. I do not see how any facts plaintiff might conceivably adduce at a hearing could affect the validity of the foregoing observations. Cf. Merchants Ind. Corp. v. Eggleston, 37 N.J. 114, 179 A.2d 505 (1962), dealing with "prejudice" as an essential ingredient of estoppel when an insurance company maintains control of the defense of a liability action against its insured, and later denies coverage. In that connection the court said (Id. at 129, 179 A.2d at 512): "Indeed some courts speak of a 'conclusive' presumption of prejudice, doubtless because, since the course cannot be rerun, they believe it futile to attempt to prove or to disprove that the insured would have fared better on his own."

Procedurally, entry of summary judgment for defendant at this time would be supportable since defendant did earlier make a motion for summary judgment before a different judge which was denied, and he repeats the request for that relief on this appeal. This Court has the right to assume original jurisdiction in order to bring the litigation to a conclusion, R. 2:10–5, and plaintiff has been fully heard on the issues.

NOTES

(1) **Consent to Impairment.** As the court recognizes, the rule of UCC 3–606(1)(b) can be varied by agreement. See the promissory note on page 49, supra. For a case holding that consent to "the release of . . . collateral" amounted to consent to the impairment of collateral, see Executive Bank of Fort Lauderdale v. Tighe, 54 N.Y.2d 330, 445 N.Y.S.2d 425, 429 N.E.2d 1054 (1981), refusing to distinguish "a release from a failure to file on the basis that the former is a deliberate act at a future time whereas the latter is a negligent act which occurs at the threshold of the transaction."

(2) **Release of Co-Surety.** In Provident Bank v. Gast, 57 Ohio St. 2d 102, 386 N.E.2d 1357 (1979), William Gast obtained a bank loan by signing a $54,000 promissory note that was cosigned by Gerald and Beverly Tonkens. Hamilton and Ruth Gast, William's parents, signed a separate instrument guaranteeing William's indebtedness to the extent of $15,000. On William's default, the bank demanded the

$47,479 balance from the Tonkens and the $15,000 from William's parents. The Tonkens sued the bank alleging various wrongdoings and as part of the settlement of this suit, the bank released the Tonkens from any liability on the note. The bank then sued William's parents. (William, being bankrupt, took no part in the suit.)

The Supreme Court of Ohio held, four to two, that the release had discharged William's parents to the extent of $7,500, the amount of their loss of contribution against the Tonkens. It concluded that UCC 3–606(1)(a) was ambiguous as to whether the discharge was total or partial, and relied on the Restatement of Security to support the conclusion that in enacting the Code the legislature "intended to limit the discharge of a non-consenting co-surety to his right of contribution." The court noted that "the critical phrase, 'to the extent that,' also modifies [UCC 3–606(1)(b)] dealing with a discharge wherein the holder 'unjustifiably impairs any collateral,'" and drew support from cases from other jurisdictions, including Langeveld, holding that the extent of discharge under that provision "is limited by the extent of the injury or impairment of the collateral."

The dissent read the language "to the extent" in UCC 3–606(1) to mean to the extent that the other party is released rather than to the extent that his right of recourse is not preserved. "There is no qualification in [UCC 3–606(1)(a)] to the discharge of a person in the Gasts' position other than to the extent that the person against whom he has a right of recourse is released. Such limited discharge is provided for in [UCC 3–606(1)(b)] where collateral is unjustifiably impaired, in which case the discharge only goes to the extent of impairment. If a limited discharge were intended in [UCC 3–606(1)(a)], the statute would so provide by stating that the discharge is to the extent that the right of recourse is impaired."

(3) **Applicability Where No Suretyship.** Suppose that there are two ordinary comakers (such as Richard and Walter in Fithian v. Jamar, supra), who have a right of contribution against each other. If one is released, does UCC 3–606(1)(a) apply to discharge the other to the extent of that right, even though no suretyship relation is involved? True, UCC 3–606 nowhere mentions the word "surety," and a right to contribution seems to be a "right of recourse" as required by paragraph (1)(a). But Comment 1, which says that discharge is "available to any party who is in the position of a surety" suggests that a suretyship relation is required. And there is case law supporting this position. See Hooper v. Ryan, 581 S.W.2d 237 (Tex.Civ.App. 1979) (UCC 3–606 "applies to sureties and not to co-makers").

Could not the same argument be made in the case of two accommodation comakers (such as Connie and Janet in Fithian v. Jamar, supra)? If one is released, does UCC 3–606(1)(a) apply to discharge the other to the extent of the right of the second to contribution from the first, even though the second is not a surety for the first? And if this question is answered in the negative, was not the court wrong in

Provident Bank v. Gast in applying UCC 3–606(1)(a) as between co-sureties?   For a case holding that "where the two sureties are joint and several obligors and an extension of time is granted to one surety *but not to the principal debtor* . . ., the better rule is that such extension is a personal contract between the parties and does not have the effect of discharging the other surety," see Cusick v. Ifshin, 70 Misc.2d 564, 334 N.Y.S.2d 106 (1972), affirmed mem., 73 Misc.2d 127, 341 N.Y.S.2d 280 (1973).

*

INDEX

References are to Pages

†